EARLY CHILDHOOD EDUCATION 80/81

Judy Spitler McKee, *Editor*
Eastern Michigan University,
Ypsilanti

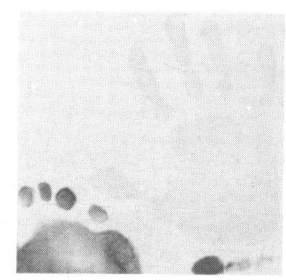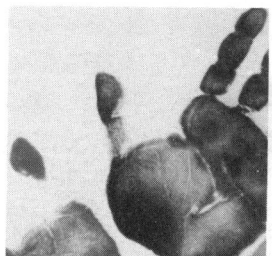
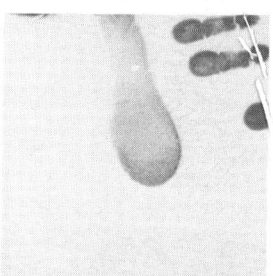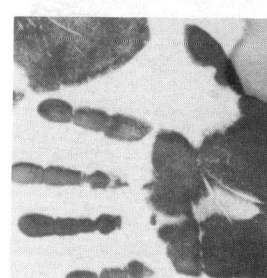

Cover photo: "Handprints and Footprints" by J. Baker.

ANNUAL EDITIONS
The Dushkin Publishing Group, Inc. Sluice Dock, Guilford, Ct. 06437

Volumes in the Annual Editions Series

- Abnormal Psychology
- ● Aging
- ● American Government
- ● American History Pre-Civil War
- ● American History Post-Civil War
- ● Anthropology
- Astronomy
- ● Biology
- ● Business
- Comparative Government
- ● Criminal Justice
- Death and Dying
- ● Deviance
- ● Early Childhood Education
- Earth Science
- ● Economics
- ● Educating Exceptional Children
- ● Education
- Educational Psychology
- Energy
- ● Environment
- Ethnic Studies
- Foreign Policy
- Geography
- Geology
- ● Health
- ● Human Development
- ● Human Sexuality
- ● Management
- ● Marketing
- ● Marriage and Family
- ● Personal Growth and Adjustment
- Philosophy
- Political Science
- ● Psychology
- Religion
- ● Social Problems
- ● Sociology
- ● Urban Society
- Western Civilization
- Women's Studies
- World History
- ● World Politics

● *Indicates currently available*

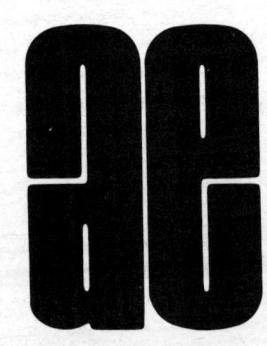

© 1980 by the Dushkin Publishing Group, Inc. Annual Editions is a Trade Mark of the Dushkin Publishing Group, Inc.

Copyright © 1980 by the Dushkin Publishing Group, Inc., Guilford, Connecticut 06437

All rights reserved. No part of this book may be reproduced, stored, or transmitted by any means—mechanical, electronic or otherwise—without written permission from the publisher.

Fourth Edition
Library of Congress Catalog Card Number: 77-640114

Manufactured by George Banta Company, Menasha, Wisconsin, 54952

ADVISORY BOARD

Members of the Advisory Board are instrumental in the final selection of articles for each year's edition of *Annual Editions*. Their review of articles for content, level, and appropriateness provides critical direction to the editor and staff. We think you'll find their careful consideration well reflected in this volume.

Louise Beem
College of DuPage

Doris Dittmar
Wright State University

Jean Emerson
SUNY Agricultural and
  Technical College,
Cobleskill

Andrew Gilpin
University of Northern Iowa

Bradley Glanville
California State University,
Chico

Barbara Mahler
California State University,
Chico

Betty Rowen
University of Miami

Naida Sievert
Montana State University

Ida Santos Stewart
University of Houston,
Houston

Tom Yawkley
The Pennsylvania State University

AND STAFF

Rick Connelly, Publisher
Ian A. Nielsen, Program Manager
Celeste Borg, Editor
Addie Kawula, Acquisitions Editor
Brenda Filley, Production Manager
Cheryl Kinne, Permissions Coordinator
Charles Vitelli, Designer
Jeremy Brenner, Graphics Coordinator
Bertha Kinne, Typesetting Coordinator

CONTENTS

1
Perspectives

Topic Guide	1
Preface	3
Overview	5

1. **How Could Early Childhood Education Affect Families?** Marilyn Smith, *Young Children,* September 1978. — 6
   The Executive Director of the National Association for the Education of Young Children argues that early childhood educators may have been asking the wrong questions about families and that responses have been directed more towards economic crises than to providing programs and services for children. She outlines purposes, settings, appropriate experiences and their potential to assure that children reach their developmental birthrights.

2. **What Is Basic for Young Children?** Lilian Katz, *Childhood Education,* October 1977. — 14
   The Director of the ERIC/ECE Clearinghouse outlines seven propositions on the central question of "our responsibilities for the quality of the daily lives of all of our children." She relates these to the "Law of Optimum Effects."

3. **What's Basic About the Curriculum?** Arthur W. Foshay, *The Education Digest,* December 1977. — 18
   A scholar of curriculum theory and history analyzes the question of what in life is basic enough to be incorporated within the curriculum. He concludes that coping skills, social development, citizenship, and private realization are interwoven basics, and that overlooking any one will weaken the other three.

4. **What Is Early Childhood Education? Some Definitions and Issues,** Norma R. Law, *Childhood Education,* February/March 1979. — 21
   A formulation of early childhood education terminology is presented from the standpoint of the consumers: children, parents, teachers, and society. Persistent issues identified include care and education, government and professional controls, socialization, cultural pluralism, early concept development, learning materials, and evaluation.

5. **How Early Should They Go to School?** Raymond S. Moore and Dennis R. Moore, *Childhood Education,* October 1973. — 26
   The authors argue that young children should not be sent to school. Instead they advocate a home teaching program staffed by mothers.

6. **Early Childhood Education: A Perspective on Basics,** Annie L. Butler, *Childhood Education,* October 1973. — 29
   Unlike Moore and Moore in the previous article, Butler argues that early childhood education is distinct from early childhood schooling.

7. **Four Who Cared,** Monroe D. Cohen, *Today's Education,* February/March 1980. — 32
   Four female child developmentalists offer their cumulative expertise and convictions about the intricate dynamics of learning in young children. Each emphasizes the importance of multiple observations and mindful interactions with children to grasp more completely their ways of functioning.

8. **Making the Day Care Decision,** Ron Haskins, Dale C. Farran, and Joseph Sanders, *Parents,* April 1978. — 36
   Recent social science research on the effects of group day care on the intellectual development, social behavior, mother-child relationship, and health of children is summarized. The authors caution, however, that the research is based on model day care centers of high quality and is, therefore, not generalizable to low-quality programs with a high adult-to-child ratio or high staff turnover.

9. **Day Care Policy: Some Modest Proposals,** Edward Zigler and Susan Hunsinger, *Day Care and Early Education,* May/June 1977. — 40
   This article presents a series of proposals by a former director of the U.S. Office of Child Development on how best to appropriate our many existing resources and how to recognize the child care bureaucracy at the federal level.

10. **Infant Day Care: Toward a More Human Environment,** Arminta Lee Jacobson, *Young Children,* July 1978. 43
This author reviews research identifying characteristics of infant caretakers who foster competence in their children. Personality factors, attitudes, and behaviors of the caretaker are summarized.

11. **What Young Children Need Most in a Changing Society,** An Interview with David Elkind, *Parents,* July 1977. 47
An eminent psychologist argues that many young children are experiencing severe pressure to achieve in academics and organized sports. Concurrently, although pressures are escalating, many parents are no longer child-centered in their approach.

2
Childhood and Society

Overview 51

12. **Our Disconnected Child,** William Kessen, *Harper's,* April 1978. 52
The definitions of childhood and its purposes have changed as a result of historical events, economic factors, and philosophical viewpoints. The works of Freud and Piaget have produced a current view of the child as propelled by internal dual processes of instinct and cognition.

13. **A Mother's Day Message: What We Can Do Now for Our Children's Future,** Margaret Mead, *Redbook,* May 1979. 54
A posthumous article taken from the distinguished anthropologist's notes offers a humane beacon of hope for greater commitment to children and their families. Too many children live in frightful circumstances of poverty, neglect, abuse, or alienation, and correspondingly fail to develop their potential.

14. **An Educational Forecast for the 1980s,** Harold G. Shane, *The Education Digest,* October 1979. 57
Educational prognostications for the 1980s by this well known futurist include increasing emphasis on early childhood education, developmental programs, and education for handicapped children as well as a demand for more teachers. An "inventory of education's tomorrow's" includes greater emphasis on direct experiences, increased use of technology, teacher militancy, and greater federal participation in educational endeavors.

15. **Proposition 13 and Early Childhood Education: Wave of the Future or Bad Splash?** Annie L. Butler and Natalie P. LeVasseur, *Childhood Education,* January 1979. 59
A somber scenario from 1999 outlines the major cutbacks in funds and their consequences for social services, particularly education. If only bare essentials are to be provided, there will be pervasive and interwoven effects on children, families, and teachers.

16. **Raising Children to Make a Less Violent World,** Benjamin Spock, *Redbook,* November 1979. 63
Renowned pediatrician, Benjamin Spock, asserts that the major causes of societal violence are neglect and physical abuse of children. He suggests that learning to care about and get along with people, as well as creativity and problem-solving are the keys to changing values and behavior concerning violence.

17. **Schools vs. Television,** Edward B. Fiske, *Parents,* January 1980. 65
Since a number of researchers have found that overdoses of television viewing have negative effects on children's school performance, educators and parents are cooperating to limit children's viewing time and habits. Five guides to sensible television viewing are offered to ensure that positive values are developed.

18. **Signals of Child Abuse,** Vanessa Vigare, *Day Care and Early Education,* Spring 1978. 68
Four major areas of child abuse and their signs are discussed. The author reveals that all reporting individuals are protected by law whether they give valid or erroneous information to police or welfare officials.

3
Development and Educational Opportunities

Overview		71
19.	**A Perfect Baby,** Virginia Apgar and Joan Beck, *Parents,* November 1975.	72
	The authors present information to young couples for increasing their chances of having a healthy baby.	
20.	**Growth: 45 Crucial Months,** Barbara Wyden, *Life,* December 17, 1971.	77
	Recent research indicates that nutrition in the prenatal period and the first 45 months after birth can have a permanent effect on the child's mental and physical growth.	
21.	**Your Child's Mind,** Burton L. White, *American Baby,* April 1976.	80
	A Harvard psychologist advocates that the educational developments occurring at around eight months of age are the most important factors in a child's experiences for later competent development.	
22.	**The Baby's Elastic Mind,** Jerome Kagan, *Human Nature,* January 1978.	83
	A long standing belief was that certain critical experiences in infancy had long lasting effects on the personality of individuals. A Harvard psychologist argues that this assumption may be erroneous, and that humans are more "elastic" than was previously believed.	
23.	**The Care of Infants and Toddlers in Group Settings,** Judy I. Schwartz, *Childhood Education,* November/December 1979.	89
	Since families are usually the best caregivers for their infants and toddlers, under what circumstances are group care programs justified? Criteria for cognitive and affective design of quality care programs are taken from the theoretical frameworks of Piaget and Erikson.	
24.	**Ecology of Infant Day Care,** Richard Elardo, *Day Care and Early Education,* January 1974.	97
	Using a stage analysis, the author presents rules for the establishment and maintenance of a quality day care program for infants and toddlers. Episodes should be short and pleasant, for maximum benefit.	
25.	**Piaget's Theory of Child Development and Its Implications,** Robbie Case, *Phi Delta Kappan,* September 1973.	100
	Piaget's interpretation of intelligence, termed the cognitive-developmental view, states that mental growth is a function of internal organization, commerce with the environment, and internal construction of reality. Implications for curricula content, assessment procedures, readiness, and active learning are discussed.	
26.	**Misunderstandings About How Children Learn,** David Elkind, *Today's Education,* March 1972.	107
	The topic of how children learn includes at least five misconceptions. The author feels that these misconceptions derive from a current emphasis on intellectual growth rather than concern for personal and social growth.	
27.	**The Truth About Sex Differences,** Susan Muenchow, *Parents,* February 1980.	109
	To the dismay of believers in unisex treatment of children, researchers argue that there are fundamental and fascinating differences between boys and girls—some determined by genes, hormones, maturational rates, and brain organizations; others related more to environmental conditions. Sexual differences in verbal, spatial, and visual ability account for differing academic successes or difficulties for boys and girls.	
28.	**Sex Roles in the Nursery,** Laura Carper, *Harper's,* April 1978.	113
	When young children engage in dramatic role playing, sexual role stereotyping is usually very apparent. According to the author, as children band together for same-sex dramatic play, they are establishing their sexual identity, and rigidity of sex roles is much more common than is role reversal, despite the phenomena of working mothers or Women's Liberation.	
29.	**When Kids Explore Sex,** Arlene S. Uslander, Caroline Weiss and Judith Telman, *Parents,* August 1977.	115
	Children of all ages are prone to engage in sex play as a result of normal growth and maturation of body and mind. Suggestions are offered for dealing with brother-sister sex play, dirty jokes, and masturbation so that children do not experience excessive fear, guilt, or abnormal sexual curiosity when they explore the roles of sexual identity.	
30.	**Aggression and Hostility in Young Children,** Bettye M. Caldwell, *Young Children,* January 1977.	118
	A psychologist and researcher notes that children's aggression is difficult to control. She summarizes research supporting nine practical suggestions for teachers and others who must cope with children's aggression.	

31. **Mother-Child Interactions and Competence in Infants and Toddlers,** Shirley Moore, *Young Children,* March 1977. 126
    In trying to find the optimum effects of out-of-home environments for very young children, the author surveys three relevant studies of mother-child interaction and their relation to children's competence at various stages.

32. **The Individuality Factor,** *Redbooks' Parent & Child,* 1976. 131
    The findings from a twelve year longitudinal study of 135 children indicate that youngsters are born with an inherent temperament, a basic behavioral pattern that is predictable when identified. Since the eight types of behavior are basically persistent and consistent during early and middle childhood, teachers and parents need to be cognizant of the meaning of individuality in children.

33. **Play Isn't Just Kid Stuff,** Brain Sutton-Smith, *Parents,* August 1978. 133
    A cognitive psychologist and scholar of folklore and games offers specific suggestions for healthy ways of playing with children from birth to fifteen years.

34. **Worlds of Play,** Donald Baker, *Childhood Education,* March 1977. 136
    A British educator offers three antidotes to the stresses and diseases of isolation, dulled sensitivity, and loss of contact with other persons: space for play, time for play, and people for play. Examples are drawn from the play of children in the West Indies, Malaysia, Western Europe, Africa, and the United States.

4
Child Rearing and Parent Education

Overview 141

35. **Whatever Happened to the Walton's?** Richard L. Isakson, *Instructor,* September 1979. 142
    The changes that the American family undergoes—major changes in size, function, and meaning—are reflected in children's school behavior and personality development. Experts offer insightful suggestions for school personnel to help fragmented or stressed families by providing a network of support services.

36. **The Consequences of Early Childbearing,** Joseph H. Stevens, Jr., *Young Children,* January 1980. 144
    Twenty percent of babies are born to women 19 years and younger, radically altering their present and future circumstances and aspirations. The major consequences for them are related to family support, educational attainment, income levels, marriage, subsequent childbearing, and their children's overall development.

37. **When Mommy Goes to Work . . .,** Sally Wendkos Olds, *Family Health/Today's Health,* February 1977. 152
    Research indicates that children of working mothers do not necessarily experience emotional problems. The author lists some guidelines for parents to follow.

38. **Crisis in the Classroom,** Joan B. Kelly and Judith S. Wallerstein, *Working Mother,* March 1980. 155
    The high incidence of divorce has precipitated divorce-engendered stress in children, adversely affecting their learning receptivity, concentration abilities, and academic attitudes and skills. The authors argue for changes in teacher attitudes, curriculum and instruction, and after-school care.

39. **Black Child/White Child,** Alvin F. Poussaint, *Parents,* October 1976. 161
    A psychiatrist offers advice for parents of all races to enable them to raise children to be free of racial prejudice, to be themselves, and to permit freedom to others. Excessive parental protection from the realities of a racially pluralistic society usually shortcircuits a child's coping abilities.

40. **How Can I Help My Children Do Better in School?** Edward Stranix, *Teacher,* September 1978. 164
    In response to the most persistent questions asked by parents of teachers, the author presents twenty-five suggestions for augmenting children's success in school experiences. Home-school cooperation is underscored in these teacher-tested recommendations.

41. **The Myth of the Vulnerable Child,** Arlene Skolnick, *Psychology Today,* February 1978. 167
Psychologist Skolnick analyzes research on child-rearing approaches to test the influence of specific techniques on personality development. She concludes that despite the ominous warnings of many professionals, parents have considerably less influence over their children's destiny than they think or have been led to believe.

5

Children with Special Needs

Overview 171
42. **The LD Syndrome: How to Recognize and Deal with It,** Joan Harwell, *Instructor,* November 1979. 172
Since Public Law 94-142 mandates that all learning disabled children be identified and planned for in an individualized manner, the author outlines characteristics of learning disabled children and methods for helping them. Informal and formal evaluation procedures are listed so an accurate diagnosis can be made.
43. **"Learning Disabled" or "Slow Learner"?** Margaret Jo Shepherd, *Teacher,* March 1975. 176
A learning disabilities specialist differentiates between children who manifest symptoms of learning disabilities and children who display signs of being slow learners.
44. **The Young Gifted Child,** Susan Schwartz, *Early Years,* February 1980. 178
Despite the fact that gifted children are usually physically, mentally, and emotionally healthier than their nongifted peers, the gifted child may be especially prone to particular types of problems. These include peer ridicule, finding friends, belligerence, monopolizing teacher or class time, indolence, boredom, under-demanding parents, lack of tolerance of others, or self-expectations for perfection.
45. **Let's Go Slow on Acceleration,** Joanne Yatvin, *Today's Education,* March/April 1976. 182
An elementary school principal discusses the pros and cons of advancing children in school or providing specially sequenced formal instruction for them.
46. **Mainstreaming: Valuing Diversity in Children,** Kathleen H. Dunlop, *Young Children,* May 1977. 185
The history of programs for children with special needs dates back more than a century and professional interest, research, and practice have changed from exclusion, to segregation, to mainstreaming in the public schools. A summary of the characteristics of a successfully mainstreamed classroom is provided.

6

Behavior and Guidance

Overview 191
47. **How to Discipline with Love,** Fitzhugh Dodson, *American Baby,* January 1979. 192
According to this noted psychologist, parents can more easily discipline their infants and toddlers with love and humaneness if they understand the developmental task of each stage and govern their behavior. Rapport with the child and respect for temperament or behavioral style of response are crucial principles to remember.
48. **Anxiety and the 3-to 5-Year Old,** Kit Bakke, *Day Care and Early Education,* Winter 1977. 194
Since young children are cognitively egocentric, they often feel confused, guilty, and anxious in situations that would not upset most adults. The causes and symptoms of anxiety in young children are discussed and suggestions are made for facilitating the development of coping skills.
49. **How to Understand Your Child's Distress Signals,** Paul Ackerman and Murray Keppelman, *Redbook,* April 1979. 197
Normal children send out non-verbal, behavioral messages to their parents to convey feelings or needs that cannot be easily communicated through words. Some of the signals that carry hidden meanings include temper tantrums, fantasy friends, fantasies, and bed wetting, each of which can be dealt with positively through adult problem-solving.

50. **Classroom Discipline Problems? 15 Humane Solutions,** Marjorie L. Hipple, *Childhood Education,* February 1978. 201
A preschool teacher addresses the perennial problem of humane and effective guidance of children so that they can move toward self-discipline and self-control. The 15 suggestions, with accompanying vignettes, are based upon child development, learning theory, and pedagogical principles.

51. **Behavioral Blockbusters!** Hugh Carberry, *Instructor,* March 1979. 205
A school psychologist identifies specific techniques for working with four types of troubled learners: the negativistic child, the impulsive child, the passive-dependent child, and the anxious child. Although each of these youngsters will manifest school difficulties, the symptoms are different from those of the learning disabled or mentally retarded child.

7
Programs and Curricula

Overview 209

52. **Humanizing the Curriculum,** David Elkind, *Childhood Education,* Feburary 1977. 210
A Piagetian scholar and curriculum critic interprets three approaches to humanizing the curriculum: adding to it, subtracting from it, and transforming it. Three current trends analyzed include affective education, back-to-basics, and open or informal education.

53. **Bilingual/Bicultural Programs for Preschool Children,** Soledad Arenas, *Children Today,* July/August 1978. 213
Two of the most burdensome tasks besetting a non-English speaking child are those of socialization and learning to conceptualize in a new language. While no single approach to bilingual/bicultural preschool programs exists, common elements can be noted in effective, high-quality programs.

54. **Developing Socially Valued Behavior in Young Children,** Esther D. Callard, *Education Digest,* May 1979. 217
The author proposes three child-rearing conditions for developing pro-social experiences in growing children: gratification in the early years, modeling and reinforcement of prosocial behaviors and developing a sense of the child's worth.

55. **10 Teaching Aids for Reading,** Roach Van Allen, *Early Years,* November 1979. 219
Ways to improve the reading attitudes and skills of children that focus on the reader, not the reading program are presented. The emphasis on reading as a symbolizing set is the Language Experience Approach to reading instruction, which requires changes in teacher attitudes and strategies.

56. **Language Development: It's Much More Than a Kit,** Patricia L. Hutinger, *Day Care and Early Education,* Spring 1978. 223
The language development of the infant and young child progresses from one word sentences (holophrases) to the use of irregular nouns (mouses and ghostes), and compound, complex sentences. Sensitive and knowledgeable teachers can use many tested strategies to provide an array of curriculum opportunities to enhance both the quantity and quality of children's language utterances.

57. **Piaget, The Six Year Old and Modern Math,** Ethel O'Hara, *Today's Education,* September/October 1975. 226
According to Piaget, children's thinking is qualitatively different from adults who write textbooks intended for instruction. Analyzing children's errors shows that children's logic leads them to different conclusions about arithmethic problems than the adult authors intend.

58. **What Your Child's Art Is Telling You,** Stewart Alter, *Parents,* December 1979. 230
Children's art offers clues to their progressions through stages of perceptual and intellectual development. The caution is made that generalizations about a child's personality cannot, however, be based on only a few pictures.

8

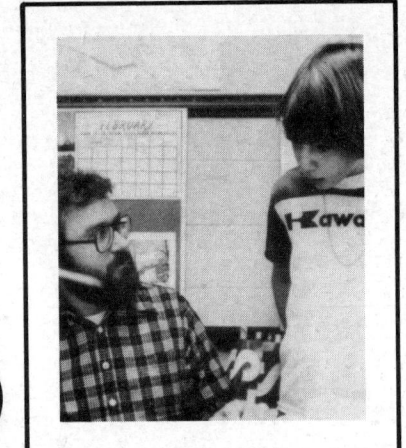

Teaching and Evaluation

59. **America's Head Start Program: An Agenda for Its Second Decade,** Edward F. Zigler, *Young Children,* July 1978. 233
A former Director of the Office of Child Development examines the often conflicting research on Head Start and concludes the programs have had important, lasting effects, not only for children, but for parents and school programming. Recommendations are made regarding Head Start's future directions, offensive posturing, comprehensiveness of program offering, and political agenda.

Overview 241
60. **The Satisfactions,** James L. Hymes, Jr., from *National Association for the Education of Young Children.* 242
The field of early childhood education offers many satisfactions. The author outlines four of them.
61. **The Meaning of Teaching,** Leland Jacobs, *Childhood Education,* April/May 1978. 244
A children's author captures the quintessence of three kinds of teachers: the schoolkeepers, the instructors, and the composers. Transactions, engagements, and the art of "growing together" with children is articulated.
62. **Teacher's First Words,** Mary K. Weir and Patricia J. Eggelston, *Day Care and Early Education,* November/December 1975. 249
Talking to children is not as easy as it seems. This article is a guide for teachers and caregivers who must learn to talk with children.
63. **Teachers, Be(a)ware of Sex-Stereotyping,** Barbara Simmons, *Growing Free: International Association for Childhood Education,* February 1976. 253
Concrete suggestions are presented to implement a non-sexist curriculum at the early childhood level. Changing of stereotypes held by teachers is a first step.
64. **Evaluating Settings for Learning,** Thelma Harms, *Young Children,* May 1970. 256
According to the author, adults should look at child care environments from the child's viewpoint. She includes some important environmental components in her discussion.
65. **The Persistence of Preschool Effects: A National Collaborative Study,** Shirley Moore, *Young Children,* March 1978. 258
A long-term follow-up of fourteen infant and preschool experimental curriculum models indicates that there have been positive effects on "the general intellectual function of children at post-test time and for one, two, and possibly three years" subsequent to intervention. Both children and parents in the experimental groups report positive experiences and effects from the varied programs.
66. **The Abt Report of Follow Through: Critique and Comment,** Shirley Moore, *Young Children,* September 1978. 264
Evaluation data of the national Follow Through program suggest that curriculum models vary greatly from place to place and from teacher to teacher, and program outcomes are related to program goals, objectives, and strategies. Despite methodological limitations of the study, the data raise serious research and philosophical questions about educational intervention and experimentation.
67. **The Diagnostic Teacher,** Barbara Somach, *Early Years,* February 1978. 269
The author poses old and new definitions and functions of tests and measurements of children and their educational progress. Depending upon the information and behavior to be tested, observation is considered a highly useful testing technique.
68. **The Role of Testing in the Educational Process,** Lois E. Burrill, *Early Years,* Februry 1978. 272
The diagnostic teacher, as explained in this article, is an informed "child-watcher" who systematically observes youngsters in a variety of school situations. Hypotheses are then made about the most useful instructional strategies to help each child learn different concepts and skills.

Who's Writing and Written About 274

Index 275

Article Rating Form 277

TOPIC GUIDE

This topic guide can be used to correlate each of the readings in *Early Childhood Education 80/81* with one or more of the topics usually covered in early childhood education books. Each article corresponds to a given topic area according to whether it deals with the subject in a primary or secondary fashion. These correlations are intended for use as a general study guide and do not necessarily define the total coverage of any given article.

TOPIC AREA	TREATED AS A PRIMARY ISSUE IN:	TREATED AS A SECONDARY ISSUE IN:	TOPIC AREA	TREATED AS A PRIMARY ISSUE IN:	TREATED AS A SECONDARY ISSUE IN:
Achievement Motivation	5. How Early Should They Go to School? 26. Misunderstandings About How Children Learn 38. Crisis in the Classroom	44. The Young Gifted Child 45. Let's Go Slow on Acceleration	Day Care	8. Making the Day Care Decision 9. Day Care Policy 10. Infant Day Care 24. Ecology of Infant Day Care	47. How to Discipline with Love
Accountability	9. Day Care Policy 52. Humanizing the Curriculum 67. The Diagnostic Teacher 68. The Role of Testing in the Educational Process	1. How Could Early Childhood Education Affect Families? 4. What Is Early Childhood Education? 66. The Abt Report of Follow Through	Discipline and Guidance		
Basics of Education	2. What Is Basic for Young Children? 3. What's Basic About the Curriculum? 4. What Is Early Childhood Education? 6. Early Childhood Education	7. Four Who Cared 52. Humanizing the Curriculum 54. Developing Socially Valued Behavior in Young Children	Emotional Development	30. Aggression and Hostility in Young Children 47. How to Discipline with Love 49. How to Understand Your Child's Distress Signals 50. Classroom Discipline Problems? 51. Behavioral Blockbusters	37. When Mommy Goes to Work 47. How to Discipline with Love 50. Classroom Discipline Problems? 51. Behavioral Blockbusters
Bilingual Education	53. Bilingual/Bicultural Programs for Preschool Children	25. Piaget's Theory of Child Development and Its Implications 42. The LD Syndrome 44. The Young Gifted Child		5. How Early Should They Go to School 18. Signals of Child Abuse 30. Aggression and Hostility in Young Children 33. Play Isn't Just Kid Stuff 38. Crisis in the Classroom 39. Black Child/White Child 48. Anxiety and the 3- to 5-Year Old 49. How to Understand Your Child's Distress Signals	
Biological/Genetic Factors	19. A Perfect Baby 20. Growth: 45 Crucial Months 27. The Truth About Sex Differences 32. The Individuality Factor		Gifted	44. The Young Gifted Child 45. Let's Go Slow on Acceleration	
Brain Research	27. The Truth About Sex Differences		Government Policy	9. Day Care Policy 14. An Educational Forecast for the 1980s 15. Proposition 13 and Early Childhood Education	
Child Neglect and Abuse	16. Raising Children to Make a Less Violent World 18. Signals of Child Abuse		Head Start	59. America's Head Start Program	
Cognition (Cognitive Development)	21. Your Child's Mind 22. The Baby's Elastic Mind 25. Piaget's Theory of Child Development and Its Implications 26. Misunderstandings About How Children Learn 31. Mother-Child Interactions 65. The Persistence of Preschool Effects 66. The Abt Report of Follow Through	8. Making the Day Care Decision 23. The Care of Infants and Toddlers in Group Settings 58. What Your Child's Art Is Telling You	Imagination	28. Sex Roles in the Nursery 33. Play Isn't Just Kid Stuff 58. What Your Child's Art Is Telling You	
			Infancy	21. Your Child's Mind 22. The Baby's Elastic Mind	44. The Young Gifted Child
			Infant Programs	10. Infant Day Care 23. The Care of Infants and Toddlers in Group Settings 24. Ecology of Infant Day Care	25. Piaget's Theory of Child Development and Its Implications 47. How to Discipline with Love
Cultural Diversity	39. Black Child/White Child 53. Bilingual/Bicultural Programs for Preschool Children	4. What Is Early Childhood Education?	International Programs	5. How Early Should They Go to School? 34. Worlds of Play	31. Mother-Child Interactions 47. How to Discipline with Love
Curiosity and Creativity	33. Play Isn't Just Kid Stuff 58. What Your Child's Art Is Telling You	24. Ecology of Infant Day Care 55. 10 Teaching Aids	Intervention: Models and Effects	4. What Is Early Childhood Education? 5. How Early Should They Go to School?	54. Developing Socially Valued Behavior in Young Children 21. Your Child's Mind 22. The Baby's Elastic Mind 52. Humanizing the Curriculum

TOPIC AREA	TREATED AS A PRIMARY ISSUE IN:	TREATED AS A SECONDARY ISSUE IN:	TOPIC AREA	TREATED AS A PRIMARY ISSUE IN:	TREATED AS A SECONDARY ISSUE IN:
Intervention: Models and Effects	6. Early Childhood Education 23. The Care of Infant and Toddlers in Group Settings 24. Ecology of Infant Day Care 59. America's Head Start Program 65. The Persistence of Preschool Effects 66. The Abt Report of Follow Through		Sex Differences	27. The Truth About Sex Differences	38. Crisis in the Classroom
			Sexism	63. Teachers, Be(a)ware of Sex-Stereotyping	
Learning Disabled	42. The LD Syndrome 43. "Learning Disabled" or "Slow Learner"	27. The Truth About Sex Differences 68. The Role of Testing in the Educational Process	Sex Role Identity	27. The Truth About Sex Differences 28. Sex Roles in the Nursery	3. What's Basic About the Curriculum? 34. Worlds of Play 38. Crisis in the Classroom 44. The Young Gifted Child
Mainstreaming	46. Mainstreaming		Socialization	5. How Early Should They Go to School? 16. Raising Children to Make a Less Violent World 29. When Kids Explore Sex 31. Mother-Child Interactions 54. Developing Socially Valued Behavior in Young Children	
Parent-Child Influences	21. Your Child's Mind 22. The Baby's Elastic Mind 23. Mother-Child Interactions 36. The Consequences of Early Childbearing 37. When Mommy Goes to Work 38. Crisis in the Classroom 39. Black Child/White Child 41. The Myth of the Vulnerable Child		Teaching: Home Programs	5. How Early Should They Go to School? 33. Play Isn't Just Kid Stuff 40. How Can I Help My Children Do Better in School?	15. Proposition 13 and Early Childhood Education 21. Your Child's Mind 54. Developing Socially Valued Behavior in Young Children 65. The Persistence of Preschool Effects
Parent Education	8. Making the Day Care Decision 21. Your Child's Mind 24. Ecology of Infant Day Care 33. Play Isn't Just Kid Stuff 35. Whatever Happened to the Waltons? 38. Crisis in the Classroom	1. How Could Early Childhood Education Affect Families? 36. The Consequences of Early Childbearing	Teaching: Professional	7. Four Who Cared 56. Language Development 60. The Satisfactions 61. The Meaning of Teaching 62. Teacher's First Words 67. The Diagnostic Teacher	4. What Is Early Childhood Education? 42. The LD Syndrome 44. The Young Gifted Child
Physical Health	5. How Early Should They Go to School? 18. Signals of Child Abuse 19. A Perfect Baby 20. Growth: 45 Crucial Months	8. Making the Day Care Decision	Television	17. Schools vs. Television	
			Testing Children	42. The LD Syndrome 57. Piaget, the Six Year Old, and Modern Math 67. The Diagnostic Teacher 68. The Role of Testing in the Educational Process	31. Mother-Child Interactions
Play	33. Play Isn't Just Kid Stuff 34. Worlds of Play	4. What Is Early Childhood Education? 26. Misunderstandings About How Children Learn	Toddler Programs	8. Making the Day Care Decision 23. The Care of Infants and Toddlers in Group Settings 24. Ecology of Infant Day Care	
Quality of Programs	1. How Could Early Childhood Education Affect Families? 2. What Is Basic for Young Children? 3. What's Basic About the Curriculum? 4. What Is Early Childhood Education? 10. Infant Day Care 23. The Care of Infants and Toddlers in Group Settings 52. Humanizing the Curriculum 64. Evaluating Settings for Learning	8. Making the Day Care Decision	Toddlers	21. Your Child's Mind 24. Ecology of Infant Day Care	20. Growth: 45 Crucial Months 47. How to Discipline with Love
			Values	16. Raising Children to Make a Less Violent World 54. Developing Socially Valued Behavior in Young Children	
Reading and Language Arts	55. 10 Teaching Aids for Reading 56. Language Development	5. How Early Should They Go to School? 26. Misunderstandings About How Children Learn 38. Crisis in the Classroom	Working Parents	35. Whatever Happened to the Waltons? 37. When Mommy Goes to Work 38. Crisis in the Classroom	15. Proposition 13 and Early Childhood Education 23. The Care of Infants and Toddlers in Group Settings 36. The Consequences of Early Childbearing

PREFACE

The year 1979 was designated as the International Year of the Child, the first global effort directed toward promotion of heightened consciousness of the special needs of children that would lead to the development of concerted action and needed programs to benefit children around the world.

Despite differing interpretations of the passing or lasting benefits of the IYC, the grassroots initiatives and responses served to focus on a multitude of concerns for children who will inhabit the twenty-first century.

For professionals in education, the decade of the 1980s represents a period of reflection and reformulation of the advances and regressions, the successes and failures of the last two decades of change and innovation. The phenomenon of over-expectancy and unkept promises for rapid results, has led to disillusionment for many, despair for a few, but, also, to renewed commitment for others.

The impact of the knowledge explosion on education has resulted in early intervention for the young handicapped child, the creation of coalitions and networks to disseminate information to a widening audience of consumers, and confusion and skepticism about the disparate advice and programs that are offered.

Contemporary educational philosophy, research, and practice are based on the findings of researchers and the experiences of practitioners from diverse, but interrelated disciplines. A survey of the backgrounds and professional training of the authors of the articles included in this fourth edition of *Early Childhood Education 80/81* reflects this panorama of fields and administrative structures. The positions taken represent those of anthropology, sociology, psychology, educational research, psychiatry, pediatrics, family life education, toy design and curriculum development.

The articles present a wide variety of points on the philosophical and educational continuum. They include the history and care of young children; terminology and classification; purposes and methods of programming; arguments for particular types of intervention models and research on their relative effects; questions of evaluation; the varied roles of teachers with children of differing ages, developmental levels, multiple degrees of health or handicaps; and changing types of family structures.

Since many issues and programs are controversial, articles representing opposing viewpoints are frequently offered. Some subjects could be identified as persistent and conventional (e.g., skill acquisition or "the whole child" concept), while others could be identified as emergent and fluid in nature (e.g., the role of teacher as parent educator, or infant and toddler programs). Thus, the reader can become familiar with the vitality, urgency, and dilemmas of the field.

Early Childhood Education 80/81 is organized by general topics and issues rather than by age, stage, or background of the children being considered. Within each section, development and education are discussed for children from infancy through age nine, which is an international definition of the scope of early childhood.

Your reactions and comments on this volume in the highly successful Annual Editions series are important and invited. With your help, we will be able to create subsequent editions which will continue to meet your personal and professional needs. Which articles were of particular interest to you? Which issues generated the most discussion or offered a different perspective? What recommendations do you have? Please fill out and return the article rating form on the last page of this book. Any anthology can be improved. This one will be—annually.

Judy Spitler McKee
Editor

Perspectives

Federal funds have been allocated for group programs for young children three times during periods of national crisis: the Depression, World War II, and the War on Poverty. The rapid expansion of programs for children under six years took place immediately after the establishment of Head Start in 1968, and many research and demonstration projects were implemented thereafter. The decade of the 1970s was a time of sobering reflection and examination of the vast amount of literature and curriculum models that had been amassed. There was a pulling back to identify what had been done, what the basic hypotheses were, and whether those organizing questions could have been subject to research or cultural biases, social class prejudices, or a feeling of "professional always knows best."

The realization dawned that the overwhelming magnitude of problems associated with poverty, emotional neglect, single parenthood, or handicaps, for instance, meant that complex, long-standing issues elude simple, short-term solutions.

The questions we ask, or fail to ask, partially determine the type of answers we can expect to find. Recurring questions are raised about what constitutes "quality," or "appropriate," or "basic educational opportunities" for young children. What is meant by "getting back to the basics"? Many traditionalists equate the basics with the 3Rs and strict teacher-dominated situations. Others argue confidence and positive motivation are basic. Still others state that food, protection, and inner security are the basic structures that precede and accompany school learning. Or, are provisions of the basics related to the type of population being served?

Questions about the what, where, when, who, how, and why of early childhood education continue to be asked, as they should be. The what refers to the question of content or subject matter. The where addresses the issue of whether educational programs should be located in special facilities, in public schools, or in private homes. The when refers to the appropriateness of timing of intervention in children's lives. The question of who has a triple focus. Who should care for and educate children: specially trained teachers, aides with high school degrees, or mothers? Who is the population to be served: all children, handicapped children, children of the poor, or neglected and abused children? Who should have decision-making powers in selecting staff, program planning, and evaluation: specialists, administrators, teachers, and/or parents? The how concerns the process of education; the instructional methods and teaching strategies used by adults with children of differing ages. The question of why is the most significant one, although too often ignored. Why should this set of opportunities be provided, for this child, at this time? Why should these objectives and methods and materials be used rather than others? Why should society care for and educate young children and work with their parents at all? Unless these fundamental, underlying questions are systematically addressed, the field of early childhood education may continue to be rampant with unnecessary conflict and arguments, thus neglecting the basic services it can provide for those who need or desire its programs and expertise.

This section offers selected responses to these questions and involves the reader in the debate surrounding the field—its historical legacy, its terminology and types of programs, its continuing struggles, successes, and promises.

Looking Ahead: Challenge Questions

When and where were the first educational programs for young children established in this country?

Are there basic differences between the provisions of early childhood education and early schooling of children?

When should intervention begin—before age three, by age five, or not until age eight?

What is basic for young children and basic in the curriculum?

Are children in day care programs less intelligent, prone to infection and disease, and less attached to their mothers than children who are at home?

What role should be taken by the federal government in providing day care programs for working parents?

What effect on children's needs do changing societal goals and personal life-styles have? Are today's parents child-centered in their outlook?

How Could Early Childhood Education Affect Families?

Marilyn M. Smith

Marilyn M. Smith, Ed.D., is Executive Director of the National Association for the Education of Young Children. She is a former nursery school teacher and college professor in early childhood development and education.

Much earlier in my professional career my statements were fraught with answers. But experience has taught me two important things. One, family and education issues are extremely complex, and I am no longer so sure about those definitive answers. Two, I have observed that people can be much more helpful by sharing with each other productive ways of thinking about an issue. Thus, this article will not attempt to offer specific answers to the question raised in the title; it will suggest different ways of thinking about families and their children.

I would like to begin by sharing a simple concept that I find extremely useful in my own thinking: The questions we ask are frequently much more important and deserve much more attention than the answers. If we are asking the wrong questions, what use is the answer?

A classic example of being misled by the wrong question is found during the initial years of Head Start when the continuation of funding for this innovative program was almost lost due to the question being asked. During those beginning years of Head Start, evaluators most frequently asked: "Will there be a significant increase in children's scores on standardized IQ tests?" We were in the midst of a comprehensive, new preschool initiative whose purposes included—

- enlarging a child's repertoire of knowledge;
- increasing self-confidence;
- promoting curiosity and initiative;
- improving verbal skills;
- providing nutrition;
- providing health/dental assessment and treatment; and
- involving parents in the education of their children.

Yet decisions regarding the continuation of the program were to be based on the answers to one question—answers concerned with the results of standardized IQ tests (which are highly suspect as meaningful measures of cognitive development in preschoolage children).

This example highlights the importance of giving increased attention to formulating relevant questions about young children and their families. Irrelevant questions can control and direct our inquiry in fruitless pursuits.

This manuscript is adapted from a presentation to the Symposium on the Family: Setting Priorities, Washington, D.C., May 19, 1978.

1. How Could Early Childhood Education Affect Families?

Are We Asking the Wrong Question?

I propose that the wrong question is being asked in the assigned title "How Could Early Childhood Education Affect Families?" This title suggests some assumptions that I consider questionable.

This society has a history of rationalizing children's programs and services by presenting them as essential to some group other than children.

What about Children?

We might be closer to a more productive question if we substituted the word *children* for the word *families*. "How could early childhood education affect *children*?" This society has a history of rationalizing children's programs and services by presenting them as essential to some group other than children. Significant government initiatives in children's programs have come in response to economic crisis rather than concern about improving the quality of life for children:

The 1930s—the Great Depression. Children's programs were initiated and funded to provide jobs.

The 1940s—World War II. Children's programs were funded to allow women to join the work force in the war factories.

The 1960s—the War on Poverty. Head Start was initiated as one of the many approaches to improve economic opportunities.

It is interesting to ponder why we as a society are still unwilling to state straightforwardly that the developmental needs and rights of young children are the reasons for providing early childhood programs and services.

What about Society?

Another concern I have about the question posed in the title is that in the process of focusing on the family as the major reason for providing educational services for young children, we will be perpetuating this society's inclination to expect families to carry the entire responsibility for child development/nurturance without assistance from the community and society.

Numerous factors far outside the control of families are having an increasingly powerful influence on the capability of families to parent constructively and competently. I would like to focus on one of the most powerful factors—economic security. Effective parenting requires money and time:

Money for the essentials of shelter, food, medical services, and education.

Time for the adult/child interactions necessary for social, emotional, language, intellectual, and physical development of infants, toddlers, and children.

Yet for American families in the 1970s, efforts to acquire the necessary money frequently result in less time with children.

For most American families the motivation to provide well for their children is not the major problem.

In a high percentage of families with children—

- both parents are working,
- parents are carrying more than one job, and
- there are increasingly more single parent families.

All of these realities contribute to less time for parenting.

For most American families the *motivation* to provide well for their children is not the major problem. Rather, the *capability to provide* may be the more productive issue to pursue. In order to do this I suggest we examine "How could early childhood education affect children?" thus assisting families in providing what they want for their children.

Early Childhood Education Defined

To pursue the question of how early childhood education could affect children, we need to establish a working definition for "early childhood education." This term has come to be used rather loosely to stand for any form of group care of young children, but early childhood *education* may or may not be occurring in group care programs.

1. PERSPECTIVES

The Purpose of Early Childhood Education

The aim of education is to facilitate development. The aim of early childhood education is to facilitate the development of young children. Note what the goal of education is not. The goal of education is not maturation. It is not the goal of early childhood education to teach growing tall. It is not the goal of early childhood education to teach conservation.

The goal of early childhood education is to facilitate—

- cognitive development,
- emotional development,
- social development, and
- motor development.

Early childhood educators acknowledge the important role of maturation in these forms of development, but accompanying this is a high degree of respect for the importance of the quality of the experiences available to children in their early years.

The Strategy of Early Childhood Education

Early childhood education, as one strategy for facilitating the development of young children, sets about to increase the availability of—

- developmentally appropriate activities,
- adult/child interactions, and
- child/child interactions,

which will facilitate rather than inhibit the fulfillment of each child's potentiality.

The Setting for Early Childhood Education

There are many settings in which developmentally appropriate experiences for young children could occur. The setting itself is not a predictor of the quality and appropriateness of the activities and interactions for any or all of the children experiencing them. It is possible for appropriate early childhood education experiences to occur in—

- nursery schools;
- the family with parents, relatives, and friends;
- group day care centers for infants, toddlers, and preschoolers;
- home-based day care;
- Head Start programs;
- parent/child centers;
- front of the television; and
- home visitor parent training programs.

Great numbers of America's children will not receive appropriate developmental opportunities during their early years unless there is assistance available to their parents to help them achieve such experiences for their children.

How Could Early Childhood Education Affect CHILDREN?

Having established the purpose, strategy, and setting of early childhood education, let's return to the question, "How could early childhood education affect children?" One way to think about this question is to examine the chances for any American child born in the late 1970s to experience developmentally appropriate activities and interactions with people.

Environmental Statistics for America's Children of the 1970s

In order to contemplate the chances for a child to obtain a good orientation and foundation for a lifetime of successful learnings, consider this list of some environmental statistics that impact on America's children of the seventies. Try to predict the potential for developmentally appropriate opportunities to occur under these circumstances.

1. Contemplate the chances of a child's mother being employed outside the home:
    - During a child's infancy and toddlerhood, the chance is one in three (Women's Bureau 1977).

1. How Could Early Childhood Education Affect Families?

- Between the ages of three and five, there is close to one chance in two (Women's Bureau 1977). During 1948, there was only one chance in eight.

- For the schoolage child, there is more than one chance in two that mother will be employed (Women's Bureau 1977).

2. What chance is there that a child will be born to a family living in poverty? One chance in six.

3. The possibility of a child spending part of his or her childhood in a one-parent family is two chances in five (Keniston 1977).

4. What chance is there that a child's mother will be in her adolescent years? One chance in five (Children's Bureau 1978).

5. Who could project the number of children living in families experiencing high degrees of stress—people troubled by economic, social, and emotional burdens?

6. What chance is there that a young child will not be immunized against early childhood diseases? Two out of every five children are not immunized, thus making them vulnerable to contracting a lifelong disability (*America's Children 1976*).

7. About twelve percent of America's children suffer from handicapping conditions, and there is a very low probability that a child's problem will be identified before entering public school (*The Role of the Family in Child Development* 1975).

It is difficult to contemplate these statistics and not conclude that great numbers of America's children will not receive appropriate developmental opportunities during their early years unless there is assistance available to their parents to help them achieve such experiences for their children.

How could society assist and support, yet not control, families as they attempt to provide developmentally appropriate experiences for their children?

Elements of Developmentally Appropriate Experiences for Young Children

Let's examine the kinds of responses, experiences, and interactions that every new human being requires to obtain a good orientation and foundation for a lifetime of successful learning. The key question throughout this description is: How could society assist and support, yet not control, families as they attempt to provide these experiences for their children?

Predictability and Responsiveness. During the early days and weeks of infants' lives, they need many chances to learn that in a number of ways their unknown world is a predictable place. These new human beings must learn that some consistent adult will respond to their signals of the need for food, warmth, turning, and dryness. Only then can newborns begin to establish a comfortable expectation of being able to control to a certain extent, as opposed to that stressful feeling of helplessness.

- The infant cries—hopefully, someone responds with food, comfort, or dry diaper.

- The child smiles—hopefully, someone smiles back.

- The baby coos—hopefully, someone coos back.

- The infant stretches for a toy out of reach—hopefully, someone brings it closer so it can be grasped.

If these "hopefullies" become "certainties," these tiny human beings will begin to develop a firm knowledge of some predictability and control which in turn encourages them to explore new situations and new people—an extremely important factor for future development.

Stimulation and Opportunities for Varied Experiences. All forms of development—cognitive, language, motor, etc.—are directly related to opportunities to practice, experience, and receive feedback.

Not long ago, I was browsing in a bookstore and became intrigued by a toddler who was moving books stacked on a low shelf from one pile to another. There was an extreme var-

1. PERSPECTIVES

iance in the size and weight of the books. At first the toddler used both hands to pick up each book. Then he began making judgments about when a book was light enough to carry with only one hand, thus being able to carry one in each hand. Then the toddler started to move a book that was the size and weight of a large encyclopedia. The book fell to the floor. He picked it up and continued to move other books. Later he came to another book the size of an encyclopedia and this time adjusted his body and exerted the necessary strength to move the book without it falling. Just imagine the inefficiency of trying to tell this child how to judge differences in weight and how to adjust his body and muscles to lift different weights and sizes. Look at the rapid, efficient learning that occurred when he simply had the opportunity to practice, experience, and receive feedback.

The point of this example is certainly not that every child needs to be taken to a bookstore to lift books, but that children cannot develop cognitive skills, concepts, and the ability to use symbols in a vacuum or a bland environment. Children need opportunities to *experience* a variety of materials, people, and places with adults or older children who can answer questions and stimulate further exploration. The young child who experiences a dull, repetitive environment, day after day, simply does not have the opportunity to exercise mind and body toward new skills and understandings. The young child who watches several hours of television every day is missing developmentally essential learning opportunities from interactions with peers, with materials, and with adults.

Just as the refrigerator light only functions when we open the door, we frequently act as though children's minds will stay turned off until we open the door with a planned intellectual experience.

The unknown factor is how many thousands of children are subjected to the crippling experience of bland, nonstimulating, nonresponsive environments. It cannot be predicted from obviously observable circumstances. Neither income level nor whether a child is in his or her own home or in out-of-home care predicts if a child is experiencing a rich, responsive environment.

Many believe that young children's major needs are for physical well-being and that intellectual development occurs only at those times when it has been planned for. Too often we view the minds of children like the light in our refrigerator. Just as the refrigerator light only functions when we open the door, we frequently act as though children's minds will stay turned off until we open the door with a planned intellectual experience. Children's minds, at least in the beginning, do not have an off and on button like the light in the refrigerator. Whatever children are experiencing, it influences the development of their foundation for intelligence, their attitudes, values, and aspirations.

Experiences with Symbolization. Competent use of symbol systems (language, gestures, numbers) forms the foundation for communication, logical thought, and manipulation of concepts. Children's development of symbol systems occurs by building bridges between direct experiences and verbal or nonverbal symbols for each experience. A crude form of symbolization at work is viewed when infants repeat the same sound to signal wanting mother or food, etc. However, in this example the infants have created their own symbol system and the adults do the translating. The challenge ahead for children is to decode the existing symbol systems of the world in which they live. Also, consider the many children who must face the challenge of learning to decode more than one language or dialect.

If anyone fails to appreciate the complexity and difficulties in gaining mastery of the world's symbol systems, just observe us as adult citizens of the United States currently trying to master the metric system. The symbol 98° Fahrenheit has real meaning to me—I can almost feel the meaning of that symbol. But 37° Celsius simply does not raise within me the same understanding. The difference, of course, is practice in attaching a specific symbol to an experience. Or recall traveling in a country where you did not know the language. Remember those feelings of uncertainty and vulnerability and empathize with the challenge that faces every infant and toddler. Appreciate the importance of assisting children

1. How Could Early Childhood Education Affect Families?

in building essential bridges between experiences and symbols. The most natural way for this to occur is for adults to provide labels when the child is experiencing something.

- The child is climbing up and down stairs, and the adult talks about up and down.
- The child is playing with the water faucet in the bathtub, and the adult provides the symbols of hot and cold at the appropriate time.
- The child is tasting different foods, and the adult labels the sweet and sour.

The key question, of course, is how much assistance will each child have in mastering this skill of building bridges between experience and symbols? Children cannot master this skill without interaction with others.

The list of experiences that are essential to development could go on and on. While these are intended as samples rather than a comprehensive listing, two other experiences children need during their formative years must be briefly mentioned.

Guidance Toward Impulse Control. There is an extremely important balance between protecting oneself and asserting autonomy, and adapting to requirements for social functioning. Perhaps this is best stated as developing respect for self which assists greatly in learning respect for others and leads to one more of the most important experiences children need from their world.

Being Valued. Good, assured feelings about self are essential to being able to immerse all of one's attention and ability into successfully mastering the abilities discussed above.

What chance is there of a significant attitude change in our society to "think children"?

How Can Children Be Assured of Developmentally Appropriate Experiences?

This is another question for which there is no answer, but I do have four suggestions to guide our thinking.

Think Children

Let's not lose, if we ever had it, the ability to put ourselves in the shoes of children and consider how it would feel to be denied the basic opportunities essential for developing our fullest potential. Isn't this a basic right of every human being? A fair shake at exercising our potential toward developing competence.

What chance is there of a significant attitude change in our society to "think children"? After all, children are no longer an economic asset providing an extra set of hands to help support the family. In fact, each child is an added economic burden. And what chance is there for a "think children" movement when children do not vote and do not have money to contribute to campaigns and causes?

This society has recently experienced a significant change in attitude resulting from the environmental protection movement. Fifteen years ago how many people were consciously aware of protecting the environment? But in just a few years, a sophisticated campaign implanted a few simple concepts in the minds of Americans. The environment cannot vote, the environment cannot speak for itself, but the environment requires nurturance if it is to serve us well in the future. If this society's consciousness was pricked to "think environmental protection," is there not even more chance that it can be pricked to "think children"? Why not a Children's Nurturance Movement, so there will be competent individuals left on earth to use this protected environment?

Think Prevention

We are a society that tends to think treatment rather than prevention—to think short-term rather than long-term. Brazelton's work with mothers and their newborn infants is a powerful example of how a small amount of preventive effort can make a great difference in the future. New mothers are helped to feel confidence and skill in observing and responding to their infants. Brazelton's work has documented significant differences in the absence of future problems of mothers and infants who experienced this preventive counseling as compared to mothers who were not in the program.

1. PERSPECTIVES

If our vision were long-term, we would immediately recognize the valid economic reasons for spending money on individuals during their early developmental years. There is really no comparison between the money it would take to enhance opportunities during the early years of life for healthy development as opposed to the money society spends supporting the millions of adults in prison, in mental institutions, those who cannot work for various reasons, etc. Critics of increased federal investment in services for families and their children contend that this will lead to a welfare state. But increased support of such programs does not have to result in loss of individual incentive—not if continued funding of these programs is dependent on successfully accomplishing the goal: that the majority of individuals become adults who are prepared to carry their own survival, are prepared for competition, are prepared to define life according to their own goals and not be limited by drastic deficiencies.

Another example of our short-term vision is that in feeling that our only responsibility is for our own children, we fail to recognize that the quality of life they will experience as adults is highly dependent on the peers they will interact with in their world. The interdependence of individuals in this society is great.

Think Community

In America today there appears to be some confusion and uncertainty about making a strong commitment to children. The Coalition of Labor Union Women Child Care Seminar compared child care services in three other countries with those in the United States (Jordan 1977). It concluded that in Israel, Sweden, and France "the national community assumed as much responsibility for the child's success as did the family. This was in marked contrast to the dominant view in the United States that the nation is a collection of individuals each of whom bears the major responsibility for his or her offspring and that furthermore the community must only intervene after a crisis develops" (Jordan 1977).

The American family is shouldering a terrific responsibility. At the same time many members of the community are searching for relevance in their lives, particularly the young and the elderly. Herein lies a wealth of resources to add to the cadre of early childhood professionals to assist in the provision of nurturance, stimulation, and care for America's young children.

Think Quality

No setting, including the family, assures children of the opportunities needed to facilitate rather than inhibit the fulfillment of their potential. The determining factor is the quality of the activities, the quality of adult/child interactions, the quality of child/child interactions. For those of us involved in the provision of developmental experiences for young children, herein lies our biggest challenge: to endeavor to achieve training, standards, ethics, and funds that will enable us to assure each child quality developmental experiences.

Conclusion

I would like to reemphasize the challenges that face us. The challenge to formulate questions that will lead us closer to finding ways to assure children of their birthright—their right to opportunities that will facilitate the development of their potential. The challenge to establish effective collaboration of the resources of families, communities, and the helping professions to better serve America's children.

Leon Chestang has eloquently addressed these issues:

> And so I ask, who, if not us will
> nurture our children?
> Who, if not us will protect them?
> Who, if not us will assume
> responsibility for them?
> And who, if not us will assure them
> of their birthright?
> Who?   (Chestang 1974)

References

Advisory Committee on Child Development Assembly of Behavioral and Social Sciences National Research Council. *Toward a National Policy for Children and Families.* Washington, D.C.: National Academy of Sciences, 1976.

America's Children 1976: A Bicentennial Assessment. Washington, D.C.: National Council of

1. How Could Early Childhood Education Affect Families?

Organizations for Children and Youth, 1976.

Biber, B. "A View of Preschool Education." In *Education Before Five*, edited by B. D. Boegehold, H. K. Cuffaro, W. H. Hooks, and G. J. Klopf. New York: Bank Street College of Education, 1977.

Biber, B.; Shapiro, E.; Wickens, D.; and Gilkeson, E. *Promoting Cognitive Growth: A Developmental-Interaction Point of View.* Washington, D.C.: National Association for the Education of Young Children, 1971.

Chestang, L. "The Black Child and the Welfare System." Paper presented to the Indianapolis Black Child Advocacy Adoption Conference, Indianapolis, Ind., February 1974.

Children's Bureau. "New Programs Planned to Meet Problems of Teenage Pregnancy." *Re: Children.* Washington, D.C.: Administration for Children, Youth, and Families, HEW, January-February 1978. DHEW Publication No. (OHDS) 78-30109.

Clarke-Stewart, K. A. "Developing the Mind of the Child." *Today's Family in Focus.* Chicago: National Congress of Parents and Teachers, 1978.

Hilliard, A. G., III. "Adapting Assessment Procedures: The Black Child." Urbana, Ill.: ERIC Clearinghouse on Early Childhood Education, 1978. ED 145 958.

Hilliard, A. G., III. "How *Should* We Assess Children's Social Competence?" *Young Children* 33, no. 5 (July 1978): 12-13.

Jordan, R. "A Commitment to Children." Report of the Coalition of Labor Union Women Child Care Seminar. Coalition of Labor Union Women, 15 Union Square, New York, NY 10003. 1977.

Keniston, K., and The Carnegie Council on Children. *All Our Children: The American Family under Pressure.* New York: Harcourt Brace Jovanovich, 1977.

The Role of the Family in Child Development: Implications for State Policies and Programs. Early Childhood Project Report No. 15, Education Commission of the States Report No. 57. Denver, Colo.: Education Commission of the States, 1975.

Shapiro, E. "Evaluation of Preschool Programs: A Brief Overview." In *Education Before Five*, edited by B. D. Boegehold, H. K. Cuffaro, W. H. Hooks, and G. J. Klopf. New York: Bank Street College of Education, 1977.

Women's Bureau. "Number of Mothers in the Labor Force Continues to Rise." *Working Mothers and Their Children.* Washington, D.C.: U.S. Department of Labor, 1977.

Zimiles, H. "Early Childhood Education: A Selective Overview of Current Issues and Trends." *Teachers College Record* 79, no. 3 (February 1978): 509-527.

What Is Basic for Young Children?

Lilian G. Katz

Lilian G. Katz is Professor of Early Childhood Education and Director of the ERIC/ECE Clearinghouse (Educational Resources Information Center for Early Childhood Education) at the University of Illinois, Urbana-Champaign.

ALL OF US who teach young children often express disappointment over not having had time to do all we had planned to in any given week, or month, or year. We cannot introduce all the topics of potential interest, all the activities that might stimulate learning, all the materials that might help develop skills. Teaching always involves choices. From among the virtually infinite variety of possible topics, ideas, skills and activities, we can only address a few.

On what bases are our choices made? Probably *tradition* accounts for a large proportion of our selections: traditional topics, materials, holidays, games and activities. To some extent the *availability of resources* determines what activities we select. Often choices are made for us by school district mandates or by central office officials, state or federal funding agencies, or boards of directors of day care centers.

Busy teachers have all too little time to reexamine the bases upon which they select the components of their programs. Most of us do well to cope with the day-to-day demands of our roles. Recently I had an experience with a group of students that caused me to step back and reflect on the underlying assumptions upon which early childhood programing might be based. I hope these reflections will help your own thinking as you look for the bases on which you make the choices in your program.

The occasion that stimulated my thinking was a seminar with a group of young, zealous students who were discussing their reactions and impressions from working in day care centers. One young woman, Susan, spoke of her experience in deeply disappointed tones. Among the complaints against the program she listed was that the director refused to let the children have small animals in the day care center. I listened appreciatively for a while to Susan's righteous indignation, and then asked her as gently as I could: "Let's speculate! What do you think are the chances that a child could develop into a wholesome adult without having had animals to play with in the day care center?"

After a few moments' thought, Susan indicated that the chances were fairly good. "What about finger paint? Block play? Can a child grow into normal adulthood without them in the day care center?" I asked. A lively discussion followed these questions, leading all of us to search for answers to the question, "What does each child have to have for wholesome development?" I want here to share with you my own answers to this question by offering seven interrelated propositions. I hope these propositions will be helpful to you as you consider how you might have responded.

The seven propositions below are built upon an assumed first principle I have dis-

---

This paper is an adaptation of Dr. Katz's keynote address to the Fourteenth National Congress, Australian Preschool Association, held at the University of Melbourne May 15-21, 1976. (Proceedings were published by the Association in a publication, *The Young Child in Focus*, edited by Forbes Miller.) Reprinted with permission.

cussed elsewhere (Katz, 1975); namely, that whatever is good for children is only good for them in the "right" or optimum proportions. Another way of stating this principle is that just because something is good for children, more of it is not necessarily better for them. This applies to so many influences on children's development that it could be called the "Law of Optimum Effects." Among the many examples of influences that should be experienced in optimum amounts are: attention, affection, stimulation, independence, novelty, choices of activities, etc. All of the latter can be thought to be "good" for children, but only in optimum amounts, frequencies or intensities.

Taking the first principle of optimum effects as fundamental, we can return to the question of what children have to have for wholesome development.

Proposition One: *The young child has to have a deep sense of safety.*

I am referring here to psychological safety, which we usually speak of as a sense of "security." Over the last twenty years or so the term "security" has come to be used as a cliché. By psychological safety I refer to the subjective feeling of being connected and attached to one or more others. Experiencing oneself as attached, connected—or safe—comes not just from being loved, but from *feeling* loved, *feeling* wanted, *feeling* significant, etc., to an optimum (not maximum) degree. Note that the emphasis here is more on *feeling* loved and wanted than on *being* loved and wanted.

As I understand early development, feeling strongly bonded or attached comes not just from the warmth and kindness of caretakers. The feelings are a consequence of the child perceiving that what he (or she) does, or does not do, *really matters* to others—matters so much that they will pick him up, comfort him, get angry and even scold him. (After all, we do not become angry with someone we are indifferent to.) Safety, then, grows out of being able to trust people to respond not just warmly but *really*.

This proposition seems to apply to all children, whether they are wealthy or poor, at home or at school; whether they are handicapped or normal, at whatever their ages, until perhaps young adulthood.

2. What Is Basic for Young Children?

Proposition Two: *Every child has to have adequate—not excessive—self-esteem.*

At first glance this proposition seems to be quite simple. But a few comments are in order. It is useful to remember that one does not acquire self-esteem at a certain moment in childhood and then have it forever. Self-esteem is nurtured by and responsive to the significant others—adults, siblings and other children—throughout the growing years.

Even more important to keep in mind is that one cannot have self-esteem in a vacuum. Our self-esteem results from evaluations of ourselves against criteria. We evaluate ourselves as having high or low esteem against criteria we acquire very early in life. We acquire them in our families, neighborhoods, ethnic groups and later on from peer groups and the larger community. Early in life these criteria against which we come to evaluate ourselves as acceptable, worthwhile—against which we judge or experience ourselves as lovable—vary from family to family. In some families beauty is a criterion; in others, neatness, or athletic ability, or toughness is a criterion. Consider that such characteristics as being dainty, or quiet, or talkative, or pious, or well-mannered, or academically precocious, etc., might constitute the criteria against which young children are judged lovable, worthy and acceptable.

Each family has of course the right, if not the duty, to establish what it considers to be the criteria against which esteem is accorded. The process and the patterns by which such criteria are implemented are most likely unself-conscious in formulation as well as expression. One of our responsibilities as educators is to be sensitive to the family's *own* criteria. We may not agree with a family's definition of the "good boy" or the "good girl." But we would be very unwise to downgrade, undermine, or in other ways violate the self-esteem values the children bring with them, even though we must help children acquire criteria that serve to protect the welfare of the whole group in our care. I cannot think of any way it could help a child to have his respect for his family and his family's criteria of the "good person" undermined.

I suggest that children have to have optimum self-esteem wherever they are, whether they are wealthy or poor, handicapped or normal, throughout their growing years.

1. PERSPECTIVES

Proposition Three: *Every child has to feel, or experience his/her life as worth living, reasonably satisfying, interesting and authentic.*

I have in mind here the potential hazard inherent in modern industrialized societies of creating environments and experiences for young children that are superficial, phony, shallow and trivial.

This proposition suggests that we involve children in activities, and interactions about activities, that are real to them, significant and intriguing to them. It suggests also that we resist the temptation to settle just for what amuses them. I would suggest as a criterion of appropriateness for children's activities that they give children opportunities to operate on their own experiences, to reconstruct their own environments and give us opportunities to help children to learn what meanings to assign to their experiences.

As I visit early childhood programs in both developed and developing countries, I wonder whether people have taken our longstanding emphasis on warmth and kindness, acceptance and love to mean: "Let's be nice to children!" As I watch adults being "nice" and "kind" and "gentle," I often speculate as to whether if I were a child in such a pleasant environment I would look at the adults and say to myself—everybody is kind and sweet, but inside them is there anybody home (Katz, 1977)?

It seems to me that children should be able to feel that their lives are real, authentic, worth living and satisfying whether they are at home, in schools or day care centers throughout their growing years.

Proposition Four: *Young children need adults or older children who help them to make sense of their own experiences.*

By the time we meet the young children in our care, they have already acquired some understandings or constructions of their experiences. Their understandings or constructions may be incorrect or inaccurate although developmentally appropriate. As I see it, our major responsibility is to help the young to improve, extend, refine, develop and deepen their own understandings or constructions of their own worlds. As they grow older and reach primary school age, we may help them with their understandings of other people's worlds. Indeed, increasing refinement and deepening of understandings is a lifelong process.

What do young children need or want to make sense of? Certainly people, what they do, what they will do next, how they feel; how things around them are made and how they work; how they themselves and other living things grow; where people and things come from. The list is endless.

If we are to help young children to improve and develop their understandings of their experiences, we must *uncover* what those understandings are. The uncovering that we do, or that occurs as children engage in the activities we provide, helps us to make good decisions about what to *cover*, or what subsequent activities to plan.

Youngsters need help in making sense of their experiences wherever they are: at home or in programs, whatever their backgrounds, throughout their growing years.

Proposition Five: *Young children have to have adults who accept the authority that is theirs by virtue of their greater experience, knowledge and wisdom.*

This proposition is based on the assumption that neither as parents nor as educators are we caught between the extremes of authoritarianism or permissiveness. Authoritarianism may be defined as the exercise of power without warmth, encouragement or explanation. Permissiveness may be seen as the abdication of power but offers children warmth, encouragement and support as they seem to need it. I am suggesting that young children have to have, instead of these extremes, adults who are *authoritative;* i.e., adults who exercise their very considerable power over the lives of young children *with* warmth, support, encouragement and adequate explanations. The concept of authoritativeness also includes treating children with respect; i.e., treating their opinions, feelings, wishes and ideas, etc., as valid even when we disagree with them. To respect people we agree with is no great problem; respecting those whose ideas, wishes and feelings are different from ours may be a mark of wisdom in parents and genuine professionalism in teachers.

The combination of the exercise of optimum power and optimum warmth implied in authoritativeness is helpful for children wherever they are, whatever their background, throughout their youth.

2. What Is Basic for Young Children?

Proposition Six: *Young children need optimum association with adults and older children who exemplify the personal qualities we want them to acquire.*

Make your own list of the qualities you want the young children in your care to acquire. There may be some differences among us. But it is likely that there are some qualities we all want all children to have; e.g., the capacity to care for and about others, honesty, kindness, acceptance of those who are different from themselves, the love of learning, and so forth.

This proposition suggests that we look around the children's environments and ask to what extent do our children have contact with people who exhibit these qualities? We might ask also: To what extent do our children observe people who are attractive and glamorous counter-examples of the qualities we want to foster? It seems to me that children need communities or societies that take the necessary steps to protect them from excessive exposure to violence and crime while their characters are still in formation.

The role and significance of adequate adult models seems valid for all children wherever they are, wherever they come from, throughout their developing years.

Proposition Seven: *Children need relationships or experiences with adults who are willing to take a stand on what is worth doing, worth having, worth knowing, and worth caring about.*

This proposition seems to belabor the obvious. But in an age of increasing emphasis on pluralism, multi-culturalism, and community participation, professionals are increasingly hesitant and apologetic about their own values. Such hesitancy in taking a stand on what is worthwhile causes us to give our children unclear signals about what is expected, and what is worth knowing and doing. When we do take a stand, we cannot guarantee that our children will accept or agree with our version of the good life. Nor do we imply that we reject others' versions of the good life. We must, in fact, cultivate our capacities to respect alternative definitions of the worthwhile life. But when we take a stand, with quiet courage and conviction, we help the young in that they can more easily see us as thinking and caring individuals who have enough self-respect to respect our own values as well as others'. Such thinking and caring adults seem to be important to children wherever they are, wherever they come from, throughout development.

In summary, all seven propositions hang together on the central question of our responsibilities for the quality of the daily lives of all of our children—wherever they spend those days, throughout the long years of growth and development.

References

Katz, Lilian G. "Psychological Development and Education in Early Childhood." In *Second Collection of Papers for Teachers*, L. G. Katz. Urbana, IL: ERIC Clearinghouse on Early Childhood Education, 1975.

———. "Teachers in Preschools: Problems and Prospects." *International Journal of Early Childhood* 9,1 (1977): 111-23.

What's Basic about the Curriculum?

ARTHUR W. FOSHAY

Arthur W. Foshay is Professor Emeritus, Teachers College, Columbia University, New York City. Condensed by permission of the National Council of Teachers of English from Language Arts, *LIV (September 1977), 616-24.*

THE "back to basics" movement has appeared and reappeared ever since the days of Progressive Education in the twenties and thirties. It is based on some reality and some misunderstanding. The reality is that a small number of students can go through 12 years of schooling and emerge functionally illiterate. The misunderstanding arises in large part from the widespread adoption of continuous promotion, in which the amount of repetition of grades was reduced and the proportion of students remaining in school until ages 16 and 18 was greatly increased. The misunderstanding could be removed easily enough if we would make passage from year to year in school, and the awarding of graduation certificates, contingent on achievement. But such measures would set us back to where we were in 1910, when the slower students were discouraged out of school. The minority who survived could read and write. They still can, and there are proportionately more of them.

What we still haven't faced successfully on a large scale is the fact that the bottom 20 percent of the population, expressed as poor achievers in school, deserve to be educated and require special treatment. They are far more expensive to educate than the more typical 80 percent of the population. Since this 20 percent tends to concentrate in the inner cities, the problem is vastly complicated by the subculture they create. We could put them out of school, and for some, this would hide the problem and part of the "back to basics" movement would also disappear.

Some of it would not, however. That part of the movement having its roots in the more affluent 80 percent of the population arises from a real difference in belief about what the schools are for. Let us consider what educationists have come to believe schools are for. The view offered here is widely shared among the professionals, and has a history at least as old as formal education. However, there is a contrasting tradition. Beginning with the Sophists, there has been a tradition that takes form to be the central meaning of academic pursuits. The formalist tradition, expressed during our time, takes spelling, handwriting, computation, and literacy to be a sufficient curriculum for the school. This view is expressed forcefully, just now, by Carl Bereiter, who reduces all formal learning to the acquisition of skills.

The first of these traditions we may call the academic. The second we may call the formalist. The academic has always sought chiefly to deal with meaning. The formalist has always sought to deal chiefly with correct expression.

Of course we want both, though not in their extreme forms. To deal with what is basic is to deal with what is at the base—the foundation under the structure. I shall deal with four aspects of this foundation, and argue that, if one is overlooked, the structure erected on such a base will be unsound. The four basics are: coping skills, character or social development, citizenship, and private realization.

The Four Basics

Coping Skills. One might say that all learning consists of the acquisition of skills. However, the coping skills I mean are those associated with the five fields of knowledge we deal with in schools: language, mathematics, science, the arts, and social studies. Unfortunately, we are so accustomed to these fields that we overlook their collective meaning. Taken as a whole, they portray to our students the array of skills and information required for them to cope with themselves and the world. Leave one field out, and the student is deprived of access to existence by just that much.

This failure to consider the meaning of the main offering underlies some confusion now appearing. There are two sources of this confusion: We confuse what is unique with what is of prior importance, and we confuse verbal behavior with all behavior. A child who does not learn the 3 Rs in school is unlikely to learn them anywhere else. This obvious fact has led many people to conclude that education in the 3 Rs is the sole, main, most important function of school. Such people consider the 3 Rs basic, which of course they are, and also sufficient, which of course they are not. The 3

3. What's Basic About the Curriculum?

Rs do not offer an adequate base for living a life. Nor are they the only unique offerings in school.

There are other basics, also uniquely offered in school. They are equally essential for coping. Here are several: the skills of social interaction—skills arising from the fact that schools offer a unique example of society to students; the skills of emotional growth; the skills of spiritual response. Leave out any of these skills and the ability of a person to cope with life is severely reduced. The coping skills embrace all the significant aspects of what it is to be a human being.

Yet skills, even viewed in this way, are not enough. To settle for skills alone would imply that education exists to make us all technicians. Learning to know *why* is, therefore, as basic to learning as learning to know *how*.

The difficulties with the present discussion of basics may now be summarized: (1) The "back to basics" movement takes a harmfully narrow view of what is basic. (2) The emphasis on skill development is reductionist. It inhibits the development of understanding—of "know-why."

Character. Equally basic in the public schools is the development of character. It is sometimes forgotten that the American public school has its origins in this objective. Character involves ethics—a knowledge and a disposition to act on a distinction between right and wrong. It involves self-direction, dependability, honest dealings, and a clear sense of justice.

Schools are social settings. If the school leaves social learnings to develop untended, children are left in charge of their own social learnings—and it is evident that children are poor teachers in this field. Children are not inherently sweet, or cooperative, or ethical. They have to be shown these qualities by precept, example, and practice. Our moral education is, in the main, negative. We are quick to forbid. We are vague and sparse in our directives about what to seek out, what to do. The children are just like us. No wonder they will say that one should not break the rules because one might be caught and punished.

Like it or not, character is a prominent result of schooling. I propose here that we resume our intentions of a century ago, and acknowledge character as one of the basics of education.

Citizenship. Citizenship is action based on a feeling of affiliation with the nation. World citizenship is based on feelings of brotherhood with the rest of humanity. Citizenship education is a process of imparting knowledge and offering direct practice in seeking such just relations at every level of social activity, to the end that students leaving high school will see their first vote as a climax of a long process of civic learning and civic action. It is of the essence of public education to develop effective citizenship. This has always been so.

To be a citizen is not only to know what the system is, but how it works. In 1950, a coal mine in Centralia, Illinois, exploded, killing more than 100 miners. Their deaths were attributable to ineffective education. They knew the mine was dangerous; they had sought help twice; but they didn't know what their next move should have been. Something basic had been left out of their education and they died of it.

Private Realization. A person is not only a public being, but also has a private, inward existence. Those who are wholly defined by the opinions of others are doomed to have no personal sense of worth. In the literal sense, they lack integrity. The idea that self-realization is basic to a liveable life is of this century. Coping skills, character, and citizenship are much older. Beginning about 80 years ago, it became apparent that people are not only social, but inward, and that private realization is basic to survival.

What is private realization? What do the schools have to do with it? By private realization, I mean to refer to that complex of understandings, attitudes, and perceptions that make up my assertion that I am. I am, apart from others and their beliefs about me. I know myself incompletely, but more fully than others know me.

Everyone who seeks to influence children has some impact on their eternal search for answers to "Who am I?" As things stand, children learn them, if they learn them at all, by accident. Since the school is such a powerful socializing influence, children are led by its neglect of self-realization to define themselves chiefly by their apparent reputations, and to diminish the importance of their inward knowledge of themselves.

We do many things to deny private meaning to people. Chief among these is our disposition to compare them, or to cause them to compete for the teacher's approval. Since the "back to basics" advocates usually want children to compete, perhaps we should consider the nature of competition in school. The dictionary says that to compete is to vie with others for a prize; someone wins it and someone else doesn't, because the prize is scarce. What is the "prize" in school? Learning, of course. But learning isn't scarce, and we say that schools exist to make learning universally available. What, then, is the prize we compete for? Something related to learning, but made artificially scarce—school grades, which are a symbol of the teacher's approval. We divert the attention of the children from learning to test-passing when we ask them to compete for grades.

The irony of this is that one of our purposes as teachers is that children shall come to love learning so that they will persist in it. When we ask them to compete for grades, we make it very unlikely that love of learning will result.

How did we get into this ridiculous situation? I think we got there because of a basic confusion of standards with social approval. The educational questions are: What are the standards children should seek to meet? Who sets them?

In a competitive school, the standards are set by the children, and thus cease being standards in any objective sense. They become mere norms—that which is typical for given groups.

Ideally, the teacher sets a stan-

1. PERSPECTIVES

dard for each child individually. This process has been approached two ways in recent years. First, there is the development of learning plans or modules to be put in the child's hands, which help self-direct the child toward the attainment of standards with a greatly reduced need for the teacher's help. Second, there is the recently developed Mastery Learning, which turns on the proposition that any normal person can learn anything, given an appropriate amount of time. This makes it necessary to allow students to go at different rates, even if through the same material. At the heart of the Mastery Learning strategy is the criterion—the standard.

The point about these two approaches is that the standard is inside the learner, and competition for grades is avoided. However, there is more to a person than intellectual faculties. There is also social, emotional, physical, esthetic, and spiritual development to be nurtured. Private realization requires that all these aspects of what it is to be a human being be attended to by all the persons and institutions that influence the child.

Here we are principally concerned with the school's part of the task. It is basic for the school to portray the whole of what it is to be human. If the school restricts itself to its intellectual functions, it misportrays the human condition. In its most extreme form, it portrays pedantry as life's ultimate goal.

A valid inward life—private realization—requires experience with many aspects of human behavior. We usually put the school subjects in an order of importance, with the 3 Rs at the top, followed by science, social studies, literature, the other arts, and hand skills and sports. To cut out any of these is to risk a malformed human being—a person who lacks a portion of what is basic to an education. When faced with a budget problem, reduce costs throughout the program and call on the community to contribute services. Don't, ever, fall into the mistaken notion that some school subjects are more "basic" than others. They are all basic.

What, then, is to be said of the "back to basics" movement? Despite the fact that it is narrowly conceived and ultimately destructive of what is actually basic, it is a response to a real problem.

The fact is that not enough students learn to read well, write well, and handle arithmetic well. The problem is not that "Johnny can't read." The problem is that there are pockets in the country where children consistently fall below their peers in other places. What follows is that we need to differentiate between the children in these pockets of ignorance and the other children.

The vision of a school we all share is of a place full of life, where people act with purpose on their own. The present "back to basics" movement in its narrow focus on a few of the coping skills, moves us away from such an ideal. What we need is a recognition of what is, in fact, basic to gaining an education and living a life.

What Is Early Childhood Education?

Some Definitions and Issues

Norma R. Law

Norma R. Law, formerly Professor of Education, University of British Columbia, served as ACEI Vice-President Representing Nursery Education (1966-68).

EARLY CHILDHOOD EDUCATION has become an umbrella term, used with varying intent by people concerned with the care and instruction of children from birth to eight years of age. It demonstrates different expectations for different age groups. Its administrative arrangements range from the simple to the highly complex. It reflects particular but quite different degrees of concern for resources, funding, hours, space, staff, curriculum, rules and regulations.

The upsurge of interest in young children that occurred in the 1960s has expanded dramatically. The number of children in day care and kindergartens has tripled. Research on early development has increased. The beginning years of life have pushed into government, technology and economics.

Meanwhile, roles and issues have become blurred. Staffing and community inequalities have become locked in controversy. The International Year of the Child dramatizes the need to ponder the meaning of the terminology of early childhood education and to take stock of current issues. What do children, parents, teachers and society itself think early childhood education is?

For Children

... early childhood education is *a place to play and to learn*. It has been organized by caring adults to provide materials and guidance within a safe and reliable environment. It may be located in a home, a church basement, a public school or a town hall. It may be for infants, toddlers, preschoolers, school-age children or a combination of these. Whatever the organizational circumstances of early childhood education, young children continue to work every minute at learning how to do things. It takes hours and hours of daily play to learn new words, experiment with interactions, test rules, practice skills and solve problems.

With remarkable tenacity and resilience, young children weather adult efforts to divert or demean the significance and vitality of their play. In urban and rural communities and in different cultures, they may perceive away-from-home play settings somewhat differently; but their yearnings have remarkable commonality. They want to be physically separate from home, yet remain emotionally attached. They reach for stimulation without giving up precious rights of choice and regression. They respond sensitively and sometimes painfully to changing atmospheres and strategies. They develop crucial mind-sets toward themselves as learners and contributors in the human community.

For Parents

... early childhood education is a *partnership in child-rearing*, help in providing daily care and stimulation, and perhaps some guidance and support for themselves in the increasingly complex tasks of parenting. Because a child may have one, two or several caregivers, many parents as well as infants may experience hurtful separations at times when being together is critical to the security of them all. The sacrifices and rewards of child-rearing are intermeshed tightly with early childhood education in all its settings and at all stages.

1. PERSPECTIVES

Parents look to school people to help them find simple yet effective ways to extend children's learnings. They turn to resources that are convenient and that respect their strengths as well as their limitations. They want to learn more about how young children grow and develop. However, they avoid being pushed into arrangements that diminish personal choice or involve territorial arguments.

The central bond of interest for parents and teachers is the child. When they understand and respect each other, the child stands to profit. When they consciously include him or her in the partnership, learnings are deepened.

For Teachers

... early childhood education is *a professional choice*. Men and women who work with young children are likely to tolerate ambiguity rather well. They are challenged by the continuity and speed of young development and by the unsteady acquisition of complex and interrelated skills. Teaching and learning in the early years are neither crisp nor orderly.

Adult job responsibilities do not fit into neat "position descriptions" either. Their diversity is reflected in the training and duties of teachers, assistants, administrators, auxiliary personnel, resource positions, consultants, government services and community workers. Because teaching and caregiving roles are so loosely defined, performance expectations often overlap or collide; and coordination on behalf of children and their families becomes a primary concern.

The availability of teachers to children and parents and colleagues in open settings inevitably increases public demands. It also diminishes personal privacy and authority. Members of the early childhood education team are likely to respond to these circumstances in quite different ways, depending on their several and varying preoccupations. Some are not only disciplined professionals but also mothers and fathers with families of their own. Others are missionaries intent upon saving the world. Still others are daily workers under contract. Yet all are members of the total enterprise. Trusting relations in the operation of a successful center are worth working for. When team members make sense to each other and hold each other accountable within the resources and limits of their community, the program functions effectively.

For Society

... early childhood education is *a cost*. Demands for child care are seen by some to be the result of social changes they don't like, the breakdown of the traditional family and an increasing number of latchkey children. Moreover, voters differ in their degree of willingness to accept responsibility for other people's children and future generations.

Society neglects young children at its peril. They are the heartbeat of every community. Their care and education are global investments as well as specifically local expenditures. Affluence and birth control have resulted in fewer and fewer children in the so-called developed countries of the world. This condition has been viewed with varying degrees of alarm, not all centered upon reverence for the child or celebration of the human potential.

Society, on behalf of young children and itself, needs early childhood education:

☐ to promote health, physical growth and motor development
☐ to increase independence in meeting and solving problems
☐ to strengthen emotional control
☐ to recognize reasonable limits and influence growth toward self-discipline
☐ to encourage self-liking and self-confidence and self-understanding
☐ to foster security with adults
☐ to stimulate liking for children of different ages and backgrounds
☐ to promote language skills
☐ to free self-expression in art, music and dance
☐ to broaden intellectual horizons
☐ to help children to observe, investigate, seek and secure information and to think critically.

Despite their differences in defining early childhood education, children and parents, teachers and society have few disagreements about these overarching goals, no matter how inarticulate they may be in expressing them. Contradictions do arise, however, about methods for achieving these goals. Deeply rooted values are likely to be challenged as they relate to daily routines, program planning, administrative decision-making or face-to-face transactions.

SOME CURRENT ISSUES IN EARLY CHILDHOOD EDUCATION

It would be strange indeed and unhealthy

4. What Is Early Childhood Education?

for early childhood education if complete conformity were obtained for rearing and educating the young. Of necessity the field is alive with critical issues. Only a few are touched upon here—"to stimulate thinking, rather than advocate fixed practice" in CHILDHOOD EDUCATION tradition. Several reflect the strengths as well as the shortages of the late 1970s. How they are resolved is bound to influence the work of all teaching adults in whatever setting they work with young children in the future.

Care and Education

Integral to deciding who cares for the young child, for how long and under what circumstances are such social realities as mother-child relations, the employment of women, the changing roles of fathers, the interventions of government and the separatenesses of families. Various types of service in child care and education are being sought in city, suburban and rural areas. For families with infants and toddlers as well as older children, some features of both home and group care are required, with highly flexible arrangements between them to match a range of developmental needs.

Many young parents are finding that both husband and wife have to, and indeed want to, take jobs away from home for all or part of the day, in order to pay for rising living costs. For some, the opportunity to have another mother with young children look after an additional child in her own home seems just right. For others, more formal group care for part or all of a day by a trained staff is desirable.

Whatever the setting, all parents and children are concerned with the quality of caregiving, the stimulation and experiences provided and the meshing of family and institutional values.

Care and education cannot be separated, any more than opportunity, encouragement and readiness can be separated from learning to walk. No home divides its time into custodial and instructional blocks. No school wedges itself into the 3 Rs without regard for the equally important Rs of respect, responsibility, relationships and relevance. No early childhood service is without educational consequences.

Government and Professional Controls

The role of government or professional organizations in setting standards and in certifying personnel has been hotly debated for decades. Care was welfare. Education was schooling. Gradually these identities have been merging.

Consistency in adult preparation, for instance, has become unlikely in view of the varying models for which staffs are being prepared and the wide range of differing responsibilities required of the early childhood education team. Other considerations are varying combinations of time and money and potentialities needed for reflective study, essential field work and interdisciplinary explorations.

The "match" of teacher-child style, background, personality, so earnestly wished for in many educational situations, is more likely of attainment here. Yet early childhood education programs often lose this advantage through inequalities of remuneration, through misunderstandings of the complexities and nature of certain teaching tasks and through bureaucratic requirements.

Socialization

Whether children are eight months or eight years old, being cared for in a private home or a public school, by their mother or a certified professional, the children's reach for other people is primary. Their total development and learning are intermeshed in their transactions with adults and other children. Social exchanges sharpen their knowing, expand their language and deepen their self-regard as well as their regard for others. To the alert adult, these exchanges carry messages of home and school values, of children's expectations in the educating situation and of society's restrictions on personal choices. When a five-year-old announces "in the 'big' school you whisper" or when the policeman on the beat remarks "Little kids belong at home with their mothers" or when the school principal complains "After-school programs sure mess up the schedules," readily apparent are the opposites that have to be reconciled for early childhood education in becoming a social force.

Cultural Pluralism

"Starting where the child is" requires that the teacher of young children fully respect their family membership and the cultural lifestyle in which they are being reared. Generalizations borrowed from sociological

1. PERSPECTIVES

research, sometimes helpful, can be dangerous if they harden stereotypes or assume problems where none exist. Each segment of the population has as wide a range of possibilities and problems as the subgroups or individuals within it. Sometimes parental troubles have deep psychological and political roots: teacher insights can halt premature judgments, and redirect energies to finding appropriate resources or providing wanted supports.

Earlier "melting pot" drives for conformity, even though frequently appreciative of cultural differences, crushed out much that was socially nourishing. Similarly, the preoccupations of the '60s with the deficits of poverty in early childhood, even though well-intentioned, disregarded many family identifications and positive inputs. Both viewpoints sought to guarantee too much for the future. The promise of early childhood education is for *now*—at two or four or seven. All children need a safe, carefully planned and flexible environment *now* in which to explore an expanding world of activities and materials, children and adults, feelings and ideas. Most of all they need a warm, enthusiastic, knowledgeable and caring teacher who respects and has sympathy for their cultural folkways, their home language and the family concerns they bring to the new learning situation.

Early Concept Development

Current investigations of early concept development have respected and used the contributions of many disciplines. They have given particular attention to the findings of Piaget based on observations of his own children.

Piaget has insisted that until age eight, young children need freedom and encouragement to explore and discover how they feel about the world and about other people gradually perceived as distinct from themselves. Fleeting and often casual sensory connections and cause-effect relationships come to be distinguished from their own wishes, fears and fantasies. Raw materials and social events have to be manipulated over and over again until modes of thinking and feeling become differentiated. Language and object exploration proceed simultaneously through play.

Yet neither leads automatically to conceptual understanding, which necessitates the insightful observation, talk, explanation and responsiveness of a thinking adult. Varying confrontations are needed with concrete examples to which the developing concepts apply. Such learnings are diverted when mindless pressures occur to get going and to achieve.

Learning Materials

The content of early childhood education does not lend itself to packages. Learning materials for young children should encourage them to touch, smell, taste, ask questions, laugh and share critical observations. And yet much of the market has been flooded with sensory toys, "discovery" kits and project workbooks, designed to program young children into single answers.

Under fire, several professional educators have undertaken the strenuous tasks of helping thoughtless and moneymaking adults see that a child needs work opportunities at his or her own level of interest and competence and understanding. In trying to articulate the use of concrete materials and everyday utensils to an interested public, early childhood people themselves have become more adept at scrounging and recycling discards and at substituting raw materials for inappropriate publications and packages. They have found also that with careful sorting and testing, many commercial products can be used imaginatively with individual children when purposefully introduced.

Evaluation

Early childhood education issues in evaluation invariably focus on goals that do not lend themselves to quantitative measurement, on criteria for development that are insufficiently specific and on the risks of subjectivity and poor documentation.

Kindergarten-primary school teachers are particularly vulnerable, tied in as they very often are with behavioral objectives and standardized tests designed for use with older children. The responsible teacher needs to know through what stages the children have come, where they find themselves at present and toward what developmental sequences they are moving. Careful and often bulky record-keeping is time-consuming but necessary, involving as it does samples of children's work, classroom and playground observations, notes of choices and activities,

4. What Is Early Childhood Education?

assessments of interests and performance and reports to parents.

Galloping inflation and diminishing births added to the above seven issues presently have governments and educators at a crossroads. The opportunities of having fewer children to care for and to educate are immense. More personal adult-child ratios become possible. Improved child health care and nutrition can be maintained. Social priorities can be rediscovered, gains consolidated and mistakes corrected. The efforts of parents and teachers, citizens and politicians, can be united in ways that really respect the strengths and needs of the children themselves.

On the other hand, retrenchment in early childhood education inevitably means the irreplaceable waste of human capital. Too many young children crowded into small quarters. Home and school adults concerned with their own needs for time and money first. Youngness bruised with boredom or overstimulation. If children are the future, their beginning years are precious to everyone. A rich society has vital opposites to reconcile in their care and education. Its basic convictions are on the line.

We want your advice.

Any anthology can be improved. This one will be—annually. But we need your help.

Annual Editions revisions depend on two major opinion sources: one is the academic advisers who work with us in scanning the thousands of articles published in the public press each year; the other is you—the person actually using the book.

Please help us and the users of the next edition by completing the prepaid article rating form on the last page of this book and returning it to us. Thank you.

Article 5

How Early Should They Go to School?

**RAYMOND S. MOORE AND
DENNIS R. MOORE**

Raymond S. Moore is president, Hewitt Research Center, California and Michigan, with headquarters at Berrien Springs, Michigan.

Dennis R. Moore is a graduate student at Andrews University and Research Associate at the Hewitt Research Center.

There is much talk these days, stimulated partly by accident and partly by design, that a young child cannot normally be fulfilled and optimally developed unless he goes to a good preschool. It is commonly inferred that a parent who does not give his child such an experience is depriving him. And in many cases of disability or handicap such an inference may be reasonable. Yet, for most children, correlated research findings overwhelmingly point in the opposite direction: For highest and best cognitive, affective and physiological development, we should do all we can to develop a wholesome home and keep him there—a place where the child can grow in an undisturbed environment, sharing the freedom and chores of the home with one or two adults (preferably his parents) in a warm, close, consistent and continuous relationship. These conclusions are reached on the bases of research and analyses by many of the world's foremost psychologists, psychiatrists and physiologists.

For more than 150 years increasing attention has been given to the development of the young child. Important advanced steps have been made in early childhood education, particularly in the last ten years. This attention and progress may be seen in important efforts by planners in California, New York, Washington, Maryland, Ohio, Michigan, Rhode Island, Tennessee, and in fact in nearly every state and the federal government. Furthermore, the American concern is being reflected around the world from Japan and Taiwan to Portugal and Germany, and from Australia and New Zealand to Britain and Canada. It is because this movement has developed into a massive trend toward earlier schooling that we reexamine its rationale.

Full documentation for the positions taken here may be found in the basic manuscript, "Early Schooling for All?" published in the CONGRESSIONAL RECORD, Vol. 118, No. 167, October 16, 1972, pages E8726-E8741; or it may be obtained from the ERIC-ECE Center, 805 West Pennsylvania Ave., Champaign, Ill. 61801.

Defining Terms

Early childhood education (ECE) is commonly viewed as a general term equated with the years before kindergarten and primary school. On the basis of a recent research review we conclude that perhaps it should include birth through age seven. We see ECE programs as including but not limited to early schooling (ES) and to day care. We believe that all children should be provided training or education from birth, but that it should be far more affectively than cognitively oriented, and wherever possible should be in the hands of the parents until age seven or eight. Equally important, we believe that optimal prenatal preparation should be made—in terms of the mother's nutrition, physical and emotional environment, etc.

We assume with California ECE Task Force and the New York Board of Regents that clinical and other therapeutic intervention in school or clinic or other environment may often be indicated. Many children are handicapped beyond the ability of the parents to provide therapy; where practicable all children should be screened to identify learning disabilities and parents should be involved at every step. We also believe that this view implies a much larger, though possibly less academic, responsibility for educators than many of us apparently yet envision. Day care, for example, must be provided for those youngsters whose parents are physically, emotionally or financially unable to care for them. And educators can do much to improve the quality of this care. But we do not find replicated research evidence for generalized early schooling programs down to ages three and four.

Reviewing Research

Replicated research evidence assembled from reputable researchers (e.g., neurophysiologists, psychiatrists, pediatricians, psychologists, sociologists, and other educational and medical personnel) leads us to conclude that efforts should not be made to induce or to legislate early childhood education out of the home and into schools for all young children in the range of ages three or four to five as currently proposed, for example, in California and New York and as under serious consideration elsewhere. To take such action is to accommodate the separation of the family and to reduce family responsibility, instead of to educate parents to retain their primary privilege and responsibility in an era when complete parenthood is urgently needed and to be supportive of the school when the child is ready to enroll. And such action clearly threatens the welfare of the child.

Bear in mind that, despite California ECE reference to "academic" development (1971:1) and New York's optimistic ECE use of "formal education" (1967:5), we assume that such early schooling proposals envision the most advanced of educational programs, with optimal freedom for children. Yet research overwhelmingly points to the *home*, not the *school*, as the desirable environment for most young children and to the undesirability of placing children younger than eight in programs of cognitive emphasis that require consistent reasoning of which they are not capable.

Early Schooling for All?

Some critics believe that such research analyses will preclude necessary early stimulation in school. Some insist that *all* children should have such intervention as is now provided for the disabled, arguing that such stimulation is a preventive measure against learning disability, delinquency and other ills. Child psychiatrist Dale Meers (1972) says that this is like prescribing methadone for all because it works for the addicted.

Some tend to assume that to deny such intervention to the average child would be educationally, psychologically and economically unsound. But they make one basic assumption which research indicates is untrue; namely, that the rapid development of the typical young child's intellect suggests the need for stimulation apart from and in addition to a wholesome home life.

Again, we agree that children should be carefully screened for physical, psychological, emotional and other abnormalities, and where disability is noted there should be intervention as soon as practicable. But while research

5. How Early Should They Go to School?

stresses the rapid early growth of the child's intellect, it does not support the so-called stimulation of children in general.

Interpretation of Intelligence
Much of the intuitive idea of early stimulation has found comfort in Benjamin Bloom's famed research review. He concluded that, "in terms of intelligence measured at age seventeen, from conception to age four the individual develops 50 percent of his mature intelligence" (1964:88).

But the Bloom conclusions are plagued with problems. A number of early childhood education researchers, whose data he used, say his conclusions are not sound. These include University of California (Berkeley) early childhood specialist Nancy Bayley (1970:1186) and her colleagues who believe that Bloom has misused their findings.

Yet his analysis constitutes perhaps the most frequently underscored "fact" on which much of the federal, state and local preschool planning has recently been made.

In the *first* place, Bayley and Honzik note the probability from their basic data that Bloom's figures are exaggerated. *Second*, even if his figures were accurate, a child's "mature intelligence" at this period is not necessarily synonymous with perception or understanding or ability to reason. It is rather a *potential* ability to reason or to perceive. *Third*, if he were to make the best use of this new ability, home is in most cases a more likely place than school. He needs a simple environment with few distractions and with relatively few people—adults or children—around. And *fourth*, he cannot yet make appropriate use of systematic instruction in reading, language study and arithmetic.

The early stimulation theory is much like rushing a thoroughbred colt onto the track as soon as he can run, in order to make greater use of his heritage of speed. Or it is like forcing open a rosebud, beautiful in its potential and perfect in its immaturity, but not yet ready to fully bloom. No matter how delicately you open it, you end up with a damaged rose.

Risks of Speeding Up Children
We agree with Heffernan, that we may be "warping children to satisfy adult demands" (1968:496-97). And we suggest with Piaget that "the problem of learning is not to be confused with that of spontaneous development even though spontaneous development always comprises learning" (1966:iv). Phillip reports that Piaget calls the speeding up of the development of the child's brain the "American question." Piaget's answer to this question, according to Phillip, is that "it probably can but probably should not be speeded up" (1969:132).

We believe that available, replicated research evidence in any one of several ECE-related areas is sufficient to question (1) early stimulation generally for children who are not handicapped or deprived and (2) day care out of the home if not really necessary. These areas include, for example, neurophysiology, maternal deprivation, cognitive and affective development and school entrance age. Key examples of research evidence are presented in our basic paper.

Brain Development, Vision and Hearing
Neurophysiologically, the young child is not completely ready for regular tasks which require abstract or cause-to-effect thinking until he is seven or eight or older. Leading cognitive psychologists suggest the age span of seven to eleven as the time when a child becomes able to reason abstractly, as required, for example, in reading. This conclusion is underscored variously by Piaget (1966:iv), Rohwer (1970, 1972), Almy (1966), Elkind (1969, 39:319-337), Furth (1970:1,3,4) and others.

Ophthalmologists and optometrists suggest that the young child is not ready for the teaching of reading visually-perceptively until he is *at least seven years old*, and for some until age nine. This statement does not mean that the child may not learn to read on his own. In fact some children may have to be restrained from too much reading (or television) in order to avoid permanent eye damage. Similar findings have been made in auditory and in intersensory perception. Neurophysiologists have found that brain structure and function—physiological and psychological growth—are very closely related.

Value of Mothering
Maternal attachment/deprivation studies clearly demonstrate the cognitive and affective value of maintaining a warm, consistent and continuing home environment *vis-a-vis* the value of a school program, however well-planned. John Bowlby (1952, 1969) suggests that dangers from maternal deprivation may exist *until eight years of age* or older. Even though the empathetic, informed mother does not formally teach, her child will likely be physiologically more mature and coordinated, more adaptable, sociable and more advanced in language skills.

A kind of synergic factor appears to enter here. Note that when the research in these areas is correlated there is a remarkable similarity of findings, and they become much more powerful when brought together than when moving in each of their areas separately. As is true with most scientific analyses, we may on occasion be faulted by the specialist. But, if we divest ourselves of special interests, look at the larger picture systematically, and grasp the larger developmental concepts implied, we will be less likely to nit-pick at the details. Only thus will we develop responsible conclusions and make sound progress in planning and implementation.

From another area of experimentation, comparative studies of early and late school entrants overwhelmingly indicate that later entrants generally excel in achievement, adjustment, leadership in general, social-emotional development and motivation. These studies have been made at high, middle and low socioeconomic levels; and measurements have been taken at virtually all grade levels with substantially the same results. Halliwell, in his "Reviewing of Reviews on School Entrance Age and School Success," concludes that

> The analysis of the review on entrance age and school success in the elementary school indicates conclusively that despite the plethora of prominent individuals and organizations which maintain that the research on early entrance supports the position that early admission results in no adverse effects, early entrance to first grade does result in lower achievement throughout the grades when comparisons of achievement with control groups of later entrants of similar abilities are made.
>
> ... In view of the facts, that at any grade level the early entrant is approximately seven months behind his control in achievement, that despite an extra year of schooling the early entrant is only three months superior in achievement to the regular entrant at a particular age, and that other approaches to acceleration have resulted in superior achievement for younger pupils both in terms of age and grade, the conclusion of the present reviewer is that the advantages of postponing early entrance to first grade programs as they are presently conducted are very real (1968:65).

Rank correlations from Husén's (1967) study of mathematics teaching in thirteen countries were analyzed by William Rohwer (1970). He found essentially that the earlier children went to school the more negative their attitudes toward schooling. Husén agrees, as indicated in a 1972 personal communication to the authors.

If these findings are valid, then one wonders why we suggest schooling at ever earlier ages, instead of using our resources to strengthen the home.

Intuitively the argument that women want their freedom too much to be concerned or that parents will not respond to their children's developmental needs certainly appears to be so. But research does not agree. A number of studies indicate that parents when carefully informed of what is best for their children and how to meet these needs in uncomplicated ways (as parents, not teachers) will respond. In other words, there is evidence that adults who will support the challenge of the environment—polluted streams and air—will also respond to the concerns of human ecology, especially their own children.

It is certainly more convenient to move along with the massive trend to early schooling and other programs (1) that would provide maternal freedom at the expense of the child and (2) that would threaten the integrity of the home. We have repeatedly asked for facts to support this movement, but apparently replicated research does not support this course. Several points should be specifically noted:

1. Some of the leading scholars in the nation advise us that they believe that research evidence in favor of generalized early schooling does not exist, certainly not in any substantial amount.

2. Some of them are deeply concerned at the indifference of many educational planners to the findings of research. Says Schaefer:

1. PERSPECTIVES

... Although much of this [ECE] research data has been generated during the last decade, earlier studies of intellectual development have motivated the current volume of research. Unfortunately, interpretations of the significance of this data, although they have guided the course of research, have as yet had minimal impact on educational planning ... (1971:18).

Rohwer provides an excellent example of research's contrast with existing early schooling trends and practices in terms of ages three to six:

> Young children find concept-learning and tasks that require combination and manipulation of concepts to be extraordinarily demanding. Research studies have shown that reading and arithmetic require conceptual abilities that many youngsters do not achieve with ease until they are close to 9 years (1972:1).

Such discrepancy between research and practice is hard to understand. Certainly our society would not be advanced technologically (planes, cars, computers, etc.) if our planners had not given implicit attention to reasearch. Should we do any less for our children?

3. A number of leading ECE authorities are modifying or reversing their positions, or have reported that they have been forced to deny their research hypotheses favoring general early intervention outside the home.

4. Sheldon White, who has recently completed a comprehensive study of federal ECE spending, is concerned that, from the way it is going, the early schooling movement "will work itself into so much trouble within six years or so that it will wipe out the gains special education has made and possibly ruin the future of early childhood education" (1970:62).

Not a single replicated experiment has clearly demonstrated the desirability of early schooling or day care for the normal child who can enjoy the security of a reasonably good home. Russia and the iron curtain countries are having second thoughts about mass day care and preschool. In England and on the continent such programs are commonly accepted. But they remain unproven. They appear to be financially feasible but their ratios of children per adult are commonly more than 40 to 1. No studies have shown that *elective* day care or preschool develops the larger potential in a child. There is no evidence that they make him a more stable, sociable, responsible and higher-achieving citizen. But many studies clearly support the contrary view.

Parents and Home Projects

A number of researchers, scholars and planners have been experimenting successfully with ECE growth programs centered in the home. These include Susan Gray, Ira Gordon, Merle Karnes, Phyllis Levenstein, David Weikart, and others. According to Gray (1971:48:3, 127-29) and Schaefer (1972), they find this more cost effective than intervention through schools. They are encouraged by the thinking and experiments of such researchers and scholars as Mary Ainsworth (1967), Urie Bronfenbrenner (1971), Robert Hess (1968:127, 128), Samuel Kirk (1972), Dale Meers (1970), Glen Nimnicht (1972), William Rohwer (1970), Burton White (1972:612-13) and Sheldon White (1970). Some, such as Blatt and Garfunkel, Kirk, Meers, Schaefer and Nimnicht, are making important modifications or even reversals of their earlier thinking. Nimnicht, formerly a chief psychologist for Head Start, now suggests that

> The early years are crucial in the development of a child's potential.... But there's no evidence that a young child needs to go to nursery school. It's my hunch that twenty minutes a day playing with his mother does a preschooler as much good as three hours in a classroom (1972:118; also confirmed by personal communication).

The implications of parent-home education are many and substantial. Where necessary, the skillful intervention in behalf of even one child in the home can work as a yeast throughout the entire family, benefiting remaining children. Instead of being encouraged to abrogate their responsibility, the parents should be helped to see their children's developmental needs and to meet them constructively. They should be taught gradually to involve children from infancy in the best possible attitudes, values, chores and other responsibilities in the home. If they do so, they will likely pass on to the school youngsters who are more stable, optimistic, self-respecting, better-disciplined and more highly motivated. The results will be integrative instead of divisive from the family point of view and hopefully provide the child the warm, unbroken environment he needs from birth through the age of six or seven.

More often than not such parent-home education will also gain parental understanding and support for the school. Where many now are urging parental participation in preschools, we suggest that wherever possible the educational community center its efforts on the home, rather than the school, for at least the child's first seven years.

We reemphasize that we recognize special educational needs for the handicapped, broadly speaking, and we are aware of the need for child-care facilities where parents are disabled or *forced* to work. Even in such cases, however, research indicates that wherever practicable the therapy and care should be carried on in the home or in an environment simulating or identified as closely as possible with the home.

Unfortunately, the early childhood education planner in general has not been as faithful as he could have been in developing the facts of research and organizing them for legislators and administrators. In part the researchers themselves are to blame. They often fail to interrelate their findings with other ECE research, and thus lose much of their potential impact on planning. Nor is their language simple enough for the planner. Often it is actually confusing.

Perhaps the time has arrived for us to become like a little child; to put away biases, to be eager for simple truths, and to speak and act accordingly. If we do this, there is some reason to believe that we will be more guarded about rushing our toddlers out of the home and into school. And for those whose homes are impossible, we will do our best to provide a homelike environment without any serious attempt at academic stimulation.

Early Childhood Education: A Perspective on Basics

Annie L. Butler

Professor of Early Childhood Education at Indiana University, Bloomington, is President of the Association for Childhood Education International

Confusion about early childhood education is rampant—about what it is and what it is not, about what it can do and what it cannot do, and even about whether it should exist at all. I can think of no better example to illustrate such confusion than the article by Moore and Moore appearing in this issue of CHILDHOOD EDUCATION. The variety of early childhood programs devised during the past ten years has often bewildered those with sufficient experience and understanding of the field to make an evaluation, but without this experience evaluation is impossible.

A large proportion of those of us who comprise the membership of the Association for Childhood Education International are involved with the education of children under the age of eight years. For many years we have worked either directly or indirectly as a professional body to improve educational opportunities for these children. This year we have chosen as the theme for our journal "Balancing Basics: What Is Basic?" What *is* basic for education of children under the age of eight?

In the following statement I shall attempt to develop some understandings I think are crucial for responding to that question. Although writing in direct reply to Moore and Moore's article, I shall not attempt to refute what they say point by point. Neither shall I attribute various points of view to other authors, a characteristic I believe to be a major weakness of their article. My goal, rather, is to seek clarification about some aspects of early childhood education based upon my years of experience in the field and upon my own analysis of a considerable volume of related writing and research.*

What Early Childhood Education Is and Is Not

First, we must continually stress that early childhood education is *diverse*. Programs for the education of children ages three through seven vary in the kinds of curricula offered, in the nature of their sponsorship, in the length of time children are in the program and in the staffing requirements—to mention but a few of the more significant differences. Curricular offerings range from programs highly child and family oriented to those very academically oriented and not including involvement of the families of the children at all, except in the most superficial ways. With regard to ages of children, asking whether educational programs should be provided for seven-year-olds is a very different question than asking whether programs should be provided for three- and four-year-olds. In the United States a sufficiently large number of people believe in the advisability of including programs for essentially all six- and seven-year-olds and for an appreciable number of the five-year-olds as a part of the public school system. Additional programs for children below the age of six have been developed in accordance with need as seen by groups of parents, philanthropic institutions, public and governmental agencies, and private individuals. A "regular" school day from early morning to mid-afternoon is generally accepted for children six years and older, but below that age the length of time the child spends in the program varies from about two hours per day, two days per week to almost ten hours per day, five days per week. Staffing needs also vary widely with the age of the children, with the younger children requiring a smaller ratio of children to adults. All these factors, among others, make a difference in the quality of educational offerings available. Even the most ardent advocates of early childhood education deplore some of the existing circumstances. Although many of these advocates have written expressing their concerns, we clearly cannot generalize—as I believe Moore and Moore do excessively—that such writers are opposed to *all* early childhood education, but only that they question certain practices.

For example, many of us find it unacceptable to call early childhood education either "early stimulation" or "early schooling." Unfortunately the term "early stimulation" found its way into the literature in connection with the push to combat cultural deprivation and as applied largely to a type of sensory stimulation believed by some to assist the learning of infants and children of lower socioeconomic levels. We have since learned that the performance of poor children is due to much more

---

*Editor's Note: For amplification of these comments, see Dr. Butler's article on "Areas of Recent Research in Early Childhood Education" (CHILDHOOD EDUCATION. December 1971, Pp. 143-47) which provides an overview of two extensive research surveys on early childhood education. See also the ACEI Position Paper on "The Child's Right to Quality Day Care" (CHILDHOOD EDUCATION, November 1970).

1. PERSPECTIVES

complex factors than mere sensory stimulation. The latter term too often connotes placing excessive pressures on children. Completely unacceptable to me personally is the idea of deliberately pushing a child beyond the point where his own pace of development indicates he can function easily. "Pushing" is quite different from providing for a child experiences to help him make optimal use of his developing abilities.

I find even more objectionable the term "early schooling." It implies an overemphasis on teaching of academic skills, combined with the idea that providing programs for children as young as four years will orient the children toward academic skill acquisition. Indeed, frequently decried in the early childhood literature is a danger reflected in later learning disabilities and attitudes toward school that can arise from the wrong kind of school experience. For many young children "early schooling" is equivalent to mis-education. *What then are some basics for quality early childhood education programs?* Minimum essentials are a safe and carefully planned and equipped physical environment in which the child spends part of his day, intellectual stimulation, opportunities to develop a healthy personality and acquire social proficiency under the guidance of competent staff. Omitting any of these elements or using unacceptable procedures in trying to accomplish them affords reason to reject the program. Early childhood programs should fully utilize the child's motivation for learning as well as his developmental abilities. Such programs should help children conceive of themselves as people who can solve problems, gain information, learn skills, and relate to other people effectively. Social and intellectual differences must be appreciated, and children be helped to become aware of their own capacities to learn. This kind of growth can only occur in situations where the atmosphere is warm and open and in which adults like, respect and relate positively to children. Steps from the home into the school environment should be gradual; but if the program is flexible and responsive to the children, I am convinced that most youngsters can benefit from it. In a forced choice—such choices are always relative to many factors—of course I would prefer no program to one damaging to children. Formalized programs, in which the curriculum is relatively fixed and where the expectation is based on the curriculum rather than on the abilities of the child, decidedly fall into the category of the potentially damaging. Such programs push some children and offer essentially no challenge to others.

What Early Childhood Education Can and Cannot Do

Quality early childhood education can provide a good educational experience for a child *now*. Early childhood education cannot give a guarantee for the future although it may increase the odds in the child's favor. The past few years have provided ample opportunity to discover the fallacy of attempting to guarantee the child's educational future by an educational program prior to six years of age. Several factors that confuse the real issues are glossed over by Moore and Moore's analysis.

One of our most urgent problems lies in how we evaluate early childhood programs. Before we can really talk about the value of programs, we must be clear about what we are trying to accomplish by them. Through the years we have planted educational programs for a wide variety of goals. Particularly at the youngest end of the age scale we have not often clarified our objectives. With the six- and seven-year old children we have stated our goals broadly, but in actual programs we have usually emphasized academic skills and we have usually evaluated only academic skills. Project Head Start is a prime example of the confused thinking that exists. Head Start at its outset was described as a comprehensive program with many kinds of goals relating to the children, their families and the communities in which they lived. Despite this fact, the program has been rejected by some critics as a failure because it did not produce hoped-for IQ gains or because the gains made tended to fade over a period of time. If, on the other hand, we were to evaluate Head Start on the basis of the contributions it has made to the health of the children, the involvement of parents and on provision of work opportunities, unquestionably the program has been a success. These factors offer great promise of an improved quality of living for children and adults alike.

Many people place a halo around the word "research." Those who design and carry out complex studies in the area of early childhood and related areas have contributed much to our knowledge. From a practical point of view, however, we must acknowledge problems in interpreting findings. Some problems arise from the nature of research, which requires the isolation of measurable bits of behavior. Some problems arise because educational researchers are usually more interested in exploring a particular theoretical problem than in the application of findings in a practical classroom situation. Indeed, one of the most difficult of educational tasks is to try to take findings that apply to any aspect of child development or early childhood education and interpret their meaning for classroom practice. We do have a great deal of research indicative of caution that should be observed in early childhood programs, but whether one views this research as meaning early childhood education programs are harmful per se is a matter of interpretation. Much of what we believe and do in early childhood education is not based on research at all. Rather it is based on theory and experience. As a general rule, many widely accepted practices are not widely researched. Because there seems to be little reason to research that which is already widely accepted, the gaps in our knowledge are glaring and apt to stay that way.

Using research in an ethical and professional way is extremely difficult; it requires both extensive knowledge and understanding of the research and of the field in which the research is done. Personal values have a way of slipping in; and generally they determine what we feel is important or not important, what we include and/or leave out of a report, and sometimes how we interpret the researchers' findings. As one long involved in research analysis, I do not in any way wish to downgrade research, but only to point out that its applications and interpretations are not always as objective as might be.

Again, *it is basic* to ask what kind of experiences a child needs at any particular time within the three to eight age range. In other words, what can early childhood education do for him now? To answer this question we need to be able to observe the level at which the individual child is functioning and we need to know what behavior occurs next in the developmental sequence. Fortunately, much research is available from which it is possible to determine the developmental sequence of a good many behaviors in the affective and cognitive as well as in the psychomotor areas of development. Children need to practice the abilities they are acquiring. Appropriate educational programs can provide this experience.

Early Childhood Education: Supplement or Threat to the Home?

Early childhood education, especially programs for children under six years of age, has always been viewed within the field of professional study as a supplement to the home. Many programs maintain close contact with the home and try to create as consistent an environment for the child as possible. Of all childhood educators, those concerned with young children are the least inclined to question the value of mothering and the seriousness of maternal deprivation. A number of educators do question the long hours that some children must spend in day care; but even under these circumstances, the question of deprivation depends on the quality of the home environment as well as that of the day care center. The experience of a child in even poor programs of day care is vastly different from the experience of one who is institutionalized. It is unbelievable that any parent would equate two to three hours spent in a good educational program with maternal deprivation. We have learned that most parents want to do well by their children, even parents previously thought not to care. Helping parents be better parents is completely consistent with advocating quality early childhood education programs.

I agree with Moore and Moore that encouraging results have been achieved by some projects that have involved working with the parent and child in the home along with providing an educational program for the parent. These programs have implications not only for ways that homes can be improved, but also for better utilization of early childhood education resources to strengthen the family's contribution to its young children. Such programs should be a supplement to, and in some cases an alternative to, early childhood education programs. Increasingly, it has become apparent that involvement of parents in their children's education is important in providing consistency and in helping the parents realize what they can do for their children along with helping the teacher understand the children better.

A potential threat to the family *can* exist when the early childhood program is based on values different from those of the home. Differences in the cultural values of social classes and religious groups to which teachers and families belong may be primary sources of this kind of conflict.

All the more then, it is basic that the two institutions most concerned about the child work together *cooperatively* for his welfare. The younger the child, the more this principle holds true. A high degree of flexibility has to be allowed in how the cooperation is to be achieved. The bulk of our experience so far has been with the youngest children through such programs as Head Start, Parent and Child Centers, day care and cooperative nursery schools. We need to explore new ways of working together, particularly in public education.

Conclusion

With so much confusion in regard to the meanings assigned to terminology in early childhood education, it is difficult to sift out those kinds of experience that can be considered basic for young children. One, no doubt, is a stable, secure home situation. A second is an educational program that provides the maximum opportunity for development. Homes, unfortunately, are just as diverse in their abilities to provide adequately for the needs of children as are schools. Just as one cannot assume that all schools are bad, one cannot assume that all homes are good. The basic question is how we balance the responsibility of the family with the responsibility of the society to provide for the education of children.

Some families choose early childhood programs on the basis of assumed advantages offered thereby to their children either in the present or in the future. Admittedly, some parents find early childhood education a convenient way to have their children taken care of. On occasion it may be to the parents' credit that they realize that someone else will do a better job. Some parents do not relate at all well to their youngest children while they may make much better parents of their older children. School is the most stable experience in the lives of many young children. Despite the Moores' insistence on the effectiveness of the home with children until age 8, this conclusion can only be inferred from limited data from other countries. In the United States we currently have less proof of the effectiveness of the home, exclusively, in working with the child for the first seven years than we have of the effectiveness of the school and the home as partners in working with the child for the first seven years.

References

Butler, Annie L., *Current Research in Early Childhood Education: A Compilation and Analysis for Program Planners*. Washington D.C.: American Association of Elementary Kindergarten-Nursery Educators, 1970.

———, and others. *Literature Search and Development of an Evaluation System in Early Childhood Education*, ERIC numbers Ed. 059780-784, July, 1971.

Hunter, Madeline. "Public Education for Four-Year-Olds: 'To Be or Not To Be.'" *Childhood Education* 49, 8, (May 1973): 403-07.

Keyserling, Mary Dublin. *Windows on Day Care*, New York: National Council of Jewish Women, 1972.

Roby, Pamela, Ed. *Child Care—Who Cares?* New York: Basic Books, 1973.

Senn, Milton J.E. "Early Childhood Education for What Goals?" *Children* 16, (Jan.–Feb. 1969): 8-13.

Weber, Evelyn. "The Function of Early Childhood Education," *Young Children* 28, (June 1973): 265-74.

Zigler, Edward. "Is Our Evolving Social Policy for Children Based on Fact or Fiction?" *Early Child Programs in the States*, Report of Conference of Education Commission of the States, Denver, Colorado, 1972.

FOUR WHO CARED

Join me on a personal odyssey. To set up a backdrop for the planning of this special edition, I first talked with many teachers and reviewed the comments of others from the most recent NEA Survey on Teacher Instructional Needs. From their remarks, I learned that teachers want to inquire into the dynamics of learning—our own learning as well as that of children.

All of us who have taught young children know that the energy expended in struggling to get them to go where we want them to go is vastly different from the tremendous satisfaction and joy we experience when we build on what they bring. How can we develop a sense of mutuality, of possibility, learning from and with children?

My quest for counsel in dealing with these concerns led me to another series of interviews, this time with some of the leading child developmentalists of our time. Four of these mentors share a particular interest in observing and assessing longitudinal aspects of growth; each of them has had significant influence on teaching practice. I invite you to share fragments of our conversations.

MONROE D. COHEN

Freelance Writer; Editor; Educational Consultant; Former Director of Publications for Childhood Education International and Editor of Its Journal Childhood Education.

A chat with Lois Barclay Murphy is always a special treat. It is sure to be wide-ranging and yet topically up-to-the-minute. It is likely to be interlaced with vivid personal reminiscences, often dating back many years, of children she has worked with—as a teacher, perhaps, or at the Menninger Clinic, or at Children's Hospital in Washington, DC, where she is a research consultant. During such a chat, nearly eight years ago, I jotted down one of her prize comments:

We need to go beyond concern about teachers' method and content to get to the children themselves, their individual styles and pace of learning, their interests, motivations, mental furniture, points of taking hold, sources of pride.[1]

Recently, I brought these words back to her attention.

In view of the current pressures on teachers, particularly in regard to children's academic achievement, would you make such a statement today?

Attention to such matters is even more needed now. My granddaughter, for example, shares with me her woes about working in special education. Often, she feels mechanical duties—the endless reports, the pages and pages of detailed "ratings" to be written—take up too much of her time. Once she gets beyond these demands, she finds her margin for creative thinking is exhausted.

I tell her, "When you need to take a fresh look at your classroom, begin by remembering that there is no such thing as a perfectly normal child. Every child is a checkerboard of potentialities, strengths, and weaknesses. One may be especially strong at taking in things visually, another through hearing. We need to choose means of instruction that make use of the strengths and give special practice in the weak areas.

All children in a group don't have the same interests either, so we need to use different materials if we want to involve them. Take attitudes toward animals, for example—one child may adore horses, another may love dogs, another may be totally absorbed with a litter of kittens. As much as possible, we need to build on existing interests as well as introduce new ones. We need to make the best possible use of the energy that goes into learning.

You have always stressed this need to personalize teaching. Could you elaborate a bit more?

Lots of children are bored to death with much of the material in elementary school—but they needn't be. Teachers can make drill and routine vivid, rhythmic, even fun, when we adapt the drill to the children's interests. We need to develop a profile of the range, patterns, and limitations of each child's interests, along with a profile of his or her abilities.

We also need to recognize that children have very different tolerances for routine tasks. Some children are physiologically more fatigable than others—just as some are more distractible than others. Therefore, we need to vary the time we require children to work on a task and how we structure a task, taking their differences into account.

Cultural differences also affect the way children approach their work. One classic study relates to a group of American Indian children who were classified as slow learners. A sensitive investigator, Otto Klineberg, found in an experiment on testing that no matter how much he urged the Indian children to go faster, they refused to do so. They wanted to do the tasks exactly right. He found that the Indian children were considerably more accurate in their work than a control group of White children, who would zip through problems that the Indian children painstakingly sought to carry through to perfection.

Lois Murphy has contributed a long series of classic studies about learning from and with children. One example is her early research on the development of sympathy in children. Some others are—

Life and Ways of the Seven-to-Eight

Year Old (with Barbara Biber and others). Basic Books, 1952.

Personality in Young Children (two volumes). Basic Books, 1956. Paperback.

The Widening World of Childhood: Paths to Mastery. Basic Books, 1962. Paperback.

Vulnerability, Coping, and Growth:— From Infancy to Adolescence (with Alice Moriarty). Yale University Press, 1976.

This last, now available in paperback, gives highly readable accounts of how children deal with problems.

My second conversation led me to New York's City College for a visit with Lillian Weber. *A screeching subway ride and pleasant, pungent stroll past fruit stands and bodegas off upper Broadway brought me to her office in Shepard Hall.*

Here is housed the famous Workshop Center for Open Education, which Ms. Weber founded in 1972 and has directed ever since. With a characteristic broad smile, she beckoned me in. We moved to a long table in one of the Center's three narrow rooms. All about us were child-made and teacher-made charts, maps, sketches, photographs, aquariums, terrariums. Our conversation began in earnest and spilled over into another session the next morning. Key points recurred again and again.

Open Corridors, as I understand the term, is a way of helping teachers deal with the vastness of a large school by organizing it into manageable places that permit both teachers and children to interact with one another.

Recently the Open Corridors program celebrated its tenth birthday. What do you consider the most significant changes that have resulted from your work during this period?

A real breakthrough has been that the isolation of teachers in the schools with which we work has been considerably diminished. Teachers have come to see the whole ambience of the school as supportive in a number of respects and to see themselves as part of the developing life of the school.

When this new pattern of relationships exists, even if it is not fully developed, teachers are able to work in a way that recognizes that they are not just mechanics whose job is to carry out prescribed programs, but people who can contribute to decision making on change.

Many who come to our Center are not in Open Corridor setups. We try to help them realize that although the school's institutional assumptions hamper them, they must not abdicate their responsibility to exercise judgment. Teachers remain at the core of relationships with children. If teachers are supported in their humanness, it becomes more likely that children will be supported in their humanness.

We of the Workshop Center and Advisory did not really remove the school's institutional prescriptions—we had no such power—but sought to help teachers understand and criticize such received wisdom. We would say, "Even though you're in a bind, find some way to make adjustments to do what you can."

How have you and your colleagues at the Workshop Center reacted to back-to-basics pressures?

We never left the basics. We never departed from substance, but we acknowledged a commitment to raise more intelligent questions about classroom content—and the nature of reading and of quantification.

A great many teachers who have worked with us have developed more conviction about encouraging children to use context in finding the meaning of what they read. With teachers, we have thought and talked about the ways children think and acquire language. New forms of reading assessment grew out of these discussions.

Politicians' reactions to public budgetary concerns, inflation, revulsion against anything that sounds as if it's extra have led governing bodies to renege on the commitment to public education and to push around lots of school people. They have not critically affected our own work yet, but the squeeze on money can of course go on to diminish basic supports.

You've been quoted as saying, "Too many teachers are too busy testing and scoring instead of interacting with children." Would you elaborate?

You learn from children where they're at. There's no point in pushing content that doesn't matter to them. If you want to build a curriculum, you must see where it fits. You must listen hard and then connect piece to piece. You must connect to each child's history where he or she was before. Those who impose knowledge without connections, who break the continuity of the child, make learning harder. Engaging with the child's purpose, you

7. Four Who Cared

confirm the child in what he or she *does* know.

One time my grandson Teddy, who lives in California, was visiting me in New York. I had planned to go with him on his first trip up the Empire State Building. I thought he'd be so dazzled—he's almost eight.

But Teddy had his own connections. Do you remember the classic picture book by Hildegarde Swift and Lynd Ward, *The Little Red Lighthouse and the Great Gray Bridge?* All the way from the airport Teddy kept saying, "Is that the Great, Gray Bridge? Is that it? Is that?"

Way atop the Empire State, as I tried to point out the various sights, Teddy was saying, "But where's the Little Red Lighthouse?" When I pointed to a space below, in the shadow of the George Washington Bridge, he asked, "But how do I know that's it? I can't tell what size it is from here; I can't see the red color." In effect he was asking, "Am I supposed to take it on blind faith from you?"

Seeing the bridge and the lighthouse remained the most important event for Teddy in the next two busy weeks. When we walked as close as we could to the lighthouse, he sighed, "Oh, it has deteriorated!" What he felt about the Great Gray Bridge and that Lighthouse was what mattered for him.

Again, you learn from children where they're at and confirm in them what they know. Listening, observing—and responding: That's how, from a mishmash of beginning perceptions, teachers and children alike come to an understanding of how the world works.

What is the basic belief or principle that has guided your work through the years?

I've become clearer and clearer about the nature of the essential teaching act. As a teacher, you have the training and responsibility to use your position in this intergenerational world as an expert available to the child. You've lived longer; you have some controls built up.

Then, to use Susan Isaacs' words, "in the interest of helping the child grow," you use this knowledge as a contributor to the world of others. You stress interaction, not just the individual atom.

To do this, there is no other way than to observe and interact with children—and then to reflect about that

33

1. PERSPECTIVES

interaction. This is different from a diagnostic-prescriptive approach that looks only for the child's deficits and for ways to get the child to take in a world you set. The second approach may interfere with other aspects of your job as teacher—interacting with children and creating, extending, and adapting the environment in response to your observations.

Lillian Weber's scholarly yet personalized book, *The English Infant School and Informal Education* (Prentice-Hall, 1971), provides a valuable undergirding for many of these ideas.

The next interview I did not conduct personally but participated in vicariously, by way of Insights, *the excellent newsletter published by the Center for Teaching and Learning of the University of North Dakota.*[2]

Marie Hughes works with graduate students and conducts seminars at the University of New Mexico, where she is now Professor Emerita. She might well be called a comrade-in-arms of Lillian Weber. They share a lifelong interest in the study and application of research on young children, with particular concern about language acquisition and development. Both have been deeply involved too with intergroup education and with studying the nature of teaching.

This talk with Marie Hughes was conducted by a former associate of hers, Mavis Martin, who is now the permanent resource colleague for the University of North Dakota Follow Through Program at Zuni Pueblo, New Mexico. What follows are only a few excerpts adapted from an extended dialogue.

It seems that some of the things you demand for children would call forth very dramatic changes in schools. These cannot be just a little patch on a temporarily flat tire. I've heard you say that we have enough information today to demand a genuine revolution at the school level. What are you talking about, Marie?

A good current example is the relatively new information on the brain and how it works. Many things are not known, but we know enough to demand some changes.

We know that the brain matures at different times in different individuals, just as do other parts of the body. The lungs do not have full capacity in the beginning; the heart is smaller at first. There is a time when a young child really can't walk; he moves in a running style because he must move on the ball of his foot until the tendons lengthen. The brain itself matures, and as it does, there are new capacities available to the individual.

But when a child is introduced to material beyond his capacity—beyond his brain readiness, if you are willing to use a word which is anathema to some people—the child cannot understand. At such times he is not capable of utilizing the material.

Do you think this is one reason it appears that so many children are not learning to read: They get off on the wrong foot if we start them when their brain is not ready?

Yes, our timing may be wrong. Also, however, we start children in ways that prevent them from knowing what is going on. You see, the child is busy, as all of us are really, making sense out of our world. So when we deliberately take a young child and introduce him to heavily structured material for which he has no basis whatsoever, then he shuts off on us.

When we say that 85 or 90 percent of children's reading difficulties are made by school instruction, this is a very conservative estimate. We introduce instruction in ways that make no sense to the learner. And as soon as something makes no sense to a child, he has to turn off.

How do you feel about back-to-basics?

Oh, I feel the back-to-basics movement is one of the most vicious things that can happen in education. It allows nothing that can truly nurture the mind of a child.

It has nothing to say about the great capabilities of the human mind. It has nothing to say about the individual child and his interests. It has nothing to say about the time the child needs for maturing or the scope of experiences that he needs. It has nothing to say about the quality of the people who are working with the child.

It is a very vicious thing. And it guarantees nothing—not even that the child will learn to decode. But decoding, even if it were accomplished, does not mean the kind of reading with comprehension that children need to do.

What kind of steps do you recommend for teachers who want to grow professionally?

Well, I don't know how best to get at that, because every human has his own life experiences, and it is very hard for another to enter that frame of experience. But we have to remember we do not choose, control, or even know the past experiences of the child we have at school. So this is one thing: We have to gain great respect for the potentiality of any human.

Then if you are going to be a teacher, you have to study children as a professional, that is, with a certain amount of objectivity, as well as great caring. I think too many teachers have not truly *seen* children, have not found ways in which to study children. If they learn to study children, then they can study their own response to children so as to find their own ways of working.

I was working with a couple of teachers the other day, for example, and they were reading to me some of the conversations they had with children. In too many cases, the child would cease to speak to them, and I was struck by the fact that neither one of those teachers had *evoked* any response. That is, their responses to the child had been evaluative or in some other way had cut off the child; these adults had not learned the process of eliciting a response.

If you can elicit responses, it shows that you are truly interested in a child; your response draws a response from him. "Then what happened?" "How did you feel?" "What would you have done?"

We must observe our own behavior and what the child does in response to our behavior. I have never understood how a teacher could give out the same type of worksheets to the children day after day and have the same children respond incorrectly day after day. What is there about us that we have so little concern for their feelings, so little caring, so little knowledge of how children learn and live?

How can teachers overcome their fears that children will not learn unless forced to do so?

The more we observe and reflect on children's reactions to their environment, the more we learn to trust them. They do their own learning.

Probably we cannot teach anyone. We now know that each one builds his own mental contents and strategies

34

7. Four Who Cared

through an active process of construction.

You are saying, then, that there is a theory of instruction in our interactions with children?

Not a whole theory, by any means. Let me remind you, for example, that we still don't know exactly how a child learns to read.

But new information is constantly made available. We don't need to base our actions on folklore—we can continue to test our hypotheses through our own work with children.

The last of my interviews led me back to New York, to a small, tree-lined street, incongruously squashed in amid the high-rise apartment jungle of the East Bronx. There in a small, cheerful flat full to bursting with paintings, books, recordings— and file after file of research notes—I found the pale but still vibrant Dorothy H. Cohen. *My visit came just six weeks before her untimely death this past summer.*

As a member of the senior faculty of the graduate programs at Bank Street College, Dorothy Cohen inspired many adult learners to improve their skills of child study. One of her books, Observing and Recording the Behavior of Young Children *(written with Virginia Stern), remains the all-time bestseller among the publications of Teachers College Press.*

What is your response to the spread of negativism among parents and teachers, the talk of "burnout"?

Why do we have more and more parents—and teachers—bitterly unhappy about the education of their children, feeling cheated?

Granted, the problems in the big cities especially are considerable. The government took over much of the funding once provided by the Ford Foundation and others, with few discernible changes in schools as the result of the influx of large amounts of money.

But we do have a number of good programs in existence without large amounts of money. We need to ask: "What do children need?" We find that like all of us, they need *responsible* adults. We don't hear about these teachers, because they are doing the job they should be doing, and that's what makes good programs.

As for teacher burnout, the strength of the teacher's role is wholly related to teachers' perceptions of themselves as adults. If teachers are to function capably in classrooms,[3] they must reject at long last the insulting and humiliating nonsense of those administrators, educational psychologists, and textbook and materials manufacturers who presume that teachers are too stupid to know what to do unless a plan of action is carefully laid out for them in easy steps. Before they can function independently, teachers—of whom approximately 70 percent in the elementary schools are still women—must debunk the popular assumption on the part of largely masculine leadership that educational materials need to be created primarily for the purpose of thwarting the natural ineptitude of teachers.

Teachers who do not trust themselves or their intelligence cannot develop good informal classrooms. Each classroom must be built by the teacher and children in it. This does not mean reversal of the familiar teacher domination and control to domination and control by the child. The teacher does not abdicate the role of the adult in the process of altering her role as teacher.

I know of course of your deep faith in teachers and also of your conviction that they must come to know more about the processes of children's learning. Many of us share your concern, however, that few educators in positions of leadership have themselves learned the techniques of observing and recording children's behavior, except by trial and error.

It is good that you are writing a new book to help teach those skills more effectively [to be published posthumously, with the help of some of her Bank Street colleagues]. **Could you comment about the place of child study in improving the schools?**

I believe strongly that most teachers care about children and want them to succeed, so teachers want information that will help them carry out their task. They want perspective and understanding. They want more solid evidence of growth or regression than their intuitive understanding or the limited scope of standardized tests gives them.

They want documentary evidence for their conferences with parents and consultations with psychologists or educational directors. It is not the negative things about their children that parents fear; they know their children are not perfect any more than we adults are. But unfair statements by people who do not know their children or care about them yet pass judgment upon them are painful, and parents properly resist them. Learning to observe children objectively and to record what is observed with the same objectivity is the real answer to the anxiety and criticisms of teachers and parents alike.

Sometimes fear clutches the heart of a really loving teacher who assumes that objectivity must mean coldness. What needs to be clear is that warm, loving feelings are good for children and that good teachers are honest about their feelings, even their angry feelings. The objectivity we're asking for is about the child's feelings, which may be very different from an adult's.

In addition to her writings about observation, Dorothy Cohen provided a panoply of insights about children through the whole span of the elementary school years (see, e.g., The Learning Child, *Pantheon, 1972, or* Kindergarten and Early Schooling, *written with Marguerita Rudolph, Prentice-Hall, 1977). Her prophetic discussion of the "children of technology" pointed to misuses of the mass media that ignore the need for human interaction.*

You can provide your own summary of these four conversations. To me what binds them all together is what Lillian Weber has called an unswerving faith in "the intelligence of teachers and the educability of children." Echoed throughout is a vision of teachers and children as co-learners— taking risks, enlarging perceptions, reflecting, growing, pursuing explorations that can bring about self-discovery.

---

[1] First reported in *Childhood Education* 48: 56; October 1971.

[2] *Insights* 11: Numbers 6 and 7, March and April 1979 (Center for Teaching and Learning, Corwin Hall, University of North Dakota, Grand Forks 58202).

[3] Although the ideas in the following two paragraphs were discussed in our interview, I have, on the suggestion of Dorothy Cohen, excerpted the precise wording from a paper she first presented at a conference at the State University of New York at Cortland in 1973. The entire paper, "The Role of the Teacher in the Informal Classroom," is included in a provocative series of essays, *On Teachers and Teaching* (edited by Charlotte Winsor, Bank Street College of Education, 1979). Reprinted with permission.

MAKING THE DAY CARE DECISION

**Ron Haskins, Ph.D.,
Dale C. Farran, Ph.D.
and Joseph Sanders**
Frank Porter Graham Child Development Center,
University of North Carolina at Chapel Hill

■ The day care decision. More American parents are considering it than ever before. Some with a baby on the way are looking ahead to day care. Some parents with children already in day care wonder if they made the right choice, and so do some parents who have decided to keep their children at home.

As with other important decisions, you will want to get all the facts available before making up your mind. What kinds of child care arrangements are available to working parents... what are some of the misconceptions about "typical" child care arrangements... what can we learn from social science research concerning the effects of day care on children's health and development?

Types of Child Care Arrangements

It's wise to recognize that most public debate and social science evidence is focused on centers with relatively large numbers of children. There is little discussion, and even less reliable information about the effects of in-home care, either by non-relatives or relatives, or about family day care homes in which only a few children are cared for at a time.

This is quite unfortunate because less than ten percent of working mothers with children under six use center-based care. About 60 percent of working mothers arrange to have a relative care for their children, mostly in their own homes. And the remainder—about 30 percent—make various other arrangements for the care of their young children while they're at work.

Though a number of social scientists are now attempting to learn more about non-center-based day care, we are currently forced to apply knowledge about center-based care to other types of day care. Parents should understand that this must be done with caution.

Myths About Child Care

Most of us still tend to believe that the "ideal" American family consists of a father who works and a mother who stays home rearing the children. Today, however, our work force includes about 37 percent of all the mothers in our country with children under six—more than five million women—and 33 percent of the mothers with children under two. And the percentage of working mothers is steadily rising.

Even many of us who are well aware of the changing role of child-rearing patterns in our country, still believe that the "natural" and best way to raise children is at home under a mother's full-time charge. Historically, the facts indicate something else. In most societies and at most times, child care has been shared with a network of blood kin and friends who provided needed practical and emotional support to the mother. The practice of isolating women and their children at home is of very recent origin, and would still be thought unusual—and very inadequate—in many other societies.

Finally, even in our country, day care is not a new phenomenon; there have always been families who made such arrangements for their children. The use of day care in the United States has tended to peak during times when women were needed in the work force—usually during major wars.

Naturally, it is more difficult for parents to reach an objective decision about day care if they believe that it is a recent fad which violates both the ideal and normal family pattern. Once day care is put into its proper perspective, parents can proceed to consider the most important question: What are the effects of day care on children's development and health? We have selected four primary areas which are of concern to parents and about which research information is available. These areas are: children's intellectual development; their relationship with their mothers; their social behavior with other children and adults; their physical health.

Intellectual Development

There is abundant social science evidence concerning the effects of day care on intellectual development. Studies show that day care programs designed specifically to promote intellectual growth can raise the IQ of many children from low-income families, but the gains may disappear in the early school years if no follow through is provided. There is, however, some evidence that gains in achievement and motivation may persist, given the proper circumstances.

On the other hand, studies of children from middle-income families in day care have not consistently shown either a positive or negative effect on intellectual development. No study has reported substantial and lasting differences of any kind—either for the better or the worse—in the intelligence of these children. It is simply not justified to support day care or to attack it on the basis of any impact it may have on the intellectual development of the child.

There is evidence, however, suggesting that the characteristics of particular day care programs can have at least a temporary impact on intellectual development. Some research indicates what common sense should tell us—that a low staff turnover, a high staff-to-student ratio, and mixed-age grouping among the children may all stimulate intellectual development. In other words, children seem to learn best in a stable social environment, when they have a substantial amount of contact with adults, and when they play with both older and younger children.

In addition, the frequency and type of interchanges between the staff members and the children may influence intellectual growth. Children's intellectual and language development appears to be slowed down when adults talk infrequently to children or when they talk to children only to give them directions ("pick up your toys," "put on your shoes"). So the characteristics of the particular center a child attends can make a real difference.

The Mother-Child Relationship

Although relations among all fam-

8. Making the Day Care Decision

ily members are significant when considering the effects of day care, studies have examined only the effect of day care on children's relationships with their mothers. In particular, researchers have focused on the close and special bond—as they call it, the "attachment"—which develops between an infant and his mother. Many parents and researchers have feared that day care might disrupt the attachment bond, with serious damage to the child's social and emotional development.

In attempting to discover whether day care has disrupted this bond, psychologists have examined the quality of the relationship between mother and child as revealed in mutual play or other typical situations, and as also shown by the child's response to separation when taken to nursery school by the mother.

Two general conclusions can be drawn from such studies. First, most research shows that children attending day care are just as secure and confident in their relationship with their mothers as children not attending day care. Only one study found any evidence of a negative effect of day care, and a number of similar studies failed to support this finding. It is interesting that children apparently do not form the kind of bond with the day care teacher which might disrupt their primary bond with their mothers, even when day care begins in infancy.

One of the authors of this article—Dr. Dale C. Farran—working in collaboration with Dr. Craig Ramey provided, in a recently completed study, concrete example of the kind of evidence used to evaluate the impact of day care on children's attachment to their mothers. The youngsters who took part in the study were between nine and 31 months of age, and had been attending the Frank Porter Graham day care program since they were three months old. In the study, each child entered a room facing a male stranger. Also in the room were the child's day care teacher, his mother and some toys. Measures of behavior included the child's first approach to any of the adults, the child's nearness to, and contact with, each adult, and the amount of sharing toys with each adult. Overwhelmingly, the children preferred to be near their mothers, spending 75 percent of the session near them as opposed to their teachers or the stranger. In addition, they interacted more with their mothers by sharing toys, touching them or asking to be held by them.

At the end of each session, the child was given a clear, locktop plastic box containing a cookie. It was then noted to whom the child turned for help in opening the box. Of twenty children given the problem, fifteen wanted help, and all fifteen turned to their mothers. Although these chil-

---

HOW TO FIND HIGH QUALITY CARE

by Gwendolyn Morgan
Day Care and Child Development Council of America

■ To find out what's available in your area, first contact the following sources:
- The agency which licenses child care in your state. This is usually under the jurisdiction of the Welfare Department or its counterpart, but occasionally it is under the Health Department, an Office of Child Development or a Department of Licensing.
- The elementary school principal in your district. He or she may know of the nursery schools and day care centers in the neighborhood of the school, although probably not about family day care.
- The Community Coordinated Child Care (4-C) organization or local Council for Children will have complete information if they exist in your area.
- A parent-organized central information and referral system, such as the Switchboard in San Francisco, the Gathering Place in Tomkins County, New York, or the Child Care Resource Center in Cambridge, Massachusetts.
- The Yellow Pages listing of "day care," "child care" and "nursery school."

Here are some of the things to look for whether your choice is a center, a family day care home, a babysitter, or a relative:
- Does the care giver respect the fact that you are the central person in your child's life, and will he or she support your values and supplement your care?
- How much attention is paid to the actual act of physical separation? There should be a concern each day to make the two transitions (away from the parent and away from the care giver) easy and natural for the child.
- Is the care giver a warm and loving person, sensitive in dealing with children? A care giver who either permits any kind of behavior or who is very restrictive is unsuitable. The quality to look for is the ability to negotiate with children.
- Is the care giver stimulating? Will he or she read and talk to the child, and encourage curiosity, asking questions which call for thoughtful or imaginative, rather than yes or no, answers?
- Will the care be isolating for your child or will there be the opportunity to meet a variety of people, perhaps to see something of the world?
- Will your child have the opportunity to play in a number of different ways? There should be a variety of materials, including props for make-believe play, and freedom from constant direction on the part of the adults. Play is the basis for all aspects of development.
- Does the center or home seem friendly or inviting?
- If there are two or more adults, do they seem to like working together and do they help each other?
- Is there a way your child can get a little privacy, either in a small private place or by climbing up to a platform where the group can be observed without involvement? Children need time and space to be by themselves sometimes, or with just one other adult or child.
- Is there a feeling of comfort and "softness" to the place? Children need soft pillows, furry animals, water, sand and clay to play with, messy things like mud and finger paint, warm things like laps and hugs. If it's all hard, linoleum and tables and chairs, it won't meet young children's needs to experience things with their senses.
- Is the place physically safe? Check for sharp edges, unprotected radiators, uncovered wall plugs, poisonous cleaning supplies or medicines within reach, unsanitary bathroom or kitchen conditions, traffic in outdoor play areas.
- Are there few enough children so that the children and adults there can get to know each other well?

For more information on child care:
write to the Day Care and Child Development Council of America, 622 14th Street, N.W., Washington, D.C. Their day care publications are the most complete of any organization. They are opening a Children's Embassy in Washington to speak up for children's needs in the nation's capital, and are seeking more members and support.

A new book on child care has just been released by the Carnegie Council on Children which has been studying public policy in support of families. This book, by Alison Clarke-Stewart, is called *Child Care in the Family: A Review of Research and Some Propositions for Policy*, and is published by Academic Press. Your local library might want to make it available to parents. Another interesting new book, by Ellen Galinsky and William Hooks, is titled *The New Extended Family: Day Care Programs at Work*, published by Houghton Mifflin.

A good parent guide is *Checking Out Child Care*, available from the Day Care and Child Development Council of America.

1. PERSPECTIVES

dren were accustomed to seeking help from their teachers while in day care, the teachers apparently had not replaced their mothers as the preferred source of assistance.

Social scientists are vigorously pursuing the study of day care and attachment. They are examining situations different from those studied so far; whether or not the age of entering day care makes a difference; and possible long-term effects that might not reveal themselves until the child is older. For now, however, parents can be reassured that research does not support the fear that day care disrupts the attachment between mother and child. However, parents should be aware that children placed in day care after about eight months of age may undergo some upset—as they would with any major change in life routine. But it seems that this is a brief and passing disruption, which apparently leaves no serious aftereffect on the child's development.

Social Behavior

If infants and children spend a great deal of time with other children their own age during the preschool years, it is possible that they will behave more in accord with their peer-group values than adult values. If so, children in day care, contrasted to those raised at home, might be expected to be more aggressive toward others of their age and adults, and more resistant to adult direction. At least two studies suggest that children with extensive day care experience are, in fact, more aggressive and less cooperative than children without previous day care.

In the earlier study, researchers found that children with longer attendance in preschool had more negative interactions with their teachers during the first grade than children with fewer years of preschool attendance. The second study, conducted at Syracuse University by Dr. J. Conrad Schwarz and his colleagues, found that three and four-year-olds who entered day care between five and twenty-two months of age were rated as more aggressive with peers and teachers, more active and less cooperative with adults than children who had no previous day care experiences. Furthermore, these differences persisted after eight months of day care attendance, thereby implying that the effects can be traced specifically to early day care experience.

These studies have caused concern among some social scientists who fear that children in day care may be slow to acquire adult values. However, not all studies support this conclusion, and perhaps more than in any of the other areas discussed here, the research is inadequate to support firm conclusions. It seems wise, however, for parents to carefully examine their day care arrangement to be certain that staff members do interact frequently with the children, do provide desirable models of adult behavior and do set standards which the children are required to meet.

These studies also provide striking examples of how research results should be interpreted by parents according to their own values. The reason that children with day care experience have more negative relations with other children and with their teachers is because they are more assertive, strong-willed and independent. Those parents who value assertiveness and independence in their children, even if the children are somewhat aggressive as well, may not find this a deterrent.

Health

Important questions related to children's physical health and well-being are also raised by day care attendance. After all, if children are brought together in close physical proximity, it seems likely that they will be exposed to more germs and viruses than if they were kept at home.

Several studies have tried to find out whether or not children in day care catch more of the common childhood illnesses—colds, diarrhea, ear infections and so on—than children reared at home. The results have been conflicting. Some studies found more sickness among children in day care, others did not. Our own studies at the Frank Porter Graham Center found the incidence of illness generally the same for children in day care and those at home, especially when the home-reared children had older siblings in the public schools. It seems that waves of illnesses move through a community, affecting children everywhere.

No study has found evidence that day care increases the incidence of serious illnesses such as polio or meningitis. Most studies also found that it doesn't help much to keep children home once they get sick in order to control the spread of illness, because children expose other children to infectious bacteria and viruses before they, themselves, have any symptoms. Once the child is obviously sick, he has already exposed others to the illness. These studies are also in agreement that illness rates in large centers are not higher than those in family day care where only four or five children are enrolled.

Unanswered questions about illness and day care will give researchers something important to study for years to come. For now it is probably justified to say that some children may get a slightly greater number of *minor* illnesses if they are in day care, though not any more at a large center than in a small home. In addition, if the child feels well enough to go to the center, you need not fear spreading the illness. It is also clear that day care centers following poor sanitation practices in toilet use and food handling can increase the rate of illness among their children. For this reason, parents would be wise to check carefully the sanitation practices of the center or home attended by their child.

Summary of Findings

The findings from social science research can be summarized as follows. First, there is little clear evidence that day care permanently enhances or slows intellectual development. Second, day care can be used, even from earliest infancy, without damaging the mother-child relationship. Third, there is some evidence that children attending day care are aggressive with peers and adults, and somewhat resistant to incorporating adult values. Fourth, day care may lead to a slight increase in minor illness among children, but the exclusion of ill children from day care is not an effective means of reducing the spread of sickness. Taken together, we believe that these findings do not provide strong or consistent evidence that could be used to deter the use of day care by most families.

Keep in mind, in reaching your decision that most of the studies have been made in model day care centers characterized by low adult-to-child ratios, good nutrition programs, excellent sanitation practices, some staff training and low staff turnover.

If the particular day care setting you have in mind is not of high quality, you would do well to seek an alternative to it.

Second, and this point can hardly be overemphasized, even for a child in day care there are many influences in his development besides that one. The warmth and acceptance of the child's parents is paramount; the kind of family medical care and nutrition provided is also vital. Important, too, is the safety of home and neighborhood, the age and number of brothers and sisters, the quality and variety of social relationships experienced by the child. Each of these factors is bound to have a considerable influence on a child's development, and each may also influence how the child responds to day care.

Finally, parents should reconsider the nature of their relationships with professionals. In earlier times families did nearly everything for themselves. They raised or procured their own food, provided education for their children, for the most part took care of the health needs of family members. In short, families solved their own problems. As society became specialized, we began to turn more of these duties over to professionals—

8. Making the Day Care Decision

teachers, doctors, psychologists, psychiatrists, social workers Like so many aspects of so-called progress—this had its disadvantages and defects as well as advantages and benefits. While it is no doubt true that various professionals know and can do many things to help children and families, such help has often tended to undermine a family's self-confidence. Professional service has often made the recipients feel incompetent or stupid. Some professionals tend to make parents feel that only they, the professionals, know enough to make important decisions about the health, education and welfare of our nation's families.

People will always seek professional help, and they should. But in most cases, we feel the professional's role should be limited to providing specialized information and services. Important decisions about how to live as a family should always remain the right and the responsibility of the parents, who, in turn, share their thinking with their children and take their views into account, when the children are old enough to take part in family discussions.

The evidence and opinions offered here should be considered as a few among many elements that must be weighed by parents in making the day care decision. Only parents are in a position to weigh the research evidence in the light of their own work and financial situation, the personalities of their children, the availability of satisfactory day care. Finally, if parents elect to place their children in day care, they should demand a central role in determining practices followed in the day care program. To do less would constitute a surrender of the rights and responsibilities of parenthood.

Day Care Policy: Some Modest Proposals

**EDWARD ZIGLER
AND SUSAN HUNSINGER**

Edward Zigler, former director of the U.S. Office of Child Development, is Sterling Professor of Psychology at Yale University. Susan Hunsinger, also at Yale, is a journalist now specializing in child development.

Now that day care seems to have some friends in the White House, it is crucial for advocates to re-examine their own proposals. What is needed is not a monolithic system of federally administered day care centers with look-alike programs and professionals. The current variety of day care services —ranging from family day care to babysitting cooperatives to centers run by corporate franchises—is a potential strength in a country built on pluralism, where no single child-rearing philosophy prevails. Nor should the new administration simply try to regurgitate the Mondale-Brademas bill, with its complicated delivery mechanism and its tendency to overlook the day care functions already played by the states.

What is needed rather is a reorganization of the child care bureaucracy at the federal level and a better use of existing resources at the local level. To upgrade and expand day care will require help from all government levels, as well as from the private sector, and all but the most indigent families should pay partial fees. Some of these steps recommended here could be implemented in communities immediately at relatively little cost.

Provide more after-school care

The American school system represents a tremendous untapped source for providing day care. Two-thirds of the day care needed is for school-age children, yet most public and private programs serve only preschool children. Thus, while teacher union leaders, most notably New York's Albert Shanker, try to convince the public that day care for preschoolers is "a job for the schools," they overlook a much more obvious and appropriate task for the school, namely before- and after-school day care for school-age children.

The cost-effectiveness of this proposal, particularly at a time when many schools are under-enrolled, is beyond dispute. In Newington, Connecticut, near Hartford, a group of parents this year were able to secure an empty classroom to provide before- and after-school care. It's particularly important to families with kindergarteners, who only attend school two and one-half hours a day. "I couldn't find a reliable babysitter to pick up my son at school and watch him until I got home," says Kathy Cochefski, a parent who helped organize the program. "Now I don't have to worry about whether he gets on the school bus or what happens until I get home."

Upgrade existing family day care

If we could upgrade and pull together existing family day care arrangements, we could go a long way toward forming the nucleus of a total system. Family day care has the merit of most closely approximating a child's own home. Many of the problems with family day care —the caregiver's insufficient training, isolation from other adults, and low and unsteady income—can be overcome through public support and organization. At least 17 states now have family day care associations. And, a number of cities have family day care networks which provide in-service staff training, toy lending libraries, regular salaries, and substitute care when a caregiver needs a day off. Networks have been tried with success in Pasadena (Community Family Day Care Project), in New York City (The Family Day Care Career Program) and in Philadelphia (Associated Day Care Services).

Expand infant care

Although good day care for infants is inevitably expensive, the U.S. can no longer ignore the need for more of it. One-third of mothers with children under three now work; yet, very few day care programs will accept infants or toddlers. Day care for infants, the most vulnerable age group, is not only the least available; it is also the least regulated. Present federal day care standards do not even specify a staff-child ratio for children under three, requiring only that state standards be followed.

As a result, we have seen centers, breaking no law, that left one caregiver in charge of nine infants. In the event of a fire or disaster, one caregiver would have difficulty even carrying three of these infants to physical safety.

Many industrialized nations handle the infant care problem more sensibly, according to Dr. Shelia Kamerman who directs cross national studies for Columbia University School of Social Work. France offers every mother with children under two and one-half a choice: day care if she works, or a family allowance that amounts to half of what she would earn if she stays home. At the least, the U.S. should implement a part-paid maternity leave option so that mothers could stay home for the first six months of a child's life.

Train more personnel

The cost of any national day care system is so great that any responsible advocate must continually seek ways to minimize cost without sacrificing quality. Since 75% of day care costs are personnel costs, we will never have a viable day care system if we continue to assume that the care of four or five children in one's home or ten children in a center requires a B.A. degree. We must begin immediately to develop a large cadre of day care workers who are certified on the basis of their performance competency, not on the basis of the number of hours they have spent in a classroom. The Child Development Associate program is already training such day care workers, but the program should be enlarged. The CDA program could also be an important quality control mechanism, by helping to ensure that every individual certified as a CDA would have at least some knowledge of children and how to work with them.

Fund care more equitably

Under our nation's current day care policy, more implicit than explicit, the children of welfare parents get clustered in publicly funded programs, while slightly better off families shun the programs because they bear the stigma of poverty.

How could the federal government fund day care more equitably, so that all families, regardless of income, have a real choice? One suggestion is to distribute money directly to families, rather than to programs. This could be done through day care vouchers or income tax credits or reimbursements. Congress recently passed a tax reform bill which makes a step in this direction. Under this new legislation, families will be able to subtract directly 20% of the cost of day care, whether conducted in a center, a family day care home, or even by a relative in their own home. The maximum possible tax saving per child under this new reform will amount to $400 a year, only a small fraction of the cost of care. But we applaud this tax reform as a potentially non-stigmatizing method of funding day care.

Set realistic standards—enforce them

Most current state and federal efforts to license day care are an exercise in futility. Over 90% of family day care is unlicensed or monitored by any public agency. While most centers are licensed, state licensing requirements tend to be too lenient, particularly on the staff-child ratio, with some states allowing one adult to care for as many as ten children regardless of age.

Part of the problem is that the 1968 FIDCR are more in the nature of guidelines than they are enforceable statutes. In 1972, the Office of Child Development drafted some more specific standards, which provide for the special needs of infants, toddlers and school-age children. But, although then Secretary of HEW Elliot Richardson approved the new standards, they were never implemented, and instead disappeared in the Office of Management of the Budget, where they are still languishing.

But the standards are only part of the quality control problem in day care; the even thornier issue is enforcement. We cannot expect federal agencies to effectively monitor all the day care facilities needed. A system of sufficient federal personnel to monitor day care would cost as much as the day care itself. Instead, we must build into the day care system more mechanisms to encourage monitoring by parents and local agencies. In addition, we need to provide more incentives for day care providers to, in fact, comply with standards. Incentives to comply would include registry in a community referral agency, access to group insurance plans, and help with securing public funds. Finally, as former HEW Secretary Wilbur Cohen says, it is unrealistic to expect day care homes or centers to comply with new standards overnight. There must be a grace period in which licensing laws are not used to drive day care settings out of existence, but rather to aid these settings in upgrading their services.

Set up community referral agencies

Part of the problem with day care in the U.S. is that there is no central place to find out about the day care that does exist. A local community agency, separate from welfare and other social services, could help refer families to reliable day care providers of various types. In Kansas, the Witchita Child Day Care Association receives about 30 to 40 calls daily from parents seeking day care. Each caller is referred to three day care providers and advised on what to look for in a good day care program. The referral system acts as an incentive for day care programs to comply with standards on quality. The agency, which serves as a conduit for public funds, also ensures that each day care facility has a mix of fee-paying and publicly-subsidized children.

Reorganize federal child care bureaucracy

Little will happen on the day care front until the day care responsibili-

1. PERSPECTIVES

ties, now spread across a dozen federal agencies, ranging from the Small Business Administration to the Department of Agriculture, are united into a single agency. Although the federal funds for day care have increased dramatically, the principle of federal responsibility for day care quality has yet to be firmly established. Despite the existence of the Children's Bureau and the creation of the Office of Child Development, no single federal agency has been granted the power of the purse strings necessary to coordinate this maze of day care, much less enforce standards of quality. Indeed, in a perfect example of bureaucratic nonsense, fiscal control of the largest federally funded day care program, under Title XX of the Social Security Act, is not vested in OCD at all but rather in the Community Services Administration of HEW. The Children's Bureau personnel in the OCD, while theoretically charged with guaranteeing the quality of Title XX day care, have no fiscal power to make such review meaningful. If we are ever to have day care of dependable quality in the U.S., the same agency which sets day care standards must have the fiscal power and responsibility to implement them.

What can the Carter-Mondale administration do about day care? None of the above recommendations calls for an instant or by any means "free" national day care program. Nor do they call for a vast increase in federal funds and administration. But the federal government should try to upgrade the quality of existing day care and to distribute public dollars for day care more fairly.

Infant Day Care:
Toward a More Human Environment

Arminta Lee Jacobson

In planning optimal environments for infant day care, the human element is often minimized. Desirable caregiving competencies which can be used as a basis for evaluating day care personnel are derived from research findings.

What implications for infant caregiving in day care can be drawn from mother-infant interaction research? Few studies have been done on interpersonal caregiving competencies or the effect of discrete caregiving variables on infant development in day care settings. Yet the spiraling increase of out-of-home care for infants demands research attention, both for professionals concerned with infant day care and for parents needing such services. The following discussion examines mother-infant interaction research in order to delineate current areas of exploration and to synthesize findings into a helpful format for administrators, educators, researchers, and others interested in upgrading the quality of infant day care.

Importance of the Primary Caregiver

The importance of the primary caregiver in an infant's development is often overlooked, although several research studies have given evidence of the relationship between early caregiving experiences and competencies in later childhood. In a longitudinal study of environmental determinants related to human competency upon entering school, White and Watts (1973) found that ratings of competency of children at age six varied very little from ratings of competency of those children at age three. Further investigation pinpointed the period of 10 to 18 months as the most crucial in determining a child's later competency, especially in the areas of social skills and attitudes.

Yarrow et al. (1973) studied the relationship between mothering experiences during the first six months of life and selected intellectual and personal-social characteristics at 10 years of age. For boys, the Wechsler Intelligence Scale for Children IQ and several aspects of a child's relationship to others at 10 years of age were related to variables of maternal behavior at six months of age. In another study (Yarrow et al. 1972), the social environment was shown to be highly significant in influencing infant functioning, independent of dimensions of the inanimate environment.

In a report by Bayley and Schaefer (1964), results of an analysis of data collected in the Berkeley Growth Study between 1928 and 1954 showed maternal and child behaviors to be intercorrelated over an 18-year span of growth. The relationship to maternal behaviors was more significant for boys. Coping capacities of older children were found to be significantly related to early mother-infant interactions in a study by Murphy (1973) of 31 children and mothers. These studies and others contribute to the growing recognition of the impact of human relations in the earliest years of development.

Research studies of mother-infant interaction have varied in the type of interrelationships studied as well as in research design, data collection, and analysis. Categories of maternal and infant variables chosen to enter into relationship models have only gross similarities among investigations. Study of interpersonal behavior by its very nature requires direct observation of behavior and is susceptible to subjectivity in measurement. Behavior patterns are often quite complex, and interrelationships not included in the research model are often overlooked. Although infants have a limited repertoire of relationship responses, adult transactions are practically unlimited in variety and complexity. Nevertheless, important information discerned from such studies helps to identify those interrelationship variables which effect optimal development in the early formative years.

Although the mother-infant dyad has been the focus of most research seeking to explain social determinants of infant behavior and development, findings from such research can easily be generalized in terms of appropriate behavior for any adult serving as a primary caregiver of an infant, even for a limited part of the day, as in a day care setting. What is conducive to optimal development in one setting could logically be conceived as appropriate in another setting.

An exception which must be made in generalizing research findings of mother-infant interaction to day care is the area of attachment of infant to caregiver. In a series of ongoing studies of mother-infant relations, Ainsworth and Bell (1972) have pinpointed quality of attachment between mother and infant as being related to other aspects of infant and maternal behavior. Mutual attachment of infant and caregiver cannot be assumed in a day care setting. Nature and degree of attachment of primary caregivers and infants in day care have not been investigated and would be difficult to study due to the common instability of such relationships over time and the confounding effects of other adults and infants.

Areas of Adult Influence

Given the limitations of research methodology and generalizations, what evidence from recent research can serve as guidelines for infant day care personnel in providing an optimal human environment for infants?

Infants' physical, emotional, social, and cognitive development is shaped to a great extent by the behaviors of the primary caregivers in relation to the children. Primary caregivers can be conceived of not only as determinants of infants' physical survival but also as social agents against which infants test their growing competencies and

1. PERSPECTIVES

conceptions of self and the world. The extent to which adults initiate interactions with or respond to infants, the affective nature of those behaviors, their content and context, all have an influence on infants' developing responses and behaviors and the context within which different facets of their development emerge.

Infant Competence. Personality characteristics, control, involvement, responsiveness, and attachment are some of the many types of maternal influences found to be related to infant development. In a study of the mother-infant dyad (Stern et al. 1969), a sequence of relationships between personality characteristics of mother, modes of maternal behavior, and responses and development of the infant was defined. The nine factors resulting from this composite appear to be distributed along a continuum ranging from child-centered to mother-centered maternal functioning. Effective mothers were defined as those whose infants were lovingly responsive to them and accelerated in development. The characteristics these mothers seemed to have in common were: (1) attentive, loving involvement with their infants; (2) high levels of visual and vocal contact; and (3) play involvement. The mothers producing the more accelerated infants were characterized as self-confident and skilled in their caregiving and individualistic in style.

White and Watts (1973) found that infants assessed in their study as highly competent had mothers who differed significantly from mothers of infants judged less competent. Mothers of the more competent infants involved themselves in more mother-infant interactions. Even when their infants were as young as 12 to 15 months, these mothers spent more time with "highly intellectual" activities and used interaction techniques which taught or were facilitative in nature. These mothers decreased their use of restrictive techniques as children grew older while mothers of the less competent infants increased their use. From the analysis of attitudes and values of mothers in the study, characteristics related to optimal development of children included a positive attitude toward life in general; enjoyment of infants in the one-to-three-year age range; an acceptance of the incompatibility of infant needs and preservation of posessions and household order; and the willingness to take risks for the sake of infants' curiosity and development.

Ainsworth and Bell (1972) studied infants' competence in direct dealing with the physical environment as measured by developmental competence on the Griffiths Scale. Positive relationships were shown between infant competence and maternal factors of sensitivity, acceptance, cooperation, and the amount of floor freedom allowed the infant. Amount of playing with the baby by the mother was also positively correlated with developmental scores of the infant. Frequency of punishment was negatively related to infant competence.

Level and variety of social stimulation (Yarrow et al. 1972) provided by a primary caregiver in the home have been found to be positively related to functioning of five-month-old infants. Infant functioning which related significantly to social stimulation included goal-directed behaviors, reaching and grasping, and secondary circular reactions. Adult responses, contingent upon infant distress, were found to be significantly related to goal-directed behavior in the infant.

Other studies (Murphy 1973; Stern et al. 1969) exemplify findings which support an optimal level of interaction, reporting a curvilinear relationship between development and degree of attention. In studying the development of coping ability in young children, Murphy (1973) found that optimal early mother-infant interactions were characterized by a balance of attention and autonomy, of interaction and letting the infant alone part of the time. Too much or too little attention, body contact, and talking to infants were found to be not good for infant development. These findings concur with findings (Stern et al. 1969) which characterize mothers of slow-developing infants as exhibitionist, vigilant, and including both high and low levels of physical contact. Murphy (1973) also found that patterns of mothering were related to individual infant temperaments in different ways, indicating the need for flexibility in interaction patterns.

Infant Vocalization. Mother responsiveness and infant vocalization have been examined in several studies. Clarke-Stewart (1973) reported a high relation of responsive maternal speech and children's competence in a longitudinal study of infants from 9 to 18 months of age.

Responsive mothers—those who ignore few episodes and respond with little delay—have infants with more variety, subtlety, and clarity of noncrying communication. During the second, third, and fourth quarters of the first year, infants of responsive mothers cried significantly less than infants of unresponsive mothers. Beckwith (1971b) also reported a positive relationship between mothers' ignoring of infants and frequency of infant crying. Infants who cried little had a wider range of differentiated modes of communication than did infants who cried often (Ainsworth and Bell 1972). Amount of maternal play behavior has also been found to be positively related to amount of infant vocalization (Clarke-Stewart 1973).

Perceptual-Cognitive Development. In the last decade, perceptual-cognitive development of very young children has interested researchers and parents. A study of perceptual-cognitive development in infants 12 weeks of age (Lewis and Goldberg 1969) also stressed the importance of maternal responses which are contingent upon the infant's behavior. Perceptual-cognitive development was found to be moderately related to the overall response of mother to infant's crying and vocalization and the amount of touching, holding, and smiling exhibited by the mother, and highly related to the amount of looking by the mother. These findings concur with other studies (Stern et al. 1969; White and Watts 1973) which characterize effective mothers as being very responsive to and involved with their infants.

An investigation of the relationships between maternal behaviors, infant behaviors, and individual differences in infant IQ (Beckwith 1971a) was made with the same infants at two interviews, during age ranges from 7.2 to 9.7 months and 8.5 to 11.3 months. This study revealed that low maternal verbal and physical contact within the home were significantly related to lower IQ on the Cattell Infant Intelligence Scale. Maternal restriction of infant exploration was found to be related to decreased interest in attaining speech during the last quarter of the first year and was significantly related to lowering of IQ scores.

Clarke-Stewart (1973) also reported maternal restrictiveness to be negatively related to scores on the Bayley Scale of Mental Development at 18 months. In this study the Bayley measure was highly correlated with the mother's nonphysical stimulation—looking and talking. Responsiveness of the mother was also related to the child's Bayley score and to the child's speed of processing information, schema development, language, and social and emotional competence. Stimulation by mother to promote achievement has also been found to be related to Cattell IQ scores at six months of age (Yarrow et al. 1973).

Ainsworth and Bell (1972) have studied cognitive development in White middle socioeconomic status (SES) infants and Black lower SES infants in terms of development of the concept of object permanence and scores on the Griffiths Development Scale. Infants who had harmonious interactions with mothers sensitive to their signals and who had developed attachment relationships of normal quality tended to develop the concept of person permanence in advance of object permanence. At 8 to 11

10. Infant Day Care

Table 1. Characteristics of Competent Infant Caregivers.

Desired Caregiver Characteristics	Cues to Desirable Caregiver Characteristics
I. Personality Factors	
A. Child-centered	1. Attentive and loving to infants. 2. Meets infants' needs before own.
B. Self-confident	1. Relaxed and anxiety free. 2. Skilled in physical care of infants. 3. Individualistic caregiving style.
C. Flexible	1. Uses different styles of caregiving to meet individual needs of infants. 2. Spontaneous and open behavior. 3. Permits increasing freedom of infant with development.
D. Sensitive	1. Understands infants' cues readily. 2. Shows empathy for infants. 3. Acts purposefully in interactions with infants.
II. Attitudes and Values	
A. Displays positive outlook on life	1. Expresses positive affect. 2. No evidence of anger, unhappiness, or depression.
B. Enjoys infants	1. Affectionate to infants. 2. Shows obvious pleasure in involvement with infants.
C. Values infants more than possessions or immaculate appearance	1. Dresses practically and appropriately. 2. Places items not for infants' use out of reach. 3. Reacts to infant destruction or messiness with equanimity. 4. Takes risks with property in order to enhance infant development.
III. Behavior	
A. Interacts appropriately with infants	1. Frequent interactions with infants. 2. Balances interaction with leaving infants alone. 3. Optimum amounts of touching, holding, smiling, and looking. 4. Responds consistently and without delay to infants; is always accessible. 5. Speaks in positive tone of voice. 6. Shows clearly that infants are loved and accepted.
B. Facilitates development	1. Does not punish infants. 2. Plays with infants. 3. Provides stimulation with toys and objects. 4. Permits freedom to explore, including floor freedom. 5. Cooperates with infant-initiated activities and explorations. 6. Provides activities which stimulate achievement or goal orientation. 7. Acts purposefully in an educational role to teach and facilitate learning and development.

months these infants were also advanced in the level of object permanence achieved. Harmonious attachment relationship, as well as floor freedom, were highly related to development scores.

Infant Play Behavior. Another area of consideration is the development of infant play behavior. According to findings by Clarke-Stewart (1973), the best single predictor of play behavior in infants was the amount of stimulation with toys and objects received from the mother at home.

Other researchers have studied quality of investigative behavior and exploratory play and its relation both to maternal behavior and to the quality of infant-mother attachment relationships (Ainsworth and Bell 1972). They found a significant relationship during the last quarter of the first year between frequent harmonious transactions with the mother, mother responsiveness to infant-initiated interaction, and the infant's greater exploration of toys and advanced behavioral schemata in play.

Social Development. Social development and play appear to be enhanced by some of the same maternal behaviors. In studying relations between the mother's behavior and the quality of the child's attachment, Clarke-Stewart (1973) found a number of nonlinear relationships. Optimally securely attached children—those able to use mother as a secure base from which to explore the environment and to which to return periodically at times of stress or for reassurance—where associated with homes where there was not constant exposure to a great number of people and where mothers were socially stimulating, responsive, and affectionate. In particular, the children's attachment was highly related to frequency of maternal social behavior.

1. PERSPECTIVES

In studying the use of mother as a secure base from which to explore, Ainsworth and Bell (1972) studied quality of infant attachment in relation to maternal ratings. Infants rated as highest in actively seeking proximity and interaction with mothers all had mothers above the median in sensitivity to infant signals, acceptance, cooperation, and accessibility.

The early manifestation of infant obedience indicates progress in social development. In a study by Stayton, Hogan, and Ainsworth (1971), maternal variables of sensitivity, acceptance, and cooperation were all highly intercorrelated with infants' compliance with commands during the last quarter of the first year. Frequency of verbal commands, frequency of physical intervention, and amount of floor freedom permitted the infant were not found to be related to compliance with commands.

Happiness. An obvious measure of effectiveness in interpersonal relations with infants is the degree to which positive affect or happiness is observed in the infant. Smiling and vocalizing and the absence of crying and fretting are seen as evidence of happiness. An infant's expression of happiness has been found to be most closely related to the mother's expression of positive emotions (Clarke-Stewart 1973). Mothers who vocalize and smile frequently have been found to have infants who vocalize and smile frequently. The more positive the maternal behaviors, the less frequently the infants fret and cry (Lewis and Wilson 1972). Infant fretfulness has been observed to be related to maternal rejection and self-control. Lower levels of infant fretfulness are associated with maternal effectiveness in physical, social, and instrumental behaviors (Clarke-Stewart 1973).

Implications for Infant Day Care Workers

Despite the inconsistency of focus and the nebulous nature of desirable maternal behaviors, mother-child interaction studies provide a sound research base for determining desirable caregiving attributes. In view of the empirical evidence on the importance of human interactions to infant development, it is clear that infant day care workers must be highly competent in interpersonal skills for quality caregiving. It is imperative that day care administrators hire and train infant caregivers on the basis of their attitudes and behaviors in interpersonal relations with infants.

Table 1 represents a synthesis of characteristics which provide an optimal human environment for infant caregiving, as generalized from the research findings. The categorization of caregiving behaviors can be used for further development of competency profiles for infant caregivers. Administrators of infant care centers will be most interested in those items helpful to selecting and evaluating infant caregivers; characteristics reflected in Table 1 provide possibilities for structuring interview or evaluation schedules. More specific attention to developmental levels of competence within behavior indexes could lead toward individualized training experiences for infant day care staff.

Further research, directed toward specification, assessment, and integration of infant caregiving behaviors, is needed, since only through delineation of these important human behaviors can child care personnel plan knowledgeably for the optimal care of infants.

Other implications for the placement of caregivers in day care settings come from research findings which highlight cultural, racial, and SES differences in maternal expectations for infants and in mother-infant interaction behaviors (Goldberg 1972; Lewis and Ban 1973; Lewis and Wilson 1972; Tulkin and Cohler 1973). Developmental differences in infants have been associated with caregiver differences. Consideration should be given to placing caregivers in day care settings where their cultural and SES values and expectations are similar to those of the families served.

Recognition of wide variations in caregivers' attitudes, sensitivities, and behaviors should also prompt day care professionals to work cooperatively with parents in setting caregiving goals for infants. Parents can help caregivers define the infant's nature and needs and the kind of environmental variables most effective in maximizing the infant's potential.

The crucial importance of the earliest experiences of life need continual emphasis and investigation. It is hoped that persons responsible for planning day care experiences for infants will be creatively sensitive to ways in which the quality of life for infants can be improved.

References

Ainsworth, M. D. S., and Bell, S. M. "Mother-Infant Interaction and the Development of Competence." ERIC Document Reproduction Service No. ED 065 180, 1972.

Ainsworth, M. D. S.; Bell, S. M.; and Stayton, D. J. "Individual Differences in Strange-Situation Behavior of One-Year-Olds." In *The Competent Infant: Research and Commentary*, edited by L. J. Stone, H. T. Smith, and L. B. Murphy. New York: Basic Books, 1973.

Bayley, N., and Schaefer, E. S. "Correlations of Maternal and Child Behaviors with the Development of Mental Abilities: Data from the Berkeley Growth Study." *Monographs of the Society for Research in Child Development* 29, no. 6 (1964), serial no. 97.

Beckwith, L. "Relationships Between Attributes of Mothers and Their Infants' IQ Scores." *Child Development* 42, no. 4 (1971a): 1083-1097.

Beckwith, L. "Relationships Between Infant's Vocalizations and Their Mother's Behaviors." *Merrill-Palmer Quarterly* 17 (1971b): 211-226.

Caudill, W., and Frost, L. "A Comparison of Maternal Care and Infant Behavior in Japanese-American, American, and Japanese Families." ERIC Document Reproduction Service No. ED 057 153, 1971, Honolulu, Hawaii.

Clarke-Stewart, K. A. "Interactions Between Mothers and Their Young Children: Characteristics and Consequences." *Monographs of the Society for Research in Child Development* 38, nos. 6-7 (1973), serial no. 153.

Goldberg, S. "Infant Care and Growth in Urban Zambia." *Human Development* 15 (1972): 77-89.

Lewis, M., and Ban, P. "Variance and Invariance in the Mother-Infant Interaction: A Cross-Cultural Study." ERIC Document Reproduction Service No. ED 084 006, 1973, Princeton, New Jersey.

Lewis, M., and Goldberg, S. "Perceptual-Cognitive Development in Infancy: A Generalized Expectancy Model as a Function of the Mother-Infant Interaction." *Merrill-Palmer Quarterly* 15 (1969): 81-100.

Lewis, M., and Wilson, C. D. "Infant Development in Lower-Class American Families." *Human Development* 15 (1972): 112-127.

Murphy, L. B. "Later Outcomes of Early Infant and Mother Relationships." In *The Competent Infant: Research and Commentary*, edited by L. J. Stone, H. T. Smith, and L. B. Murphy. New York: Basic Books, 1973.

Stayton, D. J.; Hogan, R.; and Ainsworth, M. D. S. "Infant Obedience and Maternal Behavior: The Origins of Socialization Reconsidered." *Child Development* 42 (1971): 1057-1069.

Stern, G. G.; Caldwell, B. M.; Hersher, L.; Lipton, E. L.; and Richmond, J. G. "A Factor Analytic Study of the Mother-Infant Dyad." *Child Development* 40 (1969): 163-181.

Tulkin, S. R., and Cohler, B. J. "Childbearing Attitudes and Mother-Child Interactions in the First Year of Life." *Merrill-Palmer Quarterly* 19 (1973): 95-106.

Tulkin, S. R., and Kagan, J. "Mother-Child Interaction in the First Year of Life." *Child Development* 43 (1972): 31-41.

White, B. L., and Watts, J. C. *Experience and Environment: Major Influences on the Development of the Young Child*. Englewood Cliffs, N.J.: Prentice-Hall, 1973.

Yarrow, L. G.; Goodwin, M. S.; Manheimer, H.; and Milowe, I. D. "Infancy Experiences and Cognitive and Personality Development at Ten Years." In *The Competent Infant: Research and Commentary*, edited by L. J. Stone, H. T. Smith, and L. B. Murphy. New York: Basic Books, 1973.

Yarrow, L. G.; Rubenstein, J. L.; Pedersen, F. A.; and Jankowski, J. J. "Dimensions of Early Stimulation and Their Differential Effects on Infant Development." *Merrill-Palmer Quarterly* 18 (1972): 205-218.

What Young Children Need Most In A Changing Society

An interview with the renowned child psychologist, David Elkind, on loving and learning in family life today.

Q. Dr. Elkind, you are well-known for relating child development theories to the actual practice of child rearing, and for putting these theories into useful perspective for parents and teachers. What, then, are the implications for parents and teachers of children's normal stages of development?
A. For one thing, we can relate developmental stages to changes in the way children learn at different age levels. Learning begins with observation and manipulation as in early childhood. Then labeling and classification follow in early and middle childhood. And finally, careful experiments and development of theories can be observed in adolescence. We shouldn't expect a child to function in a way more advanced than his age-related mental structures will permit.

Q. Does it seem to you that this runs counter to some current practices among parents and teachers?
A. It does. We often try to force children to learn things which are inappropriate to their stage of growth. In an article I wrote for *Parents'* magazine some years ago, and in other articles, I've discussed the possible harm in putting too much stress on academic achievement in the preschool child.

Preschool children are often pushed into reading, although reading requires the use of complex concepts (like the fact that letters can have some elements of similarity and difference at the same time). But the average child only begins to understand that one thing can be like something else and different from it at the same time, at the age of six or seven. Only the brightest children comprehend this at age three or four.

Parents and educators should respect the child's intellectual limitations and not attempt to bypass them and push on to learning beyond his or her attained level. We shouldn't try to force the child to use mental structures that haven't developed in order to meet some outside standard of achievement. At each stage of development, the child has limits as to what he or she can learn that cannot be ignored.

Q. When do different mental abilities develop?
A. Rote memory develops and matures early; the structures for language and perception seem to be mature by the middle of childhood; and reasoning reaches its final form in adolescence. These periods are critical, and the child needs the appropriate stimulation during each stage. But the limits are flexible and it takes extreme and prolonged overstimulation or deprivation to seriously injure a child.

Q. How do children respond to stimulation in learning?

A. It depends upon the kind of learning. When children are acquiring new mental abilities, as opposed to acquiring skills or concepts, one can observe children actually seeking stimulation, which nourishes further growth. A child pulls a toy, it moves, and he or she wants to pull it again, because the movement is nourishing the abilities being developed. When the child finds something that nourishes his or her mental growth, and is enjoying it, other stimulations that might be distracting are tuned out. Once the child has acquired a new mental ability he or she reaches the stage of intellectual play, and tests the limits of the newfound ability.

Q. What are some of the major trends in child rearing today, or changes from the way parents felt in the fairly recent past?
A. Parents today seem more concerned about the child's intellectual abilities than they were a few years ago. They seem to think their own parents were too anxious about their "adjustment," or emotional well-being. Children today are under great pressure for academic achievement— to learn more, earlier. While this can lead to intellectual independence at a younger age, it can also result in more children who suffer from emotional problems because of school failure.

If a child thinks his worth is related to what he achieves, instead of who he is, failure in school can cause a serious emotional upheaval. This danger probably will grow in the United States because the trend toward smaller families puts even

Reprinted with permission of *Parents' Magazine*, July 1977. Copyright ©1977 by Parents' Magazine, New York.

1. PERSPECTIVES

greater pressure on children, and means more competitive only children in the population. By the way, we are also pushing children into organized sports at earlier ages as well. It is part of the same syndrome.

Q. What other trends do you see in the United States today?
A. We are losing our predominantly child-centered approach to family life. Until a few years ago, the child's wants and needs took precedence over the parents'. Mothers, in particular, would sacrifice their own development for the sake of the children. Now the child is no longer viewed as the center of everything; his or her needs are more likely to be seen as equal to, but not greater than, those of the parents. This can lead to early emotional independence, with both good and bad possibilities.

The necessary separation from the family that begins in adolescence can become less harsh today because both parents and children already have interests outside of the family. When the young person is ready to leave home, the mother isn't as likely to feel that her world has collapsed—she may be deeply involved in a life apart from the children. This emotional independence also means that parents may get a divorce more readily if the marriage does not meet their needs; formerly they might have stayed in an unhappy marriage for the sake of the children.

Q. Statistics indicate that approximately eight million mothers in the United States are bringing up children in homes where the fathers are absent. What effect does this have on the child?
A. If one of the parents leaves home, the effect on the children depends on many factors. One of them is timing. If the father leaves when his children are quite young, it can be traumatic for the children, especially boys. At this age, boys see themselves as rivals to the father and have fantasies about getting rid of the father. If the father really leaves, the child may think that his fantasy created reality, and that he is responsible for the divorce. This could be a source of emotional problems related to guilt.

If a father dies, however, the child can deal with it more readily than if the father leaves home—there is a sense of grief with death, but that is a more positive feeling than rejection. The mother's sense of separation, rejection and anger can also be communicated to the children, and cause emotional difficulties. Our society should provide more counseling help for families struggling with the problems of death and divorce.

Q. Statistics also show that many more women with young children are now working than ever before. How does this influence child development?
A. The most significant factor is the quality of the substitute child care. This is important at any age, but it is most important in the first two years of the child's life, and crucial in the first year of life. There is no evidence that the mother must be the main caretaker; but the child does need mothering, and the ratio of children to caretaker should be no more than three to one, for children under two. As children grow older, quality care is still of great importance, but the ratio can be higher, say ten children to one adult. These ratios are rough estimates, and will vary with particular circumstances. With quality day care, there is no evidence that children are in any way harmed by being reared partially out of the home.

Q. When parents are thinking about a divorce, or if a mother is working, what kind of special help might be provided for the children?
A. When divorce is being considered, children as well as parents should be prepared for the forthcoming emotional trauma by counseling or at least by open discussion. Children need as much or more support during a divorce than the parents. If the mother of an intact family is working, or involved in interests outside the home, the father could spend more time with the children, although this may not be a realistic expectation—the increased pressure for outside achievement on women has not diminished the pressures on men.

Q. What do you see as a major need in families today?
A. Contemporary parents should be more concerned about the emotional needs of their children, and the quality of the time spent with them.

Q. What other trends do you see in family life?
A. The contemporary adults' loss of faith in reason, in science, in technology, even in the possibility of a better world, has had a profound effect on our children. We continue to be busy with our work, but our children pick up our loss of faith.

Young people today are searching for faith, something true, beautiful and abiding to believe in. This is a necessary framework within which to form a sense of personal identity. Since many adults have lost values, or so it seems to our children, they feel the lack of support in forming an identity. They feel they need an anchor to grasp—something like a religious crusade or the occult to make up for the moral weakness of adult society. Children need to know that we adults believe in something. We should share our faith and our values with them.

Q. In addition to your studies of preschool children, you've been engaged in clinical work with adolescents, and have written extensively about their needs. Is women's liberation causing great changes in interests among adolescent girls?
A. Despite women's lib, many adolescent girls are still mainly preoccupied with boys, with becoming mothers and having homes—although there is increasing consideration of other careers and of becoming persons in their own right. We still haven't resolved the problems women face in forming an identity apart from family roles. Social change has to fight the tremendous inertia of social habit.

Q. What are these problems?
A. Some of them develop from family dynamics. Men and women seem to arrive at a sense of their identity in different ways. To begin to form your own identity, you have to differentiate, to see yourself as distinct from something or somebody else.

Initially, the child attaches himself or herself to the caretaker—usually the mother—and makes the primary identification with the mother. In the preschool years, when the boy begins to conceive of himself as a certain kind of self, a boy, he has to begin the process of breaking away and differentiating from his mother and gradually identifying with his father.

When the preschool girl realizes her femaleness, however, she doesn't have to differentiate or break away from the primary caretaker. She continues to identify with her mother and maintains an unbroken history of identification with her. The kind of detachment and assertion of self that a boy first experiences when he breaks away from his mother, may not take place for women until they are married, perhaps not until after their own children have left home, when the woman must form a sense of herself as a person, and not as someone's daughter, wife or mother.

Changes in our culture are accelerating this process of differentiation and identity formation for women, however. Today, many women do not marry, and have to form identities apart from family roles at an earlier age, or women marry and have no children, or stop having children at a younger age. On the other hand, more women today do have a strong sense of themselves—an identity apart from family roles—and face difficulties in integrating their sense of self into family life.

Creating an identity is even more complex now because identity presupposes stable values. There are few social frameworks to help a woman build her own identity apart from family roles as yet, or to help a

11. What Young Children Need Most

woman find a harmony between personal identity and family roles.

Q. How about your own family life; is your wife following a career outside the home?
A. Sally, my wife, recently completed a four-year program in music, and received a performing degree in piano. She now teaches at home and at school.

Q. How do you and your wife reconcile your careers and your children's needs?

A. We share in child-rearing tasks. I get the boys off to school in the morning. And we spend time with the children that is their time. The truism that the quality of time spent with the children matters more than its quantity is borne out by experience. Paying attention to a child when you're with him counts most.

Q. What is your attitude toward parenthood?

A. I think it's important that a parent *be* something to the child, because children learn by example. Be the kind of person you want your child to be, be honest about your feelings with your children and they will learn to be honest with you. And, when a child demonstrates responsibility, give him other freedom to do what he is able to do—we grow through the freedom to act responsibly. Good parenting is not easy, it means you have to work at it and to keep growing and learning along with your children.

We want your advice.

Any anthology can be improved. This one will be—annually. But we need your help.

Annual Editions revisions depend on two major opinion sources: one is the academic advisers who work with us in scanning the thousands of articles published in the public press each year; the other is you—the person actually using the book.

Please help us and the users of the next edition by completing the prepaid article rating form on the last page of this book and returning it to us. Thank you.

Childhood and Society 2

Philosophers maintain that the litmus test for a civilization is in its treatment of and provisions for the most needy and vulnerable of its citizens. How well is America doing, accordingly, in its provision for young children? The pervasive effects of rapid social change are mirrored in the lives of young children. They are invariably the winners or the losers when society-at-large, families, or educational programs experience profound change and disruption.

The issue of whether Americans generally like children as children, treat them with respect and consideration, and tend to their basic needs for food, protection, stimulation, guidance, and encouragement draws contrasting responses. Some argue that an examination of earlier historical periods shows the ways in which children were mistreated, treated as miniature adults, or treated as inherently evil requiring religious purging. This argument continues, that, consequently, more of today's children not only physically survive childhood, but emerge from it emotionally secure and intellectually adept. Others point out that thousands of children, because of pronounced and prolonged difficulties, become troubled, marginal societal members and generally do not live up to their birthright as human beings.

This section also addresses child abuse. Some children are hurt so severely that damage is done not only to their present lives but to their future coping and learning skills as well. Violence against children is being recognized as an appalling and hideous fact of life affecting many children in every economic strata.

Educators are increasingly called upon to advocate for children—advocate for their rights as people and their societal place as future adults. Educators can join in the debates about the meaning of societal change and the implications for today's young children. They cannot afford to be either pollyannas or cynics since either position offers blind spots and inhibits the capacity to help others.

Just as societal ills and conflicts abound, so do the human abilities possessed by many to transcend adversity; and so does the dedication of a few to work to counteract and reduce the suffering, ignorance, disease, and poverty through the provision of quality care and education.

This section contains articles on global influences on children's lives. By comparing recollections of childhood to the ways in which childhood is portrayed in the articles, the reader is given the opportunity to decide on an optimistic or pessimistic view of the future destiny of today's young children. Selected solutions are offered to a myriad of problems facing our nation.

Looking Ahead: Challenge Questions

What were the most prevalent attitudes and practices toward children a century ago? What progress has been made?

How "rosy" or "grim" is the picture of current American family life? What are the consequences for children of divorce, break-down in communication between families, and working mothers?

What projections can be made for education's future in the 1980s? What are the causes for optimism or pessimism?

What effect does television viewing have on children's learning abilities and study habits? What happens to family life when television time is limited?

What can be done to help children become less violent, more self-controlled, and more considerate of others?

What are signs of child abuse? What can teachers do about child neglect and/or child abuse?

Our Disconnected Child

William Kessen

William Kessen is chairman of the department of psychology at Yale. He is the author of several books, including The Child.

Consider, that you may Perish, as young as you are; there are small Chips as well as great Logs, in the Fire of Hell.
—from an eighteenth-century primer

Damnation lay fore and aft the American child two hundred years ago. Primers began with the words "In Adam's Fall, We Sinned All," and the danger of a sin-filled death was proclaimed from every pulpit. Everyone lived under the twin threats of imminent mortality and a fall from grace. The alliance of children and grown-ups in the fear of Satan and the hope of salvation was mirrored in the social organization of the time. No one doubted the unity and strength of Church and State, and the family was seen as "a little Church, a little Commonwealth." Children dressed much like adults and played many of the games that adults played (more frequently, of course, in Europe and the colonial South than in rigorous New England); they lived in the workaday world of adults as smaller colleagues, and they shared in the major and minor rituals of the larger group—weddings, burials, punishments, and gossip. In remarkable measure, the continuity of the community was matched by a continuity of generations.

A short history of children in the United States can be sketched on the theme of their steady separation from both continuities, the story of the child severed from his past and increasingly a traveler from one specialized setting to another. In Europe, where children had been full participants in adult life from a very young age, the segregation of parent and child was under way before 1700. Philippe Ariès, the French historian, has shown that children's games and children's clothes began to differ from those of adults precisely in synchrony with the establishment of schools. (By 1800, children of the middle class were being dressed in the costumes of the lower social orders—little boys wore sailor suits with long, soft trousers, instead of the breeches worn by their fathers—just as their nineteenth-century counterparts wore peasant tunics and children today wear overalls and blue jeans.)

The first specialization of the child, in America and Europe, was Child as Student. The school remains the strongest agent of the child's separation from the world of adults. In school, we learn adult values: clock time is truer than body time; order is more to be valued than fooling around; hierarchy is essential for a proper democratic society. With the growth of schools, American children were also gradually drawn away from the world of adult work. At first chores went on, especially in rural areas; but for many children—and in urban areas, for most—the move to school was a move away from the everyday lives of their fathers.

The redefinition of childhood had its philosophers and polemicists in Europe, and their influence was soon felt in America. In 1699 John Locke published *Some Thoughts Concerning Education,* with advice to parents about their children's early training. Locke was as dubious as any colonial preacher about children's ability to grow up well without strict restraint ("children should be used to submit their desires, and go without their longings, *even from their very cradles*"), but he severed them from their demonic origins and held out the possibility of *changing* their behavior. Locke would have had fundamental disagreements with modern behaviorists like B. F. Skinner, but he started us on our way toward behavior modification when he wrote:

> Rewards . . . *and Punishments must be proposed to Children, if we intend to work upon them. The Mistake . . . is that those that are generally made use of are ill chosen . . . Esteem and Disgrace are, of all others, the most powerful Incentives to the Mind. . . .*

Rousseau's *Emile*, published in 1762, opened another door through which American cultural ideology would run. For Rousseau, the child was not only free of original sin, he was also a being of *Nature*, pregnant with unsuspected possibility. Childhood was not a time set aside for adults to finish God's work by bringing the child into closer match with adult behavior; it was a time important in itself. "Leave childhood to ripen in your children," Rousseau

---

> In medieval society the idea of childhood did not exist; this is not to suggest that children were neglected, forsaken or despised. The idea of childhood is not to be confused with affection for children: it corresponds to an awareness of the particular nature of childhood, that particular nature which distinguishes the child from the adult, even the young adult. In medieval society this awareness was lacking. That is why, as soon as the child could live without the constant solicitude of his mother, his nanny or his cradle-rocker, he belonged to adult society. . . .
> —Philippe Ariès, *Centuries of Childhood* (1962)

12. Our Disconnected Child

wrote; "... the child's individual bent ... must be thoroughly known before we can choose the fittest moral training." The child, no longer a passive recipient of instruction, had become a busy, and alert, explorer.

More than a century later, Darwin published *A Biographical Sketch of an Infant*. With chatty scholarship, Darwin offered up the child (his own) as a fit subject for scientific study, a representative of the species' capacity to perfect itself by selective transformation. Before Locke, the child had stood for the stability of family and church. After Darwin, the child became the emblem and the agent of radical change in culture—even radical change in the nature of man. In 1876, the Reverend W. F. Crafts published *The Coming Man in the Present Child; or Childhood, the Textbook of the Age*. By 1900, the new era was welcomed as the century of the child, the century of limitless growth, renewal, and transformation, the century *led* by children.

Between 1830 and 1880, technical and scientific advances—factory industry, the locomotive, germ theory—had prepared the way for Darwin's vision of man as infinitely perfectible.

Children enjoy the present because they have neither a past nor a future.
—Jean de la Bruyère (1645-1696)

These developments required the recasting of the American family. Women, who had been partners in labor and in caring for most colonial and early federalist families, were assigned new roles and new chains. The process of change began in the earliest years of the century. Work, particularly commerce and high industry, became man's province—ugly, aggressive, morally diminishing; home, hearth, and heaven became woman's —pure, incorruptible, and pallid. Of course, women kept their children with them in the cloister: somehow, these hopes of the age, these transforming young folk, had to be guarded and enfolded by maternal purity. Children were sweet untroubled innocence, precious and fragile. According to the popular literature of the time, it was better for a child to die than to join the foul world of adult males. The cultural isolation of women and children approached psychological imprisonment.

For nearly one hundred years, Americans have taken hesitant steps toward restoring children to a richer humanity. Wordsworth's romantic belief that "heaven lies about us in our infancy" received rough treatment from Freud, who showed us the dark side of human nature. A general intellectualization of the culture in the mid-twentieth century prepared us for Jean Piaget, with his view of the child as *cognitive,* as cool thinker. Both philosophies make the child into a creature more complex than ever before; both define him primarily in terms of internal processes that shape his development. It is one of the significant ironies of our time that Freud, who stressed the role of instinct, and Piaget, who has focused on pure mind, have come together in their separation of the child from the influences of history and community.

Our formal institutions preserve the child's isolation. School not only serves to teach order, rank, and merit; it is the agency of rigid age-segregation, with children marching through their lives in phalanxes one year wide. The State and the professions have taken on more and more of the work of the familial community, so that decisions about food and clothing and jobs are made far from both the child and his parents. Television can even separate the child from his own experience: what American child sees, in his personal world, the excitement and gore and simplicity of life on TV?

Today, as in colonial times, there is a profound congruence between the definition of childhood and the social order. Our disconnected child—a mosaic of roles, a wardrobe of quick-change social skills—is, unfortunately, fit for our age. He is healthy, independent, preeminently *adaptable,* generally secure from the cruelties of disease and enslavement. Yet somehow, the apotheosis of freedom has become separation from one's own history. We should take a tough look at the modern form of damnation that confronts our children, and ask ourselves not only "Have you hugged your child today?" or "What has your child learned today?" but also "Have you thought what your child will be like when he's forty years old?"

A MOTHER'S DAY MESSAGE: WHAT WE CAN DO NOW FOR OUR CHILDREN'S FUTURE

MARGARET MEAD

When Margaret Mead died, in November, 1978, she left notes on many subjects that she planned to discuss in her monthly columns for Redbook. The column that follows, based on Dr. Mead's notes on the celebration of the International Year of the Child, was organized and edited by her long-time friend and fellow anthropologist Dr. Rhoda Metraux, a Redbook contributing editor. This is the last of Margaret Mead's columns for Redbook. —The Editors

In May of 1979, when we in the United States will be celebrating Mother's Day as usual, many American mothers will be deep into another, world-wide celebration. The year 1979 has been proclaimed by the General Assembly of the United Nations as the International Year of the Child, to mark the 20th anniversary of the UN Declaration of the Rights of the Child and to assess what we have been doing for our own and the world's children.

Here at home in May, we shall have heard early reports from our own National IYC Commission, which is scheduled to make a final report to President Carter in April of 1980 on the condition of children in the United States. We shall have heard from a great many of the more than 200 nongovernmental organizations and innumerable local groups that have been meeting and talking and planning programs to honor our American version of IYC. And along the way we shall have encountered enough programs and projects about children in other parts of the world to bring home to us the fact that this year-long event concerns not only our own children but also all the children in the world, and is being celebrated by all the peoples in the 141 countries of the United Nations.

This is all very good, and it should be very exciting.

But I wonder. Have you asked yourself: What is *my* contribution to this year of the child? Have you taken a fresh, informed look at all the different children living in your neighborhood or town? Are you pleased with what you see, or are you troubled by the great needs of some—perhaps many—of the children? Are you a passive onlooker in this celebration, or are you actively working as a volunteer or a professional woman with a group that is trying to assess and meet such needs? Have you given thought to the problems of children elsewhere in the world? Have you asked your own children how they feel about growing up in the world we have made for them?

These aren't simply rhetorical questions. They are, I am convinced, questions every one of us must ask ourselves and each other, questions we must ask in our own community and every other community, wherever we can, at home and abroad. Asking questions helps one to focus one's attention, and that is the first, essential step to useful action.

But isn't it enough simply to celebrate the well-being of so many of our children?

No, it is not. It is critically important that each of us act—that we become involved. IYC has to do with something like one third of the world's total population of 4 billion people, among them about 66 million citizens of our own country. As a group they are both vulnerable and, unless we act for them, relatively helpless, for they are the world's children under 18 years of age. But potentially they are also very powerful. By the year 2000—only 21 years away—they will have become the women and men who are taking charge everywhere on earth. How they will then live together on our planet and, looking ahead, what they will then plan for their own future will depend a great deal on what we do—and on what we neglect to do—for the world's children today.

In my own childhood, English-speaking children learned Robert Louis Stevenson's verse:

> "Little Indian, Sioux or Crow,
> Little frosty Eskimo,
> Little Turk or Japanee,
> Oh, don't you wish that
> you were me?"

And thereby learned both that children around the world were very different from one another and that some—they themselves—were far more privileged.

Today this has changed profoundly. The needs of children that are crying to be met in other, poorer countries—the need for health care and education and protection—exist among our own children as well. And because radio and television have brought us closer together—at least superficially—children all over the world are not so different from one another as they once were.

Theirs is a unique generation—the first generation that has always known a world with a network of immediate communications reaching the most remote places on earth and with swift means of travel to those most distant places. Because of these international connections, this generation everywhere, not only in a few sophisticated centers, could benefit by the best understanding we have of what children need to grow in health and to realize high life expectations. Already, wherever they are, children are beginning to share some of their life experiences.

In the 1960s, when I returned to Manus, in the Admiralty Islands of Papua New Guinea, teen-aged schoolchildren were singing the Beatles' songs. And today, almost everywhere, you can hear very *little* children singing the *Sesame Street* songs. What this means is that these girls and boys, though they may never actually meet, will forever share a kind of imagery, a way of learning and

13. A Mother's Day Message

a view of the world that belongs to their whole generation.

Surely this new sharing is worth celebrating! But it is no more than a beginning. So much depends on what we are willing to do—whether we will work to improve the chances of all children or will shrug off the opportunity, not caring that people who have shared some experiences must be doubly aware of the less-positive circumstances in their lives that set them apart.

So many Americans have said to me: "Of course, we are a very progressive people. Children are the future and we have always put the children first!" We certainly have believed this, and not too long ago it might have been true, at least as a dream—a hope—that drove many parents to the hardest work so that their children would have fuller, more satisfying lives than they themselves had had. It was a dream that brought young people to America from the ends of the earth and was part of the adventure of opening the whole continent.

Today most parents still hope that their own children will succeed in life. But the dream that *all* children will share alike in a better, more satisfying life seems to be fading. We still speak the words, but do we share the belief? Are we willing to work for it?

In fact, the belief is embodied as an ideal for the whole world in the Declaration of Rights of the Child, adopted by the United Nations in 1959, which states that each child has the right:

- to affection, love and understanding
- to adequate nutrition and medical care
- to a free education
- to the opportunity for play and recreation
- to a name and nationality
- to special care, if handicapped
- to have a chance to become a useful member of society and to develop individual abilities
- to live in peace and universal brotherhood
- to the enjoyment of these rights, regardless of race, color, sex, religion, national or social origin

But when we look at the children in our own country alone, we find that a great many of them live in circumstances that reflect something very different from the rights set forth in the Declaration. We find that in some ways we are retreating from our clear social responsibilities although we are in a better position than ever before—at least in terms of our understanding of children's needs—to implement them.

It is impossible, of course, to legislate "affection, love and understanding." But we *can* work toward communities of caring people, communities in which there are resources to which adults and children in troubled families can turn for help and on which parents and children can depend when, inevitably, some adults can't make it and some children break down in despair or rebellion.

A BEACON OF HOPE

In a darkened world beset by the fear of nuclear holocaust, degradation of our soil and air and imbalance of population growth that threatens to strangle our human settlements, the Year of the Child stands like a beacon of hope. We must see that its light guides us and gives us direction for preparing a livable, sustainable, beautiful world for our children—those who have been born, those who have been conceived but not yet born, and those children of the future not yet conceived. By keeping our eyes steadily on the pressing needs of children we can determine what needs to be done, and what can be prepared for but accomplished later. For babies cannot wait.

—Margaret Mead
(1901-1978)

From the "Preliminary Report to the President," U.S. National Commission International Year of the Child 1979. Washington, D.C., November 30, 1978.

Instead, we are faced with a growing number of single-parent families—an outcome in part of what we euphemistically call our "welfare" system. We are discovering that a vast number of small children, perhaps as many as 1 million a year, suffer from extreme neglect and from physical or emotional abuse by the very adults on whom they depend for survival. Accidents, so often related to child abuse or neglect, are now the leading cause of death of children under 14 years of age. The rate of child suicide is going up: Among boys between 10 and 14 years of age it has doubled and among boys between 15 and 19 it has tripled since 1950. And every year the number of child runaways grows, and we are discovering new forms of abuse as these children are drawn into pornographic displays and both boy and girl prostitution. And how many safe places have we provided for children who fear to go home and fear for their lives in the streets?

We could, if we decided to do so, legislate shelters for abused or homeless children; we could legislate adequate health care for all our children, including preventive care for well children and the special kinds of care for handicapped children that would open the way for most of them to a mature and independent adulthood. We could supplement the diet of pregnant women, babies and children in their growing years so that they would have a good chance to do well, physically and mentally.

More than one third of our children under 14 years of age are not fully protected against preventable childhood diseases and almost one third of all children under 17 have never been treated by a dentist. And not all these children live in families that cannot afford medical care, nor are all under- and over-nourished children in families too poor or too ignorant to give them proper nourishment.

We are making some fresh beginnings, based on better knowledge, in our methods of care for children with different kinds of handicaps. In the past, too many handicapped children could receive some education and training only by leaving their homes and living for months and years in special institutions, where they were cut off from play with well children and from the everyday life of a community of families, adults and children of all kinds. Legislation has been passed. But as yet how many children with handicaps have open to them both the special help they so urgently need and education in the company of other children? How many teachers are we training to carry this additional, complex educational load?

It would be possible to go on with an analysis of this kind related to every one of the declared rights of children. We know very well, for example, that in spite of the turmoil about schools, there are many schools so inadequate and many pupils so grossly neglected that it has been demonstrated that they cannot read a want ad, fill out a job application properly, make sense of a driver's license manual or follow the simple instructions on a frozen-food package.

Too many people have come to believe that a good education for all children is too expensive for a community to provide. But how much more expensive is it to cope with the inadequacies, frustrations, depression and angry destructiveness of children growing into adults who are essentially illiterate in a world that depends on sophisticated literacy?

We know a great deal about what must be done to bring up a generation that can put the world into better order. But we also deny that it *can* be done. All around the United States, citizens are protesting against the cost of caring for people—adults as well as children—other than themselves. They are, in the newest cultlike phrase, "fiscal conservatives." They are, in fact, using this label as a mask for an ancient evil —social irresponsibility.

I think it is true that in some respects we have been spending money—and using our most precious resources in people and knowledge—unwisely. But the answer lies not in removing ourselves from the scene, hardening our hearts, closing our minds and simply taking back what once was given.

The answer—or at least the first steps to some answers—lies with every one of us. Each of us needs to commit herself to work with intelligence and caring concern in her own community—for adequate child-care centers, particularly for the children of working mothers, and for after-school programs for older children; for supplemental nutritional programs for those who need wholesome food,

2. CHILDHOOD AND SOCIETY

sponsored by local schools and churches, hospitals and clinics; for schools that teach and teaching that will include handicapped children as full members of the school community. We need to make sure that there are in our communities resources for the protection of abused children, and facilities to which teen-aged girls—expectant mothers and mothers of young babies—can turn for care and counseling. We need to broaden the possibilities for foster care, especially for children threatened by a family crisis.

Where we can, each of us needs to work *in* such programs: as teachers' aides, as helpers in hard-pressed clinics and shelters, as planners and clerks, sometimes even as envelope-stuffers for those organizations that are working for the good of children and of the community. By involving ourselves within our communities, I believe, we shall also begin to reach out, seeing what we do as part of a national and a world-wide effort.

Over the last generation we have turned far too much over to professionals with whom we are out of touch. We need those professionals—indeed, we need far more women and men who are professionally informed. But equally we need people at every level of community life who are involved because they are both caring *and* informed. We need, in fact, volunteers with energy, clear minds and strongly beating hearts. And who can they be but you yourselves?

Talk with your own children. Who better can convince you?

And then if you and your children together will agree to treat Mother's Day as a day of commitment—a commitment to be renewed each year—our thinking and working will go on *long after the end* of this International Year of the Child and there will be bright hope in the future for all the world's children—and that means for all of us.

Are Better Times Ahead for Teachers and Learners?

An Educational Forecast for the 1980s

Harold G. Shane
In Today's Education

Harold G. Shane is University Professor of Education, Indiana University, Bloomington. Condensed from Today's Education, LXVIII (April-May 1979), 62-65.

As the present decade draws to a close, it seems clear that history will preserve memories both of its distinctive traumas and of the turbulence it inherited from the 1960s. At best, the 1970s seem to have been a time of troubles. But what of the 1980s? What will the decade bring to education? Because of the protean developments in our society, some educationally relevant forecasts merit our attention as we look ahead to the 1980s.

Early childhood education, which elbowed its way to the footlights in the 1970s, should continue to star. Especially if the possibility of an echo of the 1950s baby boom becomes reality, or if inflationary pressures continue, the number of mothers of children aged five or younger who work outside their homes could increase even further. Already more than tripled in 12 years, nursery level enrolments could extend to include at least half of our three- to five-year-olds.

Despite notable opposition, prenatal intervention and the pursuit of alternatives to the natural course of conception and gestation will increase. Social disapproval of pregnant women who expose the unborn to alcohol and narcotics will be only part of this story. The very early months of life promise to become the object of more intensified study than at present. Doctors and scientists will probably make greater efforts to provide whatever therapy a fetus needs as life begins.

Day care is likely to include a greater emphasis on helping children develop. Purely custodial care merely clogs early education's arteries without carrying much enrichment to young learners. In the 1980s, programs for young children are likely to focus more clearly on guiding human development.

Prospects for the 1980s look something less than cheerful for postsecondary education in the humanities and in the preparation of teachers. The U.S. Bureau of Labor Statistics foresees a "surplus" of 2.7 million graduates with the Bachelor of Arts degree by 1985, and a Mellon Foundation inquiry concluded that by 1990 there would be a "surplus" of 60,000 Ph.D. recipients in the humanities.

A study by David Clark and Egon Guba suggests a continued decline in teacher education enrolments and in funding. At least temporarily, these researchers conclude, the support for quality programs will deteriorate. Their views were reinforced late in 1978, when the U.S. Department of Labor's *Occupational Outlook Handbook* reported a six-year drop-off of nearly 9 percent in teacher education enrolments. Business and engineering schools are likely to continue to graduate more students for at least several years, while fewer students will major in history and English.

Because of the needs of a postindustrial society, postsecondary education as a whole will not languish. Unless they serve a new clientele, however, schools may lose even more of their one-time monopoly to other educational agencies. These might include instructional programs directly sponsored by the federal government, training ventures sponsored by the federal government, training ventures sponsored by business and industry, and training in vocational skills with "transfer value" provided by the armed services. Secondary schools and universities can attract the growing crowd of potential students among the adult and elderly by cutting red tape and modifying admissions requirements for those who seek to bring their knowledge up to date or to broaden or deepen it.

The spread in the age ranges of children, youth, and mature learners at the same grade level or in similar areas of study is likely to increase during the coming decade, thus adding to a demand for more teachers. The holding power of the schools has been increasing steadily. More and more young people stay in school after age 16. The decline in scores on mass standardized tests and pressures for "competency-based" diplomas seem to reflect the presence of a large number of slower-learning students who will take longer than others to finish their schooling. Especially as opposition to "social promotion" builds, more pupils may spend at least 13 or 14 years rather than 12 in school. The schools will, therefore, need more teachers. Furthermore, educational theory will probably continue to support the designing of instruction to give students continuous progress in nongraded, personalized instructional blocks.

2. CHILDHOOD AND SOCIETY

The Education for All Handicapped Children Act (PL 94-142) will encourage the schools to initiate long-overdue educational practices designed to prevent problems for all children. More liberal policies on the age of students at admission, more careful grouping, individual educational plans (including greater heed to the needs of bilingual students), and greater understanding of and consideration for human differences will, perforce, begin to permeate more classrooms.

At the same time, however, considerable turmoil can be anticipated as PL 94-142 has an impact. This turmoil, already evident, can be expected to carry over into the early years of the coming decade. The way in which the severely handicapped are brought into the school will continue to pose dilemmas in regard to locating, placing, and safeguarding them; paying for their education; recruiting teachers competent to help them; and designing the mandatory written, individualized educational plans for as many as 8 million students who may eventually be classified as handicapped under the present broad federal definition.

Concepts of what constitutes a basic education will move along two diverse but compatible tracks. A decline in mass standardized test scores beginning in the middle school years, the parental concern reflected each year in opinion polls, and legislated requirements will accelerate trends toward achieving the "educational excellence" which became a slogan in the early 1960s and helped start the curriculum reform movement of that era. In addition, however, the problems of a threatened biosphere will require the teaching of new basics: the knowledge that will help the next generation work to restore equilibrium between humans and their environment.

The quest for ways to motivate youth to learn will increase in both scope and tempo. A need to improve students' motivation has occurred because of two developments. First, provisions for human welfare have reduced the threat of want which goaded an older generation to work. At the same time, many youth have begun to recognize that there isn't enough affluence to go around as human aspirations and numbers make ever-greater demands on the earth's finite and dwindling resources.

An important task of education in the home and at school, it would seem, thus becomes the creation of a self-image in U.S. students that is focused on the future. If learners have hope that they can fulfill satisfying personal and vocational prospects, they will seek to build skills and talents that make them useful to themselves and to society. Giving them this motivation won't be easy, but the importance of the task will certainly be more widely acknowledged in the next decade.

Probabilities for Tomorrow

Space limitations preclude a complete assessment of the forces and trends which will create issues and sharpen educational problems during the 1980s. However, the following probabilities clearly merit a place in an inventory of education's tomorrows:

• Action (direct experience) learning and service (community improvement) activities may bring new vitality and validity to schooling.

• Despite the limitations on the amount of money schools can spend on hardware, technology should become increasingly significant to education in the 1980s. Look for the use of tiny integrated circuit modules (already available) for programming hand-held computers, sophisticated educational materials that can be coupled to home or school television screens, and the first practical use of holography—projection of three-dimensional images in the classroom by means of laser beams.

• It is highly likely that teacher militancy will increase if inflation continues to threaten the profession's economic security. Jeopardized pension plans, in particular, will become an increasingly hot issue if the cost of living doubles between 1979 and 1989—and it will, if present trends continue.

• A substantial increase in federal participation in funding local school districts can be expected. State legislators will attempt to mollify voters by supporting more conservative taxation policies. Patently, the federal government will be under greater pressure to pay more of the costs of quality education as local resources diminish.

One might infer from all this that the 1980s will not be a happy decade for schooling in the United States. Such a conclusion, I think, is dangerous nonsense.

There are excellent reasons for looking to the 1980s with confidence. For one thing, our profession has enormous human resources in the form of highly educated professionals with a great deal of intellectual wattage. Enrolments at the elementary school level may or may not begin to increase by the mid- and late 1980s and recreate the market for large numbers of teachers. In any event, there remains an enormous opportunity to increase the quality of U.S. education.

Among many other things, the teaching profession has learned a great deal as it coped with the educational problems of the 1970s. Educators are constantly seeking ways to eliminate the decline in test scores while striving to retain the schools' proud record of continually increasing their holding power. The value of alternative forms of schooling has been recognized; generally, these forms have not been left outside of public education but have become a part of it. The importance of early childhood education also has begun to be recognized, and programs for young children have become more widespread.

In short, despite possible shoal waters ahead for the schools, the 1980s can bring better times for both learners and teachers. Because of the increasing scope of their clientele, educators have a number of new opportunities. These include, for example, making education more "special" and personalized for all children—not just for the handicapped; endeavoring to meet the needs of mature and senior learners; and strengthening the concepts of genuine multiethnic and multilingual education in our pluralistic society.

Proposition 13 and Early Childhood Education:
Wave of the Future— or Bad Splash?

Annie L. Butler and
Natalie P. LeVasseur

Annie L. Butler, a former President of the Association for Childhood Education International, is Professor of Early Childhood Education at Indiana University, Bloomington. Natalie P. LeVasseur is a doctoral student and graduate assistant, Department of Elementary-Early Childhood Education, Indiana University.

On June 6, 1978, the voters of California supported Proposition 13, the Jarvis-Gann Amendment, by a two to one margin. Their vote authorized legislators to slash property taxes to one percent of the 1975-76 assessed market value and to impose stiff obstacles against raising local or state taxes to make up for lost revenue.

Because public education throughout the United States is largely supported by taxes, educators the country over immediately expressed alarm about the effect the Amendment might have on the schools.

Since much of early childhood education is outside the public schools, however, speculation about the effect of Proposition 13 on early childhood education has not received due publicity. We urgently need to take a close look at some of the many ways today's trends might be expected to affect tomorrow's children.

A SOMBER SCENARIO

The time is 1999, the setting an urban center in the midwestern U.S.A.

Alice Freewald, concerned about being late for work for the second time in a week, feels her temper rising. Tom, her four-year-old, has refused to leave the house until he finds his red, white and blue tricorn hat. Thank goodness that Rebecca, now in third grade, can walk to school on her own! Alice would like to be able to put Tom on the America First Preschool bus, but the school is already too expensive without paying that additional fee. And it seems that the school is always selling something else—the school tee-shirt with a flag on it for Tom to wear on field trips, the America Needs You lunchbucket that he just *can't* live without, health insurance, liability insurance, accident insurance. The latest thing the school is pushing is life insurance for its young children!

This extreme commercialization of day care dates back to the American Tax Revolt of the late 1970s, beginning with Proposition 13, the Jarvis-Gann Amendment in California. During the next few years, similar laws were passed in most states and at the national level. Funds for social services that most taxpayers had taken for granted began to dry up. Schools lost most of their special services and personnel. School nurses, psychologists, aides, and art, music and physical education teachers lost their jobs. State and federal monies for lunch programs disappeared, school cafeterias closed, and children went back to brown-bagging it. Mandatory kindergarten was eliminated in most states.

The public schools are now back to the bare essentials and no money is available for the education of children outside the public schools. The loss of government money has had a particularly disastrous effect on the nonprofit day care centers. Unable to keep their rates at a reasonable level, a great many have been forced to close. Meanwhile a number of megabusinesses have seen a chance to make a profit through franchises, production-line techniques, and sophisticated advertising campaigns. Able to finance professional lobbyists, these business conglomerates have had many laws written to their advantage. Teacher-pupil ratios have been raised, fewer professionals are required, building codes have become less stringent and inspections less frequent.

Owners of the chain and franchise preschools have found it both economically fea-

2. CHILDHOOD AND SOCIETY

sible and more efficient to hire professional educators to write a curriculum to be used nationwide. While professionally trained teachers are occasionally hired from the swelling ranks of the unemployed, these schools find it more profitable to hire untrained people, put them through six weeks of training, and pay them the minimum wage. In addition to being less expensive, such staff members are more willing to follow the prescribed curriculum, resulting in schools that are "standardized." If your child goes to an America First School in New York, you know just what to expect from an America First School in New Mexico or Louisiana or Illinois. It is easier to sell the product!

Many people cannot afford to put their children in these overly expensive day care centers. Therefore family day care programs, sometimes excellent but more often than not poorly regulated, have proliferated. After-school day care programs in the public schools have been dropped, and the number of latchkey children has risen once again. Unsupervised children, long a problem in inner-city areas, have become a suburban problem, too.

Back to Tom and Becky

Red, white and blue tricorn hat at a rakish angle and America Needs You bucket in hand, Tom finally consents to get into the car. Alice had some initial reservations about sending him to the America First Preschool, but it is on the way to work and their television advertising has really had an impact on Tom. (He could sing the school song long before he had ever been in the school!) Alice regrets that the United Community Preschool, which Rebecca once attended, closed several years before. The times she volunteered there had been so enjoyable for her and her daughter. She has never felt as welcome at Tom's school. Rebecca misses her old preschool, too. Her only comment about third grade and about the elementary school in general is that "They never do anything that's any fun!" Becky, who loves art, has shown considerable talent; but the elementary school no longer has an art teacher, and her classroom teacher has neither the time nor the materials to encourage her interests. Consequently, Alice's Saturday mornings are devoted to driving Becky across town to lessons at a private children's studio and finding some way to entertain Tom until the lesson is over.

Tom's Teacher

"Well, he's only a few minutes late," thinks Susan Weaver, Tom's teacher at the America First Preschool. "It's really hard to plan anything, let alone follow the school's lesson plans, when the children can show up at just any time," she sighs, recalling the scene the previous afternoon when one little girl arrived in angry tears during naptime. Susan, a certified learning disabilities teacher, had intended to work with middle-school-aged children. While she feels lucky to have a job, *any* job, the America First Preschool's brief training course has left her poorly prepared for the realities of dealing with up to 20 three- and four-year-olds at a time. A wave of frustration passes over Susan as she thinks of Jacob, a child who had had some behavior problems six months ago when he entered her class. Susan never has enough time or help to give Jacob the attention he needs, and now she can almost count on him to create an incident during any group activity. With longing, Susan remembers her student teaching days, the calm, quiet experience of working with just one or two children at a time, the feeling of really accomplishing something. How she wishes she had that same feeling of competence with her preschool class!

A DEPRESSED PROFESSION

The above alternative future is one we would not like to see. Such a decline of quality in education and reduction of services could lead to frustration and discouragement on the part of both parents and professionals. If early childhood education should lose some of the gains it has very slowly made over the past decades, it would be a very depressed profession indeed.

Impact on Children

Opportunities for children of all income-levels have never been equalized in early childhood education, although progress toward that end has been made. Programs *have* been available for children whose families can afford them and for children whose families are in the lowest income-levels or who need help because of special family circumstances, but little has been available for the vast number of children whose fami-

15. Proposition 13 and Early Childhood Education

lies fall in between the extremes. Although a diversity of quality programs has coexisted under various kinds of sponsorship, opening the door to extreme commercialism is unlikely to lead to improved education or greater availability of programs to all children regardless of income.

The impact of a taxpayers' revolt will have the greatest effect on the children of some of these same taxpayers! As cutbacks are put into effect, classes will inevitably become larger and less able to provide for individualization of instruction. Pressures will become greater to follow a "ready-made" curriculum, which is being grossly oversold as being appropriate for all children. It will be increasingly impossible to make adaptations for geographical locations and for ethnic differences unless children are segregated by ethnic background. The socioeconomically disadvantaged will most likely suffer most, since they cannot afford to pay for any program. Even those who *can* afford to pay are likely to suffer because of a decline in the quality. Although large tuition fees may be paid, a high percentage of the money may go into profit—instead of into teachers' salaries, equipment and supplies, and upkeep.

Admittedly, our present schools are far from perfect. But many of them make an honest effort to provide an environment conducive to learning as well as to the feeling that school is a place where one is accepted and treated with dignity.

Impact on Families

The impact of a taxpayers' revolt on families will also be felt in many ways. In fact, the family may pay even higher costs for services once taken for granted. Psychological and social services and training in art, music and other special areas, now available through many schools, are likely to disappear at the same time that pressures on children within the classroom increase. Free immunizations and other health services will also disappear—although the need for these services will not change. The impact of lowered services would be greatest on single-parent and low-income families least able to help themselves.

Involvement of parents in the schools could be at either of two extremes. School personnel might look to parents to provide the services and staff they are no longer able to buy, and thus involvement could greatly increase. However, much more likely, communication and involvement with parents may decrease as pressured teachers come to feel that their time and energy should be directed exclusively toward teaching the children.

Impact on Teachers

Conceivably, large numbers of qualified early childhood teachers could lose their jobs if financing were reduced. Those teachers remaining would have larger classes and less adequate teaching materials and equipment. Qualified teachers could be replaced by unemployed teachers of older children, or by unqualified people willing to work for low wages. The all-too-prevalent belief that anyone can teach young children would be perpetuated. And the status of early childhood education as a profession could be lowered from its current somewhat precarious level.

The education of early childhood teachers would thereby suffer a serious blow. Many colleges and universities, seeing early childhood education as a growing field, have instituted teacher education programs, some of which are still small and struggling by comparison with programs for the education of teachers at other levels. Drops in enrollment could spell disaster to such programs. After all, why prepare more early childhood teachers when all that is needed is to offer a three-credit workshop for other unemployed teachers! Colleges and universities have already sustained cuts in teacher preparation programs; further reduction of their funding could easily lead to the complete demise of early childhood education from the curriculum.

Financial problems have long plagued early childhood education. The necessity of providing quality programs with limited budgets is familiar to many longtime workers in the field. Nobody wants the situation to deteriorate from its present level.

In fairness, commercial interests are not *necessarily* bad—but if the profit motive becomes more important than the provision of quality programs, early childhood education will be in bad trouble. If curriculum becomes more stereotyped, if teachers have so many children that just keeping them safe requires all their energies, if less well-qualified teachers are employed, early childhood education could lose a lot of hard-won professional ground.

2. CHILDHOOD AND SOCIETY

A HOPEFUL FUTURE???

Obviously the solution to the problems cited above is not simple. Indeed, the issue is larger than early childhood educators alone can tackle. Society as a whole has to come up with a solution. If we are to provide children with the quality education they need, we will have to re-examine our priorities and change some of them. Parents could have a tremendous impact. Thrusts are needed from many directions both within and outside the profession.

Some Action Proposals

Early childhood educators, in conjunction with other supporters of early childhood education, could mount an all-out effort to counteract the potential effects of Proposition 13. Together, they could:

- ☐ Educate the public about what is good and bad in early childhood education.
- ☐ Help parents become educated consumers in the child market by training them to recognize quality in early childhood programs and demand it.
- ☐ Build community interest in early childhood programs by being more responsive to community needs for children.
- ☐ Use early childhood professional organizations to develop materials for use with the public.
- ☐ Seek the cooperation of other professional and community organizations on joint projects on behalf of children.

Such actions are but a few of the obvious steps that can be taken. If these efforts are to have real clout, however, they must spread outside the profession.

In sum, we who believe in supporting early childhood education still have the ability to influence the course of future events. To insure an open public debate and analysis of the possible effects of Proposition 13 on the welfare of children and their families, let's be sure our voices are heard *now*, before the "somber scenario" becomes dismal reality.

Raising Children to Make a Less Violent World

Benjamin Spock, M.D.

Benjamin Spock, M.D., is a contributing editor of Redbook and writes a regular column for the magazine. His well-known book "Baby and Child Care," first published in 1946, was revised in 1957, 1968, 1974 and again in 1976. It has sold over 24 million copies, has been translated into 26 languages and is probably the most widely read and highly regarded book in its field. He and his wife, Mary Morgan, make their home in Rogers, Arkansas.

The following article by Dr. Benjamin Spock is the basis of a presentation at the National Assembly on the Future of the Family on November 19, 1979, in New York City. The presentation is part of a seminar on violence in the family. The assembly is sponsored by the Legal and Education Fund of the National Organization for Women (NOW). Panel subjects range from marriage contracts, a family bill of rights and the rights of children to problems of housing for contemporary families. Redbook's editor-in-chief, Sey Chassler, is a member of the National Advisory Committee for the assembly.

Of all species, human beings are unique in the wide span between their gentle lovingness and their cruel hostility. They remain devoted to their children, and to most of their other relatives, as long as they live. Many have enough love of humanity to make sacrifices, through gifts to the needy, through the kind of work they choose to do, through some of the causes they espouse—all this to help others.

But under certain circumstances—particularly when a nation is insecure and being exhorted by demogogic leaders—people will hate and attack others of their own kind because of differences of religion, skin color or political philosophy or in rivalry over territory. In war, people are ready to kill as many of the enemy as they can get their hands on. No other species shows such behavior.

It is a grisly fact that the majority of murders in civilian life are of relatives or of lovers, such is the capacity of human love to turn to hate. The beating of wives and children is another example.

Although all human beings are born with the potential for lovingness and creativity as well as for hostility and violence, the particular balance of these qualities in individuals as they reach adulthood depends on the influences found within their particular families as they were growing up and on the influences in their particular societies. We all know families that glow with love and mutual respect. We also know families that are tense with hostility.

The most powerful cause of violence today, as in the past, is neglect and physical abuse of children. This usually turns children into aggressive and often criminal adults. Their parents might have had no love for them and might have expressed only resentment. Or the death, desertion or illness of a parent or parents might have made it necessary to farm out the children. These children often land with foster families that show them no love, that give only abuse.

Mistreatment of children can occur at all economic and educational levels. Even in so-called "nice" families, love for children can be counteracted by an unusual degree of parental rage, this expressed as physical or mental abuse. There is also a great deal of "casual" mistreatment of children, especially in the United States. Several years ago two American women who had lived abroad for several years each told me that the thing that struck her most unpleasantly when she returned to the United States was the everyday abuse of children she saw in public: the hitting of children in supermarkets, the angry yanking of children along the sidewalk, the frequent irritable shouting at children who had done nothing particularly wrong.

Children subjected to a lot of abuse become adults who in turn beat their spouses or children, thus passing on the unfortunate pattern. This is because all human beings have an inclination to repeat what was done to them, whether good or bad, unless serious efforts are made to counteract the destructive tendencies. The reason for this: All of us spend our childhoods trying to learn how to become like our parents. Another reason: The anger we felt in childhood and did not dare to express waited to find an outlet in future, similar situations, these often involving our own children. It has been observed that conscience—whether in childhood or adulthood—tends to condone what was done by our parents before us.

A subtle but powerful influence to which so many subscribe and with which so many boys are indoctrinated is the "macho" ideal—men must be tough! This ideal, which exists in many parts of the world in different forms, favors aggression and violence in men. As in the United States, the indoctrination begins early in childhood. Girls are allowed to cry when hurt or disappointed, but boys must not show fear or pain or sorrow. Boys must hit back when they are hit. Boys must be willing to take all kinds of chances. Such prohibitions and obligations encourage boys and men to be aggressive whether they feel like it or not. In fact, the more frightened they are, the more they may try to cover their fear with aggressive behavior. This doesn't have to be. There are societies where males are brought up to be as tender, sensitive and kindly as females.

In the 20th century, radio, television and the movies have added significantly to the reservoir of violence in the so-called "developed" nations, especially in the United States, where programs are selected by advertisers on the basis of what they think will sell cereals, shampoos and other consumer products. Money is made through the exploitation of brutality, in stories about crimes, in Westerns and in scenes of aggressive sex.

In recent years more and more scientific evidence has shown that watching violence on film and television brutalizes everyone, children and adults alike. (Participation in war does the same thing.) This brutalizing influence has a subtle effect even when children are brought up to be kind. The most tragic impact is on those children who are neglected or raised without much affection or respect and on those who suffer a lot of physical abuse. Yet it is very hard for most of us to take action against these influences because the violent films and television programs are shown so regularly and have been shown

2. CHILDHOOD AND SOCIETY

for such a long time that they seem to be a part of normal American life.

Industrialization, the concentration of more and more people in large and impersonal cities, the breakup of the family, the tendency of people to move often, tend to weaken the positive ties between people and to release their antisocial impulses. In rural communities and small towns, especially in earlier times, everybody knew nearly everybody. Young couples were apt to settle down near their parents and other relatives. Each individual felt a certain responsibility toward others and functioned as part of a supportive family and community network. The individual also felt a certain concern and protection on the part of family and community toward him, which helped keep aggressive impulses under control. In addition, religions and other spiritual values, which were much more influential in the past, counteracted the drift toward aggression.

A majority of Americans think of themselves and their nation as distinctly on the friendly side. Europeans I've known have spoken of Americans as outstandingly amiable. But we in the United States have a tradition of violence going back to the pioneers' repeated betrayal and murder of Indians (and we've kept on breaking treaties and robbing them to this day). We've brutally abused Blacks. In international affairs, as we've become increasingly powerful, we have intervened militarily (or through the conspiracies of the CIA) in more and more countries, beginning in Latin America but more recently around the world.

We must try as citizens to check violence and immorality where it occurs in our politics and in our society. And there is much we can do as parents and family members. When there are greater-than-average tensions between husband and wife that seem to be affecting our children, we can seek counseling at a family social agency, mental-health clinic, private psychiatrist's office or marriage counseling bureau, even if only one parent is willing to go. The same applies to parents who find themselves getting inappropriately angry with their children. Children who suffer a great deal of anxiety or are overaggressive can be helped by their attendance at a child-guidance clinic.

In seeking jobs, parents can pay less attention to questions of money and prestige and more to friendliness of atmosphere and possible enjoyment of the work. They can shy away from corporations that transfer their junior executives every two years, a process that tears up the roots of every member of the family and robs them of the comforts that come from being a permanent part of a community.

Parents can refuse to give young children war toys. They can absolutely forbid the viewing of TV programs that go in for violence—crime-story violence, violence in Westerns and cartoons. Children will plead and cry for a while, but they will quit if the parents act sure of themselves.

In place of so much television viewing it would be good for parents to spend more time reading to young children who can't read or who can't read fluently. Parents can also read to older children or ask them to read to the family. Reading aloud gives pleasure. It increases vocabulary and the ability to write—skills that are decreasing today. But most important, reading aloud brings family members closer together and gives children and parents opportunities to fall into discussions about their ideas and experiences and their feelings about such moral issues as violence.

The main purpose of schooling should be to help children to mature in all respects. The learning of academic skills such as mathematics, reading and writing is of course essential. But it is even more important to learn to care about other people and how to get along with them; to learn to think for oneself and how to find the truth in an issue; to learn to take initiative, to be creative; and to learn how to solve the problems of a community, whether it be a classroom or a city.

As parents we can use our influence to help make all this possible. We can work through the PTA. We can use our votes in school-board elections—to lessen the highly competitive spirit that exists in the classroom and to elect school board members who favor the teaching of social studies and good human relations in addition to "the basics."

We can speak out vigorously against corporal punishment and against those teachers who do not treat children kindly.

We can try to encourage those athletic programs—including "little leagues"—that emphasize fun and skill over winning. We should work for dismissal of those coaches who encourage brutality and who abuse players when they make mistakes.

Most important—within the family—is having a father who doesn't sneer at gentleness in boys or other men or at the gentler occupations for men; a father who shows respect for the women and girls in the family, not so much in old-fashioned forms of chivalry as in avoiding terms and jokes that belittle women, in paying full attention to the views and interests of their wives and daughters and in sharing fully in the housework and child care.

Schools vs. Television

Researchers are finding that those hours your child spends in front of the TV are jeopardizing his chance to do well in school, but your school can help you fight back. Here's how . . .

Edward B. Fiske

Three years ago Jerri Groncki and her family were, as she put it, "addicted" to television. "Sometimes we would sit there with one channel on all night," she recalled. "We wouldn't even bother to find out what else was on."

About that time the Baltimore parent-teacher association became concerned about the negative effects of overdoses of television viewing on children's performance in school. The organization began publishing a family viewing guide and encouraging families to hold weekly "planning sessions" so that TV viewing would become a selective rather than an indiscriminate exercise. Among those who joined in were the Gronckis.

"It was like an awakening," said Mrs. Groncki. "The children began to choose to play games. Randy, who had never read any more than he had to, is now into novels. I became more involved in hobbies and community activities. I guess we all began to realize that our time is valuable and that we should spend it on things that are important to us."

The "awakening" of the Groncki family is one fruit of the growing willingness of schools, PTAs, and other educational groups to go on the offensive against what Kenneth Keniston, chairman of the Carnegie Council on Children, calls the "flickering blue parent occupying more of the waking hours of American children than any other single influence—including *both* parents and schools."

There seem to be two points of view about what bears the primary responsibility for the negative effects of television. Marie Winn, author of the controversial book *The Plug-In Drug*, believes that the culprit is the "one-way transaction that requires the taking in of particular sensory material in a particular way"; Lynn Janek of the New Jersey Coalition for Better Television Viewing believes that, "The important thing is to be a selective consumer, just as we are selective about the foods we eat." However, neither view necessarily excludes the other, and neither supports the concept that current TV-viewing habits are beneficial to anybody other than the sponsors and networks.

In fact, the extent of the problem is far greater than many parents realize. Writing in *Teacher Magazine*, children's author and reading specialist Nancy Larrick cited research showing that preschool children spend an average of 54 hours a week, or nearly two-thirds of their waking time, in front of the television set.

"By the time the child goes to kindergarten, he or she will have devoted more hours to watching television than a college student spends in four years of classes," she stated. "And by the time the youngster graduates from high school, he or she will have spent roughly 11,000 hours in school compared to more than 22,000 hours in front of television."

Unfortunately, this time spent in front of the set is not just time away from more productive pursuits, it has a negative impact all its own—so much so that, according to a blue-ribbon panel named by the College Entrance Examination Board, television is widely believed to be a major reason that Scholastic Aptitude Test scores have been falling since the mid-1960s. This impact is also reflected in the fact that colleges are now having to offer remedial work to entering freshmen in basic subjects such as writing.

One of the most noticeable—and debilitating—effects TV has on school-age children is fatigue. "Two years ago we took an informal survey and asked our kids what their favorite TV shows were," said Camille Faith, who teaches at the Gunpowder Elementary School in Baltimore. "Some of them listed programs that come on after the 11 o'clock news." She added that many students come to school tired, and it's no surprise the late shows are cited most by students having academic difficulties.

Many teachers believe that in addition to causing fatigue, television also contributes to tension, suspicion, and aggressive behavior in social relations among young children. Harry Blanchard, for example, head of the faculty at the Kimberton Farms School in Phoenixville, Pennsylvania, has observed that, "Elementary-level students who watch a great deal of TV tend to be hyperactive, nervous, and somewhat antisocial."

Educators frequently observe that long hours in front of the tube tend to dampen spontaneity and imagination, both in the classroom and on the playground. Linda Lombardi, former admissions secretary of the Waldorf School, says that the play activities of heavy television watchers tend to be "loud, active, full of short bursts rather than sustained activity, and very repetitive.

"You have the impression that they are replaying the most violent highlights of the Saturday-morning cartoons," she says, "the karate chops, the monster faces, the jumping and screaming, rather than thinking up imaginative situations of their own."

With regard to the subject of imagination, Frank Withrow, chief of the educational-technology-development branch of the U.S. Office of Education, emphasizes that young children watching TV are often confused about where fantasy leaves off and reality begins. The consequences of this confusion are not just psychological, since a child who believes that he, like Superman, can *really* fly, may actually try it. "When the Pink Panther jumps off a 500-foot cliff, that isn't reality," Withrow says. "And," he adds, "it might be a good idea to point this out." This is especially true because, as Lombardi says, "Children don't have the life background, and hence the experience or defenses, of an adult, and so everything they see affects them more than we may realize."

Another effect of TV viewing that Lombardi has noticed enables her to spot heavy watchers even in as brief a context as an admissions interview: "Young children are usually open and wonder about things they have never seen before," she says, "but the heavy watchers—including those who watch *Sesame Street* and other educational programs—will either not

---

"Schools vs. Television," by Edward B. Fiske, *Parents' Magazine,* January 1980. Reprinted with the permission of the author.

2. CHILDHOOD AND SOCIETY

notice something or they will immediately label it with a name. There's no personal reaction."

Lombardi also observes that, in children of all ages, "The ability to think and write clearly is weakened by habits unconsciously acquired from TV jargon. Also the ability to sustain a train of thought, to work concepts through, is perceptibly weaker in students whose thoughts and impressions are numb from bombardment by TV."

Finally, schools report that heavy television diets tend to give students unrealistic expectations of teachers. "Kids are so used to being entertained by personalities on TV that they expect teachers to do the same," said Blanchard. "And," he adds, "it affects study habits. If the teacher gives a homework assignment, the kids think ahead and say, 'I have to watch so and so.' They resent homework. They see it as an infringement of their right to see television."

Larrick offers one reason why teachers are coming to think of television as an unfair competitor. "One half-hour show," she says, "contains more excitement, adventure, and violence than the average person experiences in a lifetime."

With evidence mounting about the negative effects of television on the school climate, it is no wonder that many schools have begun taking steps to educate parents about viewing habits in order to help them control their children's television viewing.

Some schools are asking parents to keep children away from the tube entirely; others are setting limits of, say, an hour a day. Still others have asked parents to sign nonbinding "contracts" that include a promise to keep television from interfering with homework.

One of the most far-reaching programs is that of Kimberton Farms school, which has 320 students from nursery school through twelfth grade. It has a long tradition of trying to limit television viewing, and for the last five years this has taken the form of written guidelines. These call for no television at all for youngsters up through the first grade, while children in the second grade and above are urged to stay away from the tube on school nights and to restrict weekend viewing to three or four hours total.

Kimberton Farms is convinced that the guidelines have made a dramatic difference. "You can observe the effects with some youngsters almost immediately," says Blanchard. "Three days after they turn off the set you see a marked improvement in their behavior. They concentrate better, and are more able to follow directions and get along with their neighbors. If they go back to the set, you notice it right away."

The Waldorf School gives new parents a pamphlet asking them to limit their children's viewing to half an hour a day for those in the third grade and above and no TV for kindergarten through second grade. Administrators make a point of discussing the school's views of television during the admissions process. "If TV is a major part of the family's life, if the set is on all the time, we tell them they probably won't get much out of being part of our school," said Lombardi.

Other schools have shied away from schoolwide rules but have taken steps to educate parents about the effects of television on academic performance and have tried to encourage them to develop their own family policies. In Littleton, Colorado, for example, the Parent-Teacher Organization and the Littleton Education Association have teamed up to produce a sixteen-page *Kid Vid Guide*, whose cover asks the question, "Tele-viewing or Tele-vouring?" The booklet offers advice on choosing programs, setting time limits, and developing a critical attitude toward what families do decide to watch.

The New Canaan Country School in Connecticut sent out a statement stressing the importance of verbal competence in our society and asking parents to protect their children from "the temptation" of TV addiction. "There are some extraordinary programs, and from time to time the faculty suggests and assigns them," the coeducational elementary school states, "but to allow television-viewing as a reward for homework completed is to invite hurried homework and to limit the opportunities for your child to find himself an engrossing book. We can see no valid reason for a child to have a television set in his bedroom."

An obvious problem, of course, is what to do with time that would otherwise be spent in front of the flickering box. Many schools try to help parents by suggesting alternative activities. In its letter asking parents to work out a "definite limit to the amount of television watched," the faculty of the Horace Mann School for Nursery Years in New York City suggests that parents provide their children with art materials—such as paints, clay, and Play-Doh—and toys—such as puppets, stuffed animals, dolls, and dollhouses—that encourage imaginative play. The faculty also asks parents to work with their children to nurture a love of books and reading.

"We know that this will require more time out of your busy lives," the faculty continues, "but believe that it will pay off in the development of the children's ability to play creatively, independently, and with greater concentration."

At the Rye Country Day School in New York, Barbara Goldfarb encouraged her fourth graders to turn off the television on most school nights and to limit viewing to 45 minutes on others and to two hours on Saturday and Sunday. In doing so, she and the students made up a list of alternative activities. She says that more than a year later over half of the students watch only a minimum of television. Dawn Cano, one of the students, said that having the list of alternatives was a big help. "I found out how boring TV was, how many other things there are to do," she declared. "Now I do things from the list. I read, I go places, I draw."

A more extreme approach has been the so-called "Pull the Plug" campaigns in which schools ask parents and students to put their television sets away for one or more weeks. Parents are then asked to judge the results for themselves and, if they like them, to find ways of continuing the experiment on a modified basis through limits on TV watching.

Following this line of action, the Parent-Teacher Organization in Norwalk, Connecticut, organized 80 families to boycott television for two weeks. "You could tell the difference right away," said Walter Reck, principal of one elementary school. "The kids weren't tired in school. They got their homework done, and the parents said they were into crafts and a lot of other things they had never thought about before."

Bonnie Rising, a mother involved in the program, recalled, "It went a lot easier than I expected. The first couple of days were tough, but then they began to read and play games. They seemed to get on a lot better together, maybe because they needed each other to play with. Bedtime became easier because they didn't want two more minutes of some program."

Mrs. Rising reported that, following the two-week moratorium, she turned the set back on but established a one-hour daily limit. "We're much more selective about what they watch now," she said. "Also, the lack of background noise is a real pleasure. You don't realize how the constant drivel gets to you until you turn it off."

With this in mind, many schools have undertaken educational campaigns aimed at directing students toward quality programs. The Baltimore PTA, for example, contacts local television stations and publishes lists of programs that seem suitable for family viewing. A major thrust of this effort is to encourage parents to approach television with the same selective attitude that they would apply to the movies, which often results in parents' setting their own limits to time in front of the tube.

The Baltimore group has also begun an experimental project in four elementary schools designed to promote what is coming to be known as "visual literacy." The assumption is that television programs as well as books can be used to teach literary skills such as identifying plots and characters. Often this is done by obtaining scripts of programs and studying them before the show is aired.

Programs like *Alice*, which deals with the life and problems of a single mother raising a son, are brought into discussions of family life in social-studies classes, and some teachers use television-program content to raise social issues. Rosemary Potter, a teacher in Florida who has done much to encourage the development of "critical viewing skills," tells of a student who wrote to comedian Jerry Lewis saying that he liked his programs but asking, "How is it that in your shows there are no blacks?"

In the final analysis, the success of schools in minimizing the negative effects of television on their academic programs depends almost entirely on whether the parents share this goal. Many efforts to incorporate "educational" programs, such as *Roots* or a *National Geographic* special, into classroom instruction have failed because of Dad's refusal to turn away from *Monday Night Football* or some other paternal favorite. Likewise, the sight of parents' plunking themselves down to watch whatever happens to be served up by the tube at that moment will hardly inspire children to be selective in their own viewing.

As Linda Lombardi points out, in the 1950s many parents felt they were depriving their children of something important if they didn't give them a TV set. Today, we're beginning to realize we're doing our children a favor when we take the TV set away, at least for a while every day.

---

17. Schools vs. Television

> **A Guide to TV Viewing**
>
> **1. Know what your children watch and when.** A log of how much time they spend in front of the tube will often speak for itself about whether TV is playing too large a role in their lives.
>
> Be alert to the content, of course, including commercials, but also notice ways in which viewing affects your children's behavior. Do they become transfixed after watching for a while? Or does viewing make them tense and lead to fighting? What effects does it have on family communication when you all watch together?
>
> **2. Choose what to watch.** Don't leave it to chance. You wouldn't put a refrigerator in a young child's room and allow him to eat whatever he wanted. Why should you use any less control in guiding his intake with regard to the personalities and ideas he encounters on television?
>
> Learn to turn the set off when the program that you choose to watch is over. By making television viewing a process of *choice*, you will gain control of the set.
>
> **3. Set limits.** Many parents find that talking over a set of guidelines with their children and then following the routine they establish will go a long way toward bringing television viewing under control.
>
> In setting limits, however—such as one hour a day or none on school nights and three or four hours total over a weekend—it is important to be reasonable, accommodating such circumstances as illness with a revised schedule.
>
> A ban on dinner in front of the TV set isn't a bad idea—for parents as well as children! And some parents have rules against TV when playmates are over.
>
> **4. Join your children in watching and be alert to possible negative effects of certain programs.** When watching with younger children, be sure to point out what is real and what is fantasy.
>
> Shirley L. O'Bryant and Charles R. Corder-Bolz, two scholars who have studied the effects of parents' viewing with children, suggest scrapping the usual rules of decorum altogether when watching television. "When something is presented on TV that is in opposition to the family's value system, or offends it in any way, we advocate loud verbal reactions and exclamations of disapproval—even hissing," they say. "Similarly, when a program is in accordance with the family's views, members should approve of its content verbally—and applaud loudly."
>
> **5. Use the time spent in front of the tube for maximum benefit.** Television can be a rich source for vocabulary development. Parents can list television terms such as *bionic,* and then encourage children to look up the meanings of the words and use them in conversation.
>
> In addition, many popular television programs are tied to books that children may want to read, such as the "Little House" series or the "Hardy Boys" and "Nancy Drew" mysteries.
>
> Television programs can also serve as a springboard for conversations with teenagers on such sensitive topics as drugs, rape, or teenage pregnancy.

SIGNALS OF CHILD ABUSE

VANESSA VIGARE

Jimmy lived in a nice house. Its estimated cost was $250,000. He attended school regularly, he was well fed, and he had dozens of toys. However, when he was at school he was sometimes apathetic and withdrawn, and then at other times he would overreact or misbehave to attract attention. It seems that Jimmy's parents felt he was a nuisance who interfered with their lives. And when Jimmy came home from school, he was forced to eat, sleep, and play in the closet.

Jimmy lived in this type of environment for two years, until one of his teachers who was aware of the signals of abuse brought it to the attention of the local police. There are one million children similar to Jimmy who are abused in the United States each year. And child abuse ranks number five in the causes of death among children.

Because of the alarming number of children being abused in this country, law-enforcement agencies are trying to inform professionals who work with children about the signs of abuse. At a meeting sponsored by the San Diego Crime Prevention Division, Detective Robert Plumbley told teachers and parents the signs to look for. Plumbley has worked with abused children for several years in San Diego County and has found that most people are not aware of the signs or are afraid of involvement.

Plumbley stressed the fact that anyone who reports a possible case of child abuse is not held responsible even if the report turns out to be false. If a case of child abuse is suspected, Plumbley said for a person to report it to the juvenile division of the local police force. He also said that the person should not try to take care of the matter personally.

Sexual Abuse

There are four major categories of abuse. The most common form of abuse is the one which is least talked about. It is also one of the hardest to spot. It is sexual abuse. The signs are as follows:

1. Complaints of genital irritation.
2. Signs of venereal disease (painful urination; genital swelling, discharge).
3. Semen present on the child or the child's clothing.
4. Remarks made by one child to another (a child will usually tell a classmate something which he or she wouldn't tell a teacher).

Physical Abuse

The second most prevalent form of abuse is physical abuse. This form has signs which can be spotted more easily.

1. Injuries such as cuts or bruises on a child's body which occur too often to be accidental.
2. Bruises which are in different aging stages, noticeable by the variation in color.
3. Bruises which are thin and long, indicating a beating with a belt.
4. Imprints of objects such as a belt buckle on a child's skin.
5. Often parents who beat their children are careful to hit the child on areas which are hidden by the clothing. However, injuries can sometimes be assumed if the child's movement seems to show pain or soreness.
6. Uncontrolled violence by a parent can show itself by scratches, bruises, and red marks on a child's face.
7. Burns. (a) Burns which form a glove-like coloration on the buttocks signify that a child has been forcibly held down in scalding water for a period of time. (b) Raw blisters in the center of burns signify that a child has had a hot liquid poured on him or her. (c) Small circular burns indicate that a child has been burned with a cigarette. Small circular scars indicate the same thing.
8. A child who is overly afraid of adults may be indicating that he or she is abused.
9. Finally, a child's parent who refuses the child adequate medical care is probably trying to hide something.

Deprivation

Deprivation is another type of abuse and neglect which can be spotted easily. However, the reason for this type of abuse is usually different from the other types. In these cases, the parents are usually alcoholics, dependent on drugs, or mentally disturbed. They can hardly take care of themselves, much less their children. A lot of signs of deprivation are in the home, but some can be found outside the home.

Signs appearing on children include:

1. Dirty clothing.
2. Unwashed hair, hands; body odor.
3. No lunches provided or money supplied for food or school supplies.

Signals in the home include:

1. Unsanitary conditions; human excreta present.
2. Fire hazards in the home.
3. Uncomfortable sleeping arrangements (several people crowded into one bed, or a child who is forced to sleep on the floor).
4. A large number of insects in the home.
5. Meals not prepared regularly.
6. Spoiled or decayed foods in the refrigerator.

Emotional Abuse

The fourth form of child abuse, which many people do not think of as abuse, is emotional assault. Children who suffer from this kind of abuse have parents who express neither anger nor happiness toward them.

"Signals of Child Abuse," Vanessa Vigare, *Day Care and Early Education,* Spring 1978. Reprinted by permission from Human Sciences Press. Copyright 1978.

18. Signals of Child Abuse

This type of parent belittles the child, gives inconsistent responses, makes unreasonable demands, or may make the child feel he or she is responsible for the happiness of the marriage. A child who is treated in this manner may show any of the following signs (these signs could also indicate any of the other types of abuses already mentioned, since signals often overlap):

1. A child who has no appetite.
2. A child who is not thriving normally, who is withdrawn or apathetic.
3. A young child who is involved with drugs or alcohol.
4. A child who tries too hard to get attention from adults may be neglected.
5. A child who makes repetitive rhythmic motions signals a mental disorder.
6. A parent who shows no interest in a child's educational activities may be abusing him or her.

Obtaining Help

Detective Plumbley told the group of parents and teachers that it was the duty of every citizen to be aware of the rights of children. Local police and the welfare agencies will be glad to check out a possible abuse case, and it is better to report it if there is any chance that the crime is taking place. Plumbley also stated that although the children are of major concern, such agencies will also help the parents to straighten out their lives.

More information on this subject can be obtained from local law enforcement officials, who will be happy to set up special meetings to educate the concerned citizens in your area.

Development and Educational Opportunities

From its scientific beginnings in the 1920s, child psychology and child development have attracted researchers from many disciplines: medicine, nutrition, genetics, psychology, anthropology, sociology, and family life. In the last two decades, new fields of endeavor have emerged, devoted to the study of prenatal and neonatal development, childbirth procedures, screening, and genetic counseling. Infants have become a prime focus of research, and findings indicate that even newborns are more highly complex processors of information than was previously believed.

Early childhood education is a recipient of research information gathered from experimental studies. The enormous task educators face is to take the often conflicting research results and translate them into practices that are scientifically based, humanely oriented, and acceptable to a widely diverse audience. Individualization according to special situations and explanations to parents and administrators must then follow the development of any educational program.

Educators continue to look to the prodigious works of Jean Piaget for an understanding of the evolution of intelligence and what to expect, and not to expect, from children in different developmental stages. What most educators are displeased with, however, is that over the last fifteen years, preoccupation with the child as predominantly a cognitive creature has resulted in an overemphasis on intellectual growth and a diminished concern for personal-social habits and growth.

Lively debate continues over the causes, extent, and implications of sex differences. Reasons offered include actual brain differences and sexist cultural conditioning in childhood.

A major topic for research and discussion recently has been children's play and the way it reflects or contributes to children's learning, growth, and development. Educators find themselves continually having to rationalize the uses of play in programs to administrators and parents who fail to see the educative functions served by play. New conceptualizations and vocabulary have appeared concerning the characteristics, types, and purposes of play, and the ways in which play can be used to diagnose a child's healthy functioning, or lack of it, in specific areas.

Programming for infants and toddlers is rapidly growing across the nation and is fraught with emotional and value-laden viewpoints. For some, programs for infants sound like 1984 or a shirking of parental responsibility; others maintain that working mothers or mothers under stress need such services if their children are to grow healthfully.

Educators often cannot give straightforward, informed responses to many questions posed by administrators, parents, or the lay public because development and education depend on the complex dynamics of many interwoven factors, some of which may be unknown. What specific types of learning occur, what areas of development are most affected in an individual child over a certain time span, or how these can be accurately measured cannot be easily answered. Education and development always depend on a complex network of causative factors and multitude of contextual variables that work to facilitate or restrict development and forward progress. This section addresses some of those factors and variables upon which education and development depend.

Looking Ahead: Challenge Questions

What should women in the childbearing years know about increasing their chances of having a healthy baby?

Which periods in the child's life are critical for the development of intelligence? What roles should adults play in developing children's competence?

What are the identifying characteristics of the sensory-motor and pre-operational stages of intelligence?

What should parents look for to determine if an infant or toddler program adheres to high quality standards of programming?

Are there verifiable differences between girls and boys? What does brain research offer as evidence for sex differences?

What causes young children to engage in aggressive behavior? Is this related to their fears?

What can children of differing ages learn about their world through play?

Do children play the same way in other societies? What are the possible consequences for children who are deprived of a play life?

A PERFECT BABY

VIRGINIA APGAR, M.D., M.P.H.,
and JOAN BECK

Much more is known today than ever before about the diseases and abnormalities, inherited and acquired, that cause birth defects. There are still great gaps in our understanding, of course. But if all the knowledge now available could be put into use by physicians, by public health officials and especially by men and women who are still to become parents, probably more than half of the birth defects which now occur could be prevented.

The prevention of birth defects should begin long before a baby is born—ideally, even before he is conceived. For example, a man or woman who thinks that a close relative has a disorder which might be hereditary should take advantage of genetic counseling. This consultation should be obtained before marriage, but certainly before the conception of a child. It is particularly important for parents who have already had an infant with a genetic disorder.

Many people worry for years about the possibility of passing on to children a defect which has affected a parent or grandparent, an uncle or cousin, niece or nephew. Yet, very often, genetic counseling can prove such fears groundless or greatly exaggerated.

Often, the defect that a person fears transmitting is not hereditary at all, or is caused by a combination of hereditary factors with something that goes wrong during prenatal life. Even if a family disorder is hereditary, a genetic counselor may be able to determine from a family medical history that a particular individual could not possibly be a carrier of the abnormality. Or, if the prospective parent could be a carrier, the counselor may be able to suggest specific laboratory tests which will confirm or deny this possibility. For carriers, a genetic counselor can spell out in percentages how much risk each child would face.

A genetic counselor is also a good source of information about ways in which some birth defects can be diagnosed early in prenatal life, while the pregnancy can still be terminated if the prospective parents so decide. The counselor can also report on new treatments that may make the risk of having a baby with a specific birth defect seem less devastating to potential parents.

A considerable number of couples faced with the risk of having a baby with a major birth defect decide not to bear children but to form their family by adoption.

As more studies are done, researchers note a definite connection between the timing of pregnancy in the lives of parents and the occurrence of birth defects, prematurity, and stillbirths. Recent findings indicate that the ideal age for a woman to bear children is between twenty and 35. If possible, it is best not to begin having babies before the age of eighteen and to complete childbearing before 40. Countless mothers younger than eighteen and older than 40 have given birth to perfectly normal healthy babies. But young girls who become pregnant often do so in circumstances which make it unlikely they will have good prenatal care from the beginning of pregnancy. Many such girls are not adequately nourished, and many are exposed to other conditions which are associated with prematurity, high infant mortality, and an increase in certain birth defects.

Mothers older than 40 run greatly increased risks of having a child with a chromosomal abnormality, particularly Down's syndrome.

Many physicians now suggest that for women who become pregnant after 40, amniocentesis—an examination of the fluid in the amniotic sac—be used to discover if there are any chromosomal errors in the unborn infant's cells. New techniques make it possible to diagnose these conditions in time to terminate the pregnancy if the mother wishes.

From *Is My Baby All Right?* by Virginia Apgar M.D., M.P.H. and Joan Beck. Copyright © 1972 by Joan Beck. Reprinted by permission of Simon & Schuster, a Division of Gulf & Western Corporation.

19. A Perfect Baby

It's desirable for a man to father his children before he reaches the age of 45. The chances are somewhat greater that a baby will be stillborn or have a congenital malformation if the father is older than 45, regardless of the age of the infant's mother. However, the risks to the baby are not as great with an older father as with an older mother.

Ideally, there should be an interval of at least two years between the end of one pregnancy and the beginning of another. The shorter the time period between pregnancies, the greater the likelihood of birth defects and obstetrical difficulties. The younger the mother is, the greater the risks to which she exposes her offspring by having them too close together.

The more children a mother has, beginning with the third, the fewer the chances that each will be born healthy and normal. In part, these risks are related to factors such as the increasing age of the mother, short spacing between pregnancies, and poor living conditions.

When a couple plans to conceive a child, intercourse should take place at intervals of no more than twenty-four hours for several days just preceding and about the time of ovulation. Some birth defects occur because the ovum is fertilized late in the monthly cycle, just as it is beginning to disintegrate. This delayed fertilization greatly increases the likelihood of chromosomal abnormalities and miscarriage.

The chances that conception will occur and that the resulting infant will be normal and healthy are greatest when the uniting sperm and ovum are both fresh. Frequent intercourse during the time when conception is possible is thought to increase the odds that neither sperm nor egg will be "overripe" at the time they join.

It can be difficult to determine precisely when ovulation takes place during a particular menstrual cycle. It is usually estimated that ovulation occurs approximately fourteen days before the beginning of a menstrual period, but this varies from one woman to another and, sometimes, even from one month to another in the same woman.

One method of approximating the day of ovulation is for a woman to take her temperature every morning when she wakes up and to keep a chart of the readings. In many women, the temperature increases by a small percentage of a degree at the time of ovulation and remains higher until the beginning of the next period. If conception occurs, the temperature stays at the higher level. This method is not completely reliable, however.

A few women are aware when ovulation occurs because they feel a pain in the lower abdomen when the tiny follicle containing the maturing ovum bursts to release the egg cell. This pain or discomfort, about midpoint in the menstrual cycle, is called "mittelschmerz."

Because a mother provides the total prenatal environment for an unborn baby during the first, most critical period of his existence, her health and wellbeing are inextricably linked with his. There is much a woman can do—not only during this crucial nine months, but before—to make this environment healthy, nourishing, and free of the hazards that can produce defects in her unborn baby.

Ideally, the kind of medical care that helps a woman provide a healthy, nourishing environment for her unborn child begins long before pregnancy. Before she marries, a woman—and her future husband—should be given adequate information about family planning in accordance with their needs and beliefs. Their family histories may suggest the need for genetic counseling, not so much because it might influence the decision to marry but for its relevance in planning ahead for children.

When she is ready to have a baby, a woman should have a medical checkup before conceiving, to make sure that she has no infections, nutritional deficiency, or physical abnormality that might interfere with the baby's development or safe birth. At this pre-pregnancy checkup, a woman should be warned against the dangers of drugs, radiation, and infections during the earliest weeks of pregnancy. Her doctor should make sure that her immunizations are up to date, to protect her and the baby she hopes to conceive against as many viral infections as possible. Medical conditions which might harm an unborn infant, such as thyroid deficiency, venereal disease, tuberculosis, and diabetes should be checked for and, if present, treated before pregnancy begins. Disorders like sickle cell anemia and heart disease, which are more hazardous to a pregnant woman than to her unborn infant, should also be evaluated before pregnancy starts.

If either the husband or wife has a history of occupational exposure to radiation, or if either has been taking drugs, the doctor may decide that an examination of their chromosomes is desirable to detect any possible abnormalities. A few studies link the father's exposure to radar equipment within a few weeks prior to conception to an increase in mongolism in their babies.

Regular checkups are essential during pregnancy, too, even if they seem routine and unnecessary. This medical monitoring provides an early warning system to detect the possibility of conditions such as toxemia, Rh incompatibility, premature separation of the placenta, and premature birth. It can also alert the physician to the presence of twins, which place extra strain on the mother's body and complicate delivery.

To encourage prenatal care, most obstetricians and family doctors arrange a fee in advance to cover prenatal supervision, delivery, hospital visits, and postnatal checkups. The fee remains the same, even if the mother requires more of the doctor's time than usual because of a complication during pregnancy or at the time of birth. Often, medical insurance plans cover most of these costs, or the physician may work out an installment type of payment program if a couple wishes.

City, county, and state health departments often provide free or low-cost prenatal care in neighborhood clinics, along with health and nutrition information. Many hospitals, especially those affiliated with a medical school, often give free prenatal services and obstetrical care. The U.S. Children's Bureau has made grants of many millions of dollars to help finance these municipal

3. DEVELOPMENT AND EDUCATIONAL OPPORTUNITIES

and hospital services. In many states, some prospective parents are also eligible for Medicaid funds for prenatal and obstetrical care.

There are several sources prospective parents seeking free or low-cost prenatal care can contact for information. These include: local, county, or state health departments; the nearest office of the U.S. Department of Health, Education, and Welfare; the closest clinic or chapter of The National Foundation—March of Dimes; the nearest hospital, particularly if it is connected with a medical school; the local community referral agency or Community Fund headquarters.

No woman should become pregnant unless she is sure she has had rubella (German measles) or has been immunized against it. This cause of serious birth defects can now be eliminated completely by means of a vaccine, but such protection must be assured before pregnancy begins.

The rubella vaccine contains live virus, greatly weakened so that it is not strong enough to produce a full-blown infection but will still trigger the body to manufacture antibodies as protection against the disease. No one knows whether these attenuated viruses could harm an unborn baby if a prospective mother were vaccinated early in pregnancy. Physicians, therefore, won't give rubella vaccine to any woman who might possibly be pregnant, or who might become pregnant within two or three months. To make sure that no woman in early pregnancy is inadvertently vaccinated, most doctors will not immunize any adolescent girl unless she is known to them as a regular patient. Women are immunized only if a physician can be sure they are using a reliable method of birth control and understand the necessity for avoiding conception for at least two months following vaccination.

Before the rubella vaccine was developed, it was estimated that about twenty percent of women reached adulthood without ever having had the disease. Their unborn infants were thus in danger should they be exposed to the virus during the early months of pregnancy.

With the development of a simple blood test for rubella antibodies in 1966, doctors discovered, however, that a large percentage of women were mistaken about whether or not they had had the disease. Many women who assumed they were immune to rubella had apparently had a brief illness with a mild rash caused by another virus. Antibodies were found in the blood of another large group of women who were sure they had never had the disease, indicating that they must have had such a light case that there were no noticeable symptoms at all.

Because it is so easy to be mistaken about rubella, a woman should either have the vaccination or a blood test proving antibodies are present before she becomes pregnant.

From the very beginning of pregnancy, a woman should do everything possible to keep herself in good health and to avoid exposure to contagious diseases. This is particularly important during the first three months of pregnancy, when all of the new baby's organs and body structures are being formed and when the hazards of malformations are greatest.

An unborn infant, particularly during the first eight to thirteen weeks of pregnancy, is very vulnerable to certain viral infections. Destruction of just a few cells in his tiny body so early in his development can cause major malformations or disorders, while a similar loss in an adult would not even be noticeable. Even viruses which produce only brief, mild symptoms in an adult, can result in severe and lifelong handicaps for an unborn child.

To protect an unborn infant against the hazards of viral infections, a woman should make sure she is immunized, not only against rubella, but also against whooping cough, measles, mumps, polio, diphtheria, and smallpox before she becomes pregnant. During pregnancy, she should avoid exposure to any persons who might have a viral infection. Should she become ill during pregnancy, she should consult her physician immediately. Avoiding illness also lessens the likelihood that she might need medication during pregnancy—another hazard to the unborn child.

All during pregnancy, a woman should avoid eating undercooked red meat or contact with any cat which might be the source of a toxoplasmosis infection. Toxoplasmosis is usually a mild disease in adults. Many individuals may have it without even being aware of it, although it may produce a brief rash, cough, swollen glands, and other symptoms much like the common cold. But if a woman has toxoplasmosis during pregnancy, the organism may also attack her unborn baby. The mother recovers quickly from the disease. The unborn infant may not, but may continue to have active infection all during the months before birth and afterward.

Of the unborn infants who have toxoplasmosis during pregnancy, about twenty percent are born with major defects, including mental retardation, hydrocephalus, epilepsy, eye damage, and hearing loss. Some may also be premature.

A pregnant woman should not take any drugs whatever unless absolutely essential—and then only when prescribed by a physician who is aware of her pregnancy. This prohibition is particularly important during the first two or three months of pregnancy when the unborn infant's body and organs are developing. The reason this ruling has to be so strict and inclusive is that scientists now think many birth defects are caused by the action of a drug taken by a pregnant woman on the vulnerable tissues of her unborn child whose particular, individual, genetic make-up makes these tissues susceptible to damage.

Most drugs—over the counter as well as those sold by prescription—are tested on experimental animals under laboratory conditions before they are given to human beings. But the unborn offspring of laboratory species do not consistently react the same way to medications as unborn human children. So this kind of research cannot provide enough answers to protect all infants.

Drugs, in this sense, include not only medicines, such as aspirin, sleeping pills, tranquilizers, but also such things as nose drops and sprays, laxatives, mineral oil, douches,

19. A Perfect Baby

reducing aids, and even baking soda, vitamin supplements, and other common remedies for various conditions. Spray-can insecticides are also forbidden, along with other potent substances which can be inhaled.

X-ray examinations or radiation treatments should not be given to a pregnant woman; this warning applies particularly to the abdominal area during the first three months of pregnancy.

So hazardous is radiation to an unborn infant during the earliest weeks of his life that many physicians and hospitals make it a rule not to X-ray the abdominal area of any woman of childbearing age except in serious emergencies or during the first ten days following the start of a menstrual period. There is much less danger to an unborn child during the last part of pregnancy, after all of the infant's organs and bodily structures have been formed. X-rays at this stage may be essential to diagnose the condition of the unborn infant, or to help ensure his safe birth.

Another hazard of radiation during pregnancy is the possibility of damage to genes and chromosomes in the egg cells already formed within the tiny body of an unborn baby girl. This kind of abnormality would not show up for at least another generation, until this girl herself began to have children or perhaps for several generations.

It's best to avoid cigarettes during pregnancy. The babies born to mothers who smoke average about half a pound less in weight than the infants of women who don't smoke.

Researchers aren't sure precisely how cigarette smoking affects an unborn infant. They theorize that the growth retardation may be caused by the nicotine, which is known to pass through the placenta into the body of the developing infant, or by the high level of carbon monoxide in the mother's blood which reduces the amount of oxygen the blood brings to the unborn infant.

A nourishing diet, rich in proteins, vitamins, and minerals, and adequate in total calories, is essential during pregnancy. It is also important all of the years of a girl's life before she has children.

The body of an unborn infant must be built out of the nutrients in his mother's body. If she is gravely undernourished, her child will be, too.

In the United States, there are still many prospective mothers who do not have an adequate diet. Poor nutrition in pregnancy usually reflects a lifetime of undernourishment due primarily to poverty, but also to lack of information about good nutrition and sometimes to cultural customs.

Poor women are not the only ones who are inadequately nourished. A woman who diets too strictly during pregnancy for the sake of her appearance may be exposing her unborn infant to unnecessary risk, too. According to a three-year study by the National Research Council's committee on maternal nutrition, severe caloric restrictions during pregnancy may have harmful effects on the unborn baby's neurological development and may make his birth weight hazardously low. Ideal weight gain during pregnancy should be twenty-four pounds, or a range of twenty to 25 pounds, the Council concluded.

A prospective mother who is Rh-negative should make sure her physician takes the necessary steps to protect her unborn baby and subsequent children from Rh disease.

An Rh-negative woman who has never been pregnant with an Rh-positive baby and who has never received a transfusion of Rh-positive blood can now almost always be protected against the danger of having a child with Rh disease. All that is necessary is to have an injection of a special gamma globulin containing antibodies against Rh-positive blood within 72 hours after she's given birth to an Rh-positive infant. The Rh antibodies in the vaccine attack any Rh-positive red blood cells which might have entered the mother's circulation at the time of birth and destroy them before they can trigger the mother's own immune system to produce antibodies. Should she become pregnant again with an Rh-positive infant, she will not have any of the dangerous antibodies which could destroy the baby's red blood cells before birth.

It is essential, however, that every Rh-negative mother receive the vaccine following the birth of every Rh-positive infant, every miscarriage, or every abortion, spontaneous or induced.

Unfortunately, the Rh vaccine cannot help an Rh-negative mother who has already begun to produce antibodies because she had an Rh-positive baby or an abortion or a miscarriage before the vaccine was developed. If she becomes pregnant, her physician should monitor the well-being of her unborn infant carefully by checking the level of antibodies in the mother's blood and, if necessary, by amniocentesis. If the baby is in danger, he can often be helped by an intrauterine blood transfusion.

Every precaution should be taken to prevent a baby from being born prematurely. This caution applies to all weighing less than five-and-a-half pounds at birth.

The handicaps of prematurity extend from subtle forms of learning difficulties and behavior problems in the almost-normal ranges of birth weight to severe retardation, blindness, hearing loss, and even death in the tiniest newborns. Prematurity is often linked, too, with cerebral palsy and retarded physical development.

Prematurity is related to many direct and indirect causes: poor nutrition, illness of the mother during pregnancy, poverty, lack of good prenatal care, too short an interval following a previous pregnancy, cigarette smoking, anemia, the mother's age, unfavorable living conditions, and twins. Most of the recommendations already made will help to reduce the possibility of prematurity.

Good, regular, prenatal care is probably the most important of these recommendations, for there is much a physician can do to prevent prematurity. He can prescribe supplementary proteins, irons, and vitamins, if necessary. He can treat toxemia, bleeding, anemia, infections and other disorders in the mother before they become a serious threat to her unborn child. Sometimes, he can stop a premature labor so that the pregnancy can continue until close to full term. He can diagnose the

3. DEVELOPMENT AND EDUCATIONAL OPPORTUNITIES

presence of twins and advise the mother to get extra rest, especially during the last three months of pregnancy, to help postpone labor as long as possible.

A good physician also knows how to balance any need the mother may have for pain-relieving drugs with the safety of her child. For all of the medications given to the mother also affect her infant as long as blood is circulating through the umbilical cord. Normally, the processes of labor and birth decrease the amount of oxygen that reaches the infant; too much anesthetic or anesthetic given at the wrong time can cause brain injury or even death from the drastically lowered oxygen supply. Medications such as muscle relaxants and depressants given to the mother during labor also affect her child. Because they don't wear off as quickly in the baby as they do in the mother, their effect can be an extra handicap for the newborn who is struggling to survive on his own immediately after birth, especially if he has other handicaps.

Education-for-childbirth classes which teach a prospective mother what to expect during labor and delivery are beneficial to many women. By easing tensions and fears about the unknown, this instruction can help to reduce the amount of anesthetic a woman needs, show her ways to cooperate with her physician, and teach her how to work with the powerful muscular forces of her body—all important to the safety of her baby.

An infant changes faster during these first nine months than he ever will again. He is more vulnerable to injury before birth than he ever will be after.

Following these recommendations may seem tedious and unnecessary, especially to women who have already given birth to healthy children. But each pregnancy is different. Each child has a unique make-up. No effort is too great to increase the chances that a baby will be born without handicaps.

Information about family planning, prenatal care and genetic counseling can usually be found by contacting a large medical center or university-affiliated medical school, or from The National Foundation—March of Dimes, 1275 Mamaroneck Avenue, White Plains, New York 10605.

Growth: 45 crucial months

Barbara Wyden

We tend to think of human physical growth as a leisurely 16- to 18-year process. Implicit is the notion that if a child falls behind in his development because of illness, deprivation or any other cause, he'll have a second, third or even fourth chance to catch up.

But he won't. Recent research breakthroughs have confirmed and reconfirmed that the first 45 months—from the moment of conception until 3 years of age—determine whether or not a child will be able to live up to his genetic potential. And the factor which can most influence a child's development during the 45 months is nutrition. A series of landmark studies, conducted in this country, Great Britain, Latin America and Africa, has pointed to the nutritional status of not only the child but also the pregnant mother as the key to that development. Some researchers are even beginning to speculate that the baby's temperament, degree of energy and many other characteristics may be affected by the dinner the mother ate the night she conceived.

A child's growth begins at the very moment of conception, when the male and female gametes come together and form the DNA (deoxyribonucleic acid)—the genetic endowment that determines a person's physical and mental characteristics. To some degree, growth is a lifelong process, but the sheer velocity of this first period is never again matched. The brain and skull, along with the eyes and ears, develop first. Then the rest of the body—the heart and lungs, the digestive organs, the kidneys, the arteries, the blood, the skeleton itself—forms and develops at an only slightly slower pace than the head.

For most of the body, these first months are crucial. The only important exception seems to be growth in height. Scientists have recently discovered that children who have not reached their full height because of illness or undernourishment or other trauma can gain their genetically indicated height if they are treated with growth hormone.

After birth, the infant continues to grow and starts to develop skills. He gains control of his body so he can roll over, sit, creep and eventually walk. He learns how to manipulate, to hold on to his father's finger, to grasp a rattle, to tear things. He coordinates his hands and eyes in such skills as piling blocks on top of each other or scribbling on paper with a crayon. He makes noises and then forms words, phrases and finally whole thoughts. And he develops the ability to relate to people—to smile, to be aware of others (sometimes to be afraid of them), to imitate, to be a social being. Whether or not the individual child reaches his full capacity in all these areas depends in large part on how his brain developed between the time of conception and 18 or 24 months of age.

The brain develops in four successive stages. Early growth—intrauterine growth—comes from the division of cells. The brain grows bigger as the cells divide and divide again. After birth, there's a transition period when the cells divide less rapidly and existing cells start growing in size. Then, somewhere around the end of the first year, the cells stop dividing altogether. All growth now comes from an increase in cell size, not number. The fourth and final stage is the forming of connections between the nerve cells. Each normal cell has some 10,000 of these connections and it may be that the number of connections between nerve cells is even more crucial than the number of cells.

Nutrition, or more precisely malnutrition, has a direct effect on the way the brain grows: if a fetus does not receive enough nourishment, the rate of brain cell division slows down. A seriously deprived fetus may have 20% fewer brain cells than normal. If a newborn is seriously undernourished during the six months after birth, cell division is also slowed down—again by as much as 20%. If an infant should have been malnourished both in utero *and* after birth, the arithmetic is tragic. The brain may be 60% smaller.

"The brain never gets another chance," says Dr. Myron Winick, director of growth and development at New York Hospital-Cornell Medical College, one of the leaders in brain-growth research. "We found that cell division stops at approximately the same age in both undernourished and well-nourished children."

A report Dr. Winick made last year on starving Chilean babies under 6 months of age demonstrates the no-second-chance aspect of growth. These infants were brought to a hospital when they were so close to death that it was impossible to tell which babies would die and which would survive. Despite the most attentive medical care, nearly half died. The survivors then came under intense scrutiny. They were fed balanced diets, checked weekly by social workers, nutritionists and pediatricians, and tested by psychologists.

Preliminary findings showed that help had come too late for most. Ninety percent of the survivors had been irreparably damaged and were limited in their ability to "cope with their environment," the researchers reported: 51% were educable, but needed special teaching; 36% were only "trainable" to do simple tasks; 3% required custodial care. When these youngsters were compared with similar children who had not suffered from malnutrition, it was discovered that even if the survivors caught up to normal weight for their age and body build, their head circumference (one way of measuring brain size) was less than that of the youngsters who had been well nourished from birth. They were also retarded in motor skills.

Scientists are not willing to say that small brain size indicates lessened intelligence. They hesitate because it is not known how much of the brain we actually use, nor is it known exactly how and to what degree malnutrition slows down cell division in different areas of the brain. But all the evidence points inevitably to the conclusion that children

3. DEVELOPMENT AND EDUCATIONAL OPPORTUNITIES

with underdeveloped brains cannot function to their full genetic potential.

The rest of the body—heart, lungs, muscles, kidneys, etc.—develops the same way as the brain. The timing differs but the pattern is roughly similar. Studies have been made of rats who were undernourished in utero. Examined just before birth, these rats had lungs which were only 62% of normal weight, and hearts 84% of normal.

While poor sanitation, lack of education and substandard housing can also affect a child's growth, most researchers agree that nutrition is probably the crucial component, the one factor in the growth formula where dramatic improvements would yield dramatic results. Statistics show that prosperous mothers as well as low-income mothers suffer from protein deprivation. Women who snack on empty calories (soft drinks, salty tidbits, sweets), who get a significant proportion of their daily calories from alcohol, fats and carbohydrates rather than proteins, vegetables and fruits, or—at the other extreme—women who diet to neurotic excess do not provide the healthiest environment for a naturally greedy fetus.

"I can't emphasize how important it is for the mother not to just trust that her body will somehow have the reserves that are needed for her infant," says Dr. Merrill S. Read, director of the Growth and Development Program of the National Institute of Child Health and Human Development. And a mother's nutritional reserves, he says, cannot be suddenly accumulated during pregnancy. These assets are the cumulative result of a lifetime, Dr. Read says. "Getting ready to be a mother during a woman's adolescence is almost as important as the actual time when she's a mature woman and pregnant. It is particularly important before and during pregnancy to balance a diet with a variety of foods from the four basic food groups: meats, milk and dairy products, fruits and vegetables, breads and cereals." Dr. Read feels that special attention should be given to foods rich in iron—liver, eggs, dark-green leafy vegetables. A woman should control her caloric intake, he says, by limiting fats and carbohydrates and make everything she eats count nutritionally. "Vegetarians who exclude cheese, milk and eggs from their diets will have problems satisfying their protein needs during pregnancy when the fetus needs high-quality proteins," he said. "A mixture of cereal grains, beans, nuts, etc. may provide the essential amino acids, but it requires very careful food selection."

Dr. Michael Alderman, acting director of the Division of Community Medicine, Cornell Medical Center, feels that animal protein is essential to balanced nutrition. "The body is not capable of making nine essential amino acids, and the only way to get them is to ingest them. Meats are the major source of those proteins. Other proteins, from peanuts, beans and other vegetables, do not serve the same purpose. If a prospective mother relies solely on them she will be more likely to produce a baby with a low birth weight, increasing the risk of not surviving the first 28 days of life." A macrobiotic diet, whose main ingredient is brown rice, may be so lacking in protein that a pregnant mother might have difficulty in carrying her baby to term.

One immediate result of the new findings is that doctors are changing long-held ideas about optimal weight gain during pregnancy. The National Research Council recently alerted obstetricians that the current medical practice of limiting women to a gain of only ten to 14 pounds may be contributing to the high infant mortality in the United States. Restricting the pregnant woman's diet can be harmful both to the developing fetus and to the mother, and while no one is positive exactly what the optimal weight gain should be, there are new general guidelines. "We should probably be thinking in terms of 24 to 25 pounds," says Dr. Howard N. Jacobson of Harvard Medical School, a specialist in intrauterine development and a member of the National Research Council.

After the baby is born, overfeeding him can be almost as devastating as underfeeding. Overfeeding encourages a speedup in fat cell production, just as underfeeding produces a slow-down in brain cell production. Encouraging a baby to gobble up his formula to produce an impressive growth chart is dangerously old-fashioned. A recent study by Dr. Jerome Knittle of New York's Mt. Sinai School of Medicine and Dr. Jules Hirsch of the Rockefeller University has proved that infancy-formed fat cells stay in a person's body for life, although the amount of fat a cell is storing varies from month to month. Their experiments with newborn rats showed that rats who became fat on mother's milk remained fatter than normal-weight rats when both groups were allowed to eat whatever they wanted. Even when the fat rats were starved down to skin and bones, they still had a gross excess of fat cells—storage units of fat.

Applying the principle to humans, Dr. Knittle then turned to 200 children who had been obese since infancy and found 2-year-olds with twice the number of fat cells as a normal-weight child of that age, and 5-year-olds with twice the number of fat cells as a normal adult. The doctor's findings suggest that, for the rest of his life, someone who is overweight at age one is going to have a more difficult time than most other people when he tries to stay trim.

Although some specific recommendations for infant feeding do exist, most experts simply advise the mother to use her common sense and "don't stuff the baby." Doctors will confirm that it simply doesn't matter nutritionally or emotionally whether a baby is breast-fed or bottle-fed as long as mother and baby are pleased with the system they've adopted. Many pediatricians also feel that children should be fed only "modest" amounts of animal fats and eggs after 2 years of age. Animal studies on many species have proved that substituting polyunsaturated vegetable oils for butter fat makes a real difference in the amount of blood cholesterol in the young—just as it does in the human adult. And there is circumstantial evidence that the same is true of human infants. But doctors are not yet sure what to do about this. They do recommend that most children be switched from whole milk to skim milk at the age of 2 (although not before).

The traditional three-meal-a-day pattern for children is also coming in for criticism. Dr. Samuel J. Fomon of the University of Iowa Medical School says, "Too many parents feel their kids are really growing up when they get them to adapt to our current three-widely-spaced-meals-a-

20. Growth: 45 Crucial Months

day routine. Children really prefer snacking and it seems better for them—as long as the snacks are nutritious."

A sliver of white chicken meat, a dab of peanut butter on an apple slice, a carrot stick are nutritious snacks. Lollipops and cakes don't have the same nutritional values. Home-baked oatmeal cookies with raisins and nuts are fine within limits; chocolate cookies made with white sugar, fats and flour are not. Most American parents don't follow such guidelines and most American children are getting a lot of food, but of distressingly poor quality. A 15-state study of 3,444 preschoolers—ranging from lower- to upper-class economic backgrounds—showed that a significant number in all groups lacked proteins, vitamins and minerals in their diets. Another huge survey showed that nearly half of these preschoolers suffered from iron deficiencies. Although both studies were fact-finding efforts and the researchers did not attempt to analyze the effects of the dietary deficiencies, the children were noticeably susceptible to fatigue. They tended to tire in their play and it was expected they would probably tire in later years in their schoolrooms.

Given the solid foundation of good nutrition, each child will follow his own course of physical development. The patterns of physical growth of healthy children have such a wide range of variability that the calendar is a poor measurement of a child's progress. As every pediatrician has long been preaching, whether a baby starts walking "early" or "late," by age 3 there's no significant difference between his ability and that of another youngster. So there is absolutely no point to the perennial mothers' competition over whose baby walks first or talks first or is toilet-trained first. This needless race is prompted by our obsession for "firsts." Jean Piaget, the Swiss psychiatrist and educator, calls it "the American question": how can we make things happen faster? Piaget's answer is, "What's the advantage?" When children are ready to walk, they will walk. Or talk. Or use the toilet.

Youngsters who turn up at either end of the normal range are often given a rough time. For instance: the big 3-year-old who could be taken for a 5-year-old—and is expected to act as if he were 5; the small 5-year-old who could be considered 3—and often is, to his intense frustration. Precocious physical development often misleads parents to their expectations; precocious language development leads them to expect muscular coordination to match. The fact is that a child with the physical development usually attributed to age 3—he's toilet-trained, can feed himself completely (well, usually) with a spoon, can put on his shoes, can run and dance and jump—may have an emotional maturity of age 2 and a language ability of age 5. That's nothing to worry about if parents are conscientious about taking the child for regularly scheduled shots and check-ups and calling to the pediatrician's attention any concerns they have about their child's development, so that the doctor can determine if these problems indicate any serious retardation.

After age 3 the various aspects of a child's development will be more coordinated. By then a child is set on his biological track for life. Barring serious disease or accident, he is proceeding inexorably along the growth channels that are now set, and how well he does, how far he goes toward reaching his inborn potential, depends to a large extent on how he has been fed during the first 45 months of his life.

//
YOUR CHILD'S MIND

"The educational developments that take place in the year or so that begins when a child is about eight months old are the most important and most in need of attention of any that occur in human life."

So says Dr. Burton L. White, the country's leading expert on early childhood.

Dr. Burton L. White

When the child enters the stage between eight to fourteen months of age, the parent assumes a new, challenging, and considerably more significant role. Whereas most families in this country today get their children through the first six to eight months of life reasonably well educated and developed, I have come to the conclusion that relatively few families, perhaps no more than ten percent, manage to get their children through the eight- to thirty-six-month age period as well educated and developed as they can and should be. This statement underlies my dedication to the subject of education in the first years of life.

Not all professionals agree with me. There are people in child psychiatry, for example, who think that the first weeks of life are the most important and that prospective parents must be educated in the best way to establish a healthy mother-child relationship. My response is that I am as much an advocate of love and a close emotional relationship as anybody, but I do not believe that there really are very many parents who do not establish a good solid relationship with their children in the first months of life.

There is a good deal of information that suggests that sometime during the middle of the second year of life, children begin to reveal which way they are headed developmentally. We have also come to the conclusion that to begin to look at a child's educational development when he is two years of age is already much too late, particularly in the areas of social skills and attitudes. We find the two-year-old is a rather complicated, firmly established social being. We find it not uncommon that a two-year-old is already badly spoiled and very difficult to live with, or in more tragic situations, alienated from people, including his own family. We have seen these phenomena over and over again. On the other hand, we rarely see an eight-, nine-, or ten-month-old child who in any way seems to be spoiled or particularly well differentiated socially. Up through eight months, a child is, comparatively speaking, a very simple social creature.

You can trace your child's evolution as he goes from eight to twenty-four months of age by keeping a step-by-step journal and taking movies of him, preferably sound movies, if possible. This will confirm the fact that the twenty-four-month-old child is as different from the eight-month-old as the eight-month-old is from the newborn. Human growth is a remarkable process.

EDUCATIONAL GOALS

Over the years, three useful ways of describing educational goals of the period from eight months through three years have emerged. One deals with the child's major interest patterns. We have found that all healthy eight-month-old children seem motivated by three major interests aside from the fundamental physiological needs such as hunger, thirst, freedom from pain, etc. These three major interests are: the primary caretaker, exploration of the world as a whole, and mastering newly emerging motor abilities. These interests have obvious specific survival value. They start out vigorous and in balance in all healthy eight-month-old babies. When development goes well, they each grow steadily, and the balance is maintained. Very often, however, they develop unevenly between eight and twenty-four months of age, and the results are mildly or severely debilitating.

A second way of discussing educational goals is to talk of emerging competencies of special importance. These competencies are by no means guaranteed to develop well. I'm referring to the pattern of intellectual, linguistic, perceptual, and social competencies our research has found typical of beautifully developed three- to six-year-old children.

Toward the end of the first year, children begin to realize that older people can be helpful. They begin to deliberately seek assistance from them. This behavior we call using an adult as a resource. Shortly after the first birthday, two other very important social potencies emerge. Seeking approval for a simple motor achievement or for "cute" behavior seems to indicate the first feelings of pride in achievement. Finally, at about the same time, children begin to manifest simple make-believe or fantasy behavior. Common examples are "talking" on a toy telephone or pretending to be driving a toy truck, car, or airplane. Each of these emergents seems to play a special role in educational development.

The third way is to emphasize four key goals which are commonly accepted by most people knowledgeable in early human development. These goals are language development, the development of curiosity, social development, and nurturing the roots of intelligence.

LANGUAGE DEVELOPMENT

We have seen that while children may respond to words in some simple fashion during the first six or seven months of life, there is no indication whatsoever that they understand the meaning of those words. Their response is really an affair that involves the sound qualities of the words—the association of particular patterns of a mother's voice, for example, with the pleasure in her presence. But they do not respond differently to their own name or to some other name. They do not know, for example, that the word "Mommy" means only one person. But at about seven or eight months of age, they begin to learn language.

By three years of age, experts estimate that most children understand most of the language that they will use for the rest of their lives in ordinary conversation. Notice I said most children understand most of the language they will use in ordinary conversation. There is an important difference between the growth of understanding language and the growth of producing language. Children begin to learn to understand language earlier and at a more rapid rate than they learn to use it orally. The first five or six words should be fairly well understood by the time a child is nine or ten months of age. But he may not say five or six words until he is two years of age or even older. Nevertheless, in both cases he may be a very normal child.

From the book *"The First Three Years of Life"* by Dr. Burton L. White, © 1975 by Burton L. White. Published by Prentice-Hall Inc., Englewood Cliffs, New Jersey. Appeared in the April 1976 issue of *American Baby*. Reprinted by permission.

21. Your Child's Mind

Language, like so many of the issues we will talk about, is interrelated during the first years of life with other major developments. There is no way that a young child can do well on an intelligence test at three or four years of age, for example, unless his language development is good. You can usually predict a child's IQ once he gets to be three or four years of age with reasonable accuracy from any reliable assessment of his language skills.

Over and above language's fundamental role in the development of intelligence, it plays an extremely important part in the development of social skills. So much of what transpires between any two people involves either listening to or expressing language. And so, in a very significant way, good language development underlies good social development.

THE DEVELOPMENT OF CURIOSITY

Nothing is more fundamental to solid educational development than pure, uncontaminated curiosity. One cannot help but be impressed by this curiosity, which shows itself in a love of physical exploration as soon as a baby can move his body through space. This behavior is highly predictable except in those children who are ill or seriously damaged.

It seems logical that in the course of the hundreds of hours prelocomotive children spend looking about at distant, unreachable objects, they build up quite a head of steam with respect to an interest in exploring the rooms within which they live. Regardless of whether or not such speculation is true, you can expect the crawling infant to explore if given the chance.

Things that most adults would find totally uninteresting absorb a baby. Do not be surprised if you find your child swinging a kitchen cabinet door several dozen times for several dozen consecutive days. Do not be surprised if small pieces of dust that are picked up from the floor intrigue him. Do not be surprised if he is fascinated by the cellophane wrapper from a package of cigarettes. At the same time, of course, razor blades will interest him, along with anything else that he can inspect closely, particularly if he can handle the object and bring it to his mouth. You can therefore sense the dual nature of curiosity. It is the motivational force underlying all learning and development and achievement; at the same time, it is the source of many childhood accidents and tragedies and certainly causes a great deal of normal anxiety on the part of parents.

NURTURING THE ROOTS OF INTELLIGENCE

The child of eight months has turned a corner wherein he leaves behind his early introduction to the world and to his own basic motor skills and starts to focus on the world of objects. The year or so that follows is a period of active exploration of simple cause-and-effect mechanisms; of the movement patterns of objects; of their texture qualities, shapes, and forms. This is an incredibly rich time during which the child's mind is undergoing basic development with respect to the prerequisites of higher forms of thinking. Surely, as far as education is concerned, few things are more central than the substructure of sensorimotor explorations upon which higher levels of intelligence are built.

THE PRIMARY CARETAKER'S ROLE AS CONSULTANT

You can be quite confident that if you have provided your child with a safe home and a few stimulating materials, he will explore and find things that interest and occasionally excite him. In addition, from time to time he will find himself in situations that frustrate him or cause him modest pain. Should any one of these occasions arise—excitement, frustration, or modest pain—you can be assured that in some fraction of those cases the child will turn to you for assistance, shared enthusiasm, or comfort. At this point, when the child approaches you, you have what I consider to be your second primary opportunity to really establish yourself as your child's educator.

What a baby is interested in during this stage of his life is relatively easy to see, and see accurately most of the time. If you have a child who comes to you excited by something pleasurable or aroused by something in the way of a difficulty, you have a motivated child. If you know what he is focusing on, you have the ideal learning circumstance. What we have seen effective mothers do in this regard is, first of all, be available for such experiences. If mothers take a full-time job, they are not even going to have a chance at these experiences. Second, effective mothers pause and react to the baby as soon as they can, as often as they can. They do not keep the child waiting while they continue a phone conversation.

Once the appropriate response is made, effective mothers pause to see what it is the child is interested in. They identify the subject, then usually provide whatever is needed by the child. They also provide a few words related to the topic in question, using language that is at or slightly above the child's apparent ability level, and they express a related idea or two. For example, if the child comes to you with what looks like a little animal figure with unusually large feet, you might suggest that, "Those feet are really large. Daddy has big feet, too, doesn't he, and you have small feet." The particular content of your words is not terribly important at this stage, provided that you refer both to the topic at hand and also to something else that the child is familiar with and has a chance of understanding in a concrete way. Once the assistance or the comforting and the language have been given (and of course, you do not always have to use language), the next part of the process is to let the child leave when he wants to. Effective mothers do not bore their children.

In this pattern of response I believe we have a beautiful mechanism for effective education of a young child. First of all, the child is learning to use another person as a resource in situations that he cannot handle for himself. That is a vital social skill, one which will serve him well in the years to come. Second, he is beginning to learn a little bit more about the nature of other people, and that will stand him in good stead when he begins to interact with people other than those of the nuclear family. Third, he is learning that someone values his excitement and the satisfaction of his curiosity. Fourth, he gets language tuition, because someone is providing language that is relevant and makes sense to him. Fifth, his intellectual world is being broadened by the content of the information. Sixth, in cases when he asks for assistance, he is learning about completing simple tasks. Seventh, on those occasions where he is attempting something that simply will not work, like wrapping a kitten's paw around its tail two or three

3. DEVELOPMENT AND EDUCATIONAL OPPORTUNITIES

times, he is being taught realistic task limitations as well. As you can see, the issue of how to respond to overtures from your child is a topic of central importance.

In the role of consultant you will find it both natural, easy, and generally enjoyable to nurture the emerging social competencies. Some of your child's overtures will be requests for assistance. Your natural inclination will be to help. Do so! But be careful as the child passes his first birthday not to let yourself become the child's all-purpose tool.

THE PRIMARY CARETAKER'S ROLE AS AUTHORITY

In the homes we have studied where children are developing well, as contrasted with homes where children are developing poorly, we have always seen mother run the home with a loving but firm hand. The babies in these home situations rarely have any question about who is the final authority. In homes where children are not doing very well, however, there is often ambiguity with respect to the setting of limits and the determination of who is going to have the final say on disagreements. You need not fear that if you are firm with your infant, if you deny him things from time to time on a realistic basis, or even occasionally on an unrealistic basis, that he will love you less than if you were lenient. Children in the first two years of life do not become detached from their primary caretakers very easily; even if you spank them regularly, you will find they keep coming back to you. This is very probably due to the absolutely vital need they have for close attachment to someone.

Be firm. You do your child no favor by yielding to him, especially if it is a first child, because that child is going to have to learn some of the harsh realities of life when the second child comes along, or when he leaves the home and enters into the non-nuclear-family world. A child who has not been dealt with firmly during late infancy is considerably less well prepared to cope with life situations than one who has.

DISCIPLINE

It is important to get a pattern of solid and effective discipline established during this age in order to prepare for the more difficult job when the child gets to be a bit older. We have very rarely seen the most effective mothers repeat anything more than once in the way of a restriction or a control sentence. If a child did not respond in the desired way after the message was repeated once, the mothers acted, either with a slight pat on the behind or arm, or more commonly with physical removal of the child from the situation that they wanted him to abandon. Distraction is also an effective tactic. But the main thing is to avoid such ambiguous kinds of discipline as, for example, when you insist that the child stop doing something, and then you do not follow up when he does not stop. Such behavior is very common and only lays the foundation for later problems.

THE BABY'S ELASTIC MIND

Both life and laboratory research could undermine the Western belief that a baby's experiences determine the course of its adult life.

JEROME KAGAN

Jerome Kagan *is professor of human development at Harvard University, where his research is concerned with the issue of continuity and change in human development, as well as with intellectual and emotional development during early childhood. His Ph.D. is from Yale University, and he was formerly chairman of the Department of Psychology at Fels Research Institute, Yellow Springs, Ohio. Kagan is author or co-author of* Birth to Maturity, Change and Continuity in Infancy, Understanding Children, *and* Child Development and Personality. The Place of Infancy in Development, *which discusses the effects of group care on infants, will be published in the spring of 1978 by Harvard University Press. He is a fellow of the American Academy of Arts and Sciences and consulting editor to several journals in the human sciences.*

Assumptions about the nature and development of human behavior and the forces that promote psychological change have been transformed during the past 20 years. Western scientists used to believe, for example, that infantile autism, a form of childhood psychosis, could develop simply because a mother rejected her baby, and that any response could be taught to any organism. New knowledge has reduced our faith in these and in many other ideas.

One assumption, however, remains as vital today as it was years before the American Revolution. Many still believe that most of an infant's experiences have effects that reach many years into the future. The belief that development is continuous and cumulative leads parents to conclude that in order to prevent undesirable behavior and to promote desirable conduct, caretaking adults must provide the baby with a certain recipe of encounters. If adults fail in this mission, the infant will not develop its potential or will be vulnerable to future unhappiness.

Accordingly, we have awarded certain early experiences a mysterious power, a tonic young children need if they are to attain society's highly valued prizes. As a result, middle-class parents worry about providing sufficient stimulation to their month-old infant or wonder whether failure to unite the newborn with its mother immediately after birth might have harmful consequences.

These assumptions antedate the accumulation of firm supporting evidence and were based originally on intuition. Although intuition is sometimes a reliable guide to truth, it cannot always be depended upon. Recent evidence, from studies that have followed children for many years as well as from the laboratory and from other cultures, seems to contradict this ancient belief.

However, this new information is based on relatively crude methods. In addition, the existing studies usually measure those psychological qualities that are relatively easy to assess and remain indifferent to subtle or complex aspects of a child's development because precise assessment tools do not exist. Hence it is proper to retain a cautious attitude toward the new information. Nevertheless, it is reasonable that we at least begin to question our cherished assumption, while not rejecting completely the possibility of select islands of continuity in human development that are yet to be discovered.

Let us first consider the historical bases for the belief in long-term continuity. Two centuries ago clergy and statesmen regularly affirmed the critical importance of the child's early years, urging mothers to stay at home with their infants and to treat them tenderly. "Were man able to trace every effect to its cause, he would probably find that the virtue or the vice of an individual, the happiness or misery of a family, the glory or the infamy of a nation had their source in the cradle, over which the prejudices of a nurse or mother have presided," wrote Samuel H. Smith in 1796.

John Locke's metaphor of the infant's mind as a blank tablet and the desire of many 17th Century intellectuals to make experience primary in the creation of knowledge are among the fundamental sources of this idea. For Locke and others who believed in egalitarianism, it was useful to assume that political equality among all citizens was more easily attained if infants were relatively similar at birth. If experience were the primary—but not the sole—determinant of differences among human beings, society could arrange for all of its children to have equivalent experiences, thereby guaranteeing that they would all become free, equal, and independent as adults. Since four-year-olds are so different, egalitarians wanted to conclude that early experience was the main cause of the variation.

A second historical force behind the emphasis on early experience comes from the maxim that one must prepare for the future. Just as each person prepared for salvation through good deeds, parents were supposed, through proper nurture, to prepare their young children to be psychologically healthy adults. From colonial days, American clergymen, statesmen, and intellectuals, most

3. DEVELOPMENT AND EDUCATIONAL OPPORTUNITIES

of them egalitarian Protestants, implied that a mother's devoted care for her child was not unlike gathering wood in August to prepare for December's frigid winds.

A third contribution to the doctrine of early infant determinism comes from the biological materialism of modern psychology. Psychological experience presumably causes changes in the neurons and their synapses, like marks on a tablet, and it is easier to assume that the marks are fixed rather than transient. The modern metaphor for the mind becomes reels of tape in a tape recorder. The iron filings on the fresh tape are permanently altered by a baby's early experiences, and if no one erases the message, it will be preserved with fidelity for an indefinite period.

A fourth factor that tempts us to have faith in the stability of early experience lies in the words we use to describe human behavior. We use adjectives like *passive, irritable, intelligent,* or *emotional* for infants, children, and adults as if the age of the person described were irrelevant to the meaning of the terms. A mother is "loving," "rejecting," or "coercive" whether her child is six months or 16 years old and regardless of whether we observe her action in a home, a church, or a supermarket. The permanence rooted so deeply in our descriptive language may contribute to the belief that early experience sculpts attitudes, fears, and behavior that are extremely resistant to change.

A final reason for awarding power to early experience is the inevitable consequence of certain entrenched practices in our society. Every parent knows that his child will be evaluated for ability and character at the end of kindergarten. Those evaluations will influence the quality of education the child will receive through elementary and high school, the probability of admission to a good college, and by implication, future success, happiness, wealth, and dignity.

Few societies practice severe grading of young children with such efficiency and zeal. In most communities, children receive responsibility when they are ready, not when they attain a particular age. Moreover, children usually are given assignments they can master, such as carrying water or caring for younger children. Their status in the community is attained in adulthood by hard work, loyalty to the village, and the acquisition of land or livestock. Relative competence in motor or language skills at five years has little effect on their lives.

But because the industrialized West needs less than a third of its youth to assume positions of high responsibility or to master complex skills, we send the best-trained adolescents to professional schools. Selection usually occurs when the child is 10 or 11, and once made, the child's motivations become relatively fixed and his place in the rank order becomes relatively stable.

Most parents either know or sense this sequence and try to make sure their children are as talented and motivated as possible when schooling begins. They assume that the obvious differences among five-year-olds are the result of what happened earlier in the family. Hence parents want to guarantee that their children have the richest set of early experiences. The belief that early experience was the primary determinant of adult success was satisfying because it resolved uncertainty, provided parents with anxiety-reducing rituals, made material encounters between the child and the environment the basis for both positive and negative results, and above all, was rational.

Laboratory research on animals during the last 25 years confirmed, at least initially, the importance of early experience. A duckling, fresh from its shell, will follow the first moving object it sees and will tend to follow it in preference to all other objects. Fortunately, that first moving object is usually the mother. It used to be assumed that the first object the duckling followed, or imprinted upon, could not be changed. But recent studies by Eckhard Hess indicate that the early imprinting can be altered. Additionally, William Mason and M. D. Kenney have switched a monkey's attachment from a member of its own species to a spayed female dog. And Harry Harlow and his colleagues have been able to rehabilitate, in less than six months, extremely withdrawn monkeys who spent their first half year in complete isolation.

Although it is difficult to find equally commanding demonstrations of dramatic changes in human development, individual strands of evidence, each too weak to bear the burden of proof, can be woven into a fabric with some persuasive power. After World War II, for example, American families adopted homeless children, most of them from Greece and Korea, who had led uncertain lives during the war. When 38 of these children, whose ages ranged from five months to 10 years, arrived in the United States their progress was followed by a team from the Judge Baker Guidance Center in Boston.

Soon after the children came to their new homes, they showed signs of many problems: overeating, sleep disturbances, nightmares, and of course, excessive clinging to their new parents. But eventually these symptoms vanished, the vast majority made good progress in school, and there was not one case of serious learning disability among them. When Constance Rathbun, Letitia Di Virgilio, and Samuel Waldfogel assessed the children, they wrote: "The degree of recovery observed in most cases could not have been predicted from the writings of those researchers who have studied the effects of separation most carefully. The present results indicate that for the child suffering extreme loss, the chances for recovery are far better than had previously been expected."

A study of 141 Korean orphans by Myron Winick, Knarig Meyer, and Ruth Harris produced similar results. These girls were adopted when they were between two and three years old by middle-class American families. After six years in their foster homes all were in elementary school, and their scores on IQ and school-achievement tests were comparable to scores made by the average American child.

Recently, linguists at the University of California and psychologists at the Los Angeles Children's Hospital have been following the development of a girl named Genie who was taken from her home when she was 13½ years old. Genie had been immobilized and isolated from contact with others for most of her life. When she was discovered she was malnourished, unable to stand erect, and

22. The Baby's Elastic Mind

without language—a victim of unprecedented deprivation.

After only six years in a normal family environment, Genie has developed some language, learned social skills, can take a bus to school, and has begun to express some of the basic human emotions. Surprisingly, on some of the performance scales of the Wechsler Intelligence Scale for Children she obtained scores that approached average ability. Although Genie is still like a child in many ways and markedly different from an average California 20-year-old, she has grown remarkably in a relatively short time. These results suggest that the mind may have some of the qualities of an elastic surface, easily deformed by shearing forces, but able to rebound when those forces are removed.

Genie represents a single case, but there are more systematic studies. With Howard Moss, I assessed a large number of working- and middle-class adults who had grown up in intact homes in southwestern Ohio. The results of this project, summarized in *Birth to Maturity*, related evaluations of the children at various periods during their first 14 years to their psychological status as adults. With few exceptions, we could find little relation between psychological qualities during the first three years of life—fearfulness, irritability, or activity—and any aspect of behavior in adulthood.

Not until a child was six to 10 years old was there any firm evidence that his or her behavior foretold the kind of adult the child would become. At that time, predictions began to approach correlations of 0.5, a figure that indicates a moderate but not stunning degree of continuity.

In a subsequent investigation we followed 140 Caucasian firstborn infants, assessing them at four, eight, 13, and 27 months. We evaluated the attentiveness of the babies, their vocalizations, smiling, irritability to a variety of sights and sounds, and the tempo of their play. Variation on any of these qualities observed at four or eight months bore little relation to the child's display of similar qualities at 27 months.

We recently retested 65 of these children when they were 10 years old. There was no relation between behavioral differences in the first year of life and differences in either reading ability or IQ. There was a suggestive relation, but only among girls, between a four-month-old's tendency to smile at masks of human faces and a reflective disposition at 10 years.

Most recently, Richard Kearsley, Philip R. Zelazo, and I studied children who were either attending a day-care center or being reared only at home. We evaluated them on eight occasions, first when they were three and a half months old and the last time at 29 months. We found even less stability over the first two and a half years of life than in the earlier project.

A baby's reactions—attentiveness, vocalizations, smiling, or fretfulness—to interesting events during the first year predicted no significant behavior at two and a half. Although there was great variation among the infants, who came from both working- and middle-class homes, their behavior from seven months to two and half years showed little continuity. For example, a baby who showed anxiety with an unfamiliar child at 13 months might or might not be fearful a year and a half later.

Nor was there any long-term stability in a baby's tendency to protest when his mother left the room. We found no evidence that a child carried a generalized disposition one might call fearfulness across the first two and a half years of life—a finding that is in accord with the results of other investigators.

In an extensive study of the stability of temperament, known as the New York Study and carried out by the N.Y.U. School of Medicine, researchers used interviews and observations to evaluate such qualities as passivity, adaptability, responsiveness, intensity of reaction, and mood. Data were gathered continually during the infancy of 136 children and again during their preschool and early school years. Although preliminary data suggested some threads of continuity, more recent reports reveal no relation between ratings of temperament during the first year of life and a variety of behavior at age five. According to Michael Rutter and his colleagues at the University of London, who conducted the follow-up study, "Behavioral ratings in the first six months of life are of no predictive value in relation to the child's temperamental characteristics as shown during the school years."

A final and more controversial source of support for resilience in growth comes from our investigation of children growing up in small, isolated, subsistence-farming villages in western Guatemala. In one of these villages, San Marcos La Laguna, infants typically spend their first year confined to a small, dark hut. They are not played with, rarely spoken to, poorly nourished, and they suffer from respiratory and gastrointestinal distress for much of the year. Thus their experience is limited, their opportunity to practice maturing skills restricted, and their health poor.

When compared to American babies of the same age, the Guatemalan infants are retarded. Some of the major developmental milestones, such as the ability to recall past events, the belief that objects continue to exist when they are out of sight (object permanence), symbolic play, and language appear from two to 12 months later than they do in American infants.

For example, a baby is given a toy and allowed to play with it for 20 to 30 seconds. The toy is taken away, and a few seconds later the baby is shown two toys—the one he has just handled and a new one. By six to seven months, the typical American infant will shift his gaze back and forth between the toys several times before he chooses one of them. This action suggests he is comparing the two objects and indicates he remembers the earlier toy. A typical San Marcos infant does not behave in this way until he is 10 or 11 months old.

In a test of object permanence the examiner, an Indian woman, hides an attractive toy under a cloth. If the baby searches for the toy, we infer he remembered its being hidden and could coordinate that knowledge with action. If he does not search, we assume he "forgot" the event; some psychologists would conclude the toy no longer exists for him. American infants usually solve this

3. DEVELOPMENT AND EDUCATIONAL OPPORTUNITIES

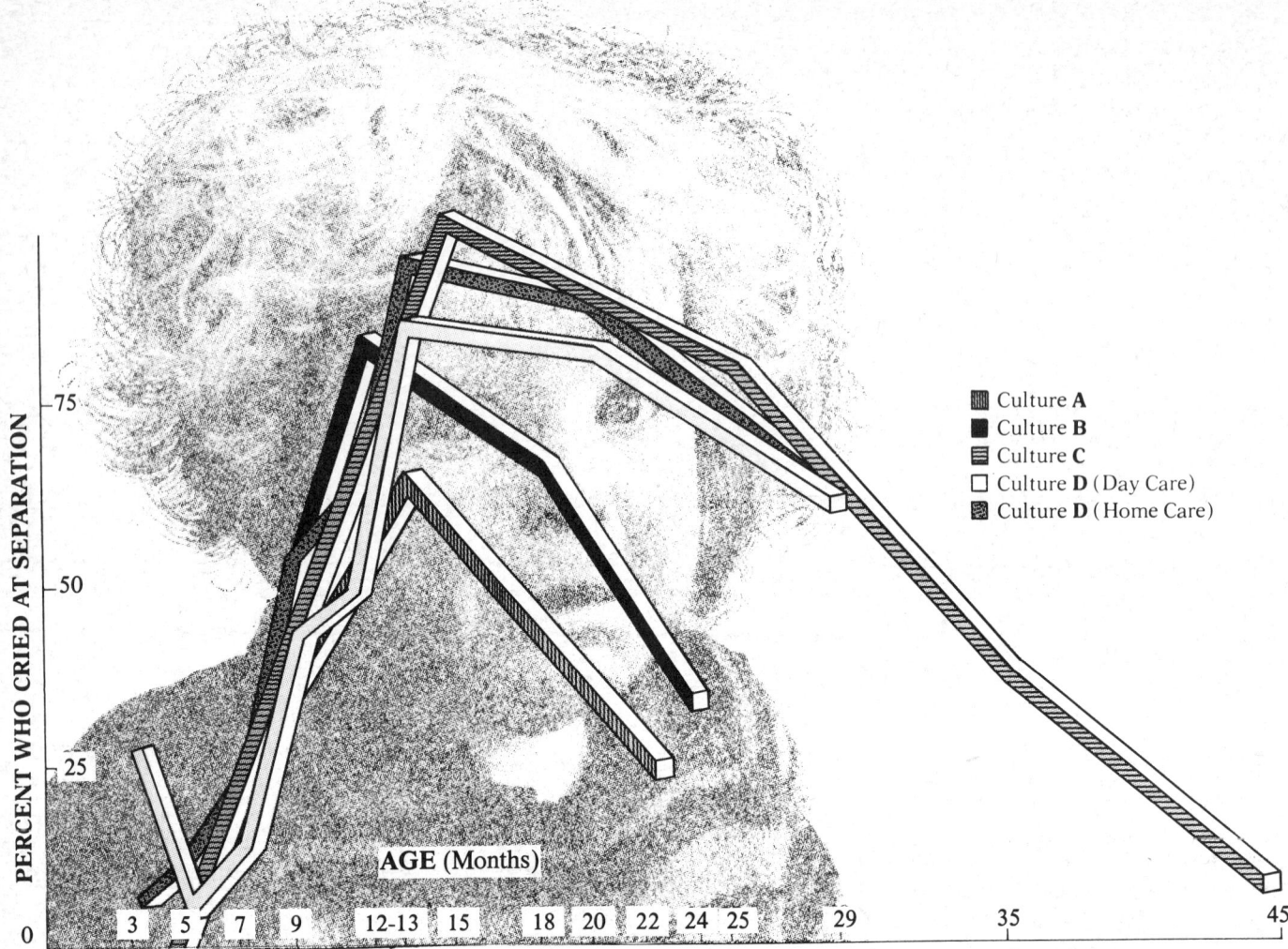

problem by the age of eight months; the San Marcos child does not retrieve the toy until he is 11 months old.

Pretend play with objects usually appears in American children around 12 months, but such imaginative play is delayed several months among San Marcos children. Finally, American children begin to speak their first words about the middle of their second year; San Marcos children do not begin to speak until the middle or end of their third year.

By the second year, life changes for San Marcos children. They are allowed to wander outside the hut and encounter the rich variety of the world. By the time they are four or five, they play with other children, and by eight or nine the boys and girls have adult responsibilities, which include working in the fields, caring for infants, cooking, and cleaning.

Our research team has made two separate assessments of the intellectual abilities of San Marcos children. In the

Different cultures treat babies differently, and each relationship between mother and child is unique. But when large groups of children are studied, a similarity in development appears. Babies under seven months rarely cried when left in an unfamiliar setting, and more children showed distress at their mother's departure between the ages of 12 and 15 months than at any other time.

first, we found that before age 10, the performance of San Marcos children on special tests of perceptual analysis, memory, and reasoning is clearly inferior to that of children in the United States. What is more, their performance is also inferior to that of children living in a nearby village who are not so severely restricted during their first year. However, by adolescence, San Marcos children perform nearly as well as American children on these tests.

Recently we returned to San Marcos and administered more difficult memory tests. For example, in one procedure we presented a series of 12 pictures that illustrate familiar objects. The child tries to recall the 12 pictures in the order in which they are presented. All of our middle-class Cambridge children were able to remember the order of all 12 pictures by the time they were eleven years old. Only 10 percent of the San Marcos 11-year-old children performed as well. But by late adolescence 58 percent could recall the order of all the pictures. Thus San Marcos adolescents can handle some difficult intellectual tasks at a level that approaches that of children who have grown up in more varied and challenging settings.

The retardation of the San Marcos infant does not preclude the continuous enhancement of his mental talents. Although the 10-year-old San Marcos child is not as proficient as the typical American 10-year-old, this difference is

22. The Baby's Elastic Mind

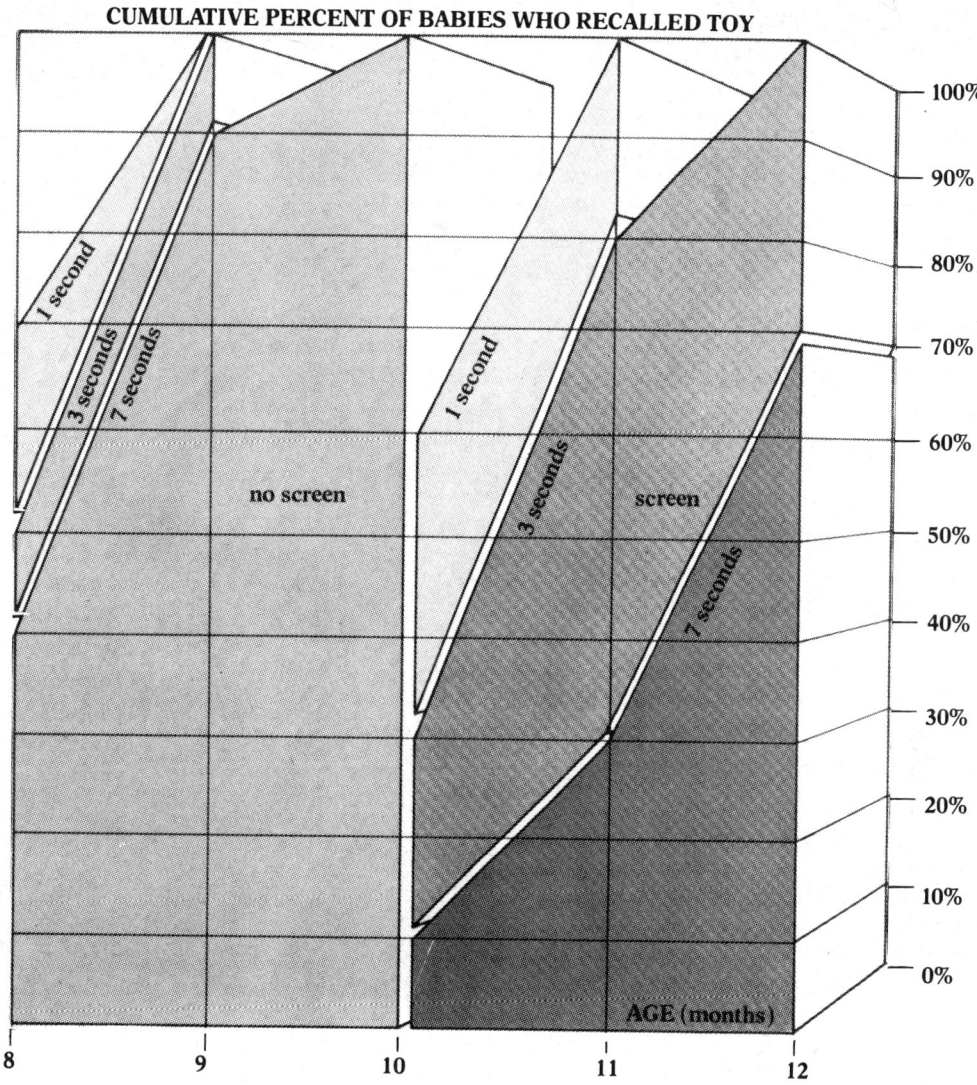

Short-term memory improves near the end of the first year. Babies watched a toy being hidden under one of two cloths but were kept from reaching for it for one, three, or seven seconds. Sometimes a screen blocked their view during the delay. By 10 months, all babies located the toy after seven seconds when no screen was lowered; by a year 70 percent found it even with the screen present.

as likely to result from continued cultural isolation and poor schooling as from the lack of varied experience and good nutrition during the first year. As in the case histories discussed earlier, change and growth seem to be characteristic of psychological functions.

The apparent lack of impressive predictability from infancy to later childhood may at first be difficult to understand, but consideration of the way a child develops suggests the reasonableness of this conclusion. Many of the infant behaviors assessed by psychologists show a lawful course of growth: a time of emergence, a period of plateau, and often, a decline. The appearance of new functions and the loss of old ones often result when new competences mature. Major maturational changes in early development may be one reason for the lack of impressive stability.

A baby enters the world prepared to attend to change in physical stimulation. Contrasts in light, motion, sound, smell, touch, and taste attract his attention. When objects in his field of vision differ in the amount of black-white contrast, for example, the infant typically looks at the place of greatest contrast. Infants also respond to differences in wavelength, as though they perceive green, blue, yellow, and red exactly the way adults do. In short, a baby is prepared to discover the dimensions of the external world and does not have to learn how to locate the information. Nature has awarded him small clues to help him ferret out the prizes she has hidden.

An important early ability is the detection of similarity between a present event and a related one experienced in the past. This experience permits an infant to form a new idea or to alter an old one in a way that takes into account the relation between the new perception and the older knowledge.

By as early as 10 weeks, babies seem to possess this ability. Sights and sounds that differ a little from an infant's prior knowledge—discrepant events—alert him and lead to new awareness. Such events are most likely to catch and hold his attention. Thus, during the first six

3. DEVELOPMENT AND EDUCATIONAL OPPORTUNITIES

months, the contents of a baby's mind change as he is exposed to events that are related to what he knows but are not immediately understandable.

As the infant approaches eight months of age a new set of behaviors emerges, suggesting the maturation of new abilities. One of these is increased attentiveness. Toward the end of the first year, a particular discrepant event will hold a baby's attention for a longer time than it did when he was six months old. The older infant also displays an obvious motor inhibition to discrepant events. A baby under seven months typically reaches at once for an unexpected, novel object. But an 11-month-old shows a short but obvious delay before reaching for the new object.

Another major change that occurs at this time is a dramatic increase in the likelihood of signs of apprehension, including crying, to a discrepant event. The consequences of a baby's encounter with an adult stranger have been investigated many times in the last 30 years, usually with the same result. Infants rarely show apprehension at a stranger's appearance before they are six months old; after that, signs of fear grow dramatically until 12 to 13 months, and then decline.

The appearance of separation distress (the tendency to cry and stop playing after the mother or primary caretaker leaves the baby in an unfamiliar place) is also similar among children raised in a variety of settings: American cities, Latin American barrios, Israeli kibbutzim, or !Kung San bands in the Kalahari. Such crying usually emerges when babies are about eight months old, rises to a peak in the middle of the second year, and then declines in all these cultures. Moreover, as Selma Fraiberg has shown, separation distress appears, peaks, and declines in a similar way among babies who are blind from birth.

The nearly simultaneous appearance of increased attentiveness, motor inhibition, wariness, and distress to discrepant events appears due, in part, to the emergence of an enhanced ability to remember. Specifically, after eight months the infant is better able to recapture representations of past experience with a minimum of cues and to hold the past and present in short-term memory for a longer time. This amplification in memory gives him more time to attempt to resolve the discrepancy between present experience and prior knowledge. If he cannot, he becomes uncertain. Fear of strangers or distress at mother's departure seems to occur when the baby does not resolve the uncertainty generated by failure to understand the relation between a discrepant experience and his store of knowledge.

Recent long-term studies of children in both the United States and isolated villages in Guatemala indicate that a baby's short-term memory is enhanced dramatically between eight and 12 months. A group of infants followed regularly at that age watched an adult place a toy under one of two identical cloths. Sometimes the infant was allowed to reach for the toy almost at once, sometimes he had to wait seven seconds. Also, on some trials a screen was lowered during the delay. There was steady improvement with age in successful retrieval of the toy. No eight-month-old could remember the toy's location when the screen was placed between him and the toy for seven seconds, while 70 percent of the one-year-olds solved that problem easily.

Seven seconds may seem a short time, but an adult can hold a telephone number in short-term memory for only about 20 seconds. If he has just looked up the number and is interrupted before he can dial it, he will find that it has slipped from his mind, just as the toy's existence vanishes from the mind of the eight-month-old.

I believe that, if the delay between the event and the time of recall is more than a few seconds, the infant under eight months has great difficulty in retrieving fresh experiences as well as in holding the retrieved information on the stage of short-term memory for a prolonged time. But the infant of less than eight months is perfectly capable of recognizing many events following a long delay because the world supplies him with a clue to help him "locate" what he knows.

It appears that enhanced retrieval memory may be the direct consequence of maturational changes in the central nervous system, perhaps involving the ascendance of forebrain mechanisms. It is probably no coincidence that the proportion of quiet sleep, which is relatively constant from three to six months, shows an increase at 10 to 11 months. Moreover, during the last half of the first year, recordings of the brain's electrical activity show a sharp drop during Stage 2 sleep in the number of sleep spindles, bursts of fast brain waves in the 12- to 15-cycle-per-second range. Since many physiologists believe that control of sleep shifts from the brain stem to the forebrain during the first year, it is reasonable to suggest that the diverse behavioral changes that suddenly and rather uniformly appear by the end of the first year are due to structural and/or biochemical changes that are an essential part of human development.

These discoveries about the infant imply that his first experiences may be permanently lost. The fears and joys of the first year seem to be part of nature's script for development, not harbingers of adolescent anxiety or prophetic signs of childhood happiness. I suspect that it is not until a child is five or six years old, when he has begun to crystallize a symbolic conception of his personal qualities and to establish consistent expectations and styles of interacting with friends and family, that we get a more reliable preview of the future. The infant's mind may be more like a sandy beach on a windy day than a reel of recording tape.

For further information:

Curtiss, Susan. *Genie: A Psycholinguistic Study of a Modern-day "Wild Child."* Academic Press, 1977.

Emde, R. N., and Stephan Walker. "Longitudinal Study of Infant Sleep: Results of 14 Subjects Studied at Monthly Intervals." *Psychophysiology,* Vol. 13, 1976, pp. 456-461.

Fraiberg, Selma. "Parallel and Divergent Patterns in Blind and Sighted Infants." *Psychoanalytic Study of the Child,* Vol. 23, 1968, pp. 264-299.

Hess, E. H. "Imprinting in a Natural Laboratory." *Scientific American,* Vol. 227, 1972, pp. 24-31.

Kagan, Jerome, and R. E. Klein. "Crosscultural Perspectives in Early Development." *American Psychologist,* Vol. 28, 1973, pp. 947-961.

Kagan, Jerome, and H. A. Moss. *Birth to Maturity.* John Wiley & Sons, 1962.

The Care of Infants and Toddlers in Group Settings

Judy I. Schwartz

"If the family is the best unit of child care, when and under what circumstances is group care justified? What constitutes quality group care?" Judy I. Schwartz provides some answers. The author is Associate Professor and Coordinator of Early Childhood Education, Queens College of The City University of New York, Flushing.

INTRODUCTION

THE FAMILY is quite simply the most efficient, effective and enduring child care system ever devised. When it functions well, the family can do for the developing child what no other entity can do. Family members can know a child better and can create more mutual responsiveness between themselves and the child than can any external caregiver. Even the modern family—debilitated possibly, changed certainly from earlier times—remains the best source of nourishment and nurture for a growing child.

This nuclear unit is not a product of chance. The family has evolved in humans and other species as the best mechanism to accommodate the needs of the young, providing a close, protective environment over the long period of development from helplessness to independence.

Is this position controversial? Does it run counter to any significant body of empirical or theoretical knowledge? Are there organized special interest groups that would find it untenable? The answer is *no*. Perhaps because the family is almost universally seen as the best source for the nurturance of young children, the specter of external child care leads again and again to claims that a conspiracy is at work to a) undermine the already weakened nuclear family and/or b) communize children by subjecting them to the influence of group care. Moreover, it is argued, the outcome of such care, especially for the very young, will hamper or even damage the child's development. A recent popular book, for example, refers throughout to Child Care Industries, Inc., in capitals, as an embodiment of this insidious trend.

Such arguments are usually exaggerated. They are often drawn in an almost classical scheme of the Hegelian dialectic: pro-family as the thesis; pro-external child care as the antithesis. What is characteristically omitted is the essential third element, the synthesis or amalgamation of the two polar positions into a harmonious compromise. Is such a synthesis possible? If the family is the best unit of child care, when and under what circumstances is group care justified? What constitutes quality group care? I shall try to answer these questions by looking at group care for infants and toddlers from three perspectives: pragmatic issues, theoretical schema and empirical strands.

PRAGMATIC ISSUES

Most of us cherish certain myths about the family. We like to believe that in an earlier time families were extended and stable. The facts, however, do not bear this out. From the earliest days most American families, for example, were

3. DEVELOPMENT AND EDUCATIONAL OPPORTUNITIES

nuclear, not extended; the mobility we associate with modern times has always been a feature of American culture (Keniston et al., 1977). But there have been real and significant changes.

The American Family Today—Some Statistics

Today's family is no longer the economically self-sufficient unit it once was. In the past, children contributed to the family's capital and economic self-sufficiency as part of its work force. Today, they have moved from the credits to the debits column in the family's economic balance sheet. In many ways, children themselves have replaced their economic potential as the family's only product.

Another important area of change is in the composition of the family. One out of every six American children under 18 lives in a single-parent home; this rate is increasing most rapidly for children under 6. The largest category of single parents is divorced women, followed closely by women under 25 who have never married (Gross, 1977). Today, approximately one out of every three marriages ends in divorce, an increase of about 700% from the turn of the century. Statistics indicate that four of every 10 children born in the 1970s will spend part of their childhood in a single-parent household. And, let's not forget that ubiquitous family member, television. It is estimated that by the time the average child reaches 18 he/she will have spent more time watching TV than attending school or simply being with parents (Keniston et al., 1977).

The model of a mother who stays at home with her youngsters until they reach school age and is there waiting for them when they return from school is fast disappearing—in fact if not in ideal. In 1948, 26% of married women with school-age children worked. This figure rose to 54% employed full time in 1976. The increase is still greater for married women with preschool children; 13% worked in 1948, 37% in 1976 (Keniston et al., 1977).

Limited Access to Adults

Today it is typical for a school-age child to have a mother who works full time. Thus, more and more children have increasingly limited access to adults. In addition, the 1977 report by Keniston and the Carnegie Council on Children estimates that 1/4 to 1/3 of all American children are born into families with financial stress so great that they will suffer basic deprivation. They report that 75% of white children under 6 in female-headed households lack access to basic essentials. For black children in such households, five out of six grow up with less than the minimum essentials.

One result of these changes is that children now enter group settings outside their families at a much earlier age. The estimated number of available day care slots in 1974 was 1 million. Yet, in that same year there were approximately 6½ million children under 6 whose mothers worked and needed day care services for their children (National Council of Organizations for Children and Youth, 1976). The number of infant and toddler programs is much smaller, as reported in a 1973 survey that found a total of only 58 such programs (Balzer, 1973). By 1978, however, Cohen and Zigler found that infant and toddler programs were increasing faster than any other sector of day care. These estimates do not account for the majority of child care arrangements which are of a more informal nature, such as babysitting and most family day care.

In this charged and stressful new world, the altered family shares many of its functions—even the care of its youngest children—with external agencies. For many, this is a matter of necessity, not choice. For example, in the federal Work Incentive Program (WIN) a mother is obligated to work in order to receive benefits. She must, therefore, use child care services. What do we know about the effect of group care on infants (birth to 18 months) and toddlers (19 to 36 months)?

Effects of Home vs. Group vs. Institution

Many of the arguments raised against group care of infants and toddlers are based on early studies of maternal attachment and the effects of institutionalization on the child's development. The Bowlby report published by the World Health Organization in 1951, which summarized findings on the long-term development of children reared away from their own homes, is frequently cited. Bowlby concluded that group care is detrimental to the young child's growth and development because it does not allow for the care of the child by a single caregiver. Hunt (1961) also concluded from a review of the research that young children separated from their mothers are deficient on most measures of social development and intellectual and physical growth.

It is important to note that these conclusions were drawn from studies of children reared in orphanages or foster homes. A series of studies published by W. Goldfarb in 1949, for example, showed contrasting patterns of intellectual functioning in a group of adolescents reared in institutions up to the age of 3 and then placed in foster homes, and a group placed in foster homes shortly after birth. The group that spent the most time in institutions was deficient in many ways compared to the group placed at an early age in foster homes. Likewise, Dennis (1973) reported on a study conducted in Lebanon that found that children adopted before 2 years of age overcame the effects of their early institutionalization, while children adopted after 2 years of age did not.

Are the effects of group care on infants and toddlers comparable to those of orphanages and similar institutions? Although a few reports have attributed such problems as an increase in anxiety to group care (Blehar, 1975; Lippman and Grote, 1974), the majority of studies find no effects similar to those associated with institutionalization. Some studies even indicate that a quality group care program may have a beneficial effect on development or may prevent the developmental decline in intellectual functioning that might otherwise have been expected in certain children (Caldwell, 1972; Horowitz and Paden, 1973; Robinson and Robinson, 1971; Starr, 1971). For example, a five-year longitudinal study by the state of Pennsylvania used a sample of 170 low-income children between 12 and 20 months of age who were enrolled in a center-based program for a period of two years. Statistical analyses of pre- and post-test data on an extensive battery of test measures found center-based children scored significantly higher than comparable home-reared children (Dusewicz and O'Connell, 1975).

Most studies do not report such positive results. But they do not report negative results, either. In sum, the majority of studies have found that group care for infants and toddlers is not harmful to the development of young children if individualized, consistent and good nurturing care is provided by the caregiver to each child (Caldwell *et al.*, 1970; Keister, 1977; Lally, 1974; Saunders, 1972; Schwartz *et al.*, 1973). An example is a report by Kagan, Kearsley and Zelazo (1973) of a longitudinal study involving Chinese and white children between the ages of 3½ and 30 months from working and middle-class homes, who were enrolled in a group care program five days a week. The major control group consisted of children reared totally at home who were matched with the center-based children on ethnicity, social class and sex. A wide range of eight separate assessments was made on perceptual-motor, cognitive and linguistic performance and on social development. The data revealed little difference on any of the measures between the day care and the home-reared children. The authors of the report concluded: "Attendance at a day care center staffed by conscientious and nurturant adults does not seem to sculpt a psychological profile very much different from the one created by total home rearing" (p. 37).

Do these findings constitute positive proof of neutral or beneficial effects of infant and toddler group care? They do not. Reviewed critically, the studies yield a tentative trend that must continue to be studied vigorously. It is important to note that most researchers emphasize the critical importance of *quality care* in their findings.

THEORETICAL SCHEMA

As we have seen, studies of infant and toddler group care have not yet given us definitive evidence of the effects of such programs on young children. Similarly, there are no theories of child development which, in themselves, support group care for infants and toddlers. However, consistent theoretical schema compatible with sound early childhood practice can be helpful in defining *quality* group care. Piaget's theory of cognitive development and Erikson's theory of emotional development, both of which meet the criteria of compatibility and consistency, are particularly useful.

According to Piaget (1952), intelligence begins to develop during the sensorimotor period, which spans infancy and toddlerhood. The scource of this intelligence is the child's interaction with the environment and the observation of changes effected on the environment. Infants cannot be taught skills that are inappropriate to their stage of development. But one can enhance an infant's development by so arranging the environment that he/she can practice the skills typically exhibited at a particular stage of development. The infant begins to perceive reality through the manipulation of objects in the natural world. The child's encounters with the environment should be rich, varied and just novel enough to pique curiosity and to challenge but not discourage exploration.

There are obvious applications that can be

3. DEVELOPMENT AND EDUCATIONAL OPPORTUNITIES

made from this information in developing quality programs. Honig (1974), for example, lists the following activities that help exercise the child's intelligence in the sensorimotor period:

☐ *Prehension skills:* reaching for toys; shaking toys; hitting and pulling suspended toys; squeaking toys; grasping and handling objects of different shapes and sizes.

☐ *Object permanence* (understanding that an object exists independent of one's own actions): playing peek-a-boo; horizontal following of toys; finding toys after their visible displacement; finding toys after invisible displacement; putting toys into containers; finding toys under containers.

☐ *Means-ends* (using objects to attain goals): reaching over an obstacle for a toy; using a support such as a pillow to obtain a toy placed on top of the support but out of reach; using a string horizontally (and vertically) to obtain a toy tied to the string; using a stick to obtain an object.

☐ *New-schema in relation to objects* (finding ways of acting on objects and using materials appropriately): hitting two toys together; patting a toy animal; making a doll walk; stretching an elastic bracelet; drinking from a cup.

☐ *Causality* (seeing the distinction between an act and its outcome): bringing an unseen object to sight; ringing a bell to make it sound; turning a key to make a mechanical toy run; working a jack-in-the box.

☐ *Construction of objects in space* (understanding space as a single continuous area within which all objects are contained and inter related): finding a toy by its sound; following the trajectory of a thrown ball; nesting several boxes; rolling objects down a plane; creeping around a barrier to retrieve an object.

☐ *Gestural imitation:* imitating a familiar, visible gesture such as pat-a-cake; imitating an unfamiliar, visible gesture such as crooking a finger; imitating a familiar, invisible gesture such as tilting the head back and forth; imitating an unfamiliar, invisible gesture such as an eye wink.

☐ *Verbal learning:* imitating baby sounds; imitating unfamiliar sounds such as "la-la"; labeling objects and experiences; listening to stories; carrying out verbal requests.

☐ *Physical development and exercise:* stretching and flexing legs; rolling a ball; bouncing to music; bending to pick up objects.

☐ *Sensory development:* listening, touching, kinesthetic, visual and tasting experiences.

☐ *Classification and seriation:* choosing and grouping similar items; picture of similar items; polar concepts, or extremes (*e.g.,* hot-cold, high-low, soft-hard, smooth-rough, wet-dry); seriation with perhaps three items such as nesting three boxes.

According to Erikson (1956), every stage of emotional development contains its own inherent conflict that must be resolved if the individual is to move on to the next stage. According to this hierarchical design of emotional development, trust is the basic emotional learning in the child's first year of life. If the infant is to develop trust, he/she must have a sensitive and responsive caregiver, one who meets the baby's needs in a consistent manner. If this is the case, the child learns that there is an order and predictability in the world. The child gains confidence in his/her abilities by seeing that his/her actions have an impact on the world. In the toddler period of development, Erikson's conflict is one of autonomy versus shame and doubt. To develop the child's autonomy, the setting must be safe yet challenging to help the child explore, meet problems and solve them successfully.

The theories of Piaget and Erikson provide an excellent foundation around which to build the cognitive and affective design of a quality group care program. The implementation of the design occurs as a natural and organic part of the ongoing activities and routines of every day—feeding, playing, diapering, napping and so on.

EMPIRICAL STRANDS

Until recently, infants were regarded as helpless organisms, basically indistinguishable one from another, to whom the world was a great buzzing confusion and on whom the environment would make its indelible mark. Research, particularly in the last decade or so, has dramatically altered this picture. Several strands of empirical data on infant characteristics and development are particularly significant for group care programs. These are studies of *individuality, competence, reciprocity, attachment* and *stimulation*.

Individuality

Far from being homogeneous, infants—even newborns—demonstrate great differences in temperament, as noted in a number of recent studies (Brazelton, 1969; Chess *et al.,* 1972; Korner, 1973; Thomas *et al.,* 1968). An example of one type of difference is in infants' arousal levels. There are wide variations, all of which fall within the normal range, in the intensity of stimulation required to trigger a reaction in individual infants. Some babies will be up and responding to a sound or a movement that elicits no noticeable reaction in other infants. Thus, even from the earliest days, infants demonstrate different (i.e., *their own*) response thresholds.

This behavioral individuality has urgent implications for infant/toddler group programs. First, there must be a sufficiently low ratio of adults to children to permit individualized caregiving. The most frequently cited ratios are 1:3 for infants and 1:4 for toddlers. Second, equipment and spatial arrangement must accommodate individual needs. For example, a baby with a high arousal level should have his/her crib located in the most quiet spot in the nap area. Finally, caregivers must observe, understand and respond appropriately to children's differing cues. The caregiver must know that when Susan has had too much stimulation she shows this by averting her eyes or turning her head, while Bobby generally gets fussy or cries. What constitutes too much stimulation, moreover, is different for each baby.

Competence

In the past, the infant was seen as a passive, reflex-bound, undifferentiated organism. Today we know that very young babies have real competencies and are capable of responding to and acting on the environment. For example, it has been found that a fetus can hear even before birth (Appleton *et al.*, 1975). We now know that newborn babies can see quite well (Mauer and Mauer, 1977). Infants can even be taught to modify their behavior, as shown in the work of Gregg *et al.* (1976) who increased infants' visual alertness and Dodd (1972) who increased the amount of infant babbling. Rheingold (1956) was able to induce more frequent smiling in institutionalized babies. As Yarrow *et al.* (1975) observe, there is continuing evidence of the infant's capacity to respond to a wide range of stimuli.

Given these facts, a group setting that fails to go beyond safe and sanitary is unacceptable. Quality care must be more than custodial care. Given the infant's capacity to be aroused, to attend to people and objects in the environment and respond selectively to stimuli, the setting must stimulate these capacities. Quality group care for infants and toddlers must motivate exploration and mastery of the environment, and teach the child to be adaptable and flexible in his/her behavioral responses.

Reciprocity

As Lewis and Rosenblum's 1974 book *The Effect of the Infant on Its Caregiver* attests, it is naive to view the infant as a passive recipient of environmental influence. The infant is capable not only of being affected by the environment, but of exerting his/her influence as well. Not only can the infant be changed, but he/she is also capable of producing change. The pattern of back-and-forth behavior between infant and caregiver is a kind of mutual adaptation between the two participants. Each learns to recognize and understand the other's cues or signals or sequences of specific behaviors that are necessary to elicit interaction or to trigger modification in each other's behavior.

Thrift (1976) likens this process in the mother-infant dyad to a prelinguistic conversation. Brazelton *et al.* (1974) see a parallel heightening and lowering of each member's *arousal level* as an important feature of this reciprocal interaction. The partners vocalize, gaze and gesture to each other to maintain the optimal arousal level. Ainsworth and Bell (1972) associate affective responsiveness of the mother to the infant's signals with the development of critical aspects of cognitive development. They found, for example, that maternal responsiveness to crying in the first quarter of the infant's first year was inversely related to the amount of crying the infant did in the last quarter of his/her first year. They also found at the end of the first year that babies who had decreased their amount of crying developed a more varied and sophisticated signaling system. As another index of the importance of reciprocal interaction, Beckwith and Cohen (1975) report that the frequency of mutual visual regard at 8 months between infant and mother was correlated significantly with cognitive development at 9 months.

What are the implications here for group care? First, the caregiver must understand that infants are responsive beings. He/she must also provide opportunities for the infant to influence the caregiver's behavior. This can be done by engaging in meaningful mutual interaction with the baby, as in a game of peek-a-boo. The caregiver must be careful to observe the infant's response repertoire and to respond appropriately to the infant. For example, the caregiver must recognize each infant or toddler's cues in a feeding situation—sucking, coughing, averting eyes, turning away, spitting up. These cues may indicate the effectiveness or ineffectiveness of the caregiver's feeding behavior. Many adults, perhaps most, are skeptical of the capacity of the very young child to respond meaningfully. They

3. DEVELOPMENT AND EDUCATIONAL OPPORTUNITIES

are apt to miss a baby's subtle cues, and be too quick to act without taking note of what the baby is telling them. They do things *to* the baby, they do things *for* the baby, but they miss doing things *with* the baby in a very real sense. One way to counteract this tendency is through *continuity of caregiving*. Reciprocal interaction is facilitated by continuity of care because both baby and caregiver have the time to learn each other's cues and become skillful in eliciting desired responses in each other.

Attachment

By the time a child is about 7 months old, he/she has formed a definite attachment to the primary caregiver. The infant's response to separation is the criterion used to determine this. Babies younger than 6 to 7 months usually do not display the distress at separation from mother that infants who have passed this critical age do (Ainsworth, 1972). In addition, in the second half of the first year other attachment behaviors manifest themselves. The infant smiles at the mother frequently, attempts to keep her as near as possible through continuous visual and auditory contact and searches for her visually and auditorily when she is absent (Cairns, 1972). However, even babies as young as 3 or 4 weeks have been found to respond selectively to their mother's voice (Wolff, 1963). This bonding relationship between infant and primary caregiver is essential to the development of a healthy personality. The pattern of reciprocal interaction noted earlier figures importantly in the development of attachment. Fraiberg (1977) says the "... early dialogue of 'need' and 'answer to need' becomes a highly differentiated signal system in the early months of life; it is, properly speaking, the matrix of human language and of the human bond itself" (p. 57).

The separation of the infant from his/her mother is at the heart of the controversy over infant/toddler group care. Do these programs engender separation anxiety and distress in children? As noted earlier, there is no clear-cut evidence of this effect. What can quality programs do to reduce the possibility of such effects?

First, it is very important to provide as home-like an atmosphere as possible to reduce the discontinuities the child experiences between home and center. One advantage of family day care programs is that their home settings avoid the institution-like appearance of many center-based programs. Second, caregivers must regard themselves as assistants to and not substitutes for the child's parents. Caregivers must take their cues from parents in working with the children. Bromwich (1977) says, "Infant intervention should have as its primary goal the maintenance or encouragement of a positive attachment between mother and infant" (pp. 77-78). Third, consistency and continuity of caregiving are essential. To build trust and self-confidence in the child, to provide regularity in the child's world that he/she can anticipate and influence, there should be a specific individual assigned for primary caregiving for each child.

Stimulation

In the 1960s, at the height of intervention program activity, it was generally held that certain children were deprived of necessary stimulation, sensory and otherwise. It was further agreed that the job of the intervention program was to make up or compensate for these deficiencies by supplying the needed stimulation. Today, many have rejected this deficit theory. In addition, a growing awareness of research findings has led many to question the "more is better" hypothesis in regard to stimulation. As has been noted, an infant has the ability to discriminate among and respond differentially to different kinds of stimuli. It is likely that this competence results from biological maturation rather than environmental manipulation.

Occurring simultaneously with *neurological maturation* is another process called *neurological integration*. Neurological integration is a process in which inhibitory brain mechanisms are activated and developed to help control such things as random movements and the change from one emotional state to another, such as when an infant becomes able to stop him/herself from crying. While this is happening, too much stimulation can be as harmful as too little. The type, intensity and timing of stimuli should be determined by the child's developmental level and individual characteristics (Korner, 1974). As Bruner (1973) observes, intervention and stimulation are actually very passive processes in which the child is acted on by an external agent. Such practices ignore findings about infant/toddler characteristics and development. On the other hand, programs that encourage exploration, provide reasonable problems for

---

Editor's note: Your attention is called to these ACEI publications in the area of infancy: (1) *Understanding and Nurturing Infant Development* (1976), which presents six provocative papers from the 1975 Texas Conference on Infancy; (2) *Developing Programs for Infants and Toddlers* (1977), a further extension of the Texas Conference on Infancy, which focuses on practical applications of knowledge about infants and parenting in both center and home.

solving, heighten the reciprocal interaction between child and caregiver, and gear all phases, including stimulation, to suit individual needs are more in accord with what we know about very young children.

CONCLUSION

Let's return to a question posed at the beginning of this paper. When is group care for infants and toddlers justified? I believe the answer is twofold. Such programs are justified when there is a need for them and when they can meet the vigorous criteria of standards of excellence.

To make those women who are compelled to work for economic reasons, or who have chosen to work for psychological or social ones, feel guilty because they do not live up to an idealized view of motherhood is senseless and cruel. Surely, their children will not benefit from making them feel inadequate.

It is just as counterproductive to force into the job market those women who would prefer to be at home full time by creating unfair and poorly conceived public assistance regulations, or by prescribing an image of the modern woman to which all must conform. Let us, instead, use our energy, our intelligence and our expertise to develop the best possible group programs for infants and toddlers. Let us also work with such groups as the Carnegie Council on Children to develop comprehensive and universally accessible public service programs that support families rather than replace them in the rearing of children. Parents must be able to choose among an array of high quality alternatives in child care whenever they are needed.

References

Ainsworth, M. D. S. "Attachment and Dependency: A Comparison." In J. L. Gewirtz (ed.), *Attachment and Dependency*. New York: Wiley, 1972.

Appleton, T., *et al.* "The Development of Behavioral Competence in Infancy." In F. D. Horowitz (ed.), *Review of Child Development and Research*, Vol. 4. Chicago: University of Chicago Press, 1975.

Balzer, F. "What About Tomorrow—Directions for the Future." In L. L. Dittmann (ed.), *The Infants We Care For*. Washington, DC: National Association for the Education of Young Children, 1973.

Beckwith L., & S. E. Cohen. *Early Cognitive Development of Full-Term and Premature Infants: Infant Studies Project Home Data*. Paper presented at a meeting of the Society for Research in Child Development, 1972.

Bell, S. M., & M. D. S. Ainsworth. "Infant Crying and Maternal Responsiveness." *Child Development* 43 (1972): 1171-90.

Blehar, M. "Anxious Attachment and Defensive Reactions Associated with Day Care." In U. Bronfenbrenner and M. Mahoney (eds.), *Influences on Human Development*. Hinsdale, IL: Dryden Press, 1975.

Bowlby, Jr. *Maternal Care and Mental Health*. Geneva: World Health Organization, 1951.

Brazelton, T. B. *Infants and Mothers*. New York: Delacorte, 1969.

Brazelton, T. B., *et al.* "The Origin of Reciprocity: The Early Mother-Infant Interaction." In M. Lewis and L. A. Rosenblum (eds.), *The Effect of the Infant on Its Caregiver*. New York: Wiley, 1974.

Bromwich, R. "Stimulation in the First Year of Life? A Perspective on Infant Development." *Young Children* 32 (1977); 71-82. Reprinted by permission from *Young Children*, Vol. 32, No. 2 (Jan. 1977), pp. 71-81. Copyright © 1977 by the National Association for the Education of Young Children, 1834 Connecticut Ave., NW, Washington, DC 20009.

Bruner, J. S. "Organization of Early Skilled Action." *Child Development* 44 (1973); 1-11.

Cairns, R. B. "Attachment and Dependency: A Psychobiological and Social Learning Synthesis." In J. L. Gewirtz (ed.), *Attachment and Dependency*. New York: Wiley, 1972.

Caldwell, B. M. "What Does Research Teach Us About Day Care for Children Under Three?" *Children Today* 1 (1972): 6-11.

Caldwell, B. M., *et al.* "Infant Day Care and Attachment." *American Journal of Orthopsychiatry* 40 (1970): 397-412.

Chess, S., *et al. Your Child Is a Person*. New York: Viking, 1972.

Cohen, D. J., and E. Zigler. "Federal Day Care Standards: Rationale and Recommendation." *Young Children* 33 (1978): 24-32.

Dennis, W. *Children of the Creche*. New York: Appleton-Century-Crofts, 1973.

Dodd, B. J. "Effects of Social and Vocal Stimulation on Infant Babbling." *Developmental Psychology* 7 (1972): 80-83.

Dusewicz, R. A., & M. A. O'Connell. *The Pennsylvania Research in Infant Development and Education Project: A Five-Year Perspective*, 1975. ERIC document no. ED 110-181. ERIC Document Reproduction Service, P.O. Box 190, Arlington, VA 22210.

Erikson, E. H. *Childhood and Society*. 2d Ed. New York: Norton, 1956.

Fraiberg, S. *Every Child's Birthright—In Defense of Mothering*. New York: Basic Books, 1977. © 1977 by Selma Fraiberg.

Goldfarb, W. "Rorschach Test Differences Between Family-Reared, Institution-Reared and Schizophrenic Children." *American Journal of Orthpsychiatry* 19 (1949): 624-34.

Gregg, C. L., *et al.* "The Relative Efficacy of Vestibular Propioceptive Stimulation and the Upright Position in Enhancing Visual Pursuit in Neonates." *Child Development* 47 (1976): 309-17.

Gross, D. W. "Improving the Quality of Family Life." *Childhood Education* 54 (1977): 50-54.

Honig, A. S. "Curriculum for Infants in Day Care." *Child Welfare* 53 (1974): 633-42. Reprinted by special permission of the Child Welfare League of America from *Child Welfare*, Vol. 53, pp. 633-42.

Horowitz, F. D., & L. Y. Paden. "The Effectiveness of Environmental Intervention Programs." In B. M. Caldwell and H. N. Riccuiti (eds.), *Review of Child Development Research*. Chicago: University of Chicago Press, 1973.

Hunt, J. McV. *Intelligence and Experience*. New York: Ronald Press, 1961.

Kagan, J.; R. B. Kearsley; and P. R. Zelazo. *The Effects of Infant Day Care on Psychological Development*. 1975. ERIC document no. ED 122 946. ERIC Document Reproduction Service, P.O. Box 190, Arlington, VA 22210.

Keister, M. E. *The Good Life for Infants and Toddlers*. Washington, D. C.: NAEYC, 1977.

Keniston, K., & the Carnegie Council on Children. *All Our Children—The American Family Under Pressure*. New York: Harcourt, Brace, Jovanovich, 1977.

Kohlberg, L. "Early Education: A Cognitive Developmental View," *Child Development* 39(1968): 1014-62.

Korner, A. F. "Individual Differences at Birth: Implications for Early Experience and Later Development." In J. C. Westman (ed.), *Individual Differences in Children*. New York: Wiley, 1973.

———. "The Effect of the Infant's State, and Level of Arousal, Sex, and Ontogenetic Stage on the Caregiver." In M. Lewis and L. A. Rosenblum (eds.), *The Effect of the Infant on Its Caregiver*. New York: Wiley, 1974.

Lally, J. R. *The Family Development Research Program—A Program for Prenatal, Infant and Early Childhood Enrichment-Program Report*. Syracuse, NY: Syracuse University, 1974.

Lewis, M., & L. A. Rosenblum, eds. *The Effect of the Infant on Its Caregiver*. New York: Wiley, 1974.

Lippman, M., and B. Grote. *Socioemotional Effects of Day Care, Final Report*. Bellingham, WA: Western Washington State College, 1974.

Mauer, D. M., & C. E. Mauer. "Newborn Babies See Better Than You Think." *Psychology Today* (1976): 85-88.

Piaget, J. *The Origin of Intelligence in Children*. New York: International Universities Press, 1952.

Rheingold, H. L. "The Modification of Social Responsiveness in Institutional Babies." *Monographs of the Society for Research in Child Development* 2 (1956): 1-48.

Robinson, H. B., & N. M. Robinson, "Longitudinal Development of Very Young Children in a Comprehensive Program: The First Two Years." *Child Development* 42 (1971): 1673-83.

Saunders, M. M. *Some Aspects of the Effects of Day Care on Infants' Emotional and Personality Development*, 1972. ERIC document no. ED 067 166. ERIC Document Reproduction Service, P.O. Box 190, Arlington VA 22210.

Schwartz, J. C. et al. "Effects of Early Day Care Experiences on Adjustment to a New Environment." *American Journal of Orthopsychiatry* 43 (1973): 340-46.

Senate Finance Committee, Child Care Data and Materials, 1974. Cited in *America's Children 1976*. Washington, D.C.: National Council of Organizations for Children and Youth, 1976.

Starr, H. "Cognitive Development in Infancy: Assessment, Acceleration and Actualization." *Merrill-Palmer Quarterly* 17 (1971): 153-86.

Thomas, J., et al. *Temperament and Behavior Disorders in Children*. New York: New York University Press, 1968.

Thrift, J. C. "Reciprocal Interactions Between Infants and Mothers." In M. D. Cohen (ed.), *Understanding and Nurturing Infant Development*. Washington, DC: Association for Childhood Education International, 1976.

Wolff, P. H. "Observations on the Early Development of Smiling." In B. M. Fass (ed.), *Determinants of Infant Behavior II*. London: Methuen, 1963.

Yarrow, L. J., et al. *Infant and Environment—Early Cognitive and Motivational Development*. New York: Wiley, 1975.

Ecology of Infant Day Care

Richard Elardo

Dr. Elardo is an assistant professor and research associate at the Center for Early Development and Education at the University of Arkansas College of Education.

The ideas on the subject that follow have been derived from the experiences of many people who have been involved with the education of infants at the Center for Early Development and Education in Little Rock. The basic rules are these:

Rule 1. Make learning time a fun time—keep it light and easy. Don't push if the child isn't interested. Try another activity, or try again later. Don't feel bad if the child doesn't want to play.

Rule 2. Continue the activity only as long as the children remain interested in it. This may be one minute or 20 minutes but seldom longer.

Rule 3. Concentrate on praising the children's accomplishments. Smile, laugh, look proud if he does what you are trying to teach him to do. Don't scold him if he doesn't do it.

Rule 4. Show the children how to do each activity.

Rule 5. Talk to the children a lot. Don't forget to imitate the sounds and words that the children themselves make.

Rule 6. Say each child's name often. Say a child's name when you praise him—"You did it, John. That's good!"

In order to understand better how and what to teach infants of various ages, a brief environmental outline and a list of sample activities for various age levels are included below. The activities have been selected from the following sources, which should be consulted for additional suggestions: I.J. Gordon's "Baby Learning Through Baby Play" (1971); G. Painter's "Teach Your Baby" (1971), and Bettye Caldwell *et al* "Home Teaching Activities" (1973).

Developmental Characteristics

Infants at this age are able to roll over completely (back to stomach), although there are wide variations. Some infants begin to crawl more during this time and others can stand with help. Between 6 and 9 months about half of all infants show stranger anxiety. Children will sometimes cry and become upset when a new person enters the room. However, a wise stranger will keep his distance and only gradually move toward the infant. Anxiety about strangers is normal and shows that an infant has formed a strong attachment to his caretakers.

At these ages infants like to engage in the same activity over and over again; adults usually find this boring, but the child is continually learning from the repetition. Infants are becoming more social and enjoy engaging in imitation games using gestures and sounds. Imitation is a social game where infants imitate adults and adults imitate the infant, particularly the sounds he makes. Infants can begin feeding themselves at this age using a spoon; they are always quite messy when they do this because feeding is a very difficult task for them. They have not quite learned where their mouths are. The way they learn is by lots of practice.

> **"From 6 to 9 months, an infant may show stranger anxiety. This shows only that he has a strong attachment to his caregivers"**

Infants engage in solitary play except for their interactions with adults, and sharing is something that occurs rarely. They usually bang many objects together whenever they have an opportunity; again, this is the way they learn about their environment. They also love to play a "drop" game in which they drop things off the table and adults pick them up. Although this may be annoying at times, infants are learning about spatial relations when they do this.

Suggested Activities

Language/Thinking

1. When an infant makes a speech sound, act pleased. Smile, laugh, and imitate his sound.
2. Read out loud to the children individually or in small groups each day. Remember, how you read is important—be excited about the book.
3. Talk to the infant constantly. Tell him what you are doing. Say "See, let's roll the ball," "Up we go," "This is your nose," etc.
4. Encourage imitation. Get the infants to "do what I do" Clap your hands, sit down, point to the light.

Motor

1. Place an attractive toy just beyond infant's reach so he will creep to it.
2. Provide small blocks for infant to grasp. Show him how to stack them.
3. Show infant how to drop blocks into a cereal box.

"Ecology of Infant Day Care," by Richard Elardo, *Day Care and Early Education*, January 1974. Reprinted by permission from Human Sciences Press. Copyright 1974.

3. DEVELOPMENT AND EDUCATIONAL OPPORTUNITIES

4. Place a different object in each of child's hands. See if he can hold and manipulate two objects at a time.

Personal/Social

1. Show infant his image in a mirror at his height level.
2. Play games with infant's hands and feet (such as "This little piggy went to market" or "pat-a-cake").
3. Stand behind the infant and ring a bell. Let him find it by turning his body toward it as it is rung. He will learn that his body can be used to find objects.

Age: 9 to 12 Months

Developmental Characteristics

By 10 months some infants have reached the point where they can recognize themselves in a mirror. This represents quite a step in social awareness. Imitation is becoming more frequent, and infants enjoy engaging in simple games such as pat-a-cake. The understanding of single words is apparent and babies can point to a few things when given the word: "glass," "show," "book."

Infants are very interested in smaller objects now. Most of the time they are exploring and learning about their environment by putting everything in their mouths. Some of them may begin walking during this period, but the variation is very large (8 to 20 months). Most infants can take a few steps with help between 9 and 12 months. They are becoming more interested in their body parts and upon request some show adults "ear," "eye," "hand," et cetera. At this age they may still have trouble finding their mouths, but adults must remember that the resulting messiness is far less important than the fact that the infants are learning so much while feeding themselves, especially if an adult is giving them attention.

Infants love to play hiding games with adults; this type of game must be simplified by the adult. The adult must allow the infant to see where the object is being hidden and then give him the opportunity to find it. Infants can attend to pictures in books and can turn pages in large books.

Suggested Activities

Language/Thinking

1. While child watches, cover a toy part way with a handkerchief and say, "Find the_____."
2. Collect different objects from outside (sand, leaves, sticks, rocks, pine cones). Let the child explore each object as you tell him about it.
3. With child watching, place his favorite toy in a bag, then help him get it out.
4. Put your hand over your mouth and say "wah wah." Now try to get the child to do this.

Motor

1. Give the child a length of string with a toy tied to the other end. Show him how to pull the string to get the toy.

2. Build a pyramid with blocks or cans. Knock it down and encourage the child to imitate you.
3. Fill a jar with objects and screw on the lid. Help child get it off.
4. Show child how to drop clothespins into a cup.

Personal/Social

1. Let the child eat while looking into a mirror.
2. Let child see himself in mirror with funny clothes on. Take a funny hat off your head and put it on him.
3. Help him drink from a cup.
4. Play hide and seek with the child.

Age: 12 to 18 months

Developmental Characteristics

Upon entering this period, infants can usually say single words that refer to something the child wants, such as "bottle," "mama," "dada." Children at this age usually engage in "sentence play"—putting sounds together in the same rhythm as a sentence. These strings of sounds have no meaning, but are the way infants imitate the adult. During this time infants love to manipulate small objects and will do this for long periods of time (20 to 30 minutes).

By this time children have usually begun to walk. They now love rhythm games and dancing. In new situations they are very cautious and will usually cling to their caretaker. When they feel more at ease, they may begin to explore the new environment or approach the new person. Children of this age are action-oriented. They love to play with large toys such as wagons, trucks, large dolls, etc. The most exciting development during this period is the child's beginning use of language. The child can now comprehend some of the adult's language, although he is not able to produce much speech himself. At first the child speaks in single words, then two-word sentences, and then sentences of numerous words. Children at these ages show interest in picture books if an adult is attentive and responsive.

Suggested Activities

Language/Thinking

1. Go on a walk outside. Keep saying things like "See the bird," "Feel the grass" and "Listen to the cars."
2. Play "which hand is the toy in." Let the children try to find the toy as you switch it from one hand to another.
3. Let the children listen to records while they play with drums and bells.

Motor

1. Allow freedom to walk around and to push objects such as a tricycle, large box or a chair.
2. Play ball with the child.
3. Show him how to roll over and do a somersault.
4. Provide things to climb on, such as stacked mattresses.

24. Ecology of Infant Day Care

5. Show the child how to scribble on a piece of large paper with a crayon.
6. Blow bubbles and let the children try and catch them.

Personal/Social
1. Show child pictures of people. Get him to say, "baby," "mama," "dada," etc.
2. Give the child a doll. Show him how to give it a kiss, comb its hair, rock it, love it, etc.
3. Help the children learn to point at things.
4. Help the children throw away garbage from snack or lunch. Provide a convenient garbage pail. Let them help wipe the table.

Age: 18 to 24 Months

Developmental Characteristics

Now children enjoy learning to name objects in their environment and also to describe certain situations—"new shoes," "want drink," "read book." By 24 months children can at times speak in several full sentences. At this point they can sit and listen to a story, point to the characters, name the colors, and talk about the story line. Usually children love to hear a story over and over again.

The child at this age engages in many large-muscle activities. He is forever exploring his environment and finding out how things work—faucets, drawers, telephones, etc. It is likely the child may leave a project before it is completed. Children find quiet activities fun also and can spend many minutes sitting and discovering how small objects work.

Lots of dramatic play is indulged in by toddlers who love to imitate adults. This is a good time for adults to facilitate language by becoming a part of a socio-dramatic episode—"Oh, I see you are making supper (child is playing in a toy kitchen). What are you fixing? Sure looks good."

Toddlers are not usually able to engage in cooperative play but can engage in parallel play—playing alongside a playmate.

By 24 months children are almost toilet-trained.

Suggested Activities

Language/Thinking
1. Get the children to pretend to serve dinner with toy plates and to pretend to drink from a toy cup.
2. Attach balloons to the children's wrists with string.
3. Put substances with different odors in baby food jars (garlic, perfume, cloves, mint, etc.). Pass the jars around and discuss the different smells.

Motor
1. Help children make a tower with blocks. They should be able to stack 4 to 8 blocks.
2. Play record and practice marching backwards.
3. Help children to make a straight line with a crayon.

Personal/Social
1. Help children make human-shape figures out of clay. Name and compare body parts.
2. Cut a large picture of a person out of a magazine and make a three-piece puzzle out of it.
3. Help children name different objects in their room

Age: 24 to 30 Months

Developmental Characteristics

Children are now able to relate experiences in simple language with prompts from adults. Some can tell their name and age. This period in a child's life is very important for language development—some authorities say it is the most important. Children should be encouraged to verbalize whenever possible. Snack and mealtimes are good times for stories and discussions of stories.

A child's movements are becoming more coordinated. The child can make representations of the world through such media as paints, clay, and dramatic play. Children can spend long periods of time playing as if they were adults. They engage in the routines of everyday life—cooking, getting dressed, going shopping, etc. However, a young child does not understand how the real world operates. Children should be encouraged to engage in socio-dramatic play (pretending), and this type of play becomes even more meaningful if adults invest their interest in the child's activities.

Children are growing more independent and many can dress themselves with some assistance.

Suggested Activities

Language/Thinking
1. Poker chips and three cans can be used to teach children to sort all the red chips in one can, etc.
2. Show children pictures of common objects and ask them to name what is pictured.
3. Ask each child to show you different things. Say, "Where's the door . . . the window . . . the table," etc.

Motor
1. Play "Ring around the rosey" and "London Bridge is falling down."
2. Play "Walk between the strings." Use two strings placed on the floor, far apart at one end, close together at the other.
3. Show children how to draw a circle.

Personal/Social
1. Make hand puppets from old socks. Let the children make them dance and talk to each other.
2. Let children take turns helping you set the table and serve snacks.
3. Play "dress up" by putting old adult clothes on the children.
4. Encourage the children to pretend they are dogs or cats—get down on the floor and start barking!
5. Make a life-size picture of each child. Let him draw in the details.

PIAGET'S THEORY OF CHILD DEVELOPMENT AND ITS IMPLICATIONS

A succinct description of Piaget's pioneering studies—studies that brought the great Swiss psychologist into direct conflict with American behaviorists—and their meaning for education.

Robbie Case

Should the elementary school curriculum be overhauled? Should formal instruction in reading be delayed until the third grade? Is didactic pedagogy at all suited to the natural reasoning processes of young children? Are conventional IQ tests invalid?

Questions such as these are not new in education. What *is* relatively new is the extent to which educators are basing their answers on the work of Swiss psychologist Jean Piaget. The purpose of this article is to summarize Piaget's research and theory, and to take a critical look at its implications for education.

Philosophical Foundations

In order to put Piaget's work in perspective, it is worthwhile to point out that it stems from a very different philosophic position from the work of many American psychologists. The latter, particularly the behaviorists, draw heavily upon the philosophy of the British empiricists, Locke and Hume. Both Locke and Hume were concerned with formulating ideas about the way in which man comes to acquire knowledge of the world. They both came to a conclusion that, although somewhat heretical at the time, seems almost commonplace now: Man acquires his knowledge of the world not from God or from logic but from the impressions he receives through his various sense organs. At birth, man is essentially a "blank slate," but as sensations are etched into this slate, he acquires knowledge of the world. The process by which this knowledge is acquired is essentially that of association: the association of one set of sensations or stimuli with another.

By contrast, the work of Piaget was based on the writings of the German philosopher, Immanuel Kant. Although Kant was impressed by much of what Locke and Hume asserted, he decided that their conceptualization of the knowing process was imcomplete.

One of the main dimensions of human knowledge on which Kant focused was its organization. He concluded that, while it is true that human beings cannot acquire any knowledge of the world *without* their sense organs, it is impossible to explain the universal organizational properties of their knowledge by assuming their sense organs to be the *only* source of this knowledge. All human beings have certain basic notions—of space, for example, and of time—which they do not simply "receive" from their senses but which they in a way possess already, and which they use to give order and meaning to what they *do* receive. Consider the simple fact that objects have a permanence independent of our own sensations. For Kant this truth could not simply be "etched in" to our minds by sensation, since it refers to something which must by definition always lie *beyond* our sensation. Rather than being a perceivable fact, then, it is a precondition which is necessary for what *is* perceived to have any meaning, or coherent organization. The human mind does not accept the registration of total chaos, as a blank slate might. In effect, it *demands* that the world be organized, and it has the inherent capacity to make that demand come true.

When Piaget began his pioneering studies, it was with this basic philosophic perspective. Like Kant, he assumed that human beings are not blank slates which passively receive the world; rather, that they actively structure it. Like Kant, he assumed that the structure of man's knowledge depends on certain universal notions which he is never explicitly taught: notions concerning space, time, causality, the permanence of objects, and so on. What Piaget became interested in was the *development* and *origin* of these basic notions. As he himself described it, what he became interested in was *genetic epistemology*. Perhaps because the notions Piaget was interested in *were* so very basic, and were so "taken for granted" by adults all over the world, the results of his investigations were often quite surprising.

25. Piaget's Theory of Child Development

Experimental Findings and Theory

The Sensorimotor Stage—From the first days of life, the infant exhibits basic reflexes when confronted by certain stimuli. If a nipple is placed in his mouth, he will suck; if something enters his hand, he will grasp; if a shape moves into his field of vision, he will track it. But his appreciation of causality, or of the permanence of objects, does not appear to be as inborn as these basic reflexes. In fact, it does not appear to be really *finely* developed until he is about two years of age.

Consider the following simple facts. If an interesting object enters his field of vision, even the youngest infant will track it. However, if it goes out of his field of vision repeatedly and then immediately returns, he will not wait for it: His glance will move to other things. Time does not appear to be represented the same way for a child as it is for an adult. When something is out of sight, it is out of mind.

When he is somewhat older, the infant's glance *will* linger in a situation such as that mentioned above. In other situations, however, he will still act as though that which is not immediately present does not exist. For example: Hold a rattle out to a six-month-old child. Then, as he starts to reach out, conceal it behind something he could easily move, such as a handkerchief. All his signs of intention will vanish and he will not try to retrieve it. In fact, he may not try to retrieve it even if it is only *partially* hidden.

When one thinks about it carefully, one can appreciate that a half-hidden object does not look exactly the same as one that is completely in view. How is the child to know it is no "half-made," as it were? When one thinks about it carefully, one can appreciate that a covered object is not present to sensation at all. How is the child to know it has not been completely *un*made? Piaget's interpretation is that this is exactly how infants do see the world—things are made and unmade, and a half-hidden object is only half an object.

Consider another example. There is a stage in the first year of life when a baby will make no attempt to rotate a baby bottle that is presented to him bottom first instead of nipple first. Once again, how is he supposed to know that they are the same object? The bottom certainly doesn't look like the top. The knowledge that an object looks different at different times but is actually a constant thing seems to be one that the infant has to *develop*. In short, the world as we see it is not something that is automatically *given* to the infant by sensation at all; it is something that he has to construct.

In constructing his world, the small child seems to follow a definite series of steps, or successive approximations, to the world we know. When he is just beginning to toddle, one can hide his favorite toy under a bright red handkerchief (in his full view) and he will remove the handkerchief with great glee. Aha, you say, he has learned that an inanimate object continues to stay where it was put. But has he? After you have played this game a few times, place the favorite toy, again in full sight, under a yellow handkerchief. Then watch as he looks under the red one again and appears baffled that the toy is not there. What he appears to have learned is only a first approximation—that when someone causes something to disappear, it will always continue to exist under a red handkerchief.

Piaget invented a number of these sorts of "trick" situations, and he found that it was not until about the age of 18 months to 2 years that the child ceased to be fooled by any of them. Piaget's inference was that it is not until this time that the child has a really strong intuitive notion of the fact that objects have a permanence independent of his perception and that cause and effect can operate independently of his willing them.

How does the child acquire this knowledge? If you watch an infant, you will note that he is continually exploring things with his mouth, his hands, his eyes, and so on. At first these explorations occur independently of each other; later they are coordinated; and finally they are extended to include shaking, throwing, and other actions. Such exploration and testing may not be too easy on parents, but the indications are that it is universal.

For Piaget, this activity is the key mechanism by which an organized view of the world is constructed. An action, even if it is a reflex, is represented in the brain by some sort of plan. You could call it a program. You could call it a neural impulse: the firing of some cells in the brain. It doesn't matter. Piaget calls it a *scheme*. Consider what happens when the child looks at his bottle or a matchbox. The visual configuration of the top activates something in the brain, called a *schema* by Piaget, and the child then acts on the object himself by manipulating it. Presto! A brand new visual configuration appears. Furthermore, when he manipulates the bottle again the first configuration reappears.

In Piaget's terminology, the first schema, or the representation in the brain of the top of the box, is assimilated by (or actually incorporated into) the scheme representing the child's action. Then the reciprocal event occurs: The second schema or visual pattern is assimilated by the same action scheme. As this happens time and again, a compound schema is built up, composed of all the various ways the matchbox can look (all the various shemata) and bound together, as it were, by all the ways it can be acted upon (the schemes). Thus the top of the box is no longer a floating, isolated pattern. It becomes part of a series of patterns, which are intimately connected by virtue of the fact that any one can be produced from any other by simply acting on it. It becomes part of a coordinated whole. Because Piaget sees the product of the child's first two years of life as the result of this sensorimotor integration, he labels this first phase of the child's development the sensorimotor stage.

3. DEVELOPMENT AND EDUCATIONAL OPPORTUNITIES

Preconceptual and Intuitive Thought—The toddler now uses the achievements of the first stage of his life as building blocks to reduce the chaos of the world even further. Now that objects are perceived as entities, and reflexes are integrated into coordinated movements, they can be given names. A little later they can be grouped together in different ways and the whole group can be named.

However, once again, none of these accomplishments occurs overnight. To begin with, the child's language reflects that his psychological units are still objects very different from adult units, which tend to be concepts. At first he seems very uncertain as to the difference between particular objects (for example, his brother), and whole classes of objects (for example, boys). He is not always sure if objects are actually in the same group. When he does build rules about general categories, they tend (as with the rules built in the sensorimotor stage) to be only first approximations to the ones used by adults. They tend to focus on only one attribute of a class and then not necessarily on the adult one. We are all familiar with the child who delights his parents by labeling a dog as "doggie," and who goes on to label a cow as doggie, a cat as doggie, and maybe even his younger brother as a doggie too. By degrees, of course, the child's organization and classification of the world becomes more refined. By the age of 5 or 6, although he cannot yet answer such tricky questions as whether there are more red roses or more roses in a flower bowl, he does appreciate that all the flowers are roses, and that some are red and some are white.

According to Piaget, the mechanism at work is very similar to that in the first stage. By forming things into classes and dividing them again, by calling a certain pattern a cow at one time and an animal at another, the child's mental activity begins to tie together the separate labels and the separate groups into an organized hierarchical framework. At first, during the preconceptual stage, a moving object is gradually tied together with other similar moving things until they all may be called cows. Then, in the intuitive stage, cows are tied together with cats and put into the category of animals, and the whole classification system is bound together as a whole.

In short, between the second and seventh year of his life, the child builds on objects to form concepts and on concepts to form classes of concepts. He does this by grouping things together, regrouping them, naming them, and continuing to explore. By the age of 7 or 8, he is capable of making some remarkably sophisticated observations about the world. His thinking begins to take on quite a logical character. However, it still depends heavily on interacting with the concrete world and it is still different from adult thought in many interesting respects.

Concrete Operations—The building blocks are now not just individual objects or people but classes of objects or people. Not only does a lump of Plasticine remain in existence when hidden but it remains Plasticine, able to be differentiated from other similar objects such as mud by certain properties, and itself containing subcategories depending, say, on whether or not it will harden overnight.

Once more, by acting on the world, the child begins to reduce the remaining chaos. He begins to extract higher-order features of groups that do not change, even though the groups change drastically. For example, having learned by the age of 5 or 6 to classify objects as long or short, heavy or light, and so on, and to relate perceptual properties of objects by using categories like more and less, he begins to appreciate that there are such higher-order categories as length and amount, which remain constant even though the perceptual input (on which the classification is originally made) may change drastically.

Probably the most famous of Piaget's experiments concerns just this sort of achievement. Take your bright-eyed little 5-year-old daughter who has just learned to count. Have her count out five beads in one row, then five in another row right beside it, and ask her if there are the same number in each row. She will tell you—perhaps proudly—that there are. However, spread out one row a little farther so it looks longer and ask her if there are still the same number in each row. Again, perhaps proudly, she will tell you that there are not, that there are more beads in the long row of five than in the short row of five. What we see once more is that her first understanding is only an approximation of the adult one and that it is based more on changing sensations.

By age 7 she will no longer make this mistake. However, her understanding will not yet be complete; once again it will proceed in definite steps. If we take two balls of Plasticine that she agrees are equal in size, and roll one into a sausage, she will not think that the long one has more Plasticine than the short one, but she *will* still think that the long one weighs more.

Although the kind of activity taking place is no longer one of sensorimotor manipulation, or of grouping and naming, Piaget sees the mechanism by which these higher-order adult constancies are introduced as essentially the same as the mechanism operating in the first two stages. The child learns that although one can always transfer two arrays of five into states where they appear different, the number you get by counting each array will still be five. Furthermore, you can always conduct the reciprocal operation: You can always transform them back into a state where they *are* in one-to-one correspondence. Once again, then, the various possible perceptual configurations of "five" all get tied together into an organized whole, connected by the internalized operations, the mental schemes. The result is that one label can eventually be applied to any array of the same number, no matter how different they look.

25. Piaget's Theory of Child Development

Formal Operations—With such higher-order concepts of the properties of objects as number, quantity, and weight, with a good intuitive grasp of causality, and with an understanding of the various possible ways things can be transformed, the child is ready to begin creating an order that is more formal. He is ready to begin relating things—for example, such concepts as mass and number—in terms of invariants which are of a higher order still, such as scientific laws. In addition, his activity in noting the things that actually happen in the world and in producing changes appears to enable him to begin thinking about what *might* happen and to envision all the changes that are possible. It enables him to reason without visual props. This in turn enables him to deduce an appropriate method for scientific procedure.

Consider the following problem: A spinning wheel has holes of various sizes in it and marbles of various sizes on it. A child is asked to figure out why some marbles fall off before others and then to test to see if he is correct.

The child who is in the concrete stage can classify the holes quite accurately and can even cross-classify them. He can see that there are big and small holes and that in both categories there are some near the center and some near the edge. He also has an intuitive notion of causality. However, he appears restricted to noting what actually occurs. If you ask why the big one fell off first, he will say, "Because it's bigger." Then, if you arrange them so that a small one falls off first, he will sometimes say, "Because it's smaller," without being overly upset by the contradiction. If you ask him to *prove* that big ones fall off first, he will not always bother to keep other things constant.

For Piaget, this child has not internalized a system in which *any* relevant attribute may vary and in which many different combinations of possibilities can all produce the same result. The child sees a big marble in a small hole near the edge and concludes that it fell off so soon because it was big. He does not imagine that one could put a small marble in a small hole near the edge and that it might fall off too, so he does not see the need to control other factors before he draws a conclusion about size. In short, although he has an internalized classification system, it is still bound to the concrete things he sees before him. The organization of his knowledge is not yet complex enough to represent conditions of the world accurately which are not before him.

In describing the sequence of stages, I have been referring with confidence to *the* child rather than to *some* children. This is because a remarkable uniformity has been found in the things children can and cannot do (the knowledge they have and don't have) and in the order in which they learn to do them. The exact age at which an individual child may begin to appreciate that weight does not change if nothing is added or subtracted may vary, but it never occurs before he learns that objects have a permanence or after he learns that all other things must be equal in a scientific experiment. Within substages the same is true; a child will always learn the conditions under which weight remains constant before he learns the conditions under which displaced volume remains constant and after he learns the conditions under which number and amount remain constant. We may thus talk about *the* child, since in these most basic interactions with the world and in the constructions of reality, all children achieve an identical series of accomplishments in an identical order.

What Piaget has described, then, is a series of stages through which all children develop. What he has postulated is that the process which propels them through these stages is a highly active one: At each stage the child starts with a world that is ordered in some respects and chaotic in others. And at each level, by acting on the world, by executing transformations, by reversing these transformations, and so on, he builds some further element of order into it. He constructs something that remains unchanged in the face of change—a coordinated whole.

I would now like to turn to the influence Piaget's theory has had, or is having, on education.

Educational Applications and Influences

Basis for the Content of New Curricula—One of the first applications of Piaget's theory, dating back almost a decade, was to suggest the content for new curricula. The reasoning of the curriculum developers probably went something like this: If these are the stages of development through which a child passes, if the abilities he acquires are really the crucial ones from a cognitive viewpoint, and if one of our jobs as educators is to assist in intellectual development, then maybe we should start providing some assistance to the child in precisely the processes and achievements which Piaget has concentrated on. Furthermore, since one stage appears to be built on the prior stage and to incorporate its achievements, maybe we should start this assistance at an early age. Whether or not this has been the precise reasoning, a number of different curricula have been developed, all aimed at providing activities to assist the preschool or elementary school child in representing number, space, and time, or to help him in classifying the world around him. Curricula have also been developed for elementary and high school students to better prepare them to understand formal and experimental reasoning in science. Particular attention has been paid to making these programs suitable for disadvantaged children. It is felt that such children may benefit more than others from programs aimed not at specific rote skills or the acquisition of factual knowledge but at broader cognitive development.

Exciting as it may seem on the surface, however, the attempt to make Piaget's stages the basis for new curriculum content is not one which, in my opinion, should be accepted uncritically. When one sees how

3. DEVELOPMENT AND EDUCATIONAL OPPORTUNITIES

painfully inadequate (by adult standards) is the knowledge of some children, there is a great temptation to rush out and prove that one is a really good teacher: that one can teach the child what he doesn't know or, at least, "help him in his attempts to teach himself." There is an equally strong pull to take something new and exciting and clearly intellectual and, because it *is* all these things, put it in the classroom. But, even if we assume that intellectual development is important—which I *do* assume—I submit that this extension of Piagetian theory into classroom practice can be justified only on the basis of one of two further assumptions: that children would not achieve the stages of development unless they had our help or that (if they *could* achieve the stages without our help) they could not achieve them as early.

Let us consider these assumptions separately. There is some evidence to suggest that not all adults reach the stage of formal operations. Estimates of adults who do not reach this stage very between about 30 and 90%. The people trying to teach formal operational skills would seem, then, to be on the right track. Assuming that these skills are important and that 50% of the people in the world never achieve them, here is a definite task in which the schools might help.

But what about concrete operational activity and the insights about the world that result from it? Here the evidence (literally, from around the world) is very different. Children appear to acquire these insights and skills on their own almost universally. Why, then, should we expend effort and money teaching them these skills in the classroom?

The only possible justification I can see is the second assumption: that for some reason children should learn these things a little earlier. But this assumption cannot be accepted simply on faith. What reasons are there for rushing a child toward a goal he will reach in a year or so anyway? The only reason I can think of is that the skills in question are somehow necessary for success in the *other* things that the school must teach and that the child who is missing them will therefore be handicapped. Yet, although I stand to be corrected, I know of no evidence to indicate that this is the case or that any conventional elementary school subject cannot be taught until children have reached the stage of concrete operations. I have seen studies quoted which suggest that children often learn to perform certain kinds of arithmetic problems at the same time as they learn to solve certain concrete operational problems, but this is obviously not the same thing.

A crucial study would be to take a group of children who were low in general development, to accelerate or broaden their development with a Piaget-based curriculum, and to show not only that they could *now* learn the required material or generalize it to the required variety of situations, but also that they could do so with less effort than a group for whom the same amount of time had been spent teaching the specific lower-order subject skills prerequisite to mastering the later material. Until such a study is done, I see no reason to support the investment of money in Piagetian elementary school curricula other than in the hope that they *might* help the children and might be fun. But similar reasoning could support the abolition of curricula completely.

Basis for New Assessment Procedures—A second school-related use to which Piaget has been put has been the development of a new intelligence scale. So far, the results have correlated well with those obtained on regular intelligence scales. The Piagetian items, although they probably can be influenced by specially enriching experiences, are said by those developing them to have the advantage of being linked to a theory of intelligence, which normal IQ tests are not. Also, they are said to draw on experience which varies less widely from subculture to subculture; they do not appear to depend on linguistic sophistication, for example, or on any particular knowledge unique to middle-class North Americans.

The attempt to construct and validate an intelligence scale based on Piaget's tests seems to me to be a basically worthwhile one. The only comment I would offer is that any decision as to which sort of test should actually be used in a school should depend on which sort of test proves to be the most useful. This means that criteria other than those of academic or developmental psychologists have to be invoked. Is the test any better at predicting school success? Does it arouse any less hostility in the community at large? Does it provide any more clues as to what help should be given to a child whose poor school performance is associated with a low IQ, and so on?

Justification for a "readiness" Approach—A third educational influence I feel Piaget is having is that of providing people who believe in "readiness" with some additional ammunition for their arguments. This influence is not so easy to demonstrate as the first two I mentioned. I cannot point to particular teachers or particular programs and say, "There. They are doing that because they believe in readiness, and one of the reasons they believe in readiness is clearly Jean Piaget's work." Yet in the discussions I have had with teachers and have seen in the literature on Piaget's discussions with teachers, his developmental findings are often cited in precisely this connection.

The argument generally goes something like this: The stages of intellectual development have been discovered across a wide variety of tasks. Furthermore, they have always emerged in a definite order; the consolidation of activity and knowledge at one stage is clearly a prerequisite for the progression to activity and knowledge at the next. Since the base of these stages *is* so broad, since one stage *is* the prerequisite for the next, and finally, since the child must actively restructure his

25. Piaget's Theory of Child Development

world at each stage *for himself*, one should therefore not try to lead the child too much. The best that a school can hope to do is to offer an environment that maximizes readiness-related experience; then, when the child appears to be ready, the teacher can introduce him to those activities that will produce the desired learning. "We can get more mileage from five minutes of teaching at this time than from five hours of teaching before he is ready" is the kind of argument put forward by proponents of readiness.

However, once again, arguments using Piaget to support a laissez faire approach should not be accepted uncritically. Ironically, one can uncover exactly the same unsupported assumption in them as is present in the arguments of those who advocate acceleration. That the achievements of one stage normally depend on massive general experience is probably true. That the achievements of one stage are prerequisite for those of the next stage may also be true. One can even assert the opposite of that which is claimed by those who have developed Piagetian curricula: that the school cannot provide a program which is much superior to normal general experience from an intellectual point of view. However, even if one assumes all three of these propositions, it does not follow that one should avoid teaching a child some specific subject (for example, reading) until he has reached a certain developmental stage—unless one also assumes that some general level of intellectual development is vital to achievement in this subject. And, as I have mentioned already, there is really no strong evidence either way on this point.

Given the pressures inherent in our present system—the stigma and frustration, for example, that are attached to not being able to read until grade five—it would seem that the greatest short-term payoff for our children would be to adopt a chain of reasoning something like this: If some children do not appear "ready" to profit from our current teaching methods, let us not stigmatize them by waiting four years to teach them. Let us find out what specific skills they can be taught so that they *will* be able to profit from our methods. Either that or change the methods.

Justification for Activity-Learning and Self-Discovery Approaches—A fourth use to which Piaget's theory has been put is similar to the third, in that it is not easy to demonstrate and also represents an attempt to justify a teaching method in which—perhaps for other reasons—people already believe. Since early in the century, "progressive" educators have believed that children should learn from their own spontaneous activity, that they should discover facts about the world for themselves, and that education should not be some tight little ticky-tacky compartment set off from the rest of children's experience. Renewed life has been added to this philosophy recently, with student unrest, with liberal criticism of our mechanized, uncreative way of life, with the advent of open plan schools, and so on. One of the bodies of evidence to which people interested in alternative education have turned has been the work of Jean Piaget.

Their reasoning has been roughly as follows: Piaget has shown that the child's own activity is what is responsible for his intellectual development, that he has to rediscover what the adult world already knows. It is therefore a mistake to make him enter a classroom, sit down in one of five rows of eight desks per row, and absorb facts for 15 years, as though he were a blank slate. In so doing, conventional education, like conventional psychology, is employing an understanding of human knowledge that has not evolved since the time of Locke and Hume. What we should be doing is encouraging activity or discovery learning.

The only comment I would make on this point is that one must be very careful about what one means by "activity" and "discovery," and one must be very precise in one's thinking about goals, before one can come to a decision as to whether Piaget's work is even relevant to this argument. Piaget's point, as has been stressed by Vinh Bang (his colleague most closely connected with education), is that when school children do learn something that really becomes a part of their view of the world or their way of thinking, it is by internalized activity. In the early years this activity must have a concrete base, but, nevertheless, it is still internalized, i.e., thinking. This would certainly imply that if one's goal was to produce such learning, one should not merely talk to young children or have them recite rules. However, this probably happens (even in traditional schools) much less often than liberal educators think. Teachers have got the message that rote learning is not the most desirable kind. Rote learning is not at issue.

What is at issue is whether, by setting tasks for children, especially tasks that are done at desks and in which the goal is not to discover something but to demonstrate or apply it one can really bring about this sort of "constructive" mental activity—whether one can get the child to rediscover what one has just told him and to make it a part of himself. What is at issue is not the *nature* of thought, which would certainly appear to be active, but whether children can genuinely be stimulated to think without being left on their own, taken to the zoo, told to choose a project, or asked to discover a principle. My suspicion is that they *can* be stimulated to think and that this is what good traditional schools have always attempted to do. However, what is needed to answer this sort of question is a Piaget-type study about concepts that are taught in school rather than concepts that are never taught in school.

Even if this type of study were conducted, however, the implications for education would not be automatic. Let us suppose it was discovered that a proper mix of didactic instruction and interaction with concrete props

3. DEVELOPMENT AND EDUCATIONAL OPPORTUNITIES

produced a greater amount of mental activity and a greater depth of conceptual understanding than an activity or discovery method. This finding could still not be used as sufficient evidence to argue that traditional methods are more desirable than progressive ones. A question of desirability like this—like the one about IQ tests—simply cannot be answered purely on the basis of psychological investigations. All that can be shown is that A does or does not produce X, not whether X is or is not desirable. It could well be, for example, that although a discovery method turned out to be inferior at eliciting scientific understanding, it might nevertheless be more desirable than a lecture method from other viewpoints—perhaps motivation, recall after 30 years, training in independent work, absence of anxiety, sense of controlling one's own destiny, and so on. And these other standpoints might well be more important to parents, students, and teachers alike than scientific understanding.

Questions of desirability do not depend only on empirical facts about their consequences. They also depend on value judgments about the desirability of those consequences. And one simply cannot ask psychology—or, for that matter, science—to make these value judgments for one.

Summary

The research and theory of Jean Piaget takes as its point of departure the philosophy of Immanuel Kant—in particular, Kant's proposition that some knowledge of the world is universal and inborn in the human species and not stamped in by sensation. Piaget has shown that, while a certain kind of knowledge is indeed universal, it is not present at birth but is, rather, constructed in a series of stages over the course of the first 16 years of human life. Piaget has also theorized that the mental process through which these stages are achieved is a highly active one, with origins in the first reflexes that the human infant exhibits.

Since one of the universal functions of education is to ensure that the younger generation does not lose the knowledge and perspective that the older generation went to so much trouble to acquire, it would be hard to argue that any theory related to the nature of that knowledge or the processes by which it is acquired could be dismissed as irrelevant. However, what I have attempted to show is that most of the current "applications" of Piaget's work actually go a good deal beyond what he has established empirically, or even what he has theorized. At a deeper level, most of them depend for their justification on an additional set of assumptions, which are either untested as yet, or inherently untestable.

Misunderstandings About How Children Learn

DAVID ELKIND

As Montessori said: "Play is the child's work." In play, he learns through engaging in real actions involving tangible objects.

Recently, a young mother of my acquaintance said with some pride: "I insist that my four-year-old daughter watch *Sesame Street*—even when she prefers doing something else." Concerned about the intellectual development of her child, this mother believes that *making* the girl watch the program will eventually help her do better in school.

Many mothers today are pressuring their preschool children to learn numbers, letters, shapes, and so on. Unfortunately, this parental concern for children's intellectual development often seems greater than their concern for children's feelings, interests, and attitudes. What many parents fail to understand is that attempting to force young children to learn specific content may produce an aversive attitude toward academic learning in general. This attitude of distaste may have such serious long-range effects on young children's academic achievement that it completely outweighs the advantages of being familiar with letters, forms, and numbers today or next week.

The foregoing example illustrates one of several common misunderstandings about the thinking and learning of young children that seem to be current today. In this article, I briefly describe five such common misunderstandings that hold particularly true for young children—and a few for older ones as well.

One of the pernicious misunderstandings about young children is that they are most like adults in their thinking and least like us in their feelings. It is just this misconception that prompted the mother mentioned earlier to command her daughter to watch *Sesame Street*. The same woman would not think of insisting that her husband watch a program she thought might "do him some good." Rather, she would realize that this kind of approach would be a sure way to turn him against the program. And yet, because she believes that children's feelings are different from those of adults, she uses a technique with her child she knows would never work with a grown-up.

Parents and teachers are equally prone to regard a child's thinking process as similar to their own. When, for example, a child asks, "Why is the sun hot?" his father is likely to explain that the sun gives off light and that it takes heat to produce the light. The relation between heat and light is not obvious, however, and the young child would hardly understand. Indeed the real intent of the child's question has to do with the *purpose* of the sun's heat. An appropriate reply would be "to keep us warm" or "to give us a suntan." These answers are not entirely incorrect and they correspond to the young child's underlying belief that everything has a purpose.

Because young children are often so capable linguistically, adults often overestimate their capacity to think.

A second misunderstanding about young children is that they learn best while sitting still and listening. This misconception arises because parents tend to generalize from their experiences as adults. It is true that we adults often learn by listening attentively to a lecture or reading a book.

The young child is, however, not capable of mental activity or thinking in the same way as an adult. He learns through engaging in real actions involving tangible objects, such as blocks or dolls.

3. DEVELOPMENT AND EDUCATIONAL OPPORTUNITIES

Thanks to the work of the famed Swiss psychologist, Jean Piaget, we now know that the child's actions upon things are what facilitate his mental activity or thinking. The young child's actions are progressively miniaturized and interiorized until he is able to do in his head what before he had to do with his hands. This internalization of action comes about gradually during early childhood and is completed at age six or seven.

To illustrate this internalization, observe a four-year-old and a six-year-old performing a simple pencil maze. The younger immediately puts pencil to paper and tries to find the right path. The older, in contrast, studies the maze and only after he has mentally decided on the right path does he put pencil to paper.

Accordingly, when we say young children are "active" learners, we must take this in a literal sense. Montessori said: "Play is the child's work." In play, the child is practicing the various actions that he will eventually internalize as thought.

Therefore, however convenient it may be for grown-ups to think that children learn while sitting still, what they learn in this way is likely to have little lasting value. In contrast, *what children acquire through active manipulation of their environment is the ability to think.*

A third common misunderstanding about young children is the belief that they can learn and operate according to rules. Many parents have had the experience of telling a young child over and over again not to hit his little brother or not to take toys apart or to say thank you when he receives something. Because a young child has not yet internalized thought, he cannot internalize rules either. Consequently, while the child understands the prohibition against hitting his brother and against breaking toys in particular instances, he is unable to generalize to new instances. This is true for learning to say thanks.

The young child's inability to learn rules has special implications for the educational programs prepared for him. We have already noted that the young child learns best through playing with and manipulating materials in his environment. His inability to learn general verbal rules supports this observation and argues against his formal education (involving verbal instruction, a curriculum, and educational objectives). Formal education, whether we speak of reading, arithmetic, or spelling, presupposes the inculcation of rules and thus is inappropriate for the majority of preschool children.

On the other hand, many activities are appropriate educational enterprises for preschoolers. Writing and printing letters is a case in point. Both Montessori and Fernald have pointed out the importance of these for later reading.

Writing as preparation for reading makes good theoretical as well as pedagogical sense in light of the ideas offered earlier. Thinking is an internalization of action, so reading can be regarded, in part at least, as deriving from the internalization of writing actions. Obviously, reading involves much more than the ability to reproduce letters but such reproduction is an appropriate prereading activity for children not yet ready for formal instruction in that skill.

Another widespread misunderstanding about young children is that *acceleration* is preferable to *elaboration*. Many parents, for example, spend a great deal of time trying to teach their young children to read or do mathematics. These parents seem to believe that if children have a head start in these special skills they will have a head start generally. The opposite is more likely to be true.

A child who elaborates the skills he does have, such as the ability to arrange materials according to size on a wide range of materials (blocks, sticks, dolls, dogs, and so on), is likely to be better prepared for future learning than a child who has learned a great deal in a short time but who has not had the chance to assimilate and practice what he has learned.

The situation is not unlike that in which one student crams for a test and another studies regularly throughout a semester. While the two may not perform too differently on an exam, the one who has been studying regularly is likely to be better prepared for future courses than the one who makes cramming a regular practice. Parents who try to teach their young children special skills and content are, in effect, teaching a cram course, and the results may be as short-lived for the preschooler as for the college student who crams.

A last common misunderstanding about the learning of young children should be mentioned—one involving the belief that parents and teachers can raise children's IQ. To be sure, IQ is affected by environment, but most middle-class children have probably grown intellectually about as rapidly as their endowment permits. Further enrichment is not likely to have marked effects upon their intellectual ability, although it may affect how they make use of this ability.

Children who have been intellectually deprived can, however, make significant gains in intellectual performance as a consequence of intellectual enrichment. Just as a child who has grown up with an adequate diet will not benefit much from dietary supplements and a child whose diet has been deficient will, so an intellectually well-nourished child is not likely to benefit markedly from further intellectual enrichment whereas a deprived child will.

In large measure, all of these misunderstandings derive from a contemporary overemphasis on intellectual growth to the exclusion of the personal-social side of development. Although I know it sounds old-fashioned to talk about the whole child and tender loving care, I strongly believe that many problems in child rearing and education could be avoided if concern for a child's achievement as a student were balanced by an equally strong concern for his feelings of self-worth as a person.

The Truth About Sex Differences

Susan Muenchow

Susan Muenchow directs public-education activities at Yale University's Bush Center in Child Development and Social Policy.

> The differences between the sexes are real — and fascinating, according to current research — but apart from reproduction, boys' and girls' potentials are not restricted by their sex.

In the age of unisex hair salons, integrated Little League teams, and bikini-clad weight lifters in *Esquire* magazine, parents may wonder if there are any real, innate, unalterable differences between boys and girls.

Few would dispute that more girls play house and with Barbie dolls; more boys, superheroes and karate. The controversy concerns how many of the behavioral differences result from nature and how many from nurture. Over the last decade, while the women's movement has been stressing the similarities between the sexes and attributing most of the remaining differences to the way parents and schools bring children up, the pendulum among researchers—including some women—has been swinging toward a new interest in the biological basis for some sex differences. The pink and blue blankets do not account for all the differences between boys and girls, they find. Differences in genes, hormones, the rate of maturation, and even the organization of the brain also play their parts.

It is important to stress that the new research does not add up to a vote for biology being the exclusive, or even the primary, determinant of sex differences. "When it comes down to the biological imperatives that are laid down for all men and women," according to Johns Hopkins University researcher John Money and journalist Patricia Tucker in their book, *Sexual Signatures*, "there are just four: Only a man can impregnate; only a woman can menstruate, gestate, and lactate." As for all the other differences between men and women—from height and weight, to verbal ability, to who scrubs floors or puts on makeup— Money says there is a tremendous variation. And, according to Yale professor of psychology Edward Zigler, the range in physical stature and intellectual aptitudes is far greater *within* each gender than it is between the genders. Furthermore, apart from the reproductive differences, most of the other traditionally sex-related behaviors that are integral to our images of men and women are so small in absolute terms that they could be overcome by cultural factors.

With these qualifications in mind, the thrust of recent research is both intriguing and subtle: anatomy is not destiny, but certain sex differences do appear to have some biological basis.

Consider one of the most frequently cited sex-linked behaviors: the tendency for boys to engage in aggressive, rough-and-tumble play. Day-care teachers observe that it is more often the boys who roughhouse and play boisterously; parents trying to teach their children nonviolence find that their sons have a disturbing propensity for pistols. As an indication that aggression might have some biological basis, clinicians have long noted that treatments with androgens, the male hormones, increase aggressive behavior in both adult men and women. But Johns Hopkins researchers Anke Ehrhardt (now at Columbia) and John Money have found that, even before birth, a higher proportion of androgens influencing the developing male fetus may make boys more prone to play roughly.

Interestingly, the clearest evidence for the relationship between androgen and aggression comes from girls.

"The Truth About Sex Differences," by Susan Muenchow, *Parents' Magazine,* February 1980. Reprinted with the permission of the author.

3. DEVELOPMENT AND EDUCATIONAL OPPORTUNITIES

Ehrhardt and Money studied a group of girls whose mothers took a synthetic hormone similar to androgen during pregnancy in order to prevent miscarriage. As a result of the masculinizing effect of this hormone, the girls, while genetically female, were born with ambiguous genitals. After corrective surgery, the girls appeared perfectly normal; they differed from a control group only in their strikingly tomboyish behavior, preferring cars, trucks, and guns to dolls and, as they grew older, liking to play football and baseball with the neighborhood boys. Similarly, Erhardt and Money have found that some boys, whose body cells cannot make full use of the androgens in their bloodstream, are quieter and less ready to engage in competitive sports.

But the link between androgen and aggression is far from simple. No parent should conclude that a little girl who prefers a fire truck to a baby doll has excessive androgens, or that a three-year-old boy who likes to dress up in a spangled ballerina costume is suffering from a hormonal imbalance. While research on hormones might seem very straightforward, University of California psychologist Jeanne H. Block points out that it is never easy to separate the effects of biology from the effects of the environment.

John Money himself is careful not to oversimplify the role of sex hormones. First, he stresses that normally everybody has some of all three sex hormones—androgen, the male hormone; estrogen, the female hormone; and progesterone, one of the hormones that help prepare the uterus for pregnancy. According to Money, boys and girls differ only in their relative proportions of these hormones, both before and after birth. Furthermore, Money explains that the effects of the hormones on the developing fetus are subtle. They do not create new brain pathways, he cautions, but rather just "lower the threshold so that it takes less of a push to switch you on to some behavior." For example, the fact that boys generally get more androgens before birth than do girls may help explain why, years later, after watching a violent cartoon on television, more boys than girls have been found to get into fights with playmates. But this speculation hardly warrants the conclusion that androgens predestine men to positions of leadership and women to staying barefoot and pregnant in the kitchen. While the prenatal hormone balance may make boys slightly more prone to roughhouse, culture plays a far greater role in determining who runs for president and who runs tea parties.

Research findings concerning which is the more active sex are also complex. Again, nursery-school teachers have long observed that when children have to stay inside, it is usually the boys who almost visibly start to climb the walls. But, again, efforts to explain the apparent higher activity level in boys have been hampered by the difficulty in separating inborn from environmental factors. Even parents of newborns have been found to talk to and hold girl and boy babies differently.

Recently, some researchers have tried to reduce the cultural bias that affects studies of infants by setting up a study in a hospital nursery where observers did not know the sex of the baby they were watching. Nameplates were covered, and each baby's hair was combed in a neutral fashion. According to the study by Adelphi University psychologist Sheridan Phillips and co-workers, newborn boys are awake more than girls, they wince more and wrinkle their foreheads more frequently, and they kick their feet and thrash about more often than the girls. According to a study done for the National Institute of Mental Health by psychologist Howard A. Moss, on the average, infant boys are also fussier and harder to calm than infant girls. From his research, Moss concludes that there is a circular effect operating, whereby the infant shapes the mother's behavior, as well as the converse. This means that, while parents may be culturally predisposed to cuddle little girls more than little boys, the girls, by being easier to calm, also reinforce the cuddling.

Some infancy studies suggest that from very early on girls may have a slight edge toward more nurturant behavior. In what some researchers consider a primitive form of empathy, newborn girls have been found to cry more frequently than boys in response to the cries of another infant in the hospital nursery. Infant girls also do more reflex smiling, perhaps as a forerunner of more sociable behavior later on. Finally, not only do girls speak sooner than boys, but infant girls also seem to have more of a knack for nonverbal communication. They are more sensitive to touch, light, and sound, particularly the sound of their mothers' voices, observes Washington, D.C., neurologist Richard Restak in his new book, *The Brain: The Last Frontier*. Girls also seem "more attentive to social contexts: faces, speech patterns and tones of voice," according to Restak. By four months of age, many girls will babble in response to a parent's face, appearing to recognize the parent as a person, while boys at this age usually still fail to make a verbal differentiation between mother and a crib toy, babbling away equally to both.

Skeptics may well argue that the capacity for nurturance is a rather sophisticated quality to attempt to measure in a newborn baby. Crying in response to the cry of another infant seems a long way from true empathy. And it is also difficult to say whether differences in tactile sensitivity or infant responsiveness to a parent's face really shed any light on why a four-year-old girl might use a towel as a doll blanket, while a four-year-old boy might use it as a superhero cape. The problem is that, by the time patterns of play are clearly established, children have already had several years of lessons in behavior appropriate to their gender.

Even the research on sex differences in physical traits has an unusual twist: while boys are usually stronger, girls are innately sturdier. According to Josef Garai and Amram Scheinfeld, in *Genetic Psychology Monographs*, boys are generally longer and heavier than girls at birth, and these differences in height and weight persist. Furthermore, these sex differences in height and weight hold true across races and cultures. Thus, while the average woman in some parts of Africa may be taller than the average American male, she still tends to be shorter than her African male counterpart. Although environmental factors, such as nutrition and exercise, certainly affect height and weight, sex differences in these physical traits are under genetic control and, consequently, are unlikely to be altered by cultural factors alone.

Still, there is absolutely no physiological basis for treating girls as if they were more fragile than boys. If anything, girls really are the sturdier sex, and parents should be more wary of bouncing their baby boys in the air. Not only are more male fetuses spontaneously aborted be-

27. The Truth About Sex Differences

cause of organic defects, but, according to Garai and Scheinfeld, nearly one-third more boys than girls die in the first year of life from all causes, ranging from congenital malformations to pneumonia and meningitis. Boys simply seem more vulnerable to stress and disease. Or, as Money and Tucker say, nature seems to prefer Eve. Twice as many men as women die of coronary heart disease, three times as many from suicide, and twice as many from accidents, although these statistics also reflect environmental factors, such as smoking and the cultural support for daredevil behavior among boys. Girls also mature faster: they not only talk but walk earlier, and they reach puberty sooner. And the difference in the rates of development, which are themselves under endocrine-gland control, may, in fact, help explain many other differences between the sexes, from who learns to read first to who appears to be more sociable.

By far the most controversial research suggests that there are very real differences in the way men's and women's brains are organized. Neurologist Restak ventures so far as to say that, "Boys think differently from girls." Researchers have long observed that more girls than boys excel in verbal ability, generally do better in foreign languages, and have fewer speech defects. Stuttering is two to four times more prevalent in boys than in girls. Then again, boys tend to excel at tasks requiring visual and spatial ability, from physics and map reading to engineering. But it is only recently that researchers have begun to find a neurological basis for these frequently observed differences in aptitudes.

It is important to note that recent findings do not show sex differences in the size of the brain or its component parts. What the research does show is that the left hemisphere of the brain, the primary center for speech, develops more quickly in girls, while the right hemisphere, the chief regulator of spatial and visual abilities, develops more quickly among boys. There is also evidence that boys have a greater degree of "hemisphere specialization." This means that a right-handed man generally has his speech center firmly located in the left hemisphere of the brain and his visual and spatial skills in the right, while a right-handed woman is more apt to have verbal and spatial capacities located in both sides of the brain.

When it comes to tasks involving spatial ability, this greater degree of hemisphere specialization is a plus for men. For example, as Restak explains, "When boys are involved in tasks employing spatial concepts, such as figuring out mentally which of three folded shapes can be made from a flat, irregular piece of paper, the right hemisphere is activated consistently." Citing studies using electroencephalogram (EEG) measurements of the electrical activity inside the brain, Restak goes on to say that, "Girls are more likely to activate both hemispheres, indicating that spatial ability is more widely dispersed." Some researchers speculate that one reason that many women have trouble fixing things—apart from the traditional lack of encouragement—may be that their brains function relatively inefficiently in solving spatial and visual problems. Many women try to solve the problem with words, thereby making it more complicated; men, on the other hand, generally find it easier to isolate mechanical difficulties without involving words, because their visual and spatial abilities are so firmly rooted in only one hemisphere of the brain.

Sometimes, the lesser degree of brain specialization among women turns out to be to their advantage. For example, after suffering a stroke on the left side of the brain, women show much less severe losses in speech than men. In one study, by Jeannette McGlone, M.D., at University Hospital in London, Ontario, no matter which side of the brain was damaged, the women were less disabled and recovered more quickly. Presumably, because of the lack of hemisphere specialization, the women were better pinch hitters; the right side of the brain could help compensate for damage done to the left.

Just showing the differences in male and female brain functioning does not, however, *prove* that these differences develop according to a genetic blueprint. "Although nothing in the environment will turn a vagina into a penis," quips Edward Zigler, "many environmental factors may affect brain specialization." After all, each of us uses only a small part of his or her total brain capacity, and practice clearly improves intellectual performance. Perhaps girls develop verbal superiority, and the associated left hemisphere, because they are rewarded for their expertise in communication skills. Similarly, boys, whose fathers want them to be "fixers" and whose mothers admire their capacity to see the whole world as a big machine, may just try harder at spatial problems and develop the right hemisphere of the brain accordingly. Anthropological studies do indicate that cultural factors influence brain functioning considerably. According to Stanford psychologists Eleanor Maccoby and Carol Jacklin, co-authors of *The Psychology of Sex Differences,* in cultures where women are subjugated, their visual-spatial skills are especially poor; where independence is encouraged among women, as among the Eskimo, the sex differences in visual capacity are much less apparent.

Assuming that some of the brain differences between boys and girls are genetically based, what are the implications for schools and parents?

Restak thinks the sex differences in spatial and verbal ability are so significant that the primary-school curriculum should be revamped accordingly, to use different approaches for boys and girls. But many psychologists, like Jeanne Block, disagree. While they applaud the use of new teaching methods to suit individual differences in learning, they see no reason to categorize these differences according to gender. To redesign classroom instruction along gender lines, Block fears, might encourage teachers to look at boys and girls in terms of deficits. As a result, the expectation that boys are poor with words, girls with numbers, would become a self-fulfilling prophecy.

If parents want to increase their children's opportunities for development, research suggests that they should discourage some of the traditional sex differences. Maccoby and Jacklin observe that bolder, more assertive, and more active girls tend to do better in school. Still more striking, they note that "training a girl to be 'feminine' in the traditional, nonassertive, 'help-

3. DEVELOPMENT AND EDUCATIONAL OPPORTUNITIES

less,' and self-deprecatory sense may actually make her a worse mother" because she won't be a good problem solver.

But parents need not take a sledgehammer approach to nonsexist child rearing, for that, too, may have a negative effect. "Waah! I don't wanna be a building contractor," protests the preschool girl in G. B. Trudeau's *Joanie*, a book of "cartoons for new children." Moreover, while supporting the move toward more independence and assertiveness among women, some psychologists fear that neither sex will receive enough encouragement for nurturance, warmth, and expressiveness. "The problem," says University of Michigan psychologist Lois Wladis Hoffman, "is that the shift in the role of women who work is more clearly documented than the shift in the role of men toward parenting." While the women's liberation movement has been stressing that little girls should be raised more like little boys, perhaps society would be better off if little boys were raised more like little girls.

On balance, many psychologists seem to approve the relaxation in gender stereotypes, where Tarzan helps change the baby's diapers and Jane, if not exactly leaping from trees, is free to choose to work both outside as well as inside the home. But there is one biologically based sex difference—the most obvious one, in fact—that many psychologists think we should emphasize now more than ever. Children should be proud of their genitals as a promise of future manhood or womanhood, say Money and Tucker. At a time when all the traditional ideas of men's and women's places are in transition, Money thinks that, "The best insurance of emotional security we can give [our children] is to help them base their gender schemas firmly on the genital and reproductive differences between males and females." If boys and girls are secure about these differences, they will be freer to pursue their own interests and capabilities without regard to stereotypes. And, as they grow older, Money believes they will be able to "wash dishes or shovel coal, tend children or run for public office without straining their confidence in themselves as masculine or feminine."

To sum up, while research is beginning to show some biological basis for sex differences, it certainly does not offer a prescription for child rearing. In fact, the research primarily serves to underscore the vast variation and individuality in the human species, male or female. As my six-year-old daughter replied when asked which sex prefers to play with trucks, "It depends on what kind of girl or boy you are."

Sex Roles in the Nursery

Laura Carper

You should have seen what a fine-looking man he was before he had all those children.
—Arapesh tribesman, quoted by Margaret Mead, *Male and Female* (1949)

While supervising one of the playrooms in the nursery school where I work, I overheard this dialogue between two four-year-old children:

"You stay here with the mommies and the babies. I'm going fishing," Gerald said to Judy as he trotted off.

"I want to go, too," Judy called, running after him. Gerald turned and repeated, "No, you stay with the mommies and the babies!"

"But I want to go fishing!" Judy cried.

"No," Gerald insisted, "But when I come back I'll take you to a Chinese restaurant."

Judy was mollified. She turned back to the dolls.

I reported the incident to Gerald's mother, who now runs a business in downtown Detroit with several other women. That year she was at home full time, but she assured me that Gerald was not mimicking his parents' behavior; the only time her husband had gone fishing the rest of the family had gone too. Dramatic play is not necessarily a replication of direct experience. It is an early form of abstract thought, a young child's way of sorting out experiences and trying on opinions drawn from various sources.

Another play scene I observe now and then goes like this: three or four little boys seat themselves around the play table in the play kitchen. The boys start issuing orders such as "I'd like a cup of coffee" or "Bacon and eggs!" or "Some more toast!" and a girl runs back and forth between stove and table cooking and serving. In one such scene the boys got completely out of hand, demanding cups of coffee one after another while the girl, Mimi, was racing around in a frenzy. She finally gained control of the situation by announcing that there was no more coffee. Apparently it never occurred to her to sit down at the table herself and demand coffee from one of the boys.

Sexist behavior among the very young is hardly a new phenomenon; viewing it as a problem is. It obsesses the other teachers and school directors whom I meet at workshops on preschool education; and it plagues the parents of my charges, who are sincerely trying to raise their children free of sexual bias. They carefully screen out books in which mothers mostly tie shoelaces and bake cookies; they buy trucks as well as dolls for their daughters and dolls as well as trucks for their sons. But as soon as the children start to play together the girls pretend to be mommies, nurses, or schoolteachers, while the boys are busy perfecting a karate chop or flying around like Batman. The parents wring their hands and wonder what they are doing wrong.

In my view, this sort of role-playing is part of a normal and useful developmental stage. Its origin lies in the child's struggle to understand his sexual identity. One of the prime tasks facing the preschool child is the establishment of a sense of self, and a sense of one's sexual identity is part of selfhood. Banding together with other children of the same sex for games where there are "no boys allowed" or "no girls" appears to be reassuring for many preschoolers.

The roles boys and girls choose when they are involved in dramatic play are determined in part by the culture. As soon as children are old enough to observe, they begin making generalizations that may or may not be accurate. Timmy, for example, went with his mother for a checkup at a large medical clinic when he was two-and-a-half. As they were sitting in the waiting room a man in a white coat walked by. Timmy said, "Hi, doctor." A moment later another white-coated man came by, and again Timmy said, "Hi, doctor." Then a woman in a white coat walked past. "Hi, nurse," Timmy said.

"How do you know who is a nurse and who is a doctor?" his mother asked.

"Doctors are daddies and nurses are mommies" was Timmy's confident reply. Yet Timmy's own pediatrician, who has cared for him since birth, is a woman.

All preschool children are as confused about sexual distinctions as they are about the world in general. At two-and-a-half, boys and girls alike will wheel a doll carriage and announce "I'm the mommy" or "I'm the daddy," regardless of their own sex. But their play at this age is based largely on observations of their mothers. The boys are as fascinated with the play kitchen and the dolls as the girls are. Little girls are convinced they will grow up to be mommies, but in my opinion *so are little boys*.

That a young boy should aspire to be a woman is not so odd. There is a powerful drive in all of us to do unto others as has been done to us. The mother who nurtures a child in earliest infancy is his first love, and he identifies with her; perhaps the most difficult accommodation of his first few years is separating from her, and learning both to recognize himself and to act as an individual. Yet it is primarily through the mother that he perceives adult life and forms impressions of daily adult tasks; it is chiefly, though of course not exclusively, through her that he learns what it is to be human. It is very hard for him to draw clear distinctions between what she does and what he can ultimately accomplish.

3. DEVELOPMENT AND EDUCATIONAL OPPORTUNITIES

One three-and-a-half-year-old boy I taught, whose mother was pregnant at the time, exasperated his older playmates by insisting that a baby was growing in *his* stomach. (The mother had told him, "We are going to have a baby.") A two-and-a-half-year-old betrayed deeper confusion about the idea of pregnancy: his mother, who also happened to be pregnant, told him he couldn't have the puppy he wanted until he was older. A few days later he came to her and said, "Is a puppy dog growing in my stomach?" A third mother told me how sadly her four-year-old son had said, "I can never have a baby," and then added wistfully, "can I?" Certainly a little girl has her problems, but at least she can mature with full confidence in her ability to follow in her mother's footsteps. A little boy cannot. He identifies with a woman, but he must become a man. He suffers from what, for want of a better name, I shall call uterine envy.

Margaret Mead, Bruno Bettelheim, and others have provided strong arguments that womb envy occurs in many preliterate cultures. The couvade (from the French word *couver*, to hatch) was once a fairly widespread practice, described in the *Encyclopaedia Britannica* as

> the custom of the father going to bed at the birth of his child, complaining of labor pains, observing dietary restrictions or otherwise acting like a woman in confinement. In its extreme form, the mother returns to work as soon as possible after giving birth, often the same day, and waits on the father; thus the roles of the sexes are reversed.

The couvade was common to a variety of ancient, not so ancient, and primitive cultures, and was observed in the Baltic states and Holland as recently as the early years of the twentieth century.

Little boys do not seem to have a clear view of growing up to be daddies. The father's biological role in making babies is far less evident than the mother's. And in the ordinary household, the father's daily role in life is performed outside the home, away from the child's view. How is a young boy to imagine spending his days as an insurance agent, when he hasn't the vaguest notion of what that is? The best he can do is pick up a briefcase and say, "I'm going to the office," or pretend to get in a car and say, "I'm going to the shop." The game stops there. Even if he pays the office or the shop an occasional visit, it cannot be as familiar to him as what mommy does at home or what Superman does on television. So he weaves a masculine image from television, where men run the world; from the supermarket, where a man runs the store; and from what he has been *told* his father does, which is to earn the money whereby the family lives. He must work very hard to play the man.

It has been argued that television gives children a false concept of masculinity that they strive to emulate; but when I was a child in the Thirties, boys were playing "cops and robbers" and "cowboys and Indians." That came from the movies. In the nineteenth century it was tin soldiers. The young boy grasps at an all-powerful male image to compensate himself for his terrible loss. Since he had previously assumed that he would grow up to be like his mother and has learned that he dare not, he builds a fortress of maleness lest his deepest inclination turn him into a woman.

Ideally, the little boy would like to have the best of both male and female worlds. He aspires to go out and prevail like Batman, but he also yearns to stay at home and nurture children. This conflict tears him apart and he tries to resolve it in his play and fantasy life. Maurice is a case in point. Shortly after the birth of his younger sister, Maurice picked up his lunch bag at lunchtime in school, stuck it under his polo shirt, and strutted around the room looking for all the world like a woman in her ninth month. Several other boys followed suit, and the game soon became a popular ritual. During this same period Maurice also became deeply involved in another game. The first thing he did upon entering the nursery was to go to one of our small building toys and construct imaginary guns. He would stick a gun in each of his pockets and carry a third. Yet his mother reported that he said, "When I grow up, I'm gonna marry all the women in the world. I'm gonna have a lot of babies to take care of when all those women go out to work." Maurice's mother is home full time.

Like Maurice, many boys in my nursery are often involved in gun play. If they are shooting up a room reserved for quiet play and I tell them that no guns are allowed in that room, they will convert their imaginary pistols into fire hoses or flashlights, to play firemen or "going on the prowl." I have noticed, however, that on those rare occasions when a father is assisting me in the nursery the boys' play often changes. They seem to lose interest in these compensatory phallic symbols and are drawn easily into whatever activity the father initiates, whether it is playing kickball, walking a balance beam, or painting.

I have taught preschool children in the Head Start program, children from working-class, middle-class, and upper-class families, and children whose mothers have sophisticated, though often part-time, jobs. In all of these settings, I have often seen children assume stereotyped sex roles when they are acting out their fantasies or experimenting with adult roles. In all of these settings, too, it was the mother who had nurtured the child in infancy. If men were free to share equally in the raising of children, a different picture might emerge.

When Kids Explore Sex

Arlene S. Uslander, Caroline Weiss, and Judith Telman

There is probably no other area in adult-child relationships that gives rise to more in-depth self-examination, or creates more inner conflict, than that of imparting sex-information to children. Among the major concerns of many parents is the fear that by telling their children about sex, they will encourage the children to become preoccupied with it. But generally, the contrary is true. Sexual curiosity and experimentation, although engaged in by almost all children (not just teenagers or pre-teens, but young children, too) is more intense and more frequent as a result of ignorance, rather than knowledge.

PLAYING DOCTOR

Part of the natural learning process for children takes place in a hit-or-miss exploration of everything about them, and adults are usually quite helpful in guiding, directing, advising and answering questions along the way. When this curiosity extends to examining the child's physical self, or that of a brother, sister or friend, there is a breakdown in the process. In our culture, there is a separation of the facilities for boys and girls—public washrooms, physical education classes, health classes and so on. And this separation extends to the home, as well, with children seldom having the opportunity to see members of the opposite sex undressed. Since anything unknown teases the imagination and arouses interest, children tend to seek ways in which to discover that which is hidden from them.

Many a five or six-year-old boy has gained his knowledge of the female anatomy by secretly poring over the pictures in a girlie magazine he has found. Some boys are satisfied by this method, others are not. Girls have even less opportunity to satisfy their inquisitive natures, since male anatomy pictures aren't as readily accessible. More than once we, as teachers, have seen a cluster of giggling seven-year old girls crawling on all fours, pretending to be looking for a lost object outside the boys' washroom.

One method children use to help satisfy their need to know about sex is role-playing. They choose the game which does just what the child wants to do—examine the human body. They play "doctor."

For toddlers and preschoolers, the game is usually confined to listening to the heart with a makeshift stethoscope, and administering candy pills for a variety of make-believe ills. As children mature, however, new aspects are added to the game. I remember a mother who said, "The other day I went into my daughter's room to see what all the giggling was about. There were my daughter and her friend completely naked, and the little boy from down the block was examining them."

And there was the playground supervisor who reported: "During the morning recess I noticed an unusual gathering of the children in a far corner of the school grounds. When I asked some of the other children what was going on, they just shrugged and looked away. So I decided to find out for myself. When I got closer, I could see that there was a veritable clinic in progress. The 'doctor' and 'nurse' were entertaining the onlookers by the public administration of physical examinations. All the onlookers were offering suggestions in accordance with experiences they had had in their own doctor's offices."

Other parents have mentioned having walked in on a "childbirth delivery." The methods the children used were sometimes based on factual knowledge, but sometimes were very fanciful, depending on the knowledge of the participants.

How parents react to such situations is crucial to the success of future relationships between the children involved, with their parents and even in future boy-girl relationships. Accusations and shame-producing recriminations solve nothing but simply add to the anger and frustration of the moment. The children are left confused, baffled and guilty.

It is wiser, although more difficult, for the adults to remain calm and cool. If, in fact, they were to be completely honest with themselves, and delved into their own childhood memories, the parents would undoubtedly recall having engaged in comparable explorations.

A sense of humor is invaluable at a time like this. The adult could say something like, "Sorry, doctor, I must be early for my appointment. May I see you in the outer office?" Or, "There's an emergency that needs your immediate attention. Could you please step over here?" In some cases, parents prefer to quietly close the door and walk away, waiting until a later time to discuss what they witnessed or overheard.

Such action gives the parent the opportunity to recover from any initial shock and confusion he or she may feel. And it serves another purpose. Often, children are already suffering discomfort and guilt when involved in sex play and would actually prefer to be doing something else, but they are unable to extricate themselves from their situation without losing face with their peers. An understanding reaction on the part of the confronting adult will allow the children to emerge from their game with dignity.

The situation should not be ignored or forgotten, however. Sex play is an indication that children want to know more about themselves. They are seeking direction and emitting signals, loud and clear, to which an adult, sensitive to the needs of children, should be prepared to respond. When we hear youngsters excitedly relating that one of their peers showed his or her "privates," we know that the time has come to explain why a child would do such a thing, and to offer reassurance that this kind of behavior is not unusual in children of their age.

If parents or teachers have established a pattern of enlightened sex education in the home or classroom, they will be able to accept sex play as a common experience of childhood, and to deal with the discovery of their children's experimentation calmly and maturely. A mother may, for example, capitalize on her discovery by explaining the value of privacy to her child, saying that some things are private, others are not. She may want to talk to the child about her own experiences at the same age, acknowledging a similar curiosity, and understanding the need to have it satisfied.

3. DEVELOPMENT AND EDUCATIONAL OPPORTUNITIES

Problems arise when children, outside the family or the classroom, have been involved in the game. The sensitive adult doesn't want to impose his beliefs or attitudes on other parents, nor does he wish to upset someone else's child by telling the youngster things that might be opposed to what his own parents have told him. It is wisest for the adult involved to say and do nothing which might cause confusion in the child's mind.

Those parents who have succeeded in building healthy attitudes for their children by personal example, shared love, mutual affection, pride in one's self and one's body will have relatively little difficulty in accepting the sex play of their children in a matter-of-fact manner. But parents who are hampered by sexual inhibitions, fearful of overstepping traditional modesty, and therefore are unable to deal honestly or comfortably with the sexual explorations of their children, should make a conscious effort to overcome their feelings so their children will be better able to cope with our increasingly more open society.

BROTHER-SISTER SEX PLAY

There is another method of sexual exploration in which children engage, which might be considered an extension of "playing doctor."

Children quickly realize they may be severely chastised if discovered cavorting in the nude with a friend. Therefore, youngsters may devise other means to satisfy their curiosity concerning the opposite sex, using resources close at hand. Many parents who come from large families, will be able to recall instances of brother-sister sex play—brothers and sisters who had to give up their beds for a visiting relative and sleep together for a night, and managed to learn a great deal about the opposite sex by fondling and touching while "asleep."

Under the guise of brotherly or sisterly affection, the older sibling may offer to help a younger one. While assisting a little brother or sister to undress or prepare for bed or bath, the opportunity may present itself to examine, visually or manually, the younger child, particularly in the genital area. Generally the youngster will enjoy the attention and interest, submit passively to the examination and not voice any objection. If discovered by the parent, the "explorer" can claim innocence and proclaim the desire to be helpful, while the youngster, not wanting to endanger the relationship with the older sibling, will usually be supportive of the story.

In such instances, parents should not jump to the conclusion that the child is a deviate, who is unduly concerned with sex. If such events are merely occasional, not habitual, and the child is happy, active, and interested in all of the things children are, not just sex, the parents should recognize that this sibling sex play is merely one way for the child to satisfy his curiosity.

DIRTY JOKES

After teaching sex education for many years, we have come to the conclusion that there is a third certainty in life which should be added to death and taxes—the inevitability of the dirty joke. As children reach the age of six, they are initiated into their peer culture by hearing their first off-color story. It is then their obligation to repeat it at the first opportunity so that the heritage can be perpetuated. This ritual has been in existence since language began, and the jokes and their variations have been the same for generations.

"Want to hear a dirty joke?" a first grader will ask. And before you can respond, he will tell the joke. "A boy fell in a puddle of mud." Ancient, unfunny, but to a six-year-old it is the most laughable thing he has ever heard. It is, perhaps, his first attempt at social humor. Even though adults would not classify this joke as "dirty," rest assured that as soon as a child comprehends the joke, he will know the difference between it and one we would categorize as "dirty." And from this innocent beginning, the child soon moves on to the "bathroom" jokes. These usually involve slang terminology for elimination and the parts of the body.

Parents are likely to be apprehensive when young children begin to tell us these jokes. The idea that a child is going to repeat a dirty joke in our presence usually makes us feel uncomfortable. But this anxiety soon dissipates as we listen and realize that the jokes related by very young children are completely different from those told by adults.

But by the third, fourth and fifth grade, the tone and substance of dirty jokes takes on sophistication and sexual undertone. Now, when Tommy says he's going to tell a dirty joke, he probably is.

Through the years, those who teach sex education, like us, have learned to control our personal disapproval when dirty jokes enter the conversation. Instead, what has been said, the feelings of the storyteller and the reaction of the people to whom he speaks are discussed quietly. Parents confronting their children when they have told a dirty joke should do the same, speaking of the effect the joke may have on others, and the importance of having respect for another's feelings. It's nice to place emphasis on what has been said rather than on who said it to help the storyteller save face, and try to relieve some of the guilt he may be experiencing.

When children are provided with accurate sex information, they tend to tell fewer dirty jokes. Because they have a more extensive sexual vocabulary and have a better understanding of the body processes, the shock value of jokes is eradicated. We saw this clearly demonstrated when a child, entering school in the middle of the term, told a joke about "Daddy's car going into Mommy's garage," as a way of establishing a relationship with his peers. In a few minutes, he realized that he would have to resort to other means to achieve his ends because the response was not what he had expected. The laughter that he thought would be forthcoming was not there. Instead, his classmates listened in silence. When he had finished, one of them calmly stated, "That really isn't funny. We call that sexual intercourse." This is an example of how sound sex education can influence a child's behavior and his relationships with the people around him.

ANOTHER METHOD OF SEXUAL EXPLORATION —MASTURBATION

Even the adult who has been able to successfully establish open and honest communicative channels with his child regarding most aspects of sexual development may find himself unprepared, threatened and upset if he discovers that his child is masturbating.

Masturbation is one of the ways in which a young child begins to discover and accept his body as pleasurable (and by which an older child tests and becomes acquainted with his sex organs and the sensations he is able to experience by manipulating them). Masturbation is a common practice rather than an unusual one.

As parents, we can better determine our course of action regarding masturbation in children if we understand what it is and why it is practiced. For the young child, examining, touching and fondling of the genitals is a natural part of self-discovery. Parents should guard against showing negative reactions which might cause the child to feel that what he is doing is shameful or degrading.

As teachers we have observed that masturbating activities increase, primarily and more obviously among the boys, preceding a testing period or before an event such as an interschool sports competition. Girls, too, become more fidgety and do more shifting on the edges of their chairs during similar periods of stress. There is a measurable decrease in this type of activity when outside pressures have passed or been dealt with to the satisfaction of the individuals involved.

Because people generally have been conditioned to believe that masturbation is wrong, the need to keep the

29. When Kids Explore Sex

activity hidden or to lessen its frequency becomes paramount in the mind of the child involved. Disappointment with an inability to kick the habit compounds guilt feelings and may lead to more serious problems. In this event, the services of a professional clinician should be enlisted to help determine the cause for the excess.

How one determines what constitutes excessive masturbatory behavior is difficult to say. If this practice follows the pattern of most excessive activity, the child will be hard-pressed to keep the need to masturbate hidden and confined to private quarters. He or she may begin to engage consciously or otherwise, in genital fondling or pressure in the presence of others. **Sympathetic understanding and compassionate guidance on the part of the parents are essential to the child's future, positive psychosexual development.** Verbal abuse or physical punishment, such as tying a child's hands, hitting, isolation or similar actions can be damaging to the child's emotional health.

Above all, it is important to recognize that both professional and lay people should have full and accurate information about masturbation, so that they can intelligently relay this information to youngsters. We will have to separate ourselves from the myths that plagued us up till now, and initiate discussions in clear, nonjudgmental terms that both adults and children can understand and be comfortable with.

Children eventually have to adjust to an environment outside their home. It is easier for them to make the transition if they are raised in an atmosphere free from fear and guilt. They are then also better able to cope with the changes that take place as their bodies develop through the various stages of maturation and growth.

Aggression and Hostility in Young Children

Bettye M. Caldwell

Bettye M. Caldwell, Ph.D., is currently Professor of Education and Director, Center for Early Development and Education, University of Arkansas at Little Rock. Previously, she was Research Associate, Department of Pediatrics, Upstate Medical Center, State University of New York, Syracuse; and Professor of Child Development and Education at Syracuse University. Her areas of experience include research in mother-child interaction; work with developmentally retarded children and their parents; design of early enrichment programs; day care; elementary education; and research on home factors associated with favorable development.

I have been active in early childhood education for half a generation now, and during that time I have seen my own professional interests turn almost 180°—from a primary concern with cognitive development (though that was never my only concern in working with young children) to an overriding obsession with how to foster the development of other-oriented, altruistic behavior in young children. This turnaround might not have occurred were it not for my personal style of working, namely, to be right in the thick of the action with teachers and children.

But what is there about my present life that has catalyzed this metamorphosis? For the past five-and-a-half years I have been the director of the Center for Early Development and Education. This is a research project funded during the first five years by the Office of Child Development and sponsored jointly by the University of Arkansas and the Little Rock School District. This year our funds come from the Carnegie Corporation; the Rockefeller Brothers' Fund; Title XX of the Social Security Act; plus financial support from our sponsors, the University of Arkansas at Little Rock and the Little Rock School District. The project originated out of my strong conviction that the experiences a child has during the first five years determine to a great extent later success or failure and the concomitant conviction that in the case of intervention with low socioeconomic children, there must be continuity between those first five years and later school experience if the early gains are to be maintained. We are housed in a Little Rock public elementary school, and our program of day care, health and family services, and home intervention is directed toward all children ages six months through fifth grade who attend Kramer School. Within that larger context, the particular experience which is most responsible for my own metamorphosis is that of being a public school principal—these three years have had tremendous and far reaching consequences in my way of viewing early childhood education and child development.

Just how has this way of life so significantly altered the way I feel about children and the process of education?

For one thing, I am now convinced that those of us in early childhood education have been unduly arrogant in our attitudes toward elementary education. There was certainly great arrogance (although perhaps unwitting and implicit) on my part in the thinking that led to the development of the Kramer Project. I was saying in effect, "Those of us who represent early childhood education could take care of America's children if you uncreative people in elementary education just wouldn't mess them up when we have finished with them."

The author's work is supported in part by Grant No. SF-500 from the Office of Child Development and by grants from the Carnegie Corporation and the Rockefeller Brothers' Fund; additional support comes from the Little Rock School District and from the University of Arkansas at Little Rock.

30. Aggression and Hostility in Young Children

Also I was saying—and there was nothing implicit in this, for I said it openly—"The techniques that we use in early childhood education would help to 'humanize' the schools if you would just watch us and learn from us. (Why lines, physical punishment, schedules to go to the bathroom, desks in a row?)" One of the things I have learned is that every one of those seemingly "inhuman" customs had its origins not in the emotional pathology of a distorted teacher but most likely in the gropings of a highly dedicated teacher trying to minimize the careless accidents and deliberate provocations that can be caused by children who have not, during earlier developmental periods, acquired sufficient self-control as to render such seemingly archaic customs unnecessary.

For another thing, I am persuaded by authors such as Toffler (1970) that changes are occurring in our society at an unassimilable rate, and that children are not exempt from the impact of these changes. For example, they are not immune to the impact of the media with its change in acceptable themes. The media demonstrate that "good guys" don't always win, and that quarrels are usually resolved by aggression and cunning. What does "All in the Family" teach about family life? Or about the equality of the sexes? What do children learn from the daily news? They learn that Whites and Blacks are fighting in Boston, but they do not learn that 20,000 children are being bused in Little Rock (where, supposedly, it all started) without incident.

There are many other opportunities for indirect or incidental social learning also—from Watergate, from the words emanating from a thousand songs that demand instant gratification, from such slogans as "do your own thing," from meetings in which adults might not be able to speak because of being shouted down, from direct and indirect forms of racial discrimination that persist in every segment of life, and from international indications that one can only settle disputes by resorting to aggression. While we need to be concerned about aggression and hostility in young children, we need even more to be concerned about these same behaviors in adults, and about the omnipresent indicators that ours is a society that apparently values such behavior.

What Do We Know about Aggression in Young Children

It is always disturbing to have someone say something like, "We really don't know too much about aggression and hostility in young children"—especially when you live with it every day. I am certain that every teacher and every aide is more of an expert on this subject than most of the researchers. But we necessarily have to say that about aggression, especially in young children, for a semantic reason if no other—namely, aggression is usually defined as behavior (verbal or physical) that has injury of a person or object as its *intent*. It can sometimes be very conjectural to try to assign intent to a young child's behavior. Did the baby who bit another child "intend" to hurt the other child, or was it to soothe aching gums? Did the toddler who pushed another child down in her eagerness to obtain a toy, causing the other child to cry, "intend" to hurt the pushed-down child or merely to get the toy? Does the child who calls his teacher a dirty name intend to defame her or to study her reaction for future reference or to try out words in an attempt to understand their meaning? Obviously, determination of intent is very difficult when we are concerned with very young children. Thus more people now are willing to define behavior as aggressive if it merely has the capacity to hurt or injure or damage, regardless of intent. The word hostility is even more difficult to define with reference to children, but most of us know what we

3. DEVELOPMENT AND EDUCATIONAL OPPORTUNITIES

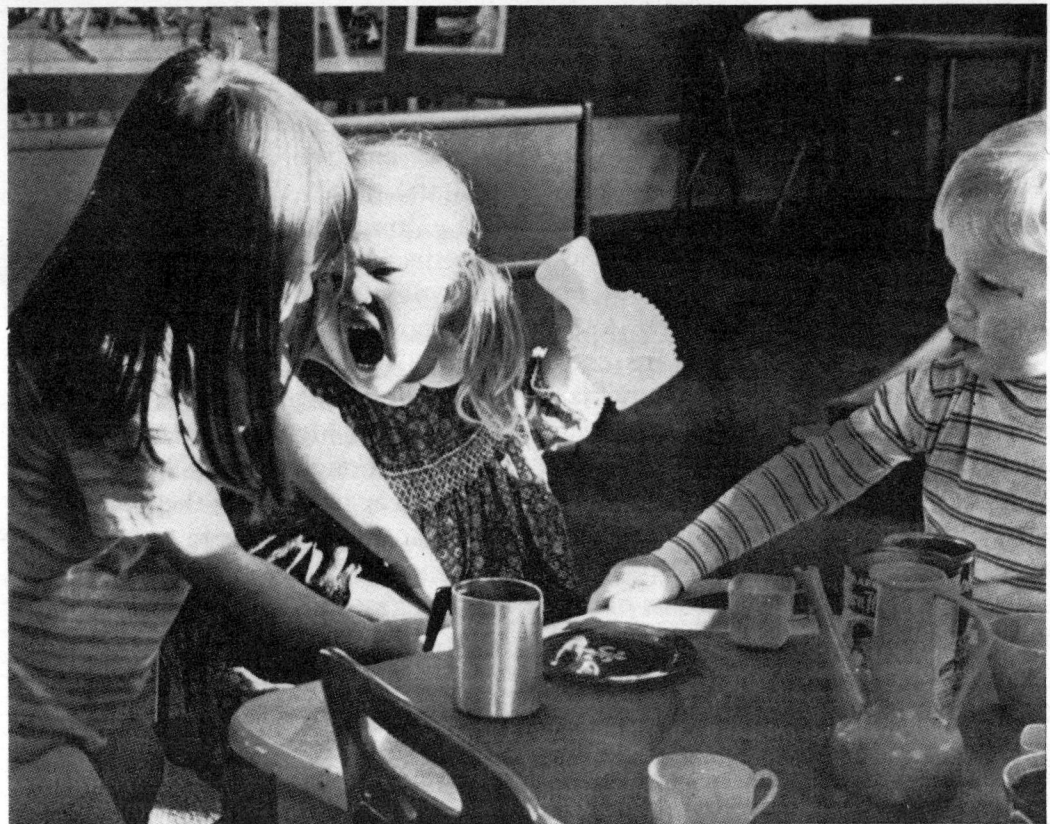

mean by the term—the angry child whose behavior leaves little room for doubt as to its intent.

Although I do not like to labor too long on definitions, I think one more distinction is worth making. This is what Feshbach (1970) has called the difference between instrumental and hostile aggression. Instrumental aggression is the sort which is aimed at the retrieval of an object, territory, or privilege, i.e., that which results when a goal is blocked. Hostile aggression, on the other hand, is oriented to another person, as a person, following some sort of ego threat or a perception that another person has behaved intentionally: "He did it on purpose."

There is some evidence (Hartup 1974) that of these two forms, instrumental aggression is far more common in young children. In fact, the decline in overall aggression with age is largely a function of the decline with age in instrumental aggression. In one of the older studies concerned with children's aggression (Dawe 1934), most of the aggression shown by children from about eighteen months to almost six years of age was instigated by disputes over possessions, with the tendency most prevalent among the younger subjects. During these years person-directed, retaliatory, and hostile outbursts increased with age.

Another finding from these skimpy developmental studies of aggression was that the most aggressive children are sometimes the children who also show the greatest amount of prosocial (positive) behavior. This suggests that some children are simply more actively social than others; they engage in more of all types of interpersonal behavior. In spite of scattered "facts" of this sort, we still know precious little about age changes in aggressive behavior. Even more important, we know very little about time trends in incidence of aggressive behavior.

I think one thing we need to do in order to better understand aggression in young children is to develop some new ways of thinking about it. Because of the semantic problems centering around intent, I think it would be better to look at aggression as another manifestation of self versus other. That is, quite apart from whether the biting baby wanted to hurt his victim, we know that he was concerned with gratification of a self-based need. The child who suddenly took a toy from another might not even have noticed that another child was at that moment playing with it, so focused was she on her own desire to possess and manipulate the toy.

We need to be as concerned about the development in children of a healthy "other" concept as we do about the development of a healthy "self" concept. But how many of us are concerned with this task in our curricula? Not enough, I fear. We desperately need suggestions as to ways to help children develop empathy and concern for others, and our good thinkers need to be giving weight to this need equal to that of the importance of the self-concept.

Practical Suggestions for Those Who Must Cope

Those of us working with children cannot wait until all the data are accumulated and our good thinkers have reached their final conclusions. We are forced to deal with aggression daily and to use whatever bits and pieces of evidence are available to us at the present time—whether or not it is still inconclusive. We must evaluate the data as it comes in and do the best we can to wisely choose our methods of coping with the aggression expressed by the children in our programs. Therefore, I want to discuss some practical guidelines for all of us who must deal with aggression daily. Some of the guidelines are fairly well supported by research findings; others are based more on my personal way of viewing the problem and my attempts at seeking a solution.

Physical punishment of aggression is not the answer. One generalization that emerges with consistency is that there is a close relationship between high use of severe physical punishment by parents and high incidence of aggression by their children. "Spare the rod and spoil the child" is not borne out by data. However, it is difficult to get causative data. Though the two variables, physical punishment by parents and aggression by children, are closely related, it is still somewhat open to debate whether physical punishment "causes" the higher incidence of aggression. It might be possible to argue that high aggression on the part of the child causes more severe punishment by the parents and not vice versa. At this time we simply cannot say. We do know, however, that they are correlated. Further, it seems logical that the adult who uses physical punishment to deal with physical aggression is communicating: "You are just not big enough to get away with it and I am." The adult also is demonstrating to the child a certain belief in aggression as a viable solution to problems.

Ignoring aggression in children is not the answer. This is something I encouraged students and teachers to do for years. Ample testimony to my approach could be found by counting the number of times children at Kramer have been heard to say, "Mrs. Caldwell won't do nothing to you." I am now convinced that this is the wrong thing to do. Ignoring aggression will not make it disappear. The danger, it seems, in not responding to a child's aggressiveness is that the child may regard the watching adult's failure to deal with the aggressive behavior as adult approval of those actions. Siegel and Kohn (1970) have conducted an experiment which seems to support this interpretation of an adult's permissiveness by children. Working with pairs of preschool age children, they allowed half of the pairs to play with various toys for two sessions in the presence of a permissive (and noncondemning) adult; the other half of the pairs played in a similar setting but with no one else in the room. Most of the children in the adult-present condition exhibited more aggression in the second session than in the first; all of the children in the adult-absent condition decreased in aggression in the second session. The adult's permissiveness apparently was viewed by the children as approval of their aggressive behavior and therefore that behavior increased rather than decreased.

Permitting aggression or hostility to be expressed, and assuming that this will "discharge" the tension, will not work. Much of our current popular psychology, however, continues to promote this viewpoint. An article in a popular magazine recently listed the following consequences which can supposedly result from ignoring anger: taut, angry muscles; malfunctioning internal organs; migraine headaches; hives; pimples; itchy rashes; common colds; problems both mild and serious with the bladder, the stomach, and the bowels; ulcers; colitis; heart attacks; being accident prone; disastrous love affairs; and depression. Advice to openly express your anger and hostility in order to remain healthy and happy has been given for years and is still being given by some. Not only is the expression of anger and hostility supposedly preventive but it is also viewed by some as curative.

Yet this position is questionable in light of recent research findings. Berkowitz (1974) after an extensive review of research conducted on controlling aggression in young children concludes:

> He [the child] should not be encouraged to attack someone to express his hostility in the hope that he will drain some hypothetical energy reservoir. The catharsis notion is an outmoded theoretical conception lacking adequate empirical support which also has potentially dangerous social implications. Violence ultimately produces more violence. (p. 135)

With this principle in mind, there is one hint as to when "punishment" (but not aggressive punishment) should occur. According to a study done by Walters, Parke, and Cane (1965), it is most effective to punish or rebuke a would-be aggressor immediately after the aggressor has initiated the aggressive behavior rather than after the attack is completed or the goal is obtained. In their study, Walters, Parke, and Cane rebuked one half of a group of boys each time they reached for an attractive toy. For the other half of the boys, punishment (again in the form of a verbal reproof) came after the toy had been touched. Later the boys were allowed to play in the room with the desired toy but this time with the punishing agent absent. Those boys who had been rebuked before touching the toy demonstrated a greater ability to resist the temptation when left alone with the forbidden toy.

In order to minimize aggression, we need parent cooperation. One of my colleagues, Richard Elardo, and I conducted a study designed to determine whether or not teachers in day care programs and the parents of the children enrolled held differing values with respect to various areas of children's behavior. According to our research, one of the few important differences between parental values and teachers' values was in the area of aggressive behavior. Parents tended to believe that young children should be aggressive and fight in school, so others will not think they are sissies or cowards.

I have seen evidence of this attitude on the part of parents at our own school. We have had parents pick their son up from school and then drive around the school campus looking for another child who supposedly had insulted their son—in order that when the other boy was located, the son could get out of the car and beat the boy up. Similarly, we had a child whose parents had "dared" him to come home from school without having beaten up the little boy who threw sand in his sister's eyes while they were playing together the previous weekend.

Unfortunately, the school will remain ineffective in its efforts to control aggression in children as long as the parents support and even encourage such behavior in their children. If we are to minimize aggression, the school and the parents must work together.

In order to control aggression, we must strengthen altruism; we must emphasize helpfulness and cooperation as highly valued behaviors. In order to do this, however, we must have a society committed to these values. In 1974 I was a member of a U.S. delegation to the People's Republic of China. Our delegation spent most of its time observing in the Chinese kindergartens, which are for children between the ages of three and seven years. I saw no incidents of aggression on the part of the Chinese children. They did not push, shove, hit, kick, or in any way show hostility toward other students; further, there were no verbal attacks made against one another. The children were helpful and cooperative toward their classmates. At first I was somewhat amazed, but later such behaviors seemed the natural consequence of the societal values. The motto which guides the Chinese is "Serve the people!" and, as far as I could tell, the motto had become a way of life. The highest virtue is service to another person or to the collective, and the worst offense is selfishness.

Our society, I fear, lacks this emphasis on service and concern for other people. We, as a society, value competition and self-advancement. We profess belief in helping others, but usually it is considered secondary to the belief that people must help themselves. If we are to foster altruism in children, our society must esteem this quality. Even if the school and the individual parents agree, little will be achieved until the whole society values helpfulness and cooperation, and other attitudes which are inconsistent with aggression and hostility.

Non-permissiveness in our attitudes toward aggression may be as important as punishment for aggressiveness. We need to learn to communicate the attitude that says, "That sort of behavior is simply not going to be tolerated here." This was one of the major findings of the longitudinal study conducted by Sears, Maccoby, and Levin (1957) on patterns of child-rearing.

> Our findings suggest that the way for parents to produce a non-aggressive child is to make abundantly clear that aggression is frowned upon, and to stop aggression when it occurs, but to avoid punishing the child for his aggression. Punishment seems to have complex effects. While undoubtedly it often stops a particular form of aggression, at least momentarily, it appears to generate more hostility in the child and lead to further aggressive outbursts at some other time or place.... Thus, the most peaceful home is one in which the mother believes aggression is not desirable and under no circumstances is ever to be expressed toward her, but who relies mainly on nonpunitive forms of control. The homes where the children show angry, aggressive outbursts frequently are likely to be homes in which the mother has a relatively tolerant (or careless!) attitude toward such behavior, or where she administers severe punishment for it, or both. (p. 266)

From my experience, I think the statement above would be just as true if we were to go back through it and every time the authors use the word "home" we were to substitute the word "classroom" and every time they use the word "parents" or "mother" we were to substitute the word "teacher." In our schools, we must communicate to the children a low tolerance of aggression while also using nonpunitive techniques for controlling it. Certainly this will not be an easy task. But all the evidence we have on the subject indicates that this is the most effective means for achieving our goal.

We must help children de-escalate their aggressive behavior. This is for

3. DEVELOPMENT AND EDUCATIONAL OPPORTUNITIES

me a relatively new concept which is of importance in helping to minimize aggressive behavior in children. It was born in this practical life I lead —observing the children at their play and observing how it is that most of the aggressive behavior develops. I couldn't begin to count the number of times I have seen a group of children running after each other, playing "monster," or "superman," or any of the other chasing games. Eventually one of the children gets knocked down, or trips, and gets hurt. The child becomes angry and blames a playmate—and the play becomes a fight. The same pattern is typical of play in the sandbox. The children begin innocently making pies, cakes, etc., until someone breaks a cake or pie and the "baker" gets mad and another fight occurs. Whenever these incidents occur and the question "why?" is posed to the children someone will answer, "We were just playing." Think how many times you have heard that explanation. I have come to realize how very often that is correct. Play, which began as positive social interaction, simply escalated too fast and in a manner not anticipated (and often not desired) by the children involved.

Our mistake is that we ususaly read intent into the resultant aggressive behavior and reason: "The child should not get away with such behavior; he should be punished." We build intent into their actions, even though it might not have been there with the children (the tripping of a child or the breaking of a mud pie from the children's viewpoint were unintended accidents resulting from too much enthusiasm). If we can avoid being judgmental and simply help the children de-escalate back to the level of play, we will possibly have helped more than if we mete out punishment.

Children need to learn different alternatives to problem situations. It is relatively common for a child to tell me, "I hit him 'cause there wasn't nothin' else to do." Children do have a

Elaine M. Ward

more limited repertoire of behaviors than adults. But it is up to us to work at providing more desirable alternatives for them. Unless we can help a child realize there are a variety of options, some more desirable than others, we cannot expect behavior to change.

We need to be more willing to play with children and to help them learn to play. How many children in your school know all the verses to London Bridge? How many jump rope to the verses we chanted as children? (All their memorization is taken up with commercials.) Or how many of you rationalize that children need to be alone during free play time? The more adults withdraw from children, the more they expose them to peer influence. And the more children interact in the absence of adults (whose behavior they could model), the more likely they are to engage in fights and quarrels over property and privileges.

Summary

Our number one objective as teachers should be to facilitate the development of children's behavior that is cooperative and supportive of one another, altruistic and prosocial rather than aggressive. Those of us who work with children know that we must cope with a great deal of aggressive behavior, which is essentially self-centered. Although this is a phenomenon of our age and our culture, it is quite possible that we have been contributing our share to the apparent increase in such behavior. The isolation of our educational endeavors from schools for older children has in the past deprived us of the opportunity to follow the careers of children and obtain the necessary feedback we should have to enable us to adapt our own techniques to the realities of life histories.

For over a generation now we have been taught essentially to let children express their aggression both to "get it out of their system" and to prevent the development of symptoms of emotional dysfunction. As we now look at this practice, it appears to have been misleading. Aggression breeds not contentment and subsequent cooperation; aggression breeds more aggression. Severe punishment for aggression—especially punishment that mirrors the aggressive act itself —apparently does little to decrease the frequency of such behavior.

Nor does ignoring such behavior help; unfortunately, it does not just go away, and there is very little evidence that a child "grows out of it." Apparently children simply grow into more sophisticated manifestations of aggressive behavior, unless the environment in which the child is developing (home, school, community, nation) communicates that such behavior is not valued, and will not be tolerated. If that environment values cooperation and service to others, and if all segments of society support one another in that valuation, apparently children can learn to develop self-control and concern for others.

We, as parents and teachers, need to give some thought to helping children learn to de-escalate their aggressiveness back down to the level of play, where much of the behavior starts. De-escalating play is different from defusing the hostility which is often theorized as causing aggressiveness. As part of this de-escalation, a plea was made for more, rather than less, involvement of adults with children in their play. The price of liberty is supposed to be eternal vigilance. Vigilance by and extended contact with adults who model nonaggressive behavior is indeed one necessary precondition for the development of children who can cooperate with one another and with adults—and be happy in the process.

References

Berkowitz, L. "Control of Aggression." In *Review of Child Development Research, Vol. III*, edited by B. Caldwell and H. Ricciuti, pp. 95-140. Chicago: University of Chicago Press, 1973.

Dawe, H. C. "An Analysis of Two Hundred Quarrels of Preschool Children." *Child Development*, 1934, pp. 139-157.

Elardo, R., and Caldwell, B. M. "Value Imposition in Early Education: Fact or Fancy." *Child Care Quarterly*, 1973, pp. 6-13.

Feshbach, S. "Aggression." In *Carmichael's Manual of Child Psychology*, edited by P. H. Mussen, pp. 159-259. New York: John Wiley & Sons, 1970.

Hartup, W. W. "Aggression in Childhood: Developmental Perspectives." *American Psychologist*, 1974, pp. 336-341.

Sears, R. R.; Maccoby, E. E.; and Levin, H. *Patterns of Child Rearing*. Evanston, Ill.: Row, Peterson, and Co., 1957.

Siegel, A. E., and Kohn, L. G. "Permissiveness, Permission, and Aggression: The Effects of Adult Presence or Absence on Aggression in Children." In *Child Development and Behavior*, edited by F. Rebelsky and L. Dorman, pp. 234-242. New York: Alfred A. Knopf, 1970.

Toffler, A. *Future Shock*. New York: Random House, 1970.

Walters, R. H.; Parke, R. D.; and Cane, V. A. "Timing of Punishment and the Observation of Consequences to Others as Determinants of Response Inhibition." *Journal of Experimental Child Psychology*, 1965, pp. 10-30.

Mother-Child Interactions and Competence in Infants and Toddlers

Shirley Moore,
Research Editor

Shirley Moore, Ph.D., Professor, Institute of Child Development, University of Minnesota, Minneapolis, Minnesota.

A movement to establish day care programs for infants and toddlers is upon us and we are alarmingly unprepared for such a movement. Although there has been an enormous increase in psychological research on early development during the past five years, prior to that time there were few studies of the first two years of life. Consequently, it will be some time before we have the extensive body of knowledge about this period of life that we need to make sound decisions about out-of-home environments for very young children.

One fruitful approach to the study of early development involves the observation of mothers and infants in their homes for the purpose of relating home milieu factors in general, and mother-child interactions in particular, to infant development. From such studies we can begin to identify aspects of the caregiver-child relation that may be critical to the development of competence in the first year or two of life. In this report, three recent home observation studies of infants and toddlers will be reviewed, conclusions will be drawn, and implications for day care will be discussed.

STUDY I. Inanimate and Social Environmental Factors

Yarrow, Rubenstein, Pedersen, and Jankowski (1972) studied infants 5-6 months old and their mothers (or other primary caregivers); the subjects were 41 low-income and 7 middle-income Black mothers and their babies. Each mother-child pair was visited at home for two three-hour observations approximately one week apart. Observers time-sampled or rated the *inanimate environment*, the *social environment* (mother's behavior), and the *child's development* on a number of dimensions. By assessing the inanimate environment independently of the mother's behavior these investigators were able to study the relations of each to the child's development.

The inanimate environment, including toys and other objects available to the child, was rated for variety (different kinds of things), responsiveness (feedback potential from moving parts, changes in shape or contour, etc.), and complexity (number of different features, colors, etc.). The social environment was rated for the variety and level (amount and intensity) of mother stimulation during caregiving, the extent to which mother was responsive to the child's positive vocalization and calls of distress, and the amount of positive affect she showed. The child's development was assessed through observation and testing. The Bayley Mental and Motor Scales were used as well as several other measures of cognitive/motivational behavior including problem solving, exploratory behaviors, and the goal directed behaviors of reaching, grabbing, and repeating interesting actions (Secondary Circular Reaction). The child was also observed for positive vocalization, fussiness, manipulative play, and attention to mother.

The evidence from this study indicates that the inanimate environment and the social environment each contribute independently to predictions of infant competence. The characteristic of the inanimate environment that related most consistently to infant development was the variety of objects available to the child. Children with more variety in inanimate objects scored higher on both Beyley Scales, were more goal directed and better problem solvers, and explored more than infants with less variety. Responsiveness of objects also related positively to the child's cognitive and motor development but not as consistently as variety. Complexity of objects in the environment did not relate directly to cognitive development, but it did predict the child's preference for novelty, reaching and grasping, and repeating interesting actions—behaviors which would appear to keep the child involved with the environment.

Mother behaviors also related positively to the child's cognitive development. The variety and level (amount and intensity) of maternal social stimulation correlated with the Bayley Mental Scale. Cognitive-motivational infant behaviors including persistence and purposefulness, and the repetition of interesting effects were also related to variety and level of maternal stimulation, as were mothers' expressions of positive affect. It would appear that mothers and other primary caregivers mediate cognitive development not only by making objects available to the infant, but by becoming socially involved with the infant as he or she interacts with the environment and by expressing pleasure at the child's pleasure. Consistent with this picture is the fact that the exploratory behavior "manipulating novel objects" is related to mother's positive affect, and to mother's contingent responsiveness to positive vocalization from the infant.

Positive correlations were found between mother's "contingent response to distress" and Mental and Motor Scales of the Bayley, and to all aspects of goal-directed behavior. Here too mother appears to be an important mediator of development by attending to her child when the infant is distressed. Presumably such attention makes it possible for the child to recover more rapidly from brief crises and renew his or her involvement with the environment. It may also reassure the infant that the world is a reasonably safe place despite the occasional hurts that occur from the child's own actions with objects in the environment.

As might be expected, the level and variety of mother social stimulation also predicts the child's more purely social (versus cognitive and exploratory) responsiveness, as does her show of positive affect toward the child.

STUDY II. "Optimal Maternal Care" Behaviors

Clarke-Stewart (1973) studied 36 firstborn children and their mothers from low-income families. The children, which included an equal number of boys and girls, and Black and White infants, were approximately nine months old at the beginning of the study. Home observations were made seven times over a nine-month period, or until the children were about eighteen months old. Observers recorded information about the infant's history and daily schedule; asked about the mother's child-rearing philosophy and knowledge of child development; completed developmental checklists of the child's language behavior, play behavior, and response to mother; assessed the stimulus properties of the environment; made a descriptive record of the activities that occurred during the observation; and completed a rating scale on mother and child activities.

In addition to the observations and ratings, the children were given two administrations of the Bayley Mental and Motor Scales, one near the beginning of the study and one near the end. Cognitive development was also assessed by administering Uzgiris-Hunt items in which the child was asked to name or point to familiar objects and to perform simple manipulations with objects. Mother's language competence was assessed by administering the Peabody Picture Vocabulary Test and mother's personality characteristics were assessed using items from the Cattell Sixteen Personality Factor Questionnaire. The children and their mothers also participated in a laboratory social play session during which the infant's reactions to a new place, new toys, and to an adult stranger were assessed.

The results of this investigation are numerous and complex; consequently selected major findings will be presented here and the reader is directed to the original monograph for a more detailed treatment. Clarke-Stewart concludes from her investigation that competence during these early months is a global characteristic—one that is apparently related to the child's feeling of well-being. Child measures that are positively correlated with each other include cognitive and language competence, motivation to act in new situations, interest in and involvement with the environment, expressions of joy, and attachment to mother. A cluster of maternal behaviors called "Optimal Maternal Care" related the most consistently to child competence. Optimal Maternal Care includes maternal warmth, and loving versus rejecting care—but also stimulating and enriching maternal behaviors. The mothers of competent children facilitate their child's involvement with objects in the environment, talk with their infant about the child's ongoing activities, and express a playful attitude toward their child. One important mother variable that is positively related to Optimal Maternal Care is the mother's own intellectuality and vocabulary which, in turn, is related to the child's intellectual competence (particularly language competence) and to the child's intellectual growth over the nine-month period of the study.

Optimal Maternal Care mothers not only structure the physical environment for their child, they also respond readily to their child's social overtures and to signs of distress; their children, in return, are low in fretfulness, a finding that confirms the Yarrow et al. data. Optimal Maternal Care mothers and their children appear to have a "mutual admiration pact." The mothers spend time with and enjoy their infants and the infants express positive emotion and thrive. In fact, one of the best predictors of infant competence toward the end of this study was the mother's social attentiveness to her infant during the early months of the study. Clarke-Stewart, in discussing maternal behaviors toward competent children, suggests that the mother's responsiveness (much of which is appropriately contingent on the child's abilities and interests) might arouse in the child an expectation that the child can control his or her own destiny which, in turn, motivates the child toward mastery. Observations show that although mothers did not spend endless hours looking at and attending their infants, mothers and infants were usually in the same area of the house and mothers interacted with or looked at their infants in 36 percent of the observations during the child's wake time. Mothers of the more competent children appear to spend more time interacting with their infants and toddlers than mothers of less competent children.

Some interesting differences were observed in style of interaction—and related differences in infant development—between White mother-child pairs and Black mother-child pairs. Although the total amount of time Black mothers spent with their children did not differ from that of White mothers, Black mothers spent relatively more time in physical care and controlling behaviors while White mothers spent more time talking and playing with their infants. The Black infants were more physically attached to their mothers, smiled and vocalized less and moved about the home less. Black infants were competent during the early months but by 17 months of age they scored lower on most measures of competence. Given the relation between infant competence and mother's general interest in her child's active involvement with the environment, one could speculate that the style of mother-child interaction of the Black mothers (with its emphasis on physical care and control) served the child well during the early months of life but did not provide enough intellectual and verbal stimulation during the later months.

STUDY III. Prediction of Competence and Environmental Correlates

White and Watts (1973) studied and compared a group of 22 infants and toddlers who were expected to be especially competent at age six (A children) with a group of 9 children who were expected to be lower in competence at age six (C children). Predictions of competence were made by assessing the older siblings and the family milieu of the target children prior to studying the target children themselves. Consequently this is a study of prediction of competence in children as well as a study of environmental correlates of competence.

For this project some children were observed from 12 to 24 months of age and others from 24 to 36 months. As in the previous studies, standardized tests of intellectual competence were administered to all of the children and extensive observations were made over a period of many months.

These investigators concluded that although there were some errors in classifying children, in general, competence at age three can be predicted quite early. A children were already more competent than C children on most measures by the time they were 24 months of age. In fact, some differences had emerged by 12 months of age; for example, A children were already linguistically more competent than C children at that age. Also by 12 months, A children were better at getting the attention of the adults and using adults as resources for learning. By 24 months of age A children performed better on measures of general intellectual competence and these differences were more marked by 36 months of age (using the Bayley Mental Scale at 12 to 24 months and the Stanford-Binet later). By the time these children were three years of age, A children imitated adults more, were more cooperative and compliant with adults, pretended more in their play, and gained more information through listening.

In assessing the environment of A and C children (including mother-child interactions) these investigators observed that the "stream of experience" of the two groups of children was not markedly different from 12 to 24 months. Most of the activity of both groups of children was nonsocial and involved wandering around the house, scanning the environment, and manipulating objects in the environment. They do note, however, that A children spent more time interacting with their mothers than C children at all ages and that A mothers engaged in more intellectual (verbal) behavior at all ages, particularly at the older ages. A children asked for more help from mother, and C children showed more clinging to mother.

One particularly interesting finding is that under age two, A and C mothers are equally likely to encourage and discourage their children, but after age two, A mothers encourage about three times as many activities as before, while C mothers discourage about twice as many activities as before. This difference in A and C mothers is reminiscent of the finding by Clarke-Stewart that the mothers of competent children stimulate and respond positively to their child's activities compared with the more controlling and restrictive mothers of less competent children. The results of this study should be considered suggestive only, since the number of children (especially C children) in some comparisons was very small and the reliability of the findings is difficult to assess.

Conclusions and Implications

Given the combined evidence from these studies, what can we say about the childrearing correlates of competence in infants and toddlers? One thing seems clear—competent infants are likely to have mothers or other primary caregivers who give them more than nurturant physical care. The mothers of the most precocious children interact with their babies contingently—that is, with the child's abilities and interests in mind. They see to it that their children have objects around to manipulate and play with, they encourage rather than discourage exploration of the environment, they talk to and play with their babies, they express their affectionate feelings for their babies, and they attend their babies when they are distressed.

One suspects from these observations that the mothers of competent children do not have mothering skills that other mothers lack; none of the behaviors they display would appear to require a high degree of social skill or expertise. But they do require a "mind set" about mothering in which the mother is conscious of her part in nurturing her child's budding intellectual and social competencies as well as in caring for her child's physical needs.

What precautions and qualifications should be considered in interpreting these data? First, it should be recognized that we do not know how well competence during the first two or three years of life predicts later competence—of the kind that leads to school success, for example. In the past our measures of infant intellectual competence have relied so heavily on sensory motor behavior that they did not predict later intellectual competence very accurately. Whether studies of the kind reported here, in which the data base is more extensive and varied, will predict more accurately is hard to say. Longitudinal studies in which the same children are followed from infancy into the school years will help to answer questions about the continuity of competencies from infancy to later childhood.

A second precaution involves the fact that these studies are correlational rather than experimental. (For obvious reasons childrearing cannot be studied experimentally except under the most unusual circumstances since we do not "randomly assign" children to mothers and to childrearing environments.) Correlational studies tell us what things go together—for example, what kinds of mothering goes with competence in infants—but they do not tell us about causes. It is certainly reasonable to hypothesize that optimal mothering will have a positive effect on a child's development. It is also reasonable, however, to hypothesize that children who are bright and capable bring out the "best" in their mothers, or that mothers who use optimal childrearing practices are themselves bright and capable and have passed that capability on to their children. In fact, probably all of these are true. Competence in children almost certainly has multiple causes. Whether one is assessing genetic or environmental correlates of competence, correlations are never so compelling (in the sense of accounting for differences in competence) that there is no room for other factors to exert their effect. The correlations between mother behaviors and infant or toddler competence in these studies are rarely above .50, indicating that indeed other things must also be predictors of competence in children. Some of the more likely factors, of course, would be physical health and nutrition, genetic endowment, father behaviors, and sibling influences, none of which are considered in these studies.

So what do we do? We use our best judgment in the light of the evidence we have. One can hardly survey the total childrearing literature without concluding that in all probability the quality of care that a child gets makes a difference. Our common sense tells us the same thing. The studies reviewed here leave one with a strong hunch that certain mothering behaviors contribute to competence during the early years of life. We should have confidence in that hunch and act upon it.

What relevance do these studies have for the movement to enroll infants and toddlers in day care? The implications for day care are indirect, but important. The competent infants in these studies had a capable and interested childrearing agent available to them—sometimes the biological mother and sometimes another primary caregiver. We do not know how important a *single* caregiver is to the early establishment of a secure bond between adult and child. The directors of one of the most carefully planned demonstration programs for infants and toddlers (Willis and Ricciuti 1975) make the point that the assignment of a specific caregiver to each child in the program is important to the child's development (even though, as in the home, others at times give care and attention). These program directors further suggest that no caregiver should be assigned to more than four infants, and even then extra help is occasionally needed. Under these circumstances, children do appear to establish an attachment to their caregivers in the center and still maintain their attachment to their mothers—and thrive in the process.

Our experience with programs for very young children is limited—but encouraging. Our best guess at this time is that we will be able to provide adequately for infants and toddlers if programs have an adequate staff of stable rather than transient caregivers—so that children can develop secure relations with the adults. Further, caregivers must be aware of the more subtle aspects of the caregiver-child relation and the complex array of caregiving behaviors that appear to be so important to optimal early development. We should not be satisfied with less for the children in our care.

References

Clarke-Stewart, K. A. "Interactions Between Mothers and Their Young Children: Characteristics and Consequences." *Monographs of the Society for Research in Child Development*. Chicago: University of Chicago Press, 1973.

White, B. L., and Watts, J. C. *Experience and Environment: Major Influences on the Development of the Young Child. Volume I.* Englewood Cliffs, New Jersey: Prentice-Hall, 1973.

Willis, A., and Ricciuti, H. *A Good Beginning for Babies: Guidelines for Group Care.* Washington, D.C.: National Association for the Education of Young Children, 1975.

Yarrow, L. J.; Rubenstein, J. L.; Pedersen, F. A.; and Jankowski, J. J. "Dimensions of Early Stimulation: Differential Effects on Infant Development." *Merrill-Palmer Quarterly* 18 (1972): 205-218.

Article 32

THE INDIVIDUALITY FACTOR

Children never conform
to a mythical average;
each one has a distinctive—
and lasting—behavior pattern

Jimmy's random eating and sleeping patterns had his parents completely upset. He didn't sleep for the same length of time on any two days. He didn't eat the same amounts at the same intervals—ever. No one could count on his reaction to the most familiar routine. In fact, his mother's day was so chopped up by his unpredictable ways that she couldn't plan for anything but Jimmy.

Eric's mother found herself overwhelmed when her very active and intense son started talking and walking. She couldn't slow him down. Unable to control her distress, she punished her son, which made her feel miserable but didn't affect Eric. He grew noisier and more active than ever, and more stubborn.

Carla worried her outgoing parents because she was so unreasonably shy. She wouldn't try on a new dress or sample a new food. When her father gave her a tricycle for her birthday, she cried and refused to go near it. At nursery school she made no friends, but played alone day after day.

All three sets of parents looked back with nostalgia to the easy days when their children were infants and much more "normal." They wondered what had happened, if they were in any way to blame and how they could eliminate their children's newly-emerged quirks.

Child psychiatrist Stella Chess, associated with New York University Medical School, says this parental reaction occurs all the time—but it's wrong.

"There wouldn't be any friction if these parents paid attention to a few basic facts," says Dr. Chess. "The most important is that those so-called ''childish quirks'' are really a part of their children's behavioral pattern."

According to Dr. Chess, behavioral patterns are as much a part of a child as the color of his or her hair and eyes—and just as enduring.

Dr. Chess, along with her psychiatrist husband, Dr. Alexander Thomas, also at New York University Medical School, and the late Dr. Herbert Birch, a research professor of pediatrics, studied 135 children over a period of 12 years. The children were only a few weeks old when the study began. A third of them developed problems their parents considered serious enough to tell the researchers about. Because the researchers kept records of both parent and child behavior, they were able to trace each child's troubles to their sources.

The doctors found that problems began when parents expected or demanded behavior the child could not deliver. When parents changed their aims and methods to suit the temperament of the child, the child began to suit himself and settled down to normal growth. When parents did not, the child's problems worsened.

Most parents are aware that every child has his or her own special ways, according to Dr. Chess. Up to a point they adapt to these ways without even realizing it. A mother may take her three-year-old son's blanket along when they go visiting, although she never did that for her older son. The younger child is different, obviously.

Although parents respond to simple differences in their children, they don't always accept the distinct individuality of each child as a fact. What the doctors' study showed, and what Dr. Chess would like to impress upon parents, is that each child is born with a tendency toward a certain kind of temperament which he expresses in his behavior.

Normally, the behavior style or temperament a baby shows in his first days stays with him and colors the way he acts through nursery school, kindergarten, first grade—forever.

Jimmy's infant reactions, for example, were probably much like his later ones—he ate and slept on his own schedule—but his parents expected this in a newborn. Eric cried noisily and expended his energy by kicking in his crib and splashing around in his bath, but then his mother regarded it as "cute." Carla was just as shy as an infant, preferring one toy to all others and seldom looking up at the visitors who hovered over her crib.

Drs. Chess, Thomas and Birch list nine kinds of behavior in which babies show clear and lasting differences. You can use them to establish your child's behavior profile. They are:

Activity: Some babies are more active than others. Some kick and squirm vigorously when being diapered; others lie still.

Regularity: Some are born with a built-in alarm clock. They eat, sleep, wake and eliminate at the same time daily. A small minority never do the same thing at the same time twice.

Approach-withdrawal: Some babies are unperturbed by new experiences. Others shy away from changes.

Adaptability: The adaptable child adjusts to change, no matter what his reaction to it may have been. The opposite type takes a great deal longer to get used to change.

Intensity: Some babies whimper while others scream, given the same stimulus. Some laugh when they are pleased; others smile faintly.

Responsiveness: It's harder to get a response from some children than from others. One child hears a distant footstep; another doesn't hear a door slamming beside him.

Quality of mood: Most children are more sunny than stormy, but some are born with a dark outlook. Nothing pleases them.

Distractibility: Some babies are oblivious to people talking, shadows across their faces, visitors tickling their feet. Others look up and smile whenever someone comes within their line of vision.

Persistence: The child who won't stop playing with his toys is typical of the persistent child. The less persistent child is one who gives up quickly after an unsuccessful attempt to

From *Redbook's Parent & Child,* 1976. Reprinted by permission.

3. DEVELOPMENT AND EDUCATIONAL OPPORTUNITIES

stand up in his crib, or who cries only intermittently when hungry.

Is there an ideal? The baby who is moderately active, regular, adventurous, adaptable, intense, responsive, positive, distractible and persistent could qualify. He makes life easy for his parents. In fact, he's such a good-natured baby that he gets lots of attention and affection and thrives on it. But even if he doesn't get what he wants he won't be upset, because he's pleasant and amenable by nature.

At the other end of the spectrum is the difficult child. He's constantly fussy. He cries but it doesn't mean he's hungry. He sleeps seven hours one day and wakes every hour the next. He is sensitive, intense, negative. He resists change and is slow to adapt when change is thrust on him. He displays an irregular, negative, nonadaptive intensity.

The easy baby makes his parents and others feel pleased with themselves and with him. The apparent unresponsiveness of the difficult child makes him hard to warm up to. His problems affect his parents, who don't realize that the child's behavior is simply his style. The parents alternate between devotion and resentment—and that's where real trouble begins.

A difficult child needs three things to help him—extreme consistency, cool assurance and skilled attentiveness. A nervous mother or an irate father can't provide them.

Dr. Chess points out that social pressures often contribute to the difficulty parents have with their children. For the most part, the problem children are negative, slow to warm up to new experiences, places, people and things, distractible or unusually active or quiet. These are all traits that don't fit the stock picture of the successful adult. The successful adult is generally educated, agreeable, sociable, well-liked, strong but not aggressive. Let a child fail to match this model, and parents worry. They visualize their irascible or flighty child lagging behind in school, missing out on college, unable to get a decent job—in short, a total failure.

Besides, parents usually suspect that they have done something wrong when children don't conform to an ideal mold. Such guilt feelings don't help the relationship between parent and child.

According to Dr. Chess, the climate of the times encourages parents to get to work to change their "unusual child," be he or she aggressive, overactive, shy or whatever. Parents are tempted to push and pull to make children over or, sometimes, to shield them from experience in order to avoid coming to terms with them, hoping that with the passage of time, they'll outgrow their "symptoms." Either method works hardships on parents and child alike.

Shielding a child who has trouble being sociable makes it harder for her in the end. She doesn't learn how to relate to others. For example, Carla's mother shielded her. When Carla pushed away a new food, Mother never served it to her again. If she didn't want to play with other children, Mother let Carla stay at her side. She never gave Carla a chance to stretch her capacity or to glimpse a wider world.

Pressing a child for quick results is also a mistake. Jimmy's mother was so anxious for her son to make friends that she tried to do it for him. She invited children home after school and Jimmy merely ignored them. Finally his mother stopped pushing, and in a few months Jimmy began bringing first one classmate, then another, home from school. He'll never make class president, but he is not without friends.

The most difficult trait in a child is distractibility. According to Dr. Chess, ours is a task-oriented society. A child who doesn't pay attention, finish what he starts, keep track of belongings, remember dates or get to places on time stirs his parents to fears of ultimate failure as nothing else can. They make the mistake of reminding him over and over about his obligations. Finally, the child shuts his ears completely or rebels by doing nothing at all right.

Reminding a child beyond a certain point relieves him of responsibility. He does what he's told while he's being told, but once out of his parents' sight he goes his forgetful way. He may fail because he didn't do his homework, but he won't see it as cause and effect. He'll see it as something that just happened—maybe his parents didn't make him study enough. He is so used to having others do his planning that he doesn't think the failure had anything to do with him.

Let a distractible child take the consequence of his casual ways and he begins to learn better. He may not be expected to find a time and place for homework, but given a regular time and quiet in which to work, the rest should be left up to him. The results—praise or censure, A's or C's—are all his, and he'll begin to appreciate the value of concentration.

Dr. Chess and her colleagues stress that the only way to change a child is to start with the behavioral endowment he was born with and stick to facts in handling him.

The range of normal behavior is very broad. Children don't all go through life conforming smoothly to a mythical average—happy, outgoing, obedient, agreeable. And difficult children are not headed inevitably for failure. The wonderful thing is that all children have a built-in wish for growth. This stimulates them to adapt with time and experience. A child who is encouraged by being taught according to his or her own capacities will prosper.

Article 33

Play isn't just kid stuff

Children learn many lessons through play. Here's a year-by-year guide to help you stimulate your child.

Brian Sutton-Smith

Some years ago my wife and I wrote a book called *How To Play With Your Children—And When Not To*. Since then we have been confronted by three kinds of people. Those who say, "Why did you have to write a book about it? Everyone plays with their children. Everyone knows that already. It is instinctive." Then there are those who say, "It's a nice dream but it is useless for the urban poor. They never play with their children." Indeed, it is true that some parents have never heard of more than two or three of the 200 or so plays and games described in the book. Finally, there are those who have found the book useful.

There are quite different ways in which we can raise children. Children have not always played a great deal throughout history. Often their work has been necessary to the survival of their parents. We were recently on the Island of Mauritius in the Indian Ocean. We visited one household where both the mother and father worked all day in a sugarcane plantation. The seven-year-old girl was cooking the family dinner; the four-year-old was minding the two-year-old. That family had no room for play.

Indeed, there is little play in societies where adults perform only routine jobs. In those cases, children are expected only to learn the passive requirements of the job, too. Imagination and creativity are not part of their lives.

But as civilization has grown more prosperous and more complex, there has been much more for them to learn, from reading to computers, and they have had to be active in that kind of learning. You can't teach people to make decisions without giving them lots of opportunities when they are young to make choices.

Play is the way of life for children who must grow up to be active and decisive in their own affairs. It is a way of life in the past restricted to those of wealth and status who carried on their games and play while the rest of us worked—hence their belief that it is "instinctive." But now play is necessary for any children who are to have an active leadership role in modern society.

There are two kinds of play: exploratory and inventive. Exploratory play is like the act of discovery. Here the child who meets people, goes places, has other children to play with, things to investigate and a private space to play in is the one who gets to learn most about the world. Children with the most appropriate toys in the first year of life are those who are the most curious and investigatory at nursery school several years later.

Adults don't appreciate the inventive kind of play—it is often the invention of nonsense and hilarity. It grows out of exploring and is a combination, in novel or ludicrous ways, of the things learned while exploring. For the past several years we have been collecting stories from two-year-old children. At first they took our requests quite seriously. Cathy, who is a rebellious little girl with parents who are both artists and separated, first told stories like this:

Batman dig
He went to bed
Him come right up
Then him Mommy said
Go back to bed
And Batman got woke up again.
And him Mommy said
Go right to bed
Him Mommy smack him bum
He went away
And then he went home
I finished.

As the first year went by and she grew rather expert at exploring her anger against her mother through Batman, she began to play more with the story itself. A year later the same girl gave us this story:

There once was a cat
And then he didn't want any
He ate dog doo but he didn't want any more
Then he said I don't like what I'm eating
And he said I don't like dog doo doo
But I'm eating dog doo doo
Cha cha cha
Choo choo choo
Koo koo city I ooh,
Coon glong glong
Shi sha sha
Glin gong
Tah tooo chit tee
Caw caw
Choo choo
La la
Lingah
Soo soo
Ka ka
Dong dong
Fellee
Sardines
Cookie
Dis sa
Fingally.

Reprinted with permission of *Parents' Magazine*, August 1978. Copyright ©1978 by Parents' Magazine, New York.

3. DEVELOPMENT AND EDUCATIONAL OPPORTUNITIES

Here she is both rebelling against conventional content (dog doo doo) and conventional story form (fingally); but she is also exploring alliteration and rhyming effects. This is the exploration of what you and I would call nonsense, but at this age there is also the learning of poetic effects. If they aren't discouraged, three-year-old children will spend much time in such exploration and invention.

Both of these kinds of play will make the child more active, but one has more to do with mastery and the other more to do with invention. At each age there are appropriate forms of both, as follows:

THE FIRST YEAR

Children who have "interesting" or stimulating parents become more capable of coping with the nursery school world later on. Of course, it may be that those who are born able to cope are also born more interesting. But we assume that the stimulation of the parents leads to the coping of the children.

Oddly enough, it seems to be babies from birth to six months old who first seek to evoke this stimulation from their parents. They attend to us more if we are more interesting. If we make unexpected funny sounds, noises or faces (if we are clowns), they take more delight in us. The major principle of their learning is that they keep responding to things (toys or people) that make interesting things happen. Each new response on their part means that new learning is also increasingly possible.

The better their attachment to us (and they are more attached to us if we are more interesting), the earlier they will begin to explore objects by themselves and learn about their properties. Some babies, however, seem to learn more from objects and others learn more from people. They should have access to both. This is probably why giving infants appropriate toys makes them more competent later on.

Appropriate toys at this age are rattles, mobiles and balls. Parents who sing to their infants have children with much earlier control of pitch, rhythm and intervals in their own singsong musical babbling. Competence, intelligence and sensitivity only come out of a richly provided and interesting environment that includes singing, talking, dancing, tickling, clowning, rock-a-bye on your knee and peek-a-boo with your baby.

While we hate to make anyone feel guilty about not doing these things, there seems little doubt that they are the beginnings of a more interesting life, giving infants more desire to be in this laughable world. Yet it's even more important to remember that infants need care, kindness and security, and that good human beings—if perhaps less interesting ones—can be produced with these alone. And it is certain that all the stimulation in the world is not worth much if care and love don't come first.

THE SECOND YEAR

By now the baby is up and walking; by the end of this year he is running. But the baby still needs stimulation from you. You can play on the floor, "read" picture books, "pretend" to be animals, laugh as towers of blocks fall over, pretend approval and disapproval with great caricature, play hide the slipper, chase each other on all fours, tug-of-war, pretend to fall over, and talk, talk, talk about everything.

Explain the world in simple terms, which implants the belief in discourse and explanation long before their substance is grasped. We all learn the outward forms before we learn the inner truth, and children are the least exception to this rule. From all of this they learn the value of words, the value of books, how to relate to and enjoy people, how to explore for things and how to examine shapes, sizes, textures, colors and graphic meanings.

But two-year-olds need more than you. Just as they needed toys in the first year, now they need space to move about. There needs to be a range of floor space from room to room or in the backyard, and cupboards to get into and out of. It's time to move the valuables up out of reach and make sure that there is nothing sharp to fall on. There should be a play corner or room for blocks, containers to fill and empty, four-wheel pull vehicles which can hold things and be emptied, big balls, play dough, crayons and a sandpit.

Two-year-olds' new principle of learning is that they can organize their world. They stack, insert, couple, array, connect and disconnect, heap, empty and fill. Most of us don't realize the extent to which we do the same; that we live with machines, washers, dryers, cars and computers, and that today's child must imitate us by exploring toy miniatures of machines.

Children don't wait until three years until they become interested in other children. The interest comes even in the first year of life. Certainly, however, by this second year they like to play with other children, giving each other things. But they can do this most easily if parents of both children are present. Then the children feel safe to move forward and explore with each other.

A tip to parents: have as much coffee with your neighbors as you can stand. It's the best experience for your two-year-old.

THE THIRD YEAR

This is where pretending enters children's play. Until now, children have played with toys, dolls and trucks, but they haven't pretended to be people. That now becomes possible and they say they are mothers and fathers. You can also pretend to be other people for them—visitors, old people, babies. They learn that you can be flexible. In traditional cultures children did not learn this. Roles weren't flexible. But today's chairpersons, presidents and salespersons must be many faces to many people. They began to get their versatility in their childhood play by quickly shifting roles. Play has more to do with life than with academic learning alone.

Playing with other children is a passion for three-year-olds. They learn how to succeed in life, testing social responses out at their own level of competence. You can't give them this as a gift, as many an unfortunate parent of an only child has found out. The happiest child always has others with whom he can play throughout childhood. The maladjusted adult of every kind is most often the one who could not make it with friends when young. The creative adult is also the one who had much privacy and often much solitariness when young. The luckiest child has access to others, and also has a private world of his own where he can withdraw when he desires.

THREE TO SIX YEARS

At these ages, children can play roles with mock emotion—as angry parents, for example—and can also develop imaginary characters. They can have silly telephone conversations, read fairy tales, play with puppets, be a mimic and get excited together over gifts, birthdays and toys. They like doing things with other children, creating order out of their anarchic dispositions. They can play games, construct buildings, sing and dance to music or simply run madly about the playground.

Some new research shows that the imaginative child in this age group is less aggressive, happier, more flexible, skilled with words and sensitive to others than are children without much imagination. It is simply not true that disturbed people are more imaginative; in fact, disturbed people frequently tell you about their unimaginative hallucinations, while healthy people keep them to themselves.

In these years children are becoming public beings. They are beginning to be able to leave the family and its special protection and observe the rules in a number of other societies, including those of their friends, school, clubs, church and lessons. It is so much easier to master these if they have lived among people who show this flexibility in both their real lives and in their play. In their real lives they discuss alternatives and consider possibilities among themselves and with their children. And in play they show with their faces, bodies and words that they can be many people.

Play prepares them for considering choices. It doesn't necessarily make them ready for specific learning; rather, it makes many kinds of learnings available. Whether children choose to use them depends on what happens in real life. But at least if they've played, they have the choices in their repertoire. The most important law of learning for this age is perhaps the law of personal variability. This is the time when children must adapt to many rule systems. What play gives them is the confidence to invent others of their own.

33. Play Isn't Just Kid Stuff

SEVEN TO TEN YEARS

Play now becomes more recognizable in adult terms. It no longer deals largely with basic information about the world of adult roles and physical effects. Instead, children begin to take up the symbolic world which we are more familiar with—numbers, letters and words. These involve educational games, board and card games. Many teachers use them and they have become a standard part of the educational process. Children do learn basic concepts from these games.

What we tend to forget in this new acknowledgment once again is that children don't only need to explore these games; they need to create their own. There is much to be had in riddles (word meanings), secret languages (letter meanings) and trick arithmetic (numbers). The most important learning of this age is the learning of double meanings.

ELEVEN TO FIFTEEN YEARS

About the age of nine, fortunate children spend as much time with their friends as they do with us. They show a new capacity to organize their own societies. Those who have learned to take imaginative roles may now make imaginative societies. These can be game playing, performance giving or fund raising, and they should be encouraged. These children still need fair-minded parents who support both their autonomy and responsibility. Their minds by these ages are usually not able to work with great abstractions and multi-layered organizations. As a result, the children need to talk and talk their way into varying permutations of mental organization; and they need you to listen and listen as they practice these novel forms of organization upon you. Your playfulness about most things and firmness on the few that are fundamental for you will teach flexibility of thought and democracy of ideas.

We are suggesting that play makes possibilities for life, not mainly for schooling. Life is larger than schooling—in the kinds of knowledge we need to succeed. We must adapt to others as leaders, partners, followers; we must control business, organize materials and artifacts, keep schedules, create machines, order and reorder abstractions.

High schools and universities are playgrounds for practice in manipulating abstractions and categories, as well as for giving serious practice in fundamental skills. Play is mockery as well as mastery. It is folly and disorder. We must have more than one point of view to fully comprehend anything. Play permits our children and ourselves just that set of possibilities. It is a variable feast—and a feast of variabilities.

Worlds of Play

Donald Baker
Donald Baker is Principal Lecturer (Professor) in English and Drama at Weymouth College of Education, Weymouth, England.

SOCIAL ANTHROPOLOGY may seem a bit remote from early childhood education, yet a comparison of children's play activities in various parts of the world reveals some interesting aspects of play that are fundamental to a sound philosophy of education for the under-fives. Play is a universal phenomenon of human life. Even a cursory glance at worlds of play in the West Indies, Malaysia, West Africa, Europe or the U.S.A. is likely to indicate common elements that once formed part of Western culture but that have now been submerged beneath the inexorable tide of technology and urbanisation.

Two elements, spontaneity and structure, are evident in all play activities. We play as we *experiment* and *ritualise*, improvising when we meet new environmental experiences and establishing behaviour patterns from the responses we make to them. In play, we *become persons*, as the numerous personae, masks or roles we adopt in different social contexts are fused into that intangible something called a "personality." In play, we discover how to live in a particular society and on what terms (with what conventions, morals and mores) that society will accept us. Moreover, in play, we learn how society itself functions and on what socio-religious principles it is based. The ethos of a traditional or tribally structured society is preserved in its myths and legends which at one time were transmitted in dance, song and oral literature. Many of these activities still take place in Africa and Asia today—and, coupled with different attitudes towards the place children occupy in a traditional society, determine the kind and quality of children's play.

Perhaps the simplest and most objective means of comparing children's play in various parts of the world is by noting ways other cultures implicitly regard the use of space, time and people for play. In doing so, I believe we can discover certain basic factors that should make us question assumptions about the nature of play currently underlying our concept of early childhood education, especially in the Western world.

Space for Play

A major influence on the physical structure of play is climate. Climatic rather than overtly cultural differences between the tropics and Britain, for example, affect the availability of space that is unrestricted by adverse weather conditions. Quite simply, a child in Britain and in some parts of the U.S.A. often has to remain in the house because it is either too wet, windy or cold to play outside. This is not the case in the tropics.

In Malaysia, West Africa or on a West Indian island, the outdoors environment is generally available to children for use and exploration. Families live much of their time in the compound or street outside the confines of the home. The beach or bush may be close at hand. In Jamaica, for example, there is a tree to climb and to transform imaginatively into a ship swaying so violently in the high wind that children actually feel sick rather than pretend to be.

Admittedly, children in Britain play in a similar way, especially in rural areas where there are trees to climb. On the other hand, many of the play activities in tropical areas are not play at all but "for real." In some

34. Worlds of Play

cases, it would be difficult if not impossible to determine whether an African child helping mother with the home chores is playing or working. We will not go into subtle and controversial arguments here over the question as to whether the one who plays is aware of his playing; but without doubt fantasy and reality have fine and frequently imperceptible distinctions, especially for the very young child of whatever culture or clime. In the West Indies, for example, children actually go fishing, cook the catch and eat it. Play and work are fused.

In general, children from urban areas in Britain and America do not have this kind of opportunity as a natural and regular possibility, but only in special circumstances such as "outings" and "visits." Thus for most British and American children fishing is a play activity. Moreover, toys in the tropics are fabricated from natural materials like coconuts and cowrie shells or anything the environment provides rather than what an expensive toy manufacturer offers in the form of impeccably "educational" objects. And, incidentally, a lesson many adults fail to learn is that the toy accurately representing the real thing often has far less educational value than a natural object that can be imaginatively transformed into *any*thing.

Compound, beach, forest or any open areas easily accessible for play contrast sharply with the restricted or nonexistent spatial opportunities for play with which an urban child in Britain or the U.S.A. is very often confronted. Streets are traffic-logged and unsafe. Gardens in Britain have often shrunk or disappeared, and the only space for play may be a corner of a room or the tiny balcony of a flat or apartment. Consequently, physical constraints have produced emotional frustration, which in turn has frequently led to general learning problems. In the interests of efficient housing, straight rows of buildings and high-rise apartment blocks have appeared as ubiquitous monuments to "civilisation." Competition was once relatively unknown by American Indian children. Today, as a result, an Indian child is at a great disadvantage in the highly competitive society of the United States. The emotional problems of young American children, adolescents and parents have increased drastically—as every social worker knows only too well.

Spatially, play in the urbanised Western world has been reduced from a village square surrounded by field and forest to a city street and ultimately to a room with a box and screen instead of a view. Yet the urge to play remains: to express the energy of emotions in a physical way, to do something with one's body and voice. In these activities a child discovers not only his own potential, but also something about the people and things that occupy his widening world. Unfortunately, his world is usually not particularly wide and the emotional stress placed upon a child because he lacks physical space in which to play is readily confirmed by zoologists' research into caged animals. Almost invariably, animals kept in restricted surroundings display uncharacteristic aggression directed towards other animals and spectators. And it may well be that the explosions of violence in a large school or block of flats, or under any circumstances in which living creatures are herded together in anonymous numbers, is a natural result of being treated as if they were nothing more than inmates in an old-fashioned zoo.

To compensate for this deficiency of space at home, playgroups, day care centres and so on offer opportunities for physical play within their limited resources. They thus provide, albeit artificially, a space for play that at one time would have been part of the environment itself. In some parts of the world, playing space and living space are identical, a fact with considerable significance for the whole philosophy of play in early childhood education. This point comes into sharper focus when we turn to a second issue raised in worlds of play; namely, time for play.

Time for Play

A child in the tropics plays until he gets tired or hungry. But in the Western world, obsession with time is often the cause of temper tantrums as mother or father sweeps away the objects a child had been playing with. It is rather like switching off the TV just five minutes before the end of a gripping programme. The frustration and annoyance I experience when called to the telephone at a crucial moment in a TV drama reminds me that children are equally disturbed whenever their play sequence is suddenly and sometimes rudely interrupted.

Our notion of time is tied in closely with the work/play dialectic, in which play is

3. DEVELOPMENT AND EDUCATIONAL OPPORTUNITIES

regarded as an alternative to work. But watch a four-year-old working physically hard as he carries buckets of sand from one part of the beach to another. Years later, his movement of sand will be timed and costed; and the playful carrying of buckets will become a tedious task. Somehow, we need to prevent the leisure/labour, play/work dichotomy from arising too early. Ideally, we all need to maintain the element of playfulness throughout the whole of life, so that play and work, time for play and time for labour, are never separated. This integration may be an impossible dream, but reference to the play of children in various parts of the world indicates an alternative attitude to work that has important implications for the kind and quality of play activities we set up for our children.

Two practical points emerge from a consideration of time for play. *In the first place,* we need to identify with children in their play, to treat them as adults and helpers, not as "actors" performing "roles" in a "playtime." The play of children in other lands demonstrates that this involvement of children in the adult world and vice versa can be and is being done. And it begins at home, not in a playgroup.

Margaret Mead has drawn attention to the aimless tasks Western children are sometimes set, on the assumption that they are being encouraged to engage in creative or imaginative play. In fact, we may very well be inducing the distinction between the attitudes towards work and play that we should be trying to avoid as long as possible. "Samoan children," Mead writes, "do not learn to work through learning to play. . . . From the time they are four or five years old they performed definite tasks which have a meaning in the structure of the whole society." Comparing Samoan with American children, she states that "The difference lies not in the proportion of time in which their activities are directed and the proportion in which they are free, but rather in their different attitude." Because of this difference, she suggests, Western children make false distinctions among work, play and school.

A five-year-old, on being taken by his playgroup supervisor to his new first school in England, commented to his future teacher: "I'll come in the mornings. Then I'll go home and play with my toys." Rightly or wrongly, school had for him already become a tolerated interruption in the course of serious play. For play is always serious. Thus it seems to me that the first thing to do is to give children meaningful tasks that are, in fact, part of the total play/work worlds of child and adult. In home and playgroup, children must have real tools, real dough to bake, real woodwork, so that the actual world is, indeed, the world of play. A child knows no such distinction. What a pity that adults have to discover it at all!

In the second place, play, whether in a playgroup, home, day care centre or wherever, must avoid giving the impression of being "time out," an interruption in the flow of a child's everyday life or a period when a grownup is freed from work. The difference between play in Samoa, the West Indies and West Africa—and even the play of my own childhood—and the play or lack of it these days is in attitude and has much to do with our concept of time. I was especially fortunate in being allowed to try out adult tasks like papering and painting, cooking and cleaning, all "for real." But then the grownups had time for me; the task took longer and no doubt had to be done over again, but for me it provided involvement in the adult world. Though what I was doing may have been, strictly speaking, "play," as far as I was concerned it was serious work. Or *was* it play? A West African child does not pretend to fetch water; he fetches it. A Malaysian does not have to engage in make-believe home play; he or she helps to keep house by performing actual necessary tasks. In the Western world what we have to realise is that, for the young child, a time for play and a time for work is one time. As a four-year-old once remarked: "I'm playing at work!"

People for Play

One of the most remarkable features of modern life is the loss of face-to-face contacts. The intrusions of TV, radio and the telephone have disrupted a basic biological behaviour pattern: the response to visual signals given in facial and bodily gestures. Even our formal handshake has degenerated into an indefinite waft of the hand accompanied by an equally vague "Hi!"

In an overcrowded world, people physically draw back from each other, with a resultant failure to make emotional and even intellectual contact. We do not listen and we do not understand. The appearance of encounter groups—"group gropes" as they are cynically called—is a symptom of the spreading disease of isolation and loneliness so prevalent in the Western world.

But urban isolation is at least partly our own fault. A Japanese girl once described to me how in Japan a new family is welcomed into the community of the street with a party. In West Africa, the first thing to do is to announce one's arrival by calling on the neighbouring families; visits will then be returned and contact made. Once upon a time and place, we knew these conventions ourselves; and, in Britain, the street with its shop on the corner was the focal point for community and gossip. Unfortunately, as living space has contracted to a room and TV, time for play has been reduced to a time when the workaday world is set aside, and a child's play is no longer viewed as an involvement in adult activities that were once available in the extended family of aunts and uncles, cousins and grandparents living around the corner.

Furthermore, retreat from people is only one aspect of a more general retreat from the world of sensations. To encourage children to touch, to taste, to smell, to see and hear, literally to bring them into direct and immediate contact with the world with all its wonder and delight, is more important than the current emphasis on technological aids, concept-forming and teaching them logical thought. We cannot express what we do not feel.

Conclusion

Partly as a result of technological intrusion, then, we of the Western world spend more time watching TV than with any other leisure "activity"; and partly from physical overcrowding, which has forced people to seek a privacy they physically need but emotionally should avoid, we have lost or are in danger of losing the warmth and humanity of physical encounters. Even stories are now told on tape and TV and not by a live adult. Yet a Malaysian girl recalls that stories are what the old people tell the young, and a West Indian describes how stories are told to anyone who comes to sit under a tropic moon and listen. Maybe we can't do the equivalent and sit under a sodium street lamp; but, in education for the under-fives, the concept of communal listening face-to-face with the storyteller is fundamental.

Thus a playgroup, day care centre or kindergaten should become a family for a morning or even a day. Here, actual tasks can be undertaken, and people sit and listen to old tales retold. Nothing replaces the face of the storyteller, which needs to be seen, its animation reinforcing the lilt and pitch of voice.

Space for play, time for play, people for play, these are antidotes to the diseases of isolation, dulled sensibility and loss of contact with each other. To reach out and touch the world, the world that is still available and accessible to us, these are needs we have to meet, artificially if we must, but actually if we can. The play of children in other countries and of other cultures suggests that, in a child's mind, the activity we call "play" need not be separated either in time, or place, or people from the daily round and common task. Play is, at least in early childhood, an integral and inseparable part of them.

"Worlds of play" may imply worlds apart. In fact, it is our "estranged faces that miss the many splendoured thing." As an under-five observed, having heard the word "infinity" described as meaning "forever," "I want to play for infinity." His world had become a universe in which time and place and the distinctions between work and play had no meaning. He had discovered Utopia; and as Neville Scarfe has so aptly remarked, "A Utopia is a place where work is play."

Editor's note: British orthography has been retained to preserve the flavor of the original manuscript.

References

Mead, Margaret. *Coming of Age in Samoa.* New York: Morrow, 1971. Reprinted by permission.

Scarfe, Neville. "Play: An Agent for Learning Social Values." *Play: Children's Business.* Washington, DC: Association for Childhood Education International, 1974.

See also:

Baker, Donald. *Understanding the Under-Fives.* London: Evans Bros., 1975.

Ebbeck, Frederick. "Learning from Play in Other Cultures." CHILDHOOD EDUCATION (Nov. 1971): 69-74.

Strom, Robert. 'Parents and Teachers as Play Observers." CHILDHOOD EDUCATION (Jan. 1975): 139-43.

Child Rearing and Parent Education

Families, according to anthropologists, are the core of human society. What impinges on the family and its healthy functioning affects not only individual members, but society as well. As the number of families living in poverty increases, as more teens are having babies without benefit of stable partnership, as divorce rates climb, and as restrictive economic realities shatter the hopes of many families, the lives and destinies of children often suffer.

The responsibilities of raising children are met with mixed emotions and strengths by most parents, ranging from joy and amazement to bewilderment, loneliness, and despair.

Historically, early childhood education has included contact with parents since the 1890s social welfare movement in urban areas. Federal programs such as Head Start and most research and demonstration projects have had varying levels of parent participation which ultimately affect program effectiveness.

Rumors that the American family is collapsing coexist with reports that families, although changing, mobile, and stressed, are surviving, if not always thriving. Clearly, patterns of family structure and role definitions are in flux, as is the ability of many to deal with new expectations and demands.

The experimentation and changes in families have been accompanied by the production of a vast supply of materials and resources for parents and educators. With more than fifteen hundred books on child rearing available, adults can find highly contradictory information and advice—some well-documented, some merely unwarranted opinion, and some condescending in tone. The type of advice that seemed adequate barely a generation ago seems strangely naive and simplistic when measured against the endless complications of today's pressures felt by working parents, mothers with feminist leanings, or the special problems faced by teenage and single parents.

Educators, despite their training, experience, or personal preferences, will increasingly be pressed into service to communicate current information to parents on a wide range of topics: child development, health and nutrition, and the services of social agencies. This additional role of parent educator is usually faced with reluctance, or met with insecurity and apprehension by most teachers.

One tested rule for honest and effective communication is to take the same sympathetic non-judgmental view toward parents that is taken toward a group of young children.

A primary goal of parent education is to try to make parents feel more relaxed and free to enjoy child rearing. A secondary goal, also vital, is to enable children to feel that a genuine bond of cooperation exists between the home and the educational program; that parents and teachers are not working at cross-purposes.

No firm answers or tried and true laws can be offered to parents that will fit even the majority of situations existing in a culturally pluralistic society with widely divergent family patterns. What many parents seem to appreciate most is up-to-date information about their child, presented objectively and complemented by practical suggestions, and a nonevaluative listener who will respect their privacy and life-style.

This section presents issues concerning the effects on children of working mothers, teenage mothers, and single parents. Contrasting issues about the relative influence of home and school are included so that readers must examine their own beliefs and experiences.

Looking Ahead: Challenge Questions

As more mothers are entering the work force, are there guidelines to ensure that children will not be automatically uprooted and traumatized?

Why are so many teenage girls having babies and raising them by themselves? What are the economic and educational prospects for these young mothers?

What types of programs have been instituted by schools to support and educate parents?

What does research indicate concerning the effects of divorce on children's emotional needs, school performance, and personality changes? What can school personnel do to help both divorced parents and their children?

What do black and white parents need to know about prejudice so that their children can be raised to function with tolerance and understanding in a pluralistic society?

How much influence do parents actually have over their children's future chances for happiness and success? How vulnerable or resilient are children to parental influence?

Whatever happened to the Waltons?

Changes in the American family and how they affect the kids you teach

RICHARD L. ISAKSON

Alice Davis teaches six- and seven-year-olds in a major city. She spends an increasing amount of class time discussing her students' home life. Of 20 sets of parents, 17 are divorced or separated.

"A few years back," she said, "children would come to school, tell me about something that happened at home, and then dive into their work. Today, that's not possible. Children need more time to sort out things that happen at home. They need more attention and servicing in school."

As far too many educators have discovered, it is the elementary teacher who has been left to do the servicing. While not intentional, this situation has come about by default and is a result of changes in the American family.

What are these changes? How do they affect kids? What can teachers and parents do to strengthen the family structure? In the past teachers rarely asked these questions. But today's teachers must ask them before the start of this school year.

Prior to the 1800s life was centered around the family. Fathers worked at home mainly as farmers or tradesmen. Parents nurtured their children, educated them, and taught them a trade. In 1642, for example, there was a law in the Massachusetts Bay Colony whereby parents could be fined for failing to educate their children.

With the Industrial Revolution, fathers began leaving home during daytime hours, and children were no longer around both parents. Education shifted from the home to the school. By 1873 most states (except those in the South) reported average school attendance ranging from 50 to 80 percent for children five to 15 years of age. Society thus became compartmentalized. The home became the consuming unit, the factory a producing one, and the school a socializing center.

In 1900 two-thirds of all Americans lived in rural areas. But as industrial centers grew, families left small towns and villages to be near centers of work. However, if sons found work close to where they grew up, it was still possible for people to live near their extended families—grandparents, aunts, uncles, cousins.

Since the beginning of the twentieth century, our society has been going through major upheavals and technological revolutions, which affect family life. Today, pure economic survival—plus the American dream of getting ahead—means family members move more often and are separated from each other. In the pursuit of jobs, education, the good life, families change their location more than ever. Only half of all families have extended family members near them. Grandparents and other relatives are no longer around to provide role models for children or support for parents.

At the same time, the nuclear family has become smaller. Fewer children in the home means fewer older children providing young ones with links to other generations. An increasing divorce rate means more children are growing up in families with one parent. While in divorces of the past the fathers left home, today, a new trend is developing: Mothers are leaving home, too. Motherless families have increased in the last few years. It is estimated that up to 42 percent of all children born today will spend some portion of their lives with a single parent.

Also, more and more mothers work outside the home. Forty percent of those mothers with children under six are employed and 51 percent of those with children ages six to 12.

Finally, a startling number of children are born out of wedlock today—15 percent.

What are the effects of these changes on today's kids?

While family experts warn people against romanticizing about the past, the fact remains the family has changed. With fewer adults in the home and more working mothers outside the home, sociologists ask: Who is rearing America's children? In many cases, parents have turned over their responsibility for young children to day-care centers—from 1965 to 1975 the number of children enrolled has doubled.

Also, many older children return from school to empty homes and are what the British have labeled "latchkey" children.

35. Whatever Happened to the Walton's?

Urie Bronfenbrenner, noted child expert, identifies the empty home as one of the reliable predictors of trouble for children. According to Bronfenbrenner, the young person today "feels uninterested, disconnected, and perhaps even hostile to the people and activities in his environment." Bronfenbrenner attributes this alienation to the disorganization of the family.

Whether this is the cause of woe or not, statistics indicate children are in trouble. Increasing numbers are running away. The National Center for Health Statistics now estimates that one out of ten children between the ages of 12 and 17 will run away from home. Also, juvenile delinquency cases have risen sharply in the last 20 years. If the present rate continues, one out of every nine teenagers will appear in court before age 18. And during the last decade suicide has become the second leading cause of death among teenagers. The loss of a parent—through death, divorce, or separation—often occurs before a suicide.

Some educators blame the drop in reading scores directly on the changes in the family structure. Ruby Nelson, a vice principal in Rochester, New York, observes that those children born in recent years to young unmarried teenage women are now appearing in schools with decidedly less oral ability and preparation for reading.

The family has traditionally been essential for the socialization of children—to pass on knowledge, skills, and values necessary to help them feel competent and productive. If youngsters do not get these from their family they turn to the school or their peers. And today, at every grade level, children are identifying more strongly with their peers than they did ten years ago.

What can teachers do?

They must be careful not to blame parents who very often are victims of contemporary economic and social forces. But teachers can recognize the strengths in families and capitalize on those so that they can get on with the business they were trained for—teaching. There are several options.

One of these options is to join others in becoming child advocates. Many experts on the family are calling for an intensification of the services social agencies offer families. They claim families need more marriage and family counseling, more economic support, more programs like big brother and big sister, more funding for daycare centers, and even a cabinet-level Department of the Family in Washington. For some families, particularly young ones, increased support from social agencies may be the only means of survival.

Teachers should not take over the role of parent or attempt to become a second parent. They can, however, work to take the family into account in numerous ways and act in alliance with other institutions to strengthen the family, complement it, and, thereby, be able to carry out those functions teachers are trained to perform.

Teachers can become child advocates in their own community. They can speak, write, organize, and work with others to get the entire community involved in the care of children. This has been one of the major thrusts of the International Year of the Child in the United States.

Another option for teachers is to work to expand the school's role to meet the needs of today's children. Schools in Massachusetts and Illinois, for example, are lengthening their school day to provide increased services for children—offering after-school programs, music classes, and other recreational activities.

Teachers can arrange for children to spend part of the day observing adults in various roles outside of school. They can also help kids get involved in challenging responsibilities within the school and community that will promote connections to other generations. Teachers can set up programs so that kids care for the ill, the aged, the very young, and tutor younger students.

Dorothy Rich, founder and director of the Home and School Institute, recommends schools provide a family room so parents can visit teachers on an informal basis and bring their preschool-age children with them. Parents, in turn, become supportive of teachers, administrators, and school programs as well as help in the classrooms.

Rich also suggests schools have a "Featured Family of the Week" program highlighting one family with pictures and background information posted on a school bulletin board.

Field trips for the entire family provide time for families to interact. And children can, of course, be made aware of their origins through family history projects.

M. Donald Thomas, superintendent of the Salt Lake City, Utah, schools, proposes all children receive parenthood education so that future parents are aware of nutrition, the effects of drugs, and the problem-solving skills needed for family living today.

What can parents do?

Parents, too, can do more to strengthen the family, and teachers can give them suggestions, thereby acting as a catalyst. John J. Conger, author of several textbooks on child development, urges parents to continue to teach those values they believe are fundamental and non-negotiable. He suggests parents open their communication channels with children to eliminate sources of parent-child conflict.

This can be done by providing the kinds of settings Bronfenbrenner suggests in which young and old can simply sit and talk. "The fact that such settings are disappearing and have to be recreated deliberately, points to both the roots of the problem and to its remedy," he states.

Kenneth Keniston, author of *All Our Children*, urges parents to simply be more responsive, loving, and consistent, and to spend more time with their children.

Some parents are already making a deliberate effort. Herbert Otto describes their attempts in *Marriage and Family Enrichment: New Perspectives and Programs*. With help from their churches, families are organizing into family clusters. Three to five families form a unit to overcome isolation often experienced by the nuclear family today. Families meet together on a regular basis to have fun together, work, celebrate, and provide support.

Family camps and family weekends are two enrichment experiences that get parents and children away from daily routines and stresses and make it possible for them to talk, relax, and play together. Families are also setting aside one evening a week to be together to discuss problems, tell stories, plan events, play games, and make decorations.

In the final analysis, teachers cannot and do not want to take over as parent for a child. But they can remember that how a child learns may be a result of what is going on in his homelife. The American family is not changing by some conscious design on the part of parents. Thus teachers need to be supportive of both parents and children caught in the transition. A teacher is likely to find that increased sensitivity and understanding of the new patterns taking shape *will* help students be more productive in school.

The Consequences of Early Childbearing

Joseph H. Stevens, Jr.

Joseph H. Stevens, Ph.D., Associate Professor, Department of Early Childhood Education, Georgia State University, Atlanta.

The family is the crucible for the development of children. Its ability to nurture and respond decisively to meet the developmental needs of its children affects how they will function as adults. The very young mother and father are generally less able than their older counterparts to perform these functions because of attenuated education, more limited incomes, greater marital disruption, and more offspring. This review will examine how early parenthood can result in fewer resources with which to nurture and care for children, and will discuss the implications for needed support services to teenagers.

The Magnitude of Early Childbearing

In 1975 one birth in five was to a woman 19 years of age or younger. The number of births to girls 15-17 years of age increased 22 percent from 1966 to 1975. In 1976, 1,100,000 teenage pregnancies resulted in 570,672 live births, 378,500 abortions and 152,000 miscarriages or stillbirths (Tietze 1979). There are more teenage mothers among whites than among Blacks, but the birth rate among Black teenagers is higher than among white teenagers. Black teenagers are more likely than whites to have premarital sexual intercourse and then become pregnant (Zelnick and Kanter 1978).

Many of the large number of sexually active teenagers use contraceptives inconsistently and ineffectively. Other factors helping to bring about pregnancy among young girls include early and frequent social activity; early menarche; lack of knowledge about fertility, conception, and birth control; and early election of parenthood as a career. Social and cultural factors help determine how the pregnancy is resolved and the long term consequences of early childbearing and parenthood. For example, Blacks choose abortion and adoption as alternatives much less frequently than whites. Ethnic and cultural membership, social class, and family structure help shape the outcome of early parenthood for both parent and child.

Educational Attainment

Early parenthood often shortens educational attainment for women and men, and the attenuation is greater for women than for men (Card and Wise 1978). Moore (1978) found that women having their first child at age 15 completed two years less schooling than women who were still childless at 24. These younger women did not catch up during their young adulthood. For all women 22 to 34, those who had children when they were age 15 or younger completed fewer years of school than those having children even at age 16 or 17. White teenage mothers lost more schooling than Black women; however, substantial educational setbacks occurred for both groups.

Furstenberg's comparable data (1976) indicated that women who became teenage parents early completed two fewer years of school than a comparison group of classmates. Only half of the teen mothers were graduated from high school by the end of the five-year followup, compared to more than 80 percent of their classmates. More nonpremaritally pregnant classmates completed high school and enrolled in post-secondary education than did teenage mothers. Even those comparison classmates who experienced a premarital pregnancy later in adolescence were more likely to have completed high school and to have enrolled in post-secondary education than were the very young teenage mothers. These young teenage mothers' school careers were, however, uneven. They did not uniformly drop out of school without ever returning.

Personal and familial characteristics such as support from family members, academic ambition, and academic competence were related to amount of schooling completed. An index of educational ambition, which reflected educational goals, desire to return to school, educational expectations, and educational goals in relation to their friends, strongly predicted educational attainment. Teen mothers with high educational ambition were much more likely to complete school than mothers with low ambition (85 percent versus 8 percent).

Academic competence was also related to schooling completed; those girls who were at or below grade level were more likely to drop out. Adolescent mothers who perceived themselves as more competent students were more likely to complete high school. Mothers' expectations of their teenage daughters significantly influenced the girls' completion of high school. Less than one-fifth of the women whose mothers had high educational expectations for them dropped out of school, compared with over two-thirds of the women whose mothers had low expectations.

Economic Consequences

Delay of childbearing is associated with dramatic economic consequences, especially for women. Card and Wise (1978) reported that adolescent mothers had significantly lower incomes and were more likely to work in less prestigious jobs than women delaying childbearing. However, teenage fathers' incomes were not significantly different than those of classmates deferring fatherhood, though teen fathers were more likely to be blue collar workers.

Moore (1978) estimated that women at age 27 who had delayed having their first child earned about $153 dollars more per year for every year of delay. Further, women delaying their first pregnancy tended to reside in households where other earners contributed approximately $1,220 per year in additional income for each year of delay.

Half of the Aid to Families with Dependent Children (AFDC) funds distributed in 1975 were directed to women whose first child was born when they were adolescents (Moore 1978). This totalled 4.65 billion dollars, not including Medicaid (estimated at $161 per child), food stamps (estimated at $286 per household), or prenatal care and delivery (estimated at $1,135 per pregnancy).

One additional finding from Moore's study illustrates the complex interrelationships of these factors of adolescent pregnancy, educational attainment, and economic consequences. For all teenage mothers living in AFDC households, those that completed high school were less likely to receive AFDC subsequently than those not completing high school. Young mothers who completed high school were more likely to live in households receiving AFDC than were older teenagers completing high school. Thus welfare support may have enabled very young teenage mothers to achieve greater economic independence. Educational attainment was a potent predictor of economic well-being.

Teenage mothers who go on welfare often become independent later. In Furstenberg's study (1976), a third of the women who reported being on welfare earlier were not receiving support five years after the baby's birth. Over the course of the longitudinal study, about two-thirds of the mothers received welfare at some time. Other research supports a pattern of moving from job to welfare, to employment and non-welfare, and back again. Those teenagers most vulnerable to being on welfare were unmarried, with more children.

Most of the women in the study reported wanting to work. Educational status was a strong predictor of employment; mothers with more schooling and higher educational aspirations were more likely to be working

4. CHILD REARING AND PARENT EDUCATION

than those with less schooling and lower educational ambitions. The economic position or the structure of the family of origin (for example, female-headed versus two parent household) did not affect the probability of working. However, family size was negatively related to the chances of working; teenage mothers with more children were less likely to be employed than were women with smaller families. The relationship of marriage to working was less evident.

What were the patterns of economic support used by Black teenage parents in Furstenberg's study? Five years after the child's birth, the modal source of major income was the teen mother's own earnings (for about 25 percent of the mothers). Income from husband's employment and from welfare were the two most frequently reported major sources after the mother's own earnings. Three out of five teenage mothers were self-supporting or were the nonworking spouse of a working man. Sixty percent of the mothers reported some income from more than one source (own employment, husband's employment, welfare, parents, child's father, unemployment, social security). Nearly all (95 percent) reported receiving some money from their families.

Early parenthood increases the likelihood that one will be on welfare for a portion of one's life. Two-fifths of the respondents received some of their income from welfare, and proportionately more of the teenage mothers than their classmates indicated that more of their income derived from welfare than from other sources. Seventy-five percent of the classmates were supporting themselves in contrast to 45 percent of the teenage parents.

Working mothers were better off economically than those on welfare. Teens living with a working spouse were better off than those unmarried; those who reported more sources of income seemed to be better off than those reporting fewer. However, about half of all mothers were earning incomes below the poverty level.

Marital Stability

McCarthy and Menken (1979) analyzed data from more than 7,000 women in the 1973 National Survey of Family Growth. They looked at Black women and white women who were either 20 years and older at first birth or under 20. Most teens in both groups were married within two years of the first birth. About 68 percent of the teen parents reported marrying within nine months of conception, while 81 percent of the 20 year and older respondents married in this period. The likelihood of marriage varied significantly along ethnic lines. Whites were much more likely to marry prior to the child's birth than were Blacks. Among post-birth marriages, marriage within the three years after the child's birth was much more likely for white teens than for either white adults, Black teens, or Black adults. The high unemployment rate among young Black males, the high numbers of incarcerated Blacks, and the large number of Blacks killed in Vietnam may make marriage less of an option for Black women.

Furstenberg (1976) found that the single most potent predictor of marital success among the teen parents was the economic viability of the male. The probability that marriages would dissolve was significantly lower in those unions in which the male was a high school graduate and/or was a skilled worker, as compared to those in which he had not completed high school and was an unskilled laborer. Marital stability was greater in those families where men improved their economic status. Unlike the previous study where age appeared to be positively related to marital stability, Furstenberg found age was unrelated. He suggested that for Blacks, age alone does not improve employability or economic success (and thus account for greater marital stability). Economic viability of males may explain McCarthy and Menken's (1979) other major findings: Marriages among teens have high dissolution rates (these rates are higher for Blacks); and white teens are more likely to remarry than are Blacks.

Subsequent Childbearing

Teen mothers have slightly higher fertility rates than do adult mothers even when age at first birth is controlled. Moore's data (1978) on women who were between 35 and 52 years of age revealed that those who were 17 or younger at first birth had about five children while those age 20 years or older had approximately three children per family. The fertility rate decreased as mother's age increased. This relationship was stronger for Blacks than for whites.

Furstenberg's data also support increased fecundity among adolescents who became parents. At the last followup, teen parents had both more pregnancies (2.11) and more children (1.66) than did their classmates (1.00 and .69 respectively). Single adolescents gave birth to a second child more quickly than did single control group classmates. No differences in the timing of the second pregnancy were observed between the very young adolescent parents and their married classmates.

Trussell and Menken (1978) found that women who were age 15 to 17 at first birth had 36 percent more later-born children than did women age 20 to 24 years. When Blacks and whites are equated for age at first birth, differences in fertility disappeared. Prior to 1965 the pace of childbearing was greater for Blacks than for whites, but this has been reversed (Trussell and Menken 1978).

Parenting and Children's Development

More infants of teenagers begin their lives at risk than do those of adults; greater incidence of low birth weight, of infant morbidity, of mental retardation, and of birth defects has been found among teenagers' infants (Venturo 1977; Niswander and Gordon 1972). Yet the evidence about the long-term developmental consequences is contradictory. In a study of Black women, Field (1979) has reported some behavioral differences between teen and adult parents and between their offspring in the early months of life. Longer labor and more obstetric complications were observed for teenage mothers than for adults. This was particularly true for teen

36. The Consequences of Early Childbearing

mothers having preterm infants. Few of the variables examined (obstetric, behavioral, anthropomorphic, and attitudinal) significantly differentiated adult from teen parents or their children. Teenage mothers of term babies expected their infants to attain certain developmental milestones later than did adult mothers. However, teen mothers of preterm infants expected these milestones would appear much earlier, and their general childrearing attitude was more punitive.

At four months of age, babies of teenagers weighed less and were shorter. The mothers' perception of infants' temperament differed significantly. Infants of teens were rated less optimally by parents in their adaptability, approach to stimuli, distractibility, and level of activity. Face-to-face interactions of mother and infant were observed to be less optimal among teens.

Teenage mothers who participated in a parent education intervention program manifested more optimal interactive behavior than parents not in the program. Infants were developmentally more advanced on the Denver Developmental Screening Test. Their mothers had more accurate developmental expectations and rated their infants as having more desirable temperaments. Similar differences in favor of the intervention group were observed again at 8 months of age (Field, Wilmayer, Stringer, and Ignatoff 1979).

Others have also reported that teenage parents' expectations for their children's development are not accurate ones. Epstein (1978) reported that, among Black teen mothers, late developmental expectations were negatively related to awareness of the developmental significance of observed child behavior and parent-child interactions. For more than three years, DeLissovoy (1973) interviewed and observed a group of married white teen parents from a rural working class background. He reported both mothers and fathers had early expectations for normative behaviors. They were described as insensitive to, as well as intolerant of and impatient with, their infants.

In contrast, Dryfoos and Bellmont (1978) reported the absence of consistent data indicating an association between

4. CHILD REARING AND PARENT EDUCATION

poor social-emotional development and teenage parenting. However, they have reported small but positive relationships between maternal age and children's intellectual development among Blacks, but not among whites. Children of Black teenagers performed slightly less well on the Wechsler Intelligence Scale for Children.

Maracek (1979) reported similar results with a largely Black sample. She examined intellectual functioning and social development among the children of teen and adult mothers at 8 months of age, at 4 years, and again at 7. At 8 months no differences in motor development were found; small but significant differences due to age of mothers were found in mental development. Some differences were detected in spontaneous play, exploratory behavior, and social responsiveness in favor of children of the older mothers. At age 4, group differences in Stanford-Binet performance were not significant. At age 7, children of adolescent mothers scored an average of 2 Verbal IQ points and 5 Performance IQ points below the children of adults. Boys evidenced a larger difference than girls. There were also differences in school achievement. Children of adolescent parents were three times more likely to fail first grade. And at age 7, 12 percent of the adolescent mothers reported learning difficulties among sons, versus 4 percent of the older mothers. However, no information about comparability of the Black adult and teen groups in terms of income or family structure was reported. Should such differences be present, they may explain some of the above findings. Ratings of children's social behavior by project staff at ages 4 and 7 suggested greater maladaptive behavior among the offspring of adolescents, especially among boys.

The Major Consequences of Early Childbearing

Education	Both teenage mothers and fathers, but especially mothers, complete fewer years of school.
Income	The incomes of teenage mothers are lower than those of mothers who delay childbearing. The incomes of teenage fathers may differ little from those who father children later in life.
Marriage	Most teenage mothers whether Black or white marry within a few years of their first birth. These marriages are more likely to dissolve than are those among adults. The economic viability of the male was a strong predictor of marital success among Blacks.
Subsequent childbearing	Women who begin their childbearing careers early have more children than those delaying their first birth.
Children's development	Consistent and substantial differences in intellectual and personal-social functioning of the children of teenage parents and those of adults have not yet been confirmed. Some evidence has suggested earlier marriage, earlier childbearing, and larger families for the children of teenage parents.
Family support	Support from the extended family enables the single teen mother to complete school and become economically independent.

Furstenberg (1976) found that maternal age at first birth was unrelated to five-year-old children's performance on the Caldwell Preschool Inventory. Measures of children's ability to defer gratification, of efficacy, of trust, and of self-esteem revealed no differences between the children of younger teens and of their classmates' children.

Card (1978) examined the long-term consequences of adolescent parentage for cognitive functioning and for personality development. When background characteristics of race, socioeconomic status, and birth order were controlled, initially significant (but small) differences in both cognition and personal-social behavior in favor of the children of non-teenage parents disappeared. Being reared by a teenage parent was unrelated to the cognitive and personality development of offspring in adolescence. Note that the offspring of adolescents in father-mother households had higher academic aptitudes; those in parent/step-parent families were the next highest; next were the single-parent children and last the children in households headed by adults other than the parent. Card also reported that the children of adolescent parents were more likely to marry early, have children early, and have more children.

Family Help

The transition to parenthood for many boys and girls is a heavy burden, especially for the young single girl. She is most likely to experience educational setbacks and obtain marginal income. Initiating motherhood early in life may result in parenting as a career choice which results in slightly larger families. Marriage, especially to one who completed high school and was stably employed, diminished the negative economic consequences (Furstenberg and Crawford 1978).

Support and help from the family of origin substantially reduced the possible detrimental effects of early parenthood. Single teenage mothers who continued to live with their family of origin were more likely to return to school, graduate, and secure jobs, and were less likely to end up on welfare. Conversely, single teen women who moved out of the family home more frequently permanently dropped out of school. More were unemployed and on welfare.

Single parenthood and an out-of-wedlock pregnancy may not doom a young female to poverty and welfare, especially when the extended family provides help and support. Such help from the family network is especially forthcoming in Black families (Furstenberg 1976), though this is also likely to occur within other ethnic and social groups, especially Hispanics and white ethnics.

Implications

Early parenthood makes optimal child-rearing substantially more difficult. Teenage families are less likely than older parents to be able to support the optimal development of their children, especially in the child's early years. There are, however, teenagers who are skillful parents. What then are the implications of these data for services to teenagers?

36. The Consequences of Early Childbearing

First, for primary prevention, educational programs about sex, conception, contraception, and parenthood are essential for teens and their parents. Effective education for parenthood courses in junior and senior high schools probably are potent preventive measures. Community-based media campaigns such as television and radio spots may be another. Yet if present trends continue unchecked, Tietze (1979) has estimated that 34-39 percent of all of today's 14-year-old girls will have at least one pregnancy before age 20. Twenty percent will give birth; 15 percent will obtain an abortion; and 6 percent will have a stillbirth or a miscarriage. However, if all adolescents became consistent users of contraceptives rather than occasional users, the number of premarital pregnancies could be reduced by another 40 percent (Zelnick and Kanter 1978).

Next, for secondary prevention, support programs for teenage parents should be established. Continuation of schooling, particularly completion of high school, is directly related to employability and income—especially for women. Schools will need to plan with the pregnant teenager and her family for the completion of schooling. While programs designed to support teenage parents in returning to school may be more successful with teenagers who are highly ambitious educationally and those having family support for continued schooling, other teenagers also must be targeted for help. Feasible and realistic combinations of vocational education, academic coursework, and parenting education, reflective of the mother's and the father's abilities and interests, will have to be developed. This may suggest expansion of work-study programs developed by the school and local industry.

Inexpensive, convenient, and effective child care services will need to be developed. Secondary schools may be appropriate sites. Schools can facilitate the development of child care systems providing center care, family day care, or outreach training programs for the relative who cares for the child in the home. Such services will need to avoid disrupting and displacing the child care services provided by the teenager's ex-

4. CHILD REARING AND PARENT EDUCATION

tended family. For many families this care will be preferable. Instead, early educators can work to complement and strengthen the work of these parent surrogates. For teenagers choosing center or family day care, these child care workers will need to develop a willingness to communicate with and involve all those with major responsibility for the child's care in the home: grandparent, mother, father, aunt, uncle, or great-grandparent.

Comprehensive service programs for teens can no longer target just the mother and include only discussion of the mother-child relationship. Further, where appropriate, programs can support and strengthen the older adult and teen-parent relationship so that it becomes a mutually supportive and growth-fostering one. The program can help the teen maintain, build, and constructively utilize a network of helping relationships with a variety of significant others. In addition to the father, this may include both the mother's and the father's families of origin. If the skill, knowledge, and resources of the members of the teenager's social network can be enhanced, it is likely that the child's development will be strengthened.

The content of the parent education component of a comprehensive service program for teenage parents is critical. Important objectives are the development of realistic behavioral expectations for children, as well as sensitive, reciprocal patterns of adult-child interaction. It may be that group training programs for adolescent parents that use other teen parents as peers may be more effective than individual consultation programs alone. Parent education programs for teenagers enhance parents' behavior and children's development (Field, et al. 1979; Badger, Elsass and Sutherland 1974).

The U.S. Office of Adolescent Pregnancy has mounted a national effort in secondary prevention. Recently, Congress enacted Titles VI, VII, and VIII of the Health Services and Center Amendment Act to fund comprehensive community service programs for teenage parents. These programs must furnish an array of "core" or direct services and of "supplementary" or coordinated services including: pregnancy testing and maternity counseling; family planning; primary and preventive health/nutrition services; sex and family life education; educational vocational counseling/ training; and child care. A few programs were funded in the fall of 1979. Whether this federal program is expanded with additional appropriations, as expected, will soon be evident.

The increase in births to very young teenagers is a sobering challenge to early educators. One important contribution we can make is to design and implement appropriate child care services and parent education programs. Yet to establish the array of comprehensive services which are needed by teenage families demands that we work collaboratively with a variety of institutions and professionals.

I would like to thank Russell Irvine, Cecelia Sudia, and Ralph LaRossa for their very helpful comments on an earlier draft of this review.

Single reprints are available for $1 from NAEYC, 1834 Connecticut Avenue, N.W., Washington, DC 20009. For multiple copies, request permission to reproduce from NAEYC.

References

Badger, E.; Elsass, S.; and Sutherland, J. M. "Mother Training as a Means of Accelerating Childhood Development in a High Risk Population." ERIC Document Identification No. ED 104 522.

Cannon-Bonventre, K. and Kahn, J. "Interviews with Adolescent Parents: Looking at Their Needs." *Children Today* 8, no. 5(1979): 17-19.

Card, J. J. "Long Term Consequences for Children Born to Adolescent Parents." Mimeo. Palo Alto, Calif.: American Institutes for Research, 1978.

Card, J. J. and Wise, L. L. "Teenage Mothers and Teenage Fathers: The Impact of Early Childbearing on the Parents' Personal and Professional Lives." *Family Planning Perspectives* 10(1978): 199-205.

DeLissovoy, V. "Child Care by Adolescent Parents." *Children Today* 2(1973): 22-25.

Dryfoos, J. G. and Belmont, L. *Intellectual and Behavioral Status of Children Born to Adolescent Mothers.* Progress Report. New York: Alan Guttmacher Institute, 1978.

Epstein, A. "Adolescent Parents and Infants Project: Preliminary Findings." Mimeo. Ypsilanti, Mich.: High/Scope Educational Research Foundation, 1978.

Field, T. *Early Development of the Premature Offspring of Teenage Mothers.* Miami, Fla.: Mailman Center, University of Florida, 1979.

Field, T.; Widmayer, S. M.; Stringer, S.; and Ignatoff, E. "Teenage, Lower Class Mothers and Their Preterm Infants: An Intervention and Developmental Follow-up." Mimeo. Miami, Fla.: Mailman Center, University of Miami, 1979.

Furstenberg, F. *Unplanned Parenthood: The Social Consequences of Teenage Childbearing.* New York: Free Press, 1976.

Furstenberg, F. and Crawford, A. B. "Family Support: Helping Teenagers to Cope." *Family Planning Perspectives* 10(1978): 322-333.

McCarthy, J. and Menken, J. "Marriage, Remarriage, Marital Disruption, and Age at First Birth." *Family Planning Perspectives* 11(1979): 21-30.

Maracek, J. "Psychological and Behavioral Status of Children Born to Adolescent Mothers." Paper presented at the meetings of the American Psychological Association, New York: September 1979.

Moore, K. A. "The Social and Economic Consequences of Teenage Childbearing for Women, Families, and Government Welfare Expenditures." Mimeo. Wahsington, D.C.: The Urban Institute, 1978.

Niswander, K. R. and Gordon, M., eds. *The Collaborative Perinatal Study of the National Institute of Neurological Diseases and Stroke: The Women and Their Pregnancies.* Philadelphia: W. B. Saunders, 1972.

Sameroff, A. J. and Chandler, M. J. "Reproductive Risk and the Continuum of Caretaking Casualty." In *Review of Child Development Research,* Vol. 4, ed. F. D. Horowitz. Chicago: University of Chicago Press, 1975.

Tietze, C. "Teenage Pregnancies: Looking Ahead to 1984." *Family Planning Perspectives* 10(1978): 205-207.

Trussell, J. and Menken, J. "Early Childbearing and Subsequent Fertility." *Family Planning Perspectives* 10(1978) 209-218.

Ventura, S. J. "Teenage Childbearing." *Monthly Vital Statistics Report* 26, no. 5, Supplement. DHEW Publication No. (HRA) 77-1120. Washington, D.C.: Health Resources Administration, 1977.

Zelnick, M. and Kanter, J. F. "Contraceptive Patterns and Premarital Pregnancy Among Women Aged 15-19 in 1976." *Family Planning Perspectives* 10(1978): 135-139.

Article 37

When Mommy Goes to Work...

What happens to her kids' emotional development... her husband's ego... her own self-esteem?

SALLY WENDKOS OLDS

Sally Olds has three daughters, aged 15, 18 and 20, and has worked part time or free lance in public relations and journalism ever since her youngest was a year old.

It used to be easy to diagnose the problems of children whose mothers worked outside the home—a group of youngsters that today totals more than 27 million in this country alone. Is Mary overly dependent and whiny? That's because she doesn't see enough of her Mommy. Does Billy do badly at school? Poor thing, he doesn't have the loving attention of a mother who could help him with his homework. Is Freddy stealing candy bars from the corner store? He wouldn't if he had Mom's guidance at home!

Such assumptions may seem logical, but they just don't hold up when scrutinized under the research microscope. As social scientists delve more deeply into the effects on children of their mothers' working, their findings are turning out to be quite different from long-accepted beliefs.

Let's take a moment for a brief history lesson. Twenty-five years ago, only 1.5 million mothers were in the labor force. Today, 14 million are. As late as 1940, only one female parent in ten worked outside the home. Today, four in ten do. Before 1969, most women with children between the ages of 6 and 17 spent their days at home. Today, the United States Department of Labor reports that a record nine million women with children 6 to 17 years old are working. In fact, nearly three million have little ones aged three to five, and over two and half million have babies under three!

With employment patterns shifting so dramatically, it's only logical that we reevaluate our long-held beliefs about child care and babies' needs in general—beliefs that for years have kept mothers tied to their babies' cribs for fear of sparking emotional and psychological traumas later on. Most of our baby-care gospel (example: "children need a loving mother at home") is based on studies of hospitalized youngsters conducted during the 1940's and 50's. Not surprisingly, researchers found that infants in understaffed institutions, who were cut off from familiar people and places and who were cared for by a bewildering succession of hospital nurses, eventually suffered severe emotional problems. Valid as these studies may be, they tell us nothing about babies who, though looked after by competent babysitters or day-care workers during the day, are reunited with their own loving parents come evening. Fortunately, studies of the last decade have sharpened and reinforced this distinction.

In 1973, for example, Harvard University pediatrician Dr. Mary C. Howell surveyed the voluminous literature on children of working mothers. After poring over nearly 300 studies involving thousands of youngsters, she concluded: "Almost every childhood behavior characteristic, and its opposite, can be found among the children of employed mothers. Put another way, there are almost no constant differences found between the children of employed and nonemployed mothers." To wit: Researchers found both groups equally likely to make friends easily or to have trouble getting along with their peers, to excel at their studies or to fail, to get into trouble or to exhibit model behavior, to be well adjusted and independent or to be emotionally tied to the apron strings, to love and feel loved by their parents or to reject them.

Just recently, Harvard psychologist Jerome Kagan and two researchers from the Tufts New England Medical Center, Phillip Zelazo and Richard Kearsley, zeroed in on the possible effects of day care on the emotional and developmental progress of infants whose mothers worked, as compared to children raised by their mothers at home. As the yardstick for his evaluation, Kagan used three characteristics considered "most desirable" by parents: intellectual growth, social development and ability to achieve a close relationship with the mother. His results? Provided the center was well staffed and well equipped, Kagan and his colleagues were unable to find *any* significant differences between the two groups of children.

Since a mother's working per se is no longer considered a crucial factor in a child's development, what factors *are* important? To find out, let's examine the problem from a different perspective. Instead of thinking in terms of working and stay-at-home mothers, we'll divide women according to whether or not they *enjoy* whatever it is they are doing, and here we can see the differences emerge.

Back in 1956, psychologist Jack Rouman traced the progress of 400 California school children and found that the emotional problems they suffered were related not to their mothers' employment status but, rather, to the state of their mothers' emotions. He concluded: "As long as the child is made to feel secure and happy, the mother's full-time employment away from the home does not become a serious problem."

Take Linda Farber, a Philadelphia city clerk who hates her job, is bitter at her ex-husband for leaving her, making it necessary for her to work, and who feels tied down by her six-year-old son, Greg. He, in turn, is wetting his bed again, gets stomachaches every morning before school and is withdrawing from other children. On the other hand, Marjorie Gorman would love to return to the personnel office where she worked before her kids were born, but her husband insists, "It's your duty to stay home with the children."

37. When Mommy Goes to Work

According to anthropologist Margaret Mead, who has examined child-rearing patterns around the world, the notion that a baby must not be separated from its mother is absurd.

Marjorie is bored and restless. Annie, her oldest daughter, has run away from home three times, has thrown a kitchen knife at her parents and is habitually truant.

Of course, these children's problems are not triggered simply by their mothers' attitudes about work. But maternal unhappiness and resentment is easily communicated to other members of the family, and can, indeed, influence the quality of home life.

Studies undertaken by University of Michigan psychologist Lois Wladis Hoffman bear this out. She found that employed women who enjoy their jobs are more affectionate with their children and less likely to lose their tempers than mothers who are disenchanted with their daily work. Furthermore, those who are content with their situations are more likely to have sons and daughters who think well of themselves, as measured on tests of self-esteem, than are resentful workers or unhappy homemakers. Following a 1974 review of 122 research papers on working mothers and their children, Dr. Hoffman concluded, "The dissatisfied mother, whether employed or not and whether lower class or middle class, is less likely to be an adequate mother." Norwegian psychologist Aase Gruda Skard agrees: "Children develop best and most harmoniously when the mother herself is happy and gay. For some women the best thing is to go out to work, for others it is best to stay in the home."

For Ellen Anthony, staying at home to care for her small baby was stifling. "I need to work," she insists. "Without some outside stimulation and a way to discharge pent-up energy, I become bored and aggressive. Now that I'm back at my public relations post, I don't overpower my daughter and husband so much and we're all happier." Carol Brunetti, on the other hand, left a good job as a department store buyer to devote full attention to her infant son. "I haven't missed my job for a minute," she says. "I love the flexibility of making my own hours. And whenever I want to go somewhere, I just take Jason along with me."

But Mom's attitude is not the only one that must be taken into consideration. No one will argue the fact that the happiness of both mother and children also depends on the father: How a husband feels about his wife's working is crucial to the emotional climate within the home. And his attitude is a distillation of many things—whether he considers himself a success or a failure at his own profession, what the basic marital relationship is like and how willing he is to assume a fair share of the management of the household and the children if his wife takes a job.

Obviously, the woman whose husband approves of her working is lucky: Balancing job and family is never easy, but when a wife has to do the juggling herself, as well as contend with a husband's opposition, it's twice as difficult.

Happily, many a man who was originally opposed to his wife's working has discovered that he likes spending more time getting to know his children, that money problems have lessened and that he and his wife have more to talk about now that she's also exposed to new people and situations.

Although many psychoanalysts continue to stress the need for an exclusive relationship between mother and baby, recent research has shown that such relationships are probably the exception rather than the rule, even in families where the female parent does not go out to work. For one thing, most fathers today are vital figures in their children's lives. A 1974 study by Milton Kotelchuck of Harvard University found that one- and two-year-olds are just as attached to their fathers as to their mothers. And for another, the typical baby in our society is cared for by several other people in addition to its parents.

According to anthropologist Margaret Mead, who has examined child-rearing patterns in societies around the world, the notion that a baby must not be separated from its mother is absurd. Babies are most likely to develop into well-adjusted human beings, she says, when they are cared for "by many warm, friendly people"—as long as most of the loved ones maintain a stable place in the infants' lives.

There's the rub. For many working mothers, finding these "warm, friendly people" to care for their children on a long-term basis is often a frustrating and expensive proposition. Experts agree that the following scenarios are probably the most stable (and, in turn, most successful), especially for babies and toddlers:

- A father who is able to dovetail his work schedule with his wife's so that their child can be looked after by one parent or the other.
- A grandmother, other relative, friend or neighbor who cares for a child in his or her own home.
- Family day care—an arrangement similar to the one above but between people who have not previously met, often arranged by a public agency.
- A full-time babysitter who comes to the house five days a week and may perform housekeeping chores, too.
- A well-run, well-staffed day-care center.

But once the parents have made the decision that Mommy should work, what about the kids? How will *they* take to their mother's new role—and if they don't, what can you do to make them understand?

Most likely, children will have mixed feelings about Mommy's new job. David, nine, whose mother is the only working mother on the block, sometimes asks her, "Why can't you be home when I get home from school like Mark's mother? She always gives us milk and cookies." But the day David's class visited the dress factory where his mother works, he proudly explained her role in designing the clothes they saw being produced.

One woman met her child's resentment head-on. After ten-year-old Lisa had asked for the umpteenth time, "Oh, why do you have to work, anyway?" her mother stopped what she was doing, sat down with her daughter and explained just how important her job was to her. She let Lisa know that she understood the child's annoyance but she made it clear—without getting angry—how unhappy, bored and restless she would be staying home.

A group of 11-year-olds told an investigator that they loved the responsibility of using their own keys to let themselves in and out and they relished the privilege of having the house to themselves for a few hours after school.

What can both parents do to help children more readily accept their mother's employment? Child-care experts suggest that you:

- Plan your schedules so that at least

4. CHILD REARING AND PARENT EDUCATION

one parent is with the baby for half his or her waking hours during the first three years of life.
- Institute new child-care arrangements a week or so before you start a job, so that your child has a chance to get used to the new set-up.
- Don't take a full-time job for the first time or make a big change in child-care arrangements when your baby is between six months and a year old, or between one-and-a-half and two-and-a-half. Try to wait a couple of months after any major upheaval—such as a move to a new home, a long illness or the break-up of a marriage.
- Keep in close touch with whoever is caring for your child and consider her or him a partner in nurturing.
- Plan "child time" into your schedule when your youngsters can depend on having some uninterrupted time with you. It need not be long, but it should be regular.
- Let your children know how much they mean to you, and that they mean more to you than your job.

"The mother who obtains satisfaction from her work, who has adequate arrangements so that her dual role does not involve undue strain, and who does not feel so guilty that she overcompensates, is likely to do quite well and, under certain conditions, better than the nonworking mother," insists Dr. Hoffman.

In other words, it's not a matter of "whether" or "where"—but of "how" the woman who works balances the seemingly conflicting elements in her life. As one magazine editor explains, "I feel I have the best of both worlds—I love my family and I love my work, and every day in every way I feel a little better about being me."

We want your advice.

Any anthology can be improved. This one will be—annually. But we need your help.

Annual Editions revisions depend on two major opinion sources: one is the academic advisers who work with us in scanning the thousands of articles published in the public press each year; the other is you—the person actually using the book.

Please help us and the users of the next edition by completing the prepaid article rating form on the last page of this book and returning it to us. Thank you.

CRISIS IN THE CLASSROOM

Youngsters who used to sit still began to roam around. Others daydreamed a lot. An important new study observes these children of divorce in their schools and suggests ways that teachers and parents can help

Joan B. Kelly and Judith S. Wallerstein

Joan B. Kelly, a clinical psychologist, is co-principal investigator of the Children of Divorce Project at the Marin Community Mental Health Center, Greenbrae, California, and engages in private practice and consultation in Marin County.

Judith S. Wallerstein is principal investigator of the Children of Divorce Project and lecturer at the School of Social Welfare, University of California at Berkeley.

For most of an hour, Saul angrily protested the excessive demands being made on him by his sixth-grade teacher. "How can he expect me to do all this work when I'm so busy thinking of the divorce? It's not fair!" Normally a good student, Saul was unable to finish assignments or prepare for tests. When he was admonished for incomplete work, he sullenly fled the classroom. Had he explained his distress to his teacher? "No," said Saul, "my teacher wouldn't understand . . . he doesn't even *care* . . . he just wants my work!" Saul's distressed and angry preoccupation with his parents' divorce had interfered with his ability to concentrate, and now everything seemed to be falling apart.

Carol's second-grade teacher reported that the girl seemed relieved, "lighter, more carefree," after her parents' separation. Then, two months later, Carol began to whine and cry, often begging for her classmates' possessions. "She eats all her lunch by 10 in the morning," said the teacher, "then pleads for more food at lunchtime because she has nothing left." Carol told her teacher she no longer cared about her schoolwork.

Saul and Carol, and other youngsters like them, demonstrate one of the dilemmas facing the schools in understanding the children of divorce. There is no single response to divorce that can be observed in the classroom and, thus, no simple guidelines for recognizing divorce-related behavior and emotional change.

Recent research confirms that divorce precipitates a major crisis in the lives of most children, and that the stress engendered by the crisis often spills over into the academic arena. Youngsters accustomed to the structure and familiarity of the two-parent family react at first to separation and divorce with disbelief, fear and anxiety, even when their parents' marriages had been grossly unsatisfactory.

Despite the absence of single or uniform indicators of divorce-related stress, children and adolescents whose parents are divorcing do share common feelings and concerns that are complexly woven into their school behavior. These shared anxieties appear in various configurations and with varying intensities. The particular pattern of each child's response depends on his or her position on the developmental ladder, the child's unique personality and the psychological ambience of the period, particularly the amount of conflict between the parents.

The material presented here is part of a five-year longitudinal study of 60 Northern California divorcing families and their 131 children, aged three to 18 at the time of the marital separation. The children and adolescents were predominantly white middle class and, with two exceptions, lived with their mothers after the separation. A full report of the entire project appears in a recently published book, *Surviving the Breakup: How Children and Parents Cope with Divorce* (Basic Books).

REACTIONS TO DIVORCE

With few exceptions, the children in our study viewed their parents' separation and divorce as extraordinarily stressful. Fewer than 10 percent of them were relieved by the divorce decision, despite considerable exposure to intense marital conflict and physical violence between their parents. Even when their parents' marriages were badly flawed, in fact, most youngsters thought their family had been sufficiently nurturing and protective, and its collapse created intense fears about their own well-being.

Contributing heavily to the children's anxiety was the fact that many of them received less attention from their parents following the separation. Preoccupied with their own distress and efforts to cope with divorce, many parents were less sensitive to the children's distress and had little energy to deal with its manifestations. Moreover, many mothers went to work full time and so were physically less available, and fathers were out of the household. Many youngsters felt they had nowhere to turn for support, creating a loneliness that at times was overwhelming.

In this regard, the high incidence of divorce seems not to blunt the children's distress. It seems to matter little whether others in the neighborhood or classroom have also faced divorce. Each child struggles alone with the individual meaning of his or her own family disruption, and solace is not to be found in numbers.

The youngsters' fears and anxieties were myriad, but we found two important recurring themes: Who will take care of me? And will my relationship with my father and mother last? The youngest children, in kindergarten and first grade, worried about basic issues of caretaking: Who will protect me? Who will feed me? Who will love me? The older children, from nine to 12, expressed many anxieties about not having enough money for food or clothes, or just for pleasure. Several worried about their parents' smoking habits: "If my mother dies of cancer, what will happen to me?" Regardless of age, the youngsters felt they now faced a world that was suddenly less reliable, less likely to be concerned with their future hopes and needs. Their preoccupation with the newly felt unpredictability of life invaded much of their thinking and attention.

Continuity in the parent-child relationship was of vital concern. The younger children watched the marital relationship dissolve and concluded, not unreasonably, that the parent-child relationship could also come apart. In their confusion, they needed to be reassured that their parents still loved them and would still be parents despite the divorce. The young child's clinging to the parent, or to the teacher, reflected this fear of abandonment. And older youngsters worried, too, about their parents' continued concern. When a father failed to call or visited only sporadically, they feared he had lost interest and no longer cared about them. When a mother came home late from work, children admitted to fears of abandonment, fears they had not felt before the divorce. The youngsters worried, too, about their parents' physical and mental health. Some became little caretakers, reversing roles as they saw a depressed or lonely parent flounder. They monitored their parents' moods, looking for indicators that would ease their own anxieties or, conversely, cause more concern about the stability of their relationship with each parent.

Another common theme in the divorce experience for children was sadness and yearning. In the first several months following separation, more than half of the youngsters were pervasively sad and moody, often tearful. Some of these children were acutely depressed and showed it through restlessness, deep sighing, concentration difficulties, a severe narrowing of their interests and creativity and various physical complaints.

For the older children, the nine- to 12-year-olds, the loss of the familiar family structure and the continuity that had been for them somehow implicit in the intact family was a central focus. Although they sometimes expressed it directly, more often these older youngsters coped with their sense of loss by feigning indifference or covering their sadness with disdainful anger. And while family disruption was also an issue for the five- to eight-year-olds, the younger children's sadness focused more directly on the absence of the father from the household. The intensity of their yearning for his return was often profoundly moving.

The majority of the youngsters were not satisfied with the frequency of their visits with their fathers—even though 40 percent of the children and adolescents were seeing their fathers at least once a week and another 25 percent had contact two or three times a month. Certainly, the traditional visiting pattern of "every other weekend" was considered insufficient by the majority of these youngsters, and where it prevailed, either because of the mother's hostility or the father's disinterest, it created even more distress.

We found that children of all ages hoped their parents would be reconciled. These wishes can be understood as efforts to cope with the children's painful sense of loss. Such hopes for family reconciliation persisted longer than we expected and existed side by side with an intellectual recognition of the finality of the divorce.

And, finally, a rise in aggression was noted in children of all ages. Increased irritability, outbursts of temper and pushing and hitting of siblings and peers were evident in the younger school-aged children. The older youngsters, starting in particular at about nine years of age, were more prone to direct, angry, verbal attacks. Often explosive and intense, the anger of the older youngsters, especially the boys, was directed most often at the father, but frequently at both parents as well. Fathers and mothers alike complained of new and uncharacteristic rebelliousness in their children and looked for guidance in managing their growing discipline problems.

Concerned about the extent to which the divorce crisis interfered with the learning process, we undertook to study the academic and social functioning of the youngsters in our project. With their parents' permission, we interviewed the children's teachers and recorded in detail their observations of the children's functioning and behavior in the early months following the separation, noting any changes they observed. The interviews, which were fairly lengthy, focused on academic achievement and skills, peer and adult relationships, attitudes toward learning, capacity to attend and concentrate in class and any other divorce-related information the teachers volunteered. Similar interviews were repeated at two subsequent follow-up points (18 months and five years after the separation), but only the data from the initial school interviews, which were conducted about six months following the separation, are reported here.

Teachers frequently did not know that a child's parents were divorcing. It has not been the custom of our society for parents to share personal information with the school. Some parents worried about prejudicing their children's teachers against the children by labeling them "children of divorce." More prevalent, however, was the failure of many parents to understand that a major crisis in the life of the child would reverberate in behavior and performance in the school setting; nor did these parents realize that, to deal constructively with alarming changes in the child, the teacher should know about the underlying problem.

Our overall experience with the teachers was mixed. Some were marvelously sensitive to the child's distress and responded accordingly. Many were themselves divorced parents, and the increased sensitivity they gained through observing their own children often enhanced their ability to recognize and meet similar needs in their students. They seemed especially eager to learn more of divorce and its impact on children. But even within this group, individual experience could influence sensitivity and willingness to reach out to the child. If, for example, the teachers' own children were coping well, they might expect that other youngsters should also do so, without being aware of family differences.

A few teachers expected children to continue to function academically as if nothing had happened, even when they knew about the divorce. Their sharp impatience with daydreaming and incomplete work reflected the notion, supported in large measure by society, that children should be little affected by such matters and that, at the very least, they should put aside their distress during school hours.

Our own view is that teachers should be informed of such major changes in a child's life so that they can be as supportive as possible. Beyond that, we believe the education of teachers needs to be expanded to include a more comprehensive, complex view of the psychological development of children, including the effects of both temporary and prolonged stress.

BEHAVIOR IN SCHOOL

According to their teachers, about two thirds of all the youngsters showed some notable changes in school following their parents' separation. While the youngsters differed in the intensity and the manner in which they expressed their distress, responses affecting academic achievement were the most common. For more than half of the students, teachers reported a high level of anxiety—most often in the form of new and unaccustomed restlessness. Children who used to sit and do their work now seemed to roam about the room constantly, interrupting classroom activities.

Not surprisingly, along with the rise in anxiety and preoccupation with the family dissolution came new problems in concentration for many children. Nearly one quarter of the youngsters had severe difficulty concentrating on schoolwork, while for others, the interruptions in attention were evident but not totally disruptive.

Sometimes the older youngsters consciously struggled to marshal their attention, but it was clear that maintaining their usual good work took tremendous effort. A typical example was Jack, who was upset about all the reading his fourth-grade teacher assigned. "It takes me *twice* as long to read a sentence or paragraph," he told us, "and then I have to read it again because I forget what I read." He started to cry. "It's going to be a *terrible* year. . . . I don't know if I'll make it."

Parallel to the rise in concentration difficulties was a substantial increase in daydreaming. As with anxiety, restlessness and decreased concentration, we found that there were no significant age or sex differences in the youngsters who began to daydream substantially more following their parents' separation.

And, finally, teachers noted considerable sadness or depression in one fifth of the youngsters. This reaction was more evident to them with the youngest children, who showed their feelings more openly in school. And the combination of intense sadness, daydreaming and concentration problems resulted, for one fifth of the students, in a significant decline in academic achievement during the several months following the separation.

These changes in behavior seemed to be unpredictable in terms of their onset. Some teachers saw fairly immediate shifts, while others noted more gradual change. There was no relationship between the tempo of the changes in behavior and the child's age, prior academic achievements or amount of conflict between the parents. The children seemed to respond according to their own internal timetables.

Some youngsters retained their ability to function academically but lost considerable ground with classmates because they expressed their anxiety in ways that the other youngsters found jarring. Dana was unaware of her rising voice and, according to the teacher, "screeched at her friends." An only child, the tension she expressed at school with her peers reflected the intense anxiety generated by the disorganized and immature behavior of her overwhelmed mother.

Unfortunately, behavior like Dana's often alienated, at least temporarily, the very youngsters from whom the children normally received solace and companionship. Their friends had no way of understanding their bewildering shifts in behavior, and the teachers did not know how to help. While they felt comfortable calling to

4. CHILD REARING AND PARENT EDUCATION

the children's attention their classroom behavior, or comforting the children themselves, the teachers never addressed the children's now precarious interactions with their peers in such a way that the teachers' advice could be understood and, therefore, helpful.

For some youngsters, the divorce precipitated gradual changes in both academic and social life. Todd began to feel that his fifth-grade teacher did not like him. Despite his history of good grades and enjoyment of school, he thought school was "no fun" anymore. Initially sad after the separation, within several months Todd could no longer accept constructive criticism from the teacher. He became increasingly irritable and started many fist fights on the playground. In explaining his behavior to us, Todd said, "The littlest things make me mad." Todd's changed behavior was linked to an emerging depression, the result of severely diminished contacts with his adored father who was withdrawing from him following a remarriage.

More subtle changes that many teachers described very much paralleled our own clinical observations. They talked of children increasingly seeking them out, needing more attention, wanting (in the early grades) to sit beside them or on their laps. As one second-grade teacher said at a workshop, "These are the kids that are waiting by the gate when I come to school in the morning."

We found the teachers' reports particularly valuable, since they allowed us to compare the children's divorce-related behavior in a variety of settings. We were interested to find that there was no high correlation between their behavior and responses in the school, at home and in our office. Students who showed real change at school were not necessarily the same ones who expressed vigorous responses at home, or with us in the office. And some angry youngsters, newly irritable and difficult to manage at home, continued their exemplary behavior at school.

Jason, for example, was fondly described by his second-grade teacher as "a highly motivated child, scholastically. He wants to be tops in his class and he is. Jason has adjusted really well to the divorce. . . . He speaks equally of both his father and mother, which I find unusual with children whose parents are divorcing. He's entirely delightful!" At home, however, Jason's anger was spilling out in frequent temper tantrums, obscene notes left for his mother's boyfriends and disruptive dinner table scenes.

In contrast, some of the youngest children tried to be on their best behavior at home, cooperating with their mothers, helping out with chores and maintaining a generally cheerful demeanor. But their efforts to cope with stress often fell apart at kindergarten, where teachers noted episodes of crying "over nothing," frequent flareups with other children about the use of toys and what appeared to be an intense need to cling to the teacher for support and direction.

Some of the older youngsters, while upset by the divorce, continued to function both at home and at school with minimal observable disruptions. That was especially true for adolescents whose capacity to function academically had become reasonably autonomous and therefore less vulnerable to temporary disruption. But even these students felt intense personal struggles that were not necessarily evident to their teachers.

THE SCHOOL AS A SUPPORT

The school represents the most continuous institution in the lives of the many children each year whose parents divorce. Two central questions, then, are: To what extent can children in crisis use the school as a supportive network? And, to whom are which aspects of school useful, and in what respects? We found that the school served as a support system in diverse ways for different children of different ages. As with other support systems outside the immediate and extended families, however, the child's ability to use the school in a supportive way in the midst of crisis increased significantly with age.

First, it was clear that school was useful precisely because it provided structure in a child's life at a time when *the* major structure of life, the family, was crumbling. Going to school daily, being required to perform certain tasks in and out of school, having routine social contacts—all of these "structural" supports could potentially help a child adapt to divorce. It was evident that many children were supported by school in this basic way, regardless of the quality of their academic and social functioning in the classroom.

Second, there was the support provided to those children who enjoyed coming to school and whose academic achievements sustained and nourished them. Such children, who worked hard, got good grades and received praise for their efforts, were not the majority, however. Our findings suggested that school served as a good support system in this sense only to those children who were of above average intelligence, who were doing well academically to begin with and who were psychologically some of our healthier youngsters. They were not necessarily dependent on the teacher to be a supportive figure, although a good relationship was helpful.

And third, some children were helped in school at a time of high stress by their close relationship to, and reliance on, a friendly teacher. Kindergarten children climbed into the laps of teachers to receive nurturance and solace. These and older youngsters stayed close by, checking often to receive assurance that they and their work were OK. The comfort the teacher provided was important to those who sought it because it temporarily reduced anxiety and brought a small measure of security.

But such nurturance did not necessarily have staying power in terms of influencing the child's ultimate capacity to cope with the divorce. The richness of the school experience in some cases was insufficient to stave off the eroding effects of the divorce turmoil at home, or within the child. For that reason, we believe it is important for teachers who observe children's continuing need for reassurance and solace to discuss their vulnerability with their parents before the children's progress in learning is seriously compromised.

Ironically, we found that the high reliance of five- to eight-year-olds on the teacher as a support system was closely linked to their capacity to use their mothers in the same way and the mothers' ability to respond. Thus, some youngsters received support on several fronts in their efforts to deal with the divorce, while others seemed to have no one.

Youngsters nine years old and up, moreover, most often turned to teachers for support and comfort when they were turning to siblings and peers as well. In short, those who were capable of seeking out the assistance or solace of others did so in a fairly wide circle. Some older boys whose fathers did not visit them turned to extended family and a teacher as reliable sources of support.

In general, however, fewer children than we had hoped really used or were capable of falling back on the school network. And, with the exception of the youngsters (particularly girls) whose reliance on the school was linked to good intellectual capacity and performance, we found little evidence to suggest that the availability of the school as a support system really shaped the child's eventual outcome. The course of the child's future, as seen five years later, was linked much more strongly to the network and quality of support provided by both parents.

What additional support can the schools provide? While this important issue deserves its own forum, we would like to make a few observations:

☐ *Teacher awareness.* The classroom teacher who knows about and is sensitive to the indices of stress in children whose parents are divorcing is a potentially rich resource for children and parents alike. To that end, we have tried to summarize here some of the major reactions of children to divorce and point those who are interested to more detailed information.

☐ *Teacher willingness.* As crucial as awareness is the teacher's willingness to act on that knowledge. The empathic teacher, recognizing the child's distress, can provide a setting that makes the most of the child's efforts to cope. While continuing to maintain high standards and expectations, a teacher can still acknowledge the youngster's temporary difficulty in meeting classroom responsibilities. We have found that simple indications of support—"This is a hard time for you, I know"—can be the highlight of a distressed child's day.

☐ *Curriculum and attitude changes.* With more than one million children and adolescents experiencing divorce each year, it is time to formally acknowledge the widespread existence of the divorced family. As we said earlier, there is no solace in numbers. Yet the devotion, until recently, in curriculum materials to the two-parent, intact family has certainly created a greater sense of aloneness, of differentness, in many children. Classroom teaching that acknowledges and discusses the many possible variants of family life—one-parent households, father-headed and mother-headed; remarried families; two parent families; extended families—makes children feel secure with their own particular family structure.

☐ *After-school care.* With the majority of women working in the aftermath of separation and divorce, a central problem that creates anxiety for parents and potential difficulties for children is the after-school time when millions of youngsters are unsupervised and unattended. They are our new generation of latchkey children, but many of them do not have keys. Using the school facility for after-school care for youngsters up to 12 years of age is a logical solution. Some creative and successful programs incorporate town or city recreation workers and activities, charge sliding-scale fees and use the school's bus system to bring the youngsters to a central location.

☐ *Adult education programs.* In many areas, parent education groups focusing on divorce have provided helpful information and support to parents and, through them, to their children, in the midst of divorce. There is much to know and understand about divorce-engendered behaviors and feelings, as well as activities that help parents cope with their own distress, and the educational framework is an ideal one for providing such support.

The high incidence of divorce in the past decade produced profound changes in family life and structure. We have found that many children are greatly affected by the initial separation and divorce experience and the subsequent changes in parent-child relationships, economics and overall stability in their lives. When observed one year later, however, many of the youngsters in our study had coped successfully with divorce-related changes, were no longer overtly distressed and functioned quite satisfactorily in both the academic and the social spheres. Others, however, were found to be in considerable trouble—some of whom remained so from before the divorce, and some of whom were newly experiencing difficulties in learning.

Because we recognize learning to be one of the central developmental tasks for all youngsters of school age, our own concern has been the extent to which the divorce crisis interferes with the process of learning. Certainly, temporary interruption in this process may turn into significant academic problems if the child is not able to resume his or her attention to learning within a reasonable period of time. Divorce-engendered stress may compromise children's receptivity to learning, their willingness to venture into new materials, their ability to concentrate and their overall attitude toward learning and the school setting. Children in the earliest stages of mastering reading may be most vulnerable to the disorganizing effects of family disruption, but older children need a continuing sense of achievement to maintain positive attitudes toward learning.

It is critical, therefore, that teachers and principals be sensitive to the ways in which the stress of family breakup can disrupt, even if temporarily, their youngsters' ability to participate in the learning process. Such awareness, and the willingness to provide a supportive setting for the distracted youngsters of divorce, will combine to make the school more responsive to the changes wrought by a decade of divorce. In so doing, schools will continue to meet their primary responsibility—helping all children learn at the level of their highest potential.

REFERENCES

Hetherington, E., and Deur, J. "The Effects of Father Absence on Child Development." *Young Children,* vol. 26, no. 4 (1971): 233-48.

Hetherington, E., et al. "Beyond Father Absence: Conceptualization of Effects of Divorce." Unpublished paper. 1975.

Hetherington, E., et al. "Divorced Fathers." *Family Coordinator* 25 (1976): 417.

Kelly, J., and Wallerstein, J. "Brief Interventions with Children in Divorcing Families." *American Journal of Orthopsychiatry,* vol. 47, no. 1 (1977): 23.

Kelly, J., and Wallerstein, J. "The Effects of Parental Divorce: Experiences of the Child in Early Latency." *American Journal of Orthopsychiatry,* vol. 46, no. 1 (1976): 20.

Kelly, J., and Wallerstein, J. "Part-time Parent, Part-time Child: Visiting After Divorce." *Journal of Clinical Child Psychology* 6 (1977): 51.

Wallerstein, J. "Responses of the Pre-School Child to Divorce: Those Who Cope." In *Child Psychiatry: Treatment and Research,* edited by M.F. McMillan and S. Henao. New York: Brunner/Mazel, 1977.

Wallerstein, J., and Kelly, J. "Divorce Counseling: A Community Service for Families in the Midst of Divorce." *American Journal of Orthopsychiatry,* vol. 47, no. 1 (1977): 4.

Wallerstein, J., and Kelly, J. "The Effects of Parental Divorce: The Adolescent Experience." In *The Child in His Family,* edited by E.J. Anthony and C. Koupernik, vol. 3. New York: John Wiley and Sons, 1974.

Wallerstein, J., and Kelly, J. "The Effects of Parental Divorce: Experiences of the Child in Later Latency." *American Journal of Orthopsychiatry,* vol. 46, no. 2 (1976): 256.

Wallerstein, J., and Kelly, J. "The Effects of Parental Divorce: Experiences of the Preschool Child." *Journal of the American Academy of Child Psychiatry,* vol. 14, no. 4 (1975): 600.

BLACK CHILD / WHITE CHILD

Alvin F. Poussaint, M.D.

Associate Professor of Psychiatry, Harvard Medical School, co-author with James P. Comer, M.D., "Black Child Care."

"I never mention race," protested a black mother when asked how she approached racial matters with her children, ages eight and ten. She did not permit "racial talk" at home around the children because it upset and threatened her. This well-meaning parent explained that she wanted to protect her youngsters as long as she could from the pain of being black.

Unfortunately, there is no escape from the racial conflicts with which children must cope. Four and five-year-olds are already aware of the racial problems in America. Although the greatest exposure to racial topics for children is at home and in the neighborhood, children also must inevitably confront racial issues in school, on television, in the movies and through any number of their own encounters.

In trying to help children handle racial feelings, avoiding the problem isn't helpful. Too much parental protection from life's realities may hamper a child's later ability to cope with life as it is.

Black Parent/Black Child

Black parents have an especially difficult job. They must rear their children to be free of prejudice as they help them to develop a positive black identity in the face of prejudice and social handicaps.

It is important to emphasize that black children develop a sense of pride primarily through identification with their parents and other black adults. Although slogans such as "Black is Beautiful" have their place, catch phrases alone cannot do the job. If black adults are free of self-hatred and comfortable with their identities, their children will absorb these feelings of security in a natural manner.

A family life-style that reflects confidence and self-respect is the key ingredient in teaching black children self-esteem. This task is made easier if the black parent has tried to instill racial pride in ordinary day-to-day ways without shielding the child from racial realities. For instance, dolls should be of different races. Black parents, like white parents, shouldn't give their children dolls of only their own color. Black children, like white children, should have both black and white dolls to play with. All children need to grow up able to live in a world with people of many races.

How a black child faces a racial issue at the age of ten, say, will reflect his parents' child-rearing style during the youngster's early years. Much will depend on how parents respond to the innocent but searching questions that children ask. The rule of thumb in these situations is to be calm, not to overreact, and to give simple answers appropriate to the child's age. For example, one black mother went into a tizzy because her six-year-old called his skin color "dirty" and wanted to know why the dirt didn't wash off. This mother was thrown into a turmoil because she feared that her child was developing a "negative identity." She broke down in tears and screamed, "Don't you ever say that again." She succeeded in frightening the child and increasing his tension and confusion over skin color. This child was searching for an explanation, and in his own way showing curiosity normal for a six-year-old child. In this case, a simple supportive explanation is called for, such as, "People have different skin colors—brown, white, black, yellow—and you have a pretty brown color like Mommy and Daddy; it isn't dirty and it doesn't wash off." If the child asks additional questions, then the explanation should be continued until he feels satisfied.

Young black children will have similar questions about hair texture, facial features, and other characteristics. In fact, it is not uncommon for a black five or six-year-old to say, "I want to be white." The black parent, on hearing such a remark, should be calm and investigate. Some children may say it to test their parents—so don't fall into the trap by overreacting. Others might be expressing a wish to look like their friends, but this does not necessarily mean that they reject blackness. Some children may have been exposed to name-calling or other forms of racial hostility. The parent may have to question the child about such experiences. Be supportive and reinforce the fact that his skin, hair and features are attractive, though different from Caucasian characteristics. Be sure that the child is exposed to black heroes, role models and friends. This simple approach may suffice and the "wish to be white" may slowly disappear.

Many parents find it difficult to restrain an immediate emotional response when their child has been hurt by racial cruelty, but it is important to try and comfort and explain instead of reacting angrily. For example, if a black child is called an ugly word like "nigger," a black parent cannot just fly into a blind rage but must reassure the child that he is a good person and whites who call him such names are not nice people. At the same time, the parent must not encourage the child to be anti-white, but should stress instead that there are good and bad people in both races. In this situation the mother or father can help the child to be assertive, and at least say to the name-caller, "I don't like you calling me bad names and I want you to stop." On the other hand, parents should not suggest acts of violent retaliation because such behavior can damage the emotional well-being of their own children, as well as the name-callers. Attempts should be

4. CHILD REARING AND PARENT EDUCATION

made to talk out problems first, although fights among children—on any issue not just race—are sometimes unavoidable. If a situation of this type gets out of hand, parental intervention may be necessary, but children should be encouraged to try to handle such situations alone. Then, if a similar incident occurs later, he or she will be better able to deal with it.

Black parents have a special responsibility to help their children develop coping mechanisms that don't compromise their children's dignity. Black children should never be encouraged to "adjust" in ways that demean them. Fortunately, most black parents today do not have to be told that they should not raise their children to play the stereotyped roles of "Uncle Tom," "Aunt Tomasina" or "Sambo."

White Parent/White Child

White parents have different issues to face in raising their children free of prejudice, but the basic approaches are similar. The white child, like the black child, will take his cues and attitudes from the adults around him. Therefore, the first step for white parents is to examine their own attitudes toward blacks and other racial minorities. Questions that white parents might ask themselves range from the simple to the subtle:

1. Do you feel black people are inferior?
2. Do you frequently find yourself feeling hostile to blacks?
3. Do you tend to generalize about blacks, particularly in negative ways such as, blacks are violent, sexually immoral, smell differently?
4. Would you be upset if your child attended a school with blacks or had black playmates?
5. Would you object to a black neighbor?
6. Do you hesitate to invite blacks to your home for social occasions or do you include blacks among your friends?
7. Would you object if your teenage son or daughter dated a black person?
8. Are you opposed to interracial marriages?

If most of your answers to the above questions are "yes," you will have difficulty raising your child free of prejudice. However, if you hesitate only around the issues of interracial dating and marriage you have less of a problem, but you may still harbor biased attitudes that your children will detect and absorb.

It is not enough for white parents to be passive or inactive on racial issues, merely refraining from saying or doing prejudicial things. For, in such cases, their children may absorb the prejudices that are prevalent around them or grow up ignorant about other racial groups. If white parents are willing to try to understand and eliminate their biases, in order to help their children develop healthy racial attitudes, there are things that they can do for themselves and their children.

Youngsters are frequently afraid of the strange and unusual. Many white children, when they are unaware that different racial groups exist in our society, may on a first encounter with blacks see them as frightening. For example, a white mother reported that her five-year-old was afraid of black children and even became afraid of her own mother when she returned from vacation with a deep tan. The mother, who considered herself progressive on racial issues, did not know where her daughter had picked up such feelings. But on further questioning it was clear that the child had no black playmates and had never seen her parents socialize with black people. In addition, her toys, dolls and storybooks were all white or white-oriented. The parents seldom made informative comments when the child saw blacks on television or occasionally in the movies.

White parents should consciously expose their children to different ethnic groups—directly when possible, but at the very least through toys, dolls, storybooks and family discussions. This exposure will help the white child to have feelings of recognition and respect for the black children whom they encounter in school or in the playground. Unfortunately, many of our neighborhoods are so racially segregated that opportunities to mingle are few for both white and black children. This is sad, and it is one of the reasons that school integration is so crucial if we are going to raise a new generation of children with improved racial attitudes.

But even where there is community and school integration, there are likely to be problems. A frequent question from white parents is what can they do when their children have had negative experiences with black children, such as fights, for example. A mother said her eight-year-old son avoided black students at school because some of them picked on him and were belligerent. She felt her son was now beginning to dislike all black people. In situations such as this, parents must try to help their child have positive experiences with other black playmates. They should also remind the child—as black parents should remind their children when they are exposed to prejudiced actions by whites—that there are good and bad people in all races. They can also point out that there are white children, whom he doesn't like, and explain that this doesn't cause him to hate all white children. They may also point to black sports figures, TV personalities, schoolteachers and others whom the child admires.

It would also help if white parents explained that some black children have had difficult social experiences themselves, because of racial prejudice in society, and that these experiences might have made them feel angry toward whites. This is not to excuse a particular black child's behavior but to help the white child understand some of the larger social issues. In no case should white parents allow their children to accept abuse from black children because they feel guilty about being white. Relations established with blacks because of deep white guilt are usually unhealthy for both parties. Good friendships are based on mutual respect and equality and not on the subjugation of either person. Moreover, don't paint a picture of blacks as being so downtrodden that your child develops a patronizing attitude toward them. This is important to remember because white children who are unconsciously condescending become upset and confused when black children react negatively to them. The white child may feel that he's being friendly when he says, "Blacks really know how to play football and dance." However, the black child may hear it as a patronizing remark.

Such incidents call for sensitivity on the part of all parents. Should black parents encourage their children to be more tolerant of awkward attempts of white children to be friendly? Can white parents be astute enough to detect patronizing attitudes in their children and help them to change, or will they react with anger that a "friendly" gesture by a child was scorned? Patience, tolerance, respect and understanding on both sides are important if such issues are to be resolved constructively.

Often, delicate racial encounters create the most anxiety and conflict. A white father felt quite liberal because of his social activism in black causes until his fifteen-year-old daughter asked him how he would feel if she dated a black student in her class. The father was completely flustered and said he didn't think that it was a good idea. The daughter, who was testing him, was surprised and upset. The father later realized that despite his progressive racial attitudes, when it came to his own family he had drawn a line at the point of interracial dating, even though he did not intellectually condone these feelings. After this confrontation, his daughter accused him of being a hypocrite and became increasingly rebellious.

The lesson here is that under certain circumstances it is better to be honest about one's limitations and prejudices. If white parents have reservations about interracial dating, they should discuss them honestly without getting angry and defensive. If their reasons are because they believe blacks are inferior, there may be serious conflicts with their children. But if they believe that interracial couples have to endure certain social hardships (which is true), they have a responsibility to discuss these matters with their children. It may surprise some white parents to know that a great many black parents are just as opposed—perhaps even more so—to interracial dating and marriage as are white parents. In both cases, it is most important that neither white nor black parents reject their children for interracial dating or marriage. The bonds between parents and children should remain strong, particularly when children are facing outside problems. Although as it happens, our society is changing rapidly and even the difficulties for interracial couples are diminishing.

Interracial Parents

This brings me to a final point of current concern—what about the children already growing up in interracial homes? Because children of interracial couples—black-white, or black-oriental, or black-Indian, and so on—are defined by society as black —many of the approaches already discussed are the same. Interracial parents should follow the advice given to black parents. But in the case of a black-white couple, the white partner must make a special effort to understand the black experience in order to be as helpful as possible to their children.

Similar advice is in order for white parents who adopt a black child. Such parents cannot pretend to be color-blind because the adopted child will have to face a world that treats him as a black. Therefore, it is crucially important that white parents in these cases expose themselves to other blacks and learn all they can about the issues of being a black person in America.

Black parents, white parents, interracial couples, and white parents with black or racially-mixed children—all can take affirmative steps to help their children grow up with a positive identity themselves, while also remaining free of racial prejudice. We can raise children to be both humane and appreciative of the wealth of cultural experiences that different racial and ethnic groups have brought to America. Given the racial conflicts and misunderstandings which permeate our society, we cannot expect this change to happen automatically. A change in racial attitudes during the next generation will come only from our positive efforts today.

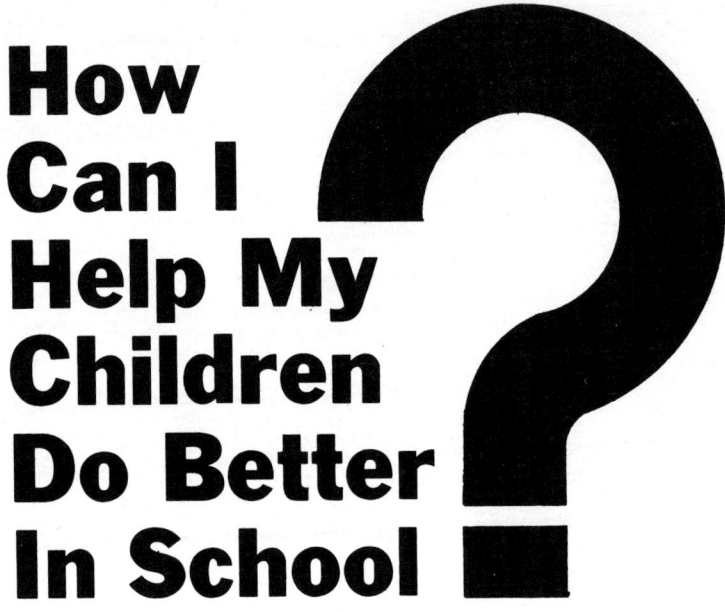

How Can I Help My Children Do Better In School?

Edward L. Stranix

Edward Stranix is house director of the Rhodes Middle School in Philadelphia.

Twenty-five clip-out suggestions teachers can give parents who ask the perennial question

How can I help my children do better in school? Teachers and school administrators have heard this question from parents since schooling began. Up to now, some standard answers have been: "Keep in touch with what's going on in your child's school life"; "Meet the teacher"; "Join the P.T.A."; "Do volunteer work at school."

All of these are good suggestions, and thank goodness for parents who are involved in school activities. But parents can do *much more* to help their children do better in school—particularly with basic reading and pre-reading skills.

Following are ways you can suggest for parents to help their children and, in the process, become partners in learning with the school. Though employing these techniques takes no educational training, it does take time. It's worth it. Some of the suggestions may seem obvious, but there's no reason to assume that most parents follow them all. If presented as answers to parents' specific questions or as general, non-condescending reminders, they can serve you well. Consider sending all parents a checklist similar to this one and include a letter to introduce it.

Twenty-five Ways to Help Your Children in School

1 Keep your children healthy. Should the school nurse or doctor inform you that your child has a health problem, discuss it. He or she can help get the assistance you need. Seeing, hearing and feeling well are essential to learning.

2 Talk with your children. Talk naturally. Don't use baby talk no matter how young the child. The more words a child can understand and say, the easier it will be for him or her to learn to read and to understand.

3 Listen to your children. Encourage them to talk about their everyday activities. Make sure you give them the chance to initiate conversation during meals and on other suitable occasions. Your children will learn to express themselves if they know you will give them your attention.

4 Praise your children. Praise and recognition reinforce learning. Reading, for example, is enjoyable, but it's also hard work for children. They need your support and encouragement. Praise them when they succeed and help them when they are having problems.

5 Be patient with your children. Even though you work with them and help them with their homework, they may make the same mistakes many times. Don't despair. Some experts say that new learning sometimes requires more than 15 repetitions before it is absorbed. It's most important that you do not become angry or impatient, since learning cannot take place in a tense atmosphere. If you find yourself "losing your cool," just stop and do something else for a while.

6 Avoid comparing your children. Each child is unique. Some children learn faster than others. If your children seem to be moving at a slow rate, don't blame them or worry them about it. It's too early to make comparisons anyway, for your children may have an as yet untapped reserve of attributes and talents. Let them know you love them for what they are and that you will continue to love them no matter how they do in school.

7 Set the stage for good homework habits. Try to provide a quiet, well-lighted place for study, and make sure there is room for books, dictionaries, papers, pens, pencils and other homework tools.

40. How Can I Help My Children Do Better in School?

8 Schedule home study on a regular basis. To succeed in school many children need a regular study time each night free of interruptions and distractions. If your children are not given a homework assignment, this scheduled time can be used for review, reading for pleasure or some type of family or learning activity. It's a good idea to provide each of your children with a notebook so that he or she—and you—will always know exactly what the assignments are. This notebook will also serve as a written record of all assignments and will help to organize review and study of previous material.

9 Set a bedtime and stick to it. Learning is hard work and requires full use of all faculties. Your children will be in the proper frame of mind and otherwise ready for learning only if they report to school each morning well-rested.

10 See that your children's school attendance is excellent. When children miss school, they may miss the presentation of new information or the mastery of a difficult concept. Once they fall behind their group, it's especially hard to catch up. Some children can never quite adjust after frequent or extended absences from school.

11 Know exactly how your children are doing in school. If you find out that they are having academic or other problems, don't wait to be contacted by the school. Take the initiative by making an appointment to talk it over with the teacher. If you can't get to school, send a note asking the teacher to contact you by telephone. Find out how you can help. Perhaps you can provide information about your children and family that will help school people respond with greater understanding to your child's situation.

12 Make family mealtimes meaningful. Mealtime can provide the ideal setting for talking together, sharing events of the day and discussing individual problems and aspirations. In a relaxed, family atmosphere, youngsters have a chance to test their debating skills in friendly arguments and to talk out their differences of opinion. Such discussions will help develop your children's self-confidence and encourage them to speak up in the classroom. Don't allow TV to interfere with this perfect opportunity for family communication.

13 Make television your servant, not your master. Children learn a lot from television—both good and bad. Help them choose appropriate programs to watch. Then watch with them and, afterwards, discuss what you've seen. This approach to television can help your children develop new interests that you can encourage them to read about.

One system for choosing programs carefully is to get the family together once a week to consider the television listings. Go over the listings as you would a restaurant menu. (In a restaurant you wouldn't order just anything.) By choosing carefully in advance, you'll help your children form the habit of considering television as only one of many entertainment/learning tools available, and you'll give them a valuable thinking and decision-making experience.

14 Take your children places. Visits to nature and science centers, art museums, train and subway stations, airports, farms, factories, shipyards, supermarkets, pet shops and so on will help broaden their experiences. Such diverse activities are vital in readying young children for reading.

15 Read with your children. It's a rare child who is not delighted to be read to by a parent or older friend, but it's important to read *with* your children, not only *to* them. Not long ago, I saw a young teacher trying to read a book to a small group of five-year-olds. The children kept interrupting with questions and comments, frequently turning back a page or two and saying such things as "Let me see the lion again" and "See the mouse with the hat?" Finally the teacher said in an angry tone, "Do you want me to read this story or not? If so, hush!" That teacher's scolding kept her students quiet, but from that point on the youngsters were spectators of the reading process not participants in it. The experience lost its excitement and the story wasn't personal anymore. It was just ink on paper.

As irritating as interruptions can sometimes become, it's important to remember that children's comments during a story signal that they are making connections between new material and something they already know—the essence of the learning process. So read *with* your children and welcome interruptions. They tell you that you are doing your job well.

16 Help your children read. If your children are beginning readers, tell them the words they can't yet read so that they can move along and maintain interest. Later, you can assist them in figuring out the harder words for themselves.

17 Have your children read to you. Encourage them to read a story to themselves before they read it to you. This practice will help give them confidence and a greater understanding of what they have read. It will also make the story more interesting to them.

18 Listen as your children tell you about what they have read. Reading is not reading unless it's accompanied by understanding. Therefore, when your child shows understanding by wanting to tell you about what he or she has read, it's extremely important to show you are interested.

19 Provide a wide variety of reading materials in your home. Children learn by example rather than by precept. If you have books, magazines and newspapers readily available and in use, your children will see that reading is a source of pleasure and information. It's infinitely more effective for your children to see you reading often than it is for you to tell them to read.

20 Give your children books as birthday or holiday gifts. Children who have books they can call their very own are motivated toward reading. The arrival of books mailed directly to your children—with their names on the labels or cartons—provides a strong inducement for reading.

21 Tempt your children with paperbacks. For a number of young readers, there is something formidable about hardcover books; for them, paperbacks are much more attractive. Also, because paperbacks are less costly, you can provide many more and a greater variety.

22 Intrigue your children with their own magazine subscriptions. Few youngsters—even those not keen on the idea of reading anything at all—can resist the appeal of the arrival in the mail of their own magazine. Reluctant readers suddenly find themselves poring over instructions for easy do-it-yourself projects, riddles, puzzles and stories. Before they know it, they're "hooked" on reading—anxiously awaiting the next issue of *their* magazine.

23 Get your children interested in daily newspapers. The writing communicates a sense of vitality and immediacy that piques children's interest. Clip articles that will appeal to them. Also point out that newspaper advertisements provide a service for the consumer—whatever his or her age. Encourage the children to read ads in the newspaper and especially in "their" magazines for products that interest them.

24 Join and use the free public library. Take your children to the library. Help them get their own cards and select and take out their own

4. CHILD REARING AND PARENT EDUCATION

books. Ask the librarian to suggest good books to suit your children's ages and interests.

25 Encourage a wide variety of reading experiences. The fact that children read is sometimes more important than what they read. For example:

Kitchen Reading. Labels on food cans and boxes can make interesting reading. The contests and free gifts advertised on labels are strong reading motivators. Reading these labels can also lead to writing contest entry letters or filling out forms for free merchandise.

Medicine Cabinet Reading. Labels on jars, bottles and boxes found in the bathroom (excluding dangerous medicines and poisons, of course) can be just as interesting as those found in the kitchen and may also include contests and special inducements.

Rock Record Reading. If your children are between the ages of 10 and 14, they probably have a collection of rock records. Listening time can also be reading time. Album jackets are filled with information about the kids' favorite rock stars, and sometimes the words to the songs are included. Many record shops sell songbooks that have the lyrics to all the new rock records. Encourage your children to read along as they play the records.

THE MYTH OF THE VULNERABLE CHILD

Anxious parents should relax. Despite what some psychologists have been telling them for years, they do not have make-or-break power over a child's development.

Arlene Skolnick

Arlene Skolnick is a research psychologist at the Institute of Human Development, University of California, Berkeley. Skolnick, who received her Ph.D from Yale, is chiefly interested in marital relationships and changes in self-concepts in later life. She has written *The Intimate Environment*, coauthored *Family in Transition* (both published by Little, Brown), and is now writing a developmental-psychology textbook for Harcourt Brace Jovanovich.

Americans have long been considered the most child-centered people in the world. In the 20th century, this traditional American obsession with children has generated new kinds of child-rearing experts—psychologists and psychiatrists, clothed in the authority of modern science, who issue prescriptions for child-rearing. Most child-care advice assumes that if the parents administer the proper prescriptions, the child will develop as planned. It places exaggerated faith not only in the perfectibility of the children and their parents, but in the infallibility of the particular child-rearing technique as well. But increasing evidence suggests that parents simply do not have that much control over their children's development; too many other factors are influencing it.

Popular and professional knowledge does not seem to have made parenting easier. On the contrary, the insights and guidelines provided by the experts seem to have made parents more anxious. Since modern child-rearing literature asserts that parents can do irreparable harm to their children's social and emotional development, modern parents must examine their words and actions for a significance that parents in the past had never imagined. Besides, psychological experts disagree among themselves. Not only have they been divided into competing schools, but they also have repeatedly shifted their emphasis from one developmental goal to another, from one technique to another.

Two Models of Parenting

Two basic models of parental influence emerge from all this competition and variety, however. One, loosely based on Freudian ideas, has presented an image of the vulnerable child: children are sensitive beings, easily damaged not only by traumatic events and emotional stress, but also by overdoses of affection. The second model is that of the behaviorists, whose intellectual ancestors, the empiricist philosophers, described the child's mind as a *tabula rasa*, or blank slate. The behaviorist model of child-rearing is based on the view that the child is malleable, and parents are therefore cast in the role of Pygmalions who can shape their children however they wish. "Give me a dozen healthy infants, well-formed, and my own specified world to bring them up in," wrote J. B. Watson, the father of modern behaviorism, "and I'll guarantee to take any one at random and train him to be any type of specialist I might—doctor, lawyer, artist, merchant, chief, and yes, even beggar man and thief!"

The image of the vulnerable child calls for gentle parents who are sensitive to their child's innermost thoughts and feelings in order to protect him from trauma. The image of the malleable child requires stern parents who coolly follow the dictates of their own explicit training procedures: only the early eradication of bad habits in eating, sleeping, crying, can fend off permanent maladjustments.

Despite their disagreements, both models grant parents an omnipotent role in child development. Both stress that (1) only if parents do the right things at the right time will their children turn out to be happy, successful adults; (2) parents can raise superior beings, free of the mental frailties of previous generations; and (3) if something goes wrong with their child, the parents have only themselves to blame.

Contemporary research increasingly suggests, however, that both models greatly exaggerate the power of the parent and the passivity of the child. In fact, the children's own needs, their developing mental and physical qualities, influence the way they perceive and interpret external events. This is not to say that parents exercise no influence on their children's development. Like all myths, that of parental determinism contains a kernel of truth. But there is an important difference between influence and control. Finally, both models also fail to consider that parent-child relations do not occur in a social vacuum, but in the complex world of daily life.

Traditionally, child-study researchers have assumed that influence in the parent-child relationship flowed only one way, from active parent to passive child. For example, a large number of studies tested the assumption, derived from Freudian theory, that the decisive events of early childhood centered around feeding, weaning, and toilet-training. It is now generally conceded that such practices in themselves have few demonstrable effects on later development. Such studies may have erred because they assumed that children must experience and react to parental behavior in the same ways.

Even when studies *do* find connections between the behavior of the par-

4. CHILD REARING AND PARENT EDUCATION

ents and the child, cause and effect are by no means clear. Psychologist Richard Bell argues that many studies claiming to show the effects of parents on children can just as well be interpreted as showing children's effects on parents. For instance, a study finding a correlation between severe punishment and children's aggressiveness is often taken to show that harsh discipline produces aggressive children; yet it could show instead that aggressive children evoke harsh child-rearing methods in their parents.

A Methodological Flaw

The image of a troubled adult scarred for life by an early trauma such as the loss of a parent, lack of love, or family tension has passed from the clinical literature to become a cliché of the popular media. The idea that childhood stress must inevitably result in psychological damage is a conclusion that rests on a methodological flaw inherent in the clinical literature: instead of studying development through time, these studies start with adult problems and trace them back to possible causes.

It's true that when researchers investigate the backgrounds of delinquents, mental patients, or psychiatric referrals from military service, they find that a large number come from "broken" or troubled homes, have overpossessive, domineering, or rejecting mothers, or have inadequate or violent fathers. The usual argument is that these circumstances cause maladjustments in the offspring. But most children who experience disorder and early sorrow grow up to be adequate adults. Further, studies sampling "normal" or "superior" people—college students, business executives, professionals, creative artists, and scientists—find such "pathological" conditions in similar or greater proportions. Thus, many studies trying to document the effects of early pathological and traumatic conditions have failed to demonstrate more than a weak link between them and later development.

The striking differences between retrospective studies that start with adult misfits and look back to childhood conditions, and longitudinal studies that start with children and follow them through time, were shown in a study at the University of California's Institute of Human Development, under the direction of Jean Macfarlane. Approximately 200 children were studied intensively from infancy through adolescence, and then were seen again at age 30. The researchers predicted that children from troubled homes would be troubled adults and, conversely, that those who had had happy, successful childhoods would be happy adults. They were wrong in two-thirds of their predictions. Not only had they overestimated the traumatic effects of stressful family situations, but even more surprisingly, they also had not anticipated that many of those who grew up under the best circumstances would turn out to be unhappy, strained, or immature adults (a pattern that seemed especially strong for boys who had been athletic leaders and girls who had been beautiful and popular in high school).

Psychologist Norman Garmezy's work on "invulnerability" offers more recent evidence that children can thrive in spite of genetic disadvantages and environmental deprivations. Garmezy began by studying adult schizophrenics and trying to trace the sources of their problems. Later, he turned to developmental studies of children who were judged high risks to develop schizophrenia and other disorders at a later age. When such children were studied over time, only 10 or 12 percent of the high-risk group became schizophrenic, while the majority did not.

Other Sources of Love

The term "invulnerables" is misleading. It suggests an imperviousness to pain. Yet, the ability to cope does not mean the child doesn't suffer. One woman, who successfully overcame a childhood marked by the death of her beloved but alcoholic and abusive father, and rejection by her mother and stepmother, put it this way: "We suffer, but we don't let it destroy us."

The term also seems to imply that the ability to cope is a trait, something internal to the child. One often finds in the case histories of those who have coped with their problems successfully that external supports softened the impact of the traumatic event. Often something in the child's environment provides alternative sources of love and gratification—one parent compensating for the inadequacy of the other, a loving sibling or grandparent, an understanding teacher, a hobby or strong interest, a pet, recreational opportunities, and so on.

Indeed, the local community may play an important role in modulating the effects of home environments. Erik Erikson, who worked on the study at the Institute of Human Development, was asked at a seminar, "How is it that so many of the people studied overcame the effects of truly awful homes?" He answered that it might have been the active street life in those days, which enabled children to enjoy the support of peers when parent-child relations got too difficult.

Psychologist Martin Seligman's learned-helplessness theory provides a further clue to what makes a child vulnerable to stress. Summarizing a vast array of data, including animal experiments, clinical studies, and reports from prisoner-of-war camps, Seligman proposes that people give up in despair not because of the actual severity of their situation, but because they feel they can have little or no effect in changing it. The feeling of helplessness is learned by actually experiencing events we cannot control, or by being led to believe that we have no control.

Seligman's theory helps to explain two puzzling phenomena: the biographies of eminent people that often reveal stressful family relations, and Macfarlane's findings that many children who did come from "ideal" homes failed to live up to their seeming potential. The theory of learned helplessness suggests that controllable stress may be better for a child's ego development than good things that happen without any effort on the child's part. Self-esteem and a sense of competence may not depend on whether we experience good or bad events, but rather on whether we perceive some control over what happens to us.

Parents Can't Be Pygmalions

Many of the same reasons that limit the effect of events on children also limit the ability of parents to shape their children according to behavioral prescription. The facts of cognition and environmental complexity get in the way of best-laid parental plans. There is no guarantee, for example, that children will interpret parental behavior accurately. Psychologist Jane Loevinger gives the example of a mother trying to discipline her five-year-old son for hitting his younger sister: if she spanks him, she may discourage the hitting, or she may be demonstrating that hitting is okay; if she reasons with the child, he may accept her view of hitting as bad, or he may conclude that hitting is something you can get away with and not be punished for.

Other factors, interacting with the child's cognitive processes and sense of self, limit the parents' ability to shape their children. Perhaps the most basic is that parents have their own temperamental qualities that may modify the message they convey to their children. One recurrent finding in the research literature, for example, is that parental warmth is important to a child's development. Yet warmth and acceptance cannot be created by following behavioral prescriptions, since they are spontaneous feelings.

Further, the parent-child relationship does not exist apart from other social contexts. A study of child-rearing in six cultures, directed by Harvard anthropologists John Whiting and Beatrice Whiting, found that parents' behavior toward children is based not so much on beliefs and principles as on a "horde of apparently irrelevant considerations": work pressures, the household work load, the availability of other adults to help with household tasks and child care, the design of houses and neighborhoods, the social structure of the community. All these influences, over which parents usually have little control, affect the resources of time, energy, attention, and affection they have for their children.

The effects of social class may also be very hard to overcome, even if the parent tries. Psychiatrist Robert Coles has written about poor and minority children who often come to learn from their families that they are persons of worth—only to have this belief shattered when they encounter the devaluing attitudes of the outside world. Conversely, middle-class children from troubled homes may take psychological nourishment from the social power and esteem that are enjoyed by their families in the community.

Science and the Family: Historical Roots

Given the lack of evidence for the parental-determinism model of child-rearing, why has it been so persistent? Why have we continued to believe that science can provide infallible prescriptions for raising happy, successful people and curing social problems?

As psychologist Sheldon White has recently observed, psychology's existence as a field of scientific research has rested upon "promissory notes" laid down at the turn of the century. The beginnings of modern academic psychology were closely tied to education and the growth of large public expenditures for the socialization of children. The first psychologists moved from philosophy departments to the newly forming education schools, expecting to provide scientific methods of education and child-rearing. The founding fathers of American psychology—J. B. Watson, G. S. Hall, L. M. Terman, and others—accepted the challenge. Thus, learning has always been a central focus of psychologists, even though the rat eventually came to compete with the child as the favored experimental animal.

If the behaviorists' social prescriptions conjure up images of *Brave New World* or *1984*, a more humane promise was implicit in Freudian theory. The earliest generations of Freudians encouraged the belief that if the new knowledge derived from psychoanalysis was applied to the upbringing of children, it would be possible to eliminate anxiety, conflict, and neurosis. The medical miracles achieved in the 19th and early 20th centuries gave the medical experts immense prestige in the eyes of parents. There seemed little reason to doubt that science could have as far-reaching effects on mental health as it had on physical health. Furthermore, as parents were becoming more certain of their children's physical survival, children's social futures were becoming less certain. When the family was no longer an economic unit, it could no longer initiate children directly into work. Middle-class parents had to educate their children to find their way in a complex job market. The coming of urban industrial society also changed women's roles. Women were removed from the world of work, and motherhood came to be defined as a separate task for women, the primary focus of their lives. Psychological ideas became an intrinsic part of the domestic-science movement that arose around the end of the 19th century; this ideology taught that scientific household management would result in perfected human relationships within the home, as well as in the improvement of the larger society.

The Limits of Perfectibility

As we approach the 1980s, Americans are coming to reject the idea that science and technology can guarantee limitless progress and solve all problems. Just as we have come to accept that there are limits to growth and to our natural resources, it is time we lowered our expectations about the perfectibility of family life. Instead of trying to rear perfectly happy, adjusted, creative, and successful children, we should recognize that few, if any, such people exist, and even if they did, it would be impossible to produce such a person by following a behavioral formula. Far from harming family relations, lowered expectations could greatly benefit them.

What is more, the belief in parental determinism has had an unfortunate influence on social policy. It has encouraged the hope that major social problems can be eradicated without major changes in society and its institutions. For example, we have in the past preferred to view the poor as victims of faulty child-rearing rather than of unemployment, inadequate income, or miserable housing. Ironically, while we have been obsessed with producing ideal child-rearing environments in our own homes, we have permitted millions of American children to suffer basic deprivations. A seemingly endless series of governmental and private commissions has documented the sorry statistics on infant mortality, child malnutrition, unattended health needs, and so on, but the problems persist. In short, the standards of perfection that have been applied to child-rearing and the family in this century have not only created guilt and anxiety in those who try to live up to them, but have also contributed to the neglect of children on a national scale.

For further information, read:
Clarke, Ann M. and A. D. Clarke, eds. *Early Experience: Myth and Evidence*, Free Press, 1977, $13.95.
Garmezy, Norman. "Vulnerable and Invulnerable Children: Theory, Research and Intervention," American Psychological Association, MS 1337, 1976.
Goertzel, Victor and Mildred G. Goertzel. *Cradles of Eminence*, Little, Brown, 1978, paper, $4.95.
Macfarlane, Jean. "Perspectives on Personality Consistency and Change from the Guidance Study," *Vita Humana*, Vol. 7, No. 2, 1964.

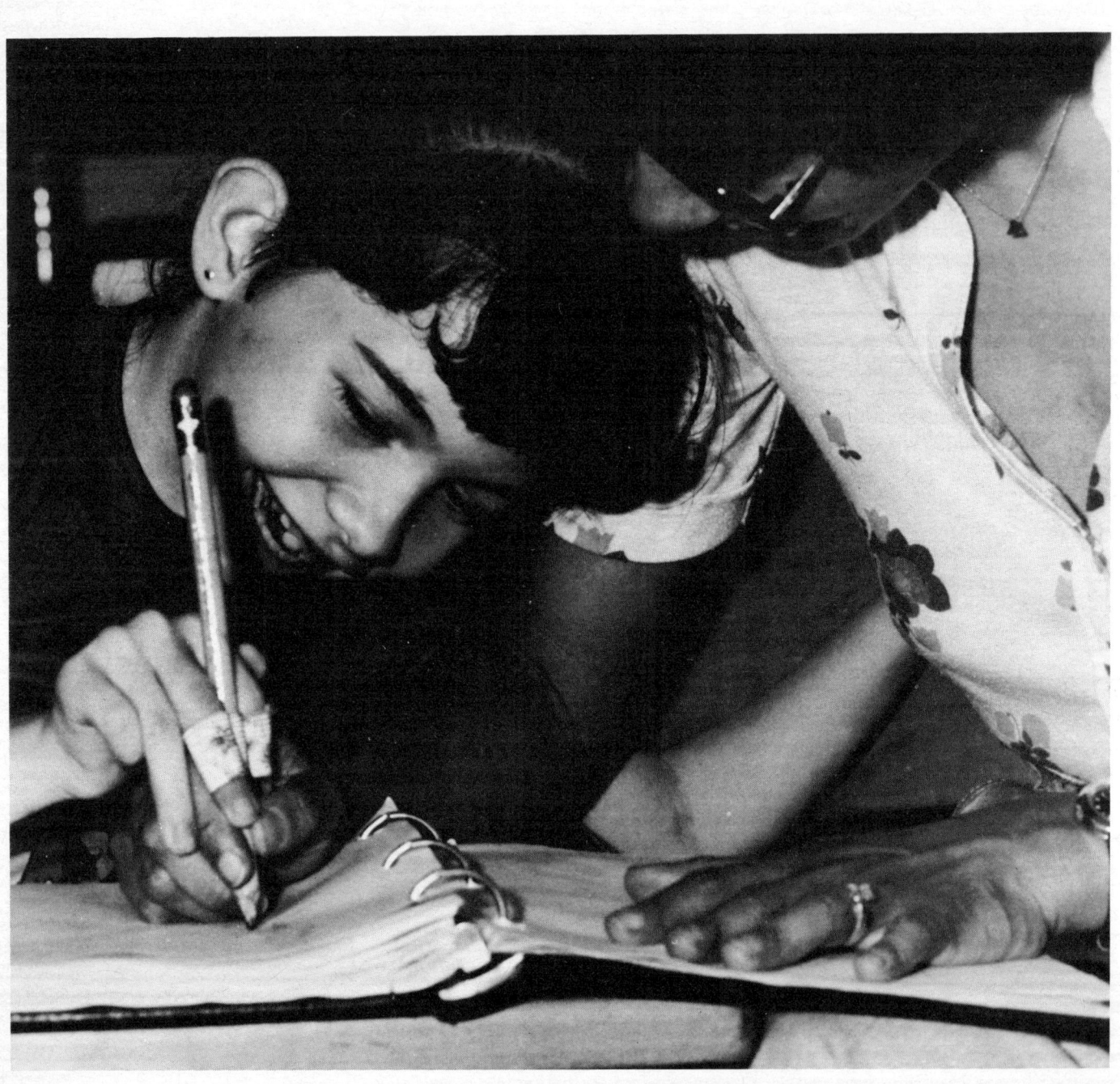

Children with Special Needs 5

In 1975 Congress passed the Education for All Handicapped Children Act, which mandated that all children be provided access to appropriate educational opportunities within the public educational system. This act and subsequent legislation on state levels produced major modifications in and additions to existing programs serving young children and their families.

Learned individuals throughout history have attested to the potency of the early years of life, referring to them as "the formative years," the "sensitive periods," or "the impressionable years." Consequently, the linkage of early childhood education and special education efforts seemed inevitable and overdue given the wide—although not universal—acceptance of the thesis that the first six or seven years of life are critical in laying the foundation for later learning, growth, and development, or lack of it.

Local school district personnel have provided leadership in a three-tier approach in implementing special education programs and in making required adjustments to regular school offerings. The three tier plan includes identification, assessment, and intervention to assure that children are not excluded, misdiagnosed, inaccurately placed, or undereducated.

The first phase, identification, includes reaching children before they are of legal school age so that their abilities will not atrophy and their needs will be met. Assessment, or evaluation, is the second phase, and may include formal and/or informal techniques with parents and professionals working together. The final phase is intervention, encompassing a range of medical, social, and psychological services employed in conjunction with the educational program. The early education component involves the planning and monitoring of a distinctly individualized program for each child.

During the past few years, there has been a much wider societal acceptance of persons with special needs. Mainstreaming is a method of integrating children with special needs into regular educational programs.

Special professional associations have become increasingly interested in children identified as learning disabled, gifted, and academically talented, who too often were unable to have their special academic and intellectual needs met in regular programs. Such efforts are highly warranted and usually welcomed by educators to redress former imbalances and inequalities in treatment. Yet, despite the differing traits, disabilities, or exceptionalities special children may display, it is helpful to keep in mind that early childhood educators have traditionally viewed *all* young children under their care, first and foremost, *as children.* This is a proposition that will be remembered and applied by wise and responsible educators and parents.

This section examines assessment and intervention focusing on children with learning disabilities, gifted children, and mainstreaming.

Looking Ahead: Challenge Questions

What is included under the label "learning disabled"? Are distractability, hyperactivity, and slow learning clear signs that a learning disability exists?

How is a "learning disabled" child different from a "slow learner" with developmental lag?

What is meant when a child is identified as "gifted"? Does he/she have special emotional or social needs that accompany the special intellectual abilities?

What are the possible negative consequences of accelerating school-aged children?

How do teacher attitudes and skills in dealing with human differences affect the effectiveness of a mainstreamed program? What are the characteristics of a successfully mainstreamed program?

The LD Syndrome:
How to recognize and deal with it

Joan Harwell

Joan Harwell is a teacher at Monterey Elementary School in San Bernardino, California.

It has been two months now since you greeted your new class for the first time and discovered—a little slowly, to be sure—that you had a learning disabled child in your class. His name is Richard, and he is but one of the 30 lively kids who entered your room back in September—kids for whom you would be parent surrogate, teacher, and friend for the next 10 months. You were alerted that Richard had a learning problem; his last teacher said he could do his work if he would, but he'd rather fidget. He constantly plays with things, bringing small toys from home or finding something at school to fool around with. The very first day, while other students were listening to you, he was opening and closing his desk lid, intently watching the hinge mechanism. His former teacher also mentioned his tendency to kiss, hug, and touch his classmates, all of which annoyed them and caused them to reject him.

How are you and Richard getting along now? Can you help him to be a more effective learner? Can you help the other children accommodate his difficulties? The next few pages will supply some clues to Richard's problem and some cues to use in your own management techniques.

Back in 1963, Dr. Sam Kirk, an authority in special education, used the term *learning disabilities* to describe youngsters such as Richard with disorders in withdrawal, concentration, reading, and speech who are not handicapped by blindness, deafness, or mental retardation. Physicians had previously called them *children with brain damage or minimal brain dysfunction*, terms that parents found difficult to accept. Dr. Kirk made his identification on the basis of performance or the ability to learn.

Today, psychologists and educators are still arguing over a single definition for the term, but in general, they agree on several things. First, learning disabled children are not usually physically handicapped or mentally retarded. Secondly, they show great discrepancies between potential and achievement not attributable to cultural deprivation. It appears also that these youngsters fail to accurately receive, process, and integrate sensory stimuli even though their sensory organs function with normal acuity.

Learning disabled children often experience multiple failures including teacher rejection and repeating a grade before anyone decides that they have an LD problem. As a dyslexic boy said, "I flunked kindergarten because I kept running into the teacher with my tricycle." And he was in seventh grade before he was identified as learning disabled!

A basic problem is that each child is unique in his deficits, areas of strength, and capacities to handle the frustration caused by his learning disability problems. Diagnosis is a tough problem, even for an experienced teacher; so you will need to know what to look for in a variety of areas.

Teacher identification

Suppose you suspect you have an LD pupil in your room. How do you follow through?

Two characteristics are almost universal among learning disabled children:

1. They have directionally spatial relationship problems and difficulty in sequencing. It may be a failure to read from left to right; in oral reading they may read all words in a sentence but switch their positions; it may be reflected in an inability to put things where they belong.

2. They have difficulty in conceptual thinking. It may be a deficiency in oral language development or they may fail to comprehend words which you assume they know.

Other symptoms often apparent in an LD child include:

- Confused perception—reversed numbers or letters; inability to copy from book or board accurately; constantly loses place; is distracted by movement or noise; cannot do fill-in-blank type activities; cannot discriminate between sounds.
- Lack of motor control—awkward and clumsy; illegible handwriting; uses scissors poorly; can't hit a baseball, catch a ball, or skip.
- Short attention span—doesn't listen; fails to complete simple tasks; insists on repeating a behavior long after the teacher feels it should have stopped.
- Poor memory—previously learned material is quickly forgotten.
- Plus or minus activity levels—hyperactivity or its opposite, hypoactivity.
- Behavior problems—withdrawals or disinterest; refusal to complete assignments; sullenness or depression; unusual aggression.

No single youngster will show all these symptoms, but when several are present a pupil will feel frustration in even simple learning situations; and other children and you, the teacher, will experience mounting pressures in your encounters with him.

A typical classroom may have from one to four children with some degree of learning disability. It appears there are more learning disabled boys than girls.

Diagnosis begins with your feelings that you may have a learning disabled child. Despite average or above average ability, he is falling behind, his peer relationships are deficient, and it is difficult to help him. Obviously, help is needed.

The first step is to create the most complete record possible. Over a week or two, jot down behavior examples; then construct your own diagnostic profile of the student. The importance of this step cannot be overemphasized. You are a professional diagnostician and you have the most comprehensive opportunities to view his behavior. One caution—seek only "to tell it as it is" in your record. You are not trying to confirm a judgment or prove a point.

Your first contact thereafter should be your principal. Share your account of the child's behavior, and if the principal is a supportive person, ask him to make his own observations and record them. Then jointly you are ready to discuss the matter with the child's parents. Depending on available facilities, your goal is that they will have the child diagnosed physically, academically, and behaviorally, plus obtain an accurate measurement of his intellectual capacities, or that they will approve such testing by the school. This may involve several discussions with the parents as well as a visit to the home.

Should parents not wish to have the child assessed, that is their right. However, their objections should be carefully documented, and don't give up on your first try. Often, refusal is reversed in a second conference, because the parents are as frustrated as the teacher and a great deal more frightened. Remind the parents that the goal of diagnosis is not to establish causes, but to develop a remediation plan.

Physical diagnosis

A child suspected of having a learning disability should be referred to a pediatric neurologist for a complete assessment of his general health. This should include a physical examination, tests of visual and auditory acuity and blood and urine. An assessment should be made of the child's gross and fine motor controls. The examination may also need to include an electroencephalogram (EEG) to determine if organic brain damage can be documented.

The school should send a letter of referral via the parent to the doctor requesting an examination and a written report of his findings, with notations of any implications that affect the child's educational program. If medicine has been prescribed which is to be taken at school, the doctor should advise dosage and any possible side effects.

In-school physical diagnosis of the child should include informal teacher evaluation:
1. Gross motor control—Can he skip? walk a line? balance on a step stool or balance beam? balance on one foot?
2. Fine motor control—Can he trace over lines, both wavy and straight? Can he reproduce a circle, triangle, and diamond without confusion? Is his daily handwriting of poor quality?
3. Activity level—Is the child constantly up and down, rarely completing an assignment? Can he participate in simple group activities?

Academic diagnosis

Academic achievement should be tested by the classroom teacher, school psychologist, or a trained therapist. Four simple-to-administer tests give a wealth of information about what a child knows and what he needs to learn:
1. Woodcock Reading Test, Form A
2. Key Diagnostic Math Test
3. General Information Section of the Peabody Individual Achievement Test (PIAT)
4. Wide Range Achievement Test (WRAT)

The first three are available through the American Guidance Service, Inc., Publisher's Bldg., Circle Pines, MN 55014.

WRAT can be ordered from Guidance Associates of Delaware, Inc., 1526 Gilpin Ave., Wilmington, DE.

All of these tests are valid for K-8 students, but use Level 2 of WRAT when testing a child 12 years old or older. Each test can be administered in 20-30 minutes and it is a good practice to keep files of them on hand.

Behavioral diagnosis

Behaviors which are counterproductive to academic progress should be charted. A situation of one adult to one child may not be a true sample of his behavior in the classroom; so he should be observed on three consecutive days for five-minute periods in the morning and again in the afternoon.

Once these practices are identified, teacher and parent can decide on one or two behavioral goals and set up strategies that can lead to modified behavior.

Intellectual capacity

With written permission from parent, refer the child for measurement of his intellectual capacity. A preferred test is the Wechsler Intelligence Scale for Children, Form R, 1974, used for ages 5-15 years, since it renders subtest scores and valuable information regarding a variety of functions. Some test items measure visual processes while others measure auditory. If the school psychologist administers the test, there should be a teacher-psychologist conference immediately following the testing so that information gained is shared.

Often the LD child may show a 20-30 point difference in scores on the verbal/performance side of the test. Such discrepancies have vast implications for the methods of teaching.

Instruction

Now that the extensive diagnosis you sought has been completed, what next? Unless it becomes the basis for the learning prescriptions you are about to prepare, the process was extravagant and of little value. You should continuously draw on the information obtained to the greatest extent. Presumably you have more data on this child than on any other in your class; but you need it, for *his* needs are more acute.

Talk over the report with your principal. Seek amplifications, especially on any part that seems to disagree with your findings. Share with the parents as much as possible. Share, too, with the child where it will help him know more about himself.

Successful teaching of the LD child comes from applying strategies that respond to specific needs, and it can happen best in a regular classroom. But you should feel free to ask for special materials and to have access to electronic equipment and learning aids that will support your efforts. You are assuming a particular responsibility that calls for the most effective learning devices possible.

Often the LD child seeks great amounts of affection, praise, and approval from adults and peers. When his needs are met by persons in his environment who are important to him, he functions with fewer behavioral problems. You and he must be jointly committed to his tasks of learning. Both of you must recognize that it may take multiple efforts for a single learning to occur and that frequent reviews will be needed to guarantee retention.

General management A few tips apply to practically all LD children, but even they should be scrapped if an alternative strategy works better. Try these six for size.
1. The LD youngster should sit near you, not isolated from the group, and his desk and accoutrements should be his and his alone.
2. Degrees of conformity should be reasonable and flexible. He may not listen when you are reading to the class, but neither should he be permitted to divert the attention of others.
3. Reproofs are best delivered privately. Small punishments or social restraints should be applied as needed and are prefer-

5. CHILDREN WITH SPECIAL NEEDS

able to allowing situations to deteriorate.
4. Always remember that you are in control. If you or the other children need relief, send the LD child on an errand, to the media center, or even for a walk around the building.
5. Sustained inner tranquillity for the LD child comes far more from a series of small accomplishments than from getting his own way. Between drill and practice periods, encourage the child to draw, work with clay, listen to a record or follow along with a book on tape, plant a flower, or do anything that represents achievement.
6. Secrets often help, especially if they are contingency measures. If Richard raises or lowers the desk top excessively, work out some alternatives with him. Then quietly suggest he try number six on his paper. Even having to stop to get out the list is a diversion.

Speech It is not unusual for an LD child to have poor speech, but the reasons or causes are diverse. The words and word patterns of others may not make an impression because of poor hearing, wandering attention, a tendency to hear beginnings and not endings, or associative hearing that causes the association rather than the original word to register in the brain. He may have remnants of baby talk, a tendency to stutter, or a lisp caused by malclusion or habit. His sound pattern may be restricted by poor breathing. He may even think one word and have another word come out.

If your school has a speech program, your LD child is a likely candidate for special instruction. Otherwise, you must follow the recommendations of the diagnosis and then seek a volunteer adult to fulfill them on a regular basis—the task is too big to add to your other duties.

In all conversations, enunciate well and look directly at the child. Correct mispronunciations in a quiet, ongoing way. Straighten out mixed-up sentences and repeat them in the correct form. But avoid such corrections in front of other children, except when helping the student to convey an idea to another child.

Language development Oral speech is a major tool but don't assume it will be the prime communication device for the LD child. He may draw pictures, use body language, or act badly to convey a message. Even withdrawal is a way of talking to you. Here are some effective guidelines:
1. Make an effort every day to talk conversationally with him. It need not be longer than three minutes, but it is important.
2. When withdrawal occurs, it is rarely advisable to attempt to introduce conversation to relieve this condition.

3. Avoid calling on the LD child in a class situation unless he shows that he wants to contribute.
4. Be warm and considerate but don't permit him to disrupt your work with another child or group because he wants to talk.
5. Avoid excessive touching or patting during a talking time. The physical stimuli outweigh the idea exchange.
6. The child should have his own recorder and be encouraged to record descriptions, stories, messages, and even protests and arguments. He should know you will listen to the tape sometime during the day it is recorded.
7. Devices such as Speak and Spell (Texas Instruments) are usually helpful. Concentrate on spelling common words accurately instead of trying to cover a wide range.

Reading Statistically, learning disabilities are manifested most in learning to read, but keep the figures in perspective. Reading is the core subject of the elementary school and everything else relates to it. If a pupil has any learning deficits, reading is likely to be involved.

From the diagnostic testing, you have a picture of both the problem areas and the student's sources of strength. An individual prescription is absolutely necessary, and if you have a reading specialist, ask for help in constructing it. If part of the testing was done by a reading expert, get help there. As a competent practitioner, don't hesitate to call on any available human resource, but also be prepared to change and modify as you go along.

Here are some cues, applicable at any grade level:
1. One reading method or source of materials is rarely adequate. Pick and choose from a variety of resources.
2. Short periods of machine learning are profitable but don't be surprised when the student starts ignoring them. Drop the practice and go back to it later.
3. Visual and auditory aids are especially important, including flash cards, use of a language laboratory, sequence cards, and read-alongs.
4. Utilize commonalities in both sounds and meanings. For associative learnings, create small packs of flash cards of fruits, colors, games, streets, even the names of the children in your class.
5. Have a minimum of two and as many as five reading practice periods a day, with at least one devoted entirely to associating sounds with symbols.

Mathematics Again, your diagnosis will reveal areas that need work and resources on which you can build. The LD child may have a poor or phenomenally good memory. He may see relationships visually, or bypass them altogether. So take the evidence to your best source of help (principal, mathematics specialist, another teacher) and use a team approach to create a prescription. You are working with an ex-

---

A DOZEN SPECIAL TIPS FOR HELPING THE LD CHILD

1. Instruction should be mostly individual or with a partner and absolutely never with more than four children.
2. Twenty minutes in one area is probably long enough, never more than thirty.
3. Most LD children need two or three practice sessions daily in skill areas.
4. Program some fun and success into each experience.
5. Insist on accuracy and attain mastery at one level before proceeding to the next.
6. Teach concrete, unchanging elements first. When these are mastered, move to exceptions. But in the beginning, don't tell students there will be exceptions later.
7. Don't encourage LD children to jump to conclusions, for example, seeing only the beginning letter of a word and then guessing the rest. Go slow enough for total visual acuity.
8. Only assign an independent written task when you are absolutely certain the student knows what to do and can do it.
9. Never assume an LD pupil has heard something unless you have him verbally feed back what he thinks you said.
10. Encourage the use of all types of props—markers, cutouts for focusing, rulers, or anything the child may devise on his own.
11. Be honest but liberal with praise and rewards in frequent intervals.
12. Provide structure with subjects always in the same order and the same adult working with the student. Never let another child take an LD child's seat.

42. The LD Syndrome

traordinary problem; don't hesitate to seek help.

Here are some practices that might prove worthwhile.

1. Combine visual and auditory in drill. Have the LD child see, hear, and say that 4 + 6 = 10 simultaneously.
2. Use demonstration, experimentation, and practice more than you do with non-LD children. Richard knows four cups equal a quart because he has poured from the cup to a jar over and over again.
3. Separate the most essential learnings and concentrate on them. Let Base 2 be something in a ballpark.
4. Provide individual flash cards and access to specialized electronic devices if possible, but avoid use of a hand calculator unless it is one with a paper tape.
5. Stress sequence and order through use of such materials as sewing cards and dot drawings.

Public Law 94-142, the Handicapped Children Act of 1975, demands that we locate all learning disabled children, plan an Individualized Educational Program which develops their potential, and mainstream them into regular classrooms wherever possible. You are going to do that and far more. Through extensive diagnosis and detailed planning, you have a workable course of action. You, Richard, and the rest of the class can and will have a tolerable and profitable year together.

We want your advice.

Any anthology can be improved. This one will be—annually. But we need your help.

Annual Editions revisions depend on two major opinion sources: one is the academic advisers who work with us in scanning the thousands of articles published in the public press each year; the other is you—the person actually using the book.

Please help us and the users of the next edition by completing the prepaid article rating form on the last page of this book and returning it to us. Thank you.

'LEARNING DISABLED' OR 'SLOW LEARNER'?

Careful diagnosis avoids false hopes

Margaret Jo Shepherd

Dr. Shepherd is an associate professor at Teachers College, Columbia University, in New York and Coordinator of the Learning Disabilities Program in the Department of Special Education. She is a senior faculty member on the staff of the Child Study Center, the department's diagnostic center for children with learning problems.

"Shouldn't our son be called a child with specific learning disabilities?" ask the worried parents of a nine-year-old boy who has finished a long day of educational testing in the Special Education Child Study Center at Teachers College, Columbia University in New York. I pause before responding no, anticipating and, for a moment, wishing to avoid the certain signs of disappointment and deepening concern the response will bring.

We will go on together to explore the difference between the learning problems affecting their son, a slow learning child, and the learning problems of a child with specific learning disabilities. Like so many others before them, these parents had read and heard about "specific learning disabilities" and had come to the Child Study Center because they wanted to be told that their child's failure in school was caused by learning disabilities.

THE LD LABEL MEANS HOPE

Learning disabled appears to be the one descriptive term that can be applied to children with school learning and adjustment problems without eliciting negative connotations. To most parents and teachers the diagnostic label "learning disabilities" has become an optimistic diagnosis. It implies that the child's educational problems are temporary, that constructive action can be taken and that the outcome will be favorable. Consequently, the identification of a child as learning disabled has a positive influence on attitudes toward that child and particularly on adults' expectations for the child. It is easy to understand why learning disabled is the preferred diagnosis of most informed parents and of many teachers and psychologists.

My intent is not to disparage the attitudes of hope and optimism associated with the term learning disabilities. The search for constructive solutions to children's learning problems, which the current interest in learning disabilities has brought about, is one of the major developments in the field of special education during the past 15 years. Further, the effort to develop effective educational programs for learning disabled children has produced a rapprochement between regular and special education that should delight even the most cynical among us.

There is cause, however, for caution against the misuse of the term and misinterpretation of the diagnostic concept. This article is a plea for caution in the use of the diagnostic term learning disabilities.

CAN WE DEFINE LEARNING DISABILITIES?

The idea that normally intelligent children, who do not have primary sensory or emotional deficits, could still have specific learning problems didn't begin to influence educators' attitudes and school policies in the U.S. until the early 1960s. Unfortunately, it has been unusually difficult to give a precise definition to the condition of specific learning disabilities. There is as much confusion today about the exact meaning of the term and about the nature and causes of learning disabilities as there was in 1968 when an Advisory Committee appointed by the U.S. Office of Education first formulated its official definition of the term.

CAREFUL DIAGNOSIS

Despite the fact that there is no real consensus about the definition of learning disabilities and that learning disabled populations vary widely, there are at least two commonly held views about the condition of specific learning disabilities that should be considered in making a diagnosis.

The first and most important of these considerations is that children with specific learning disabilities *demonstrate* normal intellectual ability. Second, these children manage to develop normally in some respects despite learning disabilities. Thus, their development and skill attainment is markedly uneven. They show learning *abilities* as well as learning *dis*abilities.

It is this combination of normal intelligence and learning strengths with learning disabilities that encourages optimism about the corrective effect of special educational techniques. When these conditions are present in a diagnosis of specific learning disabilities, optimism is warranted. But if they are not, and a diagnosis of specific learning disabilities is made, optimism may soon turn to disillusionment for parents, teachers and children.

MISDIAGNOSIS OF SLOW LEARNERS

The children who stand the greatest chance of suffering as a result of being misdiagnosed as learning disabled are those who, like the nine-year-old boy mentioned earlier, fall into that gray area between mental retardation and average or normal intellectual ability. These children are familiar to all teachers. Their school performance is consistent with their own abilities, but below the expected standard. They have obvious achievement and learning problems, but they do not qualify for special education services in most school districts. Whether it is desirable or not, these children have traditionally been called "slow learners."

Given current attitudes about specific learning disabilities, the dangers in misdiagnosis should be obvious. Resultant expectations may not be consistent with the child's ability and may cause erroneous decisions about the type of instruction a child needs, the rate at which new learning will occur and the standards of performance a child can be expected to maintain.

Perhaps the greatest danger lies in the possibility that inappropriate, long-range academic goals will be established. The slow learning child, incorrectly diagnosed as learning disabled, may be exposed to a highly specialized form of remedial instruction when the real need is for systematic developmental instruction paced at a rate consistent with learning ability.

It is acknowledged that a differential diagnosis between slow development and specific learning disabilities is often difficult to make. It is also true that when there is doubt as to which diagnosis should be made, one would always hope for and want to give the most positive diagnosis—learning disabled. But, recognizing that mislabeling is dangerous, it is important that the distinguishing features between slow development and specific learning disabilities be carefully considered when a diagnosis is made.

LEARNING PATTERNS

Perhaps the most important distinguishing feature is that a slow learner's development is even. The child doesn't demonstrate the erratic pattern in development and skill attainment that is characteristic of the child with learning disabilities.

A slow learner's language and perceptual-motor development may be immature and may reflect behavioral deficits similar to those of a learning disabled child. Both types of behavior in the slow learner, however, will be similarly immature, and developmental levels will be consistent with intellectual ability.

A slow learner's school achievement will be below that expected for the child's age level in the basic academic subjects. There will be remarkable similarities in performance levels and a discernable consistency between academic achievement levels and mental development.

An examination of the child's developmental history should reveal the same consistent pattern. This is the child who was slow to learn both to walk and talk, rather than slow to learn one set of skills but quick to learn another—a learning pattern often true of the learning disabled child.

The slow learner is the child whose performance on intellectual ability tests places him or her at the lowest point within the range designated as average intelligence. And when you examine actual performance, it is apparent that, once again, it is even. The child performed equally well on all types of tasks used to measure intellectual ability. In contrast, the learning disabled child may have attained *exactly the same score* but performed very poorly with some types of tasks and exceedingly well with others.

Observation of a slow learner is likely to reveal that once a skill has been learned and accuracy has been achieved, it is maintained. Long-term observation reveals a steady pattern of academic progress rather than a pattern of progress and subsequent regression. Erratic performance is the sine qua non of the learning disabilities syndrome.

Finally, the slow learner is less inclined to impulsivity. Attention spans may be shorter than desired or expected, and restlessness and distractibility may be present, but the tendency to respond without reflection is less characteristic of these children than of those with specific learning disabilities.

BEHAVIORAL SIMILARITIES

It is important to recognize that slow learners do demonstrate many of the same behavior patterns that are characteristic of children with learning disabilities. This is particularly true with regard to errors in letter and number reproduction—a characteristic symptomatic of perceptual-motor dysfunction. It is also true of the kinds of errors made when the child is learning to read.

Behavioral similarities between the two types of children cause diagnostic confusion. The difference is this: Behavior that appears to represent a specific deficit fits into a pattern of developmental retardation when the child is a slow learner. Behavior that appears to represent a specific deficit is usually just that when the child is learning disabled.

To sum up, a diagnosis of learning disabilities implies the probability of ultimately normal academic progress and the possibility that educational intervention may actually alleviate the learning problem. Consequently, such a diagnosis has a powerful effect on the attitudes of those who set educational goals and determine educational expectations for children. This seems sufficient reason to make that diagnosis with accuracy and caution.

The Young Gifted Child

Young gifted children can be prone to specific difficulties in their school careers—author Susan Schwartz points out the warning signals

Dr. Susan Schwartz

Susan Schwartz is Visiting Assistant Professor in the Psychology Department of the State University of New York at Oswego.

The years before entrance to first grade are critical for all children, not just the gifted, in terms of intellectual, social and emotional development. What I have presented here is some reflective thinking on the problems of young gifted children, along with some suggested interventions to help deal with those problems.

But first, the gifted preschooler has to be identified as such. The teacher of a preschool child has as much (and sometimes more) opportunity to detect giftedness than anyone else with whom the child interacts. Parents may be too busy, or unaware of special talents.

If a child in your class exhibits eight of the characteristics listed below, consistently, then further observation or testing is in order. If you can spot 12 or more, the child is most likely gifted and testing and possible intervention measures should be implemented.

Checklist for Characteristics of the Young Gifted Child

1. Has a quick and sharp memory.
2. Asks a lot of questions.
3. Is nervous about relationships with other children.
4. Learns new material quickly.
5. Easily performs difficult manual tasks.
6. Is bored by normal activities.
7. Has difficulty making friends.
8. Shows unusual talent in a special area such as music or art.
9. Shows interest and aptitude in many areas.
10. Has larger than usual vocabulary for age.
11. Prefers solitary activities.
12. Is able to verbally express ideas easily.
13. Is anxious about work being perfect.
14. Adjusts to changes easily.
15. Has a long attention span.

Problems and Interventions.

Four problem areas are considered: *Peer, Classroom Behavior, Parental* and *Self*. Each of these sections is further divided and three main interventions are proposed in these categories—Teacher/Classroom, Teacher/Parents, and Direct (self).

The interventions are described first and then the problems are delineated with possible interventions as well as specific recommendations.

Interventions

Teacher/Classroom

Grouping: This intervention may already have been used in your program if you are the teacher of a class of gifted children. However this is not the only way of grouping. If you have but a few gifted children in your class, have them work together on certain projects.

Although there are advantages to grouping there are also disadvantages. Grouping can cause alienation from the rest of the class and does not help the child become accustomed to being around others who are not gifted. Probably the best plan is to use grouping for some activities but not for others.

Special assignments: Think up special projects in special interest fields for the gifted child, or make projects more open-ended with less restrictions.

Teacher behavior: Teachers sometimes tend to praise gifted children quite a bit and there are times when

44. The Young Gifted Child

this can do more harm than good. Praise should be contingent upon performance.

Sometimes the teacher may come to expect too much from the gifted child in too many areas. Expectations that the teacher conveys to the child should be based on a consideration of all the child's abilities, talents, or lack of them.

Social Engineering: Just as a teacher's behavior toward the gifted child holds much sway, so does the arrangement, timing and management of classroom activities. Many problems may be solved with this kind of social engineering.

Teacher/Parents

The teacher is the child's link from the home to the larger environment of the school which means that parents and teachers need to communicate and communicate well. One or two meetings to exchange ideas or information may be all that is needed. On the other hand, it may be necessary for the parents and teacher to work together for a longer period of time on a special project or problem-solving approach.

Direct (self)

If a problem is too complex, or particularly stubborn, it may be necessary for the teacher to refer the parents to a psychologist or other person whose specialization may provide some answers.

Problems

Discussing problems of the gifted child may lead to the impression that gifted children have more than their share of troubles. This is not true. Short and long term research has shown that gifted individuals are as healthy as other children physically, mentally and emotionally; they may even be healthier. The point here is not that the gifted child has more problems, but that he or she may be especially prone to specific ones.

Peer

Ridicule: Children often thoughtlessly pick on others who are different, and gifted children can appear different to their peers. Since the preschool classroom may be the child's first venture into a social environment other than home, acceptance from peers can be crucial for the young gifted child. This is the period of formulation of self-esteem, and hence very critical. Names, labels or feelings of ostracism can persist and the child who others call odd may come to believe that it is true. Interventions suitable here are Teacher/Classroom—Grouping, Teacher behavior, Social engineering; Teacher/Parents and Direct (self).

Specific Recommendations

—Grouping with children of similar ability will reduce the appearance of being different.
—Try to observe what is causing the ridicule. Is it something that you as the teacher are fostering (e.g. by giving too much praise?). Is it a mannerism the child has?
—Consultation with parents or with a counselor may be in order depending on the severity of the problem.
—Arrange situations so that the child's gifts or talents are an asset to the group while working on a special project and are therefore appreciated.

Envy: Envy from peers can be a positive or negative influence depending on its severity and how it is perceived and directed. If it is severe, the gifted child can not help but perceive it. If it is severe and obviously directed at him/her then the influence will be negative. Other children may express direct anger in or out of class. Hidden envy may show up in taunting or making fun of the gifted child.

However, if the envy is moderate and/or is not directed right at the gifted child, then the influence could be positive. Other children may try to emulate the gifted child who always has the right answer, or is best in art or music. This could help raise the motivation of all the children since they may try to be as good or know as much as the gifted child. The gifted child's self-esteem may increase as he/she realizes that others desire to be as good.

Attention must be paid in this situation lest the gifted child rely too much on always being the best, or on praise from others to assess his or her own self-worth in the future. Interventions to use here include Teacher/Classroom—Grouping, Teacher behavior.

Specific Recommendations

—Grouping with children of similar ability will make the child seem "less bright" to peers.
—The teacher should be sure that an *appropriate* amount of praise and attention is being given.

Finding friends: Finding friends at the preschool level is an important and often difficult task for all children. Children at this level are becoming aware of others and of the rest of the world. They are learning to share time and ideas with others. Sometimes this is not easy. Learning about and learning to cope with a world away from home can be trying, especially to a child who is used to being the center of attention. At school there is only one teacher for many children and the children must learn to turn to each other for attention, praise, help and company. Since the gifted child might be especially used to being the center of attention at home, it may be even more difficult for the gifted child to adjust to a school situation. The gifted child may be less willing to share the teacher's time and attention and may come to resent the other children, presenting a roadblock to making friends. This may interact with a problem of level: The other children may appear young and/or slow to the gifted child, who may therefore not want to interact with others, or may assume an attitude of superiority, making the finding of friends even more difficult. Interventions to use here include Teacher/Classroom—Grouping, Special assignments, Social engineering.

Specific Recommendations

—Grouping will put the child more in contact with those of similar ability
—Even if there are not other gifted children in the class, there are probably children who share interests. Arrange for special projects to get some of these children together.
—Some children are more outgoing than others and consequently they

5. CHILDREN WITH SPECIAL NEEDS

make friends easily. Pairing the gifted child with an outgoing child will make it easier for the gifted child to be accepted and to make friends.

Classroom Behavior
Belligerence: The gifted child may be aware of superior abilities and may use them to take leadership that can lead to dominance. This is certainly an undesirable pattern. Interventions here are Teacher/Classroom—Teacher behavior, Social engineering; Teacher/Parents and Direct (self).

Specific Recommendations
—The teacher should be sure that the child is not being reinforced for dominant behavior by getting more attention (even if the attention is a reprimand and not praise, it is still reinforcing).
—Arrange group projects where cooperation is necessary for the project's completion.
—The problem may stem from home; insight and help may be available through parents.
—If the trend toward dominance is severe enough, a psychologist may be sought.

Monopolizes class or teacher time: Because of diverse interests, intense curiosities and/or superior abilities, the gifted child may command more class or teacher time. It may be easy for a teacher to fall into the habit of spending more time with a child who is exceptionally bright, but this may cause a problem for the child later when he or she must adjust to a new teacher who may not have that capability. Interventions here are Teacher/Classroom—Special assignments, Teacher behavior, Social engineering.

Specific Recommendations
—Work up special projects that will creatively engage the child's time and energy.
—Reinforce the child through attention and praise for quiet, independent activities.
—Arrange situations where peer approval is contingent upon cooperation and sharing.

Indolence: There are many reasons why a gifted child may be, or appear to be, lazy. The activities of the class may seem boring or unstimulating to the gifted child and motivation may therefore be low. The gifted child may be reading by the age of three or four. If the other children are learning the alphabet, the gifted child will be very bored and may refuse to engage in any of the alphabet learning activities. Another possibility is that the child is aware of superior abilities, and is purposely appearing slow or lazy in order to gain peer approval and acceptance. Indolence can mask gifts and talents and slow the intellectual growth of the child. Interventions to use here are Teacher/Classroom—Special assignments, Grouping, Teacher behavior; Teacher/Parents.

Specific Recommendations
—Grouping with others of similar ability can motivate the child.
—Special assignments may alleviate boredom.
—Reduce praise if there is a possibility that the child is "faking" to gain peer approval.
—Parents may be able to shed light on the cause or help in motivating the child.

Parental
Parents attitudes towards their child's gifts can have great and permanent effects of the child's growth and motivation. If the parents are unaware of the child's talents then a meeting between parents and teacher may be all that is needed. However, some parents may be aware of their child's abilities and still appear apathetic. They may feel unprepared to cope with a "special" child and may not know what they can or should do. The parents can easily convey their feelings of uneasiness to the child without even realizing it. The result can be that the child mistakes the parents' lack of praise or action as rejection, and may become unwilling or unmotivated to pursue interests and abilities. It can all add up to a stifling of the child's intellectual or emotional growth and a neglect of special gifts. Interventions—Teacher/Parents.

Specific Recommendations
—Speak with parents about child's abilities and suggest ways to capitalize on their development. Provide resource information for testing and guidance.

If on the other hand, the parents are very aware of their child's gifts and are too demanding, this can put a tremendous pressure on the young child who wants very much to please. The child may become overly concerned with perfection, nervous and unable to enjoy the activities that are forced upon him/her. Interventions—Teacher/Parents.

Specific Recommendations
—Discuss differential aptitudes with parents. Help them realize what they can and can't expect from their child; what goals are realistic for them to set.

Parents Under-demanding: Because a child seems "special" the parents may decide that special treatment is in order. Parents may feel they do not need to teach the child as much at home, or do as much to encourage mental growth and stimulation. The gifted child may seem more mature than others and parents may feel they do not have to direct the child's development as a result. The gifted child, like all children, needs parental attention, guidance and stimulation as well as encouragement and direction from parents to explore and develop gifts and talents. Intervention—Teacher/Parents.

Specific Recommendations
—Help parents see how their encouragement directly affects their child. Give suggestions for small projects for the parents to set up at home to challenge their child's special abilities.

Too much attention: If a gifted child comes from a family in which the other children are not exceptional, parents may tend to praise and give more attention to the gifted child. This can lead to sibling rivalry and a child who needs and expects a lot of attention—more than he or she is likely to get in the future. Interventions—Teacher/Parents.

Specific Recommendations
—Emphasize the problems this can

raise in terms of sibling rivalry and need for attention. Show parents how to give praise that is contingent on performance and based on each child's abilities.

Parents prefer that the child be popular: Most parents would be proud to have a gifted child, but there are some who may not place much value on the fact that their child can learn faster than others, or can play the piano very well at the age of four. They may feel that it is more important for the child to be "normal" or popular. They may try to gear the child's interest away from music, art or school, towards activities that the parents deem more "popular." It is hard to say who is right or wrong in a case like this, but it is certainly not beneficial for the child to be discouraged, and in some extreme cases, prevented, from developing a special interest, aptitude or talent. Interventions—Teacher/Parents.

Specific Recommendations

—Emphasize the uniqueness of their child and the need for special talents to be allowed to develop.

Self

Tolerance of others: It may be difficult for a gifted child to be around others who are not as bright. Boredom, restlessness or impatience may easily set in. But the gifted child must grow up and eventually learn to function in a world that is full of people who are not as intelligent or talented, and it will be easier to do so if tolerance of others is fostered at an early age. An important concept here is not only learning tolerance, but learning an appreciation of the unique self-worth of every individual regardless of intelligence or talent. The gifted child who fails to learn to interact with those who are not as bright will not only find it difficult to make friends in the future, but will probably have a hard time making a healthy adjustment to an adult life. Interventions—Teacher/Classroom: Social engineering.

Specific Recommendations

—Have children of different ages and abilities work on activities together.

Self expectation for perfection: Just as parents may place too many demands on the gifted child, the child may come to expect too much from him/herself. Everything may have to be "perfect" or "just right" and the child may become frustrated or nervous when it is not. It is hard for a child to enjoy activities if the result must always be perfection and a pattern like this that is set in the preschool years could last into adulthood resulting in unrealistic self-performance goals and pressures. Interventions here are Teacher/Classroom–Special assignments, Teacher behavior, Social engineering; Teacher/Parents and Direct (self).

Specific Recommendations

—Reduce quantity of assignments.
—Reduce expectations of what should be accomplished so that the child finds it easier to meet with success and approval.
—Provide "just for fun" activities with some easy-going children.
—Speak with the parents about providing similar kinds of activities at home and also about reducing their expectations.
—If problem is severe, direct counseling may be needed.

44. The Young Gifted Child

Boredom: Perhaps the most obvious problem the gifted child may face is boredom; boredom with the kind or pace of activities, or with peers. If the class is engaged in pre-reading activities, and the gifted child is already reading, he/she will be bored. If a storybook is being read to the group the gifted child may want to read it on his/her own and may become frustrated when not allowed to do so. Even if the material to be learned is new to the gifted child the pace may be unbearably slow. Boredom can be so severe that it causes an almost unbearable restlessness, and any interest or excitement in going to school can be quickly extinguished. This can and does often happen at an early age and the waste that can result from a non-development of talent and ability is enormous. Fortunately the problem of boredom is one that is relatively easy to handle, if only we are aware enough to spot it. Interventions—Teacher/Classroom—Grouping, Special assignments; Teacher/Parents.

Specific Recommendations

—Grouping will raise the level of stimulation.
—Involve the child in more and varied assignments including outside special projects.
—Involve the parents in outside and at-home projects.

We are all caught in a web of definitions and decisions in regard to the gifted and talented. It will probably be some time before it is all sorted out. In the meantime, the special talents and gifts of the children with which we work must be paramount.

Let's Go Slow on Acceleration

Joanne Yatvin

As an elementary school principal, the most frequent requests I get concern academic acceleration. Typically, such requests come from parents of our youngest children, who feel that formal reading and math instruction should begin in kindergarten or that a child who can read should skip kindergarten or that something is wrong when their first grader can't read a book of fairy tales by midyear.

Parents are not the only ones who want acceleration, however. Many teachers and principals, harassed by anxious parents and wanting to look good to the public, have succumbed to the pressure and are now pushing children into advanced work and esoteric subject matter. Their strategies range from trying to cover as many textbooks in a year as possible to directing a group of eight-year-olds in a Shakespearean play.

Upon reflection, it is not difficult to discover the causes of this most recent trend toward academic acceleration. One is our American obsession with competition; we are not satisfied unless our own children excel everyone else's in sports, creativity, and academics.

Another is the current economic recession, which has produced a deep and pervasive fear for our children's future. If our children are not among the best academically, we wonder, how can they get into prestigious colleges or have a chance at the dwindling number of good jobs? Still another is the well-publicized results of various standardized tests, which imply that many children are not learning as much as they should in school.

These three factors have aroused in parents a fierce determination to secure a quality education for their children, which, in turn, has given rise to acceleration programs in many schools.

Meeting the fears and desires that spring from the first two factors is clearly beyond the capability of any school. But providing the quality education parents want is and always has been the primary goal of educators and educational institutions. I certainly have no quarrel with it—only with the mistaken notion that pushing children through subject matter at a rapid rate makes for quality education. Experience has convinced me that this kind of acceleration does not benefit either bright or average students and that it can, in fact, harm them.

Let's begin with the harm. What critics of acceleration have stressed in the past is the possible social maladjustment that can result from skipping children or making them into academic grinds. Although this sometimes occurs, I have not found it a common or lasting problem, since most healthy kids learn to cope.

More serious and widespread, in my opinion—though less obvious—are the attitudes, fears, and self-images that can develop in children who are pushed. They may come to doubt their own worth or their parents' love. They may learn to value only success and successful people. They may feel guilty about wanting to play, to make noise, to act silly—guilty about being children.

Added to the possibility of psychological damage, moreover, is the danger of intellectual damage. Before academic skills can be learned, all children need a strong background of foundation skills. Unless they have (and continue to have throughout their school careers) considerable experience in moving within their environment, manipulating objects, observing phenomena, communicating with people, and formulating concepts about the world, they cannot learn to read, write, or perform various mathematical functions.

They may be able to perform some of the mechanical operations required, but they will have no true understanding and no base of intellectual power upon which to develop further competence. For this reason, children who are pushed into a concentrated program of book and pencil-and-paper tasks before they have a preacademic skill foundation are prone to develop learning disabilities in one or more academic areas.

Even if great care were taken to protect children from psychological and mental damage, however, the lack of any real benefits from acceleration makes it hardly worthwhile. Ample evidence exists to indicate that children who have been accelerated do not do any better in the long run than those who have not.

Several reading studies, for example, show that children who are given formal instruction early are frequently surpassed later on by children who start at a later age. In another vein, my impression is that most of the FLES (Foreign Language in the Elementary School) programs, so popular in this country a few years ago, have been terminated. Apparently, students who participated did not do any

45. Let's Go Slow on Acceleration

better in high school than those who began a foreign language in the ninth grade.

Children fail to benefit from typical classroom acceleration because it violates basic learning principles.

In the first place, acceleration focuses on information, not skills, although we know that information quickly becomes obsolete, that it has only limited usefulness in subsequent learning, and that most of it is soon forgotten.

Secondly, increasing the rate of instruction to cover more material each year forces children beyond the point of effective learning. Several research studies have shown that when new material is introduced too rapidly, lumped together for quick teaching, or inadequately practiced, both assimilation and retention decrease. When the emphasis in a classroom is on covering material rather than really learning it, as it is when acceleration is the goal, little attention is given to finding a rate of instruction that suits children.

A too rapid rate increases the likelihood of superficiality. If material is to be covered quickly, the easiest approach is to give everything a once-over-lightly. Letting children explore ideas takes more time than can be spared and does not produce results that will raise scores on achievement tests.

Also tied to increased rate is decreased opportunity for practice. This is unfortunate because skills deteriorate if they are not used regularly, and much of what may superficially appear to be time wasting in some classrooms or on a playground is really necessary maintenance and new applications of learned skills. Such practice activities are indeed more time-consuming than the introduce-drill-test-move-on procedure typical of acceleration programs, but they are a vital part of learning that cannot be eliminated without adverse consequences.

In addition, an acceleration program often introduces skills without regard to whether children are physically and emotionally ready for them. Certainly, five-year-olds can be taught to play chess, but, given a choice, wouldn't most of them prefer more social and physically active games? Skills that are not in tune with a child's development at a particular age are not likely to be practiced in free time and, thus, will fall into disuse.

The concept of readiness is a key issue in a more complicated way also. As Piaget's learning studies have shown, children move through stages of intellectual development, dependent on physiological growth, experience, social interaction, and previously developed mental structures.

Of course, there are individual differences, but by and large all children in a society go through the same stages in the same order at approximately the same age. Teaching that ignores these stages results only in superficial and temporary learning. For example, you can tell kindergarten children to color the sky down to the ground in their pictures, and they will do it if they remember to, but it is not until much later that they come to understand that the blue sky above them and the invisible air around them are one and the same.

Another of Piaget's conclusions sheds further light on the weaknesses of the acceleration concept. Piaget believes that children must be actively involved in order to learn: They assimilate new data through physical and logical operations on phenomena and then reorganize their own mental structures to accommodate them. Because, again, this learning process is time-consuming, it has not found favor with advocates of acceleration. It is far quicker and easier to emphasize rote memorization of facts and acceptance of authoritative opinions than it is to encourage children to think.

From a condemnation of acceleration, I return now to a consideration of our original goal: All children should receive a quality education. And on that basis, I must also condemn much of what might be termed "standard educational practice" along with the various manifestations of the "back to the basics" movement.

The perceptive reader has no doubt realized early in the foregoing discussion that much of what is wrong with acceleration is also wrong with education in general and that the ordinary classroom can wreak its own forms of psychological and mental havoc on children.

It is not necessary, I think, to belabor the often-made points about boredom and destruction of motivation in classrooms where all children must learn the same thing at the same time or to demonstrate that accumulation of information, superficiality, and passive reception of material are fairly typical characteristics of regular and "basics" educational programs.

It should be emphasized, however, that in such programs Piaget's theories of intellectual development are as often ignored as they are in acceleration programs because teaching proceeds in a pattern and at a rate that takes no account of needs or readiness. Moreover, while there may be lots of practice of the busywork variety, insistence on quiet and order in the classroom precludes children's active involvement with learning tasks.

Despite the distressing pictures I have painted, many classrooms exist that foster real learning. For average children, they provide a foundation of skills and understandings sufficient to meet the demands of future schooling and the outside world. For bright and creative children, they provide in addition, a chance to explore new fields and to move ahead at a rate compatible with their development.

Those parents and educators who are seriously determined to improve education should learn to

5. CHILDREN WITH SPECIAL NEEDS

identify such classrooms and exert their influence to help them proliferate.

How does one identify "learning classrooms"? Because they come in all shapes and sizes with widely varying amounts of equipment, noise, and clutter, it takes some time to perceive what is really going on. Essentially, a "learning classroom" is not a "teaching classroom." What children need are not instructions, explanations, lectures, and demonstrations, but opportunities to learn. Learning flourishes when classrooms have the following characteristics:

1. Foundation skills. For considerable time before the 3 R's are introduced, classroom activities focus on physical movement and control, auditory and visual reception and memory, oral expression of ideas, logical reasoning, and social interactions. Though less central in the curriculum in later school years, these kinds of activities continue throughout the education process.

2. Active involvement. Children are continually expected to manipulate, observe, experiment, make guesses, discuss, argue, explain, change their minds, and produce their own creations. Workbooks and drill materials that encourage children to fill in blanks and repeat what they've read without thinking are conspicuously absent.

3. Skills more than knowledge. Most lessons are aimed at enabling children to do things. Information is valued primarily as an aid to doing. Reinforcement activities allow children to practice, extend, and apply skills to new situations.

4. Flexible tasks and time periods. Children frequently have choices of what to do and when to do it. When there is group work, tasks are differentiated to suit individuals, and when a single assignment is given to the whole class, there is considerable latitude in the way it can be done. Although there are deadlines for some assignments, others may go on indefinitely. At times, a child may decide not to finish a task that he or she has started.

5. New experiences, opportunities, and challenges. Remembering that a classroom is a closed and somewhat static environment, the teacher tries to keep it stimulating by introducing new materials, areas of interest, decorations, groupings of children, and types of tasks. He or she also takes children out of the classroom often. The changes are not random—though they are partly dictated by the children's and teacher's feelings—but are organized to broaden experience and increase challenge.

6. Hard work (not to be confused with a large quantity of dull work). Most of the assignments demand thought and sustained effort. Careful workmanship and thoroughness are valued; so is a noble failure. Because drills, exercises, and tests do not provide any real reason for children to work hard, most assignments ask children to produce things that are real, important, and useful to them.

7. Teacher guidance. The teacher knows what each child has done and can do and is sensitive to the child's learning rate and feelings about learning and about himself or herself. The teacher suggests, guides, encourages, criticizes, and allows children to make mistakes. He or she is tolerant of occasional failures, false starts, and time wasting, but in the long run expects excellence from every child.

When a classroom has all these things—or even most of them—children can accelerate their own learning in a natural way. Guided by a wise and perceptive teacher, they can start down the road to the quality education we have, until now, only dreamed of.

Mainstreaming: Valuing Diversity in Children

Kathleen H. Dunlop

Kathleen H. Dunlop, Ph.D., is Associate Professor, Faculties of Education and Psychology, at George Peabody College for Teachers, Nashville, Tennessee. She is a former elementary school teacher and Head Start teaching coordinator.

On her way to school, Sue's second thoughts began in earnest. "Maybe I should have said no. What if the kids don't understand? Can I really be a good teacher for a handicapped child?" As she drew closer to school, her thoughts continued: "What if it doesn't work? What will the kids think? What will *Danny* think?"

Yesterday afternoon, Sue's principal had come into her kindergarten room with Danny's mother who explained that she was looking for a school where Danny, paralyzed from the waist down since birth, could work and play to his full capacities with nonhandicapped children. Danny's mother and the principal stayed for a while, watching the activities in the classroom. Just before they left, Danny's mother asked Sue how she would feel about having a handicapped child in her classroom. Sue replied that it would be fine, if the mother felt that the classroom would be a good place for Danny. She added quickly that she had no special training and had never before worked with a handicapped child. Danny's mother replied, "I'm not worried about that," and went on to say that she liked the individual nature of the activities going on and the open, accepting environment. She felt that the atmosphere of respect and acceptance, above all, was important for Danny. The principal and Danny's mother left after arranging for Danny to come the next morning about half an hour after the start of school.

I would like to acknowledge the excellent teaching and consultation of Sue Lindenberger, kindergarten teacher in the Metropolitan Nashville-Davidson County School System, Nashville, Tennessee. It was in visits to her classroom that this article had its beginnings.

Everything had happened quickly, and Sue was happy at the prospect of opening her classroom to another child. As the morning drew closer, however, her excitement gave way to anxiety. Doubts about the wisdom of having agreed to the arrangement grew, and Sue practiced parts of the discussion she planned to have with the children before Danny's arrival. She wanted them to understand and accept him, but as she practiced the discussion, her doubts grew larger about her ability to handle the situation well for everyone.

She set up the day's activities as the children arrived anxious to tell her about special things and eager to see what was going to happen that day. Just as the children sat down for discussion time, Heather called out, "Teacher! Look! There's a new boy here!" Danny—his eyes quickly exploring the room and his mouth turned up in a tentative smile so typical of "new kids"—was wheeled through the door and into the room.

That afternoon, the phone rang in an office several miles away. When I answered, Sue said, "Hi!" With scarcely a pause she said, "I just had to tell someone! I have *never* been so proud of anything in my whole life as I was of my kids today. They were great!" She explained who Danny was. "When he came in, about four kids wanted to take his lunch and put it up on the shelf for him. Two others took his coat and showed him where to hang it up. Several took turns pushing his wheelchair when we went out for recess and lunch. Somebody asked why he had a wheelchair and Danny said, 'It's because I can't walk.'" Sue continued, "I don't think everything is always going to be this beautiful, but I was so worried and they handled it so well. They were just fantastic!"

* * * * *

Thus did one teacher and 26 children meet "mainstreaming": the growing and often legislatively mandated practice of integrating exceptional children into the "regular" classroom. Children who are

5. CHILDREN WITH SPECIAL NEEDS

being mainstreamed include those with physical handicaps, such as Danny, as well as those who have been identified as having emotional problems, learning disabilities, and intellectual handicaps. When regular classrooms experience success in mainstreaming, one large element of that success is a teacher whose relationship with children is characterized by several factors: respect; understanding and acceptance of human differences; understanding of children's development; and awareness of the tremendously important role the teacher plays in setting a tone of acceptance and appreciation of human individuality.

Growth of Mainstreaming

Children with special needs have not always been a focal point of concern among educators in the United States. Although Massachusetts opened a special school for mentally retarded children in 1850 and shortly thereafter Howe (1866) advocated integrating blind children into regular public schools (so that "social competence" in all children might be enhanced), it was not until the turn of the century that even scattered efforts were made to educate exceptional children in public schools. At that time, special classes were opened in public schools in some states (e.g., Rhode Island and Massachusetts) and classes for blind children were opened in the Chicago public schools. For the most part, however, children with special needs were excluded by law and policy from public schools.

In 1922 the Council for Exceptional Children was founded and began advocacy work on behalf of children with identified special needs. It was not until the late 1940s and 1950s, however, that there was any appreciable effort on the part of public schools to provide educational services to exceptional children. The weight of federal law was added to state efforts in the 1950s with the passage of Public Law 85-926 which provided financial assistance to educate teachers to work specifically with exceptional children.

As the practice of creating special classes for exceptional children grew, so too did the research focused on ascertaining the efficacy of special class placement for the handicapped. Some research indicated that special classes provided a more supportive and sheltered social environment for exceptional children, but other researchers found that special class placement did little to increase the learning and academic achievement of children.

Lloyd Dunn, a leader in the field of special education, drew serious, widespread attention to the issue of special class placement in 1968 with the publication of an article questioning the appropriateness of special, segregated classes for many children labeled "educable mentally retarded" (Dunn 1968). The importance of Dunn's question, combined with increasing demands from the parents of handicapped children that public schools serve their children, resulted in the beginning of a movement whose major impact is just beginning to be felt today. State legislatures in increasing numbers have enacted laws requiring that public education systems provide all children with an education appropriate to their needs and levels of development. Most often, such legislation has also required that exceptional children be educated in "regular" public school classrooms wherever possible. At the federal level, Head Start programs have been under federal mandate since 1972 to insure that no fewer than 10 percent of the places in Head Start programs go to handicapped children.

Research on Placement of Special Children

If it is to work well for all children, however, mainstreaming cannot be construed as a license to place all children in a "normal" classroom and consider them a group whose goal is homogeneity. Mainstreaming cannot become a process whereby children with highly individual needs and strengths are given the same "equal" treatment. If it is to enhance each child's sense of dignity and worth, mainstreaming must be considered a way of expanding common conceptions of "normal" and of helping all educators meet the different needs of each child in a classroom. All children, in unique ways, are exceptional and special individuals.

Some research (Jones 1974) has found that children in special classes experience and dislike the stigma that accompanies the labeling which precedes placement. Others have found that children in segregated "special" classes have less favorable attitudes toward school than do equally exceptional children in integrated or mainstreamed classrooms (Gottlieb and Budoff 1972). Still other researchers have found that exceptional children in special classes do not accomplish their educational objectives at any better rate, and often have lower standards of academic achievement than do similar exceptional children in integrated classroom settings (Johnson 1962).

Not all researchers have found that special class placement has negative effects on exceptional children, however. Goldstein, Moss, and Jordan (1965), for example, found that educable mentally retarded (EMR) children in special classes took greater risks than did their counterparts in regular classes; they also found that the children's progress was rated more positively by their parents than was the progress of EMRs in regular classes. In another study which focused on the behavior of emotionally disturbed children, Vacc (1971) found that children in special classes exhibited positive changes in behavior, while regular class exceptional children registered negative changes. Many other studies have found negative factors associated with regular class placement for exceptional children. One of the most common negative outcomes has been identified as peer rejection, which can constitute a major element in the school lives of many handicapped children assigned to regular classes (Bryan 1974; Gottlieb, Gampel, and Budoff 1973; Iano et al. 1974; Johnson 1950).

Characteristics of a Successfully Mainstreamed Classroom

The presence of a skilled and sensitive teacher—one who can facilitate positive peer relations and motivate learning—is central to the success which children in *any* classroom experience. That skill and sensitivity become critical in the mainstreamed classroom, where the range of individual needs and strengths is broader than that to which many educators have become accustomed.

Haring, Stern, and Cruickshank (1958) identified four factors critical to the success of integrating exceptional children into regular classrooms: the extent to which (a) the classroom provides for all needs of the child; (b) the child can become a contributing member of the group; (c) the physical facilities of the school are amenable to the child's needs; (d) the teacher with whom the child is placed understands and accepts him/her. Wynne, Ulfelder, and Dakof refer to one of the same themes: "The ability and attitude of the teacher appear to be *the* most important factors in the success of an integrated program" (1975, p. 75).

A teacher who values and responds to the individuality of each child is central to the success of any mainstreamed classroom. Of greatest importance would seem to be the teacher's skills, sense of purpose, and attitudes of acceptance, understanding, and concern for each child in the classroom. Those attributes can be manifested in many ways. The practices discussed below are some that have characterized the plans, activities, and interactions of teachers who have made mainstreaming a success for the children in their classrooms.

Differences between children are discussed with sensitivity, openness, and honesty. Children are generally very much aware of physical and behavioral differences, and a lack of discussion about human differences does *not* minimize their awareness of those differences. It may, however, help build an attitude that differences per se are bad or, at best, unfortunate.

In successfully mainstreamed classrooms, discussions of differences occur whenever children ask questions or the teacher feels that discussion would be helpful to the growth of children's understanding. If they are to be helpful to *all* children, such discussions must convey the teacher's genuine respect for each of the children in the group and an understanding of individual children and their unique needs, interests, and abilities.

In the successfully mainstreamed classroom, children are often involved in answering the questions raised. A child who has a major difference is very often the one most capable of explaining what a difference means and how it feels. In a supportive environment, children are also often capable of giving direct answers that satisfy the need for information and contribute to building an attitude that differences, and questions about them, are normal and acceptable.

The teacher focuses intensively on the development of positive learning sets. In the suc-

5. CHILDREN WITH SPECIAL NEEDS

cessfully mainstreamed classroom, each child is given an abundant measure of encouragement and support. The teacher focuses on what children *can* do, activities for which genuine praise can be given, and areas which need positive encouragement.

The development of positive learning sets involves expectations for the attainment of realistic goals. The teacher has a tremendous amount of power—through realistic goal-setting, encouragement, and expectation—to create an environment in which each child grows to feel that he or she can do many things. When teachers assess children's needs, plan for children's progress, hold developmentally appropriate expectations for each child, and respond positively and with appropriate feedback to each child, children will thrive.

It is critical that the teacher ensure opportunity for some success on the part of each child. No one, child or adult, will long stay in a situation where the feedback on performance and personal worth is continually negative. Adults often have the freedom to leave a negative situation; children do not have the same freedom in the physical sense, but they can and often do escape by engaging in unproductive, aggressive, or withdrawing behavior. Each child must experience real success and must know that she or he is a positively valued member of the classroom.

Some time is set aside each day to evaluate and plan for the progress of each child in the classroom. One common source of distress in a classroom is children's inability to understand what is expected in work or behavior; an equally perplexing problem is work which does not challenge or interest a child. The problem in either case does not lie primarily with the child but is more likely found in inadequately conceived and implemented curriculum. Setting up time each day to evaluate children's skill levels and abilities can be a most important first step in ensuring that required and optional activities are reasonable, stimulating, and interesting for individual children.

Information about children's progress and interactions can be jotted down momentarily during the day; similar information can also be collected at the end of each day. The teacher's attention, even for a short time, can often be focused objectively and fully on one child each day and the detailed observations can be most useful in evaluating a child's needs and progress. Volunteers and other classroom aides can also be asked to make brief and specific observations.

Objective information is most important in evaluation so that children's tasks and environments are not set up on the basis of old or erroneous information. Systematic planning and evaluation can make the difference between a classroom that is "getting by" and one that is fostering learning for all persons involved.

Children are allowed and encouraged to undertake activities independently. One of the greatest benefits the mainstreamed classroom can offer all children is the opportunity to learn to work well in a group that includes children with different needs and abilities. In a successfully mainstreamed classroom, children learn that each child is capable of doing a great deal independently and that each child can offer help to another. Handicapped children are encouraged to do things for themselves whenever possible; the help of other children is valued but is not overused at the expense of the handicapped child's growing ability to interact independently in the classroom.

Whenever possible, the classroom is set up to promote independence of action. Children are encouraged to make decisions for themselves and to act independently within the classroom environment. Rules that govern the class are minimal and reasonable; they can be understood and explained by the children. When the needs of individual children require flexibility the teacher may make exceptions. The exceptions, however, are reasonable and well-explained so the children can learn to determine for themselves the roles of individual and group needs.

When limitations are placed on the behavior or activities of a child, positive and concrete suggestions for alternative activities are made. Merely limiting certain kinds of behavior ("You know you're not supposed to . . .") is insufficient. The sensitive and effective teacher establishes positive options and gives a child guidance in discovering alternatives which exist in the classroom. Clear guidance, firmness, and consistency may be needed in helping a child select alternatives, but well-planned options must exist.

Cooperative activities are planned and built into the curriculum. Just as independence is promoted and valued, healthy cooperation is also given a great deal of importance in the classroom. Activities on which two or more children can work are encouraged. Interacting on interesting tasks, children can learn more about capabilities and personalities of other children. In well-supported cooperative activities, children can begin to understand that the human experiences they each have are as important as the overt behavioral and physiological differences.

The teacher in the successfully mainstreamed classroom is alert for repeated occurrences of self-imposed or other-imposed isolation: She or he is, in short, a good observer of the patterns of social interaction in the classroom. The teacher is also aware of individuals and groups of children who are more secure and comfortable, and therefore often more able to accept and integrate isolated children into their activities. The sensitive teacher can often accomplish unobtrusively the beginnings of social involvement for a child who cannot do it alone because of lack of confidence and/or lack of consistently appropriate behavior.

Parents are involved in classroom activities whenever possible. Parents represent a rich resource and additional help in the classroom; they also are a valuable source of information about school programs for the community at large. Using parent volunteers often allows the teacher time to respond more adequately to individual children's needs.

Also, the opportunity for parents to interact with children other than their own in the mainstreamed classroom helps them see that all children, handicapped or non-handicapped, have needs and interests in common. Calming parental misgivings about the integration of "different" children into the regular classroom is often the key to helping children develop healthy attitudes toward others and accept human differences.

* * * * *

These are some of the characteristics of a successfully mainstreamed classroom. In many instances, the characteristics differ very little from the attributes of any good classroom for young children. That fact in itself may represent a critical element in successful mainstreaming. The success of mainstreamed classrooms does not depend primarily on learning a whole new set of rules and techniques for "different" children who are entering "regular" classes. It *does* depend in large part on the sensitivity of teachers, their willingness to grow and learn in response to new needs, their ability to see similarity in all children, and their willingness to value and foster diversity.

I visited Sue's class for an hour some two months after Danny's arrival, bringing along another visitor who had taught for several years. During the visit, Danny—who had become accustomed to slipping out of his wheelchair and moving about in the classroom by pulling himself around on the floor with his hands and arms—was quite involved in different activities. As we left the room, the newcomer commented to me, "I'm sorry the mainstreamed child wasn't there today. I really wanted to see how things were working out for him."

It is a tribute to Sue and to the many teachers of young children like her that there are not "normal" and "handicapped" children in successfully mainstreamed classrooms; there are children who differ in abilities, personalities, and some specific needs, but who experience an essentially similar core of humanity and humaneness. The likenesses, if we let them, far outweigh the differences. The differences that do exist should be valued and cherished, for they comprise the uniqueness which characterizes healthy human beings.

Behavior and Guidance

Parents and educators alike put guidance and discipline first when questioned about areas in which they would like more advice, support, and specific techniques in working and living with young children. Many parents depend on educational programs for the socialization of their children. It is through such programs that children often learn to get along with peers and non-family adults, and develop more emotional coping skills.

A host of vital questions are often asked by concerned, anxious, or frustrated parents about aggressive, withdrawn, compulsive, or manipulative behavior. Experienced educators and mental health specialists, however, have no easy solutions, no magic formulas that are guaranteed to work for different children in varied situations.

Until they reach the mental age of six or seven, children inhabit a perceptual world that is dominated by their subjective fantasies and desires, physical actions, and adult prohibitions. Perceptive adults recognize that young children are not reasonable, miniature adults. The ability to think and reflect on one's feelings and behaviors, or about their multiple causes and consequences, is beyond the emotional or intellectual powers of children. Such self-understanding and self-discipline require the maturity of adult logic and extensive experience.

Yet, even the youngest of children can be guided by adults toward healthy expression of a wide range of emotions, including anger and frustration, as well as profit from being redirected in their wishes and behavior when the situation necessitates it.

Psychological research conducted in individuals who are winners and achievers indicated that, very early in life, they developed consistent and pervasive feelings of inner control over their lives. Guidance and discipline of children, then, is not something adults *do to* children as much as it is the gradual process of enabling children to develop self-regulation and feelings of mastery and control over their lives when adults are not around to curb them.

People of all ages need the protection and security of consistent rules and routines, but these need not be arbitrary or demeaning. All rules need to be framed with the understanding that the promotion of positive mental health is a key goal. Still, innumerable situations arise daily when young children, aided by adults, can begin to make choices about their feelings and behavior and their developing competence. Learning that one can choose, builds towards autonomy and a healthy internalized sense of power and control over external circumstances.

Power struggles and contests between children's willpower and adults' tolerance levels are inevitable in early childhood programs. Knowledgable adults, however, who can objectively understand and interpret children's behavior and emotional reactions from the framework of developmental levels and context variables, are in a pivotal position to foster growth in mental health, self-discipline, and competence.

This section includes the work of authorities who postulate a correlation between behavior and mental health. Common behavior problems are discussed from the viewpoint of a humane and child-oriented discipline.

Looking Ahead: Challenge Questions

What does "discipline" mean for parents or caregivers of infants and toddlers? Are there underlying principles to follow with children in the infant and toddler stages?

What do temper tantrums, bed-wetting, and fantasies signify in children's behavior? How can these "signals" be interpreted and managed correctly?

Is "bad" behavior outgrown? How can adult models positively or negatively influence it?

Are there humane techniques that actually work with school-aged children? How can teachers model acceptable attitudes and habits for young children?

What techniques are appropriate for developing self-discipline in young children other than excessive reliance on adult power and limitations?

Are teachers a negative force on children's manifest creativity, especially in art work? How does the development of logical processes affect children's creativity?

HOW TO DISCIPLINE WITH LOVE

Dr. Fitzhugh Dodson

Infancy, which lasts from birth until the child begins to crawl or walk (which will vary according to the child), covers approximately the first year of life. This is the most important period of your child's life, for in infancy he is forming his most fundamental attitudes toward himself and his world. The developmental task of infancy is that of *learning either a basic trust in himself and his world, or a basic distrust,* or something in between. If your baby is fed when he is hungry, given plenty of physical cuddling, and not ignored when he cries, he will feel good about himself and his world and will develop a basically optimistic viewpoint toward life.

Most parents do quite a good job with their child during the stage of infancy, and discipline problems do not ordinarily arise at this time. Nevertheless, the child-raising problems unique to the stage of infancy are important—particularly to the first-time parent. The means by which parents handle these problems will either strengthen or weaken the discipline process that begins at a later stage.

During this stage, it is important for you to remember two things.

First, remember the importance of rapport as the foundation of discipline. Rapport is what makes you a much-loved person in the eyes of your child and rapport is what makes her *want* to obey you. And you are lucky that you have a whole year in which to build rapport by feeding her, cuddling her, talking to her, singing to her, bathing her, changing her diapers, and attending to her other needs. In doing all of these things you are building a solid relationship between the two of you. It is this reservoir of rapport and trust that you will draw upon to handle the discipline problems of toddlerhood.

Second, some children are easier to raise than others. Since each child embodies a different combination of genes, each and every child in the world has a unique biological temperament that begins to manifest itself at birth. Researchers have studied babies in their first week of life and found vast differences among them in such temperamental factors as how active or passive they are, in their rate of crying, intensity of reactions, distractibility, approach or withdrawal in response to a new stimulus, and degree of persistence in the face of obstacles.

I am stressing the fact that every child has a different biological temperament because I find it so under-emphasized in books on child psychology and child raising. Many parents seem to believe that the environment they provide for the child is the only factor in determining how the child turns out later in life. This is simply not true. It is the *interaction* of the child's basic temperament with the parental environment that decides how the child will turn out. So parents are *not* 100 percent responsible for the kinds of adults their children become.

What is the practical value of this information for parents? It is simply this: if you have a child whose biological temperament makes him easy to raise, certain discipline methods may work effectively with him. The same discipline methods may work poorly or not at all with a child whose different temperament makes him hard to raise. You may have to use different discipline methods, exert much more parental power, and develop more gray hairs raising a hard-to-raise child. But if you do, don't compare yourself with a neighboring parent who has an easy-to-raise child. Don't berate yourself for doing a terrible job as a parent. Recognize the simple fact that some youngsters are harder to raise than others and take more out of you.

Here are some of the problems that can arise in the stage of infancy.

My baby wakes up at night and then won't go back to sleep after her feeding.

Let me tell you what *not* to do. If you give in to her demand for a period of playtime after a middle-of-the-night feeding, you are giving her a payoff for wakefulness after the night feeding. Pretty soon you may be horrified to discover that she is now waking up not once but several times a night for her playtime. She needs her middle-of-the-night feeding or she wouldn't wake up for it, so give her the feeding. But she has no physiological or psychological need for a middle-of-the-night play-time, unless you, by mismanaging the situation, train her to demand such nighttime play periods.

So what should you do? Give her absolutely no middle-of-the-night payoffs. All playtime with baby is reserved for the daytime hours. After feeding her in the middle of the night, tuck her in bed, perhaps with a favorite cuddly doll or animal, kiss her and pat her lovingly, and march out of the room. Do not under any circumstances go back into the room. If she is used to having you give in to her nighttime demands, she may cry bitterly, usually for decreasing amounts of time, for several days to a week. Then she will probably stop, for she will now be convinced that there will be no playtime payoffs after her night feeding. She will either go back to sleep or amuse herself for a little while and then go back to sleep.

I'm ashamed to admit this, but there are times when I actually hate my baby.

Such feelings are normal and natural. The trouble is, nobody tells new parents ahead of time that they are going to feel this way. A parent thinks, "How in the world can I have such terrible feelings about my baby?" It's easy to answer that question with a little bit of psychological analysis. Anything or any person that frustrates us makes us feel angry. The greater the frustration, the greater the anger. And there are many, many ways in which a small baby can frustrate you and make you angry.

Consider just one example: Your baby may wake up in the middle of the night and start crying and crying. Nothing you do will quiet him. There he is, crying his little head off, and there the two of you are, groggy and desperate for sleep, not knowing what to do. At a time such as this you may find yourself getting furious at your baby, maybe even yelling at him, "Shut up! Don't you know I need to get back to sleep?"

Don't feel ashamed to admit that there are times when you hate your baby. That's normal. There are times when all parents hate their babies, when their babies frustrate them terribly. Or when negative feelings about the baby have been building up for weeks and then something trivial happens that breaks the psychological dam, and the negative feelings come pouring out. Admit your feelings to yourself, and try not to feel guilty about them.

TODDLERHOOD

Toddlerhood can be summed up in one sentence: It is the stage of exploration. No scientist will explore the world more enthusiastically than your little tyke will research her home and backyard. Very quickly she will earn her Ph.D., with a dissertation on The Underside of Things.

During the course of all this exploration, she will be working on the developmental task of this stage: *learning self-confidence* versus *learning self-doubt*. She needs to be free to explore and research her environment. If she is allowed and encouraged to do all these things freely, this stimulating environment will help her acquire feelings of self-confidence, which will become part of her self-concept throughout life.

But if your toddler is forced to adapt herself to an alien and purely adult environment, if she is surrounded by what seems to be a thousand no-nos and restrictions, then she will develop feelings of self-doubt.

Personally I find toddlerhood a delightful stage and one in which few discipline problems need arise. I think there are two main reasons why parents begin to have difficulties with their children at this time. First, they do not know "the nature of the beast," and second, they do not provide the proper environment for the "beast" to live in.

How should I handle my toddler's temper tantrums?

It is perfectly normal for a child to have tantrums at this age because his frustration tolerance and impulse control are in a very primitive stage of development. You should be aware that you cannot communicate with a child in the midst of a tantrum. So however you choose to deal with your child's tantrums, wait until a tantrum is over before trying to communicate.

If you are by temperament the kind of person who can do it, the best way to handle a temper tantrum is simply to ignore the tantrum until it has run its course. In this way, you are eliminating any payoffs. If you continue to ignore your child's temper tantrums, they will eventually disappear.

If you find it gets on your nerves too much to just sit there while his tantrum runs its course, then send him to his room to have the tantrum. Tell him he can come out when he feels better. If he refuses to go to his room, you may have to escort him there and deposit him. When the tantrum is over, then you can communicate with him.

What you should *not* do is to give him any payoff. If you do, that will strengthen the tantrum and make it more likely that he will have one again. And remember that scolding him, lecturing him, yelling at him, or spanking him are payoffs to him, so beware of them!

My toddler leaves the house in a perpetual mess!

Good! That's the way it should be with a toddler. Toddlers just aren't built to be psychologically healthy, on the one hand, and keep a neat and tidy house on the other. If you are allowing your toddler to express his healthy urge for exploration, the house will not be neat. But make it easy for yourself by tidying up the house only once, at the end of the day.

The basic secret of handling a toddler is the discipline method of environmental control. Give him an environment in which he is free to roam and explore—a childproof house and backyard—and you will find him to be a delightful little tyke. Present him with a house and backyard that are not suited to his needs, and you will find him difficult to manage.

ANXIETY and the 3- to 5-Year-Old

KIT BAKKE

Kit Bakke holds Bachelor's degrees in political science and nursing and has participated in a parent's babysitting cooperative in Berkeley, California. She is currently working as a pediatric staff nurse at Children's Orthopedic Hospital and Medical Center in Seattle. Correspondence may be addressed to the author at 2254 78th Avenue NE, Bellevue, Washington 98004.

As adults, we each have had personal experience with anxiety. We know that it can disorganize our behavior, interfere with our concentration, decrease our self-esteem, and impair our communications with others. The same is true of children. Like adults, children become anxious about events they do not understand. They get anxious when things seem out of control. And they get anxious when they feel guilty, or think they should be feeling guilty.

We cannot in many cases reduce the circumstances in the child's life which are precipitating the anxiety. Perhaps there is an impending divorce, or a move, or a new baby on the way. But we can give children some tools which may help them to reduce their anxiety themselves. Doing this successfully requires knowing answers to these questions: (1) What specific types of situations tend to make young (3- to 5-year old) children anxious—and Why? (2) What does an instance of anxiety behavior in this age group look like? (3) What specific adult interventions are likely to help or hinder a child's attempts to cope with his or her anxieties?

The Child's Point of View

The more research that is done on young children's cognitive processes, the more we realize that their patterns of thinking are quite different from an adult's. Jean Piaget, among others, has stressed several key areas: young children tend to be egocentric and animistic; they do not believe in accidents or coincidence; and they tend to adopt an authoritarian type of morality.

According to Piaget, children find it very difficult to sympathize with another's point of view; that is egocentrism. On the other hand, they tend to believe that inanimate objects have thoughts and feelings; that is animism.

Children believe that everything is motivated, that everything occurs by intent—every effect has a cause. Combined with their egocentrism, this leads children to view the world as a series of events staged primarily, if not exclusively, for their personal benefit or punishment. It is not a difficult step from these assumptions to believe that wishes can have real effects; that is, if something happens, it means someone wished it would happen.

Authoritarian morality demands justice that is swift, sure, and tough. Retribution is inescapable. There is a punishment for every crime, and vice versa, for every punishment (for instance, a rainy Saturday) there must have been a crime. If you ask a 4- or 5-year-old what they consider reasonable punishment for a given misdeed, they are apt to suggest some pretty stiff sentences—such as not getting any dinner for a week, or giving away all their toys to the kid next door.

If the world view of children is different from ours, it stands to reason that their anxieties might arise from different situations. In addition, 3- to 5-year-olds are actively involved in two crucial tasks of psychological development. They are constructing their consciences, and they are identifying and strengthening their gender roles. Both of these tasks can be highly anxiety-producing.

Conscience-building requires the child to internalize all the "shoulds" and "oughts" and "don'ts" that he or she has been hearing since birth. It is a difficult process by which all those rules (proscriptions and prescriptions) are put inside the child's head. The child must experience guilt in order to learn to obey the rules.

For instance, a 3-year-old knows that Mommy got angry at her when she unrolled a whole roll of toilet paper into the toilet. The next time she feels like unrolling a roll of toilet paper into the toilet she may remember that anger. Just the thought of that anger will produce anxiety and guilt, which the child will reduce by not playing with the toilet paper. But she still wants to do it. It will take several repetitions of the wanting and the accompanying anxiety before the child will learn to completely avoid the anxiety by not even *thinking* about playing with the toilet paper. And so a conscience is begun; but not without a process involving considerable anxiety.

The acceptance of a specific gender and body type has been discussed most thoroughly, and most adults are familiar with at least the outlines of Freudian theory: little boys notice that girls do not have penises and wonder why they had them cut off, and are afraid that it might happen to them too; little girls can wonder similar things. These are reasonable anxieties considering these children's egocentrism and strict sense of punishment. Yet when

48. Anxiety and the 3-to 5-Year Old

these young children try to discuss their worries, adults often don't want to talk about it. This can be very anxiety-producing, since it sends the message that something is probably *very* wrong, that it is so bad that it cannot even be talked about.

Causes of Anxieties

Given this backdrop, what are some examples of anxiety-producing circumstances? Disciplining is a big one. Children need to have an exact description of the specific behavior for which they are being disciplined. If it is not clearly spelled out, a child might easily conclude he or she is being punished for thoughts or wishes, or just because he or she is generally a "bad person." Children will incorporate this (mis)information into their self-image and conscience-construction, where it can have long-term effects.

Receiving double messages from adults is a situation producing anxiety. We sometimes imply a choice where we actually mean for none to exist. For instance, how many of us have said to a child: "Do you want to wash your hands now? It's lunchtime." We are not presenting the child with a real choice here, and yet we phrase it as such. Anxiety is produced by this kind of unclear communication.

Another example of a double message is the following: A 4-year-old boy climbs up the toy shelves and gets into a precarious monkeylike position. You scold the child and get him down. Later in the day, another teacher comes into the room and you relate the incident within earshot of some of the children. "And you should have seen that little monkey up there! He was so pleased with himself," you say, laughing. This time the children sense approval, whereas initially the message was disapproval. They are left confused and somewhat anxious about future guidelines.

A third anxiety-producing circumstance occurs when adults deny the meaning and strength of a child's feelings. This is not unusual, particularly when the feelings are negative. One girl says, "I hate you!" with great vehemence, and adults rush to say "Oh, no, now, you don't really *hate* Jennifer." This teaches that child that her reading of her own feelings must be inaccurate; it denies her developing sense of reality and of herself. This is anxiety-producing. It also teaches her that there is no gain in verbally communicating feelings.

Anxiety Behavior

Instances of anxiety behavior in the 3- to 5-year-old group are not hard to spot with a little practice. This age group is far more likely to communicate anxiety in behavioral or play terms than verbally, so it is important to learn to read these messages. Here are some mechanisms a child might employ to cope with his or her own anxiety.

First is "acting out"; for example, being a bully, breaking known rules, doing things of which the child knows you disapprove. Children will do this at times as a way of asking for punishment when they feel guilty or anxious over some private misdeed. Johnny may have wished that his best friend would fall off her tricycle, and when she did, he was overwhelmed with guilt and anxiety over his power to do harm. He is afraid to tell anyone, or knows from past experience that adults are often no help in these matters. So he acts out, forcing an adult to punish him; this then relieves his internal guilt. To the observer, these instances of misbehavior may seem to come out of the blue with no understandable cause.

Acting silly can be another clue to the existence of a child's anxiety. We may often pass such behavior off as simply "attention-getting behavior" and not think beyond that observation. We should be asking ourselves, Why is this particular child in such great need of attention at this particular time? It helps here, as always, to have for comparison a good idea of each child's normal baseline behavior. Anxiety alters behavior from the usual. Any changed behavior that does not on the surface appear to be adaptive or growth-producing should be considered a possible communication of anxiety.

Regression to an earlier behavioral level is a classic form of anxiety behavior. It is almost axiomatic that the 3-year-old boy begins wetting the bed or sucking his thumb or demanding to have back his baby blanket when his new brother is born. The child is anxious over the newcomer's competition for his mother's time and affection. He may wonder if he is being replaced (maybe Mom will forget to pick me up from day care one afternoon). He feels as if he has lost control.

The anxiety produced by feeling as if you have lost control can also be exhibited in ritualistic behavior. The little girl who must have her spoon and her cup just *so* before she can eat, or who must have her blanket and dolly placed just *so* before naptime, is an example of this. The child feels that her environment has become so chaotic that she must exert what power she has or else all will be lost.

Play therapists such as Virginia Axline have written and taught that children's play inevitably reflects the stresses of their current lives. While we may not be play therapists or child psychiatrists, we can all look at playing children with an eye to the possibility that any behavior might be a message from a child that he or she is trying to cope with anxiety, and may be asking for help.

Adult Intervention

So what kind of help can we give? The suggestions which follow are primarily on the level of verbal communications, and all are designed to improve a child's self-esteem. Remember, in most cases you probably cannot do much to alter the situation that is causing the anxiety, but you probably can help the child learn to cope with it better. Children, like adults, will cope more successfully if they are getting the kind of feedback that makes them feel good about themselves and their efforts.

6. BEHAVIOR AND GUIDANCE

Several authors have discussed the destructiveness of "you" messages and the benefits of "I" messages. In our context, an "I" message has three major benefits: it indicates to the child that adults have moods and feelings just like chilren; it offers an alternative behavior; and it presents a model of good coping skills.

Here is an example. A child is acting out, being loud and pushing other children around. It is late afternoon. Maybe she is anxious about going home to parents who always seem too tired to pay much attention to her. But the teacher is getting tired too and is reaching the end of her rope. She could say, "Stop it! You kids are being 'way too noisy and you're driving me crazy." This is a classic "you" message. It puts all the blame and guilt on the kids by passing judgment on their behavior.

The "I" message approach would go like this: "Oh gee, kids, I'm really getting tired right now. Let's sit over here and [read a story/get out the puzzles/do some coloring/sing our counting song/etc.]." This response allows the teacher to own her own tiredness. She does not make the kids feel responsible for *her* feelings. And she gives them an alternative form of behavior for which they can get approval (increased self-esteem). Depending on the maturity of the children and the size of the group, the teacher might even give them a choice of activities, which can further increase a child's self-knowledge and self-esteem.

A second approach which can help children increase their self-esteem is to always reinforce their sense of reality. Being careful not to deny a child's expressed feelings and avoiding double messages are examples of how to strengthen a child's sense of reality.

Let the child be the judge of whether or not a fall hurt. Don't rush in with "Oh, that doesn't hurt now" a fraction of a second after the accident. Let the child do his own inventory and decide for himself if it hurts or not.

It may also be important to acknowledge a difficult time in a child's life, if you know it exists. For instance, if you know the parents are getting a divorce, *and* you think you recognize some anxiety behavior, try to talk to the child, not about the behavior, but about the feelings which lie beneath. Do not pry or ask questions; just say, "I guess it's tough at home right now for you," or if you know more specific details, "It must be hard with your Daddy moving out." Just acknowledging the situation like this can tell the child that you are available for him to lean on, that you are not afraid to talk about it, and that it is O.K. for him to do so too.

Of course, it is important to accompany these kinds of statements with an arm around the shoulders or an available lap. Solely verbal expressions of sympathy and understanding go only so far with children (with adults too!).

Any interaction between adult and child which encourages accurate verbalization of feelings can increase self-esteem and improve coping. To be understood brings a feeling of great relief to all of us because it reduces our aloneness. So children this age should be given time and attention to let them know we think their words are important. Ask the child questions; *listen* to the answers. Restate them to check your own understanding. If *you* place value on a child's words (and therefore on his or her feelings and opinions), the child will learn to do the same.

In summary, then, we can help anxious children by recognizing that the patterns of their thought predispose them to certain types of anxieties; by noticing certain common behavioral anxiety-messages; and by responding in ways that do not increase anxieties but which, instead, give children tools to cope with them better themselves.

For Further Reading

Axline, Virginia. *Play Therapy.* New York: Ballantine Books, 1969. (Rev.)

Fraiberg, Selma H. *The Magic Years: Understanding and Handling the Problems of Early Childhood.* New York: Charles Scribner's Sons, 1959.

Mead, Margaret. *And Keep Your Powder Dry.* New York: William Morrow & Co., 1965. (Rev.)

Child Care. Vol. 4, No. 36 (October). Ithaca, N.Y.: Co-op Extension, U.S. Department of Agriculture, 1976.

Wolff, Sula. *Children under Stress.* Harmondsworth, England: Penguin Books, 1973.

HOW TO UNDERSTAND YOUR CHILD'S DISTRESS SIGNALS

Paul Ackerman, Ph.D., and Murray Kappelman, M.D.

Paul Ackerman, who has a Ph.D. in child and special education, is Special Assistant to the Deputy Commissioner of the Office of Education for the Handicapped, U.S. Office of Education, Department of Health, Education and Welfare. He is active in parent-education groups, and with Dr. Murray Kappelman is the co-author of the books "Between Parent and School" and "Signals: What Your Child Is Really Telling You."

Murray Kappelman, M.D., is Professor of Pediatrics and Associate Dean of Medical Education and Special Programs at the University of Maryland School of Medicine. He is the author of the books "What Your Child Is All About" and "Raising the Only Child," as well as co-author of "Signals: What Your Child Is Really Telling You."

At times every parent is puzzled by a child's behavior. Perhaps your three-year-old daughter has temper tantrums, during which she holds her breath so long that she passes out. Or your five-year-old son plays by himself and talks to "Chester," his fantasy friend. Or your eight-year-old daughter is shy and seems to have no friends. You notice that she spends more and more time alone.

These are signals, messages, from your child, telling you something he or she cannot express in words or through the usual family conversations. They convey a feeling or a need too complex or too frightening to talk about in the usual way. A signal is an alternate way of communicating, a method that usually says: "Please stop! Listen!"

To respond to your child in a helpful way, you, the parent, must search for the message hidden behind the outward signal. It is a search that may proceed easily or may take every bit of your intelligence, patience and ingenuity. You must enter your child's mind like a detective. You must reconstruct your child's world, consider your child's action and try to uncover what made her act the way she did.

Important things to notice: Under what circumstances does the signal occur? Does the signal repeat itself? Does it happen at a certain time of the day? Each day? If you find, for example, that a child signals every night just before bedtime, perhaps she is trying to postpone going to bed and to put off her real fear—the dark. That child may be saying a lot more than that she merely wants to watch more television, which might be a parent's first quick conclusion. The process of helping your child does not stop with finding the message, however. Once you have all the clues, you must put the pieces together and devise a plan of action. Perhaps you will need the help of a friend, your mate or a professional to do this. Whatever your procedure, when you are ready to talk to your child, try phrasing your thoughts in the *child's* language. Ask simple questions that she can understand and answer. In this way you may be able to help her find her own solution to the problem. Here are some samples of common signals children send out:

Temper tantrums. You have just told your three-year-old son Billy that he cannot have another piece of candy. He pouts and asks belligerently, "But I want it." Shaking your head, you cover the candy dish and say firmly "No." All of a sudden he hurtles his small body to the floor, screaming in a loud voice, kicking his legs and arms and rolling his body. Billy is having a classic temper tantrum. What does this overreaction mean? What is behind the signal?

Understanding the meaning behind the temper tantrum helps the parent to react sensibly to such sudden, wild behavior. The sight of your child writhing on the floor in fury can be very disturbing, and the natural tendency is to attempt to soothe him, to talk him out of the tantrum. However, this is the wrong approach, and would mean that you had not interpreted and acted upon the child's actions correctly.

The message in the tantrum Billy is throwing is uncomplicated and very straightforward. He is trying to force you to bend to his wishes by the most outrageous behavior he can think of. Remember that no actor wants to perform before an empty house. Billy is an actor; his temper tantrum is a performance. Therefore, having

6. BEHAVIOR AND GUIDANCE

understood the message, you can break up the act by removing yourself, his audience, from the room. Very quickly the screaming and the kicking will cease. The signal will be over; the message will have been received and intelligently rejected.

Temper tantrums may signal other, more complicated messages as the child grows older. Six-year-old Karl repeatedly came in from the yard where the other children were playing and stood in the kitchen, crying and banging his fists on the wall or kitchen table. Though his parents tried to soothe him, he was unreachable. The physical aspects of his anger and frustration had to ebb before he could be questioned. But then he would start to cry and run into his room. His parents were confused. What did it all mean?

Karl's parents sat down and discussed it. Clearly the episodes occurred after their son had been playing outside with the other children. The message obviously was contained in something that was happening outside. The next day Karl's father stationed himself in the corner of the yard to watch as he went out to play. The cause of Karl's signal, his angry tantrum, became obvious in a very short time. As the other six- and seven-year-olds gathered, they selected teams to play ball. Karl was excluded. His father watched as Karl pleaded to be included on one of the teams, but the other boys said he would have to be the umpire again. Within minutes, Karl had fled the play area and was back in the house, furious, beating his fists against the kitchen wall and crying. Karl's signal was one of complete frustration.

Now his father understood and could help his son. He approached the youngster and told him that he noticed the other boys would not include him on their teams. "Why?" he asked, with obvious concern. The boy looked away, embarrassed. Finally he stuttered, "Because I can't throw the ball so good. They don't want me messing up the game." His father nodded. "That must make you very angry," he said gently. Karl looked at him with appreciation. "It does," he said. His father put his arm around the boy's shoulders. "How about if you and I practice throwing and catching the ball until you're good enough to be on the team?" he asked. He hugged his son tightly. "We're friends. I don't like to see you angry. And I remember having to practice with my own dad until I was good enough."

Karl's father not only had perceived the signal and interpreted the message, but also he had reacted in a compassionate and meaningful way. He had offered his son a solution to his problem and stressed that it was not one about which he should be ashamed. As the days went by and the practice between father and son continued, Karl became a better ball handler and the father-son relationship grew into one of deep mutual affection and respect. The other children began to watch Karl play ball with his dad, and soon he was invited to play in the neighborhood games. The fist-banging temper tantrum ended.

Fantasy friends and fantasies. Gwen's mother is working in the kitchen. The house is very still. Suddenly she hears her three-year-old daughter chattering away in her bedroom. The mother puts down the dishcloth and listens. Gwen is holding a conversation with someone, talking excitedly and then pausing as if listening for an answer. But her mother knows that Gwen is alone in her room. Whom could she be talking with? She tiptoes in to look at the little girl.

Gwen is sitting on the floor in the center of the room. Seated in front of her are three stuffed animals, and Gwen's small head bobs as she speaks happily to each in turn. She asks questions, listens for answers and then talks back. Gwen's mother is amused. But then she becomes concerned. Is it normal for her daughter actually to be talking to these stuffed animals? Is there a message hidden in this signal?

There is indeed a message, and Gwen's mother's initial amused and tolerant reaction was the correct one. Fantasy friends are a normal part of many young children's lives. The world around them is so new, so exciting, that they want to share their delight. The sounds of words coming from their own mouths and the ability to get responses from the mouths of others are newly discovered miracles. Because other children her own age may not always be available, Gwen has chosen the solution of many other youngsters. They create their companions from the toys—dolls and stuffed animals—around them.

Sometimes, however, the fantasy friend can be the signal that a child is too lonely. The parent whose child has a fantasy friend can decipher the message of too much loneliness by considering the following factors:

- How many children of the same age as your child are available and how often does she have the opportunity to play with them? If the answer is "too few" (fewer than three) and "too seldom" (twice a week or less), then a message of loneliness is probably being signaled.
- How well does your child play with other children when they are available? If there are others laughing and playing outside the young child's window but she prefers to play with the imaginary friends, the message is one of alienation and loneliness and should be of concern.
- Is your child really happy in substituting these imaginary friends for the real thing? Or is she a silent, unhappy child who holds her imaginary friends tightly against her as she yearns for the company of other children, but cannot make contact with them? In that event, ways must be found to help your child.

Bed-wetting. When the frustrated mother of a five-year-old strips his bed of wet sheets, folds them and carries them down to the basement for washing, as she has done almost daily, she feels that her son's signal is very clear. He refuses to control his bladder at night and she has the irritating job of cleaning up after him. This mother is reacting to the signal of bed-wetting and not to

49. How to Understand Your Child's Distress Signals

the underlying message. The questions she should be asking are: What does the bed-wetting mean? Why is it happening? What needs to be understood so that I can act intelligently?

Sometimes the problem is a physical one. Children who have urinary-tract infections, recent or long-standing, can become bed-wetters. Parents of children like these usually will remember that the youngsters have had episodes of unexplained fever, abdominal pain, difficulty in holding urine, frequency of urination or failure to grow or gain weight properly. When a physical problem is suspected, the child should be taken to his pediatrician.

Sometimes the child has not yet developed sufficient control of his nervous system to permit retention of urine while he is asleep. This is a normal variation in the growth of the nervous system in children. There is nothing physically wrong; time is the healer. By the age of five, most children can control their bladders at night.

Often the young child needs stimulation and encouragement to overcome this problem. Parents can use a reward system to accomplish this goal. What is a "reward system?" Simply methodically rewarding a youngster for a job well done. A popular and often-successful system is the use of a gold star on the calendar for each dry morning. When a specified number of gold stars appear on the calendar, the child receives the reward. The sight of the gold stars and the pride that the child feels in his success often are reward enough. However, special treats and privileges, say for every five or ten gold stars, will reinforce the child's "gold star" success. Limiting fluids in the evenings can also help. This should be the child's responsibility, as is the whole problem of solving the bed-wetting signal. Parents should act as helpers, not policemen.

Sometimes there are psychological reasons for bed-wetting. Mrs. Stein took seven-year-old Judith to the doctor because the girl had started to wet her bed over the preceding months. The mother was honestly perplexed. "She was so easy to train. She was dry from the time she was eighteen months old. And now every morning . . . " Mrs. Stein did not have to go on. Her tone and her set jaw conveyed her intense resentment.

Together the doctor and Judith's mother tried to look carefully at Judith's signal. She had been trained. She was over five. The bed-wetting was of recent inception. She had no other urinary or physical symptoms. She was a cute, active, seemingly happy little girl with no school or social problems. No answers could be found by looking at these facts. But when the doctor probed further and asked about changes in the home, Mrs. Stein reminded him that she had a relatively new baby in the house. "Judy loves the baby. She helps me all the time with him," she quickly added when the subject was explored.

"Tell me, what do you and Judy do together these days?" was the next question. Mrs. Stein thought for a long time. "Well, we do a lot of things around the house," she said, "but mainly for the baby." To emphasize what the signal was telling Mrs. Stein, the doctor asked the next question: "But what do you do with Judy alone—just the two of you?" Judy's mother shook her head. "Not much. The baby takes up my time."

Judy was sending the "regressive" signal of bed-wetting. She was losing the companionship and, she feared, the love of her mother since the baby's arrival. Her response was a clear signal of need. And how appropriate that Judy used the most applicable one to tell her mother that if babies needed special attention, she too could be a baby. (Judy's sheets had to be washed along with the baby's diapers.) Yet Mrs. Stein, in her busy, harried day, had overlooked the obvious meaning behind Judy's actions. Judy's mother solved the bed-wetting problem by setting aside two hours each day to devote to the types of mother-daughter activities that would support and nourish a seven-year-old.

Other signals children deliver are countless. Among them are excessive shyness, running away from home, refusal to eat, sleeplessness, frequent physical complaints, refusal to go to school. When confronted with such signals of distress, parents should try to understand and deal with them—if necessary, with the help of a professional counselor or the child's pediatrician. Best of all, however, is the prevention, wherever possible, of conditions that evoke distress signals from children. Here are a few suggestions that may help.

Establish a special daily "attention time" for the entire family. An "attention time" is a period in which the whole family can be together and can participate in open and free discussion. For many families the attention time is at the evening dinner table. For others this special period may be at breakfast, before bed or right after school or work. Often the parents use this period to set family rules, but such business should be kept to a minimum. This time should be one of family sharing, when a child can speak freely. "What happened today?" is a good starting question. The attention time is when the parents really get to know their child better. The parents can listen for what is "between the lines" and discover the fascinating world of their child. And likewise the parents can share some of their own daily frustrations or joys. It is a time for discovery—of each other. The quality of the time spent is infinitely more important than the quantity.

Listen aggressively to your child. When you have listened closely to your child and she is finished, let her know that she has been heard and understood. How? You can restate what she has said in your own words or you can ask questions for clarification. Asking questions is important, because it allows you, the parent, to find any subtle messages that you might have missed. Often a simple "How do you feel about that?" will reveal hidden meanings in the child's message.

Know your child's friends. Friends often have

6. BEHAVIOR AND GUIDANCE

influence on your child. Knowing her friends can give you insight into attitudes your child may have adopted and pressures faced. Include her friends in some of your family's activities—dinner, outings, vacations, sports. As a parent you will be entering your child's world in a manner that says to her, "I care."

Establish a system of rewards and punishments. Every child needs to be rewarded and punished at various times. It is often helpful to both child and parent to know the consequences of an act, whether positive or negative. As you see your children mature give *them* the privilege of determining the rewards and punishments for some of their acts. By permitting the children to do this, you make it possible for them to take responsibility for their own actions. This is a vital preparatory step toward adulthood.

Share experiences with your child. Certainly you and your child have experiences together. But do you really share them? Do you talk about them together? Do you recall them often? Do you compare them to experiences you yourself have had? The objective in all this is to build good avenues of communication between you and your child.

Assign your child tasks that increase independence. One of the marks of his or her maturity is the child's ability to assume more independence. The parent must help the child prepare for this responsibility by asking her to perform tasks that lead to less dependence on the parent. Naturally you should exercise restraint in the amount of responsibility you demand, but there are many small tasks that can be assigned early. Simple tasks allow a child to move along the road toward becoming an independent adult.

Look at situations positively as well as negatively. There are both positive and negative elements in every dilemma, every problem and even every success. Harassed parents often find themselves seeing only the negative aspects of childhood problems. Finding positive aspects in your child's behavior can lighten the often-tense atmosphere of childhood problem solving. A good slogan to follow is "Catch a Child Doing Good."

Allow love and affection in your home. Do your children really feel the emotional and physical warmth that come from love and affection? A bedtime hug, an arm around an older boy's shoulders as you walk down the street, an unexpected smile that shows caring between you and your child, holding your daughter's hand during difficult moments—all these acts tell your children that they are loved and valued. It is also meaningful for children to see brief, loving displays of affection between their parents. This gives them a sense of security and the model of a loving relationship. Fathers must not feel ashamed to show love to their sons physically. There is nothing "sissified" about a father's spontaneously hugging his son. If we expect our youngsters to grow up believing in the importance of love in a relationship, whether marriage or parenthood, we must provide good examples.

Take inventory of yourself as a model parent. A major aspect of prevention is the presentation of a good model of adulthood to your child. The best and most accessible model should be you. Ask yourself, Do I think about the morality of my actions? Do I live by an established, consistent set of values? Do I reassess my values periodically and change them when appropriate? Do I always act like an adult? Am I a person who can solve problems by reasoning? Can I control my anger and frustration? Can I accept criticism? Am I tolerant? Consistent?

No human being has yet achieved perfection, and life would be very dull if this were not so. But these are characteristics to strive for in trying to be a good model for a child. And if in addition you are able to say, "I was wrong; I am sorry," you will be a fine model indeed.

Classroom Discipline Problems? Fifteen Humane Solutions

Marjorie L. Hipple

Marjorie Hipple is a Preschool Teacher at Bent Twig School, Gainesville, Florida.

Concern about how to guide children effectively and humanely is common to all teachers whether they are veterans or beginners, young or old, male or female. Some teachers, however, seem to have less difficulty with child guidance or "discipline," as it is often called, than do others. The reasons for the differences are no doubt varied; the personality of the teacher or the size and composition of the class, for example, can readily affect the choice of approaches used and the success of these methods. Yet there are approaches that seem to work well for many teachers and that are based upon knowledge of child development, learning theories and sound pedagogy. The purpose of this article is to suggest some of these for your consideration.

The approaches are grounded upon some basic assumptions. One is that *it is preferable to try to identify causation whenever possible in guiding child behavior rather than to treat the behavior in isolation.* We know all behavior is caused—by internal needs of the child, by external factors, or by an interaction of these forces.[1] An awareness of causation can enable us to respond more effectively and intelligently to specific behaviors. For example, if we realize that the aggression children display is the result of frustration they feel because a task is too difficult for them, we might want to modify the task rather than simply treat the symptom, aggression.

Second, it is assumed that *the use of positive or at least neutral techniques is more productive when guiding children than the use of negative methods.* Although various schools of psychology diverge on other points, most agree about the value of positive responses in maintaining productive human interaction. Self theorists claim that as we deal in positive ways with children, we bolster their self-concepts and thereby enable them to develop emotionally in growth-promoting ways. Behaviorists assert that positive reinforcement of behavior tends to increase the occurrence of that behavior. On the other hand, when we resort to *negative* techniques, including not only punishment but also the threat of punishment, we may create a mood of hostility that can transform classrooms into battlegrounds. And, once this pattern begins, we may be unable to turn it around as easily as we would like. Stated more simply, the difference between the use of positive and negative approaches often accounts for "the teacher who never scolds, but has such a good class" and "the teacher who has to yell and scream at her children, who still do not behave."

A third assumption is that *versatility in the use of guidance approaches is more effective than reliance upon any single technique.* No doubt you have experienced the frustration of using a method that works well one day only to note its ineffectiveness the next time it is tried. This inconsistency is not difficult to understand when we consider the variations of mood, motives, personality and situational factors that enter every human interaction. What works one day may fail another. What works with one child may fail with another. What works for one teacher may fail for another. Versatility—or

---

[1] For reasons of clarity and brevity, this article will deal specifically with ways to guide children. The analysis and modification of situational factors that affect behavior are also necessary when we deal with the ecology of the classroom. That aspect of management is, however, beyond the scope of this article.

6. BEHAVIOR AND GUIDANCE

eclecticism if you wish—is vital if we are to be responsive facilitators.

Finally, it is assumed that, over the long haul, *approaches that foster the development of internal behavioral controls and problem solving are more productive than those that rely upon external controls or authoritarianism to keep the immediate peace.* Said another way, our goal is to foster self-discipline.

The following approaches and illustrative scenarios are offered as suggestions rather than as prescriptive cure-alls. They are a tiny part of the universe of guidance approaches that can make teaching and learning more humane and enjoyable.

1. Accentuate the positive. If a child's behavior is unacceptable, suggest appropriate alternatives—positive substitutes—rather than focus negative attention on the inappropriate behavior.

Scenario: A child is throwing building blocks. Intervene by suggesting that the blocks are for building but that, if the child wishes to throw, he may work with bean bags or balls. Two positive alternatives are offered the child: either to build with the blocks or to throw with other objects.

2. Be a "model" model. As a teacher you are assuredly a significant model for your students—yet quite inadvertently you may model the very behavior you wish to modify. Still, it is rather encouraging to also realize that when you model desired behavior that, too, is emulated. Note how much more effective Scenario 2 is likely to be.

Scenario 1: A child pushes another child in order to cut into line. You shake her violently while exclaiming, "I won't have you pushing other children around."

Scenario 2: Having in hand a leaking paint container, you need to use the classroom sink. You ask if you may *please* use the sink out of turn rather than simply cut in front of the children who patiently await their turns. They agree to your request, and you remember to thank them.

3. Spotlight behavioral consequences. Young children are egocentric. And their egocentrism can prevent them from being able to put themselves in another person's place. You can help children move from egocentrism to socialized behavior by having them analyze the consequences of their actions. In spotlighting consequences, try to discuss the child's behavior in a nonjudgmental way and encourage him to think about its impact on people, objects and events with the intent of developing his consideration of cause/effect relationships.

Scenario: A child continually damages equipment ... take him aside for a probing discussion about "What will happen if all of the toys get broken?" Encourage him to think about the various effects of his behavior and to suggest alternate behaviors himself.

4. Send "I-messages." The use of I-messages is an approach developed by Thomas Gordon (1974) to deal with behavior that is causing problems for the teacher.[2] An "I-message" is a personal statement by you, the teacher, that has three components: your nonjudgmental description of the problem, its tangible effects upon you, and your feelings about it. The sending of "I-messages" is an intimate form of communication in that it bares your feelings in order to raise the child's consciousness about the effects of his behavior. For this reason, you may feel uncomfortable about using this technique and, if so, you may be better advised not to use it. Like the rationale for spotlighting consequences, this approach is based upon the belief that many children are unaware of the impact their behavior has upon others.

Scenario: Discuss a problem with your class concerning, say, clean-up behaviors: "When you leave the clay uncovered, it dries out and I have to mix a new batch which takes a lot of time. I really hate having to make new clay every day." Then facilitate a discussion of how the problem might be worked out.

5. Help children hurdle. Sometimes you can help a child avoid frustration or the loss of his or her self-control by simply offering a suggestion, a question or a gesture at the right time. This approach may sound alien to ears that have long received the message that teachers should encourage autonomy. Assuredly you do want to support this attribute. But you also need to foster interdependence when the situation calls for it. Everyone needs a helping hand sometime.

Scenario: A child stamps his feet in exasperation as he tries for the umpteenth time to pull on an unwieldy boot. Sensitive to his plight, give him a reassuring start with a pull on the stubborn footwear.

---

[2] Gordon espouses this technique for dealing *only* with behavior that causes the teacher problems. Behavior that is causing problems for the child (e.g., fear, worry) are more effectively dealt with in other ways which he outlines. Readers interested in learning more about Gordon's approach are urged to consult the references that follow this article.

6. **Instruct.** Children often behave inappropriately because they do not know what is expected of them. Even that which appears to be obvious or simple to you may not be at all apparent to the children. A good dictum is: When in doubt, teach them how.

Scenario: A new set of manipulative math materials arrives. In introducing the equipment, demonstrate a few of the many possibilities for its use, and then observe children using the materials to determine whether further instruction is necessary.

7. **Limit options.** Sometimes children are overstimulated by the number of choices available to them or, once they have made a choice, they may not handle it well. They may have too much time, too much space, too many materials, or too many activities on their hands. This overload is often the case with children who enter school for the first time. Ultimately children must learn to make choices and, as they mature, they do. But their immediate problems may require the limiting of those choices.

Scenario: A child has great difficulty staying with a task. He moves from one learning center to another, staying only long enough to take out materials, then moving on. Request that he choose one activity, help him get started with it, and, if necessary, monitor his behavior until the activity is underway.

8. **Divert behavior.** Some unacceptable behaviors are fleeting or situation-specific. In these instances it is often most effective to alter the social environment by diverting the child to another activity.

Scenario: Two children, best friends, sometimes rub each other the wrong way. On these occasions, step in before their conflict gets out of hand, directing each child to different activities.

9. **Ignore behavior.** Sometimes the best thing you can do is to ignore inappropriate behavior. Although this can be difficult to do, ignoring some behaviors has positive outcomes worth considering. First, behavior that is ignored is *not* reinforced. And behavior that is not reinforced tends to subside or stop. (At least one exception to this generalization should be noted: Aggressive behavior does not necessarily lessen when it is ignored. It may, in fact, increase. For this reason, it often must be dealt with directly by other methods.)[3] A second value to ignoring some behaviors is that children will often solve their own problems when left to do so, utilizing worthwhile personal or interpersonal skills in the process.

Scenario: Two children argue over the use of a toy. Silently observe them and decide not to intervene when they work out a method of taking turns that is satisfactory to them.

10. **Reinforce appropriate behavior.** Teachers continually reinforce behavior, either consciously or unconsciously, for good or ill. An important task for you is to become conscious about reinforcing behaviors you wish to see repeated. Unfortunately, if you are not aware of your impact as a reinforcing agent, you may reward the wrong kinds of behavior.

Scenario: A child who usually "acts out" during group activities interacts productively today. Immediately reinforce his long-desired behavior with either tangible or intangible rewards.

11. **Reinforce adjacent behavior.** Sometimes it is exceedingly difficult to reinforce desirable behavior because it appears so seldom. The next best approach may be to reinforce acceptable behavior of adjacent peers in the hope that the misbehaving child will imitate those peers so as to obtain similar reinforcement. This technique should *never* involve a direct comparison of one child with another (e.g., "Why can't you sit like John?")!

Scenario: Although a few children behave disruptively during a class activity, most of the children participate well. Praise the group of "good workers," commenting on the businesslike way most of them are working today. (Possibly suggest that those who complete their work might utilize the extra time to pursue activities of their own choosing.)

12. **Cue behavior.** Young children need and want a sense of order in their lives. Routines can provide the security that enables children to adapt with confidence to new situations. Everyone responds, often unconsciously, to environmental cues. Cues can be helpful in signalling fairly regular events such as transition periods between classes or activities. A flick of a light switch, a chord on the piano, or an upraised hand communicates messages in an effortless way.

Scenario: It is time to clean up materials used during the activity period. The children finish their work as they hear a familiar "Clean Up" tune on the piano.

13. **Monitor behavior.** Teachers monitor behavior in a number of ways, many of which take the form of body language or other nonverbal communication. An uplifted

---

[3] See Restraining Behavior (Point No. 15).

6. BEHAVIOR AND GUIDANCE

eyebrow or a surprised glance can sometimes relay messages to children more effectively than words. Physical proximity—placing a hand on a child's shoulder, moving about among the students, standing quietly in a potential problem area—can say, "I am here if you need my support."

Scenario: Two girls enjoy each other's company so much that they sometimes forget the task at hand in their happy socialization. A glance in their direction may clearly say, "It's time to get back to work, girls."

14. Give a breather. Occasionally it is necessary to remove a child from a provoking situation. The removal or breather is a neutralizing, tempoarary event—a time out—that is ended when the child indicates that he has the desire and control needed to reenter the group. Giving a breather is *NOT* punishing a child, placing him in a dark or otherwise frightening situation, or demeaning him. Instead it is providing him with an unprovoking alternative activity which he pursues by himself.

Scenario: Coming to school charged up with frustration, a child continually aggresses against her peers until adult intervention is imperative. Guide her to a quiet part of the room where she can work at an activity of her choice until she feels better about herself and can work productively with the group.

15. Restrain behavior. It is sometimes necessary to restrain children from continuing their behavior. When children are in the throes of anger that can make their actions potentially dangerous to themselves or others, restraint may be the only workable approach. Verbal restraints are simple, nonjudgmental statements that say, in effect, "I can't let you harm yourself or another child. You are angry now, but once you calm down, you will be better able to handle the situation." It may be necessary to accompany the verbalization by physically restraining the child. Physical restraint should never be a punitive or aggressive response: It is NOT hitting, shaking or pushing a child about. Instead the child is calmly but firmly held in a neutral way until regaining self-control.

Scenario: A playground altercation quickly escalates to a fight between two boys. Part them, but hold the one who will not stop until he calms down.

A FINAL WORD— WHEN ALL ELSE FAILS . . .

It is so easy to take ourselves too seriously, to get lost in the welter of problems, to lose our sense of humor—and our sense of perspective—especially on those days when everything goes wrong, our mood is a bit rocky, and we *know* the barometric pressure is affecting both ourselves and the children. Why not accept those days with humor rather than fighting them? Why not revise those plans so carefully made, laugh a bit, and find ways, with the input of the children, to salvage the day? After all, some days *are* like that, aren't they?

References

Galambos, Jeannette. *A Guide to Discipline.* Washington, DC: National Association for the Education of Young Children, 1969.

Gordon, Thomas. *Teacher Effectiveness Training.* New York: Wyden, 1974.

Greer, Mary, & Bonnie Rubenstein. *Will the Real Teacher Please Stand Up?* Pacific Palisades, CA: Goodyear, 1972.

Hipple, Marjorie. *Early Childhood Education: Problems and Methods.* Pacific Palisades, CA: Goodyear, 1975.

Pringle, Mia Kellmer. *The Needs of Children.* New York: Schocken, 1975.

Behavioral Blockbusters!

Do you have trouble with negativistic, impulsive, passive-dependent, or anxious kids? In this four-part article, noted psychologist Dr. Hugh Carberry tells you how to handle and help them.

Hugh H. Carberry is director/psychologist, Sterling Area Child Study Center, Magnolia, New Jersey.

THE children we will be talking about here are not learning disabled or mentally handicapped. But they do have problems, or blocks, which create situations the teacher must resolve if the learning process is going to be effective. And these problems, if not properly dealt with now, can become serious adult deficiencies. So it behooves the teacher to help these troubled children—for their own sakes and for the sake of all around them.

The negativistic child

The youngster who is negativistic typically seems sullen or antagonistic. He refuses to do what is asked, even when the request is reasonable. When he experiences failure or perceives that things are going against him, he may pout or quit. In more extreme instances, he may even become violent, sometimes inflicting punishment on himself or others.

This youngster can be a dramatic underachiever in spite of good intellectual ability. His negativism can get in the way of using his intelligence in a productive, efficient way. This tendency toward negativism can, of course, be coupled with an impulsive or anxious approach to learning, further decreasing efficiency.

The negativistic youngster is one of the most difficult to deal with and one of the easier children to get involved with in a very negative relationship. At the same time he can be a very challenging youngster. It is important to realize that the child's negativism is learned behavior and can be unlearned. Here are some things you can do.

1. Focus initially on those situations in which the child is usually cooperative; concentrate and reinforce that behavior. Usually, this will be something in which the child is interested.

2. Ignore in a very matter-of-fact way any confrontations with the child. The negativistic child has discovered that negativism very often is a sure way to gain attention.

3. Gradually introduce situations in which the child is usually negativistic, working for change. Tell the child that you appreciate that he is changing his behavior and discuss briefly with him the fact that you are working with him toward certain goals.

4. Reduce the criterion for the correctness of a task while you're working with his negativism. Reduce expectations; settle for small gains and resist constant preoccupation with success.

5. Create a predictable environment for the child in which he is rewarded for accomplishments, nonrewarded if he fails to meet reasonable demands.

6. Be prepared to modify tasks and reset expectations if the child fails or becomes negative.

The avoidance of confrontations with the youngster while rewarding cooperative behavior is the basic key to success. If you find that it is very difficult to be positive with this child, this is a good cue that you are involved in a vicious circle of will struggles and the unhappiness that goes with it.

Quite often the negativistic child will be supersensitive to any perceived "unfairness" by the teacher, and while he may not express his anger directly, he may sulk and brood. Typically, the youngster catastrophizes in an irrational way about perceived injustices. Discussions around these themes (e.g., teacher's unfairness, favoritism in the classroom, always being picked on, and so on) can help reduce angry, hostile feelings. **Listening to the child** discuss these feelings can help alleviate some of the guilt and angry feelings that the child may have. Help the child to understand that it is not the end of the world if he is treated unfairly, that teachers and parents make mistakes, too. That can go a long way in helping him become better equipped for life.

The impulsive child

The youngster who is impulsive is also a very difficult child to handle. Very often he will rush into a situation without thinking. Thought and planning usually follow rather than precede his actions. The impulsive child has not learned to control some of his behavior, and that often gets him in trouble. He often falls behind because his learning efficiency is significantly lowered by his impulsivity. How can this youngster be helped?

6. BEHAVIOR AND GUIDANCE

1. The child needs a great deal of *structure*. Take time to talk with him, to help him develop the habit of listening. For example, preface conversation with such statements as: "I am going to say something. I want you to listen, then say it back to me." Start with short phrases and graduate to sentences and later brief paragraphs. Also, give only one or two instructions at a time. Frequently the impulsive child learns best and increases his attention by being shown what to do rather than by being told.

2. Decrease permissiveness and choice making. The impulsive child typically has difficulty when faced with too many alternatives. He also needs to know clearly the rules and limits of the classroom. When he is faced with too many choices, he gets frustrated. It is better to reduce the choices. Move slowly toward helping him learn decision making.

3. Train the child in organizational skills. Impulsive children usually need help in approaching a task. Go through the process with the child in a step-by-step manner and then check the child as he accomplishes each step. For example, if the youngster needs to learn how to add a column of double figures and to understand the concept of carrying, this should be shown in detail in a concrete way.

4. Reduce stimulation in the environment. The impulsive child is often distractible. His attention is drawn quickly to other stimuli around him. It is important to reduce the possible sources of stimulation. A quiet place is difficult to find in many schools, but it's worth the effort.

5. Reduce pressure. The impulsive child has many new behaviors to learn to increase his efficiency. But you need to work on a continuum of change, giving rewards initially for very small steps. If a child can only attend for one minute, he needs to be praised for this and then moved to the next step. In our culture, we tend to value the final product more than the process, but if one of your goals is for your youngster to concentrate for 15 minutes on a project, it is important to realize that being able to do that three out of five days a week is an improvement which needs to be communicated to the child.

Finally, you should provide a model that is organized, nonimpulsive, and structured. Before you can help the youngster you have to look at your own behavior and work toward desired change. Teachers may fear that these suggestions, which decrease impulsivity, could produce side effects that decrease spontaneity. However, there is a real difference between freedom of expression that is sensitive, disciplined, and organized and the impulsive approach that at times creates problems through insensitive chaos and disorder. Structure and organization do not necessarily mean repression of impulses or a climate of fear.

The passive-dependent child

The passive-dependent child simply does not take the initiative in most situations and is a problem because he is not utilizing his full potential and quite often dramatically underachieves. Teachers often describe this child as "immature" or "not aggressive enough."

If a child continues to have this passive-dependent stance reinforced, he may develop a life-style marked by a lack of healthy assertiveness. This can be very handicapping as an adult. Reinforcement of the child's passivity and dependence breeds anger for both teacher and child. This type of child typically expresses his anger indirectly by stubborn resistance, dawdling, procrastinating, and sometimes lying and petty stealing.

Behaviorally, this is a child who rarely asks questions when he does not understand or who is always asking questions when, in fact, he probably does understand. In the latter instance, the teacher eventually finds herself getting irritated at the child because of the excessive dependency and his constant demand for attention. Identifying such a child is the first task of the teacher. It is important to remember that this may be the child's basic approach in many life situations and that change in the learning style is necessary before gains can be made. This child may be fairly good in rote memory tasks like spelling or memorizing the multiplication tables but has difficulty in tasks demanding more assertiveness like solving arithmetic problems, logical reasoning, or social interaction with peers. The goal for the teacher is two-fold: to decrease the frequency of passive-dependent behavior; and increase the frequency of assertive, risk-taking behavior.

The teacher should make a profile of the child's behavior to know what to ignore and what to reinforce. This is an essential first step. This profile should consist of actual descriptions of behavior, not attitudes. Knowing what you want is as important as knowing what you do not want. One way is to make a list of negative statements and convert them to positive statements, which then become specific behavioral goals for the child. For example, "Laura is constantly seeking reassurance for understanding simple instructions from the teacher," can be converted to, "Laura attempts assignments independently without asking unnecessary questions." Also, reward in a meaningful way any behavior that approximates assertive, risk-taking behavior. A child cannot go from one style to another in one jump.

The critical element in the success of any such plan is the teacher-child relationship. Involve the child right from the beginning directly in the change process. What is really a reward for the child can only be discovered by talking to the youngster about it. Once desirable behavior is established the teacher can then reinforce on an intermittent basis.

A child who is passive in his approach to others has a negative self-image. A teacher can be helpful by having the child write five things about himself which he sees as good. Teaching the child how to handle a compliment or to give compliments is one way of increasing assertiveness.

Again, the idea of providing a model to the child of assertive behavior is critical because so much of children's learning occurs through imitation. As teachers we find passive and conforming behavior easier to deal with than assertive or aggressive. However, the passive child tends to become the passive adult and this can complicate his life.

The anxious child

This is the child who sets about most tasks by being frightened. He decides in advance that a situation may be too difficult, and he's petrified at at-

51. Behavioral Blockbusters!

tempts to get him to try something new. Typically, he freezes or blocks, and if you are not aware of his fear he may come across as being intellectually dull. Memory and attention are also affected. As adults, we can all identify with this state of mind, for at some point in our lives we have experienced it. It is a very human phenomenon and occurs most often when we are threatened or feel inadequate in some way. This is especially true in new learning situations. If a child is allowed to withdraw and retreat from stress, he will have fewer and fewer experiences and less growth will take place. The more situations that are avoided out of fear, the more fearful the child becomes.

Obviously, the child who is fearful and anxious cannot be thrust directly into those situations which he fears. This would be too traumatizing and not effective. Teachers, however, can help in a variety of ways.

1. Reduce the criterion for success or correctness. Initially, lower standards and "settle for less." Give praise for every small effort that is made. If a child is fearful of talking in front of friends or classmates, praise him for talking to one or two individually.

2. Guarantee the child success in learning. If a youngster is fearful of reading aloud in class, for example, have him tape his reading at home and play it back to him as a way of instilling confidence. Movement along a continuum of geared activity can also be rewarding.

3. Structure any new learning situation for the child so that he fully understands the process. An anxious child will worry about what might happen, what could go wrong, and how he might make mistakes. It is important not to assume that the child knows what is to take place.

4. Reduce any sense of group competitiveness by helping the child see that he only needs to compete with his own record. In our society, we seem to be conditioned to compete with our peers. For a child who already feels inadequate this can be overwhelming. Helping him develop an attitude of self-competition can be much more realistic. Instead of letting him compare himself with the other children on a test, ask, "How does this compare with what you expected, or how you did last time?"

A child develops the attitude of "what if" this happens or that happens. This can be immobilizing and we need to help him see that usually the worst thing that happens is that we make a mistake and this only proves we are human beings.

The children we have discussed here are not exceptional, but they do have problems. And it's important you help them alleviate those problems. Make the above methods work for you and for your anxious or impulsive child.

Programs and Curricula

Curricular experimentation began on a nationwide scale in 1957 with the collapse of the Progressive Education movement and the launching of the Russian Sputnik satellite. It has resulted in profound transformations in both the schools and in the expectations of the public who support them with tax money. The War on Poverty instituted by President Lyndon Johnson created Head Start, a national program to give young children of economically disadvantaged and culturally different backgrounds a better chance for educational success.

The phenomenal expansion of programs for children under six years from all strata of society has been accompanied by an overmarketing of curriculum materials, kits, objectives, and "packages" of hardware and software, each guaranteeing success for the buyers. Many educators have suggested that innovation and production of materials be halted and replaced by examination of what has occurred in curricular undertakings. In many school systems, financial crises are necessitating cutbacks in funds for equipment, materials, and supplies.

Several educational movements are occurring concurrently, and aspects of these can be observed in both child care centers, serving a population under five years of age, and school programs for children five to nine years of age. Three movements that have received wide publicity and testing are labeled back-to-basics education, affective education, and open (informal) education. Each approach has ardent defenders and staunch detractors.

Advocates of the back-to-basics approach stress mastery of reading, arithmetic, and writing (handwriting and compositional writing), arguing that the schools have too often been ineffective in developing these skills in learners. Proponents of the affective education movement argue that children's self-concepts and understandings of themselves and others are the bases for all school learning and motivation as well as for developing a healthy personality. Individuals supporting open or informal education maintain that children's unique interests, abilities, and needs must be taken into account; furthermore, education must include an emphasis on "the whole child" and the development of responsibility, initiative, curiosity, and creativity.

Questions that continue to be at the forefront of discussion concern the proportion of time spent on formal or informal methods, teacher-dominated or child-oriented approaches, didactic-verbal or action and play models, and group or individual instruction and evaluation.

Clearly, there are no curriculum panaceas and each offering and model has both advantages and shortcomings. Some approaches work better in the short run while others produce long-lasting results. Some models work effectively because the teacher's basic temperament, style, and beliefs fit the model or because the parents reinforce that approach at home. Early childhood specialists note that approaches producing positive results with some children are not effective with others. This testifies to the complexity of factors that undergird individual differences, even within the same family.

This section analyzes trends in humanizing, compressing, and transforming the curriculum. Viewpoints on how and when to teach beginning reading and arithmetic, and how success is related to a child's cognitive stage are included.

Looking Ahead: Challenge Questions

What constitutes a *quality program* offering for young children?

What does it mean to offer "a good, basic education" for today's children who will be adults in the twenty-first century?

What is meant by adding to, subtracting from, and transforming an early childhood curriculum? What effects does each approach have on growing children?

How can socially desirable attitudes and behavior be developed? What influences children's moral development?

What approaches have been successfully used in bilingual/bicultural programs?

How should beginning reading be taught? Is reading only a perceptual task and work-attack skill, or are logic and reasoning also involved?

What concerns have been raised about present reading practices used with children prior to first grade?

What can teachers do to enhance children's language usage and understandings?

Are there stages in children's art work? What do paintings and drawings tell us about individual children?

What lessons have been learned about intervention fifteen years after Head Start? What might be its future directions?

Humanizing the Curriculum

David Elkind

David Elkind is Professor of Psychology, Department of Psychology, College of Arts and Sciences, The University of Rochester, Rochester, New York.

EDUCATIONAL PROGRAMS, of whatever kind, must meet two basic yet contradictory human needs. One is the need for *individuality*, the striving of each person to be unique and to realize his or her full powers and potentials. The other need is for human *sociality*: to relate to other people and to subordinate one's personal inclinations for the benefit of others. In the broad sense, any educational program meeting one or both of these basic human needs could be said to be "humanistic." But in a narrower sense, humanistic education might be limited to those programs providing equal opportunity for the realization of human individuality *and* human sociality. In this introductory paper, I will discuss humanizing the curriculum in the broad sense and will outline three contemporary approaches to curriculum reform. These approaches can be distinguished by their desire to *add to, substract from* or *transform* existing curricula.

Adding to the Curriculum

When an existing curriculum is regarded as not allowing sufficient opportunity for human individuality, new curricula may be added to the old. In recent years, for example, a variety of so-called "affective" curricula have been proposed and have been added to the school program at different levels. Innovations, such as classroom meetings, value clarification and moral discussions, have been implemented to help individual children understand themselves and others better. Many of these activities are indeed useful to teachers and to children. They provide an additional set of tools and procedures to be used in educational practice and thus enrich the teachers' armamentarium.

But the affective curricula can present problems as well. They can, and often do, perpetuate the same errors that are imbedded in the traditional school curricula. That is to say, many aspects of the school curricula are too difficult for the cognitive level of the children to whom they are directed. Social studies offer a case in point. As commonly pursued, teaching first-grade children about the "cultures" of the world may be a futile exercise. How can one expect very young children, who cannot fully comprehend the ethnic differences in their own community, to understand the world of Australian aborigines?

Many of the affective curricula used in the schools repeat the error of demanding tasks beyond children's level of cognitive ability. Many children of elementary school age, for example, are not really able to rank their feelings from "1 to 5"; nor are they always able to reflect upon their own thinking in ways that permit assigning clear priorities to what they want most or least. My eleven-year-old son, for example, has changed his mind five times about what he wants for his upcoming birthday. Children's priorities are shifting and transient rather than abiding or lasting. Is it worthwhile for children to go through the procedure of assigning priorities that are momentary at best?

Moreover, if the affective curricula are simply added to the school curricula, they can become a burden to teachers. The latter already have so much of the school curricula to "cover," and so little time to cover it, that the imposition of additional curricula can hinder rather than help them. And some affective curricula can backfire. A child whose parent has just died, or whose parents have just been divorced, may be deeply embarrassed or hurt by being required to reveal publicly what are legitimately personal feelings. Affective curricula that involve procedures geared to the child's level of understanding and meshed with the school curriculum can be beneficial. But if these methods and procedures are simply foisted upon the teacher as additional educational "objectives," the result may be just the opposite of what was intended.

Subtracting from the Curriculum

A somewhat different approach to curriculum reform is taken when current educational practices are regarded as not sufficiently geared to socialization—to the acquisition of tool skills required for the successful adaptation of the individual to society. The current "back-to-basics" movement reflects this approach. It argues that too much attention in education has been paid to individuality and too little to sociality. Accordingly, those who advocate "back to basics" often want to substract those aspects of the educational program that speak to human individuality; namely, the arts. Presumably, the less time spent on the arts, the more time available to spend on the fundamentals.

In my opinion, the back-to-basics movement, like that of affective education, is based on a false premise. Affective education may lead to the inference that cognitive and affective processes are distinct and have to be addressed separately. But good teaching is always affective *and* cognitive, and the successful teacher is always "half ham and half egghead." Teachers' enthusiasm for the subject matter and their respect for and good feeling for children provide all the affective education a child needs in the school setting.

The back-to-basics movement is based on another false premise of a different order than that which gave rise to affective education. It is that if children today are doing more poorly in academic subjects than they were a decade ago, then this fact *must* be due to our having been too soft and too permissive. The widely reported drop in SAT scores over the last fifteen years has most often been interpreted in this way. Critics have argued that the drop was caused by schools' not requiring children to read and to write enough and by young people's wasting time by watching television.

The belief that decline in performance must be a result of sloth is, of course, deeply imbedded in our Puritan heritage. But in this case it happens to be wrong. Just about fifteen years ago the "new" curricula, stimulated by Sputnik, hit the schools. These curricula, created by university professors, were up-to-date—with the "new math" and "psycholinguistic" reading programs, not to mention a plethora of science programs. These curricula were much more hard-nosed than the child-centered "progressive" materials that preceded them. Far from being "soft" on children, the new curricula were more difficult than many others in recent American educational history. The drop in SAT scores then may reflect the fact that the new curricula were too *hard* rather than that they were too easy.

Some evidence favors this last statement. For example, although SAT scores in math and reading went down, scores in creativity and analytic skills went up—just what one would expect if the new curricula were too difficult. In dealing with curricula beyond their comprehension, children have to be both analytical (to figure out what is going on) and creative (to find their own ways to deal with the curriculum demands). In addition, some of the curricula materials now coming out that reflect the back-to-basics philosophy are easier and more child-centered than much of the curricula of the sixties!

The back-to-basics movement, then, while it starts from a false premise, has had some positive effects. Under the guise of "getting tougher" on children, the new curricula have in fact often gotten easier. And this change is all to the good. Some recent data from the National Assessment of Academic Achievement indicates that reading scores for 9-year-olds have gone up over the last four years but that this finding does not hold for 13- or 17-year-olds. My interpretation is that these 9-year-old children are products of the new curricula, which are child-centered and concrete.

What is more negative in the back-to-basics movement in elementary education is the de-emphasis of the arts. If the aim of the back-to-basics movement is to enhance socialization, then de-emphasizing the arts is a sad mistake. The arts are social as well as individual. In a very real sense the arts are a basic means of social communication, the way individuals can share a sense of beauty. By de-emphasizing the arts, the back-to-

7. PROGRAMS AND CURRICULA

basics movement deprives children of a prime means for reconciling the conflicting demands of human sociality and human individuality.

Transforming the Curriculum

When the curriculum is regarded as not paying sufficient heed to the integration of human individuality and sociality, a different approach to curriculum reform is taken. Those who see the curriculum in this way want neither to add to nor to substract from it but rather to *transform* it in such a way that the needs for individuality and sociality can be brought into harmony. To my mind, this approach to education is best exemplified by the informal- or "open-"education movement. In many ways the open-education movement is a modern version of Dewey's "project" method, in which social adaptation and pupil interest were both taken into account in choosing curriculum materials.

The open-education approach to curriculum is too well known to be reviewed in detail here. Such programs allow for pupil choice and allow children to take responsibility for their own learning. The emphasis is upon teacher-made rather than commercial materials, and the teaching is heavily experience-based. The school day is loosely organized into large blocks of time rather than into closely clocked intervals. Great emphasis is accorded the arts as an integral part of education, particularly in providing means of expression. In all these ways, open education tries to transform the curriculum so that the needs for individuality and sociality reinforce and complement, rather than conflict with, one another.

But the open-education approach to curriculum is not without its own problems. Good informal instruction is hard work, and the teacher has constantly to fight against the temptation to institutionalize innovation. And nothing is more deadly to children than an overdone idea. The opposite danger must be faced as well. I have seen children engaged in truly innovative science or math activities that were both interesting and fun. But these activities were not integrated with the rest of the school program, and neither I nor the children could see where they were leading. In the same way, I have seen children so conditioned to asking questions that they no longer bothered to wait for the answers. Done well, open education can be a model of truly humanistic education; done poorly, it can be a disaster.

Conclusion

In this paper I have briefly outlined three contemporary approaches to humanizing the curriculum, to reconciling each person's need for individuality and sociality. Each of the approaches—affective education, back-to-basics and open education—speaks to an important need or needs. Each approach has limitations as well as virtues. We find, then, no one single answer to humanizing the curriculum. How we approach the task will depend upon our world view and our priorities with regard to human individuality and sociality. And children can adapt to and profit from each of these approaches, so long as each is taken with the children in mind. In the broadest sense, humanizing the curriculum means putting child-need and child-ability into the curriculum equation.

See also:
Hawkins, David. "Balancing Basics: The Three Rs Revisited." CHILDHOOD EDUCATION, 50, 4 (Feb. 1974): 187-91.
"Increasing and Releasing Human Potentials." CHILDHOOD EDUCATION 47, 7 (Apr. 1971). See esp. David Elkind, pp. 346-48.

Bilingual/Bicultural Programs for Preschool Children

Soledad Arenas

Soledad Arenas is director of the Head Start Strategy for Spanish-Speaking Children, ACYF.

Most 3-, 4- and 5-year-old children have much in common. They speak their parents' language; they are beginning to know what behaviors are acceptable or unacceptable at home, and they are active and curious, struggling to make sense of the world around them. For an increasing number of children, this is a time for a new experience: preschool.

When children go to preschool, their lives change suddenly. Away from their parents, they are expected to follow an unfamiliar routine while learning to function in a group with children the same age and to share practically everything with them. This is all hard enough, but for children whose cultural and language background is different from that of most of the other children, there are even more hurdles to overcome.

Two of the biggest problems are socialization and learning to conceptualize in another language.

Conceptualizing—that is, forming abstract ideas—requires language, because forming an idea involves recalling past experiences, generalizing from those experiences and giving a name to that generalization. The child who enters a preschool speaking only his or her native language or limited English will often have a difficult time. In the first place, the child brings experiences that are often culturally different from those of the teacher and the other children; his set of references are not the same. Second, the child is unable to talk with the teacher and understand instructions. As a result, the child is not able to participate fully in activities that lead to concept building and other aspects of development.

Socialization—conforming to expected behavior in a group—presents a similar problem. The bilingual/bicultural child may find that some of his or her behavior patterns are ignored or discouraged in the preschool. Often teachers not trained in bilingual/bicultural education are not aware of the different socialization patterns among cultures and they may expect, encourage or reinforce behaviors unfamiliar to children from minority cultural backgrounds. As a result, these children are likely to feel frustrated or rejected.

These and other hurdles can be overcome or eliminated with a sound bilingual/bicultural preschool program. In making the transition from home to preschool, a child must be able to blend his or her expectations and experiences at home with those of the preschool. How can we ease this transition for children from different cultural and language backgrounds? What should be included in a sound bilingual/bicultural preschool program?

No Single Best Approach

There is no single "best" bilingual/bicultural preschool program. The precise form such a program takes should be a function of the group it serves. The cultural and linguistic differences among Chinese, Native American, Spanish, Filipino and other groups are wide, and there are differences even within each group. A preschool program serving Chinese-American children in San Francisco, for example, may not be appropriate for a Chinese-American group in New York. Furthermore, several racial and ethnic groups, with or without a different language or dialect, may be represented in a particular community. Often the reality of a preschool program is that it is bilingual and multicultural. The specific style and content of each program must be tailored to the needs of the community and the groups within it.

However, there is consensus among specialists in bilingual/bicultural or multicultural early childhood program development that effective programs share some fundamental principles. Successful programs are those which:

• Provide an environment in which children can develop to their optimum potential. This requires a sound developmental curriculum, one that reflects the language and culture of the children it serves. It also requires that staff members and program resources be representative of the group's racial and ethnic mixture.

• Build on the strengths the bilingual/bicultural child brings to a new learning situation. The fact that a child speaks little or no English does not mean that he is missing something. He does have a language, and with it a rich cultural background with values and expectations. The child already has a strong base for learning.

• Continue the development of the first language and facilitate the acquisition of a second. Children should be made to feel that the language or dialect they use is acceptable—the fact that they are communicating is most important. The idea here is to show children the pleasure and necessity of communication in both languages. This is not as hard as it sounds. Children love to talk and given the chance to express themselves they will learn whatever language they need.

7. PROGRAMS AND CURRICULA

- Attend to the individual language and developmental needs of each child—in either language. Just as no two English-speaking children are at the same stage of language development, neither are two Spanish-speaking children. And what a child needs to learn in one language may not be the same as what he needs to learn in another—a child may be at a stage where he can be taught certain concepts in one language, for example, but be unable to learn those same concepts in the second language. This is why it is so important for the teacher to be able to assess each child's stage of development in either language.

- Avoid problems that may arise in conceptualization or socialization. Bilingual/bicultural children may have a different frame of reference and, therefore, different learning styles. Dr. Manual Ramirez, a professor at the University of California at Santa Cruz, has observed that bilingual children show preference for two contrasted learning or cognitive styles. Some children, because of their background, prefer to work independently, are competitive and require limited interaction with the teacher. Other children, however, prefer to work with others to achieve a common goal. They are more sensitive to the opinions of others and seek guidance and praise from teachers. Children who prefer to function in one style should be reinforced in that particular style, but they should also be encouraged to function in the style in which they have had less exposure.

- Emphasize parent involvement. A successful preschool program is one which is an extension of home. Teachers have to be aware of the child's home values and expectations, and one way of acquiring this information is by involving parents in various aspects of the program.

Simple as these principles may sound, they are not widely applied in preschool programs serving bilingual/bicultural children, for many reasons. In the past, staff training has not emphasized methods for enhancing the development of these children, nor has there been much research on the implementation of such programs and their effectiveness in promoting children's development. In addition, developing bilingual/bicultural programs means change, and change is often avoided for the easier alternative of maintaining the status quo.

Making A Commitment

Preschools which adopt these principles of bilingual/bicultural education must have an overriding commitment to persevere, for this is a new area and resources are often limited. For real communication to take place, both languages must be used in the classroom. Saying *Buenos dias* in the morning and *Hasta manana* in the afternoon is not bilingualism. Nor will it suffice to isolate the non-English speaking children for a short time each day with a special teacher. A serious program must integrate both languages into all areas of the curriculum in an atmosphere of respect and appreciation for cultural diversity. All this, in turn, must revolve around experiences which are appropriate for each child's developmental stage.

Learning two languages can become part of the learning that takes place naturally during the socialization process—children playing with other children and learning from each other. Teachers can take advantage of this natural interaction. If both languages are part of the regular classroom environment, children will help each other learn both languages. All children will benefit from understanding that there are many ways of speaking and different ways of behaving. However, the teacher must also plan first and second language learning situations in which he or she can reinforce language development and keep track of each child's progress.

The issues involved in making a preschool program biculturally or multiculturally relevant, however, are even more difficult to address than the bilingual aspect. A child's specific cultural heritage must be accepted and included as central to the preschool experience. A child's cultural background is not always manifested as concretely or tangibly as his language, but it is always there. Such formal cultural aspects as foods, music and dance are easily recognized. However, a child's deeper culture—his values and behavior patterns—are more difficult to pinpoint. Yet, in a school situation, deep cultural differences may yield behavior differences, and a teacher's understanding of culturally determined behavior is often a key to understanding the child.

Although one cannot draw up a list of cultural differences, especially one that would have relevance to all children of differing cultures, there are certain constellations of behaviors that are more common among Spanish, Chinese or Native American children than among white, middle-class children. For example, a teacher may think that a particular child is being disrespectful because he does not look her in the face when she talks to him. However, that child may have learned at home that to be respectful he must *not* look an adult in the face when reprimanded. In the child's mind, he is behaving appropriately; in the teacher's, he is not.

One way for teachers to learn about the children's culture is to go into the community where they can meet the children's parents, observe their customs and incorporate aspects of the culture into the program's curriculum activities.

A bicultural program should not force a particular culture on a child, or favor one culture over another. The goal here should be to develop an appreciation of cultural pluralism in children. This is a real challenge. Having a "culture corner" and a sombrero or a poster of an ethnic hero on the wall does not constitute a bicultural or multicultural approach. The children's culture should permeate the whole curriculum so that a child, whether involved in a structured activity or free play, is encouraged to reflect his family culture freely.

The preschool environment should provide relevant cultural experiences in all activity areas—for example, story books should depict different cultural groups and include the children's language and dollhouse areas should include furnishings and articles found in the children's homes.

Making ethnic foods instead of muffins and poached eggs can be supervised by a teacher or a parent who knows how to prepare the ingredients and furnishes the correct utensils. Above all, a teacher should try to repeat and foster the interaction that goes on among family members

53. Bilingual/Bicultural Programs for Preschool Children

at home during meal preparation time. These experiences show the child that home and school are closely connected—and also help develop socio-dramatic skills.

Some research has shown that different cultures encourage the development of different thought processess—that Anglo children tend to think deductively, while inductive thinking is fostered in Spanish families.[1]

Different types of reasoning are basically products of culture. Respecting different styles of play and learning in young children is applied biculturalism. As with language, teachers can build on a child's preferred play and learning styles and encourage the development of both inductive and deductive logic.[2]

Acceptance of a child's culture fulfills a main goal of preschool—that of developing within the child a sense of self-esteem and family pride. This goal applies equally to children of minority and majority cultures. Before a child can learn, he or she must have a healthy sense of self—and the development of a positive self-image requires an appreciation of one's individuality and pride of home and family. A sound bilingual/bicultural preschool program can help children connect the two worlds in which they live.

A successful program requires close cooperation and commitment on the part of program administrators, staff members and parents. Administrators and parents must be knowledgeable about the philosophy and approaches implemented in the program. Staff members must be trained in early childhood education and in the areas of language acquisition and development and cross-cultural communication. Although it is preferable to have all bilingual teachers in such programs, this is seldom the case. This is not to say that monolingual teachers do not have a place in bilingual/bicultural programs. Trained, sensitive English-speaking teachers can be effective in a team teaching situation when they are paired with bilingual teachers.

Parent Involvement

Involvement of parents is crucial to the successful implementation of bilingual/bicultural programs because the relationship between learning at home and at school is most intimate during the early years. Parents know what is best for their children, but the advantages of a bilingual/bicultural program may not be readily apparent to them. Parents of bilingual children need to understand why their children will start in their dominant language and gradually be introduced to the second language. Parents of English-dominant children need to understand that their children's development will not be impeded by being exposed to another language. If parents' views of bilingual/bicultural education are positive, it is logical that they will transmit this positive attitude to their children.

The success of a bilingual/bicultural program often depends upon parents. If parents are involved in the planning, acquire an understanding of the program's purposes and goals and take part in activities, they are likely to accept and endorse the program. If parents do not become involved and do not feel welcome in the school, the program is headed for failure. Why? Because parents are the best source of information about their children—both about the child's individual needs and personality, and about what constitutes appropriate behavior in their culture. When parents are involved in the classroom on a day-to-day basis, the culture of the community will become part of the curriculum and a truly bicultural program can emerge. This strengthens the bonds between home and school and will usually result in increased parental support for the program. Parents then become the program's most vocal advocates.

ACYF Efforts

Three years ago the Office of Child Development—now the Administration for Children, Youth and Families (ACYF)—initiated the Head Start Strategy for Spanish-Speaking Children to help Head Start programs implement sound developmental, bilingual/bicultural programs. Four areas are being emphasized: curriculum development; staff training; resource networks; and research.

Curriculum Development. Four curriculum models, each having as a foundation the principles of child development and the language and cultural needs of Spanish-speaking children, are being developed at Head Start centers in San Antonio, New York City, Detroit and Watsonville, Calif. Each model incorporates both English and Spanish and will also be sufficiently flexible and adaptable for use in multicultural settings.

Although based on the same principles, each model has a distinct approach to education. One program, for example, follows a preacademic approach emphasizing teacher-initiated activities. Two are based on a cognitive discovery approach, which stresses a balance between teacher-initiated and child-initiated activities, and another is eclectic, combining a variety of approaches.

Staff Training. Concurrently, four bilingual/bicultural staff training models are also being developed. Competency-based training as established in the Child Development Associate (CDA) program is integral to all four models.[3] In addition, two models are focusing on training bilingual/bicultural CDA trainers.

In these models, staff members are learning to train other Head Start staff members in developing bilingual/bicultural programs. They are also being trained to assist Head Start and local education agencies that are implementing such programs.

Resource Network. A regional resource network has been established in Denver to provide in-service training, access to bilingual/bicultural materials and assistance in implementing programs.[4] This network is intended to serve as a model that other regions can replicate.

Research. Several research projects have recently been funded by ACYF to explore issues related to the development of bilingual/bicultural children and their families.

Within the next two years, ACYF expects to make information on these projects and research studies available to communities interested in implementing the programs.[5]

Is It Worth It?

Preschool program administrators and staff members might well ask—and legitimately: "If we adopt a bilingual/bicultural approach, will the children really benefit?"

Even though research studies are limited, the results indicate that children do indeed gain from a bilingual/

7. PROGRAMS AND CURRICULA

bicultural program—and that English-speaking children, as well as bilingual children, benefit.

Studies undertaken by several researchers reveal that bilingual children use language more precisely and accurately than monolingual children.[6] Knowing two or more words for a given reality enables bilingual children to think more easily in the abstract. And a child who is able to express one thought in more than one way can move more quickly to the concept itself and not stay at the stage of just labelling the thought. In monolingual schools, the usual reinforcement for abstract thinking skills is through mathematics. The bilingual child, however, has the advantage of having a second way to acquire abstract thinking skills.

Learning in a native language does not keep children from learning in a second language. Research shows that children taught to read in their native language do as well reading in the majority culture language as children whose only instruction is in the majority culture language.[7]

Research findings also support the idea that children who feel good about themselves do better in school than children who have a poor self-concept—and children in a bilingual/bicultural educational setting have a better feeling about themselves than children whose language and culture are not part of the school program.[8]

Another benefit—not evidenced in research but implied through experience—is the effect of a sound bilingual/bicultural program on the community. Such a program, which actively involves parents, can serve as a vehicle for parents from different language and cultural backgrounds to learn about each other's values and cultures while working together toward a common goal: a quality developmental program for their children.

---

[1] Manuel Ramirez and Alfredo Castaneda, *Cultural Democracy, Bicognitive Development, and Education*, New York, Academic Press, 1974.

[2] Ibid. See also W.W. Liedtke and L.D. Nelson, "Bilingualism and Conservation," Ed 030 110, 1968.

[3] This training program is described in "Child Development Associates: New Professionals, New Training Strategies" by Jenny W. Klein and Rita Weathersby, CHILDREN TODAY, Sept.-Oct. 1973.

[4] Early Childhood Bilingual/Bicultural Resource Center, 910 - 16th Street, Suite 722, Denver, Colo. 80202.

[5] Additional information on the model projects is available from Soledad Arenas, ACYF, P.O. Box 1182, Washington, D.C. 20013.

[6] See, for example, Elizabeth Peal and Wallace Lambert, "The Relation of Bilingualism to Intelligence," *Psychological Monographs*, 76, 27, 1962; Wallace Lambert and John MacNamara, "Some Cognitive Consequences of Following of a First Grade Curriculum in a Second Language," *Journal of Educational Psychology*, April 1969; and Carol Feldman and Michael Shen, "Some Language-Related Cognitive Advantages of Bilingual 5-year-olds," Ed 031 307, 1969.

[7] Nancy Modiano, "National or Mother Language in Beginning Reading: A Comparative Study," *Research in the Teaching of English*, Vol. 2, No. 1, 1968; and Robert Lado and Theodore Andersson, *Early Reading*, Georgetown University Papers on Languages and Linguistics, #13, Washington, D.C., 1976.

[8] Ramirez and Castaneda, op. cit.

Can Children Learn to Love?

Developing Socially Valued Behavior in Young Children

ESTHER D. CALLARD

In Childhood Education

Esther D. Callard is Professor, Human Development and Relationships, College of Liberal Arts, Wayne State University, Detroit, Michigan.

FOR the past decade, we have had to face the reality that our society is beset with the tragic consequences of antisocial acts: parents' abuse of children, youth gangs terrorizing old people, children vandalizing their schools and attacking their teachers. My husband and I first identified the antisocial behavior of young children in the United States as a serious problem over 20 years ago during a sabbatical study tour in Hong Kong, Japan, and Thailand. We were struck by the contrast between the children with whom we worked at home and those we observed in the nurseries and elementary schools in these Asian societies.

We identified three child-rearing conditions which our subsequent studies have convinced us have important significance in social experience: (1) gratification during infancy and toddlerhood, (2) modeling and reinforcement of prosocial behaviors, and (3) a sense of the child's worth. Each of these three child-rearing conditions will be examined here.

Gratification in the Early Years. In traditional, nontechnological societies, mothers hold their infants close to their own bodies, nursing them on demand, responding to them in terms of their individual needs. Crying is responded to immediately, and there is virtually no expectation that infants will modify their patterns or demands in line with an externally imposed schedule.

In the contemporary United States, we find two philosophical positions that mitigate against trust-inducing, gratifying conditions for infants. First, we find a philosophy based on, "Don't spoil the child; the sooner he learns, the better." Many well-meaning parents in stable homes with ample material support in their parenting roles hold these nongratifying, trust-denying, development-stunting attitudes. Second, we find in America a philosophy of individual responsibility that claims, "If a woman chooses to have a baby, that's her problem; let her take care of it." Thus, we find mothers who may want to provide the loving care the infant needs but who may be too overwhelmed to cope with their problems and unable to find the supportive help they need. When children come, as many of our children come, from noncaring or even hurtful experiences they are quite justified in assuming that strange adults will be obstacles or threats to their well-being.

Clearly, educators face a difficult but crucial role when these children enter the classroom. We must meet their suspicion and distrust, even rejection, without counter-rejection. The earlier in their lives we can get to them, of course, the better. This is a major argument for the availability of well-staffed preschool centers. "Well-staffed" is the key term. Teachers who deal with children at this crucial time in their social-emotional development need to be knowledgeable in the area of child development, mature and experienced enough to help both child and parent, and secure enough to deal confidently with the displays of anger and rebellion of their immature pupils. It is not easy.

And what about the alienated sixth-grader or the teenage gang member? It's not easy to get through, to keep your cool, to enforce the limits with these older children. It demands more than simply having an informed, mature, well-intentioned classroom teacher. It requires administrative policies, school board support, and auxiliary services within the community, all coming together in recognition that there is a problem and that the classroom teacher cannot face it—or solve it—alone.

Reinforcement of Behaviors

Modeling and Reinforcement of Prosocial Behaviors. The nontechnological societies we observed in Asia and Africa accepted as their ideal the compliant, conforming person, one who incorporated what was, in each of these societies, a fairly homogeneous code of behavior. In the People's Republic of China, we also found a monolithic code, uniformly taught and modeled. Behavior was prescribed; deviant or defiant acts were clearly censored. This censorship was carried out in an extremely gentle, nonpunitive manner, which mirrored the ideal of nonviolence which it was trying to uphold. But

7. PROGRAMS AND CURRICULA

it carried the force of the whole society behind it: care-givers, teachers, peer group.

In the United States, we claim that we want our children to be conforming, to be "good," but we often give them a contrary message. We laugh at their misdeeds and actually brag (while we claim we are complaining) about the way they flout authority. One part of us loves the rebel and cheers the defiant. We are obviously in conflict in our own minds about our allegiance to obedience versus rebelliousness.

This message and our ambivalence is picked up by our children. It is reinforced by messages from "the street" and the media. At what is probably the most critical level—that is, in our interpersonal relationships with our own children or our students—we often use discipline techniques that model the behaviors we claim to be trying to suppress: we ridicule, we berate, and we mistreat, even to the point of physically abusing. We do this in spite of the fact that research findings indicate, as Leonard Berkowitz says, that "aggression is all too likely to lead to still more aggression."

Again, it is clear that, as educators, we play a significant role. We create a society in our classrooms and in our total school milieu that says to the child: This is the behavior that we believe in, that we practice, and that we expect you to practice. If that message is to enhance socially valued behavior, we must deal with children and with each other in a human, cooperative fashion. Our classroom must be so staffed and our tasks sufficiently manageable that we are, ourselves, not so stressed that we lose our own controls and violate our own personal and professional codes of conduct.

Beyond this, we need to believe sincerely that it is good for children to be held to a high level of social conduct, that they will find a much-desired and needed sense of security in a framework of order and personal constraint.

Sense of Worth

Sense of Worth. The third condition that we identified as contributing to the positive socialization of the child was the sense of worth bestowed on him by the society. In pretechnological societies, children were needed for their immediate services—for child care, agricultural or animal care, housekeeping, errand-running, and a myriad of service tasks. In more technologically advanced centers, such as Tokyo and Hong Kong, we were repeatedly told that each child had a responsibility toward the family and the community. It was obvious that there was an expectation that children would bring honor and substance to their families.

With the growth of technology and affluence in the United States, it has become increasingly difficult for children to feel of any *real* value. What tasks can they perform for the family in these days of electric food processors and dishwashers? How can they assume responsibility for shopping errands or even for their own transportation to school and recreation centers in our spaced-out environment? Clearly, in our economy, children are not an asset; they are a costly liability. And, clearly, in our individualistic society, it cannot be expected nor would it be accepted that they eventually will assume the responsibility of repaying the family or community that supported them in their long years of dependence.

The schools, more than any institution other than the family, have the burden and the opportunity of providing each child with a sense of personal worth and a vision of what he can contribute to others. This natural and self-reinforcing function is one that good teachers perform constantly in their own classrooms. The task is to expand the walls of the classroom so that children can experience their sense of worth throughout the community.

Our children need symbols of their value to us. They also need *substance*. One affirmation of what a society values can be found in what it insists that schools place in the curriculum. Do we place knowledge of child care and parenting on a par with knowledge and skills in woodworking, basketball, and typing? Do we even insist that schools insure that every child learn about the reproductive processes of his body, the process of birth and the means of its control, the immense importance of the decision to bring a child into the world, the responsibility of parenthood? And the joy?

What it all means is that, if we are to encourage socially valued behaviors in our children, we must, *as a total society*, treat children as socially valued human beings. It means that caring for children must be a national priority. Thus, the job of educators cannot begin and end in the classroom. We must lend our concern and our specialized knowledge to the cause of children in every sphere of their lives.

In Denmark, we found a philosophical commitment to children, *and* we found substantive programs that demonstrated that commitment. In addition to sex education and parent education in the schools, the Danish people provide a vast network of services to the pregnant woman, to mothers, and to young children.

Our own National Research Council Advisory Committee on Children recommends that the federal government take the lead in developing a comprehensive national policy for children and families. As vital components of such a national policy, they list assurance of adequate income, a broad and integrated system of support services, and mechanism to ensure their access.

Do national goals and programs seem remote from the educator's task of teaching prosocial behaviors to young children? They are not. Children are products of their total life experiences, which are bound to the welfare of their families, to the resources and behavioral standards of their community, and to the commitments and values of the society as a whole. It is simplistic to think that we can close our schoolroom doors and educate children within our own walls. There are no walls. We should celebrate this fact and join wholeheartedly in encouraging the social conditions that encourage socially valued behaviors in children.

FREE Teaching 10 aids for reading

These reading-teaching aids cost nothing and require no approvals for they focus on the reader, not on the reading program

Dr. Roach Van Allen

Dr. Van Allen is Professor of Elementary Education at The University of Arizona, Tucson, Az.

"Basic Instruction" is the name that is thrust upon what is happening in reading instruction in classrooms where I observe. Teachers work hard. They are honest in their efforts to implement programs imposed from outside. They are fearful of falling achievement test scores. I find a few who are beginning to question seriously the "industrial model" that has been equated with basic education. These teachers are asking:

Does anyone really know which are the basic ingredients of language for success in reading?

Has anyone ever produced enough "successful" products with a particular sequence of instructional modules to prove its validity?

Is the language acquisition for reading process well enough defined that it is dependable? Is it the same for all children?

Is our effort to individualize reading instruction a misconception? Don't all children eventually individualize reading?

Is oral reading in a group setting an act of teaching or testing?

What proportion of time should be devoted to teaching as compared to testing or assessment?

If children "master" aspects of phonics, structural analysis, or word meanings, does the result guarantee improved reading ability and desire to read further along the line?

Do children with high test scores choose reading more than those with low scores? Do they use reading for valid purposes with greater skill and frequency than others? What percentage of good readers are turned off of reading because of the mechanical way it is presented in the instructional setting?

Does parental support increase the desirability of a reading instructional program that is ineffective for many of the children? Do parents understand the "reading process" as well as they understand the "assembly line process?"

Are there any true alternatives to the industrial model of instruction?

In this article I will try to deal with the above questions by asking teacher-readers some other questions that relate to true alternatives to the above. There are no real answers to those questions... they are the wrong questions for anyone who has a foundation in human development and who

7. PROGRAMS AND CURRICULA

operates from a theoretical model that has human experience as the central core of the theory.

There are some human alternatives that you as a teacher might try during this school year. As you contemplate the questions and the suggestions that follow, you will see that most of them do not require any permissions or approvals. They do not require any unusual expenditure of funds. They do not demand any special assessment instruments. What they do is to add flesh to already existing structures and materials. They focus on the learner rather than on an adopted program. In the process of focusing on the language and ideas of the learner, they clarify concepts about language that are required for reading with any degree of independence. Also, they bring learners under the influence of their human and physical environments and the resources they have to offer.

Questions That Answer

1. *For improved reading programs, have you tried increasing thinking abilities by increasing awareness of human connections to:*

The sky? It is available to every child everywhere. There is as much of it over poor neighborhoods as there is above affluent ones. Nearly every author of a story says something about the weather. To be able to talk about weather is basic.

The earth? Many authors write about the earth. To be able to talk intelligently about its characteristics and its potential is basic to the development of vocabulary and concepts required throughout reading.

Water? Every reader must have some understanding of water and its connection to human life. All human beings are related to the sky, the earth, and water. To understand these connections is to understand much that is in reading.

Animals? To know and love animals is to know and love much that is basically human. Talking and writing about animals provides opportunity for the development of basic vocabulary for all reading: head, eyes, ears, hair, feet, nose, mouth, legs, etc.

Machines? Children cannot escape the influence of machines in their lives. Through their contact with and interest in machines, they come to use the vocabularies of nouns and verbs that are common in all of reading. This interest can then be extended to include descriptive categories that may not be common in language rooted in the home but which are essential for reading.

2. *Have you translated this increased awareness into:*

Role playing? Every child deserves to try on and try out new situations in a non-threatening environment. To act out—to assume a role impossible in real life—is to assure some level of comprehension of ideas that are basic and growing. It is children who cannot extend *self* beyond reality that cannot comprehend stories in reading instruction regardless of abilities they might have to recognize words.

Imagining? To see, hear, feel and say some sense of abstractness is basic to the development of language for reading. What do the clouds look like? What is in a string painting? What sense of meaning is in a blown-ink painting? This sense of awareness is critical to the development of a sense of story.

Talking? Walking and talking together can generate a sense of security in children. Many have never made the connections between *self* and all that is around them. They need to talk about things that are basic and important. Filling in worksheets on the same information is a very poor substitute.

3. *Have you ever tried publishing your own books from children's ideas and language?:*

Dictating to the teacher? A portion of each school week can be devoted to the recording of the personal language and ideas of students. This time is precious in that it affords opportunity for teacher-pupil interaction on the most personal and private basis—real language.

Dictating to parents? With very little help most parents can participate in the recording of experiences of their children. The record can be illustrated by the child or by one of the parents, bound into a simple book and shared at home and school. Parents deserve to know that their child is developing the sense of story that is necessary for success in reading.

Personal writing? When self-expression is encourged and inventive spelling is accepted at school and at home, children begin personal writing very early. In the process they come to experience the reality of the writing/reading process. They make the human connection to the whole realm of reading instruction.

Co-authorship? Teachers of very young children can invite students who are older to become co-authors of books about real or imaginary experiences. The children can work together in a variety of ways, but ones that will assure that the young students ideas and language are included in some of the final product.

Display of books by authors? As manuscripts are produced, edited, illustrated and bound into books, they need to be displayed. First they should have a prominent place in the classroom. Then some of them should be moved to the school library and made available to other children. In some communities, books by children are placed in public libraries and are checked out like any other books. Authors are congratulated frequently as they meet their readers.

4. *Have you ever provided materials for children to express their thinking in ways which do not require abilities to read and write?:*

Painting? Experiences with paints serve as launching pads for talking. This talk can be written and then read. The whole process of generating literacy is inherent in painting activities.

10 Teaching Aids for Reading

Sculpturing? The ability to organize meaningless material into something that is meaningful is inherent in sculpturing activities. It is a basic activity for all of learning. It is classified as essential to an ability like reading too, which requires that the reader take some notion of organization to the reading task. Any meaning present is dependent upon the reader as much as it is upon the writer.

Cooking? Cooking is a basic human experience. In school it can be used for social and recreational purposes or it can be used for language development. Every class of word used by human kind is inherent in cooking—names, action, description, and words of structure. It is one of the few school experiences available that assures a teacher access to the variety of descriptors found throughout literature—color, size, shape, texture, number, feelings, taste, smell and the whole range of comparisons.

Composing stories? Oral composition without the dictation process is an experience that every young child deserves. It is basic to enter into reading with a sense of story that will sustain halting recognition of words and phrases. It is one of life's great pleasures.

Re-telling stories? The use of ideas, words and phrases of good authors is basic to the development of language for literacy. Children should hear stories and then re-tell them with increasing abilities to recall details and language of the authors.

Puppetry? Acting out characters as puppets gives children from every language community a chance to try on language that is not typical of their home-rooted language. They can practice saying things they may find in their reading.

Chants and games? The chanting of language that repeats over and over provides opportunity for children to develop an ear for language like that found in reading (even though that language might be "foreign" in their homes).

5. *Have you increased opportunities for success in reading by providing a variety of media?*

Filmstrips? They provide a sequence of ideas with language provided for listening. Re-telling the stories using the sequence of frames builds confidence in developing a sense of story.

Books with tapes? These usually model excellent oral reading while children follow the print. Good models are especially helpful during periods of halting oral reading.

Study prints? Social studies and science study prints stimulate the production of words to name things, tell how they move and describe them in multiple categories.

Fine art prints? Realistic and abstract fine art prints can stimulate self-expression. Children learn that great artists want them to participate in the meanings that may be there.

Classical music? Repeating patterns and dependable passages are like those found in many selections of children's literature.

Scraps of all kinds for just "messing around" to discover an idea that can be captured. It has been in the process of "messing around" that many great inventions have been born.

6. *Have you ever invited parents and other interested citizens to share in teaching which results in expanded interests and improved reading skills :*
- a parent who will type while a child presents dictation?
- parents who will discuss their own work and interests?
- someone who will explain plant growth in a school flower bed?
- a retired teacher or other senior citizen who will demonstrate a hobby and relate it to reading?
- a local author who will talk with young authors about writing and publication?
- a parent who will listen to a child read?
- a talented reader who will read to a small group of children and involve them in repeating beautiful language in effective ways?

7. *Have you ever changed your reading instruction goals as a result of:*
- conferences with children about their feelings and attitudes toward the reading program?
- joining in as a student and letting a child be the teacher?
- asking parents for suggestions that they think will improve the program for their children?
- observing reading specialists demonstrate language development techniques?

8. *Have you ever examined your learning space to evaluate its usefulness for language development, including reading?*
- a floor space with pillows as a comfortable place for recreational reading?
- a chalkboard as an extension of a writing and editing center?
- a "Word Wall" with categories such as, Words We All Use, Words of Color, Words of Action and Words of Size as a resource for writing and spelling?
- a private place to read and reflect on reading?
- a shield from distraction which can serve as an instruction board for independent workers?
- a quiet place for personal reflection and meditation for students and for teacher?

9. *Have you ever individualized the learning process by:*
- using cross-age grouping for oral reading practice?
- using cross-age grouping for the presentation of dictation by young students?
- using peer group independent reading by assigning an able reader to each group?
- using authors of books developed in the classroom to help with the reading of those books?

10. *Have you ever expanded your program of evaluation to include:*
- children's ability to read books they have written?
- children's ability to tell stories in sequence which have setting, characters and plot?
- children's ability to write in a variey of literary forms such as the terquain, cinquain, haiku, senryu and tanka?
- observation of children's

7. PROGRAMS AND CURRICULA

reading choices in the classroom?
• observation of the extent to which those who can read, do read when completely free to choose?

Inherent in the answers to the 10 "Questions that Answer." is the well-known psychological principal that effective instruction begins with what is known. In reading instruction this means that some of instruction must relate to personal speech. That is the language that is known by each student. The known is then expanded into the unknown, not just by reading about it, but by experiencing it in mutiple ways.

Each student is honored as a person through opportunities to produce ideas and have them reflected in the learning environment. During the time that reading *per se* may be slow and difficult, students should be supported with language learning tasks that do not require excellence in writing/reading.

As children gain confidence as language producers, the whole matter of reading makes sense and becomes a natural extension of their personal language and thinking.

We want your advice.

Any anthology can be improved. This one will be—annually. But we need your help.

Annual Editions revisions depend on two major opinion sources: one is the academic advisers who work with us in scanning the thousands of articles published in the public press each year; the other is you—the person actually using the book.

Please help us and the users of the next edition by completing the prepaid article rating form on the last page of this book and returning it to us. Thank you.

LANGUAGE DEVELOPMENT: It's Much More Than a Kit

PATRICIA L. HUTINGER

Patricia L. Hutinger is Professor of Early Childhood Education at Western Illinois University, Macomb, Illinois 61455, and Director of the Macomb 0-3 Regional Project.

When those of us who work with children younger than 6 think about language development and the activities we should plan to enhance children's language development, sometimes we think only of adding more vocabulary. Although a wide vocabulary is useful for a young child, sometimes the child who is highly verbal, talking about "infinity" and other abstract concepts, is only demonstrating something Piaget calls "school varnish." It is misleading to assume that the child who has a fantastic vocabulary also has developed the underlying concepts that go with all the big words he or she uses. Language development is much more than the acquisition of new words.

While theorists do not agree about the relationship between language and thought, practically speaking, we know enough to plan activities for children that will help them develop a flexible use of language. Sometimes teachers and administrators are bombarded by educational-materials salesmen who promote their products as the answer to a language program. But language development takes people, not kits. A good language program is not as complicated as is sometimes thought.

Simple Steps

We all use the language other people in our community use to communicate all kinds of information in most of our waking hours. So do the children in our care! Sometimes we don't feel like talking. Children feel the same way! Sometimes we don't want to respond to a question with a complete sentence; instead we respond with a short phrase. We are more inclined to carry on a long, complex conversation when we initiate that conversation ourselves. Children have similar inclinations!

Probably the most effective steps teachers and other caregivers can take toward enhancing children's language development are simple ones. They don't require a cash outlay, or new curricular materials, but they do make *time* demands upon you.

1. Accept each child as a very special, worthwhile, unique human being.
2. Listen to each child when he or she talks to you (and when a child doesn't talk, listen to the *behavior*).
3. Take the time to talk to each child, using complex, elaborated language.
4. Provide rich varied experiences so that each child will have something to talk about. Then, allow children plenty of time to observe what is happening.
5. Make sure the child has many opportunities to hear language from other *people,* rather than hearing language primarily from a mechanical source (radio, television, mechanical talking toys, and head phones).

After you've looked over the above suggestions, you will probably agree that they won't cost you or your school any more money. They may, however, mean rescheduling your time and your priorities. It is *more* important that you spend time listening to what a child is trying to communicate to you than it is to separate out the language patterns that are not yet "mature," correcting the child's grammar. *Communication is far more important than whether or not the young child uses the correct verb form each time he or she speaks.*

The Development of Syntax or Grammar

When linguists talk about syntax or grammar, they are not talking about the kind of grammar you studied when you were in elementary school or high school. Rather, they are talking about a *description* of the way the child puts words together—there is no right or wrong way. The child develops his or her own grammatical system. He or she learns language by imitating some things, but there is much more involved than that. The child learns a rule system for using language, even though no one points out those rules (in fact, the child's language may develop more easily if those rules are *not* pointed out). By the time the child is 5, he or she uses most of the complex constructions that adults use, but the communications are usually shorter and contain less information. Language develops in a predictable manner in most children.

In the beginning, the very young child uses holophrases (one-word sentences)—when "mo" means "more milk," "more water," "play with me some more." Soon, the child begins to use two-word utterances for communicating a variety of ideas. Two-word utterances may differ in the meaning and/or intention of the speaker. Some examples follow: "dog cat" (*conjunction:* "I see a dog and a cat"); "John hat" (*possession:* "This is John's hat"); "party dress" (*attribution:* "This is a party dress"); "Chuck ball" (*subject-object:* "Chuck will throw the ball").

Children "operate" on their language. Sometimes you will hear a

7. PROGRAMS AND CURRICULA

child correcting himself or herself, or sometimes he or she will expand an utterance, such as "Stand up . . . dog stand up . . . dog stand up table." When this happens, the child is showing progressive operation on his or her own language (but he or she won't be able to use words to tell you about what he or she is doing). Children filter what they hear through their own rule system: when children stop and correct themselves, we can infer that they are monitoring their speech against some form of correctness.

Around 3 or 4 years of age, sometimes a little later, the child begins to use over-regularizations of inflections, even though he or she may have been using the correct (adult) verb forms earlier. These are to be expected, and will eventually be changed to correct forms. Examples occur when the child discovers that there is a way to make words express something that happened in the past—add an "-ed"! Then the child says "comed," "breaked," "goed," "doed," "feeded."

Something similar happens when the child begins to find out about the plural form. Then, he or she will generalize the plural rule to irregular nouns. Although the child may have been using "mice" correctly, when he or she begins to apply the plural rule, "mice" may become "mouses" and "feet" may become "footses." When the child acquires a flexible command of the rule for plurals, he or she will again use the forms correctly. Pay attention to what the child *means*, not the way in which he or she is saying it. Correcting may make you feel better, but it will not make much difference in the child's performance. Correcting can even be harmful to the child's sense of self-worth.

When the child begins to use negation (and it happens early!), expect to hear things like "No sit there" and "Wear mitten no." The correct form will appear without adult correction. The form the child's questions take also is interesting and will eventually be transformed into utterances that are much like adults'; but in the beginning, the child will ask questions such as "What the boy hit?" "Where I should put it?" and "What he can ride in?" Again, attend to the meaning, not to the form, or the way the child is asking a question. Questions that require a yes-or-no answer are much easier than the "Who," "When," "Why," "What" variety. The yes-no questions are usually formed correctly earlier.

Evaluation of the Child's Language Development

A measure of Mean Length Utterance (MLU) derived from samples of the young child's spontaneous speech may be more useful in diagnosing and prescribing than are scores on the various language scales of a more formal nature. Roger Brown's work outlines procedures for MLU *(A First Language: The Early Stages* [Cambridge: Harvard University Press, 1973]). The MLU and an accompanying analysis of the child's language patterns provides specific information about the child's communication. Language samples are individual measures, and are somewhat time-consuming. It is important to note, however, that an actual record of what a child *does* say gives you a lot more information for making curricular decisions than does a test score. Also of interest is the development of tests such as the *Say What I Say* test (developed by Madalene Barnett), which focuses on the child's ability to imitate various grammatical structures and also provides a fairly accurate assessment of the child's production ability as well as his or her syntactic patterns.

What Can Teachers Do?

There are several things you can do, and probably are doing already to some extent, that enhance the child's language development.

Use Expansion. When a young child makes an utterance that is not grammatically complete (for an adult), such as "dog bark," use the utterance, but expand it to an adult grammatical form: "Yes, the dog is barking" or "Yes, that dog barked."

Use Extension. Expand the child's utterance, as above, but add some new information, for example: "Yes, the dog is barking, but he won't hurt you" or "Yes, the dog is barking because he's mad at the other dog."

Use Questions That Are Open-ended (Divergent). For example, instead of asking, "Do you hear that noise?" (which requires a "Yes" or "No" from the child), ask, "What do you think might make that noise?" Ask questions that help the child begin to make predictions: "I wonder what would happen if we let these ice cubes sit here in the dish?" Practice using divergent questions, rather than those that have only one right answer (convergent).

Record Your Own Language. Use a tape recorder (or a video tape, if available) during the day, to record your own language. Play it back after school. Listen to your questions, to your sentence structure, your pronunciation. Consciously work on improving your ability to expand, extend, and ask questions. Do you use non-standard dialect, yet reprimand children when they speak in the same dialect?

Courtney Cazden is spending a great deal of time studying the language development of young children. She suggests that teachers ask themselves the following questions (the list below is taken, with some rephrasing, from her book *Child Language and Education* [Chicago: Holt, Rinehart & Winston, 1972]):

1. Is this a back-and-forth monologue on my part?

2. Are my questions open- or closed-ended?

3. Am I moralizing, that is, am I telling children how they should be thinking and feeling instead of accepting the way they do think and feel?

4. Do I really listen to children? Or do I jump in with an answer as soon as I think I've guessed what they mean, or even with an answer that fits my own preconceptions or needs for control?

5. Is my language production geared to the children's understanding, and does it at the same time expand the children's existing language, giving them new words for more complex operations?

6. Do I finish sentences, or do I leave children hanging?

7. Do I avoid using pat phrases over and over again?

8. Do I involve children in activities that lend themselves easily to promoting—and that might even necessitate—verbal interactions?

9. Is there a maximum chance for children to converse with each other?

10. Do I take action to involve children in verbal communications when there is the opportunity?

11. Is my verbal interaction related to the real world and the child's real world?

Cazden goes on to say: "Drilling children in linguistic forms can turn the kids off in a hurry, just as quickly as asking them to produce correct answers to questions. You can teach a child to use the correct words in the right places, such as 'under,' 'over,' 'around,' 'into,' 'or.' But if you want more than a mechanical repertoire of words, if you want understanding and transferability, be sure the words are attached to action or demonstrations of what the sounds actually mean in the context of the child's experiential field and are not embedded in abstractions" (*ibid,* p.116).

Finally, the most important question to ask yourself: Does the interaction between me and the child take place in the context of mutual trust and respect, based on my genuine friendliness, love, unconditional acceptance, warmth, empathy, and interest?

Some Experiences to Enhance Language Development

The activities listed below are usually a part of the early-childhood curriculum. They are simple, although they often require a great deal of planning. Nevertheless, they might be called "well-known but overlooked secrets" of language development. Classroom teachers often are doing the very things that will lead to enriched language development, yet fear that they are not doing enough directed work. Knowledge of what is expected in normal language development provides a justification for these activities.

1. Read to children every day. Be sure the stories are good ones, at the child's level. Ask the children's librarians if you need help. They have lots of good information.

2. Write down the things children tell you about their pictures. Remember, we don't talk in the same way that books are written.

3. Make books of each child's work, of photographs of the child's family, the class and its activities, and other things of interest. Fasten the pages together with rings, or sew them together. Use cloth pages sometimes. Talk about the books.

4. Take trips to interesting places: the bowling alley, the shoe-repair shop, the bakery, the zoo, a farm, a small airport and then a big airport, a trip on a train, a trip on a bus, different kinds of stores. When you get back, draw about the trip. Tell about it. Recreate it in creative dramatics. Effective trips can be quite simple but need careful planning.

5. Arrange things so that children have many opportunities to see operations from beginning to end. For example, make butter (shake up whipping cream in a sealed fruit jar, wash, add salt if desired)—it's more fun if you can visit the farm and bring back whole milk, but that might not be possible. Make applesauce from apples (better yet if you can pick the apples). Make cloth from yarn (woven, knitted, crocheted). Make peanut butter. Grow pumpkins, and make pumpkin pie or pumpkin bread, as well as jack-o-lanterns. Children often are not aware of the origins of things we take for granted.

6. Visit community affairs such as 4-H fairs, craft shows, antique-auto shows, new-car shows, farm-equipment displays.

7. Provide plenty of raw materials—paper, paint, crayons, clay, boxes—and time to work with them.

8. Encourage children to talk about whatever they are making, but don't keep asking them, "What is it?" Try Haim Ginott's "descriptive reinforcement" too (*Between Parent and Child* [New York: Avon Books, 1965]).

9. If you have a tape recorder, children can use it to communicate. Young children like to hear themselves talk when the tape is replayed. Young children's experience with CB radios can be an interesting dramatic-play starting point. Record group singing sometimes, too.

10. Encourage music activities. Children can make up their own songs as they are playing. Songs often use language in an expressive, exciting way.

Conclusion

Planning for the optimal language development of the children in an early-childhood setting requires interaction with *people*: children must be comfortable in communicating with adults and their peers. If the long-range objective is to raise children who can function in a democracy and communicate their ideas, then attention to the characteristics of developing language is important. Children must have many opportunities to use language and to have interesting experiences so that they really *do* have something to talk about. Teachers and other caregivers can provide conditions conducive to optimal language development.

PIAGET, THE SIX YEAR OLD AND MODERN MATH

ETHEL O'HARA

"When I was a child I spoke like a child, I thought like a child, I reasoned like a child." (St. Paul, First Century, A.D.)

As St. Paul said so long ago and as Piaget has been telling us for 50 years, the thinking (cognition) of children is different from that of adults. Often we adults feel that since we can think things out that children can too if they just pay attention and try or if we just drill enough and repeat enough the concepts we want them to understand. However, if we are to take seriously the theories Piaget has advanced, we must revise our attitudes and the demands we make of children.

Piaget is called a developmental psychologist because he believes that cognition develops in a set pattern and at a somewhat standard rate for all people. He believes that each person must go through each stage of cognition, that no stage can be omitted. Cultural background and intellectual ability may cause variations in the length of stages, but the cognitive development follows patterns with all children, as do teething and walking.

Piaget has described four main stages through which children develop in their thinking:

Stage one is called the sensorimotor period and refers to the way babies learn about their world through their senses and their motor responses to what they sense. It lasts from birth to about age two.

The second stage, which lasts from about ages two to seven, is known as the preoperational stage of concrete operations.

The third, called the concrete operational stage, lasts from approximately ages seven to 11. It is characterized by the ability to deal with two relationships or properties at the same time.

After age 11, most children arrive at the fourth stage, known as formal operational thought. They are then capable of abstract thinking (thoughts about thoughts) and no longer have a great need for the handling and manipulation of concrete materials.

As a first grade teacher, I will concentrate in this article on children in the second stage.

The thinking of stage-two children has many characteristics which make them interesting and delightful. It is really because their thinking is so different from ours that we find them so charming and cute.

Following is a discussion of some characteristics of the thinking of the preoperational child which Piaget has described.

Animism means that the child gives human characteristics to inanimate objects. Often dolls or teddy bears take on very human qualities. Children's books such as *Winnie-the-Pooh* are based on this delightful characteristic of childhood. The difference between children's thinking and adults' is that even if adults enjoy the story they know and accept the reality of what a teddy bear can do—children really do not.

A perfect example of this happened when I read *Ben and Me* to a group of first graders. It is a book more suited to children a few years older, but since a child had brought the book to me, I attempted to read it with a brief explanation that the story is told by a mouse who lived in Ben Franklin's house and helped Ben with his inventions. One little boy asked, "Did the mouse really write the story?" I explained that Robert Lawson had written the book but had written it *as if* the mouse were telling it.

My little friend again asked, "But did the mouse really do it?" He simply could not think about the mouse in two ways at the same time. The child would have been perfectly well satisfied with a "yes" answer—that the mouse had told the story—but my answer had been quite beyond his understanding at that time.

This inability to see something from two viewpoints at the same time is also the reason young children don't understand any but the most obvious kinds of jokes. At about age seven, the light suddenly dawns and they "get the joke." It is at this stage that they go around telling jokes to everyone and get such a kick out of them. They have discovered the secret of what's funny.

Billy at about age seven told this joke—"What do you do if you break your toe?" When no one knew the answer, he said, "Call a tow truck." Everyone laughed. Later, his little sister (age four) told the same story except that she said, "What do you do if you break a toe?" Her answer was, "Call a truck."

Her preoperational way of thinking had made her miss the point. It seems that a good test of child development could be made by telling jokes to children and evaluating their responses.

Centering is another characteristic of preoperational thought which emphasizes the child's inability to consider more than one aspect of a situation at a time. An experiment which shows this can be done with two containers, one a short, wide jar, and the other a tall, thin one. If a child takes an even number of beads, puts one bead into each jar, and continues until all the beads are gone, there should be an equal number in each jar. The preoperational child will center on one characteristic, perhaps the height of the beads in the containers and insist that there are more in the tall, thin jar than in the short, wide one. Because the children in stage two do not yet have the concept of equality and the conservation of quantity, their sensory perception (what they see) fools them.

Still another characteristic is *egocentrism*, which refers to the child's inability to take another person's point of view. This quality of egocentrism undoubtedly accounts for the sibling rivalry we have all seen, and the young child's inability to enjoy competitive games. Egocentrism makes it impossible for children to share their parents willingly or to lose a game without tears.

In the nursery school, children play side by side, talking, each in a monologue, paying little attention to the others. This kind of play in the company of other children but not really together is sometimes called *parallel play*. The talking is called the *collective monologue*— each talking in the presence of the others but not really communicating. This type of play and speech is typical of the egocentric preoperational child.

Most of us are aware of how young children confuse time, ages, and relationships. When they see the teacher's husband, they say, "Your Daddy is here." When her daughters visit, they say, "Your sisters are here."

Last year I listened while a group of second graders discussed the ages of the five adults in their room. They decided the 6'2" young man of 25 was the oldest and the 5'10" young lady of 21 next oldest. Apparently they centered on height as their criterion for determining age. They completely ignored the gray hair, glasses, and mature but short figure of the middle-aged teacher who was also there.

Since children grow taller as they grow older, they naturally associate tallness with being older. Their preoccupation with their own growth is probably what leads them to the wrong conclusion.

Their centering on one characteristic at a time is evident. Although second graders are at an age when most of them can consider two characteristics at the same time, they do not always do so.

First graders, six years of age, look like their younger siblings, and their thinking is more like that of younger children than of those older than they. When we see true believers in Santa Claus or the Tooth Fairy, we know what a different view of life they have from ours. Adults see Santa's makeup, his false beard, and the padded red suit, but the child is completely awed and thrilled at seeing Santa himself.

On Halloween, six-year-olds in their costumes are absolutely convinced that people don't recognize them. They are sure they look like pirates, witches, or whatever.

One Halloween two very little boys wearing bunny masks visited their neighbors. One neighbor said, "Why look at these two little rabbits! Put away the candy and let's get some carrots." The older boy, who was about three and a half, quickly told everyone, "We're not really bunnies. We're the boys from next door."

The six-year-olds may not be as naive as those little ones were, but they are easily swayed by appearances and are often not ready for the reasoning expected of them.

Having given some idea of what the child in Piaget's preoperational stage of development is like, I should like to relate all of this to the first graders in our schools, since by reason of age alone most of them are preoperational in their thinking.

It is my belief that many of the things included in first grade programs, particularly in mathematics, are completely unsuited to children of this age. We teachers are trying to help six-year-olds build concepts for which they are not ready.

Among the concepts that first graders find most difficult is the *associative property of number*, known as *regrouping* in first grade. Most children simply cannot follow the reasoning that goes with this example:

$9 + 4 =$
$9 + (1 + 3) =$
$(9 + 1) + 3 =$
$10 + 3 = 13$

The idea behind this regrouping is that since it is easier to add a number to 10 than to some other number, we should regroup to make our work easier. It is logical from our adult viewpoint to do this, but first grade children do not yet have the maturity of thought necessary for them to regroup on their own. When we demonstrate, using counters for 9 and 4 and regroup them by moving them to make 10 and 3, they can almost follow our thinking, but I believe that there is very little carry-over to their thinking. The whole concept remains meaningless (perhaps through second grade too) for most children.

Most of the math programs for first graders do not include the associative property concept until near the end of their first grade programs. And even then, only a few of the really bright children get something out of it, so, on the whole, it seems to me unsuited to first grade.

I find that children often understand things on a concrete level but have trouble with the written expression of the same idea. This is especially true with the chevron

7. PROGRAMS AND CURRICULA

symbols for "greater than" or "less than." If we show them a counting frame (abacus), they can see that 23 is more than 18 or less than 32. But when it comes to writing or reading the number sentences, they have trouble.

Eventually they get so they can make the chevron point to the smaller number, but then they can't read it without help. They can't remember which way the chevron points when they say "less than" or when they say "more than." It is really a complicated process, and I question its value in first grade.

Frances L. Ilg and Louise Bates Ames tell us in their book, *School Readiness,* that oblique lines are the most difficult ones for children to make. Most children before age seven cannot make the diamond ($\lozenge$) because of its oblique lines, and yet our math programs ask children to make the arrows ($<$) for less than and ($>$) for more than.

Another place that I feel we move too far in first grade is in teaching measurements such as cups, pints, and quarts. It is fine for children to use containers, to play with them, and to hear the measurement vocabulary, but we shouldn't expect them to understand concepts such as four cups to the quart.

On one of the standardized tests we give, I have found that almost all of the six-year-olds are sure they can fill six cups from a quart. When we ask how many cups can be filled from a quart, they always mark *all* of the six cups shown, and I suspect if there were more, they would still mark all of them. Yet so many of our math programs make an attempt to present this concept of changing quarts to pints and cups and so on to these six-year-olds, who, Piaget tells us, *cannot* reverse their thinking; i.e., they cannot see in their minds that four full cups can be transformed into exactly one quart and vice-versa.

I have found it frustrating trying to get these younger first graders to "know" their number facts cold. We give them much experience in counting, using number lines and folding perception cards (they look like large dominoes). After constant repetition of certain facts such as $3 + 2 = 5$ or $5 - 3 = 2$, I find that many children still must count each time they meet these facts in their work.

Newell C. Kephart, in his book, *Learning Disability: An Educational Adventure,* says, "Drill may be important . . ., but it will become important only after the concept has been developed, not before." Applying this principle to all first graders, perhaps we should expect less of our first graders.

It is startling to see young first graders always start over from one when combining addends even though they have just counted out blocks for each addend. For example, when they meet the number sentence $5 + 3 = \square$, they count out five blocks and then three more. When they are told to put them together, they cannot start from five and then count six, seven, eight. Instead, they count all the way from "one" again, indicating they are not conserving quantity.

One of the tests used to see if children do conserve quantity shows five blocks in an extended row and five in a short row in this fashion.

$\square \quad \square \quad \square \quad \square \quad \square \quad \square\square\square\square\square$

Preoperational children will insist the extended row has more blocks. They think the long row has more blocks than the small group even after counting each and finding five in each. If five blocks in a long row are more than five in a small group, then what does *five* mean to these children? Are they ready to work with numbers with any real insight?

Of all the concepts presented in first grade math programs, I believe that the missing addend is the one which children find most difficult.

For example, I gave Paul, a child almost seven years old who had completed first grade in a school where an attempt is made to teach this concept, a sheet of arithmetic equations of the type used in his mathematics program. Some were very easy and some were more difficult because of what we usually call their abstract quality.

Paul had counters (small blocks) to use. I had given him 10, since no sum was greater than 10. When he met the equation $4 + \square = 9$, he started counting, decided he didn't have enough blocks, and had to get more. After he answered with 13, I asked him to read the equation. As he read $4 + [13] = 9$, he immediately realized it did not make sense. He was quite surprised, and when we reread it as $4 + [\text{how many}] = 9$, he got the right answer.

In each case when he made an error, he was able to see the answer did not make sense when I asked him to read the equation aloud. From experience with younger first graders, I would say that, unlike Paul, almost none of them can see the absurdity of their answers.

The characteristics of preoperative children, which I feel interfere with their dealing with equations, are *centering, transductive reasoning,* and *irreversibility.*

Most six-year-olds can learn to count objects accurately. They can count to 100 by ones, twos, fives, and tens with some understanding and can add and subtract vertically:

$$\begin{array}{r} 3 \\ +2 \\ \hline 5 \end{array} \qquad \begin{array}{r} 5 \\ -3 \\ \hline 2 \end{array}$$

They can do equations such as $3 + 2 = \square$ and $5 - 3 = \square$, but almost all have great difficulty understanding equations where the unknown is in a different position as in the following:

$3 + \square = 5$ (Here they answer 8.)

$\square + 2 = 5$ (Their answer is 7.)
$3 = \square - 2$ (They answer 1.)

By checking the *wrong* answers (à la Piaget), we can see they are centering on the sign (the $+$ or $-$) and operating on the numbers without trying to give meaning to the number sentence. I have always called it a reading problem—one of comprehension—and not a math problem. Since studying Piaget, I feel that preoperational children can't understand these so-called abstract equations because they don't yet have the concrete operations of thought necessary to deal with them.

Another characteristic which may prevent six-year-olds from dealing logically with equations is an inability to see things as a whole (*transductive reasoning*). Perhaps they focus on each element of the equation separately and cannot put them together into a coherent thought. Since the elements of the equation remain separate in their thinking, the whole number sentence (a first grade term for equations) remains meaningless. This is also probably the reason six-year-olds cannot understand the associative property of number. They just don't connect the several steps in the regrouping process.

Irreversibility means that if six-year-olds see something one way, they cannot automatically see the reverse, which indicates to me that to six-year-olds it does not follow that since $6 + 1 = 7$, then necessarily $7 - 1 = 6$. Our textbooks usually present subtraction in this fashion. Perhaps, in spite of our best efforts, preoperational children do not understand the reversibility of addition and subtraction but deal with each equation or algorism separately.

Does irreversibility enter into the difficulty six-year-olds have with the equation $4 + \Box = 6$? Maybe it does, since they don't understand that they must think "how many more" (an additive approach to subtraction) when the sign $(+)$ tells them to put numbers together.

It has occurred to me that perhaps six-year-olds work on the equations they get right with the same lack of understanding they do on the ones they get wrong. They center in the same fashion on the sign $(+$ or $-)$ and fortuitously get the right answer. Teachers may thus assume they understand the equation when really they do not. This was brought to my attention when I noticed that in subtraction, although the unknown may be in the more abstract position, they get the answer right. For example:

$8 - 7 = \Box$ (ordinary position of the unknown)

$8 - \Box = 7$ (more abstract position of the unknown)

Here the sign tells them to subtract, and they get the right answer. Is it with understanding or just luck? In the equation $\Box - 1 = 7$, the minus sign does not help them, and they usually answer "6."

Some say that the missing addend is included in math programs to teach children that "+" does not always mean they should add. While this may be the eventual aim, it seems to me that it is useless to present an idea to children who are unable to understand it because their method of thinking is not yet sufficiently developed.

Some experts in the field of mathematics say that subtraction must be taught as the reverse of addition. Here, again, this is what we hope children will eventually understand when they have had enough experience with the processes of addition and subtraction and have matured sufficiently, but I doubt they can learn it that way in first grade.

The "spiral curriculum," so popular with textbook companies, is built on the premise that we introduce a concept early and then repeat it again and again every six weeks or so, each time building on past experience until eventually the children "get it." Maybe instead of building a concept slowly, we are really introducing children to failure because they are not yet mature enough to learn it. The spiral curriculum for many children may mean failure today, failure six weeks later, failure 12 weeks later, and so on with eventual success at 30 weeks or even in second grade.

Do children need this continual practice and failure? Would they have been more successful and therefore happier if we had waited to introduce these concepts?

At this time, the trend in teaching math is somewhat away from the workbook-textbook approach and toward the mathematics center or workshop with all sorts of games and materials, such as balances, weights, shapes (flat and solid), and containers.

This kind of program seems ideal for first grade, but it is difficult to administer. If the program is too unstructured, some children may try too few things and learn too little. An individual program for each child leaves very little time for each if math time is limited to 30 or 40 minutes a day. A structure that meets minimum needs for most children and allows time for them to experiment and play with mathematical toys and ideas is probably best.

"New Math" came about because educators wanted to put more meaning into math programs. I agree that math with understanding is desirable. It is fun to teach math with Cuisenaire rods and other objects which add a dimension of reality to the abstraction that is number. It is fun to catch the "Aha!" expression when a child discovers a principle. But let's not put into the math program of six-year-olds concepts they are incapable of understanding.

We cannot return to childhood and reason again as children do. We can only do what Piaget has done—observe children and try to understand their thinking. Only then will we devise programs with which they can be comfortable.

What Your Child's Art Is Telling You

It may not provide the key to his personality, but your child's art will give you valuable clues to his development and to the way he sees the world.

Stewart Alter

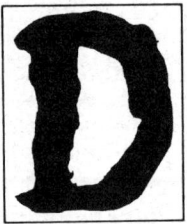

Does your child really think your legs grow out of your head just because he has drawn you that way? And how were you to know that when you complimented him on the nice rabbit he drew that you would hurt his feelings, and he would explain, "That's not a rabbit; it's a horse!"?

Even modern art movements that were once considered outrageous are now accepted and understood. But children's art still keeps many parents scratching their heads. Not only is it difficult to understand why children draw the way they do; it is also hard to figure out the right way to react to a child's artwork.

From an adult point of view, learning to draw seems relatively straightforward—a skill or technique that is learned and mastered depending upon one's inclinations and talents. Actually, the process is far from straightforward; it is as complicated as the whole process of growing up.

There are many theories about why children draw the way they do, but there is agreement among them on one key point: children are not trying to draw visual likenesses of what they see. Just because we adults assume that the "right way" to draw something is to depict it as realistically as possible doesn't mean that a child cares about or is interested in that. He has much more fundamental concepts to discover and master in his artwork, concepts that make concerns about technique or realism insignificant by comparison.

Imagine you are once again pretty much new to this world. Then think of how many mental connections you would have to make before the notion of drawing naturalistically even occurred to you. You would have to notice that the pencil you're holding in your hand can make marks on paper; that you can control the way those marks look; that you can make a connection between your world and those marks; and, finally, that you can intentionally set out to draw your world by using those marks to represent people and things you know.

It is, in fact, the process of rendering experience that is important to children, not the finished artwork. And, in this respect, a child's interest in art is clearly different from that of most adults.

"A youngster draws what he is interested in, and whatever is important to him at the time," says W. Lambert Brittain in his book, *Creativity, Art, and the Young Child*. "The act of drawing seems to be an occasion in itself, and the child is engaged in the process rather than in producing a product recognizable to an adult." Preschoolers, for instance, will frequently not end up drawing the same thing they started out to draw; they may not even recognize their own drawing if they're shown it the next day.

Commenting on the differences between adult and child art, Laurie Wilson, assistant professor and director of the art-therapy program at New York University's department of art and art education, says, "Children see things sometimes more simply. Different things hold their interest, and this is what they draw. Not perspective and space. It is more who or what is in the picture and what they remember about it," she explains. "If they saw a giraffe and all they remember is the tallness of the neck, they will draw the giraffe in that way because that's what caught their attention."

Drawing what interests them often makes children's art seem to lack reality, and adults frequently worry that the child doesn't know that the world

58. What Your Child's Art Is Telling You

Seeing evidence of his stage of development in a child's art is one thing; trying to read too much into it about his psychological well-being or self-image is another—and definitely not a good idea. "There's no question that when you know how to read pictures you can read a great deal," says Laurie Wilson of New York University. But, she emphasizes, "It takes a while to learn how to understand them." Bright colors don't necessarily mean he's happy and dark colors don't necessarily mean he's depressed. One cannot make simple generalizations about a child based on formal elements in a few of his pictures.

"A lot of parents are alarmed at horror imagery and superhero kind of stuff," says Wilson. "Many eight- and nine-year-olds do gruesome war scenes. Some kids that age love scary stories. That could be normal and within the realm of play," she explains. "Children go through phases. They may be stuck on Frankenstein, and then it will be another phase and then another phase. It's alarming only when you see it all the time and it drives away every other kind of imagery, but all the time for two weeks is not strange," she says. "Be aware of what their friends are drawing. Maybe it's just a fad. Maybe *Jaws* just came out."

Above all, it is necessary to keep in mind that children's art is important not because of what it can tell parents, but rather because of what it can do for children. A child's art is more than just a reflection of where he is in his development and thinking; it can be a catalyst for that development and thinking.

In this regard, Dorothy Johnson, national chairman of the elementary division of the National Art Education Association and art supervisor for the Volusia County, Florida, public schools, believes that art can even improve a child's capacity for learning in other apparently unrelated areas, such as math and science. "Kids have only one avenue of learning and that's through the senses—seeing, touching, feeling, and hearing," explains Johnson. "So any school activity or any activity in life that increases the capacity of their senses will naturally increase their capacity to learn as well."

doesn't look like his picture. Parents should be reassured. The simplicity of a child's drawings is deceptive; a child *does* know more than he is "telling." Just because a child draws a person as a head with legs does not mean he is unaware that people have bodies and arms, too. The truth of the matter is that children draw only what they are ready, willing, and able to "say" in the language of art at that particular time.

Making a useful analogy between the development of art and the development of language, Rudolf Arnheim, in his book, *Art and Visual Perception,* notes that: "Apart from exclamations the early speech of children consists mostly of nouns. It would be erroneous to conclude from this [, however,] that the child is more interested in objects than in happenings. Rather do these nouns represent 'one-word sentences' that stand for questions, demands, and reports at a stage at which the verbal statement has not yet been differentiated into several different words. Person, object, and action are still represented as an undivided entity through one word."

The parallel between the development of a child's art and language skills becomes even clearer when we realize that children start off each in ways that are similarly incomprehensible to adults. Babbling seems to make as little sense to us as scribbling; but, in both, free-form experimentation gradually leads to a more controlled form of expression.

W. Lambert Brittain, in *Creativity, Art, and the Young Child,* describes three definite stages of scribbling. From about one to two and a half years of age, children go through their "random scribbling" stage. After that, they move on to the stage of "controlled scribbling." Although the child's scribbles may look the same, a significant change has occurred between these two phases: "Now," Brittain explains, "instead of the scribbles being primarily a result of the physical action of the hand pushing and pulling the pencil across the paper, the child appears to have visual control over where the marks occur."

At about three and a half or four years of age children start giving names to the marks they are making. Brittain believes that this "naming of scribbling" stage is "an important step in the development of abstract thought," because it "indicates a shift away from the mere physical control over the lines to an understanding of these lines as symbols that stand for things ... the child knows."

According to Brittain, after four years of age "children's drawings begin to look more like the object that is supposed to be represented." But children still are not trying to draw visual likenesses, and Brittain cautions that "just because we as adults [can] see a recognizable form emerging, [does not mean that] young children are now attempting to draw naturalistically, and that these drawings are poor imitations of the real world and need to be corrected."

From this point on in their development, children's art becomes more complex and more representational. A five-year-old's drawings will include fewer objects floating in space, a sense of a right-side up, and a "greater understanding of the relative sizes of the objects portrayed," Brittain explains. "By six years, most children will begin to set the elements in their pictures on a base line. However, the drawing of a person is still made up of geometric forms."

It is important to remember that while all children go through these basic stages in their artwork, they do so at their own speeds and individual paces. Since these stages occur gradually and often overlap, there is no need to worry if a child who is drawing simple figures in one picture returns to scribbling in his next.

Watching the developmental stages that children go through in their artwork can help parents to understand what to expect of their children in other developmental areas, and the insight they gain in this way can be crucial in helping them to realize when they are making unfair and unrealistic demands.

Following this line of thought, Brittain, who teaches in Cornell University's department of human development and family studies, notes: "A child who is still scribbling in kindergarten is not intellectually ready to deal with factual information, to follow directional instructions, or to recognize positional differences in letters, all of which may be required in a reading readiness program designed for five year olds. No amount of scolding, extra work, or remedial help will make the child mature any faster."

231

7. PROGRAMS AND CURRICULA

Referring to art as a "discovery process, a decisionmaking process," Jerilynn Changar, arts-curriculum and workshop coordinator for the Targeted Programs Group at Cemrel, Inc., an educational research-and-development laboratory in St. Louis, points out that children are constantly called on to make decisions in art: how to use space and shape; "how much or how little paint to use; how hard, bright, or subtle the colors will be." Adults may not consider these decisions important in and of themselves, but they are important as part of the process by which the child learns how to make decisions.

Art also gives a child the chance to assimilate his experiences and state them with an emphasis on what is most important to him. As adults, we are always involved in rethinking our thoughts: How often, for instance, do we realize what we wanted to say only after we have said it? For children who are not able to use language as easily to reflect on their experience, art helps them to process what they have seen, felt, and done, and to focus—even if unconsciously—on whatever has made the greatest impression.

Moreover, as Bette Acuff, associate professor in the department of art and education at Columbia University Teachers College, points out, "If you can draw a picture of an idea you have or a memory of something you've seen or done, then you have internalized it in some way, and this gives you a new sense of owning your actions and experience."

Besides showing children that they do have some control over their experiences, to some extent art also allows them to take control: "As in dramatic play, drawing and painting are other modes in which children can use their imaginative functions to master their worlds," Acuff says. Not only can they record and synthesize their experiences in their artwork, according to Acuff; "They can make up their own rules. It gives them a chance to say, 'I'm the master of this,' and it has a psychological value there."

But what should a parent's role be in all of this? "Children should be encouraged to come up with their own drawings and say something about how they see the world and themselves," says New York University's Laurie Wilson. "They shouldn't be asked to draw one right way and their drawings should never be judged."

One additional note to parents: Wilson feels that "children should make their own pictures and color them" rather than use coloring books. "Coloring books imply children can't draw; using them becomes automatic and totally nonindividual. It doesn't challenge the child in any way and makes for a cheap, easier solution to something that could be much more exciting and more the child's own unique production. With a coloring book, all you have to do is figure out how to move a crayon on a page."

Jerilynn Changar feels it's important for the child to be given his own art corner at home where he can work any time of day. "It should be a place where if he spills or drips he won't think the whole house is going to fall apart," she says. The child also should have a regular place, such as a refrigerator, where he can show his work. "To ignore or reject his work is to show that you reject his ideas and feelings," says Changar. Parents can also provide their children with "inspiration and motivation" for art, giving them suggestions such as, "What would happen if tomorrow your dad said we could go anyplace in the world? Why don't you draw what you would like to see there?"

Another way to provide inspiration is to give children a greater base of sensory experiences. "Take them on a lot of walks. Give them a lot of things to look at," suggests Acuff. "Notice all gradations of colors, such as all different kinds of greens. Notice differences in shapes. Find all rough things and all smooth things. But focus on only one or two aspects at a time. Go out with your children and draw together." But if you do these activities, make sure you present them as "a game, a possibility, not an imposition," says Acuff.

But what do you say when your child shows you his drawing and you haven't got the slightest idea what it is?

Jerilynn Changar suggests finding something you can point to in the drawing and asking him about it. "You can say, 'Oh, I see you've used a lot of blue. Can you tell me about it?' or 'I see several different kinds of activities going on. Can you share them with me?' If he says, 'Oh, I don't know,' that's fine, even if you're not satisfied with his answer. The most important thing is that you are showing an interest in what he's done, and that it's important to you," she says.

Changar, like Acuff, also believes art can be a valuable experience for families to share. "When a family comes back from a vacation, for example, one night or one rainy day, get out a big piece of brown butcher paper, use simple materials, and have everyone draw his favorite part of the trip," she suggests.

"It's a way of telling your child that you're willing to share your ideas and feelings, a way to communicate and discover things about each other. Many times you will find out what the child liked or didn't like about the trip in an indirect way." Changar adds that family drawing sessions—like all parental involvement in children's art—"should be set up in a nonthreatening, noncompetitive way, so that the skill is not the focus, but rather the acceptance of each other and the sharing."

America's Head Start Program:
An Agenda for Its Second Decade

Edward F. Zigler

Edward F. Zigler, Ph.D., is Sterling Professor of Psychology, Yale University, New Haven, Connecticut. From 1970-72, he was Director of the HEW Office of Child Development.

As most of you know, my life has been closely intertwined with the Head Start program. I am proud that I was a member of the original planning committee for Head Start. During the years I served as the first director of the Office of Child Development, I was also the public servant responsible for Head Start. And, finally, for the past twelve years of my life, I have studied and evaluated the effects of the Head Start program.

Given my involvement with Head Start, I am troubled by the misunderstanding and confusion that continue to surround this bellwether program. Both the Associated Press and the New York *Times* have erroneously reported in the last year that Head Start has ceased to exist. In response to the New York *Times*'s error, I wrote the following letter:

> The New York *Times* erred in its assertion that Head Start is dead. Head Start, the most innovative program ever mounted on behalf of America's children, is alive and well. Your mistaken assertion is illustrative of the misunderstandings, controversy, and confusion that have surrounded the Head Start program since its inception over a decade ago. At a cost of over $400 million per year, the Head Start network continues to provide a preschool educational program enriched by a broad spectrum of social services to over 200,000 of America's economically disadvantaged children. Furthermore, over the years, the Head Start program has proven to be a valuable national laboratory for the development and assessment of a whole array of intervention efforts, such as the Home Start program, efforts relevant to the outcome and development of all of our nation's children.

Adapted from a speech given at the annual Head Start conference, May 1977, El Paso, Tex.

> Your editorial was correct in indicating that Head Start is a vulnerable program that has suffered many trials and tribulations. The history of this program has been one of moving from crisis to crisis, with Head Start people at local levels never feeling very confident that they would receive the following year's funding. Particularly detrimental to the Head Start program has been that coterie of psychologists, early childhood educators, and social policy analysts who have regularly, albeit erroneously, proclaimed the failure of the Head Start program. However, those Americans closest to and therefore most knowledgeable about Head Start, namely those American families whose children utilize it, have never wavered in their praise and support of this program. Head Start has continued to be funded because a bipartisan group in Congress has refused to turn a deaf ear to that relatively powerless segment of society that has always been Head Start's most fervent champion.

> What of Head Start's future? It remains problematic. For this reason, the Head Start program needs the active support of all those who feel that no national effort should take priority over the health and development of our nation's children.

Scholars continue to argue over whether Head Start has been a success or a failure. Anyone conducting an appropriate evaluation would have to conclude that Head Start has been a success. Why, then, is there an argument?

Let us now ask the central question: Do children who experience Head Start manifest greater gains on cognitive and personality measures than do comparison children who have not had the Head Start experience? The answer to this question is a resounding "Yes." Why then has it become fashionable to speak of the failure of Head Start? The assertion of Head Start's failure is based upon the reported finding that the advantage of Head Start children over non-Head Start children is not maintained once the children have spent two or three years in elementary school. But how is this finding to be interpreted? The raw data would appear to represent more an indictment of schools rather than of Head Start.

7. PROGRAMS AND CURRICULA

I would like to issue a serious warning against the popular "fade-out" notion. That is, the current conventional wisdom concerning the impact of Head Start is that the gains in performance obtained by Head Start children as compared to non-Head Start controls fade out a year or two into the elementary school grades. My own considered views concerning this bit of conventional wisdom are that it is more conventional than it is wise. From the Wolff and Stein report (1966), through the Westinghouse report (1969), to Bronfenbrenner's scholarly analysis conducted for OCD (1974), we have been informed that there are no striking long-term effects accruing from a one-year Head Start experience. This has been repeated so often that many now treat this conclusion as beyond question. I choose to question it. In flocking to this position, thinkers have ignored a relatively large and consistent body of evidence which indicates that the benefits of participating in a preschool intervention program have much greater staying power than currently popular views would have us believe. For those of you who are not prepared to accept that there are discernible effects accruing from Head Start attendance, I recommend that you read a recently prepared review of the evidence on this point by Frank Palmer (1975). I assert here today that besides being erroneous, the worst danger of the "fade-out" position is that it provides ammunition to those in America who feel that spending money in an effort to improve the lives of economically-disadvantaged children is a waste.

I ask decision makers not to set social policy on the basis of the conclusion that there are no long-term effects of Head Start attendance. I say to these decision makers that the evidence on this point is not as unidirectional as many currently believe. Bad science makes for bad social policy. I ask my colleagues in the research community to forego the temptation of delivering definitive pronouncements concerning the "fade-out" issue and await instead the collection and analyses of more data. Such a stance strikes me as currently being the only reasonable one if thinkers are to combine social responsiblity with the researchers' deeply-ingrained attitudes of skepticism and objectivity. (Zigler 1976, pp. 5-6)

This position, which I advanced about three years ago, not only remains valid but has been strengthened by several recent papers that have come out of the Longitudinal Research Consortium headed by Professor Irving Lazar at Cornell (see Moore 1978). The evidence is now clear that Head Start does indeed have long and important lasting effects.

I think the long-term effects of Head Start depend on two factors:

- Getting parents involved in the training of their own children, and

- Guaranteeing that schools follow the Head Start program with further intervention efforts.

These factors illustrate two types of continuity. First, there should be continuity between the Head Start program and the child's home. The parent is that wonderful lever that makes the efforts of the Head Start program mount in importance. If the parent will continue the Head Start center work at home, the effect will be greatly enhanced. Secondly, there should be continuity between the Head Start program and subsequent kindergarten and elementary schooling. We can never inoculate children in one year against the ravages of deprivation; there must be continuity. It is crucial that the schools follow the Head Start effort with a dovetailed second intervention that builds upon the gains of Head Start.

... the research issue of the next five years will not be whether Head Start is effective, but rather how to determine which children benefit maximally from the Head Start program.

In regard to whether Head Start is a success or a failure, I think the issue is beyond debate. I think the research issue of the next five years will not be whether Head Start is effective, but rather how to determine which children benefit maximally from the Head Start program.

Warnings: What Head Start Must *Not* Become

This basically positive view does not mean that we should rest on our laurels. I prefer to think of Head Start not as a static program but as an evolving concept, an effort that must continue to grow and develop. What, then, should be the future of Head Start? Head Start is essentially America's national laboratory for testing and refining our nation's efforts to improve the quality of life for our country's children. Let me begin by clearly enunciating what Head Start should *not* become.

First, I think **we must repudiate forever the view that higher IQ scores and their close correlate, elementary school grades,**

59. America's Head Start Program

are the ultimate goals of the Head Start effort. The back-to-basics movement represents a new threat to what is best about the Head Start effort. The issue here is whether we shall commit ourselves to a narrow cognitive development approach or to a wider whole-child approach. The back-to-basics and cognitive development emphasis is based on a fallacy: the now-discredited deficit hypothesis that the central problem for economically disadvantaged children is their intellectual inadequacy. The children of the poor have as much intellectual potential as the children of the affluent. When we began Head Start, scholars were publicly saying that poor children did not have the intellectual capacity to be able to store cognitively and retrieve their own names. Some of you perhaps remember that sad epoch when we were putting children's names over a mirror so they would be able to learn their own names. This is where the cognitive emphasis ultimately leads.

... the primary goal of Head Start is to promote socially competent human beings.

Let us proclaim instead that the primary goal of Head Start is to promote socially competent human beings. What do we mean by a socially competent human being? What would be the measurable indicators that we had succeeded with Head Start? The measure of social competence includes the physical and mental health and well-being of the children we serve. That is why it is so fitting for the Head Start program to serve handicapped children. Only five or six years ago, handicapped children were *not* included in the Head Start program. Today, 10 to 12 percent of the Head Start children are handicapped, and the job that Head Start people have done stands as a model to the school system of what mainstreaming is really all about. Head Start has shown that mainstreaming requires training and preparation, not just the willy-nilly placement of children together. Since the incidence of handicap is much greater among the poor than among the nonpoor, Head Start was a little slow to reach out to this segment of the population. I can only say that I take my share of the blame. But I am proud to have all of you as colleagues who at least acted better late than never.

In addition to the physical health and well-being of children, we should look at formal cognitive ability, including language and closely-related intellectual skills, in its proper place. That is the second aspect of social competence. The third aspect, which I have been talking about as long as Head Start has been in business, is to work on the emotional, motivational development of children. I am convinced that where we made our error was in ever thinking that poor children suffered from lack of intelligence. The real problem is that they frequently do not use optimally the intelligence they have. And the job of Head Start is to develop the emotional and motivational skills that are the heart of school performance and mind performance.

Three factors are particularly important in producing a socially competent human being. One is the locus of control variable: Does the child really feel in charge, that things happen because he or she makes them happen, or is the child just a passive victim of outside forces? The children who feel they can possess the necessary competence to accomplish a task will become the competent adults. I also ask you to work very closely with children to see that they develop a healthy and appropriate responsivity to adults. And finally I ask you to continue the work that has been basic to Head Start since its inception, that we do everything we can to respect the child's culture, the child's sense of home and worth. In short, we should do everything possible to develop a positive self-image among children in Head Start centers. Those emotional and motivational variables are part of the social competence we are talking about.

Now, another warning. As Head Start ages, we must guard against becoming an elitist group of self-proclaimed experts to whom parents turn over their children so the children will be raised properly. Children are raised by parents in their homes and not by Head Start personnel in centers. All the good that Head Start can do can be wiped out if we do anything to disparage the parents of the children we serve. Head Start is the only institution on the national scene that represents a true partnership between families and professionals who serve these families. It is this viable partnership that represents what is unique and revolutionary about the Head Start effort.

7. PROGRAMS AND CURRICULA

This partnership lies at the heart of our success, and we should rededicate ourselves to the basic principle that Head Start reflects the wisdom and competence of the parents who utilize its services.

In the future, **we should also not waste our energies seeking magic periods.** I have now witnessed fifteen years of this aimless search. We have one group of experts who say that the magic period is the nine months *in utero*, and that we should concentrate all our energies on this period. Then we have another group of experts who say the magic period is the first year of life, the only time period worth intervening in. Another group is still holding to the two years before school as the crucial period. Still another group of experts maintains that the first three elementary grades is the magic period. Now, believe it or not, another group of workers tells us that adolescence is the critical period in the life cycle.

This is a useless and nonsensical argument. These are all magic periods. Let us take seriously what developmental psychologists have to teach: There is a continuity to human life, one period built upon another, each period important, each period needing a special set of nutrients and programs for the child at that age. Certainly we must have good prenatal care; we also want infant programs; we need preschool and school-age programs; and we can still help children in adolescence. The problem with magic periods is the tendency to give up on children who have outgrown them. In my view, one should never give up on a child, regardless of age. There is always some kind of program that could be helpful, and it is our responsibility to deliver these programs to children, *whatever* their ages.

Analogously, in the future **we should stop viewing Head Start as a panacea required by every child whose family income falls below some arbitrary figure.** Head Start has already started to evolve from a single program into a center with a variety of programs serving the myriad needs of children and families residing in neighborhoods where the Head Start center is situated. Rather than expecting children to fit the requirements and characteristics of Head Start, Head Start should become a center containing many programs tailored to fit the needs of the childen and their families. This model of the Head Start program of the future already exists in the Administration for Children, Youth, and Families (ACYF) Child and Family Resource programs. In my opinion, this model is the wave of the future.

Recommendations: What Head Start Should Do

Now that I have briefly summarized what Head Start should *not* do, I would like to make a threefold set of recommendations for what it should do:

- We need a change in Head Start's basic stance;
- Head Start needs a substantive program agenda; and
- There should be a political agenda for those who support Head Start and those who feel that the healthy development of children should be our nation's top priority.

Perhaps some people will think me naive to try to move into the political arena. It is true that I probably know more about t-tests and multivariate analysis than I know about that land of Oz we call Washington, D.C. But, if I have learned one lesson in my twenty years of experience in this field, it is that accomplishments on the substantive program front rarely outdistance those on the political front. I'm asking you to care for children. I'm also asking you to be social activists. Let us remember our community action roots and not be bashful. Too often people who care about children think that because our cause is just we really don't have to fight for it. But other people have other agendas. We cannot compete as a lobby group with the National Rifle Association, but we *can* speak with one voice; we can be heard.

The basic stance of Head Start **must change from a defensive to an offensive posture.** After the first summer, Head Start was a smash hit; we were the "Sesame Street" of 1965. Then the Westinghouse report (1969) came along and we went from being viewed very positively to somewhat negatively. Finally, through our own efforts and the new programs in Head Start, we moved from a negative to a somewhat neutral position in people's attitudes toward us.

Why have we been so orphanlike, standing hat in hand, begging to please keep the program alive? Why have we never just sold what we had to sell?

Now I say to you, I have lived through some dark days in Head Start. Why have we been so orphanlike, standing hat in hand, begging to please keep the program alive? Why have we never just sold what we had to sell? Instead we have always pleaded for one more year, with the promise to show some "results" by then. Why did we take that stance? The nadir of the Head Start program in America probably took place about 1970 when I went to Washington to become the director of the Office of Child Development. One of the first tasks I was called upon to perform was to attend a meeting at the Office of Economic Opportunity. And what I was confronted with about one week into my Washington experience was a three-year phase-out plan for the Head Start program. The Nixon administration had decided that Head Start would go; in that period all the War on Poverty programs were being phased out and Head Start was just included in the group. Well, that frightened me, and we did what we had to do to keep Head Start alive. It wasn't a matter of more money; it was a matter of keeping the program alive. This is a story with nothing but heroes. Head Start parents came to the rescue of the program; Department of Health, Education, and Welfare (HEW) Secretary Elliot Richardson took our case to the White House. I saw Republicans and Democrats combine to say, "This is the one program that we wanted for children; let's not spoil it now."

The evidence is increasingly clear that Head Start works and can work even better if we can expand Head Start into areas in which children and families need service.

That incident indicates to you why we were so passive in our approach to Head Start. We had to be passive because we were, frankly, scared to death. But the days when we must be scared to death are over. We no longer have to stand hat in hand. The evidence is increasingly clear that Head Start works and can work even better if we can expand Head Start into areas in which children and families need service. We are taking this evidence to the Hill, and we are taking it to our friends in the administration. Now this kind of expansion cannot be done with mirrors. It will require more money. Too often in the past we at the national level have passed new tasks down to the regions and local levels and said, "Hey, do this," without a dollar to do these new things. You have all worked for less than you are worth; you have received low salaries and low prestige. Your commitment is on record. But you can only ask people to work for nothing without adjustment for inflation for so long. And we must seize the moment now to make up for the inequities that you have suffered for many years. That is my political standpoint: Change it from passive to assertive, from negative and reserved to positive and demanding.

Head Start's Agenda

What is my substantive agenda? Here I feel more comfortable than when I make political pronouncements. I am a student of child development and of the family's importance in that development. What do I see then as being important items on our Head Start agenda over the second decade in the life of this program?

First, **we must do better in the Child Development Associate program.** We must produce a cadre of workers in this country who can care for children. At the risk of appearing a little inconsistent with my stance on magic, I do believe there is some magic somewhere in Head Start and in childhood intervention. The magic is not in ages or even in particular types of programs. It is in the relationship between the adult caregiver and the child being cared for. That's where the magic is. If we want Head Start to be a success, then we need to make sure that every adult caregiver in every Head Start center in this nation has the skills and abilities to be an optimizer of the development of the children in his or her charge.

7. PROGRAMS AND CURRICULA

Now I will make a somewhat revolutionary appeal, an appeal that has divided Head Start people in the past, but I will risk your wrath. I think that the day will soon come when **Head Start will be expanded to include nonpoor children**. I have never believed in the philosophy that poor children should go to one center and more affluent children to another. Now I am enough of a realist to see that we cannot do everything overnight; we have to have some priorities. I think that besides serving children of the poor, Head Start should give the following groups priority. I think we must continue our efforts and thrust toward handicapped children whatever their family income. I think we should make a special effort in regard to non-English-speaking children. Finally, I think we should make a special effort to give some priority to children of single-parent families in which that single parent works. Somebody must care for these children, and too many of them are not cared for today.

Beyond expanding Head Start to meet these new priorities, I also think **we should expand Head Start services**. I believe that Head Start should play a very simple role in the new inoculation effort. A tragedy is taking place in America. The Center for Disease Control in Atlanta indicates that the inoculation rate in America is down 50 percent; this declining curve means illness and death for children. I am pleased that HEW Secretary Joseph A. Califano has spoken out in favor of inoculating children. I cannot believe that a nation that can go to the moon cannot get children vaccinated against polio and measles and other childhood ailments. Head Start has a special role to play in an inoculation program. In the ghettos and slums of this country and in the Appalachian poverty areas, some 70 percent of the children are probably not inoculated. Why are they not inoculated? People sound very righteous when they say, "Look, poor people can take their children to a hospital and get them inoculated for nothing. Why don't they do it?" And I say to them, "Have you ever been to one of those hospitals and seen how poor people are treated there?" That's why Head Start could play a special role, because the one thing the Head Start has that the American health system does not have is credibility with parents. If we decide to inoculate the children in neighborhoods, they are more likely to come to Head Start than anywhere else.

Some other very quick ideas for this idealistic agenda: It's time for Head Start to move into doing something about the number one killer of America's children—accidents. **Head Start should develop a formidable accident prevention program**. (See Ross and Seefeldt 1978.) Another problem is teenage motherhood. While the birthrate in this nation declines, teenage births are soaring. These young children who are trying to raise children need our help. We can draw on our experience with the Parent and Child Centers and the Education for Parenthood Program to **provide services to teenage mothers in our Head Start centers**, if we decide to do so.

Head Start centers must also become active agencies to combat child abuse, which has now reached the epidemic figure of one million cases a year. I can't believe that the National Center on Child Abuse and Neglect in ACYF cannot be coordinated with the Head Start program for the benefit of children.

In conclusion, I want to give you a brief political agenda that must be accomplished if we are going to do any of these things. There are two basic requirements. One is that we have to have a vocal and effective lobby on behalf of children and families, and you are the nucleus of that lobby. We must also have a strong and effective ACYF that can be the focal point for developing and then implementing social policy. ACYF continues to be vulnerable. It was created by Executive Order, and any time the powers-that-be would like to, they can abolish it.

We must do everything we can to support ACYF and its Commissioner, Dr. Blandina Cardenas. We must see that ACYF is legislated by Congress. We must do everything possible to see that the prestige of the ACYF Commissioner is enhanced. Dr. Cardenas has my support; I will work with her as closely as I possibly can so that she can become the very best Commissioner of ACYF.

ACYF has already suffered a very serious reversal since my tenure. When the Commissioner of ACYF was made responsible to an Assistant Secretary, that was a different ballgame than when I dealt directly with the Secretary of HEW. We should insist that the Commissioner be a presidential appointee in the same way that the Assistant Secretary for the Office of Human Development Services is a presidential appointee so that we are talking about two people who at least have the same status in their interactions.

I ask HEW Secretary Califano to stop making a political football out of Head Start. We have important work to do. You are here doing the work that Head Start people should do, becoming knowledgeable about how to help children. The children need our undivided attention; they don't need all this "where's Head Start going to be next year?" I ask Secretary Califano and I ask the White House to step forward and state unequivocally and clearly that Head Start has been a smashing success and will remain in ACYF.

I have thought about these matters and I find myself much more optimistic than I have been in a very long time. You have done a magnificent job. I am grateful to you and all I can say in conclusion is that I am very proud to be one of your colleagues.

References

Bronfenbrenner, U. *A Report on Longitudinal Evaluations of Preschool Programs*. Vol. 2. *Is Early Intervention Effective?* Washington, D.C.: Department of Health, Education, and Welfare, 1974. Publication No. (OHD) 74-25.

Moore, S. G. "The Persistence of Preschool Effects: A National Collaborative Study." *Young Children* 33, no. 3 (March 1978): 65-71.

Palmer, F. "Has Compensatory Education Failed? No, Not Yet." Unpublished manuscript, State University of New York, Stony Brook, 1975.

Ross, S. P., and Seefeldt, C. "Young Children in Traffic: How Can They Cope?" *Young Children* 33, no. 4 (May 1978): 68-73.

Westinghouse Learning Corporation. *The Impact of Head Start: An Evaluation of the Effects of Head Start on Children's Cognitive and Affective Development. Executive Summary*. Ohio University Report to OEO, Clearinghouse for Federal Scientific and Technical Information, June 1969.

Wolff, M., and Stein, A. *Factors Influencing the Recruitment of Children into the Head Start Program, Summer 1965: A Case Study of Six Centers in New York City (Study II)*. New York: Yeshiva University, 1966. Office of Economic Opportunity Project No. 141-61.

Zigler, E. F. "Head Start: Not a Program but an Evolving Concept." In *Early Childhood Education: It's an Art? It's a Science?* edited by J. D. Andrews. Washington, D.C.: National Association for the Education of Young Children, 1976.

Teaching and Evaluation

There is a deeply imbedded societal myth that not much intellectual ability or professional skill is required to work with young children. Professionals understand the fallacy and deceptiveness of such thinking.

Researchers of the teaching process identified a constellation of personality qualities and skills that characterize successful and fulfilled teachers, neophyte or seasoned.

Physical stamina is a major requirement due to the energy levels of healthy, growing children. Genuine enjoyment and a feeling of comfort in being with children is vital, since they are acutely sensitive to mannerisms or facades. Intellectual curiosity and the desire for continuous learning are essential since children's minds are opening up and they frequently pose questions that adults cannot easily answer. Emotional warmth, lack of prejudices, and tolerance of children's not-yet-adult state help the teacher to understand and deal with human differences and individuality.

Flexibility and resourcefulness in the face of upset routines and disorder help the teacher to manage the many unforeseeable situations that arise. Emotional maturity and sensitivity enable a teacher to live with children as striving, growing, learning organisms, quite unlike adults in their outlook. Finally, an attitude of playfulness and a sense of humor permit the teacher-adult to enliven children's experiences, and, in the words of Einstein, "to awaken joy in creative expression and knowledge."

Most early childhood programs have established some system of recording and evaluating children's abilities, skills, needs, and progress.

The evaluation systems used may be formal or informal, objective or subjective, standardized or makeshift, well-planned or hit-or-miss. Nonetheless, nationwide pressures have mounted for more systematic evaluation, especially for more objective, criterion-referenced measures, and for greater specificity of the goals and objectives to be measured.

The basic question being asked by many persons remains the same: Is the amount of time, money, and effort being expended in educating young children worth it or not? Does more input automatically guarantee more output?

In some programs, educators are required under various funding agency rules to administer a battery of tests to an entire group of children at specific times in the program. Long standing concerns about such practices are that young children are often unable to respond accurately and perform naturally to paper-and-pencil tests, to tests administered in a large group, or to a test examiner who is unfamiliar to them.

Contemporary alternatives to standardized testing of intelligence, readiness, and achievement levels include systematic observing and recording of children's play and class activities, or interviewing them individually (clinical method) about their perceptions and concepts. Because each of these approaches can take place in a more natural setting, they provide more valid information than more obtrusive methods and anxiety-laden settings.

This section presents an analysis of what teaching actually involves with young children. Also included are several points of view about educational accountability—an educational reality that will endure despite one's philosophical views or personal experiences with evaluation.

Looking Ahead: Challenge Questions

What are common satisfactions derived from teaching young children? Are there special skills required or could anyone perform well?

What aspects of teaching are similar to what artists or composers do in their work?

Are there specific ways of opening up children who are not highly verbal? At what times during the program are children especially receptive to two-way communication with teachers?

How can teachers become more sensitized to the sexist language and demands made on children?

What aspects of the physical, interpersonal, and intellectual environment should be noted when evaluating a program?

What has research shown about the effectiveness of the national Follow Through program? Is this similar or different from what research on the persistence of pre-school effects has indicated?

What are the purposes and limitations of different kinds of evaluation instruments?

What alternatives to standardized and group testing are there for teachers? How can systematic observation be used effectively?

Article 60

The Satisfactions

James L. Hymes, Jr

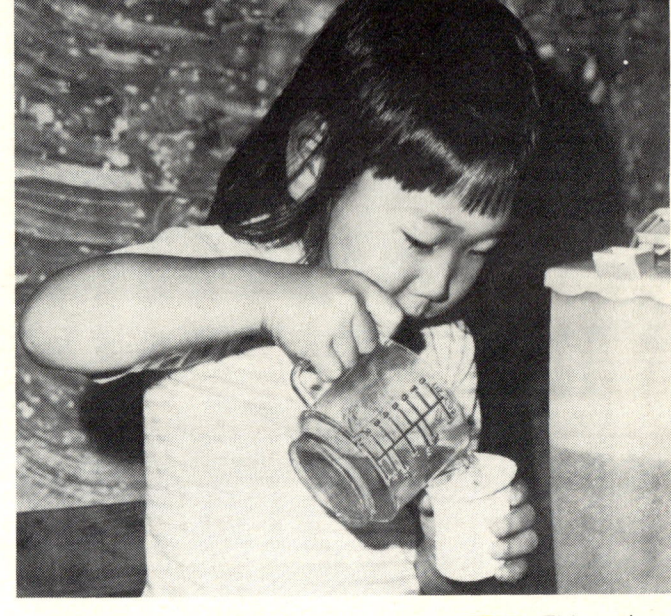

Young children want to solve their own problems.

The profession of Early Childhood Education isn't one problem after another. The field offers many deep satisfactions. One solid satisfaction—it has been the theme of much in the earlier pages—is the chance to work in a still unsettled, expanding field where there is much work to be done. Early Childhood Education is a good field for activists. It offers everyone the real possibility of contributing to the solution of problems.

A second satisfaction in Early Childhood Education is the chance to work with parents as well as children. All teachers in the field—in nursery school, kindergarten, child care, Head Start—need to work closely with parents. These adults can be good friends; they can become true allies. Associating intimately with them can be a rewarding experience. You don't work with children alone.

The main joy, however, will come from your response to the children themselves. Most people, of course, say, "I love little children." If you have worked with older youngsters, you probably "love" them too. Children of all ages are not hard to like. The best way of being sure that early childhood is *your* field is to match yourself up against the strengths that are peculiar to young children. This way you can be more sure that *young* children—not just all children—will bring you special satisfaction.

Young children—from birth—are highly imaginative, for example. Does this thrill you? They are creative, in paint and blocks and language. They are experimental, ever trying something that no one else has thought of doing. Do you get excited by freshness and innovation, or does it seem better to you when people stick to the tried-and-true?

Young children have a biting curiosity. This makes some people a little uncomfortable. How do you feel about children probing all the time? With questions, with their fingers, getting up so very close so they can be sure to see? You have to prize curiosity if you work with the early childhood age range, not want to shut it off and short-cut it.

The whole age range is bursting with ego. This is not surprising, but not everyone likes it. As babies, these children do not know they exist. Later, they have moments when it is hard for them to realize that anyone else exists. They want to try everything (even though you could do the job better and quicker). They want to solve their own problems (even though you could show them how in a jiffy). Some people work with young children because they want to tame them and civilize them and make them like the rest of us. A teacher has to have a due regard for the rights of all, but you won't get any fun out of spending time with young children unless you treasure individuality. The job at this age level is to build children up, to make individuals strong, not to knock them down and keep them in their place.

These are active children, not meant to stay put, not meant to stay seated, not meant to line up. They can work hard but almost never in one great big beautiful group. Five or six or seven or more different activities must be going on at once. Does the thought of this drive you crazy? You always have to have something up your sleeve, a ready suggestion as one small group tires of what it is doing. You can't run out of ideas. You have to think of your feet. And, because there is so much going on all at once, you have to be observant. You need eyes in back of your head, and

Reprinted from *Early Childhood Education, An Introduction to the Profession* by James L. Hymes, Jr. Pages 65-71. Copyright 1969; 1975 second edition. National Association for the Education of Young Children, 1834 Connecticut Ave., N.W., Washington, D.C. 20009.

60. The Satisfactions

sometimes you will wish that you had six pairs of hands. All the busyness and movement wears some people down to a frazzle in no time. Their great urge is to stand in front of the class and talk and be TEACHER, with everyone's eyes glued on them. How about you? How do you feel? What do you like?

There is always a lot of emotion in young children's groups. These boys and girls have strong feelings. A child may be hurt, and hate, for the moment. You see glee—it gets loud and noisy, for the moment. You see fear. Many people would rather work with older children who keep their feelings hidden. Some take it as their job to get young children to cover up how they feel or to pretend that they do not have emotions. The good teacher of young children starts on the assumption that youngsters do have feelings, and that the emotions are a real and important part of life.

You have to be smart, and very well-informed to teach young children well. Don't think of working with young children unless you do quite well in English, in science, history, math.... If you work with older children you have the textbook to protect you. Three- to eight-year-olds can pop any question at you: about dinosaurs or rockets, about China or twins or what makes a rainbow, or anything under the sun. If school work has always been a chore for you, these curious youngsters will show you up.

Of course, you can't know everything. No one can. But it is the spirit that counts. These children are in love with life. Everything around them looks so appealing and exciting and mysterious and wonderful. If you too are in love with learning, you will get a lot of satisfaction from working with your soulmates. If reading, thinking, puzzling, and asking bore you, then do watch out. A lot of people make the mistake of assuming you don't have to be very academic to work with young children. They really are off base. They probably are fooled because the good teacher of young children does not talk much at the whole group of children. You can't get through to these children with lectures and a lot of words. But these children want to find out, and they want the truth, and they ask very rock-bottom questions. You have to be on your toes to keep up with them.

One last satisfaction: You will have a lot of freedom teaching in Early Childhood Education. You are more apt to be your own boss. This is especially true in the nursery school, and this is one of the reasons why so many nursery school teachers truly love their work. But there is freedom in Head Start and in kindergarten and in child care, also. There is less chance of some confining "approved" course of study that has to be covered. Actually, there is also more freedom in the primary grades than most teachers take advantage of.

Often the teacher in early childhood can do almost what s/he pleases. This is very deeply satisfying *if* what you please is significant. The little world, the private world of your children's environment can be a laboratory in democ-

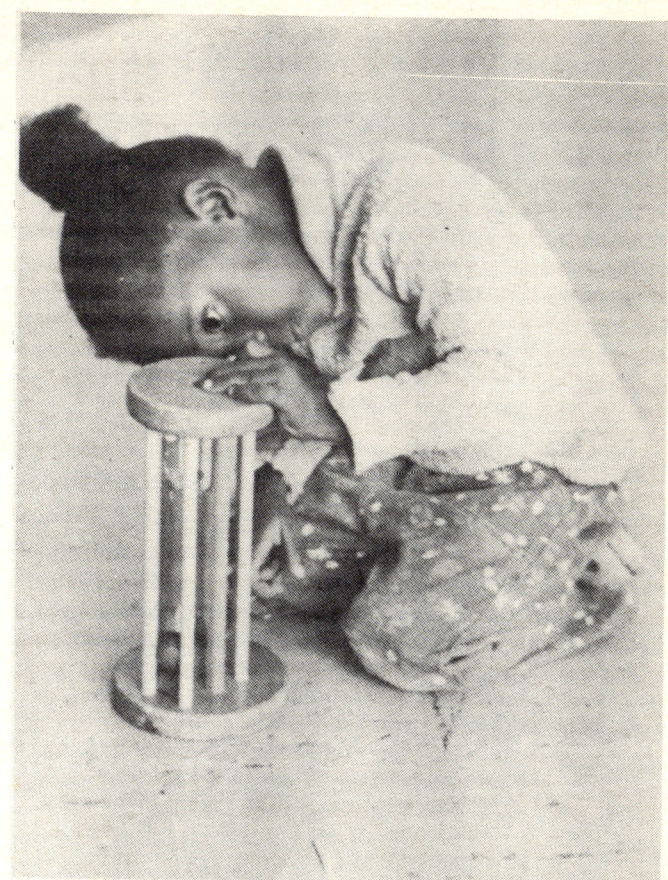

Prize curiosity if you work with young children; don't shut it off and short-cut it.

racy. It can be where young children get their first outside-the-home taste of what it means to live in America.

The way you speak to children, how you conduct yourself, your relationships, the tone and climate and spirit of your group, these can all be expressions of your best dreams for how you wish everyone would live. Guided by reason and with a respect for law. With a devotion to freedom. With a reverence for the right of all to life and liberty and to the pursuit of happiness. Where the majority have their rights but where even the single lone individual has rights, too. A place of decency, of kindliness, of warmth and friendship, a place where a child feels safe.

To teach young children well you must study children. You must study much subject matter. You also have to be a student of how this country of ours lives, and of how it could live and prosper even better. If you use your freedom to help young children grow and develop, teaching can bring great pleasure to you, a good start in life for the children, and a firm base for the future.

Article 61

The Meaning of Teaching

Leland B. Jacobs

Leland B. Jacobs is Professor Emeritus, Teachers College, Columbia University, New York City.

TODAY many of us who teach feel we are beset by dilemmas and perplexities unlike those with which any previous generation of teachers has ever had to cope. Ours *are* difficult times to do our jobs well, to be true professionals. All kinds of thorny problems—dichotomies, disagreements, challenges—come to the fore, which we must wrestle with, collectively as well as individually.

Here are some of them: accountability, competency-based programs, "thorough and efficient education," models and paradigms, career education, sex education, moral education, sensitivity training, the "right to read," linguistics and psycholinguistics, packaged curriculum programs, national testing programs, busing, community control, tenure, unionization. And—God help us!—these things all become entangled with *behavioral objectives!*

But primary to all these concerns, in my estimation, is the attention we must give to what we believe and what we know about being a teacher of boys and girls. A real problem with accountability at the present time, for example, is that we have not as a profession really been about our business to clarify what teaching means.

There's only one reason why you and I are employed—to teach. Over and over again, it seems to me, every one of these curriculum problems, these management problems, these peripheral problems all go back to what you and I believe teaching is.

THREE KINDS OF TEACHERS

Three kinds of people call themselves teachers. Without describing them too fully, perhaps we can pretty well agree on them.

Schoolkeepers

We have *schoolkeepers*—dozens of them in our profession. They keep school. They are tidy people—they water the plants every day. After the purple-passion-sheet little ducks are all cut out for March or April, they put them up straight above the chalkboard. They ceremoniously get out the handwriting alphabet in the fall and put it above the chalkboard, and in June they ceremoniously dust it and put it away for next fall. They move from one workbook to the next; their lesson plans can be put in little squares and boxes (page 21, page 32, exercise 3). They always get their reports in to the principal on time.

The greatest schoolkeeper I ever saw was in New Jersey. He used seven workbooks! The kids sat on them; they put the last one they were using under and pulled the next one out. That's one thing about schoolkeepers; they have it all in order. They pat kids into line. If children aren't doing the waddling duck rhythm the way the teacher wants them to (she may weigh 200 pounds like me!), she'll get down and say, "I want you to do it like this." Not a child in the room could *possibly* do it like that! Schoolkeepers—they bear the *name* of teacher, but they see their job as forming children—keeping them "in form."

Instructors

Instructors, the second group, so love their subject matter that they want the children to love it the same way they do—hence they sneak up on them. They seduce them with gold stars, with little airplanes on spelling charts. They use external motivation.

When I started my teacher education, some fifty years ago, authorities were more honest—they didn't call it "motivation" then. They called it "stirring up the aperceptive mass." And today I visit classrooms where instructors are still busy "stirring it up" so that children get the content they want them to have. ("Boys and girls, tell me, what kind of cookies does your

61. The Meaning of Teaching

Mama—or Papa—bake? Oh, that's nice, Helen... chocolate chip! And your Mama, Susie? That's nice, pineapple bars. You buy them at the store, Willy? What kind?") Such instructors don't give a tinker's dam what kind of cookies are being baked—because all they are doing is stirring up the aperceptive mass. ("Now we're going to read the story about baking cookies with Mama.")

Instructors: they're better than schoolkeepers, because they see their job as *informing*.

Composers

And then there are folks like us—real *teachers*. They don't add methods to content—they know that what you do and the way you do it are inextricably woven together. When McLuhan wrote *The Medium Is the Message*, every real teacher I know said, "So what?" They've known this forever. Real teachers know that teaching is a compositional act.

THE ART OF THE TEACHING ACT

The way you "compose" teaching, as I see it, is by confronting children. The job of teaching is to get in kids' way, not to get out of their way. If we keep out of their way, they may as well be out on the street. I hear educators sometimes say, "The teacher wasn't really doing anything; the children were doing it all." Nonsense! The teacher had so posed confrontations as to know when to be in and when out. Composed confrontations: we compose schooling experiences in such a way that we're sure all of the children, in terms of who they are, can encounter the content.

On to Engagement

We do not compose *umbrella* confrontations, because only two people can get under an umbrella. We compose *canopy* ones, where all can get under with their own encounters, and start some interaction. But too often in our professional literature we have talked as if that were the end of it. Not at all—interaction is just a beginning; it leads to *transaction*. And when it really works, in those glorious moments, it moves on to *engagement*. Engagement of the children in the encounter, engagement of the teacher in making that encounter the most remarkable possible experience.

Dignity of the Child's Being

Real teachers know that teaching starts first in their own minds, with the acceptance of the child as he or she is. It starts with the dignity of the child's being.

The great educational psychologist Arthur Jersild has said that a child has not only the right to be the age child he is when he comes to school; he has the right to be the kind of child he is. George Murphy, who for years was in charge of the reading clinic at Pennsylvania State University, told audiences all over this country that you have not really seen a child until you've seen "beyond the head lice and the snotty nose." And L. Thomas Hopkins told audiences at ACEI conferences that when a little fellow in your classroom isn't giving you the behavior that you want, you *still* have to say to yourself—if you are a real teacher—"It's the best behavior he has at the moment. God willing, he'll have better at the end of this year of living with me, but at this moment this is the best behavior he's got."

A child *lives*—that's where teaching starts.

Dignity of Recognition

Children come to school *alone*, too. They do not come to us as bundles of individual differences, all neatly tied up the way twigs are tied up in the Black Forest; they come wholly alone.

Oh, that worries some people, because they equate aloneness with loneliness. But we all know deep down inside that to be human is to have to live alone—alone with one's heartbeat, alone with one's locomotion, alone with one's cholesterol count, alone with one's perceptions of life. Anybody who has lived intimately with another person for many years knows that one is never totally explicable to another. And that the purpose of communion and communication is to reach from the aloneness or the "onlyness," if you prefer, of one to another.

Dignity of Recognition. Recognition in terms of interests. One can awaken us teachers out of a sound sleep and ask, "What are you doing?" and an answer trips on our tongues, "We are meeting the needs and interests of children." The terms are too broad. We should recognize that children bring at least three kinds of interest to the classroom. Some are interest curiosities;

8. TEACHING AND EVALUATION

some, interest concerns; and others, interest commitments—and they cannot all be treated the same way.

Interest Curiosities. We were in a home awhile ago where a little girl was so excited and interested in finding out about something at the dinner table. I said, "Ask it at school." And she responded, "Not on your life. I don't want to know that much!" Curiosity may lead on; we have to ask what we are doing to keep it growing.

Interest Concerns. Today's children know no more about love or affection or belonging or acceptance than did those of any other generation, so far as I can tell from working with them. But in some ways they *are* more knowledgeable. Because they watch television, they have seen the devastating effects of war and they know there are inequities in this world; they bring those concerns to the classroom. And we must deal with them, not because, in all humility, we have any better solutions but because we want sympathetically to do what we can to help them comprehend that there are human problems to be worked on.

Interest Commitments. Even very young children have commitments—they may not last very long; but, my, how motivational it can be to take them seriously. I know one little boy, Tommy, who when he was five lived in a neighborhood that had the most marvelous garbage collector. Tommy would be out to meet him every time he came, and one day announced to his own family that when *he* grew up, he wanted to be a garbage man. Don't laugh—because if you had to do without your Robert Redford or your garbage man, which choice are *you* going to make! Now, Tommy grew up to be a college professor; make anything of that you want to.

Another little boy, on an island off Massachusetts, at a very early age got curious about, and then seriously interested in, turtles. The great turtle authorities in America have heard about him. They send him brochures and they come to visit him, for they see the continuation of their work in that little fellow!

When the great storyteller Seamus McManus used to visit in America, he stopped in dime stores all over to buy things for the children of his village—and he always bought a couple of extras, for there would be new babies. He was taking a gift to that unknown child who some day would carry on *his* traditions, would sit and listen as he had to the stories that led him to become the storyteller.

You ask, "How am I going to know if the interest is a curiosity or a commitment?" If the classroom is the right kind, the children will tell you . . . provided that you listen.

Splitters and Lumpers. They come with the dignity of identity and recognition in terms of a *preferred learning style*.

In practically any classroom, some of your children are going to be *splitters* and some are going to be *lumpers*—and some will be both. Splitters take ideas, hypotheses, questions and build logically, logically, logically to a conclusion. Lumpers—they throw out a good gob of stuff and then pull out the strands to see if it works. (The test of what you are is what you did when you wrote term papers. If the professor said that you should turn in an outline of the paper and you wrote the outline first and then wrote the paper, you are a splitter. If, like me, you wrote the paper and then found out what the outline was, you're a lumper!)

Hypothetical Others. If you are doing the *real* teaching act, you are creating of each child a hypothetical other. "Given these circumstances," you surmise, "that child will behave this way." You don't *know* he's going to behave this way today; life is not that neat. Observing behaviors, we make some hunches—and we know when that hunch is wrong and the child has moved on.

Turnabout is fair play; the children have *us* all labeled as hypothetical others too. Anyone who has taught in the same school for as long as three years has a grapevine growing. "When you get into her classroom and she says, 'What will we do after we've had the study?' yell as fast as you can, 'Make books.' You're going to make books no matter what other choices there are."

Dignity of Learning

The job of real teaching is not to result in learning. Learning is all about; it no more belongs to us in schools than it does to the church, the home, the peer group. You cannot stop learning if you wanted to. When you have really been taught, you come away *knowing what you know.* Oh, somebody will

61. The Meaning of Teaching

say, "Even in learning what you don't know?" Of course—how can you know what you don't know until you know what you know? Look back at the teachers who somehow or other got to you. What they did was help you pick the stuff that remained somewhat disparate, each in its own little box, when all of a sudden they weren't in boxes any more. They'd all gone together. You knew what you knew!

Discourse and Nondiscourse. As real teachers, you and I have two ways to help children know what they know. We have opportunity to induct them into the worlds of discourse and nondiscourse.

Discourse is the realm of fact, information and judgment—and, in the negative sense, propaganda. When we're dealing with children to help them know what they know about facts and information, this material has to be built logically and linearly. It has to start with a problem, question, topic, proposal, hypothesis, assumption, and be developed to a reasonable conclusion. Then comes the test: verifying it.

Real teachers seldom use a single textbook; they push kids out to verify. They don't even want all the same kind of dictionaries in their classrooms—they want eight or ten different dictionaries. Schoolkeepers protest, "But the children are going to find that the books don't agree!" That's exactly what real teachers want.

In every classroom where we deal with American history, do you know what I'd put? At least one Canadian book. If children used that to find out about the American Revolution, they might not recognize it but they ought to hear it. Teach them to verify.

Small children know this need intuitively. If we tell them some information, they go and ask somebody else they respect, "Is it *true*?" The result of building on that intuition and of taking children into the realm of discourse is an informed intellect.

But another hallway to knowing is no less important: nondiscourse or aesthetic feeling, the realm of the arts.

Aesthetic feeling, which is to be distinguished from your own *psychological* feeling, involves projecting yourself into what you are not. It is to become one with the "elephant's child and the great, gray, green Limpopo River, all set about with fever trees."

Rather than building logically and linearly, aesthetic feeling is built relationally, from a beginning to a middle to an end. Its test is not verifiability but believability. Do you *believe* a Calder mobile? Do you *believe* the Three Billy Goats Gruff? Do you *believe* that

A goblin lives in our house, in our house
A goblin lives in our house, all the year round?

While discourse leads to an an informed intellect, nondiscourse leads to an educated imagination.

Real teachers, then, compose teaching so that children have two comparable ways of knowing. Thus children come to know the causes of the American Revolution, informationally; they also know the music of the Revolution, the paintings of the Revolution, and the story of the Revolution as in *Johnny Tremain*.

Dignity of Being Responsible

Real teaching calls for being responsibly productive. It is foolish to say, as some teachers do, "I don't care anything about the children's product, it's just the process that counts." D.E.M. Gardner, the magnificent English early childhood educator, told us the story when she was visiting here of entering a classroom where there was a "lovey-dovey" teacher, where everything in the room was "lovely." The teacher, upon approaching one child who was painting at the easel, exclaimed, "Oh, beautiful! Beautiful!" The little boy tore his picture off the easel, crumpled it up and stomped on it, saying, "Tain't either. It's the worst painting I ever made in my life!"

Another kind of teacher insists, "I don't care what the process is; it's the product that counts." A thirteen-year-old Campfire Girl, seeking to tell the difference between the way adults and children write poetry, closed her poem with these lines:

And old folks write for pleasure's sake
But children write for fame.

Product, product! But real teachers know that process and product go together.

Being responsibly productive means to *react*, to *do*, to respond to both the process and the product.

GROWING TOGETHER

What has all this to do with "growing together as professionals"? Everything! For as

8. TEACHING AND EVALUATION

I said at the beginning, responding as individuals to the clash and clamor, in our lives, of such concerns as accountability and sensitivity training and behavioral objectives requires that we clarify for ourselves just what we believe the act of teaching to be. It starts in our own classrooms, when we form deep-down reactions that say, "This I believe; this I stand for."

And having done that for ourselves, we are going to raise our voices every chance we get. "Sometimes," as Lillian Hellman once put it in an informal talk, "you stand up and raise your voice. And you may not hear another sound in the room but there are others who have been inarticulate and who will praise you for doing for them what they could not do for themselves."

In our classrooms, in the teachers' room, in curriculum meetings, we raise our voices to be heard about what we believe teaching is. We seek out others in our communities with comparable views. We form, if you will, a small political action group.

We quit being silent when questions of tenure come up and only schoolkeepers get hired. We support that maverick teacher who looks so funny to the schoolkeepers and instructors. We don't leave the decision-making to someone else; we get our word in too.

One of the great school superintendents in America said once, "Give me any day a teacher who experiments and finds out it's a blind alley, who experiments and comes back again and again, to one who sits on haunches and bewails, 'It probably wouldn't work anyway'."

Refusing to back off, we seek broader associations as in this organization of ACEI—and its professionals of courage, like Agnes Snyder and Alice Keliher and Roma Gans and L. Thomas Hopkins and Larry Frank and Laura Zirbes. Courage? You bet it takes courage. "We might get hurt a little?" You bet we'll get hurt a little. But we'll get hurt a lot more if we acquiesce, because we'll go home nights hating ourselves for not being true to ourselves.

Real teachers do not teach toward objectives; they teach toward outcomes. It doesn't all have to be done today. "You've got tomorrow and tomorrow and tomorrow," as Sylvia Ashton-Warner says. To what end? As Alfred North Whitehead said so beautifully, to the end that children leave us accepting themselves, knowing they're dignified persons, full of "activity of thought, receptivity to beauty, the humane feelings."

To the end that children know, as John Masefield says, that "the days that make us happy make us wise."

Who know, as e. e. cummings told us, "I'd rather learn from one bird how to sing than teach 10,000 stars how not to dance."

Or, as Edith Wharton said, we're going to help develop in our classrooms persons who are "incorrigible life-lovers. Life-wonderers. And adventurers."

We can grow together professionally only if we proudly say, "I'm not a schoolkeeper. I'm a real teacher."

See also:
Jacobs, Leland B. "The Teacher Asked of the Child." In *Readings from CHILDHOOD EDUCATION: Articles of Lasting Value*, p. 178. Washington, DC: ACEI, 1966.
Murrow, Casey. "Fostering Dignity in Teachers and Children." CE 52, 3 (Jan. 1976): 129-33.

Teacher's First Words

MARY K. WEIR and PATRICIA J. EGGELSTON

Dr. Weir teaches at the University of Illinois, Division of Child Development and Family Relations, 1105 West Nevada, Urbana, Illinois 61801; and Dr. Eggelston teaches at the University of Indiana, Early Childhood Education, Bloomington, Indiana 47401. Both train preschool teachers and both have worked in a variety of preschool settings.

During the early years children certainly learn language best by talking frequently with their peers and with adults about things that are meaningful in their lives. No textbook drill or exercise can supplant the routine, day-by-day flow of conversation as the most useful source of language development.

However, if children are to learn how to use language in verbal communication, caregivers must also learn how to talk to children. It's not so easy as it seems. How many times has a young trainee or inexperienced staff member reached out to a child only to be greeted by an incomprehensible silence and a blank stare?

Teacher: Your name is Billy. I'm Ms. Howard. How are you today?

Billy: (No response)

Teacher: Oh, that's such a nice shirt you're wearing. Did your mommy just buy it for you?

Billy: (No response)

Teacher: Come with me. Let's go over and play with some toys. Do you like to play with blocks?

Billy: (No response)

Teacher: Let's play catch.

Billy: (No response)

Teacher: (to her co-worker in hushed tones) Is this child deaf?

Children like Billy may be unusual cases, but establishing an easy flow of daily communication does take time, perseverance and good old teacher know-how. The results of chatting with your preschoolers may seem mundane—Cathy has a new dog, Bobby doesn't like his brother, and George wants to know why they can't do more things "like on Sesame Street"—but the cumulative effect on the children is language learning by leaps and bounds.

Encouraging children to talk is knowing, in part, that every activity during the day can be used for verbal interaction. Here are some conversational suggestions, modeled on a typical day in the life of the preschool, that will motivate children to communicate and also build a better relationship between pupil and teacher. The suggestions may be used as a way of monitoring your efforts in moving children towards verbal self-expression. Implicit in all suggestions is the assumption that caregivers and other adults should use language patterns with which they feel comfortable. Familiar language patterns reflect each teacher's personality as well as ethnic culture. Equally important is that the teaching staff respect the child's own particular language as the one that is most natural for learning.

Entering

Provide each child with a personal greeting.

Teacher: Hello, David. What a nice brown hat for this cold morning.

Comments about what children are wearing or how they look not only help them feel comfortable, but also help them notice differences, similarities, colors, or other characteristics related to their appearance. This approach also provides children with a knowledge base as well as a feeling for language.

Take time to listen and respond to the child bursting with a story to tell.

Greg: Teacher, tomorrow gramma brought the baskets and they had pink and red and blue and she gave one to me and one to Jimmie and one to Mary. They had an egg and I ate one jelly bean.

Teacher: So Gramma brought you baskets yesterday. My goodness, what was pink, red, and blue?

Greg: Jelly beans!

Teacher: For heaven's sakes! Why did she bring you those?

Greg: Because it was Easter, silly.

By taking time to listen and respond, the teacher indicates that the caregiver is interested in the child's life at home. Such informal interactions also give teachers opportunities for identifying and clarifying children's misconceptions.

Make a point of giving a special greeting to the shy child.

Teacher: Hello, Sylvia! I saw your brother last night. He said you had some new puppies at your house. (Pause long enough for response to occur.) How many do you have? (Pause again—no response.)

Teacher: Could I come to see them? Asking personal questions will help

8. TEACHING AND EVALUATION

these children make the transition between home and school. They also provide ways of obtaining something more than just a yes-or-no response, an important point to remember when conversing with children. Of course, a yes or no is better than silence.

Taking Off Wraps

Verbalize the child's actions.

Teacher: Tressie, it's really hard pulling the pants over your shoe.

One of the primary ways that young children learn new concepts and a larger vocabulary is by having the teacher verbalize their actions.

"If, on occasion, they quarrel, adults do not need to jump in and provide solutions for every instance."

This period is also a good time to start talking about what the children can do during the morning, helping to recall what they did yesterday and pointing to activities that are on tap for today. It may also be a time that a child engages staff members in extended conversation.

Breakfast

Introduce new vocabulary whenever possible.

Teacher: (showing cereal box) Guess what kind of cereal we're having this morning.
Billy: Corn flakes.
Teacher: That's right. Corn flakes. (Underlines each word with her finger as she says it.)

Variety in breakfast foods will provide many chances to explore new vocabulary words and occasionally to recognize and read words from the familiar box.

Continue conversations begun at entering and at breakfast time.

Teacher: Greg told me this morning that his grandmother brought him an Easter basket. What else was in the basket, Greg?
Greg: Well, there was green stuff you can't eat.
Teacher: Hm, I wonder what that was? What do you think it was, Lisa?

The sharing of these earlier conversations helps develop recall, brings home experiences to schools and provides a basis for children to know about one another beyond the hours of the preschool day.

Help children begin to plan for the day while building on prior experiences and introducing new ones.

Teacher: Jim's boat still needs a sail, and the material for that is on the shelf. Martha, what do you want to do with the pebbles you asked me to save yesterday?
Martha: I want to glue them.
Teacher: That sounds like a good idea. There's some cardboard next to the scissors. You might also look into the collage box if you need more.

In addition to helping individual children play, the teacher indicates to the children the activities that are available, new, and not normally a part of the daily schedule.

Free Play

During this time children are usually free to choose from a variety of activities. An uninterrupted period gives children the opportunity to talk to one another without adults interfering. In the doll corner or around the blocks, children talk spontaneously and naturally about their activities. If, on occasion, they quarrel, adults do not need to jump in and provide solutions for every instance.

Permit children to solve their own problems through language.

(Tim grabs Jerry's hat from his head. Jerry starts to cry. Teacher watches. Tim goes to dress up corner and gets another hat. Returns to Jerry and says, "Here's one for you. It's for the train.")

By allowing children to solve their own difficulties in relating to one another, language use begins to be an aid in understanding feelings and relationships among people.

Use language to help children develop concepts.

Carol: Look teacher, I've mixed these all up.
Teacher: Good, what colors did you use?
Carol: Red and this one.
Teacher: That's blue. I really like this new color. Do you know its name?
Carol: Yes, that's purple. My momma's new dress is purple.

Through language children begin to understand concepts that are embedded in the variety of materials with which they work. The concept of position in space is illustrated when children build high and low with blocks; textural differences are found in the doll corner when some of the dolls are hard, some are soft. Speaking to children about these concepts is a way you help children learn.

Find time to talk personally with each child during the day about important events or experiences in their lives.

Johnny: (work bucket in hand, playing with pipes and pipe fittings in the sand pile) The pipe goes under the ground, I saw it on the way to school.
Teacher: Yes, some pipes are under the ground. What do you think they put in the pipes?
Johnny: I don't know.
Teacher: What were they putting in them this morning?
Johnny: Lots of water.
Teacher: Yes, that's one thing that goes in pipes.

Billy and Teacher are reading from a children's book about a boy who has become temporarily separated from his mother.

Teacher: Have you ever been lost from mommy in the store?
Billy: I cried.
Teacher: That is a scary feeling. Did someone help?
Billy: No, I found her all by myself.
Teacher: I bet that made you happy. No more scary feelings that day.

There are many opportunities to relate individually with one or two children. You may talk informally, read a story, play a game, or have a tea party with them. The personal nature of this contact gives comfort and security to the children.

By listening carefully to children as they work with materials and one another, you can determine what their language skills are. A child who does not talk freely with an adult may talk freely with other children. As one becomes aware of the individual language patterns of children, then the adult is in a better position to elaborate and expand their language when talking with them.

Find opportunities (by careful listening) to elaborate and expand children's language.

Jean: (a toddler) comes with book in hand to teacher and says, "Book."
Teacher: Do you want me to read a story?
Jean: (Nods head yes.)

Expanding a child's language may mean taking one word that the child is using to express a whole sentence and turning it into a sentence.

Lisa: (serves cake during a tea party in the doll corner) This cake.
Teacher: What kind of cake do you have today?
Lisa: Chocolate.
Teacher: This is chocolate cake.

Both expansion and elaboration are techniques that adults may use to help children with their developing language skills.

Snack and Juice

This period can be formal or informal. In many centers everyone sits down at the same time for juice. In other centers juice is offered during a specified time period as one of a variety of activities that occur during the free-play time. In either of these settings, conversation about the food served will aid in concept development. Important concepts to include are taste, texture, color, names of food. Whether a formal or informal style of service is provided, an adult should always sit down with a small group of children. Sitting at eye level makes it easier to talk with children.

Bathrooming and Washing

Explain your requests or demands to children so that they will understand and avoid repeating over and over what children already know.

Teacher: It's nearly time for lunch. Kevin, you and Joe please go wash your hands.
Teacher: Kevin, go wash your hands. Don't use too much soap, remember to turn off the water and use only one paper towel. When you're finished come back and sit down.

In the first example, a good reason is provided along with one simple command. In the second example, too many instructions are given to children who know the procedures and rules. In some situations it is necessary only to identify what is to happen next. The children will know what to do.

Avoid expressing shock or punishing children for asking questions about physical functions.

Whenever possible adults should use words for toileting that the children use in their homes. It is important that adults use words that describe the body functions as accurately as possible without becoming overly technical, and without being cute.

During bathroom time children express curiosity about their bodies and frequently use exploratory and toilet talk to describe themselves and their body functions. Adults have learned the proper times and places for using particular kinds of language. Most children have not yet learned this.

John: (giggling in the bathroom corner, pointing to Danny who is urinating) "Look at his thing, look at his thing."

Teacher: "Yes, that's Danny's penis."

Expressing shock or meting out punishment to children who are still learning may result in the opposite from what is desired. The undesirable language and exploration may escalate as a means of testing out the adult. Positive, open and honest answers to questions and expressions from children will help them to understand their body functions and to cope with body differences.

62. Teacher's First Words

> "Positive, open and honest answers to questions will help them to understand their body functions and to cope with body differences."

Again, bathrooming and washing up provide time for developing cognitive language skills.

Henry: (lathering up the bathroom mirror with soap, obviously enjoying the finger-painting experience) This feels good.
Teacher: What are your doing on the mirror?
Harry: Gooey.
Teacher: Yes, it also feels slippery and smooth. When its clean, wipe the soap off with paper towels.

The touch and feel of materials used in washing are ideas that children learn about when adults answer their questions and talk to them about it.

Outdoor Play

Outdoors is a natural place for rhythmical language to occur. Jumping on a jumping board or swinging on a swing is often punctuated by the child's spontaneous sing-song poems. Adults may enhance this with their own chants.

Take advantage of the natural rhythms in the out of doors with children.

Pat: (on the swings chanting)
   I'm swing ing
   I'm swing ing
Teacher: I see you. I see you. I see you.
Child: I'm swing ing
   I'm swing ing.
Teacher: You're...up...high
   You're...down...low.

Urban sounds are sometimes syncopated and rhythmical, such as the fire siren, people walking on sidewalks, jack hammers or nailing in nails. These are rhythms that children imitate verbally and that adults can point out to children.

The natural environment provides

8. TEACHING AND EVALUATION

a variety of opportunities for children to develop exploratory and observational language skills. Describing a leaf dotted with raindrops or telling a teacher about the antics of an ant are rich and rewarding experiences for the child.

Body and spatial awareness are areas that children are also sensitive to while out of doors. Adults, with their language, can help children develop these concepts.

Barbara: (on the top rung of the jungle gym) Look at me, teacher, look at me.

Teacher: You're way up high. You're higher up than I am.

Children develop an awareness of using their bodies when they are seen slowing down as they descend a slide by pressing their legs against it, or when they fit themselves into a tiny space such as a cardboard box. Adults help the child's awareness by verbalizing to them about these events.

Lunch

As during breakfast and juice or snack time, lunch is a period when adults should sit with small groups of children, talking about food and events of the morning.

Talk to children more than adults at mealtimes.

Teacher: (to other teacher at table) I bought the cutest dress for the party Saturday night. (Turns to Jessie.) Jessie, use your fork, not fingers, to eat your food. (Back to other teacher.) Will you help me pin up the hem?" (Back to Jessie.) I told you to eat with your fork.

Teacher: (to other teacher at table): Remind me to tell you later about my new dress. (To Jessie) Try eating this way with your spoon. (As she demonstrates.) That is easier than the fork, isn't it? (Turns to Cynthia.) Please pass me the bread. (Cynthia complies.) Thank you.

When adults model the appropriate manner words that are used during mealtimes, children pick these up and incorporate them into their speech patterns. When adults model inappropriate behavior, less useful patterns are learned.

Once again, children talk to one another when seated around the table. This can also be a planning time for events of the afternoon. Round or hexagonal tables seem to facilitate these kinds of language interactions among children. In order for this kind of conversation to occur, lunch needs to be relaxed and unhurried for everyone.

Naptime

Several adults in the nap room help to settle children easier and will provide times for quiet conversation.

Billy: (loudly singing a refrain from music that occurred just before naptime) I've been working on the railroad.

Teacher: (shouting from the other side of the room) Billy, you lay down and be quiet. I don't want to hear a word from you.

Billy: (loudly singing a refrain from music that occurred just before naptime) I've been working on the railroad.

Teacher: (moves close to Billy, whispering) Some children are trying to sleep. You need to sing that song very quietly, just to yourself. (She stays near Billy until his song is hushed and soft.)

Many children practice their developing language skills just before they fall asleep; therefore, quiet murmurings in the sleep room are positive signs. Having a familiar toy helps children to verbalize quietly to themselves rather than to their neighbor. When adults speak in hushed tones, children follow that pattern. Quiet background music also induces the relaxation and quiet that comes before falling asleep.

Going Home

Both adults and children are tired toward the end of the day. Special efforts directed toward those children who are there the longest will help them to wait more patiently for parents to arrive. Activities such as sitting in rocking chairs, reading quietly to one or two, working a puzzle will help end the day pleasantly for everyone. When parents arrive a special goodbye to each child by name provides a personal touch to end the day.

Share with parents something the child has done during the day.

Teacher: (to parent) Terry had such a good time making jello today. I bet he can tell you which flavor he likes best. He can probably help you make it at home.

Such sharing gives the parent something to talk about with the child and helps extend the school into the home.

So ends a language-rich day for adults and children in a preschool program.

Teachers, Be(a)ware of Sex-Stereotyping

Barbara Simmons

Here are concrete ways to implement a nonsexist curriculum. Barbara Simmons is Assistant Professor and Chairperson, Early Childhood Subcommittee, College of Education, Texas Tech University, Lubbock, Texas.

Since 1776 a revolution has occurred in American attitudes toward children and their education. Sexism, so very evident in the double standards practiced by colonists, is gradually beginning to disappear from school programs designed for older children. But a need clearly persists to restructure the early experiences of young children so as to eliminate sex-role stereotyping.

Classroom procedures that perpetuate sexism should be analyzed by teachers and paraprofessionals. Often we are unaware of the subtle, unconscious influences we have on children's self-concepts and interpersonal relationships as they are now and may become in the future. In many cases four-year-olds bring sexist behavior to school with them, causing preschool teachers to be confronted with the problem of changing these views in order to give children the freedom to dream that they can be what they want to be without restricting their aspirations to traditional sex roles.

The following are a baker's dozen of suggestions for ways to move toward a nonsexist curriculum.

Hammering and Housekeeping

Provide learning centers that give children the opportunity to select activities that interest them. Strive to eliminate any stigma that may be felt by girls as they build, or boys as they sweep or cook. When demonstrating methods for sawing wood, hammering nails, setting the table and dusting furniture, encourage both boys and girls to participate.

Divide the responsibility of maintaining a clean classroom among all the children. Distribute your requests for assistance equally and randomly to members of both sexes (say, "I need two big, strong children to help me carry this plank"—not, "two big, strong boys").

Facing the Music

Use music and dramatic play as opportunities for children to see themselves in new roles. Avoid subtle distinctions whereby girls are asked to play the quiet, small instruments such as sticks, sand blocks and triangles, while boys play loud "aggressive" instruments such as drums and cymbals. When you encourage the children to respond rhythmically to music, allow everyone to be elephants, monsters and motorcycles. Girls don't always have to be butterflies, birds, fairies and angels. Similarly, in dramatic play, Big Billy Goat Gruff need not always be delegated to a boy. Girls can easily be trolls, giants, ogres and even the Big Bad Wolf. Use puppets to give shy children security while they verbally experiment with new roles.

A combination dramatic play or make-believe corner can be equipped with hollow blocks, boards, boxes and a set of props so that children can create any setting—house, store, hospital, laundromat, subway, farm, restaurant, etc. Include a stethoscope, mail bag, briefcase, clothes and hats of various types.*

What Parents Do

When talking with children about homes and families, ask, "What do your parents do?" or very possibly, "What does your parent do?" instead of the stock, "What does you Daddy do?" As more women in our society pursue careers outside the home, hopefully men will share a larger portion of the responsibility for rearing children. Conceivably, a revised role of father may need as much emphasis as the traditional role of mother has received for years. Dolls or sewing cards in the make-believe corner should no longer be reserved for girls.

For boys who have never seen their fathers in the kitchen, it might be profitable for the female teacher to invite a male teacher or principal to present a cooking

---

* Thanks for this suggestion, and others that appear in this article, go to Jeanne Walton, Regional Training Specialist, Day Care/Child Development, Head Start Regional Resource and Training Center, University of Maryland, College Park, Maryland, and to Marlene Ross, Early Childhood Consultant, Kensington, Maryland.

8. TEACHING AND EVALUATION

activity. When fathers and mothers are themselves tapped directly as classroom resources, the information they share can be helpful; but the real reward is observing the child's delight when a parent serves as teacher.

In view of the decreasing number of children who are part of a traditional nuclear family complete with mother, father and several siblings, conduct discussions that encompass and show acceptance of a variety of lifestyles.

Curious Careers

Ask professionals who are engaged in occupations unusual for their sex to visit your school. Children would benefit from meeting and questioning a male nurse, a female doctor, a male telephone operator, a female engineer, a policewoman. Use role-playing to enhance and enrich children's understanding of information gained from these interviews.

Fair Tales

Screen carefully stories you select for telling or reading to children. Consult the "Growing Free" resource-bibliography in this issue for lists of desirable books that depict both sexes in a positive light. Picture books and poetry written for young children have been critically examined by researchers and consistently found to show boys in the more exciting and challenging roles; girls, on the other hand, are often shown to be passively demonstrating the supposedly feminine characteristics of docility, obedience and domestic achievement.(1) When you encounter conspicuously sexist stories in your classroom, explain your reactions to children. Even the youngest child can comprehend fairness and equal opportunity.

Important precaution: recognize that not every book on a list labeled "nonsexist" is necessarily qualitative literature. Move beyond labels; be alert to dangers of self-defeating censorship. The goal is to provide children a fair-minded multidimensional view of life, avoiding polarization and prejudice.

In the past, the few token women selected as subjects for biographies were often seen engaged in sex-typed occupations or married to politicians. Recently publishers have begun to provide better models, as in stories of heroines of the suffrage movement and of other women leaders of often overlooked times in history.

TV Tantrums

Analyze television programs for sex-stereotyping. The impact of *Sesame Street* is hard to measure, but the fact that so many of the lead characters are male certainly cannot positively influence the self-esteem of young females. Enough sexism is perpetrated by the television shows and commercials children view at home.

Toys and Taboos

Select play materials that extend children's options. Some parents seldom buy scientific, mathematic or manipulative toys for girls, selecting instead toys that require solitary, passive play and are overwhelmingly oriented toward domestic development.(2) Girls should not have progress in math and science retarded because they have been deprived of resources that might assist them in developing manipulative and problem-solving skills. (Mothers and female teachers should beware of such statements as, "I was always weak in math" or, "Boys are better in arithmetic.") Verbal skills do not belong solely to girls, nor are scientific abilities inherited only by boys.

Re-drawing the Lines

When organizing the classroom, avoid separating children into a "boys' line" and a "girls' line"—except perhaps for going to the restrooms. If lines are necessary, have children line up according to the color of their shoes, height or initials. ("Children with buckle shoes get your coats, then children with tie shoes"—*not* "Ladies first!")

Playing the Game

Plan a balanced physical education program that is suitable for all children. Avoid segregating outdoor play by sex. Activities utilizing the balance beam increase coordination; both coordination and strength can result from running, skipping, jumping and playing ball. Help both sexes experience the pride that accompanies physical prowess; provide equal opportunities and expectations.(3)

The very attire worn to school may determine the degree of participation in action sports. Little girls who wear frilly dresses are much less likely to run, jump and tumble—as are boys who wear new clothes their parents warn them not to dirty. Spend time complimenting children's achievements rather than emphasizing clothes and appearance. Certainly in this day of permanent press and magic cleaning potions we have no reason for allowing clothes to inhibit children's actions.

When you discuss famous athletes, remind children of the expertise of Gail Pierson and Billie Jean King as well as the more commonly touted masculine sports celebrities.

Toeing the Mark

Be alert to sex-typing when teacher-pupil interactions are observed.(4) Collaborate with colleagues by observing, analyzing and discussing each other's interactions with children to be sure that verbal transactions, physical reinforcements and discipline are fairly distributed, regardless of sex. Discipline of boys, when compared to that of girls, tends to be harsher; avoid admonishments like "Be tough" or "Big boys don't cry." The unfairness of such tactics is multiplied when we reward the quiet, conforming behavior of many girls by ignoring them.

63. Teachers, Be(a)ware of Sex-Stereotyping

Male Call

If there is a male teacher in your school or center, remember he should be helping to break down stereotypes, not to perpetuate them. Is he the "fix-it-man"? Is he in charge of the workbench? Is it his job to take the active boys outside to work off steam? Is he relieved of messy cleanup tasks and bathroom supervision? Is he preparing to become principal or director because "men are so much better at managing"?

"Can We Do More?"

In sum, we teachers and parents need to sharpen our sensitivity to sex-role stereotyping because we know that the experiences of young children can provide men and women of the future either a foundation for unfair discriminations or a basis for mutual respect. If most of the suggestions here seem "old hat" to you, well and good. Our aim has not been to give marching orders of "Do this, do that" but to acknowledge credit for doing helpful things and to suggest with a gentle nudge, "Have we noticed . . . can we do more?"

References
(1) John Stewig & Margaret Higgs, "Girls Grow Up To Be Mommies. A Study of Sexism in Children's Literature," *Library Journal* 98 (1973): 236-41.
(2) "A Report on Children's Toys," *Ms.* (Dec. 1972):57.
(3) Celeste Ulrich, "She Can Play As Good As Any Boy," *Phi Delta Kappan* 55(1973):113-17.
(4) Pauline Sears & David Feldman, "Teacher Interaction with Boys and Girls," *The National Elementary Principal* (Nov. 1966): 30-37.

Evaluating Settings for Learning

Thelma Harms

Environmental awareness is as significant to a teacher as to an artist. By recognizing that environment is an interplay between materials, people and time schedule, the teacher can create a more productive setting for learning.

It is very helpful during an evaluation to look at the environment from a child's point of view. To a child, everything that is present in a setting is a stimulus. He responds to what is really there, not only to what we as adults are aware is there. The way people treat him is as real a part of his environment as the materials on the shelves or the space provided for block building. The teacher's tone of voice, the way she walks and her facial expression contribute to the overall atmosphere. Similarly, the child's interaction with other children is an important component of the school setting. Everything present in the environment, even the spacial arrangement, communicates to the child how to live in that setting. Materials that are in good condition and placed far apart on open shelves tell a child that the materials are valued, that they are meant to be considered, and that a child may take them off the shelf by himself. When they are taken off the shelf, they leave a big, empty space so it is easy to put them back where they belong. What kind of a message does a child get from open shelves crowded with an odd assortment of materials, few with all the pieces put together? What kind of a message does he get from a closed cupboard?

Physical environment is a powerful means of communication. To sensitize yourself to physical environment, set yourself the task, every time you walk into a new setting, of reading the messages contained in the room arrangement. The room with a speaker's stand in front of rows of chairs tells us something about the predicted relationship of teacher to student, and student to student in the class. Chairs in a circle imply another kind of learning interaction.

Children respond to the messages given to them by the physical environment, the activities and the time schedule, so we must become increasingly aware of the total environment we are creating for them. Often problems occur because contradictory messages are being simultaneously sent out by the different components making up the environment. The teacher may be trying to prevent running and sliding while the large, slick expanse of floor in the center of the room is inviting the children to run and slide. Improvement in the children's use of materials in that situation might require a reorganization of the physical environment rather than improvement in interpersonal skills or changes in activities or time schedule. In another school, however, the physical environment may be well defined, the interpersonal atmosphere warm and accepting, but the children may need the challenge of more complex activities, or they may need longer periods of unbroken time to become involved in the activities offered. Each setting for learning needs to be looked at individually because it is a unique combination of children.

Suggestions for Using the Check List

The following list of questions is organized into four categories. Each category contributes in a major way to the environment as experienced by the child. The questions are meant to help you identify both strengths and problems in your own setting. Many schools have found it helpful to give each staff member a checklist to think about for several days before the evaluation meeting. Then, when the entire staff meets, each person is prepared to share his observations and suggestions.

Evaluation Checklist

The Physical Environment

1. Can quiet and noisy activities go on without disturbing one another? Is there an appropriate place for each?
2. Is a variety of materials available on open shelves for the children to use when they are interested? Are materials on shelves well spaced for clarity?
3. Are materials stored in individual units so that children can use them alone without being forced to share with a group?
4. Are activity centers defined so that children know where to use the materials?
5. Are tables or rug areas provided for convenient use of materials in each activity center?
6. Is self-help encouraged by having materials in good condition and always stored in the same place?
7. Are cushioning materials used to cut down extraneous noise—rug under blocks, pads under knock-out bench?
8. Are setup and cleanup simple? Are these expected parts of the child's activity?
9. Have learning opportunities been carefully planned in the outdoor area? Painting, crafts, block building,

64. Evaluating Settings for Learning

carpentry, gardening, pets, sand and water all lend themselves to learning experiences outdoors.
10. Is the children's work displayed attractively at the child's eye level?
11. Do the children feel in control of and responsible for the physical environment?

The Interpersonal Environment
1. Is there a feeling of mutual respect between adults and children, children and children?
2. Is the physical environment enough under control so that the major part of the adults' time is spent in observing or participating with children?
3. Can children engage in activities without being disturbed or distracted by others?
4. Do adults observe children's activity and intervene only when it is beneficial to the child?
5. Do adults have "growth goals" for each child based on the needs they have observed in each child? Is individualized curriculum used to reach these goals?
6. Do children feel safe with one another?
7. Is competition avoided by arranging materials in individual units, limiting the number of children participating in an activity at one time, insuring the fairness of turns by starting a waiting list on which the child can see his name keeping his place in line?
8. Do the adults show children how to help themselves? Are children encouraged to learn from one another?
9. Are there opportunities for children to play alone, participate in a small group, and participate in a large group?
10. When limits are placed, do adults use reasoning and consistently follow through? Are limits enforced?
11. Are the adults models of constructive behavior and healthy attitudes?
12. Is there an overall warm interpersonal environment?

Activities to Stimulate Development
1. Are there many opportunities for dramatic play: large housekeeping corner, small dollhouse, dress-up clothes for boys as well as girls?
2. Is ther a variety of basic visual art media: painting, drawing, clay, saltflour dough, wood-glue sculpture, fingerpaint, collage?
3. Is music a vital part of the program: records, group singing, instruments, dancing?
4. Is language stimulation varied: reading books, games with feel boxes, flannel boards, stories, questions and answers, conversation, lotto games, classification games? Are limits enforced through verbal control and reasoning?
5. Are there small manipulative toys to build eye-hand coordination and finger dexterity?
6. Are there some opportunities to follow patterns or achieve a predetermined goal: puzzles, design blocks, dominos, matching games?
7. Do children do things like cooking, planting seeds, caring for animals?
8. Are field trips planned to give experience with the world around us? Is there adequate preparation and follow-up after trips?
9. Are there repeated opportunities for children to use similar materials? Are materials available in a graded sequence so that children develop skills gradually?
10. Are children involved in suggesting and planning activities? How is free choice built into the program?
11. Are new activities developed by teachers as they are suggested by the interests of individual children?
12. Is the range of activities varied enough to present a truly divergent curriculum? Are there opportunities for learning through exploration, guided discovery, problem solving, repetition, intuition, imitation, etc.? Is there provision for children to learn through their senses as well as verbally?

Schedule
1. Is the time sequence of the school day clear to both teachers and children?
2. Has the schedule been designed to suit the physical plant and particular group of children in the school?
3. Are long periods of time scheduled to permit free choice of activities and companions?
4. Are other groupings provided for in the schedule, e.g., small group activities, one to one adult-child contacts, larger group meetings, etc.?
5. Is the schedule periodically reevaluated and modified? Are changes in schedule and the reasons for these changes made clear to both staff and children?

Extending Your Experience

Visiting other schools and using the checklist as an observation guide is a good way to extend your experience. There are also some helpful films and books you might want to use as resource materials. A selected list of films, books and pamphlets to extend your experience with environment follows:

Films
"My Art is Me." Univ. of California Film Media Center, Berkeley, Calif.
"Organizing for Free Play." Project Head Start, Office of Economic Opportunity, Washington, D.C.

Books
Almy, Millie C. *Ways of Studying Children.* New York: Teachers College Press, Columbia University, 1959.
Ashton-Warner, Sylvia. *Teacher.* New York: Simon & Schuster, 1963.
Pitcher, E. G., Lasher, N. G., et al. *Helping Young Children Learn.* Columbus, Ohio: Charles E. Merrill Books, 1966.
Read, Katherine. *The Nursery School: A Human Relations Laboratory.* Philadelphia: W. B. Saunders Co., 1960.

Pamphlets
"Space, Arrangement, Beauty in School." #101, Association for Childhood Education International, 3615 Wisconsin Ave., N.W., Washington, D.C. 20066.
"Let's Play Outdoors." #101, National Association for the Education of Young Children, 1834 Connecticut Ave., N.W., Washington, D.C. 20009.
"Nursery School Settings—Invitation to What?" #102, NAEYC.
"Space for Play: The Youngest Children." #111, NAEYC.

The Persistence of Preschool Effects: A National Collaborative Study

Shirley G. Moore, *Research Editor*

Shirley G. Moore, Ph.D., Professor, Institute of Child Development, University of Minnesota, Minneapolis.

In 1975 a group of investigators who had previously conducted studies on the effects of early school experiences discussed the possibilities of a long-term followup assessment of the children who had participated in their studies during the 1960s and early 1970s. The investigators were motivated by their own scientific curiosity as well as by the practical implications of knowing more about the long-term effects of educational intervention of the kind offered in current Head Start and Home Start programs. The group became known as the Consortium on Developmental Continuity. Dr. Irving Lazar, of Cornell University, became the project director of the followup effort that was sponsored by the Education Commission of the States and the Office of Human Development Services of HEW. In September of 1977 the Consortium published a report entitled "The Persistence of Preschool Effects: A Long-Term Followup of Fourteen Infant and Preschool Experiments." This column is a discussion of the major Consortium findings to date.

Participating Projects

The original intervention studies upon which the followup is based were completed by 1969, with some short-term followup extending into the 1970s. The projects were of three types: (1) home-based programs in which the parent, usually the mother, was the primary educator; (2) center-based programs with a more or less structured educational curriculum; and (3) programs with a combination of center-based education with home visits involving the parent and the child. There is no attempt in the Consortium report to assess the relative advantages of these different kinds of educational intervention, although future reports based on the Consortium data may address this issue; the purpose of this first report is to examine the long-term effects of early educational intervention as a concept—in general. Since the projects represent a variety of educational strategies and types of intervention, the Consortium data provide an overview of long-term preschool effects on a limited number of outcome measures. Data from the projects listed on page 66 were included in the followup analyses.

Data Collection

Although many different instruments had been used to assess the effects of the interventions in the original projects, the followup instruments were agreed upon by the Consortium investigators and were administered by all projects wherever possible barring local restrictions and monetary limitations. Followup measures on which analyses have been done so far include an age-appropriate *Wechsler Intelligence Scale*, a *School Record Form* with information about special education placement and retention in grade, a *Youth Interview*, in which the child was asked about his or her own educational performance and aspirations, and a *Parental Interview,* in which parents

65. The Persistence of Preschool Effects

Participating Projects and Directors

The Philadelphia Project: Dr. Kuno Beller; a center-based program for children beginning at age four offered through the public school.

Institute for Developmental Studies: Drs. Martin and Cynthia Deutsch; a center-based program for low-income children in New York City beginning during the preschool years and extending into the elementary school.

The Parent Education Program: Dr. Ira Gordon; a home-based, parent-focus for children from three months to three years of age with backyard play and activity groups added to the program when the children reached age two.

Early Training Project: Dr. Susan Gray; a center-based summer program with a home visitor winter program.

Family-Oriented Home Visitor Program: Dr. Susan Gray; a home-based program involving the mother, toddler, and other members of the family whenever possible.

Curriculum Comparison Study: Dr. Merle Karnes; preschool children attended one of five program models: Bereiter-Engelmann, traditional, Community-Integrated, Montessori, or Karnes's concept development program.

Mother-Child Home Program: Dr. Phyllis Levenstein; weekly visits are made by "Toy Demonstrators" to the homes of infants to work with their mothers on improving verbal interaction between mother and child.

Experimental Variation of Head Start Curricula: Dr. Louise Miller; preschool children attended one of four programs: Montessori, Bereiter-Engelmann, DARCEE, or a traditional nursery school.

Harlem Training Project: Dr. Francis Palmer; a one-to-one center-based program stressing either concept training or discovery activities for toddlers meeting twice weekly.

Perry Preschool Project: Dr. David Weikart; a cognitively-oriented preschool program during the two years before children enter kindergarten.

Curriculum Demonstration Project: Dr. David Weikart; preschool children attended one of three center-based programs: Bereiter-Engelmann, a cognitive program, or a unit-based traditional program, and were also visited at home by a teacher once a week.

Carnegie Infant Program: Dr. David Weikart; a home-based program for infants and their mothers to facilitate the role of mothers as teachers.

Micro-Social Learning System: Dr. Myron Woolman; a preschool program of modular learning units and a "life-simulator" play space in which children applied the skills they learned.

Head Start and Follow-Through New Haven Study: Dr. Edward Zigler; five-year-old children attended a local Head Start program and were followed through the eighth grade.

---

were asked their opinions of the preschool programs in which their children participated.

In addition to the above measures, program and control children from the various projects were compared on measures collected during the period of the original projects. Although individual investigators had assessed their own program-control differences previously, the Consortium group reanalyzed the original data, using identical procedures for evaluating each project, and finally, statistically pooling the results of the individual projects for an overall assessment of "preschool effects." The most commonly shared data included pre- and posttest Stanford Binets or Peabody Picture Vocabulary Tests on which program and control children were compared for the amount of intellectual growth they showed during the project period. (In some instances, the original projects compared different educational curricula with each other; however, this data will be treated in detail in future Consortium reports and will not be discussed here.)

A word should be said about the data from the original projects. Ideally the program and control children in studies of this kind should be carefully matched on general intellectual functioning at recruitment time so that differences found after participation in the program cannot be attributed to differences that were there in the first place. Unfortunately exact matching of program and control children is difficult to achieve in field studies since the families who enroll their children in such programs are likely to be more advantaged than those who do not. In any case, there appears to

8. TEACHING AND EVALUATION

be a small but consistent bias favoring the program children in most of the projects, though not all of them. Consequently in treating the original data, the most valid analyses are those in which differences between the program and control children in pretest performance are statistically controlled so that posttest differences—if they exist at all—can be considered legitimate program effects. Such statistical adjustments do not completely eliminate biases in the original samples but they do help and are considered to be a reasonable treatment of data of this kind. Having offered these comments, short attention will be given to the IQ data from the original studies since it is redundant with previously published reports by the individual investigators.

In general, the original program children in these projects did improve in intellectual functioning more than the control children even after adjusting for pretest differences between the groups. Of the nine projects that had designs involving pretests, five showed clear program effects on posttest Binets well beyond the 5 percent level of significance (indicating that only 5 times in 100 would such differences be due to chance). Another favored the program children at the 10 percent level of significance, and for a third project, immediate posttest scores did not differ but tests after one year favored the project children. As has been the case all along with Head Start and other intervention data, the program and control differences were maintained for a year or two following the termination of the intervention, and then differences faded. Although three of these projects did continue to show significant differences lasting beyond the second year, two of the three had pretest biases favoring the program children, making the data hard to interpret even with adjustments for pretest scores.

Sample Attribution

Before discussing the results of the long-term followup data obtained by the Consortium, the problem of sample attribution must be given attention. In following up children many years after their participation in an intervention project, the sample is bound to diminish; children move away and cannot be traced, families refuse to participate, schools refuse to release pupil information—or may simply not have the desired information to release. Finding 30 percent of an original sample in studies such as these is considered par for the course. In fact, the Consortium investigators did extremely well in finding their children. Most projects found over 50 percent of both program and control children and several found 70 percent or more. Given the number of children involved in the original projects, it is safe to conclude that the children found comprise samples that are big enough to reliably represent the original groups.

The next attribution issue to be addressed is attribution bias: Is there any reason to believe that the children found and those not found differ in any important way that might distort the extent to which they represent the larger sample? And even more importantly, could attribution affect the program and control children differently? Suppose, for example, that among the program children, a disproportionate number of good performers happened to be found for followup while the opposite was true for control children. This bias would inflate "program effects" attributing to the program differences that existed in the children prior to their participation. To assess the representativeness of the children found for followup, the Consortium looked at the comparability on pretest IQ (that is, intellectual performance prior to participation in the original project) of the program children found compared with those not found and the control children found compared with those not found. While the followup program and control children were generally representative of their respective groups, the followup sample perpetuated the biases that existed originally in many of the projects. In fact, biases favoring the program children were exaggerated in three projects such that followup program children had average pretest IQ scores that were 5, 6, and 10 points higher than their respective followup controls. Consequently, in discussing the Consortium results attention will be given wherever possible to the data from individual projects in which followup program and control children happened to be well matched for initial IQ.

IQ Data and School Performance

In an attempt to confirm or refute Head

Start's history of disappearing IQ gains, the Consortium investigators included the Wechsler Intelligence Scale (WISC) among the followup instruments. Administered in 1976 to the children from six projects (with more to be administered at a later time), overall program and control children performed similarly. Only children from the Levenstein project who were still quite young (with a mean age of 9.9 years at the time of the WISC administration) performed better than the control children from that project. Program and control children from the other projects, who ranged in age from 11 to almost 17, did not differ significantly in total WISC scores or on verbal or performance subscales (the only exception being the program children of one of the projects with a biased followup sample). These WISC scores are consistent with previous followup Head Start data in that only the younger program children continue to show advantages over control children on tests of general intellectual functioning.

In discussing the IQ data, Lazar makes the point that despite fading program-control differences over the years, the persistence of differences that favor program children over a two-year period or more would appear to represent something more fundamental than "test taking" know-how. His point is well taken. Persistent differences extending into the school years—at which point all children get exposed to tests—are likely to be due to some combination of ability and motivation.

One of the unique contributions of the Consortium project is the attention given to school performance variables not considered in previous studies, namely, special education placement and grade retention. If participation in an intervention program helped children to perform better in school through skill development, achievement motivation, parental support, or any combination of these factors, one would expect these school variables to yield different results for program and control children.

One problem, of course, is that school districts use very different standards and different criteria in assigning children to special education programs and in retaining them in grade, and some of these standards and criteria could have been applied differently for program and control children. For example, if a school district had cooperated in the original project, there might be a bias against placing a "project child" in a special classroom or retaining the child in grade. There is no evidence presented in the report (although future analyses may provide some) regarding whether or not the academic performance criteria for placing children in special classes or retaining them in grade were the same for program and control children. However, the children participating in these studies were, at the time of the followup, enrolled in literally hundreds of different schools; while criteria for special education placement and grade retention almost certainly varied from setting to setting, it does not seem likely that program and control children would have been treated *systematically* differently in so many different schools. The child's own family as a source of influence for or against special placement or grade retention is possibly the most likely source of systematic bias; however, whether the parents of program children would be *more* or *less* resistant than control parents to the child's placement in a special classroom or to grade retention is an open question.

Special Education Placement

What do we know from the followup data on special education placement and grade retention? At the time of the Consortium report, five projects in which program and controls could be compared, had provided data. Of the five, four showed significant differences (two well beyond the 5 percent level of significance and two beyond the 10 percent level) indicating that a smaller percentage of program children compared with controls had been placed in special education settings. Of the four projects showing differences, three were comparing program and control followup children who were closely matched (the fourth is suspect of favoring the program children) so that information from these projects is highly suggestive of a true program effect. Whether the program effect was actual improved school performance or some other factor (such as parental protest at the prospects of special placement for the child) is impossible to say from the data presented in this report. Hopefully data of this kind will be forthcoming from the Consortium and from other intervention projects.

8. TEACHING AND EVALUATION

Grade Retention

Data on grade retention are similar to that of special placement but not as robust. Seven projects reported grade retention data. When analyzed individually, only one of the seven is significant, but data from that project must be considered suspect because of the biased followup sample favoring the program group. Of the remaining projects, four have percentages that support the hypothesis that program children are less often retained in grade, one shows no differences, and one favors the control group. When the data are pooled across projects, the combined program effects are significant at the 5 percent level of confidence, indicating that, overall, program children were less likely to be retained in grade than control children. This effect is tenuous, however, and may not hold up with more careful matching of followup groups and with the addition of data from the other Consortium projects.

The grade retention information from the Woolman project was analyzed separately and deserves comment. This project included an especially large population of Spanish surnamed children. To assess the grade retention record of the Spanish surnamed children who participated in the preschool program, these children were compared with a random sample of Spanish surnamed children in the general school population. The program children had significantly fewer instances of grade retention—32.8 percent compared with 62.9 percent for the general population of Spanish surnamed children. Grade retention differences from this project are impressive and would not appear to be due to biases in the sample favoring the program children since 90 percent of the program children were selected from among the highest risk children in the school district.

This new information on special placement and grade retention among children who have participated in preschool intervention programs is particularly relevant to the early education movement. If program children are, in fact, performing better in school than their respective controls, the programs would clearly have served an important part of their original purpose. Sparing children the humiliation of school failure is not only humanitarian but also cost–effective given the high cost of special education and grade retention.

Two other sources of Consortium data will be commented upon, the Youth Interview and the Parental Interview. To date, only a few responses from each of these sources of data have been analyzed.

Youth Interview Findings

In the Youth Interview, program and control children were asked, "How are you doing (or did you do) in your school work; that is, overall, not just in one subject?" Data from the measure were pooled across projects. For program and control children who were at least fifteen years old, program children were significantly more likely to evaluate their own school performance as better than control children, the pooled significance being beyond the 2 percent level of confidence. Although this finding is difficult to interpret without knowing the contributions of individual projects, it does suggest that the children themselves are reliable reporters of their own school performance. As Lazar suggests, it may also be an indication of a higher self-concept on the part of program children compared with control children.

When a similar analysis was done for the younger children, differences were not significant. Younger children who have been in school for a shorter time may not have a reliable sample of their own academic performance to compare with others, or they may be less willing or able to make such comparisons even with evidence about their performance.

Concerning school status, there was a slight tendency for more control children to drop out of school and, among the drops, to drop earlier than program children, but the effect was not statistically reliable and may be due to chance or to problems of comparability of program and control children found for followup. More information on this variable will have to await further data and further analyses. Also program children did not have educational aspirations that differed from the control children.

Future followup information in this area would be of interest; it would be helpful to know, for example, whether program children are more likely than control children to get post high school training of any kind including on the job training, vocational technical training, or college work. This, in turn, could have implications for their job marketability as adults.

Parent Interviews

The last data to be discussed come from the Parent Interviews in which parents were asked if they felt the intervention program had been good for their children. Specifically they were asked what they liked best about the program, and whether they liked the location (home, center, or both) of the program activities. Data of this kind are always suspect because the most disapproving parents may simply refuse to be interviewed or to answer such questions frankly. Nevertheless, positive responses so overwhelmed the "norm" for these data that it is highly unlikely that the programs were not well received by the parents of children participating. Of the parents of children in the home-based programs, 100 percent (of 87 parents) felt the program was good for their child. The comparable figure for the center-based programs was 93.4 percent (of 412 parents) and for the combination programs, 87.8 percent (of 137 parents). Parents particularly liked that their child was learning things that would help him or her later. Parent participation was an attractive feature of the programs that involved parents, with 22.9 percent of those in home-based programs and 23.7 percent in the combination programs identifying this as the most attractive feature of the program. The most striking result, however, is that parents were overwhelmingly supportive of the particular kind of program in which their child participated; virtually all of the models of intervention were popular with parents.

Summary

The positive effects of early education on the general intellectual functioning of children at posttest time and for one, two, and possibly three years following intervention, have been confirmed. Also special education placement, and possibly grade retention, is less likely to be the fate of program children compared with control children. In retrospect, the parents of the program children overwhelmingly state that the programs were good for their children, and the children themselves report that they are doing well in school compared with the reports from control children.

The picture is hopeful, but there is still much to be done with the Consortium data. All of the projects have not yet administered all of the followup instruments, and some instruments administered have not yet been fully analyzed. Additional analyses of the available data are required for a more refined assessment of program outcomes.

The Consortium study is the first truly long-term followup of children who participated in the early education programs of the 1960s. The data from it warrant continued followup beyond the public school years of children who participated in the Consortium projects, and long-term followup of children from other similar projects.

Reference

Lazar, I.; Hubbell, V. R.; Murray, H.; Rosche, M.; and Royce, J. *The Persistence of Preschool Effects: A Long-Term Followup of Fourteen Infant and Preschool Experiments.* Ithaca, N.Y.: Community Service Laboratory, New York State College of Human Ecology, Cornell University, September 1977.

The Abt Report of Follow Through: Critique and Comment

Shirley G. Moore,
Research Editor

Shirley G. Moore, Ph.D., Professor, Institute of Child Development, University of Minnesota, Minneapolis

Abt Associates Incorporated of Cambridge, Massachusetts, published a report in 1977 on the evaluation data of the national Follow Through program (*Education as Experimentation* 1977). In April of that year, Richard Anderson of Abt presented a summary of the evaluation data at the annual meeting of the American Educational Research Association (Anderson 1977). The report was discouraging to those interested in educational intervention in the primary grades and to model sponsors who felt that the data upon which the evaluation was based were biased and somewhat arbitrarily selected from all that was available. With support from the Ford Foundation, a critique of the Abt report was prepared by experts in the field of educational evaluation under the direction of Ernest House of the Center for Instructional Research and Curriculum Evaluation at the University of Illinois (House, Glass, McLean, and Walker 1977). This column will summarize the Abt findings, discuss selected issues in the critique by House and his colleagues, and present comments by Walter Hodges of Georgia State University and Robert Sheehan of the University of Virginia, who offer a more elaborated perspective of Follow Through and its impact. (Details of Hodges and Sheehan's concerns will appear in a future issue of Young Children.)

Summary of Findings

Follow Through was an extension of Head Start to kindergarten and the primary grades of elementary schools. The program was based on the assumption that intervention through third grade was needed for high risk children even if they had attended Head Start preschool programs. As was the case with Head Start, Follow Through offered alternative models of classroom styles. Programs varied from those with highly-structured, didactic classrooms to those with flexible, open classrooms organized around individualized units of study. Although all models addressed the teaching of the basic skills of reading, writing, and arithmetic, some models also addressed broader educational goals in the areas of language and cognitive functioning, student initiative, and classroom participation. Parent participation was stressed to varying degrees by Follow Through models; for some models, direct parent involvement was the major source of intervention as a supplement to classroom activity.

By the spring of 1978, Abt Associates had spent nearly five years studying data from 17 different Follow Through models all of which had been implemented in several different sites. In their report, the school performance of Follow Through children is compared with what would have been expected of them (based on estimates of the performance of non-Follow Through children) had they been in regular classrooms. Data available to Abt included scores from four tests: the *Metropolitan Achievement Test* to measure reading, arithmetic, spelling, vocabulary, and language; the *Raven's Progressive Matrices* instrument to measure abstract problem-solving ability; the *Coopersmith Self-Esteem Inventory* to measure self-concept; and the *Intellectual Achievement Responsibility Scale* to measure school-related self-concept and student responsibility. Additional data collected by individual sponsors were not included in this national evaluation report.

What Do We Know from the Abt Analyses?

Were children in Follow Through models doing better than non-Follow Through children? Although a few of the models appear to provide better education than regular classrooms, most do not. In fact, Anderson states that "in general, across all models, all groups, and all measures, we find fewer positive effects (12.8%) than negative (19.6%) and a preponderance (67.6%) of null [no difference] effects" (p. 7). He also concludes that models that produce positive effects more often than would be expected by chance are those that emphasize the mechanics of basic skills rather than broader educational goals. The model with the best performance overall on the measures included in the evaluation was the Oregon Direct Instruction model developed by Wesley Becker and Siegfried Engelmann, a model that emphasizes individual and group classroom drill on basic skills.

In a different analysis, for which individual measures were clustered into three performance domains—a basic skills domain, a cognitive conceptual domain, and an affective domain—the Follow Through groups performed better than non-Follow Through groups approximately one-third of the time across models, the other two-thirds being instances in which there were either no differences between Follow Through and non-Follow Through groups, or in which the non-Follow Through groups performed better. (Unfortunately, the collapsing of these last two categories in presenting the data makes it impossible to assess the percentage of time that non-Follow Through was actually superior to Follow Through.)

Although Follow Through groups do somewhat better in this analysis than in the one involving individual measures, the record of Follow Through classrooms in these evaluations leaves much to be desired. As in the previous analysis, the didactic models (the Oregon Direct Instruction model and the Kansas Behavior Analysis model) do better than other models on all domains, including the affective domain. It should be noted, however, that the Florida Parent Education model—a model with very different educational strategies and goals—also contributes substantially to the positive side of the ledger on all three domains in this analysis.

Limitations of the Abt Evaluation Data

Cautions Made by Anderson. In discussing the Follow Through evaluation data, Anderson cautions against relying too heavily on the findings concerning model superiority for two reasons. First, the assessment instruments used strongly favored models that emphasized the basic mechanics of reading, writing, and arithmetic. Second, there was a wide variability within models across sites. A striking feature of the data on the over 100 model sites assessed is that a model that did very well at one site, relative to non-Follow Through comparison groups, might do poorly at another site.

If one looks at the four best performing Follow Through sites on the basic skills domain, two of these four sites involved basic skills models (Direct Instruction and Southwest Educational Development Laboratory) and two were affective/cognitive models (Bank Street and Responsive Education). The four best sites on the cognitive conceptual domain included a basic skills model (Direct Instruction) and three affective/cognitive models (a Bank Street site and two Responsive Education sites). The four best performances on the affective domain included three basic skills models (two Direct Instruction sites and a Behavior Analysis site) and one affective/cognitive model (Responsive Education). Without exception these models had other sites in which children performed below what might have been expected on these same domains.

Concerning this issue, *Anderson concludes that the clearest finding of the evaluation may be that local circumstances, attitudes, and activities not measured in the evaluation have more to do with the effectiveness of Follow Through models than their educational characteristics.*

Becker and Engelmann (1977) in summarizing the data on Follow Through classrooms compared with non-Follow Through classrooms, take strong exception to an interpretation of Follow Through data which suggests that models are equally effective (or ineffective) depending upon site; they reiterate the better overall performance across sites of the more didactic models on measures of academic school performance and on affective measures.

In discussing the seemingly poor performance of Follow Through children, Anderson raises a number of questions that suggest a clear need to reserve judgment about Follow Through. Some of the problems faced by Follow Through sponsors and their evaluators are indigenous to field studies of this kind and are difficult to avoid. Implementation of the models was extraordinarily difficult at many sites since it involved marked departures from traditional classroom practice, particularly for those models that required a close working relation between the home and the school. Also at some sites the "regular" classrooms that were used for comparison were exposed to Title I and other educational interventions that presumably benefited the high risk children in their classrooms, reducing the validity of the Follow Through/non-Follow Through comparison. At some sites a diffusion effect seemed to be operating in which non-Follow Through teachers incorporated into their own classrooms some of the Follow Through curriculum and procedures. The more extensive the "borrowing" of Follow Through program components, the more program differences due to Follow Through would be reduced.

There were also problems of high attrition (the loss of subjects in the course of the study); small site samples for some models reducing the likelihood of significant effects being detected; and problems of the "match" between the Follow Through children and their non-Follow Through controls.

Critique by the Center for Instructional Research and Curriculum Evaluation. In their critique of the Abt report, House and his colleagues address many of these same issues. They too emphasize the limitations of the analyses comparing models, given that so many important model goals went unassessed. They also comment on the statistical procedures used for comparing models with each other. In the Abt report, the number of students in a model influenced how good that model appears to be, biasing the data in favor of the didactic, basic skills models. A reanalysis of the Follow Through data, using equally defensible statistical techniques that reduced this bias, did not favor the didactic models but showed differences among models to be within the range of possible chance effects. Further, in the House reanalysis, Follow Through schooling was neither significantly better nor worse overall than non-Follow Through schooling. House suggests that the "truth" might lie someplace between the positions taken by the Abt evaluators and their own.

House and his colleagues also question the use of analysis of covariance (ANCOV) to cope with the problem of the match between comparison groups (that is, differences in the groups that exist *prior* to an educational intervention). Inasmuch as there is no adequate way to control statistically for such initial differences, results of analysis of covariance under these circumstances should be interpreted with caution and, wherever possible, should be supplemented with other analyses of the data. At the very least, all available data should be used to evaluate the Follow Through program, including the data gathered by individual sponsors wherever it meets acceptable scientific standards.

Perspective of Hodges and Sheehan. Hodges and Sheehan (1978) address this issue at some length in a paper presented at the 1978 conference of the American Educational Research Association. They documented their position with references to sponsors' data. Children attending David Weikart's Cognitively Oriented model, for example, were tested for productive language skills—an area of competence that is central to the goals of the model. The children in that model, compared with the non-Follow Through comparison children, were more fluent, used more diverse vocabularies, used more descriptive statements, and wrote better organized narratives.

Children in the Bank Street model—a model that emphasizes flexible classroom scheduling and individualized curriculum activities—initiated communication more, were better at expressing their thoughts, and were involved in more peer communication than non-Follow Through controls.

A group of children enrolled in the Parent Support model sponsored by Hodges performed better on 11 of 33 measures on the California Achievement Test compared with non-Follow Through children, while there were no differences between the groups on the other 22 measures. A number of models that emphasized parent involvement found marked differences favoring the Follow Through groups in parental attitudes about school and investment in the educational experience of the children.

These and other measures obtained by the model sponsors would certainly appear to be important model outcomes; a full description of the Follow Through project should include them. A publication edited by Rhine (in press) will present reports from several Follow Through model sponsors. The final report on Follow Through to be issued by the U.S. Office of Education will also include information on data gathered by sponsors.

What Can We Say about Follow Through?

It is unfortunate that the national evaluation report was so limited in its scope; we would do well to hold off on our final assessment of Follow Through until all of the relevant data are available for examination. It does appear, however, that Follow Through did not produce the desired effect. Even the most successful models were barely better than others—or than regular schooling. It should be kept in mind, however, that if we decide that Follow Through innovations are worthless because they are no better than regular school programs, we are left with the original dilemma of how to help high risk children to do better in our schools. We were not doing well in that endeavor prior to Follow Through. In fact, we had not addressed that problem in the primary grades before Follow Through and Title I despite the existence of the problem for many years. Follow Through and Title I are the first extensive efforts to cope with it. Only if we learn from these programs can the investment in them pay off.

What comes next?

1. We need to learn all that we can about the more illusive educational goals that were not included in the national Follow Through evaluation study. Among the more important educational outcomes are the child's ability to think, reason, and problem solve outside of the test situation; to read with comprehension and communicate effectively; and to take initiative in learning. Relevant measures developed by the individual sponsors are a good place to begin, but further instrument development will be necessary.

2. The short- and long-term effects of parent involvement and participation in the education of the child should be assessed.

3. We need to know more about the long-term effects of different models of education. Do didactic models serve the child best in the short run while other models do better over time? Or does the added time commitment given to basics by the didactic models pay off in greater preparation for later subject matter mastery by high risk children?

4. We should learn what we can by looking at outstandingly successful and unsuccessful sites, whatever the model. Are there teacher or school variables that determine, to some extent at least, the success or failure of a model at a given site? Are there schools in which almost any well-conducted model will succeed—or fail? If so, what are the characteristics of such sites?

5. Did Follow Through affect the quality of life in schools as many sponsors feel it did? Hodges and Sheehan comment on data from sponsors indicating that Follow Through teachers had higher morale and were more satisfied with their school programs than non-Follow Through teachers. Follow Through children, in turn, indicated their satisfaction in school by attending more regularly than non-Follow Through children. If the quality of life was improved for Follow Through children, why was it not reflected in academic performance? Is it possible that liking school may not enhance the child's academic performance per se, but may motivate the child to stay in school longer, learn more outside of school, and consider additional schooling beyond the point when the child no longer *must* attend school?

These and many other questions remain unanswered in evaluating Follow Through programs. Experimentation in curriculum for the primary grades for high risk children is just beginning; we should not expect to solve pervasive, long-standing problems easily or quickly. Follow Through is a base upon which we can build in the future.

References

Anderson, R. B. *The Effectiveness of Follow Through: What Have We Learned?* Paper presented at the meeting of the American Educational Research Association, New York, April 1977.

8. TEACHING AND EVALUATION

Becker, W. C., and Engelmann, S. *Comparative Results in Project Follow Through: A Summary of Nine Years of Work.* Eugene, Oreg.: University of Oregon Follow Through Project, May 1977.

Education as Experimentation: A Planned Variation Model, Volume IV. Cambridge, Mass.: Abt Associates, 1977.

Hodges, W. L., and Sheehan, R. *Ten Years of Evaluation Effort: The Work of Follow Through Sponsors.* Paper presented at the meeting of the American Educational Research Association, Toronto, March 1978.

House, E. R.; Glass, G. V.; McLean, L. D.; and Walker, D. F.; with assistance from Hutchins, E. J. *No Simple Answer: Critique of the "Follow Through" Evaluation.* Urbana, Ill.: Center for Instructional Research and Curriculum Evaluation, 1977.

Rhine, R. *Encouraging Change in American Schools.* New York: Academic Press, in press.

We want your advice.

Any anthology can be improved. This one will be—annually. But we need your help.

Annual Editions revisions depend on two major opinion sources: one is the academic advisers who work with us in scanning the thousands of articles published in the public press each year; the other is you—the person actually using the book.

Please help us and the users of the next edition by completing the prepaid article rating form on the last page of this book and returning it to us. Thank you.

Article 67

the diagnostic teacher

One way to learn how much the child knows is to observe him carefully and then plan teaching strategies which will lead to further observations

Barbara Somach

The author is an educational consultant and supervisor in the learning disabilities program at Bank Street College of Education, New York. She is a former faculty member of the early childhood department, Queens College, City University of New York.

In order to make meaningful curriculum decisions and plan appropriate teaching/learning situations, you need to answer the question "How do I know what a child knows?" One way is to become a diagnostic teacher.

What's a diagnostic teacher? Primarily a child-watcher who is involved in an ongoing daily process of observing children in the classroom, making decisions about what they should learn and implementing these plans with a variety of methods and materials.

These decisions and plans should consider the whole child. To be a diagnostic teacher, you must look at the physical, social, emotional, cognitive and language development of each child. You must be aware of what a child can and cannot do and be sensitive to how he feels about himself as a learner, remembering that the feelings a child has about himself can affect the way he approaches a task and his actual performance.

As a diagnostic teacher, you should have knowledge of child development and be able to assess the progress of individual children based on age-appropriate stages established by such theorists as Piaget, Freud, Gesell and Erikson. After getting a general reading of the child's developmental level based on these established stages, you then sharpen your vision and notice specific details.

Additional information about each child is gathered by noting: (1) physical characteristics and general health conditions; (2) motor abilities, small and large muscle development; (3) language development—ability to speak, use appropriate labels, describe familiar objects, interpret language, communicate and listen; (4) cognitive development, including general fund of information, awareness of details, memory, following directions and time and space concepts; (5) social and emotional development through interactions with peers and adults, self-concept, approach to task and handling of frustration and stress.

But be aware that your own cultural and personal biases may interact and color what you see and hear. Be honest with yourself and acknowledge this when putting all your data together for a total picture of the child.

Observing Patterns. Considering that a major task of the diagnostic teacher is to become aware of emerging patterns of children's academic performance and behavior, you'll need to look at children in many school and classroom situations—language arts, math, blocks, snack, gym, lunch, art, music, whatever. Make note of the way children seem to be taking in information, responding to directions and accomplishing tasks. Do this for a reasonable period of time so that you'll have enough information to help plan long- and short-term goals for individuals and groups of learners. Notice the time of day the child seems most alert and responsive to learning, when fatigue and frustration occur, if he's easily distracted and what he likes and dislikes about school.

Remember that information gained from observation and from any other formal or informal test should be used to help children maximize their strengths and abilities, not label them or put them into pigeonholes. A diagnostic teacher helps a child to know and understand what he can do academically and encourages him to use these strengths to support learning in weaker areas. She makes immediate adjustments in her teaching to accommodate the needs of the learner.

To help document your observations and record children's classroom performance, you might want to keep anecdotal notes in a card file, a daily diary, a check list or use audio and video tapes.

Active Role. Admittedly, all of this sounds as though the teacher plays an essentially passive role in gathering information, with the child performing in a certain way and the child-watcher simply making note of the performance (providing she's on hand to see it). In actual practice, however, diagnostic teachers play an extremely active role in gathering information.

Here, for example, is the sort of process you might use to gain

8. TEACHING AND EVALUATION

information that could help you evaluate the effectiveness of a learning situation. It relates task expectations and demands to the child's performance and requires an active involvement on the part of the teacher.

Let's say you want to find out if a child knows the alphabet. First, you must clarify and state in specific terms what you mean by "know the alphabet." Do you expect the child to match an upper case letter with another upper case letter? Point to an upper or lower case letter when you say the letter name? Say the letter name when you point to a letter? Say the names of the 26 letters in sequence? Identify in some manner the letters that spell his name? Write the letters of the alphabet in upper or lower case letters?

Second, while the child is involved in this task you have the opportunity to observe many things, including these behavioral indicators:
Temperament (how does the child approach the task?)—impulsively or reflectively, gives up or persists, passive or active.
Attentional factors—ability to focus or distractible, length of attention span, concentration.
Self-concept—works with confidence or needs constant approval.
Interactions with adults and peers—comfortable or withdrawn.

Third, if the child can complete the matching task correctly, then an assumption may be made, based on observable evidence, that the child's vision is not impaired, that the brain can perceive similarities and that differences and a level of eye-hand coordination has been established.

Fourth, if the child cannot do the task, it is important to do a Task Analysis, which means to determine: (1) the sequential steps involved in learning the task; (2) the specific behaviors needed to perform the task, and analyses of teacher language of directions and instructions, both oral and written.

For example, if the task is to match felt letters on a flannel board, the specific abilities needed to complete the task involve the ability to understand directions (receptive language); to see letters (visual acuity); to perceive distinctive features and discriminate between letters (visual perception); to look away from the letter and mentally hold on to the configuration while looking at other letters (short-term memory); to understand concepts of same and different (cognition); to pick up the letter and place it on flannel board (visual motor); to place the letter in the proper direction (integration of cognition, visual and motor).

Fifth, if the child fails to complete the task, beware of coming to conclusions based on a single experience. A diagnostic teacher understands that a task can be used for both teaching and testing and that diagnosis does not need to rely on the use of specifically designed tests. While working with the child in any learning situation, you are continually assessing what he can and cannot do or understand. When incorrect responses are made, it's essential to zero in and try to locate the point in the learning process where the errors are made. If the child cannot do the task successfully with symbolic material, then make the task even simpler and change to concrete manipulative materials.

Following Directions. If your hunch is that the child is having difficulty at the level of following directions then test it out by observing the child following directions in formal and informal situations.

Give the child a simple commission such as "bring me the book" and observe. Increase the number of commissions gradually to two—"go to the closet and put on your coat"—and then add more. Use the information gained from these observations to help select appropriate materials that will provide the child with successful learning situations. Teacher-made games and materials and commercial teaching games can help assess if the child has the prerequisite skills needed to be able to think, listen, read, write, spell and do math.

Another example of a diagnostic task is to take six letter tiles, make the words "was" and "saw" and place them on the table in front of the child. Ask the child to tell you whatever he can about them. If the child can tell you that "was" and "saw" are the same because they are made from the same three letters, but different because the letters are in reverse order, that the middle letter remains the same in both words and that the "w" is first in the word on the left and last in order on the right, then what can you assess that this child knows in terms of concepts, language and visual discrimination? What instructional plans might you design from knowledge of these strengths?

In diagnostic teaching it is necessary to consider the following steps in planning instructional programs:

1. Observe children in many situations in and out of your classroom.
2. Formulate a hunch or hypothesis about the child as a learner based on keen observation of the individual child and your knowledge of child development.
3. Test your hunch in several teaching sessions and notice the child's strengths and errors.
4. Analyze the data by looking at samples of children's work, including stories, paintings, poems and handwriting; and by listening to tapes of children reading and speaking.
5. Look at patterns of errors for clues about the way a child learns. These errors can help you figure out what and how to teach that child. Be on the lookout for verbal and nonverbal messages that kids give that tell you what they know, how they know it and how to teach them.

67. The Diagnostic Teacher

6. Make instructional decisions and implement them.

The diagnostic teaching process involves the need to observe the learner and make hypotheses; to diagnose the strategies and behaviors he uses to complete a task and how he learns; to determine what he can do and note the patterns of errors in what he can't do; to plan and teach a new task; to evaluate performance; and to make adjustments in instructional decisions. This ongoing teaching-testing procedure is essentially circular in nature, beginning with the observation of the child and returning to the observation once instructional decisions have been adjusted.

Jot down notes or keep concise records that tell you at any point in time what a child knows. With this information, you can be knowledgeable about strategies and modalities the child uses for learning different kinds of tasks. By using task analysis you can break the task down into small steps and teach the parts that are needed. By analyzing the quality of your directions, instructions and questions, you can discern if the difficulty is your sentence structure, choice of words or oral presentation.

Remember that conclusions are tentative, that another learning situation may provide you with additional information which can confound your earlier findings and be quite different from the data you already have collected. You need to integrate this new information into the learning profile you are establishing for each child.

This assessment procedure aids in evaluating all children in the classroom, but is especially helpful with high risk learners. Instructional decisions based on up-to-date and ongoing assessment of children's needs and evaluation of their performance on learning tasks, plus accurate record keeping gives you, the classroom teacher, a way to document what the child knows.

In conclusion, a diagnostic teacher is a flexible teacher who keeps an open mind about a child's ability to learn. She makes hypotheses about the best ways to help a child learn and tests them out with various materials and methods. She understands that testing and assessment is an ongoing fluid procedure that takes place daily, and contributes to effective educational decision making.

the role of testing in the educational process

Here, an in-depth look at testing and how it relates to your children and you

Lois E. Burrill

A former classroom teacher, Ms. Burrill is manager of information and advisory services, The Psychological Corporation, New York.

What is a test? What role does it play in the educational process? Perhaps you, the readers, will question whether any such role exists, but it's my belief that such a view arises from a misapprehension of what a test really is.

Permit me, then, to submit what I believe to be an appropriate definition: A test is any sample of actual behavior—particularly those samples noted in some sort of standard and defined way—and is usually collected for the express purpose of decision making.

Too often a test is considered simply as a way to *judge* how well a subject has been taught and learned—that is, to measure *success*. Important though this is, it's only part of the decision making process in which teachers are constantly engaged. Teachers must also ask themselves what is *worth* teaching—in other words, what is *important*. Having determined this, they must further decide how *best* it may be taught and learned—what is *appropriate*. We are concerned with these kinds of questions because we are members of a helping profession and our role is to help individual children and groups of children. We must therefore take action and make choices among alternative courses of action.

Our decisions are based on our evaluation of the present situation. An important part of the word evaluation is *value* and our decisions ultimately must be concerned with worth or value as shown by all those italicized words. But sound decisions depend on our being able to evaluate relevant factual information about the present situation. The more we know, the more accurate and trustworthy our information, the more likely we are to be able to evaluate and make appropriate decisions.

Now it may be clearer why I offered a broad definition of testing. Testing is the appropriate term to describe any and all methods we use to collect that information. Using this more accurate definition, any doubt about the enormous role testing must and should have in the teaching/learning process evaporates.

Indeed, it's clear that, intentional or not, testing is constantly taking place within the school setting. It would not, in fact, be totally out of line to suggest that good teaching and testing are so closely related and intertwined as to be virtually inseparable. Good teachers are constantly testing, just as they are constantly teaching, whether in the lunchroom, on the playground, in the corridors, or in the classroom!

Much testing, of course, is and should be informal. No paper and pencil "test" is necessary or even appropriate for many kinds of situations. Testing covers a wide variety of methods, procedures and techniques, and it must be stated loud and clear that formal paper and pencil testing, even where appropriate, does not, cannot, and should not be allowed to replace other effective methods of testing.

Ways of Testing. What, then, is the role of standardized, norm reference-testing in the educational process? If we accept the stereotyped view generally adopted by students, teachers, congressmen, and, it must be admitted, too frequently test publishers, this sort of "test" might well be used as sole criterion for a definition which would probably be something like this:

A paper document, developed by some unknown persons outside the local school, asking a lot of questions—each with several possible answer choices. Such a test also has a separate piece of paper on which answers are to be recorded by number or letter. That piece of paper, the "answer sheet," will then be scored by a machine somewhere outside the school and another piece of paper with lots of "scores" will be returned to the school some weeks after "testing" has taken place.

It's a shame that our minds jump to such an image, for to limit our notion of such tests to this very narrow definition precludes the positive value of such instruments as appropriate techniques to complement, supplement, enhance and enlarge information gained by other testing procedures.

The most appropriate testing technique or tool to use in each case depends in part on the knowledge or behavior you are seeking to test. Some behaviors

68. The Role of Testing in the Educational Process

lend themselves rather well to direct measurement; others are more difficult to get at. Some knowledges and behaviors can be tested both efficiently and accurately by use of paper and pencil; others may only be assessed by observation of a child's actual behavior.

Here are some of the ways we have of testing:

1. One of the teacher's first sources of information about a child may be a parent, rather than the child himself. An interview with a parent would, by the definition proposed above, be considered testing, as would the more formal completion of a questionnaire or behavior inventory.

2. Observation is probably the most important method of testing in early childhood years. There are numerous techniques of observation, ranging from the most casual noting of behavior to quite systematic and formal methods such as time samples. Observations can be extremely valuable, but they can also lack validity. Teachers need to develop skills in observing children in ways that will not encourage false impressions or lead to conclusions biased by the hopes and wishes of the observer. And many times, without special preplanning, it's difficult to observe any evidence one way or the other about many of the goals teachers deem important.

3. One way to combat certain shortcomings of the usual observation techniques is to create a situation in which the behavior for which you want to test is likely to occur. Such structured situations are particularly useful in testing for behaviors that may not occur often in the classroom or which do not usually occur spontaneously.

4. Closely related to structured situations for observation are structured work samples. The child's own products are certainly, by the broader definition, tests and should be a valuable source of information about the child's progress and current level of development.

5. Check lists and rating scales are paper-and-pencil testing tools a teacher can use very effectively. In some cases, teachers may develop their own check lists and, less frequently perhaps, rate each characteristic on a scale of one to three, five, seven or ten. However, a number of check lists have been developed by state departments of education, test publishers, textbook publishers, and other external sources, and are readily available.

6. Classroom exercises are also tests. Sometimes these take the form of informal inventories of difficulties, or informal quizzing of students on particular content of the curriculum. Sometimes, of course, especially as a child progresses through the grades, these are paper and pencil tests.

7. Textbooks often include chapter tests, unit tests and review tests. These, too, may be useful sources of information for decision-making.

8. Finally, there are published and commercially available tests. Although publishers provide materials for use in several of the categories of testing mentioned earlier, it is for so-called norm-referenced or standardized tests that they are best-known. Their importance in the decision making function of the teacher is determined to a great extent by the individual, but the fact remains that certain behaviors of children can be accurately and efficiently tested by such methods. By collecting the kinds of information that *can* be collected in this way, teachers may obtain valuable insight into many aspects of student behavior in a relatively short period of time, leaving more time for action based on the decisions the teacher makes using this information.

I think it's important at this point to return to the idea of *evaluating* and to make again the distinction between *evaluating* and *testing*. Testing, as we have defined it here, is a tool, a procedure for collecting relevant information. That information is, in isolation, quite neutral—valueless. The results of testing must be processed—evaluated—by teachers, administrators, parents and other decision makers. Testing attempts to answer the question: "What is the present situation?" It does not and cannot go beyond that and answer the questions: "So what? Is that good? Is it good enough? What do I do next?"

And it is also important to remind ourselves that not all testing is good or useful or relevant. Tests and testing are tools and tools may be poorly made. Furthermore, like most tools, it takes a certain amount of skill to use testing well.

I have dwelt at length on the role of the teacher in the testing process. What role, then, do I propose for test publishers in the teaching/learning process? I would suggest several. First, we test publishers should continue to try to develop good testing tools for use by the classroom teacher. Not only should we publish paper-and-pencil tests for those purposes for which they are appropriate but also other, non paper-and-pencil procedures for collecting relevant information about children and their development.

Second, I believe we have a role to play in helping teachers develop their own methods of testing and information gathering. Unfortunately, many of the skills necessary to the good use of test results are not now part of the teacher's formal preparation for teaching, especially in the area of using good paper-and-pencil testing information for decision making in instruction. Therefore, a third responsibility of the test publisher must be to help teachers gain proficiency in these areas.

WHO'S WRITING AND WRITTEN ABOUT

Ackerman, Paul, **197**
Allen, Dr. Roach Van, **219**
Alter, Stewart, **230**
Anderson, R.B., 265
Apgar, Virginia, **72**
Arenas, Soledad, **213**
Ariès, Philippe, 52

Baker, Donald, **136**
Bakke, Kit, **194**
Beck, Joan, **72**
Becker, W.C., 265
Bloom, Benjamin, 27
Bowlby, John, 27, 90
Brazelton, T. Berry, 11
Brittain, W. Lambert, 230, 231
Bronfenbrenner, Urie, 143
Butler, Annie L., **29, 59**

Caldwell, Bettye M., **118**
Callard, Esther D., **217**
Carberry, Hugh H., **205**
Card, J.J., 144, 145, 148
Carper, Laura, **113**
Case, Robbie, **100**
Chess, Dr. Stella, 131, 132
Cohen, Dorothy H., 35
Cohen, Monroe D., **32**
Conger, John J., 143

Darwin, Charles, 53
DeLissovoy, V., 147
Dodson, Dr. Fitzhugh, **192**
Dryfoos, J.G., 147
Dunlop, Kathleen H., **185**

Eggleston, Patricia J., **249**
Elardo, Richard, **97**
Elkind, David, 47-49, **107, 210**
Epstein, A., 147
Erikson, Erik, 92, 168

Farran, Dale C., **36**
Fiske, Edward B., **65**
Foshay, Arthur W., **18**
Furstenberg, F., 144, 145, 146, 147, 148, 149

Garmezy, Norman, 168

Hall, G.S., 169
Harms, Thelma, **256**
Harwell, Joan, **172**
Haskins, Ron, **36**
Hipple, Marjorie L., **201**
Hodges, W.L., 266
House, E.R., 264
Howell, Dr. Mary C., 152
Hughes, Marie, 34, 35
Hunsinger, Susan, **40**
Hutinger, Patricia L., **223**
Hymes, James L. Jr., **242**

Isakson, Richard L., **142**

Jacobs, Leland B., **244**
Jacobson, Arminta Lee, **43**

Kagan, Jerome, **83**, 152
Kappelman, Murray, **197**
Katz, Lilian G., **14**
Kelly, Joan B., 155
Keniston, Kenneth, 143
Kessen, William, **52**
Kirk, Dr. Sam, 172
Klineberg, Otto, 32

Law, Norma R., **21**
Lazar, Dr. Irving, 258, 262
LeVasseur, Natalie P., **59**
Locke, John, 52, 83

Maracek, J., 148
Martin, Mavis, 34
McCarthy, J., 146
Mead, Margaret, **54,**153
Money, John, 109, 110
Moore, Dennis R., **26**, 30
Moore, K.A., 144, 147
Moore, Raymond S., 26, 30
Moore, Shirley, **126, 258, 264**
Morgan, Gwendolyn, **37**
Muenchow, Susan, **109**
Murphy, Lois Barclay, 32-33

Niswander, K.R., 147

O'Hara, Ethel, **226**
Olds, Sally Wendkos, **152**
Otto, Herbert, 143

Piaget, Jean, 24, 27, 91, 100-106, 108, 183, 226-229
Poussaint, F., **161**

Rich, Dorothy, 143
Rousseau, 52

Sanders, Joseph, **36**
Schwartz, Judy I., **89**
Schwartz, Dr. Susan, **178**
Seligman, Martin, 168
Shane, Harold G., **57**
Sheehan, R., 266
Shepard, Margaret Jo, **176**
Simmons, Barbara, **253**
Skinner, B.F., 52
Skolnick, Arlene, **167**
Smith, Marilyn M., **6**
Spock, Benjamin, **63**
Stranix, Edward L., **164**
Sutton-Smith, Brian, **133**

Terman, L.M., 169
Thomas, M. Donald, 143
Tietze, C., 149
Trussell, J., 147
Tucker, Patricia, 109

Vigare, Vanessa, **68**

Wallerstein, Judith S., 155
Watson, J.B., 169
Weber, Lillian, 33
Weir, Mary K., **249**
White, Dr. Burton L., **80**
White, Sheldon, 28
Wilson, Laurie, 230, 231
Wyden, Barbara, **77**

Yatvin, Joanne, **182**

Zigler, Edward, **40**, 233

INDEX

Abt report: critique of, 266; evaluation of Follow Through program, 264-268
academic acceleration: criticism of, 182; causes of failure of, 183; causes for trend in, 182; and Piaget, 183
Administration for Children, Youth and Families (ACYF), 215, 236
aggression: alternatives to, 124; in day care vs. home-reared children, 38; as child's reaction to divorce, 156; guidelines for dealing with children's, 121-124; and hostility defined, 119-120; and media, 119; parental encouragement of, 122-123; sex differences in, 109-110; society's encouragement of male, 63
Aid to Families with Dependent Children (AFDC), 145
"American question" (Piaget), 27
amniocentesis, 72
androgens, and aggression, 109-110
animism, 226

anxiety: adult intervention suggestions on, 195-196; behavior, 195; causes of, 195; as child's reaction to divorce, 155-157; role of teacher in reducing, 207; in three-to-five year old, 194-196
art, understanding children's, 230-232
autonomy, 92

back to basics movement: 18-20, 211-212; future of, 58; harm of, 34; pressures, 33
bed-wetting, 198-199
bilingual/bicultural programs: characteristics of successful, 213-215; for preschool children, 213-216
black: parents handling racial issues with children, 161-163; teenage mothers, 144, 146, 148
brain development: importance of pre- and postnatal nutrition to, 77-79; and reading readiness, 27, 30; sex differences in, 111
Britain, and play in, 136, 137

centering, 227
certification: of day care workers, 41; of teachers, 23
child abuse: 55; "casual," 63; deprivation as, 68; emotional, 68-69; physical, 68; sexual, 68; signals of, 68-69; statistics on, 68
childbirth: classes, 76; consequences on mother of early, 144-150; drugs during, 76
child care: description of quality, 37; effect on children, 48; information available on, 37; see also, day care
child development: effect of early childbearing on, 147, 148; and parental-determinism, 167-169; Piaget's stages of, 100-103, 226; effect of working mothers on, 152-154
Child Development Associate program (CDA), 41, 237
child rearing: current trends in, 47; and parental-determinism, 167-169; quality vs. quantity of time, 49; three conditions of, 217-218

children: abuse of, 55, 63, 68-69; acceleration programs for, 182-184; anxiety in three-to-five year old, 194-196; anxious, 206-207; curiosity in, 81; day care vs. home-reared, 38; effect of death and divorce on, 48; diagnostic teaching of, 269-271; discipline of, 82, 192, 193, 201-204; distress signals in, 197-199; reactions to divorce, 142, 155-158; concept of early childhood education, 21; educational development of, 80; emotional development of, 92; environmental statistics for America's, 8-9; place in family, 48; gifted, 178-181; place in history in U.S. and Europe, 52-53; improving school performance of, 164-166; impulsive, 205-206; individual differences of, 32, 33, 131-132; language development in, 80-81; latchkey, 142, 143; learning disabled, 172-174, 176, 177; limited access to adults, 90; mainstreaming handicapped, 185-190; misunderstandings about learning in, 107-108; motivation to communicate, 249-252; negativistic, 205; parental-determinism, 167-169; parental handling of racial issues of, 161-163; passive-dependent, 206; satisfactions in teaching young, 242, 243; sexual identity in, 113-114; and stress, 168; suicide rate in, 55; of teenage parents, 144-150; effect of television on, 65-66; effect of working mothers on, 152-154; world rights of, 54-56
college education, future of, 57
community responsibility: 56; vs. family, 12
concept development, Piaget's findings on, 24; see also, learning
conception: ideal male and female ages for, 72-73; proper timing of, 73
concrete operations: 102, 226; characteristics of, 226-227
cultural pluralism, 23-24
curriculum: affective, 210; back-to-basics, 18-20, 33, 34, 58, 211-212; basics of, 18-20; humanizing, 210-212; open, 212

day care: after-school, 40; family, 40; and federal bureaucracy, 41-42; federal funding of, 41; in future, 57; vs. home-reared children, 38, 48, 90-95; infant, 40-41, 43-46; effects on intellectual development, 36; effect on mother-child relationship, 36-37, 48; myths about, 36; finding quality, 37; quality control problem, 41; referral system for, 41; types of, 36; see also, child care
Declaration of Rights of the Child, 55
depression, as reaction of children to divorce, 156, 157
diagnostic teaching, 269-271
discipline: 82; of infants, 192; solutions to classroom problems, 201-204; of toddlers, 193
divorce: effect on child's behavior in school, 157, 158; effect on children, 48; children's reaction to, 155, 156; school as support for children of, 158, 159
Down's syndrome, 72
drugs: during childbirth, 76; during pregnancy, 74

early childhood education (ECE): children's concept of, 21; cost of, 55; basic curriculum for, 14-17; definition of, 7, 26; impact of Depression on, 7; and effect of divorce on, 142, 156, 157; evaluation of, 24, 30; effect on families, 6-13, 30; effect on changes in American family on, 142-143; future of, 57; goals of, 22; home-based, 28; and IQ of children of teenage mothers, 148; learning materials of, 24; parents' concept of, 21-22; implications of Piaget's research on, 103-106; and implication of play, 136-139; possible effect of Proposition 13 on, 59-62; purpose of, 8; satisfaction with, 242, 243; setting for, 8; society's concept of, 22; teachers' concept of, 22; impact of World War II on, 7
educable mentally retarded (EMR), 187
education: and academic acceleration, 182-184; and diagnostic teaching, 269-271; effect of divorce on children's, 156-159; effect of changes in American family on, 142, 143; of gifted children, 178-181; improving children's school performance, 164-166; and learning classrooms, 184; of learning disabled children, 172-174, 176, 177; and importance of physical environment in classroom, 256, 257; satisfactions in teaching young children, 242, 243; eliminating sexism in curriculum, 253-255; and three types of teachers, 244, 245; and art of teaching, 245-247; teenage parenthood and effect on, 144, 145; role of testing in, 272, 273
Education for All Handicapped Children Act (PL 94-142), 58
egocentrism, 227

family: changes in American, 142-143; and handling of racial issues by parents, 161-163; single-parent, 9, 55, 90; support for teenage mothers, 149; today's American, 90
fantasy friends, 198
fathers, role in parenting with working mother, 153
federal government, role in day care, 41-42
Follow Through: Abt evaluation report of, 264-268; description of, 264; lessons to be learned from, 267; success of, 264, 265
formal operations, 103, 226

genetic counseling, 72, 73
German measles, see rubella
gifted children: characteristics, 178; problems and interventions for, 178-181; recommendations to help solve problems with, 179-181
government, see federal government
gratification, of infants in U.S. vs. nontechnological society, 217

handicapped children: education for, 55; and Head Start, 235; statistics on, 9
Head Start: 242, 264; expanding eligibility for, 238; in future, 236; and handicapped children, 235; and IQ test results, 6, 30, 234-235; long-term effects of, 234; misunderstanding surrounding, 233; new agenda, 237-238; importance of parental cooperation to, 234, 235; purpose of, 7, 235

infants: competency in, 44, 93; importance of consistency to, 9, 94; day care for, 40-41, 43-46, 97-99, 152; determinism, 83-88; discipline of, 192-193; emotional development of, 92; group care vs. home care of, 89-95; individuality in, 92-93, 131-132; male vs. female, 110; six to nine months, 97-98; nine to twelve months, 98; twelve to eighteen months, 98-99; eighteen to twenty-four months, 99; twenty-four to thirty months, 99; perceptual-cognitive development, 44-45; play behavior, 45; predictability to later childhood, 83-88, 128-129; importance of primary caregiver to, 43, 94, 130; reciprocity, 93; short-term memory in, 87, 88; social development, 45-46; vocalization, 44
intellectual development, during sensorimotor period, 91
IQ: effect of day care on, 36; effect of Head Start on, 6; parents' concern over child's, 47, 108
International Year of the Child, 21, 54, 55

latchkey children, 142, 143
learned-helplessness theory, and child's vulnerability to stress, 168
learning: critical periods in, 47, 236; developmental stages of, 47; disabled, 172-174, 176, 177; evaluating setting for, 256-257; misunderstandings about, 107-108; and Piaget's stages of child development, 100-103; sexual identity, 113-114
learning disabilities: characteristics of children with, 174; definition, 176; diagnosing and teaching children with, 172-174, 176, 177; helping children with, 174; compared to slow learners, 176, 177; symptoms, 172, 173
learning disabled, see learning disabilities

mainstreaming: characteristics of successful classroom, 187-190; growth of, 186; of handicapped into regular classroom, 185, 186; research on effectiveness of, 187, 188
marriage, effect of teenage parenthood on stability of, 146, 147
maternal attachment/deprivation: 27; effect of day care on, 37-38, 91, 94; compared to institutionalization, 90; see also, mother-infant interaction
mathematics: difficulties of six year olds with modern, 227-229; and learning disabled child, 174, 175
Mean Length Utterance (MLU), 224
minimal brain dysfunction, 177
mother-infant interaction: and environmental factors, 126-127; implications for infant day care, 43-46, 130; and "optimal maternal care" behaviors, 127-128; see also, maternal attachment

neurological integration, 94
neurological maturation, 94
nutrition, importance of during first three years of life, 77-79

Optimal Maternal Care, 127-128
ovulation, 73

parental control, and influence on children, 167-169
parental-determinism: criticism of, 167, 168; effect on social policy, 169; flaw in research on, 168; historical roots of, 169; limits on, 168, 169; two models of parenting and, 167
parent-child relationship, and parental determinism, 167-169
parenthood: consequences of teenage, 144-150; education, 143, 150
parenthood education, 143, 150
parenting: effect of teenage parenthood on, 147; and parental-determinism, 167-169; two models of, 167
parents: action on television viewing, 66-67; attitudes on children's sex play, 115-117; concern about child's IQ, 47; effect of changes in American family on, 143; and gifted children,

180; and handling of racial issues with children, 161-163; and helping children accept mother's employment, 153, 154; interracial, 163; need for assistance, 9, 21-22, 38-39; and parental-determinism, 167-169; setting an example, 45, 125, 260; single, 9, 55, 90; teenage, 147, 148; understanding child's distress signals, 197-200; view of early childhood education, 21-22, 30; ways parents can help children do better in school, 164-166

perceptual-cognitive development, 44-45

play: and children in Britian, 136, 137; climate and influence on physical structure of, 136, 137; effect of technology on, 139; elements of, 136; from eleven to fifteen years, 135; exploratory and inventive, 133; in first year, 134; importance of, 21, 108; and loss of face to face contact and, 138, 139; parallel, 227; in second year, 134; from seven to ten years, 135; sex, 115-116; supervised vs. free, 124, 125; from three to six years, 135; in third year, 134-135; in tropics, 136, 137, 138

preconceptual and intuitive thought, 102, 226

pregnancy: drugs during, 74; ideal age for, 72; ideal interval between, 73; importance of nutrition during, 77; and Rh disease, 75; and rubella, 74; smoking during, 75; and toxoplasmosis, 74; and viral infections, 74; x-rays during, 75

prematurity, handicaps of, 75

prenatal care: 77; cost of, 73-74; important issue of the future, 57

preschool, study on effects of, 258-263

primary caregiver: characteristics of competent, 45; importance to infant development, 43, 94; role as authority, 82; role as consultant, 81-82

Proposition 13, possible effect on schools, 59-62

Public Law 85-926, 186

Public Law 94-142, 58

racial issues, how parents should handle children and, 161-163

reading: relationship to language facility, 219-222; and teaching children with learning disabilities, 174; ten aids for, 219-222

reading readiness: and brain development, 27, 30; and Piaget's stages of child development, 105

Rh disease, 75

rubella, 74

Scholastic Aptitude Test (SAT), drop in scores, 63, 211

schools: and art of teaching, 245, 246, 247; decline in enrollment, 57-58; effect of divorce on behavior of children in, 157, 158; and eliminating sexism in curriculum, 253-255; and gifted children, 178-181; importance of physical environment in classroom, 256, 257; and learning disabled children, 172-174, 176, 177; role in day care, 40; as support for children of divorce, 158, 159; vs. television, 65-67; and three types of teachers, 244, 245; ways parents can help children do better in, 164-166

sensorimotor period: 101, 226; activities to enhance intellectual development during, 91-92

separation, and effect on education of children involved, 142, 155

sex differences: in activity levels, 110; in aggression, 109-110; biological basis for, 109; at birth, 110; in brain specialization, 111; in verbal and spatial ability, 111

sex hormones, 109, 110

sexism, elimination of in school curriculum, 253-255

sexual exploration: brother-sister, 116; children's, 115-117; and masturbation, 116-117

sexual identity, in preschool children, 113-114

single-parent families, 9, 55, 90

slow learners, compared to learning disabled, 176, 177

smoking, during pregnancy, 75

socialization, of children in U.S. vs. nontechnological society, 217-218

speech, and learning disabled child, 174

stimulation, 9-10, 94-95; effect on intellectual development, 27

stress, and the vulnerable child, 168, 169

suicide, in children, 55

symbolization, 10-11

teachers: coping with behavioral disorders in children, 205-207; "burnout," 35; certification of, 23, 41; decline in educational enrollment of, 57; diagnostic 269-271; recommendations for classroom discipline, 201-204; concept of early childhood education, 22; setting an example, 202; and gifted children, 178, 179; threat of inflation to, 58; interaction with child, 33; role in language development, 224-225; identifying learning disabled, 172, 173; instructing learning disabled, 173, 174; importance in mainstreaming handicapped, 186-187; and motivating children to communicate, 249-252; recommendations to, 34-35; satisfactions in teaching young children, 242, 243; and art of teaching, 245-247; in competition with television, 66; three types of, 244, 245

teaching: and academic acceleration, 182-184; art of, 245-247; diagnostic, 269-271; children of divorce, 159; effects of changes in American family on, 143; gifted children, 178-181; and learning classrooms, 184; learning disabled, 173-174; and motivating communication in children, 249-252; personalized, 32; and eliminating sexism in curriculum, 253-255; vs. testing, 33; young children, 242, 243

technology, impact on future education, 58

teenage mothers: black, 144, 146, 148; effect on children's development, 147, 148; consequences of childbearing on, 144-150; family support for, 149; increase in, 144; and IQ of children of, 148; and marital stability, 146, 147; prevention programs for, 149, 150; welfare, 145

testing: role in educational process, 272, 273; vs. teaching, 33; types of, 272

television: aggression on, 63; effect on school-age children, 65-66; and SAT scores, 63; vs. schools, 65-67; selective watching of, 66-67; time spent watching, 65; worldwide communications with, 54

temper tantrums, 193, 197-198

toxoplasmosis, 74

tropics, play in, 136, 137, 138

trust, 92

U.S. Office of Adolescent Pregnancy, 150

violence: removal from children's lives, 64; toward children, 63; U.S. tradition of, 64

vulnerable child: and parental determinism, 167-169; and stress, 168

welfare, and teenage mothers, 145, 146

women, personal identity vs. family role, 48-49

women's liberation, effect on adolescent girls, 48

working mothers: and effect on children, 152-154; and importance of father, 153; statistics on, 8-9, 36, 48, 90; ways to help children of, 153, 154

x-rays, during pregnancy, 75

Credits/Acknowledgments

Cover design by Charles Vitelli

1. Perspectives
Facing overview—Freelance Photographers Guild/Charles P. George.

2. Childhood and Society
Facing overview—Freelance Photographers Guild/Henry Monroe.

3. Development and Educational Opportunities
Facing overview—Freelance Photographers Guild/Sydlow. 86, 87—Joey Reinlieb © Human Nature, Inc. 107—Chris Kuhn.

4. Child Rearing and Parent Education
Facing overview—Freelance Photographers Guild/ E. Alan McGee.

5. Children with Special Needs
Facing overview—Freelance Photographers Guild/Tom Marotta/ UNICEF.

6. Behavior and Guidance
Facing overview—Freelance Photographers Guild/Peter L. Gould.

7. Programs and Curricula
Facing overview—Freelance Photographers Guild/Ben Ross.

8. Teaching and Evaluation
Facing overview—Freelance Photographers Guild/Spencer Blank. 242—Bruce Grossman. 243—Karyl Gatteno. 253—Bruce Reedy. 254—VME Smith.

WE WANT YOUR ADVICE

ANNUAL EDITIONS: EARLY CHILDHOOD EDUCATION 80/81

Article Rating Form

Here is an opportunity for you to have direct input into the next revision of this reader. We would like you to rate each of the 68 articles listed below, using the following scale:

1. **Excellent: should definitely be retained**
2. **Above average: should probably be retained**
3. **Below average: should probably be deleted**
4. **Poor: should definitely be deleted**

Your ratings will play a vital part in the next revision. So please mail this prepaid form to us just as soon as you complete it.
Thanks for your help!

Rating	Article	Rating	Article
	1. How Could Early Childhood Education Affect Families?		35. Whatever Happened to the Walton's?
	2. What Is Basic for Young Children?		36. The Consequences of Early Childbearing
	3. What's Basic About the Curriculum?		37. When Mommy Goes to Work . . .
	4. What Is Early Childhood Education? Some Definitions and Issues		38. Crisis in the Classroom
	5. How Early Should They Go to School?		39. Black Child/White Child
	6. Early Childhood Education: A Perspective on Basics		40. How Can I Help My Children Do Better in School?
	7. Four Who Cared		41. The Myth of the Vulnerable Child
	8. Making the Day Care Decision		42. The LD Syndrome: How to Recognize and Deal with It
	9. Day Care Policy: Some Modest Proposals		43. "Learning Disabled" or "Slow Learner"?
	10. Infant Day Care: Toward a More Human Environment		44. The Young Gifted Child
	11. What Young Children Need Most in a Changing Society		45. Let's Go Slow on Acceleration
	12. Our Disconnected Child		46. Mainstreaming: Valuing Diversity in Children
	13. A Mother's Day Message: What We Can Do Now for Our Children's Future		47. How to Discipline with Love
	14. An Educational Forecast for the 1980s		48. Anxiety and the 3- to 5-Year Old
	15. Proposition 13 and Early Childhood Education: Wave of the Future or Bad Splash?		49. How to Understand Your Child's Distress Signals
	16. Raising Children to Make a Less Violent World		50. Classroom Discipline Problems? 15 Humane Solutions
	17. Schools vs. Television		51. Behavioral Blockbusters!
	18. Signals of Child Abuse		52. Humanizing the Curriculum
	19. A Perfect Baby		53. Bilingual/Bicultural Programs for Preschool Children
	20. Growth: 45 Crucial Months		54. Developing Socially Valued Behavior in Young Children
	21. Your Child's Mind		55. 10 Teaching Aids for Reading
	22. The Baby's Elastic Mind		56. Language Development: It's Much More Than a Kit
	23. The Care of Infants and Toddlers in Group Settings		57. Piaget, The Six Year Old and Modern Math
	24. Ecology of Infant Day Care		58. What Your Child's Art Is Telling You
	25. Piaget's Theory of Child Development and Its Implications		59. America's Head Start Program: An Agenda for Its Second Decade
	26. Misunderstandings About How Children Learn		60. The Satisfactions
	27. The Truth About Sex Differences		61. The Meaning of Teaching
	28. Sex Roles in the Nursery		62. Teacher's First Words
	29. When Kids Explore Sex		63. Teachers, Be(a)ware of Sex-Stereotyping
	30. Aggression and Hostility in Young Children		64. Evaluating Settings for Learning
	31. Mother-Child Interactions and Competence in Infants and Toddlers		65. The Persistence of Preschool Effects: A National Collaborative Study
	32. The Individuality Factor		66. The Abt Report of Follow Through: Critique and Comment
	33. Play Isn't Just Kid Stuff		67. The Diagnostic Teacher
	34. Worlds of Play		68. The Role of Testing in the Educational Process

(continued on back)

About you

Name _____ Date _____
Address _____
City _____ State _____ Zip _____
Telephone _____

1. What do you think of the Annual Editions concept?

2. Have you read any articles lately that you think should be included in the next edition?

3. Which articles do you feel should be replaced in the next edition? Why?

4. In what other areas would you like to see an Annual Edition? Why?

EARLY CHILDHOOD EDUCATION 80/81

BUSINESS REPLY MAIL
First Class   Permit No. 84   Guilford, Ct.

Postage Will Be Paid by Addressee

**Attention: Annual Editions Service
The Dushkin Publishing Group, Inc.
Sluice Dock
Guilford, Connecticut 06437**

NO POSTAGE
NECESSARY
IF MAILED
IN THE
UNITED STATES